NetWare® UNLEASHED

NetWare® UNLEASHED

Rick Sant'Angelo

SAMS
PUBLISHING

A Division of Prentice Hall Computer Publishing
201 West 103rd Street, Indianapolis, IN 46290

This book is dedicated to all the teachers who have helped me to understand networking and life in general. May the clarity bestowed upon me help and empower you in your work.

Copyright © 1994 by Sams Publishing

Trademarks

Publisher
Richard K. Swadley

Associate Publisher
Jordan Gold

Acquisitions Manager
Stacy Hiquet

Managing Editor
Cindy Morrow

Acquisitions Editors
Gregg Bushyeager
Mark Taber

Development Editor
Mark Taber

Production Editor
Mary Inderstrodt

Copy Editors
Joe Williams
David Bradford
Keith Davenport
Mitzi Gianakos
Jim Grass
Sean Medlock

Editorial and Graphics Coordinator
Bill Whitmer

Software Development Editor
Wayne Blankenbeckler

Editorial Assistants
Sharon Cox
Lynette Quinn

Technical Reviewer
Steve Kalman

Marketing Manager
Greg Wiegand

Cover and Book Designer
Michele Laseau

Director of Production and Manufacturing
Jeff Valler

Imprint Manager
Kelli Widdifield

Manufacturing Coordinator
Paul Gilchrist

Production Analyst
Mary Beth Wakefield

Proofreading/Indexing Coordinator
Joelynn Gifford

Graphics Image Specialists
Tim Montgomery
Dennis Sheehan
Sue VandeWalle

Production
Nick Anderson
Ayrika Bryant
Juli Cook
Lisa Daugherty
Rich Evers
Dennis Hager
Kim Hannel
Angela P. Judy
Stephanie McComb
Jamie Milazzo
Wendy Ott
Rochelle Palma
Ryan Rader
Kim Scott
Michelle M. Self
Ann Sippel
S.A. Springer
Suzanne Tully
Elaine Webb
Dennis Wesner
Alyssa Yesh

Indexer
Jennifer Eberhardt

Overview

Contents

Part III System Administration

Part V Internetworks and WANs

Part VIII Protocol Analysis

Part X Troubleshooting

Part XI Appendixes

Acknowledgments

I would like to extend a special thanks to my friend Peter Kuo. He is one of the hardest working, most knowledgeable, and most dependable professionals I have ever met. He has written some of the most difficult and technical parts of this book, and he is an author in his own rights. I also acknowledge Micheal Hader, Mark Johnston, Jeff Wade, Dan Nassar, and Doug Archell. Their efforts make this book so very credible. I cannot thank each of them enough for contributing their best tips, tricks, notes, and cautions with you and with me.

My thanks are also conveyed to Steve Kalman, who is the technical editor for this monumental project. You will find his hidden influence throughout this book. Steve has been a friend for a long time; we have worked together, and he encouraged me to write my first book. He is the author of *Printing on NetWare* (M&T Books) and is a highly regarded free-lance Certified NetWare Instructor who teaches all over the country. I also thank his wife Gail, for loaning him to me for the long hours of reading and editing the manuscript.

Last but not least, I greatly appreciate Mark Taber, Gregg Bushyeager, and the production team at Prentice Hall Computer Publishing for their professional support and direction.

About the Authors

Rick Sant'Angelo, Author

Rick Sant'Angelo was one of the first to become a Certified NetWare Engineer. He has been integrating NetWare since its introduction in 1983, having installed and worked with virtually every type of LAN and NOS available. He has written two previous books on NetWare, *Optimizing NetWare Networks* and *Putting NetWare Lite OS to Work* (M&T Books), and has been a speaker at computer industry trade shows. He also develops and teaches professional seminars on NetWare Center for Advanced Professional Development. Rick's background includes consulting, system analysis and design, and training in several Fortune 100 firms, as well as in small businesses.

Rick's in-depth understanding of the mechanics of NetWare and LANs and ability to teach the subject is demonstrated in every facet of this book. His deep conviction that understanding the mechanics of NetWare and using terms consistently is the factor that makes a network simple to work with.

You can contact Rick at

LAN Tech Systems
(206) 253-6558
CompuServe ID 76366,71

Peter Kuo, Chief Contributing Author

Peter Kuo, Ph.D., is the first Canadian Enterprise Certified NetWare Engineer and a Certified NetWare Instructor. His area of expertise includes advanced NetWare topics such as network management, IBM, and UNIX connectivity issues. Peter is a SysOp on NetWire (CompuServe), supporting many advanced sections for Novell, such as Async Connectivity, IBM Host Connectivity, TCP/IP-NFS, LAN WorkPlace/WorkGroup, NetWare Management System, LANalyzer, Network Management, and NetWare 4.0. He also is a member of Novell's Professional Developer's Program.

You can contact Peter at

DreamLAN
CompuServe 71333,1700

Doug Archell, Contributing Author

Doug Archell works for a large Canadian financial institution and provides consulting services. As a Certified NetWare Engineer, Enterprise Certified NetWare Engineer, and Certified NetWare Administrator, he is quite experienced in troubleshooting NetWare, Ethernet, and Token Ring networks.

Micheal Hader, Contributing Author

Micheal Hader is president of Hader & Associates and its subsidiary, Atrium Learning Center, a company specializing in consulting and training on leading-edge computer technologies, information systems, and end-user computing. Over the past nine years, he has conducted training for every company listed in the Fortune 500 and has held seminars in the U.S., Great Britain, Canada, and Australia covering advanced NetWare and Windows topics. A leading author for Prentice Hall Computer Publishing, Addison Wesley, and IDG, Mr. Hader has written or coauthored six books on NetWare and Windows, including best-seller *Networking Windows 3.1*, *Mastering NetWare*, *NetWare Troubleshooting*, *Killer Windows Utilities*, *Killer WordPerfect 6.0 Utilities*, and *NetWare Unleashed*. More than 7,000 LAN administrators, from beginners to ECNEs and CNIs have benefited from Mr. Hader's expertise and knowledge in implementing successful NetWare environments. Mr. Hader holds a Masters in Business Administration from Pepperdine University. You can reach him at

Hader & Associates
CompuServe 76200,145
(615) 822-9002

Mark Johnston, Contributing Author

Mark Johnston is the Business Unit Manager for Cable Management Products at Microtest Inc. in Phoenix, Arizona. A professional engineer, Mark has spent 14 years in the communications test equipment field concentrating on field service applications. Mark has led teams that developed a number of significant products, including the first hand-held X.25/SNA protocol analyzer, the first frame relay protocol analyzer, and the first LAN cabling certification tool. Mark is active in the EIA/TIA and IEEE committees, participates in the ATM forum, and speaks and writes about communications test issues.

Daniel J. Nassar, Contributing Author

Daniel J. Nassar is president of LAN Scope Inc., a Philadelphia area national local area networking consulting firm that specializes in emergency network troubleshooting, network optimization and health studies, and associated training.

Dan is experienced in a extensive range of computer system areas. He is proficient in LAN layout and design and strong in all phases of LAN problem analysis and performance tuning, especially in the Token Ring and Ethernet environments. Dan also is skilled in all phases of computer system maintenance and diagnostics.

Dan is the author of *Token Ring Troubleshooting*, a joint LAN Times and New Riders Publishing work. You can reach Dan at

LAN Scope Inc.
Office: (215) 359-3573
Voice Mail : (215) 446-3831

Jeffrey S. Wade, Contributing Author

Jeffrey S. Wade has been involved in the networking and LAN-Host integration fields for nine years and holds a B.A.S. degree in Computer Systems from Florida Atlantic University. He is currently employed by IBM Corporation as a client-server networking specialist in Tallahassee, Florida and holds the Novell ECNE and CNI certifications. Jeffrey provides consulting services and conducts classes to assist customers in developing client-server LAN solutions for their businesses. He has worked previously as an instructor for the Center for Advanced Professional Development, and as an engineer for Tymnet-McDonnell Douglas Corporation.

Introduction

This book is a NetWare encyclopedia that every NetWare administrator or integrator needs for managing a 3.x or 4.x system. The authors of this book, who have a combined NetWare experience of *decades*, share their most powerful insights. This book is a helpful guide for any integrator or administrator who is caught in the whirlwind of downsizing.

Whether you are integrating NetWare for the first time or you have installed and managed systems for years, this book provides the first line of support for you to embark on any project relative to NetWare. It also gives you direction of where to go for more detailed or comprehensive material on each subject.

Who This Book Is for

This book is written for an intermediate to an advanced technical audience. You won't encounter lengthy instructions for copying disks or creating directories. It is assumed that you have a good, fundamental understanding of microcomputers and DOS.

If you have no NetWare experience, Part 1 will give you a sufficient level of understanding to comprehend the rest of the material.

If you are an experienced NetWare professional, take the time to scan the first part of this book. This book consistently uses certain terms as they are defined here–not necessarily as they are defined by Novell. You will find that the mechanics of the NetWare file server operating system, networking software and protocols, and LAN technology are presented in a simple, clear, and precise manner. Your ability to troubleshoot will be enhanced by understanding what happens inside the system.

How This Book Is Organized

This book is organized into the following parts:

Part I. Theory Behind the Practice: This chapters in this part cover the inner workings of NetWare, its protocols, and local area networks (LANs). This part goes into more detail than Novell training about how and why NetWare works the way it does.

Part II. Planning and Installation: This part is a guide for integrating NetWare 3.12 and 4.01 versions. It is full of helpful tips–gained from the authors' experiences.

Part III. System Administration: This part walks you through the basics of setting up NetWare administration and printing, including the latest additions: BasicMHS, ElectroText online documentation, and the new menu system.

Part IV. Network Management: This part is a survival guide for managing networks using available software tools. This is not a product review, such as those that you read in various periodicals, but a helpful analysis of available tools—and what they do for you.

Part V. Internetworks and WANs: This part provides simple and direct instructions for integrating NetWare in a campus-wide or enterprise-wide environment. It clarifies routing and bridging issues, and system design for internetworks and wide area networks (WANs).

Part VI. Performance Optimization: This part probes every aspect of NetWare, the underlying LANs, and the WANs that you can exploit for better performance.

Part VII. Preventing Downtime: This part explores the critical failure points, products, and available features to keep your system running nonstop.

Part VIII. Protocol Analysis: This part is a guide to analyzing NetWare and local area network protocols. It is a simple and direct beginning point for using a protocol analyzer with NetWare. This part and a protocol analyzer will help a network professional evolve into a true networking professional.

Part IX. Windows and NetWare: This part explores Windows integration and administration in a NetWare environment.

Part X. Troubleshooting: This part discusses the most likely problems that you'll encounter when something goes wrong. It also shows how to identify and solve problems.

Appendixes: Support material (including a glossary of NetWare terminology) is offered in the appendixes.

Conventions

Look for the following conventions in this book:

> **Tips**, which indicate the author's simple and direct advice, are shown in a dialog box. See the following Tip box for an example.

TIP ▶

To ensure that each user has a unique value, you can set the S_FILE environment variable to the logical station number in the system login script as follows:

```
SET S_FILE="%station"
```

Notes, which are pertinent comments that the author conveys, are indicated in a dialog box. See the following Note box for an example.

NOTE ▶

When a disk problem occurs, it might cause volume(s) on that drive to become dismounted. You can restore the volumes by running VREPAIR.NLM. See the Troubleshooting section for running VREPAIR.

Cautions, which let you know that something is very important to observe or do, are indicated in a dialog box. See the following Caution box for an example.

CAUTION ▶

NDS tree partitions should not be confused with file system partitions. NDS partitions do not contain information about the file system, only about NDS objects and their associated properties.

Program names are indicated in all uppercase. For example, the NetWare serve monitor is the program MONITOR.NLM.
Screen messages and commands typed at a system prompt are indicated in the following proportionally spaced type style:

```
COPY A:*.* C:\NET
```

Theory Behind the Practice

PART

I

Networking with NetWare

1

by Rick Sant'Angelo

The purpose of this chapter is to set a clear and stable foundation about what NetWare is and what language is used in this book. Even the most experienced NetWare users, administrators, and technicians are perplexed by some of this material, because Novell has inadvertently confused the industry by using some words inconsistently.

Technical people might have gaps in their knowledge and clouded or confused perceptions about a few basic concepts. Because this book is written for advanced NetWare users, the material presented in this chapter is discussed once and not repeated in subsequent chapters. Pay close attention to the language, however, because your clarity and understanding depend on the precise use of words in this book.

Terminology: Novell versus Industry Standards

Terminology is a problem in our industry, affecting all who work with networks. Without precise usage and understanding of terms, it would be impossible to clearly discuss any topic in this book. Enzlo's third law states that terminology is 85 percent of data communications, whereas technology only accounts for 15 percent. Terminology is addressed by industry standards organizations, but there are simply too many choices. Besides, organizations such as Microsoft and Novell apparently create new definitions for terms to conform to how they have been using them.

This book doesn't use terms loosely, inconsistently, or without precise meaning. Because this book uses terms clearly and consistently, you'll find that understanding NetWare and supplemental hardware and software is simple.

Novell can be inconsistent in terminology usage; it uses terms incongruously in manuals, screen messages, and training materials. At times, Novell applies the same terms for different meanings. If you've read several different industry periodicals, you have probably managed to adjust your understanding to a particular writer or periodical. Even if you understand a concept completely, you might not be certain about what is meant by a particular term referring to that concept.

Being inconsistent when discussing advanced concepts doesn't work well. Clear and precise terminology is required so that lengthy discussions of basics aren't necessary.

This chapter also clarifies some concepts that you should understand. Later chapters address many advanced topics that assume in-depth understanding of networking with NetWare. For these reasons, it is imperative to read this brief chapter.

When any question arises concerning terminology, you're encouraged to find the term in Appendix A, "Glossary of NetWare Terminology." If you're not certain about what is being discussed, you'll miss subtle and important details about the subject matter.

Which is the LAN?

One of the most perplexing terms used in our industry is *local area network* (LAN). The term LAN was first used in the early 1970s, in Xerox's Ethernet project at the Palo Alto Research Center. The definition described a system of computers connected over a limited distance. At the time, the Ethernet components were integrated at the system board level. Today, things are different; Ethernet and Token Ring LANs are separate entities from the computers with which they are interfaced. Though technology has changed, the definition has not.

The term LAN often is used to describe a NetWare or another type of network. However, this book doesn't use the term in that manner. Although this may conflict with common industry usage (including Novell's usage of the term), the old definition causes perplexing problems in identifying a single physical Ethernet, Token Ring, or other type of LAN. In a network using routable protocols (which include Novell's IPX, TCP/IP, AppleTalk, or OSI protocols), it is critical to identify each LAN as a separate entity.

It is imperative to know whether the entire system or just one component (such as the Ethernet portion) is being discussed. The commonly used terms in the industry don't support this clarification, because the terms LAN and network often are used interchangeably.

Definition of the Term Network

A *network*, as discussed in this book, is a generalized term that applies to an entire computing system. Therefore, a multiuser computer system based on a NetWare server is called a NetWare network (as opposed to a *NetWare LAN*).

This definition is based upon the term *network architecture*, which is used consistently throughout the industry to describe the design of a multiuser computer system. Each vendor describes hardware, software, protocols, and functions for connectivity in a network architecture, or blueprint. IBM's Systems Network Architecture (SNA), Digital's (DECnet) Digital Network Architecture (DNA), Xerox's Xerox Network System (XNS), and International Standards Organization's Open

Systems Interconnection (OSI) reference model describe network architectures. Novell calls its blueprint *Universal Network Architecture.*

Network architecture is best described by the OSI model, which standardizes nonproprietary protocols and functions in seven layers. Although this book isn't concerned with the actual OSI protocols, OSI serves as a model to compare to other networking protocols. In this book, each layer of protocol is compared to the OSI level so you can relate it to OSI or other network architectures with which you may be familiar. The OSI model is described with functions and corresponding NetWare protocols in Table 1.1.

Table 1.1. The OSI seven-layer model and functions.

OSI Layer		NetWare Layer	Function
7	Application	NLMs	Server-based applications
6	Presentation	NCP	OS function calls
5	Session	NCP	Connection establishment
4	Transport	NCP/SPX	Acknowledgment/error control
3	Network	IPX	Delivery/routing/Inter-LAN/ WAN Communications
2	Data-link	Access protocol	Intra-LAN/WAN communications
1	Physical	Physical medium	Encoding/electrical

Protocols

Protocols establish rules of communications—functions and procedures for communications at various levels.

Although the term protocol is used quite loosely by Novell, protocols have very specific duties: they carry out the functions discussed in Table 1.1. The term protocol is rarely used by itself in this book; the specific layer of a protocol is named and usually is correlated with the OSI equivalent layer.

For example, Internetwork Packet Exchange (IPX) in this book is referred to as a *network protocol* because it executes the network layer functional equivalents of the OSI Model. LAN protocols are referred to as *access protocols* and have distinctly different functions than the network protocol. They're also named by an industry standards organization. Chapter 5, "NetWare's Protocol Stack," gives a full description of how NetWare's protocols enable network communications. IPX, NCP, SPX, and other NetWare protocols are fully explored and compared to OSI layers.

Definition of the Term LAN

The term *LAN* is used in this book to refer to a specific individual Ethernet, Token Ring, ARCnet, or other type of local area network. Although the textbook definition includes computers as part of a LAN, this definition excludes computers and isolates the LAN itself as a clearly separate entity. Today, network interface cards (NICs) clearly draw a boundary between the LAN and its protocols, and other networking protocols that are employed.

Therefore, the following definition for *LAN* applies in this book:

LAN is a multipoint connectivity medium that enables communications between computers over a limited distance with high-bandwidth and low error rates. A LAN terminates at each computer in the form of a network interface card (NIC) and includes all electronic and electrical components that connect them.

The boundary of a single LAN is limited to the NICs that are connected to a cabling (or unbounded media) system, where LAN frames are propagated without the assistance of a bridge or router.

This new definition clearly isolates an Ethernet LAN from a Novell network. Although Novell and others use the term LAN to describe a network (as discussed in this book), you should keep the following points in mind: in every case (in this book), LAN refers to the Ethernet or Token Ring portion of the network only; network refers to the entire system.

This new definition is consistent with the way the term LAN is used in the NetWare server operating system screen messages. The programmers who write the operating system portion of NetWare address each logical LAN or wide-area network (WAN) as an entity. Therefore, when you view server console messages or menu selections in the server MONITOR, this definition is consistent with the definition used in this book. In manuals and training or marketing materials from Novell, the term LAN may be used to describe the entire system or the LAN, as discussed in this book.

Other Useful Definitions

A few other definitions can assist you in making some sense of your system. Although you may understand networking, taking a few moments to look at the way these terms are used in this book will pay dividends.

LAN, or Physical LAN

Frames from every node on a single *physical LAN* are propagated to all nodes on that physical LAN. In an Ethernet LAN, each node is directly connected to a single cabling segment or cabling segments joined with repeaters (including wiring concentrators, multiport repeaters, and hubs). In a Token Ring LAN, each node is directly connected to a single ring. A single ring may consist of nodes connected to multistation access units (MAUs) or control access units (CAUs) joined to a single ring.

Logical LAN

When two or more physical LANs are joined by any type of bridge (MAC-layer or LLC-layer), they appear as one *logical LAN* and are addressed as one network address. This doesn't apply to LANs joined with routers (see the following sections, "Bridge" and "Router").

Network Address

A single physical or logical LAN or WAN has a *network address*. LANs and WANs joined with bridges (not routers) appear to be one logical LAN, and therefore are one addressable entity.

Frames (LAN Frames)

Data travels across a LAN in small fragments called *frames*. Each frame contains addressing and error-control information that enables the data contained in the frame to reach its destination, provided it is located on the same LAN.

Packets

Each frame of data transports a *packet* of data that includes network protocol information and sometimes data to be transferred from one computer to another. The packet is formatted by a higher-layer protocol, such as Novell's proprietary

Internetwork Packet Exchange (IPX) protocol. A packet of data contains network information and perhaps data, and is encapsulated into a LAN frame (or WAN frame or packet) for transport across a LAN.

> **NOTE** ▶
>
> Most Novell material fails to draw a distinction between a "frame" and a "packet," referring to both as "packets." Understanding the difference and identifying which term is discussed is of key importance.

Bridge

A *bridge* joins two or more physical LANs to appear as one logical LAN. Bridges work at the data-link layer of the OSI model, acting upon information contained in the LAN frame header. A bridge is therefore ignorant of whatever type of network packet is encapsulated and does not require intelligence to deal with a network protocol.

> **NOTE** ▶
>
> Novell previously used the term "bridge" to describe the internal router. Versions 2.2 and 3.11 and later documentation correctly apply the term "router." However, you'll find the term "bridge" applied to routers in many Novell and industry publications. To understand NetWare network architecture, you must be aware of the difference between a bridge and a router.

Router

A *router* also joins two or more physical LANs; however, they are distinguished as separate logical LANs or as network addresses. A router works at the network layer of the OSI model, acting upon information contained in the network packet header (IPX in a NetWare network). A router is therefore ignorant of what type of LAN it is servicing. Its NIC driver processes and removes the LAN frame; only the packet is viewed for processing.

Therefore, a router must be capable of processing the type of network protocol employed in each type of packet required. A router can work with any type of LAN, because each NIC has a driver to enable communications.

Distributed Processing versus Centralized Processing

Previous generations of multiuser computer systems focused on centralized processing. In a mainframe or minicomputer system, all processing is contained in a central processing unit (CPU). Users have *terminals*, which are simply keyboards and monitors for accessing the CPU.

In a NetWare system, the file server is normally not used for centralized processing. Instead, *file servers* share disk drives, printers, communications ports, and perhaps other resources with *workstations*. Workstations are computers with their own processors. Processing is therefore distributed among the workstations.

Client/Server Architecture

The NetWare operating system is designed for use as a *server*, not a user workstation. The NetWare server is not generally used as a workstation also. Workstations normally don't share their devices; therefore, they are *clients* of the server.

This is in stark contrast to a DOS-based, peer-to-peer network operating system (NOS), such as NetWare Lite, LANtastic, or InvisibleNet. In a peer-to-peer network, each workstation can share its devices and use other workstations' devices. Servers are used as workstations with a less powerful stature than a NetWare server.

In 2.x and previous versions of NetWare, the file server could be installed as *nondedicated*, meaning that a server could serve double duty as a workstation. This was accomplished by allocating a DOS session under the NetWare server operating system. The DOS window is limited to 640K of memory, can't access extended or expanded memory, and cannot run Windows or other protected-mode software. Using a NetWare server as a workstation limits resources available to clients. It also reduces the server's reliability and stability because of demands placed on it as a workstation. Not all software works properly on a nondedicated server. For these reasons, it is not recommended that you use your 2.x server in a nondedicated mode except in limited situations.

> **NOTE** ►
>
> The term "client/server" is applied often to software systems in which client software interacts with a server software component, as is the case with client/server database systems. This use of the term is alternative to the way it is used in this book.

Support for DOS, Windows, OS/2, Macintosh, UNIX, and Windows NT Clients

NetWare is designed to support workstations running an operating system that differs from its own server operating system. It supports five workstation operating systems. DOS, OS/2, and Windows NT workstations use an IPX packet driver and a workstation requester (sometimes called a shell). Macintosh- and UNIX-native protocol stacks are supported by adding server-based applications. Mac and UNIX workstations don't need to load any NetWare requesters; instead they use their native networking software to access a NetWare server.

NetWare Versions

Current NetWare versions are 2.2, 3.12, and 4.01. Each of these versions is based on a different operating system. Each is divided into releases for varying numbers of users (from 5 to 1,000 users).

NetWare 2.2 is based on the 16-bit architecture of the 80286 processor, which uses 24-bit addressing. It can address up to 12M of RAM, 256M per volume, and a total of 2G of disk storage.

NetWare 3.x versions are based on the 386's and 486's 32-bit architecture. It can address up to 4G of RAM, and 32 terabytes of disk storage. Because it senses and uses the native mode of either a 386 or 486, it isn't called NetWare 386 anymore. This version features dynamic allocation of resources, automatically tuning itself for changing conditions. It also enables drivers and NetWare Loadable Modules (NLMs) to be loaded and unloaded from the console, reducing installation complexity and making it a simple and effective platform for server-based applications.

NETWARE 4 NOTE ▶

NetWare 4.x is based on the 32-bit architecture of the 386 and 486 processors. Although it's essentially the same as the 3.x operating system, several enhancements have been added to improve the operating system. It also incorporates NetWare Directory Services (NDS), an enterprise-wide service that links servers and network resources into a hierarchical, object-oriented directory.

Summary

Although many advanced users, administrators, integrators, managers, and technicians understand NetWare quite well, you are advised to study this chapter to fine-tune your understanding of the terminology used in this book. In some cases, this book's language is different than the inconsistent and conflicting terms used by Novell and by the industry.

Terminology used in this book is in direct conformity with industry standards organizations and helps to clarify concepts and mechanics of NetWare that are commonly confused—even for the most experienced NetWare users.

Whenever you are not clear about the meaning of a word, you should search in the following order:

1. The glossary of this book
2. Novell's *Concepts* Manual (supplied with your NetWare distribution kit)
3. Microsoft Press *Computer Dictionary*

Lastly, the first section of this book, this chapter included, contains important facts about NetWare and terminology used in this book. This provides a foundation for later discussions. Advanced material presented in later chapters assumes the reader has this basic knowledge. As an advanced NetWare user, you should review this chapter before going on.

Local Area Networks

by Rick Sant'Angelo

2

This chapter discusses the local area network (LAN) itself as a separate entity. In this book, the term LAN refers to Ethernet, Token Ring, ARCnet, or other types of LANs as separate subsystems, not to be confused with the other layers of networking components that are employed in a network.

One of the most common errors technical people make is to specialize in one area without understanding the basics of each subsystem with which they come into contact. Even though you may specialize in one aspect of networking—perhaps administration, computer hardware, or Ethernet/Token Ring—as a network professional, you must learn the basics of all aspects of the network, including the LAN. Despite Novell's well-developed education system, Novell-trained integrators generally lack a good working knowledge of what goes on inside a LAN. (NetWare integration is simple enough even without this knowledge.)

To understand all the layers of protocols that are employed in a network, a clear and consistent terminology must be applied to the mechanical aspects of LANs and NetWare. As discussed in the previous chapter, Novell has hindered this understanding with its inconsistent use of terms.

The insufficient clarification of the mechanics of LANs and the inconsistent use of terms contribute to a general lack of troubleshooting expertise in our industry. This brief chapter clarifies the mechanics of LANs and how they relate with the software layers of Novell's protocols. It also establishes language that is applied consistently to all parts of this book.

The information in this chapter is important for even the most knowledgeable and experienced integrator. For those less experienced with LANs, this chapter provides the basics that are necessary to understand the primary platform upon which clients and servers exist. For all readers, this chapter explains how words are used in this book, information that will not be repeated in subsequent chapters.

Overview of LANs

The first type of LAN ever developed, called Ethernet, emerged from Xerox's Palo Alto Research Center in the early 1970s. This product was an extension of an access protocol called *carrier sense multiple access with collision detection* (CSMA/CD), which evolved from the Aloha project at University of Hawaii in the 1960s. In the late 1970s, Digital Equipment Corporation and Intel joined forces with Xerox to develop Ethernet II and standardize it as a non-proprietary LAN that could be used by many developers.

The Institute of Electrical and Electronic Engineers (IEEE) formed a LAN committee, the 802 workgroup, to study and develop standards for Ethernet and other types of LANs. The workgroup developed a common set of standards to enable interoperability between various vendors' products. When customers started demanding such interoperability, developers began to use the 802 standards to create products that could be integrated with those of other vendors. Of course, the fact that Ethernet technology is public domain did not hurt its popularity. On the contrary, many vendors decided to join Digital, Intel, and Xerox in using Ethernet to link their CPUs and terminals together.

Networking evolved out of consumer demands and as a reaction to proprietary systems. The user community found that non-proprietary systems not only could be made interoperable, but that they lead to competitive products and prices.

Today, the LAN is a totally separate subsystem that can be integrated as a common connectivity medium between all types of computer systems, whether proprietary or open. LAN terminology, however, is still a tangled mass that does not allow LAN vendors to clearly distinguish themselves as a separate industry from that of networking software and operating systems. In-house integrators now most often see the LAN as another component that they can incorporate into their multivendor systems. Though some system developers prefer to bundle the LAN, networking software, operating systems, and computers as one sale, in-house integrators tend to select each subsystem separately. It is time that a new definition be used for the term LAN and that all of us recognize a LAN as a separate subsystem within a network.

Two basic types of LANs account for the vast majority of installations: Ethernet and Token Ring. A few other types of LANs that used to be popular have faded into oblivion. According to a recent International Data Corporation study, Ethernet accounted for 45.9 percent of all installed LANs in 1991, while Token Ring accounted for another 31.8 percent. Both were growing in popularity, and Token Ring was growing faster than Ethernet. Figure 2.1 shows the relative market share for each major type of LAN. These figures include Apple LocalTalk LANs, which are used almost exclusively in Macintosh-only networks. Industry researchers estimate that Ethernet and Token Ring will account for more than 95 percent of all LANs by 1995.

Analysts have projected that the market for Fiber Distributed Data Interface (FDDI) will grow, but industry-wide sales have been disappointing, totaling less than 6,000 units in 1992. ARCnet's market share is shrinking and is expected to virtually disappear within the next couple of years. The market for LocalTalk also is shrinking; its limited bandwidth is insufficient to satisfy even the smallest of client-server demands. Legal actions regarding token-passing ring patents threaten to eliminate royalties and make Token Ring even more popular.

FIGURE 2.1.

Market share in 1991 by LAN Type. (Source: International Data Corporation.)

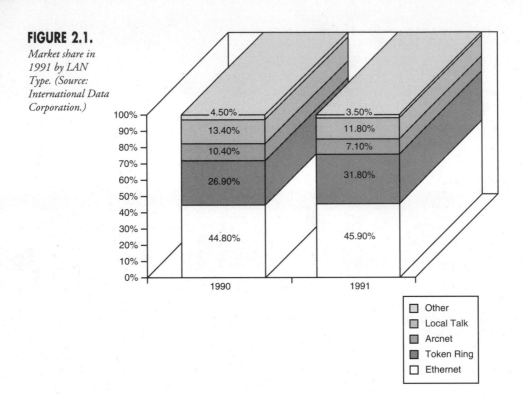

Some new 100 Mbps technologies promise to change all of our projections. CDDI, Fast Ethernet, 100BASE-VG, and TCNS have moved high-bandwidth access protocols from expensive optical fiber components to less expensive copper wire components. As these products become standardized and gain acceptance with developers, prices will come down even farther and more will be sold.

To understand the technology of LANs, first we should discuss the basics and make certain we are all speaking the same language. LAN designs consist of three components:

- Access protocols
- Topology
- Cabling

Each topic needs to be discussed in brief terms.

Access Protocols

An *access protocol,* sometimes called an access method or access scheme, defines the type of LAN. The access protocol controls access to the media and establishes the rules and methods employed to enable communications between NICs. Access protocols are employed at the LAN level, while other protocols operate at levels above the access protocol. It operates at the data-link layer of the OSI model.

Two basic access protocols account for most of the products on the market today: CSMA/CD and token-passing ring. Ethernet uses CSMA/CD access protocol, Token Ring and FDDI use token-passing ring (FDDI incorporates a few improvements on the original access protocol). Implicit token-passing bus is used by ARCnet and TCNS, and an access protocol called *carrier sense multiple access with collision avoidance* (CSMA/CA) is used in Apple Computer's LocalTalk LANs. Even in today's robust networking market, other LAN access protocols account for far less than 1 percent market share.

Topologies

Topology describes the manner in which cabling is laid out. General topologies include:

- Bus (linear or star)
- Ring (including star-wired ring)
- Tree
- Mesh

Topologies can include hierarchical and distributed variations. Tree topology is used in cable-TV networks and in broadband LANs (which are seldom used anymore). Mesh topology is employed in X.25 packet-switching public data networks (PDNs) and value added networks (VANs). Ethernet, Token Ring, and ARCnet LANs use only bus and ring topologies.

In a bus network, each bit is broadcasted to all other nodes. Ethernet and ARCnet are bus networks that can be configured into either linear bus or star bus fashion, as shown in Figure 2.2.

In a linear bus topology, electrically isolated cabling segments can be joined with repeaters, which simply repeat each bit broadcasted on any cabling segment onto all other cabling segments. In a star bus topology, the star is configured by a type of multiport repeater called a *wiring concentrator* or *active hub.* Wiring concentrators can be connected in parallel fashion to form a distributed star bus or cascaded in series to form a hierarchical star bus. Both linear bus and star bus topologies can be combined as long as each segment is dedicated to either a linear bus or single-node star bus segment.

FIGURE 2.2.

Linear bus and star bus topologies.

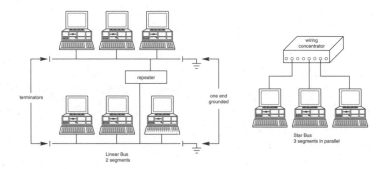

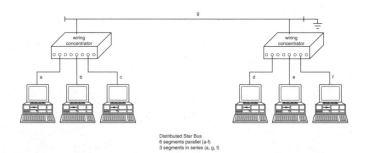

NOTE ▶

Novell and some industry writers often use both "segment" *and* "topology" to describe a physical or logical LAN (as defined in Chapter 1). This clearly constitutes misuse of these terms. A segment, per IEEE standards, is an electrically isolated portion of a physical LAN. Topology, again defined by IEEE standards, pertains to cabling layout. In this book, the term "cabling segment" is always used to describe an electrically isolated cabling segment, and "topology" is always used to refer to cable layout. In this book, the term "LAN" is used to identify a separate physical or logical LAN.

Token Ring, FDDI, and CDDI LANs are ring networks wherein each node is a repeater that transmits bits to its nearest upstream neighbor. In order to accommodate this flow of data, nodes must be configured into a physical ring. This configuration can be a simple ring or a star-wired ring.

A multistation access unit (MSAU) is a physical switching device that collapses the ring into a star-wired ring. When a node is powered off, the switch in the MSAU is closed, physically bypassing that connection. MSAUs can be connected together to enlarge the ring to form a distributed star-wired ring variation. Ring and star-wired ring topologies, as used with Token Ring LANs, are shown in Figure 2.3. Each MSAU has ring-in and ring-out (RI and RO) ports that are used to complete the ring between units. In connecting the ring-in of each unit to the ring-out of the other unit and vice versa, redundancy is established—only one cable is required to keep a ring established.

FIGURE 2.3.

Ring and star-wired ring topologies.

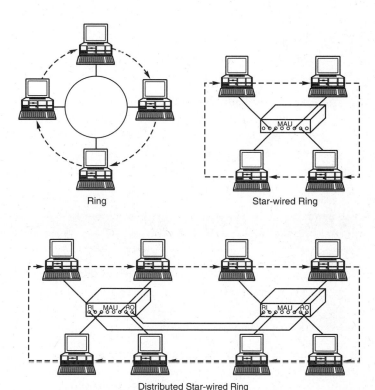

Ring   Star-wired Ring

Distributed Star-wired Ring

Fiber distributed data interface (FDDI) and copper distributed data interface (CDDI) LANs also use ring and star-wired ring topologies. FDDI specifications are formalized by American National Standards Institute (ANSI). CDDI (FDDI on copper wire) standards have not been adopted as of yet, but several vendors make products that use FDDI's access protocol over copper wire and have defined *de facto* standards.

Cabling (Media)

Media is divided into two categories: bounded and unbounded. Bounded media refers to cable, but LANs today can use such unbounded media as radio wave, laser, microwave, and infrared. IEEE standards only define cabling, but new products use unbounded media as cabling substitutes. Cabling is divided into three categories: coaxial, twisted-pair, and optical fiber.

Coaxial cable is the original LAN cable and consists of two conductors, an inner core and an outer shielding. Three basic types of coaxial cable are used for LANs and TV: 50, 75, and 93 ohm cable. You must be certain to use the correct one. Coaxial cable is very stable due to the configuration of the outer shielding conductor and inner core.

Twisted-pair cable comes in shielded and unshielded varieties of both voice- and data-grade levels. 10Base-T uses voice-grade level three unshielded twisted-pair cable, but it can also use level four or level five (data-grade shielded twisted-pair). Two or more twists per foot are required to eliminate excessive noise and to achieve the resonance that maintains the signal on the wire. Unshielded twisted-pair is easily affected by other electromagnetic sources.

CAUTION ▶

> Even if unshielded twisted-pair cabling conforms to specifications and appropriate distances are maintained, electrical characteristics may fall out of range due to electromagnetic and other sources of environmental interference. A cable tester should be used on an installed segment to see if the cable is suitable for LAN communications.

Fiber-optic cable comes in various sizes and carries light instead of electricity. This provides immunity from electromagnetic interference and extends the distance over which it can be used. It is also more secure the other kinds of cable, because data cannot be tapped by picking up electromagnetic fields generated by the flow of electricity on the cable. Thicker fiber-optic cable actually can reduce distances over which the cable segment may be used effectively due to the angle of light reflections within the cabling.

Cabling specifications are very important. Access protocols require very specific cabling characteristics to perform properly or to work at all. Cabling can be tested for five specific characteristics:

- Length
- Attenuation
- Near-end crosstalk
- Noise
- Loss

Cable characteristics are quite specific, and must fall within acceptable ranges for the type and length of cabling. "Better" cable may actually cause problems or not work at all, especially in CSMA/CD LANs where the access protocol is so dependent upon the electrical characteristics of the cabling.

IEEE Standards

IEEE's 802 committee has defined standards for most types of LANs. Much of the work that the 802 workgroup has done has enabled us to determine exactly how far we can run a specific type of cable for a specific type of LAN. As mentioned earlier, 802 workgroups were also instrumental in promoting interoperability between competing vendors' products.

The 802 model for LAN design is divided into three layers within which there are several sets of specifications, as follows:

Logical Link Control (LLC)

- Link addressing for LLC bridges
- Definition of service access points (SAPs)
- Management of the data link
- Error control
- Flow control
- Connection-oriented service

Medium Access Control (MAC)

- Access protocol
- Frame formatting
- Node addressing
- Error detection

Physical Layer

- Medium (cabling)
- Mechanical (connections)
- Electrical (encoding of signal)
- Topology
- Synchronization

Access protocols provide the foundation for IEEE standards. The IEEE 802 model, as illustrated in Figure 2.4, shows CSMA/CD and token-passing ring access protocols and their corresponding physical specifications. Physical layer standards refine how the access protocols can be implemented with various cabling, connections, and topological characteristics.

FIGURE 2.4.

The IEEE 802 Model.

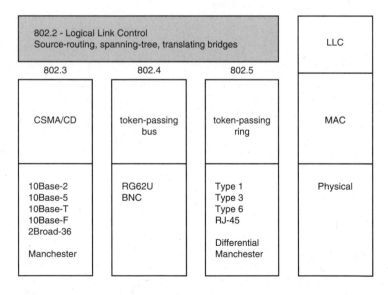

The primary 802 standards include:

- 802.2 Logical Link Control (LLC)
- 802.3 CSMA/CD Standards
- 802.4 Token-passing bus
- 802.5 Token-passing bus standards

802.3: CSMA/CD Standards

CSMA/CD is commonly referred to as "Ethernet," but this is actually a misnomer. Ethernet is a design primarily developed by Xerox that later evolved into Ethernet II at the hands of Digital, Intel, and Xerox. Ethernet II is only one set of physical and medium access control specifications under IEEE's 802.3 specifications. Ethernet II uses a slightly different frame format from 802.3 frame formatting. (Frame formatting is discussed in greater detail later in this chapter under the section "How Ethernet Works.")

802.3 standards include the options shown in Table 2.1.

Table 2.1. CSMA/CD choices.

10Base-2	Thin coaxial cable (thin-net or RG58U), internal transceivers and BNC connectors, linear bus topology running at 10 Mbps
10Base-5	Thick coaxial cable (Ethernet or thick-net), external transceivers and N-series connectors, linear bus topology running at 10 Mbps
10Base-T	Unshielded twisted-pair (voice or data grade, level 3-5) and RJ45 jacks, internal transceivers, star-bus topology wiring concentrator running at 10 Mbps
10Base-F	Optical fiber with ST or SE-type transducers, fiber optic repeater links (FIORL), star-bus topology running at 10 Mbps
2Broad-36	Broadband TV-coaxial cable with BNC connectors, tree topology broadband analog running at 2 Mbps

802.3 physical specifications also limit the number of cabling segments in sequence. Only four repeaters can be configured in series, with only five cabling segments from the near end to the farthest end. If five segments are in series, two must be unpopulated (no nodes attached to the cabling segment, only two repeaters). The standard enables up to 1,024 cabling segments, as long as no more than five segments are configured in series as discussed from any end to any other end of the LAN.

> **CAUTION** ▶
>
> LAN integrators must be careful not to violate the rule about serial cable segments. A distributed star bus configuration should be used instead of a hierarchical star bus to avoid violating this rule.

Because each cabling segment is electrically isolated from the others, the use of a wiring concentrator that configures parallel segments provides more stability than a normal coaxial linear bus topology. 10Base-T requires wiring concentrators and only one node per (unpopulated) cabling segment. If concentrators are linked together parallel to one another (that is, with a linear bus cable segment), you never need to be concerned about the serial segment rule.

Ethernet LANs use Manchester digital encoding, which requires two signal transitions per bit.

802.4: Token-Passing Bus

Token-passing bus access protocol standards were developed for General Motors' manufacturing automation protocol (MAP). Both MAP and Attached Resource Computing Network (ARCnet) use a very similar access protocol. 802.4 specifications do not cover ARCnet, as commonly believed. ARCnet is a proprietary trademark of Datapoint and shares the very same cabling rules. Token-passing bus access protocol description does apply to both, though proprietary differences eliminate the possibility of interoperability between MAP and ARCnet. Because MAP is no longer used by General Motors, and was never used elsewhere, any discussion of 802.4 standards is purely academic.

802.5: Token-Passing Ring

Token-passing ring standards only apply to Token Ring. This access protocol, originally invented by Olaf Soderblum of the Netherlands, was developed into standardized products by IBM. In a bid for open standardization, IBM published the standards, and they were formalized by IEEE in the 802.5 specifications.

These standards specify a 1 Mbps token-passing ring on coaxial cable, 4 Mbps on unshielded twisted-pair cable, or 16 Mbps on shielded twisted-pair cable. Several types of twisted-pair cable are mentioned in the specifications, but new standards are under consideration to allow voice-grade level 3 (same as 10Base-T) twisted-pair cable to be used with 16 Mbps. This proposal has been submitted to IEEE by IBM and Synoptics. It would require a special type of multistation access unit (MSAU) that re-times the signal.

802.5 cable specifications are more complex than 802.3 rules (which are not simple either). 802.5 uses matrices to specify cable lengths based on the type of cable being used and the number of nodes and MSAUs.

802.2: Logical Link Control (LLC)

LLC defines protocols and frame formats for bridging among LANs of the same or dissimilar types. This is accomplished through the designation of service access points and an additional few fields added to the end of the frame header.

LLC bridges use spanning-tree or source-routing protocols defined by IEEE. Spanning-tree protocol designates a specific path for frames to take if multiple bridges are present between physical Ethernet LANs. Source-routing provides a method for nodes to find and determine frame paths to be taken between multiple physical Token Ring LANs. A translating bridge can move frames of data from one type of LAN to another. These functions are accomplished by designating the entry point bridge as the source service access point (SSAP) and the exit point as the destination service access point (DSAP).

MAC-Layer Bridges

MAC-layer bridges, sometimes called transparent bridges or learning bridges, connect physical LANs into a single logical LAN by filtering or forwarding frames based on their destination addresses. Unlike LLC bridges, this type of bridge requires no LLC header fields. The only requirement is that the frame format used on both physical LANs must be the same. MAC-layer bridges do not work properly when multiple paths exist or when a network of bridges connect multiple physical LANs.

How Ethernet Works

Ethernet is a 10 Mbps bus LAN that uses CSMA/CD access protocol. Cabling standards include two types of coaxial: unshielded twisted-pair and fiber-optic.

CSMA/CD is a contention access protocol, meaning that only one frame can be transmitted at a time, and each node is in contention for access to the media. Access is controlled by the transceiver connected to each NIC. The transceiver enables frames to be sent when the cable is free. When other communications are detected, the transceiver does not enable the NIC to send data. If any other bits are detected on the cable during the first portion of frame transmission, a collision is detected. Under these conditions the transceiver aborts the frame transmission, waits a random amount of time (to avoid a subsequent collision) and attempts to resend data if the cable is clear.

CAUTION ▷

CSMA/CD access protocol relies heavily on using the proper cable at the proper distance. Improper or defective cabling causes undetected and/or false collisions that affect performance at high levels of network utilization. LAN integrators are cautioned to heed cabling rules for Ethernet LANs.

CSMA/CD provides immediate access to the media as long as it is not busy. One concern is that a busy node can dominate the LAN to the detriment of other nodes. The transceiver therefore implements *jabber control*, which is effective in preventing domination of the network by one node. After each frame (or 150 ms), the transceiver interrupts any transmission coming from its NIC, thereby giving another node an opportunity to take control of the medium.

Frame formatting as shown in Figure 2.5, combined with the access protocol, determines which node accepts the data frame. The frame header contains node addressing, which is controlled by IEEE standards. IEEE issues a manufacturer number which becomes part of the serial number of the NIC. Each NIC, therefore, has a unique *universal node address*. Alternatively, an NIC driver can be configured to use an assigned *local address*. The trailer contains a cyclic redundancy check (CRC). Unfortunately, unless some type of monitoring software is used, bad CRCs are not detected.

FIGURE 2.5.

An 802.3 frame format.

802.3 frame format

Preamble	start of fr del	destination address	source address	Length	data	pad	crc
7 bytes	1	6 bytes	6 bytes	2 bytes	1501 bytes		4 bytes

NOTE ▶

Ethernet II frame formatting, which is used by Digital, Hewlett Packard, Sun Microsystems, and many other developers, varies from standard 802.3 frame formatting and must not be mixed with NICs generating other frame formats. Two other frame formats exist for a total of four different frame formats used with Ethernet. Drivers can normally be configured for any of these frame formats, but they must be used consistently among all nodes that need to communicate with one another. NetWare 3.x and 4.x servers can support multiple frame formats at one time.

CSMA/CD is a simple and effective access protocol that is widely supported, performs very well, and is simple to understand. Every Ethernet integrator should understand how vital conforming to cabling rules is. Many integrators insist that TV coaxial cable can be used or that a cable is good if continuity is confirmed. Nothing can be further from the truth. Under normal conditions, CSMA/CD will work regardless of how poor the cabling plant is; however, under heavy network utilization, false collisions affect all active nodes, resulting in lower capacity.

How Token-Passing Ring Works

Token-passing ring is a 4- or 16-Mbps deterministic access protocol where access to the media is controlled by the possession of a free token. Deterministic means that control of the ring is determined in an orderly manner. Token Ring standards enable the use of several types of shielded and unshielded twisted-pair cabling. It is a ring LAN, and normally it is configured as a star-ring, whereas a physical ring is configured by an MSAU.

A token is one of the three types of frames circulated around the ring, as illustrated in Figure 2.6. The access control field simply indicates that this frame is a free token. The token is generated by the *active monitor*, which is normally the first node powered on to the ring. The token, like any frame, is physically circulated around the ring.

FIGURE 2.6.

An 802.5 token frame.

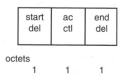

start del	ac ctl	end del

octets

1   1   1

Once a free token is received, a node can send a data frame. If the node does not need to send data, it relays the token to its nearest upstream neighbor. If data is to be sent, the data frame is copied, put on the media, and sent to the nearest upstream neighbor. A data frame is shown in Figure 2.7. When a token is captured, the node has a prescribed amount of time to send data. Multiple data frames can be sent in one time segment as time permits. As the ring becomes more heavily saturated, the amount of time allocated to each node is reduced, while the total time for a trip around the ring remains constant.

FIGURE 2.7.

A Token Ring data frame.

start del	ac ctl	fr chk	destination address	source address	data	fr chk seq	end del	fr stat

octets

| 1 | 1 | 1 | 6 | 6 | 1-17,946 (16 Mbps) 1-4,442 (4 Mbps) | 4 | 1 | 1 |

Each node receives the frame, examines the destination address field for a match with its own node address, and forwards it to its nearest upstream neighbor if the destination address does not match. When the data frame reaches the destination node, the receiving node copies the frame to its buffers, changes a bit in the trailer indicating that it has been received, and forwards the intact data frame to its nearest upstream neighbor.

At the end of one full trip around the ring, the data frame reaches its source node, where the frame is examined for receipt and accuracy, then purged from the ring. If all was in order, the free token is released. (This applies to a 4-Mbps Token Ring; in a 16-Mbps Token Ring, the free token is released immediately after the data frame.)

Each node along the ring can change a bit in the trailer, which signals an error condition, such as a persistently busy token. When a node sends data and never receives it's frame back, it initiates a *beaconing* process, wherein a third type of frame is dispatched. A beaconing node causes its nearest upstream neighbor to also beacon. If a node does not receive its own beacon within the time allotted for a trip around the ring, it concludes it is not communicating with the rest of the ring. If this condition exists, the node closes its bypass switch, taking itself out of the ring. Other beacons bypass the offending node, arriving at the source thereby indicating that all is well. This procedure resolves problems that occur from a defective NIC.

Token Ring also uses a priority scheme to establish priority reservations for subsequent use of free tokens. Three bits in the access control field establish a priority level. If the priority level in a frame is higher than the priority level in a free token, then the frame can be sent. By establishing a new priority level as a frame passes, nodes can establish reservation levels that require an equal or higher priority for using the free token. This ensures that excessive latency will not occur when network utilization reaches higher levels.

A form of error control is conducted by the active monitor. Each frame is timed and is expected to make its trip around the ring within a prescribed amount of time. If it does not, the active monitor assumes the frame was lost, purges the ring, and issues a new token. Passive monitors keep track of the active monitor. If it is removed from the ring, one of the passive monitors issues a type of frame that initiates a contention-resolution procedure, causing a claim token to be captured by another node awarding it the status of active monitor. The active monitor then issues a new free token, and the ring is reinitialized.

A token-passing ring obviously has more error-detection and resolution than CSMA/CD and relies far less on cabling for its stability. It therefore performs more consistently under load and can diagnose and eliminate faulty nodes. It was previously thought that the overhead associated with the access protocol limited its performance, but recent testing indicates that access protocol overhead consumes less than three percent of bandwidth.

FDDI and CDDI

FDDI is a standard of ANSI's Accredited Standards Committee (ASC). The ASC X3T9.5 standards are about 95 percent in place, having defined the access protocol and physical specifications. Management standards are still being drafted, and copper-wire extensions to the standards are under consideration. ANSI has representation on the International Standards Organization (ISO) and takes IEEE standards to the international level. (IEEE is a U.S. trade association.) For these standards, both groups agreed to cut out the middleman and simply allow ANSI to draft the standards.

FDDI uses a basic token-passing ring access protcol with the following key additional access protocol modifications:

- Capacity allocation scheme
- Fault management
- 4B/5B encoding
- Dual attachment of nodes
- Physical medium dependent (PMD) sublayer

Capacity Allocation Scheme

Instead of using the priority reservation system used in Token Ring, FDDI uses a capacity-allocation scheme to enable a mix of stream and burst transmissions. This is more effective for client-server applications where two-station dialogues are the rule. Synchronous and asynchronous frame types are defined. When a two-station dialog is established by normal synchronous frames, additional frames in a series can be transmitted asynchronously, even though the node's time allocation has expired. Because the token must complete its trip around the ring within a given amount of time, and because some nodes may not have used their time allocations, the free time is granted for asynchronous transmissions.

Fault Management

Instead of using an active monitor to monitor the ring, FDDI enables all nodes to monitor the ring. A different claim token initialization procedure is used that is more efficient and more stable.

4B/5B Encoding

4B/5B provides synchronization and is more efficient than either differential Manchester or Manchester encoding. While Manchester encoding requires two signal transitions per bit, and differential Manchester requires three signal transitions per bit, 4B/5B requires five signal transitions for each four bits. The signaling rate for 10-Mbps Ethernet is actually 20 million transitions per second, and for 16-Mbps Token Ring, it is 48 million transitions per second. However, the signaling rate for 100-Mbps FDDI is only 125 transitions per second. This is more effective because the bandwidth of the cable is used more efficiently. 4B/5B does not sacrifice accuracy, either; the fifth signal transition provides all the synchronization necessary to keep the signaling phase aligned.

Dual Attachment of Nodes

Nodes are categorized as Class A and Class B nodes. FDDI requires a dual counter-rotating ring. Class A stations are dual attached (that is, attached to both rings). This requires two chipsets on each Class A station NIC. Class B stations are single attached to the primary ring. In the event of a link failure between two Class A nodes on a ring, the dual attached node on each side of the fault closes a circuit between the two rings, configuring a third ring as shown in Figure 2.8.

This essentially doubles the cost of a Class A NIC, but it adds far more reliability to a ring topology. It is impractical to attach nodes to a wiring concentrator when such long distances are involved, and to extend the farthest reaches of the ring, nodes may need to be strung in a series. Dual attachment enables great distances in the overall length of the ring. The standard enables up to two kilometers between nodes, and up to 200 kilometers overall length. Up to 1000 physical attachments are allowed, combining both single and dual attached nodes. Single attached nodes should be connected to wiring concentrators.

FIGURE 2.8.

Dual attached nodes healing an FDDI ring.

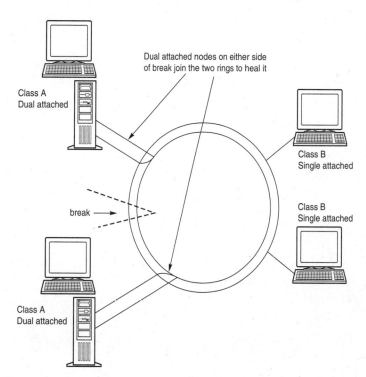

Physical Medium Dependent (PMD) Sublayer

ANSI divides the traditional 802 standards for the physical layer into two sublayers, the physical layer protocol (PHY), and the physical medium dependent (PMD). PHY interfaces with the MAC layer and provides data encoding and synchronization. PMD provides transport of bits that are specific to cabling, connectors and other electromechanical devices in use. This provides independence of the two functions and relies less heavily on physical devices for stability.

Copper Distributed Data Interface (CDDI)

FDDI standards currently only define fiber-optic media and devices. However, due to the separate PMD layer, NICs have been developed to run on shielded and unshielded twisted-pair. Two industry groups, have proposed copper wire extensions to the standard. One group lead by Synoptics, has proposed unshielded twisted-pair specifications; another group, lead by Ungermann-Bass, has proposed shielded twisted-pair specifications. These proposals have not been drafted, however products conforming to these proposals are already on the market, and a *de facto* standard called CDDI has been established. Many reputable vendors, including IBM, already produce CDDI products.

CDDI is far less expensive than FDDI. The cost of fiber-optic transducers, optical bypasses, and repeating devices drives up the cost of FDDI significantly. Dual attachment also drives up the cost. Almost all costs are doubled for a Class A node: there are double chip sets, double optical devices, and double token-passing ring royalties. Because the royalty is based on the manufacturer's selling price, the royalty for FDDI is much higher as a direct ratio to cost.

Current pricing on FDDI/CDDI NICs have fallen to about $3,000 per Class A NIC and under $2,000 per Class B NIC. Cable installation, wiring concentrators, and repeaters are also very costly. When (and if) royalties are eliminated and CDDI standards are adopted, this technology can be priced within reach of workstation nodes. Until then, FDDI/CDDI is almost exclusively used for backbone LANs and specific applications having large bandwidth requirements that are not cost sensitive. Where additional bandwidth, security, resistance to interference, or distance requirements are required, FDDI is the best choice.

ARCnet and Thomas-Conrad Network System (TCNS)

ARCnet is a more elaborate combination of a broadcast type of bus network and token-passing. Like Ethernet, ARCnet is a bus network where every bit is broadcasted over all segments to all nodes. However, like Token Ring, a token controls access to the media. ARCnet is proprietary—Datapoint holds the patents. TCNS is the very same access protocol, but very minor changes and patents make it a derivative of ARCnet.

ARCnet configures a *logical ring* instead of a physical ring as used with Token Ring. When the LAN is initialized, each node broadcasts its node address (which is set with switches instead of being assigned a universal address). Each node keeps a table identifying itself (source ID) and the next higher numbered node (next ID). The token is therefore broadcasted from the SID to the NID and is in turn relayed from that node's SID to NID. When the highest numbered node forwards the token, it goes to the lowest numbered node to start its trip around the logical ring.

When a node has the token, it can send a series of data frames. Data frames are addressed directly to the destination node and do not need to travel around the logical ring. Before transmitting a series of frames, however, the SID sends a free buffer enquiry (FBE) and expects a reply in the form of an acknowledgment (that is, buffers are free, data can be received), or a negative acknowledgment (buffers full, try again later). An acknowledgment allows the data frames to be sent, and a negative acknowledgment causes the token to be passed and data to be held in the NIC buffers until another turn comes up. Because of the FBE, ARCnet access protocol is called *implicit token-passing bus,* as opposed to 802.4's token-passing bus access protocol.

ARCnet is quite inexpensive, the royalty is not very high, and Standard Microsystems Corporation (SMC) produces and sells VLSI chips to other ARCnet vendors for as low as $10 per chip. Many brands of ARCnet NICs have been produced for as little as $100 retail per NIC. ARCnet is quite stable, enables very long cabling distances, and has no complexity to its cabling rules. Separate NICs are made for linear bus or star bus topologies. Both can be used in one LAN, but each segment must be used for one type or the other, not mixed. You are not limited in the number of repeaters in series, so configuration is simple, flexible, and stable.

ARCnet bandwidth is limited to 2.5 Mbps. Datapoint has developed 20-Mbps ARCnet, but the industry has already passed judgment on it. Thomas-Conrad's 100-Mbps TCNS has already eclipsed the 20-Mbps product, and both Thomas-Conrad and SMC, who are the two major purveyors of ARCnet, have put their efforts into marketing Ethernet and Token Ring products. It looks like ARCnet is fading very quickly. In 1991, ARCnet held 10.4 percent of the LAN market, but its market share shrunk by more than 30 percent in 1992 and is eroding even more rapidly.

Novell pushed ARCnet integration very hard. It produced RX-Net NICs, which used an SMC chip. Novell promoted ARCnet because it was inexpensive, stable and easy to install. In a small network, the limited bandwidth is not noticeable, and at low utilization its response is as good as Ethernet's. Novell's promotion of their own brands of ARCnet and Ethernet NICs pushed prices down and made network integration simpler. Novell no longer produces any NICs. It has completely dropped the RX-Net NIC, and the Novell Ethernet NICs are produced and marketed by Eagle Technologies.

Fast Ethernet and 100BASE-VG

Many Ethernet vendors, led by Grand Junction Networks, have proposed a Fast Ethernet standard retaining CSMA/CD access protocol and boosting the bandwidth on existing cabling to 100 Mbps. Under Manchester encoding, however, the signaling rate is increased to 200 million signal transitions per second.

To accommodate this signaling rate, level five twisted-pair or coaxial cable is required. Because CSMA/CD access protocol is so heavily dependent upon cabling for its collision detection, some vendors are concerned that Fast Ethernet is not a conservative enough approach. Though standards have been proposed to IEEE's 802 workgroup, the committee is taking a very cautious approach to these standards. One major concern is that normal 10BASE-T level three or level four twisted-pair will need to be replaced for upgrades. IEEE has decided that the 802.3 workgroup will draft the new standards.

An alternative product, called 100BASE-VG, has been proposed to IEEE by a group lead by AT&T and Hewlett Packard. 100BASE-VG divides the physical layer in much the same way FDDI does. This enables abandonment of CSMA/CD access protocol in favor of more sophisticated physical-medium-based technology and Demand Access Protocol.

Demand Access Protocol requires acknoledgement from a switching hub before transmitting a frame. Each cabling segment can send and/or receive data independantly of other cabling segments, thereby increasing the number of frames on the LAN at any given time. Demand Access Protocol reduces collisions, and improves traffic flow, making even better use of available bandwidth.

100BASE-VG uses normal 10BASE-T cabling standards, including level three and four twisted-pair, so no cable replacement is necessary for upgrades. In order to retain the use of level 3 cabling, 100BASE-VG uses Quartet Signalling. In this system, all four wire pairs are used, each one carrying 25 Mbps for a total of 100 Mbps. Signaling rate on each pair is therefore limited to 50 million signal transitions per second instead of 200 million. This is more stable and prudent. IEEE has decided to form a new workgroup to draft the standards.

Both Fast Ethernet and 100BASE-VG are inexpensive public-domain *de facto* standards that provide high bandwidth and low cost using common cabling. Their close alignment with traditional Ethernet makes either proposal a sure-fire winner at the retail level. Without IEEE sanction, however, consumer confidence is quite limited. Most firms depend heavily on formally standardized products to ensure future compatibility and to protect their investments.

LAN Performance Characteristics and Comparisons

LAN performance is very poorly understood at this time. LAN technology has moved ahead very rapidly, Token Ring having appeared in 1985, FDDI and TCNS in 1990, and Fast Ethernet/100BASE-VG in 1992.

Benchmark Testing

The most perplexing issue of LAN performance is the question of how it is measured. Traditionally, benchmark tests have focused on the maximum capacity of NICs running under NetWare. More recent reviews have also taken into consideration the amount of CPU utilization the server NIC consumes. Both of these considerations are important; however, most LAN traffic occurs in the very low end of network bandwidth utilization.

Network traffic tends to be "bursty" in nature, with general traffic occurring at very low levels of utilization. Typical traffic on a 10-Mbps Ethernet LAN supporting 50 to 100 users will consume less than five percent of bandwidth the vast majority of the time, but it may have spikes of up to 70-90 percent utilization for very brief moments. Because an Ethernet LAN can transfer about one megabyte of data in a second, sustained heavy loads are not realistic measures of normal performance (although testing under such conditions gives us an indication of how good the performance may be during those brief episodes.) Most benchmark tests do not tell us how good performance might be under usual conditions, when network utilization is at 5 percent or less.

Latency is a more important measure during those low utilization periods. Latency is the delay that is encountered in sending a request. Latency is the result of several mechanical factors, including access protocol delay in accessing the media, delay in copying frames on or off the media, copying packets from the buffers to workstation or server RAM, and any number of other firmware or driver-software delays in processing frames and packets of data.

Most of the commonly used benchmark tests only assess maximum capacity. Both Novell and IBM have been working on new benchmark tests that evaluate performance under real-world software operating conditions. The most prevalent benchmark tests currently used include:

- PERFORM3 (Novell copyrighted product available from Novell at no cost)
- PERFORM2 (Novell copyrighted product available from Novell at no cost)
- TESTNET (public domain, included on disk with this book)
- PC Magazine LAN Testing Benchmark (available at no cost from Ziff-Davis Labs)

PERFORM3 is a product that tests multiple workstations with incremental file save sizes. A PERFORM3 test runs for a prescribed amount of time on all participating workstations. This provides capacity testing at various packet/request sizes. Because the spread of packet sizes in a network can vary tremendously under different operating conditions, it is unrealistic to test capacity at one large request size only. This product adequately addresses the issue of testing at various request sizes, but still only tests maximum capacity. The issue of latency is partially addressed in PERFORM3's ability to test smaller packet/request sizes. Smaller request sizes are affected by latency. Few testers who have addressed this issue, however, include smaller request sizes in their benchmark results. This testing program is ideally suited for testing a server NIC for maximum capacity at various request sizes.

PERFORM2 is another Novell product that tests single or multiple workstations at once. It runs each workstation test for a configured number of iterations. However, it gives an unrealistic picture of overall network performance because some workstations complete the test before others, skewing aggregate performance statistics. Various request sizes can be tested, and tests can be configured as read or write tests and in overlaid or sequential fashion, which provides a wide variety of test circumstances. This product is better suited for testing workstation NICs one at a time.

TESTNET by Scott Taylor is similar to PERFORM2, but enables more latitude in configuring tests; plus, it is housed in a more colorful and friendly user interface. It is also better suited for testing workstation NIC capacity under varying circumstances.

PC Magazine LAN Testing Benchmark (Ziff-Davis Labs) is a test of maximum capacity at various request sizes. It works in a similar fashion to PERFORM3. It reports test results in Mbps. The other products listed report test results in kilobytes per second. The results of this benchmark should not be compared with results from other benchmarks. For some mechanical reason, it reports lower performance at higher levels of utilization than PERFORM3. It is simpler to learn and provides a greater variety of test suites.

Evaluating Benchmarks

Most test results report data from PERFORM3. Ziff-Davis Publications, including *PC Magazine* and *PC Week*, uses the PC Magazine LAN Testing Benchmark.

When reading benchmark tests, however, keep in mind that most reviews are only showing maximum capacities under various circumstances. Rarely would your real-world circumstances be similar to the benchmarks. Therefore, the benchmarks are only appropriate for gauging the horsepower of the NICs being evaluated.

CPU Utilization

In evaluating a LAN, another important factor to consider is how high your server's CPU utilization climbs. When more than one NIC is used in a server, or when server-based applications use much of your server's processing power, this may become a substantial issue.

To evaluate whether this is a problem for you, you can watch your server's MONI-TOR for CPU utilization statistics. If it never climbs above 90 percent, this is not a major consideration. However, it may surge above that level very briefly, and you may not notice. To assess that possibility, Novell provides a server-based application, STAT.NLM, which you can install on your server to monitor CPU utilization over a period of time. STAT.NLM is provided on the disk that accompanies this book. (CPU saturation will be addressed more fully in Chapter 23, "Novell Products for LAN Monitoring.")

General Comparisons of LAN Types

A few good reviews have been done on Ethernet, Token Ring and 100 Mbps technologies. *PC Magazine*'s October 13, 1992, issue contained a good review of Token Ring NICs. *PC Magazine*'s February 9, 1993, edition evaluated 45 Ethernet NICs. *LAN Times*' March 22, 1993, issue had an excellent review of many Ethernet NICs, and *PC Week*'s March 15, 1993, issue had a special report on 100-Mbps LANs. These reviews contained much data about more recent testing of many LAN types. The conclusions discussed in this section are drawn from those reviews.

Ethernet Performance Characteristics

Ethernet performs as well as any other LAN type at low levels of utilization. This is because its latency is very low. CSMA/CD access protocol is contention-oriented, and when there is no contention for access to the medium, access is immediate. Therefore latency is mostly an issue of NIC and driver efficiency, or high network bandwidth utilization. The first issue has been addressed by every vendor that makes Ethernet NICs and drivers. Almost all brands perform well. Though there may be some variations in latency among brands, the variance among brands is slight. Variations generally shows up in small-request-size tests.

Capacities at high levels of utilization vary widely, depending upon NIC and driver design. A more pressing issue, however, is the quality of your cable plant. CSMA/CD protocol depends upon cable and topology configuration characteristics to detect collisions. Therefore, cabling imperfections can reduce top capacity by increasing the number of false and undetected collisions. In most cases, network utilization limits capacity to 70 percent or so of total available bandwidth (10 Mbps), while tests that are run under perfect cabling conditions can produce 90 percent utilization with the very same NICs, server, and workstations.

Another problem with Ethernet is the lack of error trapping. The access protocol provides no mechanism for detecting or reporting bad cyclic redundancy checks, high collision rates, or lost frames due to many conditions. Ethernet is normally quite reliable, but with many common cabling problems, such as reflections from frayed connectors, kinks in cables, or defective devices, false collisions or lost data can result.

Splitting users up onto separate physical LANs can usually resolve capacity problems. Because the NetWare server OS has an internal router, interfacing multiple physical LANs is practically as simple as installing multiple NICs in your server. If you take this route, be certain to watch your CPU utilization. See Chapter 23 for a complete discussion of this topic.

In the final analysis, 10-Mbps Ethernet LANs perform as well as any other LAN type, as long as periods of high network utilization do not restrict performance. Normally, this limitation is resolved with multiple NICs in the server or moving to a more powerful LAN, such as 16-Mbps Token Ring or a 100-Mbps LAN.

Several factors make Ethernet the most popular LAN on the market. One major factor is its wide acceptance among computer developers. Ethernet is integrated into just about every multiuser computer system, including IBM mainframe SNA networks. The industry is in love with Ethernet, and even if it were bad, many vendors are now so biased, it could probably never die.

Token Ring

Token Ring has almost twice the usable capacity of Ethernet. Most Ethernet tests show about 90 percent of the usable bandwidth available under load (due to collisions) for about 1.1 megabyte-per-second throughput. 16-Mbps Token Ring, however, has demonstrated up to 97 percent utilization for capacities as high as 1.95 Mbyte/sec. Token Ring has less reliance on cable conditions, and the access protocol has provisions for detecting many types of error conditions, and provides a mechanism for reporting these conditions and recovering from them.

Token Ring, however, is more expensive than Ethernet at about $300 per workstation (counting the cost of the NIC and MSAU). Most of this cost is due to the royalty paid on the patents. The validity of the patents is being contested in U.S. federal appellate courts at this time. Eventually, the patents will expire anyway, and Token Ring prices will fall.

Two issues inhibit clear understanding of Token Ring performance. First, recent NIC design improvements have revolutionized Token Ring performance characteristics. Second, few reviews have adequately addressed Token Ring performance under favorable conditions.

Madge Networks and IBM have reduced latency issues by using busmastering capabilities of EISA and MCA design. Token Ring performance suffered noticeably greater latency at low levels of network utilization. Many new Token Ring NICs now perform as well at low levels of utilization as Ethernet NICs.

Reviews have presented Token Ring in a very unfavorable light. Token Ring capacity actually grows as the ring grows—more nodes (and therefore more repeaters) and more cable length increases the capacity of the LAN to hold more bits (and therefore more tokens). This is true of a new feature, early release of the token, that was added with the 16-Mbps Token Ring. When a frame of data is transmitted, a free token is released immediately behind the data frame(s). This provides two to four free tokens on the cabling at the same time, depending upon the size of the ring. Because the 16-Mbps Token Ring was not perfected until 1992 (in other-than-IBM products), testing has not kept pace with development.

Most Token Ring reviews (of which few are available) benchmark three to six workstations with a server. Token Ring has proven to achieve full capacity at 12 nodes. With all due respect to testers, because Ethernet can be saturated with six nodes, it seems reasonable to test the same number of nodes with Token Ring. The *PC Magazine* survey in October 1992 used only three nodes per server, thereby measuring only a portion of Token Ring performance.

Between the incomplete testing and the relative newness of the technical improvements, the full story of Token Ring has not yet been told. Token Ring is growing faster than Ethernet. Many integrators have flocked to Token Ring due to either its superiority of design or its demonstrated superiority of performance. The industry will see increasing utilization of Token Ring as this more stable, dependable technology becomes better understood and less expensive.

Because Token Ring capacity is almost twice that of Ethernet, it is recommended for accommodating more nodes on a single physical LAN or for applications that demand bursts of higher bandwidth, such as CAD/CAM, desktop publishing, and heavy printing activity.

One factor limits Token Ring even more than its price. Fewer multiuser computer developers integrate Token Ring when compared with Ethernet. Though Token-Ring-to-Ethernet translating bridges are available, direct support for Token Ring is not available in many minicomputer or mainframe vendors today.

ARCnet

Though ARCnet is fading in popularity, it is still a viable solution for small networks. Its bandwidth limits total capacity to about 300 Kbyte/sec, or less than one third that of Ethernet. Its low-end response, however, is equally as good or better than that of any other type of LAN. Therefore, when light traffic from a few nodes is present, users do not notice any difference from any other type of LAN. Just a few nodes, however, can experience moments of delay due to the saturation of the bandwidth.

One of the reasons that ARCnet has such low latency is the small frame size. With NetWare, Ethernet uses a 1024-byte packet size, and Token Ring uses a 4096-byte packet size (larger packet sizes are supported with 4.0), whereas ARCnet uses a 508-byte packet size at the frame level and up to a 4096-packet size at the packet level (Novell's Turbo RX-Net driver). Single IPX packets are broken into fragments and transported in 508-byte frame data segments. This gives better response for small packets and less latency in access to the medium.

TCNS

TCNS is currently the least expensive of 100-Mbps technologies. Last year, according to research by International Data Corporation and company sales statistics, Thomas-Conrad sold more than twice as many TCNS nodes than all brands of FDDI combined. TCNS cabling is quite simple, basically the same as normal ARCnet cabling with shorter distances. Coaxial, twisted-pair and fiber-optic NICs are available, at prices ranging from $725 to $1000 retail. Active hubs (wiring concentrators) for TCNS are also far less expensive than competing 100-Mbps wiring concentrators.

TCNS, like ARCnet, has excellent response at low levels of utilization and small request sizes, due to the coupling of the small frame size and the large packet size (as per the preceding discussion of ARCnet). Its high-end capacity is currently limited by the quality of busmastering in its NICs. A TCNS server NIC is normally limited by the server's CPU utilization. When T-C develops a busmastering server NIC as good as their Token Ring models, more capacity will be released. A single TCNS server NIC can accommodate about four times the traffic of a single Ethernet NIC.

Fast Ethernet and 100BASE-VG

To date, few products have been based on these designs; however, *PC Week*'s special report on 100-Mbps LANs compared one brand of 100Base-VG NIC with TCNS and an FDDI NIC. The high bandwidth capacity was very impressive and its cost was quite low.

At the low end of network utilization, Ethernet and Fast Ethernet apparently perform the same; but at the high end, Fast Ethernet increases capacity by a factor of nine. Its price is low, especially for a new product, starting at $595 to $995 retail. However, its limited availability and undetermined compatibility in the future are factors that ought to be considered.

FDDI/CDDI

FDDI NICs also were tested in *PC Week*'s special report. The performance level was about the same as Fast Ethernet: absolutely amazing. No testing has ever focused on its latency or response time, but it is assumed to be equal to or greater than Token Ring's, because improvements to the access protocol theoretically improve this characteristic.

Cabling choices include unshielded and shielded twisted-pair and fiber optics. Fiber-optic dual attached NICs (Class A) are very expensive, retailing from $2,700 to $3,995. Twisted-pair single attached NICs (apparently, twisted-pair can only be used on Class B nodes) start at $1,150. Wiring concentrators, however, are extremely expensive. At this time, the cost of an FDDI/CDDI LAN can be exorbitant.

Many vendors jumped on the FDDI bandwagon very early, and Infonetics Research projected 1993 sales of $1.3 billion for this product category. However, acceptance has been very disappointing. According to International Data Corporation estimates, the entire industry sold only 6,000 units in 1992.

Selecting the Right LAN

Table 2.2 has been compiled to compare the pros and cons of each type of LAN. Scores have been assigned on a scale of 1 through 5, with 5 being the highest score and 1 being the lowest. Each factor also has a multiplier based on its relative importance.

In an evaluation of your own, you would assign weight according to which factors were most important and eliminate those factors that have no bearing on your particular needs. For example, in a backbone LAN, cost may not be as important a selection criterion as performance.

Table 2.2. Weighted scoring for selection of a LAN type.

Factor to Consider (with multiplier)	Ethernet Ring	Token	TCNS	Arcnet	Fast Ethernet	FDDI /CDDI	100 BASE-VG
Performance (available bandwidth) (10)	2	3	4	1	5	5	5
Latency (10)	5	4	5	5	5	5	5
Stability (10)	3	5	5	5	2	5	5
Acceptance among vendors (5)	5	4	2	3	5*	4	4*
Availability of products (5)	5	4	2	2	2*	5	2*
Cabling choices (8)	5	4	4	3	4	3	5
Error Control/ reporting (8)	1	5	4	4	1	5	2*
Cost (7)	5	4	5	5	5	1	5
Weighted Score	233	260	259	226	230	266	271

* = information not available at this time

Advanced NetWare Operating System Features

3

by Rick Sant'Angelo

IN THIS CHAPTER

Although you may be quite familiar with NetWare, this chapter will fill you in on some subtle yet important details that even the most advanced integrators may not know. Understanding the mechanics of the NetWare system will assist you in many ways.

This chapter discusses what is in your "red box." Topics include

- The NetWare server operating system
- NetWare workstation software
- NetWare's server file system
- System fault tolerant features of NetWare
- NetWare's internal router
- NetWare Directory Services and other features of 4.x

The NetWare File Server Operating System

Unlike network operating systems that run on top of another OS, the file server portion of NetWare is both a server OS and a networking software. Microsoft LAN Manager and IBM LAN Server run on top of OS/2, and Banyan VINES runs on top of UNIX. The integration of networking functions and OS functions into a single OS makes NetWare more efficient than these other packages. A few of the unique features the NetWare OS has that other OSs do not have include

- Multitasking and multiuser design
- Dynamic allocation of resources
- Nonpreemptive processing

Multitasking and Multiuser

A good server OS must be able to multitask to provide a high level of multiuser functionality. Though OS/2 and UNIX are good multitasking OSs, they lack networking functions. NetWare, however, is specifically designed for multiuser capabilities. It was not designed as a workstation system, such as OS/2, or as a centralized CPU OS, such as UNIX. A file server provides I/O for user requests, and NetWare is perfectly suited to this task. It also serves as a platform for server-based applications. This OS is designed exclusively to be a server OS.

Auto-Tuning (Dynamic Allocation of Resources)

One of the most impressive features of NetWare 3.x and 4.x server operating systems is how they dynamically tune themselves during usage for best performance at all times. The OS monitors itself, constantly adjusting and reallocating resources as necessary to provide the best performance with the lowest overhead under widely varying conditions.

With other networking software packages, the integrator or administrator must adjust OS parameters and networking software to levels that are sufficient for specific operating conditions. The configuration levels allocate resources that are sometimes under-utilized, but they must be set at levels that are high enough to provide dependable service under maximum use conditions. Configuration levels can never be set as efficiently as desired under the widely fluctuating demands of a large network, nor is it simple to learn how to adjust server OSs to levels that are suitable for small networks.

A NetWare 3.x or 4.x OS serves small and large networks alike with equal efficiency and performance and without the intervention of an administrator. NetWare is therefore the simplest NOS to use and requires far less training for dependable, optimized operation and continued serviceability.

Nonpreemptive Processing

Although UNIX, Microsoft LAN Manager, and NT use preemptive processing, NetWare executes and controls multiple tasks (called *threads*) in a nonpreemptive mode. In a preemptive environment, each process running on the server is time-sliced and executed simultaneously—each one in a protected mode. NetWare's OS scheduler schedules each process in the most favored ring of the processor (ring 0), where there is no protection. Each process therefore cannot be preempted by any other process; it can run uninterrupted and with full processor power until finished. Each process realizes greater processing power and requires less processor utilization to control and monitor the activities of several processes at one time.

NetWare's nonpreemptive processing is executed sequentially by running each task, including the task scheduler, in ring 0. Intel 80286 and higher processors execute threads in one of four rings: rings 0 through 3. Ring 0 is termed the "most favored" ring, because it has priority over threads running in rings 1, 2, and 3. Each higher-numbered ring has sequentially lower priority. Most multitasking OSs execute code in ring 3, whereas a scheduler executes in a higher-priority ring, which gives it the capability to preempt any thread.

In most Intel-based multitasking OSs, multiple threads are *time sliced*; that is, threads take turns executing for about one-eighteenth of a second at a time. This enables multiple tasks to run apparently at the same time, though actually each task runs for a time slice and is then preempted by the next process, which in turn is preempted—rotating processor time among active threads. Also, in most Intel-based multitasking OSs, the scheduler retains control of the threads. The threads are executed in ring 3, where suspended memory is protected from corruption by other threads. This is an effective system design; however, it is quite processor-intensive. The scheduler must keep track of all resources, and contention for access to I/O devices is severe. The memory protection of ring 3 is also expensive in terms of performance.

NetWare's nonpreemptive processing yields better performance and requires less processor utilization than normal preemptive processing. Each thread is scheduled to run unbridled on the processor in ring 0. The scheduler assigns priorities to threads and stacks them for processing, but it cannot control or interrupt them during execution. Each process is designed to run for a period then relinquish the processor if not completed and wait for another turn. This enables short processes to run to completion, and it reduces CPU utilization since less processor overhead is required to control and track resources of concurrently active threads. Execution in ring 0 also exacts the very best performance available from Intel processors.

Nonpreemptive processing, however, can affect reliability. A poorly behaved disk driver, LAN driver, or NLM can dominate the processor to the detriment of other processes. If a process crashes, it can bring the OS down with it. Disk drivers, LAN drivers, and NLMs must therefore be carefully written and tested to ensure that they will not dominate the processor or crash the server.

NETWARE 4 NOTE ▶

To enhance its reliability, NetWare 4.x can execute NLMs in a protected mode "domain." An NLM can be loaded into any ring, preferably ring 3 where memory protection exists, to prevent an untested NLM from causing trouble. When NLMs prove reliable, it is recommended that they be loaded in the more powerful, unrestrained realm of ring 0.

NetWare Workstation Software

The workstation portion of NetWare includes software that enables DOS and OS/2 workstations to communicate with the server. This portion of NetWare consists of three parts:

- The *NIC driver*, which empowers an interface between the MAC layer implemented in the NIC firmware and the IPX protocol.
- The *IPX packet-driver* software, which implements IPX protocol and header information.
- The *workstation shell* or *requester*, which implements NCP protocol and header information.

Two types of workstation drivers are currently in use for DOS workstations: traditional IPX drivers and ODI/MLID drivers. Traditional drivers have provided hardware independence since Novell introduced NetWare in 1983. Novell's Open Data Link (ODI) and Multiple Link Interface Driver (MLID) specifications were more recently introduced to enable workstations to simultaneously support multiple frame and packet types. Either type of driver can be used with NetWare 3.x, but ODI/MLID drivers are preferred because they use slightly less RAM, load into upper-memory blocks more efficiently, and provide more robust networking protocol support.

[handwritten margin note: ODI/MLID to support multiple frame + packet types]

DOS workstations load terminate-and-stay-resident (TSR) software into memory that implements the layers of protocol necessary for connection to the LAN and to the server. OS/2 workstations load the same drives as SYS files. The stack consists of

- Traditional IPX drivers
- ODI/MLID drivers (versus NDIS drivers)
- The Workstation shell or requester

Traditional IPX Drivers

[handwritten note: NIC driver code + Packet-Driver object code = IPX.com]

Traditional IPX driver files must be "generated" by the installer, using the WSGEN application (supplied with NetWare 2.2 and 3.x versions). The installer must select the NIC driver, either from the list of included drivers or from a vendor-supplied disk. The driver is configured with the NIC's physical switch and jumper settings (or other configuration options). Then the NIC driver object code is linked together with the IPX packet-driver object code into a single executable file, IPX.COM.

[handwritten note: NIC driver object code is linked together with the IPX Packet-driver object code into a single executable file IPX.com]

Figure 3.1 illustrates the various layers of LAN hardware, firmware, and software involved in linking the workstation to the LAN and to the server, as employed in traditional IPX drivers.

FIGURE 3.1.

Traditional IPX drivers.

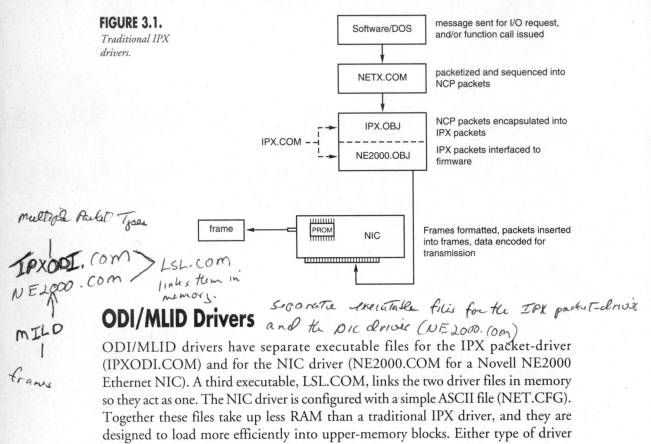

[handwritten annotations:] multiple Packet Types

IPXODI.com
NE2000.com } LSL.com links them in memory.

MILD
|
frames

separate executable files for the IPX packet-drivers and the NIC driver (NE2000.com)

ODI/MLID Drivers

ODI/MLID drivers have separate executable files for the IPX packet-driver (IPXODI.COM) and for the NIC driver (NE2000.COM for a Novell NE2000 Ethernet NIC). A third executable, LSL.COM, links the two driver files in memory so they act as one. The NIC driver is configured with a simple ASCII file (NET.CFG). Together these files take up less RAM than a traditional IPX driver, and they are designed to load more efficiently into upper-memory blocks. Either type of driver may be used with NetWare 2.x and 3.x versions.

[handwritten annotations:] MLIDs can support multiple frame formats. 802.3 - 802.2

The NIC drivers themselves are referred to as MLIDs. MLIDs can support multiple frame formats simultaneously, such as Ethernet 802.3 and Ethernet II frames. ODI packet drivers can support multiple network packet formats (such as IPX and IP) simultaneously. In order to support the vast majority of networking products and workstation environments, Novell had to develop a flexible workstation stack. In comparison, traditional IPX drivers can only support one type of packet and one type of frame at a time.

[handwritten annotation:] ODI packet drivers can support multiple network Packet formats (IPX, IP)

Figure 3.2 illustrates the various layers of LAN hardware, firmware, and software involved in linking the workstation to the LAN and to the server as employed in ODI/ MLID drivers.

FIGURE 3.2.

ODI/MLID drivers.

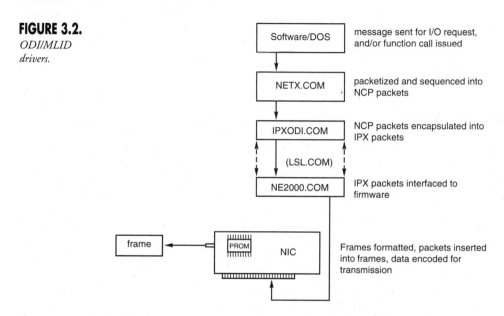

Network Device Interface Specification (NDIS)

Microsoft has a competing standard for Novell's ODI/MLID driver specifications: the Network Device Interface Specification (NDIS). LAN Manager and IBM LAN Server use this type of driver. NDIS drivers are less efficient in a NetWare environment than ODI/MLID drivers. You will find that they take up more RAM and some of the drivers cannot load into upper memory blocks. Since they are designed for interface with different networking protocols, using NDIS drivers with NetWare is like driving a square peg into a round hole. To support this option, Novell provides another TSR, ODINSUP, which supports NDIS drivers with NetWare.

The Workstation Shell or Requester

The DOS workstation shell, NETX.COM or NETX.EXE, is used to provide connection-oriented services with the server. The OS/2 Requester provides the same function for OS/2 workstations, whereas the DOS shell for NetWare 3.12 and 4.x is now called a requester. The later version DOS requester uses a new system of virtual loading modules to provide "universal client" services. NETX has been replaced by

VLM.EXE, which loads other files with .VLM extensions—similar to overlaid files. There are separate .VLM files for the 3.x shell (NETX.VLM), print services, NetWare Directory Services, and other services. Files that need to be loaded are simply placed in the working directory with VLM.EXE and load automatically; or a list can be specified of which VLMs to load in a configuration file (NET.CFG).

Universal File System, File Caching, and Name Space

NetWare's file system is an effective, high-performance system that utilizes server RAM and highly evolved algorithms for caching Directory Entry Tables (DETs), File Allocation Tables (FATs), and file blocks. This file system also provides support for file listings from various workstation OSs. Figure 3.3 illustrates NetWare's Universal File System.

FIGURE 3.3.

Universal file system.

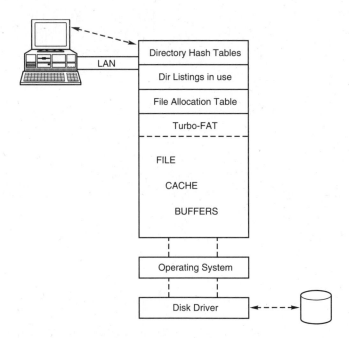

Universal File System provides several features that enhance performance and increase fault tolerance. The major features are

- Directory hashing and directory caching
- File block caching
- Turbo-FATs
- Elevator seeking
- Name space

Hashing and Directory Caching

The DETs for each volume are *hashed*, or indexed, and grouped by directory. The hash file is kept in RAM so directory entries can be found rapidly. Hashing is not necessary for a small file system, but NetWare is designed to support file systems with thousands of file listings.

When a user accesses a file, the file listings for the directory being accessed are cached. Most often, file access occurs repeatedly in the same directories. Because the file listings in the directory are cached, they are immediately available and don't require a physical read request from the disk directory listing.

File Block Caching

As a file is accessed, file blocks are read from RAM. If the requested file blocks are not already cached, physical read requests are issued to cache the blocks into RAM, and the blocks are then read from RAM. When a block is updated, it is updated in RAM. Physical read requests are given priority over physical write requests, because data written to a cached file block is immediately available. Physical write requests are postponed or given a lower priority. Updated data in a cache buffer that has not been written to the disk is called a *dirty cache buffer*. This provides rapid access to files and reduces I/O contention at the disk drive.

Algorithms based on relinquishing the Least Recently Used (LRU) blocks provide a high ratio of hits to the cache versus physical read/write requests. NetWare 4.x's SERVMAN application shows statistics indicating the percentage of hits to the cache. A long-term hit ratio of 95 percent indicates that on an average, 20 requests result in one physical request. That ratio is generally found to be attainable under normal conditions, provided the server has enough RAM.

Turbo-FATs

When a large file is accessed, a *turbo-FAT* index is built on the FAT entries. When a file is too large to fit into RAM, this reduces the amount of time required to find file segments throughout the file. NetWare automatically creates a turbo-FAT whenever a single open file contains more than 64 blocks. Turbo-FATs are shared by multiple users and remain active in RAM on the server for a short amount of time after file access has been completed. This improves search rates for records within a file, especially when several large files are concurrently accessed, as is the case in randomly sequenced relational database activity.

Elevator Seeking

Physical read requests are batched, prioritized, and placed into sequential order according to physical proximity to the current location of the disk read/write heads. This process, called *elevator seeking*, improves access rate significantly.

Combining the preceding features with normal multiuser random file access eliminates disk fragmentation as a concern. Defragmenting a NetWare volume can only improve disk performance marginally; unlike a single-user DOS file system, NetWare's file system eliminates disk access speed as the major bottleneck. (The remaining impediment is the disk transfer rate.)

Name Space

NetWare's file system defaults to a DOS-type file listing in the DET. Name Space support can be loaded on the 3.x and 4.x server to provide additional spaces in the directory listings for the longer filenames used in OS/2, Macintosh, and UNIX file listings. When Name Space is added to a volume, each 11-character DOS listing is supplemented with additional characters in a second listing (up to 128 characters). Name Space is added for each additional client OS supported on a volume.

System Fault Tolerant (SFT) Level I Features

In NetWare 2.0 and all subsequent versions, Novell incorporated two important features that improved physical disk storage reliability. Mirrored DETs, FATs, and Hot Fix redirection protect the physical file system from corruption, damage, and loss of data caused by media defects. In 1985, when these features were introduced, disk media and disk controller verification were far less reliable than today. Even today, SFT I ensures security from interruption in file access due to media defects.

Mirrored DETs and FATs

One of the most serious problems that can occur in any file system is for a DET or FAT to sustain damage. This can result in lost data and interruption of service. However, each NetWare volume's DET and FAT in RAM are mirrored to duplicate copies on the disk. For safety, DETs and FATs are written simultaneously to two mirrored sets of tables located on different parts of the drive. Mirrored DETs and FATs provide the mechanism for NetWare to automatically recover from such damage and reconstruct file access interactively by reading from the good mirrored listing with no interruption of service.

Each time a volume is mounted, the mirrored listings are checked for consistency and compared against the physical files. When a damaged DET or FAT is encountered, errors are reported at the console, and if you approve, the more recent entry is copied to repair the damage.

Hot Fix Redirection

Every physical disk write can be read-after-write verified before the corresponding dirty cache buffer is flushed. If a block of data written to the disk cannot be read back and verified accurately, a media defect is detected. When this problem occurs, the data in the dirty cache buffer is written to a special volume reserved specifically for this purpose. The Hot Fix volume is allocated during installation for each NetWare volume and serves as a safety net for file blocks that had been written to bad sectors on a disk surface. When bad blocks are encountered, they are logged in the disk drive's bad block table so they will never be used.

Disk read-after-write verification is performed by most disk controllers today. If a disk controller does not perform a hardware-level verify, NetWare can perform a software verify. This function is generally controlled by the disk driver and can be regulated by an administrator through a menu selection in the server's MONITOR.NLM.

System Fault Tolerant (SFT) Level II Features

SFT II features are currently included at no additional cost to NetWare 2.2 and all 3.x and 4.x versions. These features protect disk and file updates and include disk mirroring/duplexing and the Transaction Tracking System (TTS).

Transaction Tracking System (TTS)

TTS safeguards specified files so that they will not become corrupted if an update fails. During the updating of a file that has the Transactional file status flag, TTS keeps a transaction backout file. The updates are stored in this backout file, while the original file is left intact. When the update finishes, the backout file is appended to the original file and the process is complete. If anything stops the update process before it completes, the original file is left intact and undamaged.

All updatable OS files are marked as Transactional so that TTS can protect them. Without this feature, critical files like DETs and FATs could be damaged by problems such as a power loss to the server or a disk becoming full. You also can protect your data files by using the FLAG command, which marks files with a Transactional file status flag.

Disk Mirroring/Duplexing

Disk mirroring provides mirrored physical write requests to redundant drives. When two disk partitions are physically mirrored, every physical write request is sent to both drives. If one drive fails and the other drive is physically able to work, NetWare displays an error at the console indicating that a disk drive has failed, but work goes on as normal, with no downtime or loss of data. When the drive is replaced and repartitioned, NetWare automatically remirrors the active drive to the new drive in a background mode. User requests are processed as normal, with remirroring in the background.

Duplexing is when the two physical drives are located on separate controllers or host adapters. Duplexing adds more redundancy with duplicated disk adapters, and adds an additional element of disk I/O performance. Because two drivers need to be loaded to the separate disk adapters, NetWare automatically splits seeks, enabling concurrent read/write access to both drives. Under certain conditions, disk I/O operations can be improved substantially using duplexing. Figure 3.4 illustrates mirroring and duplexing.

FIGURE 3.4.

Disk mirroring and duplexing.

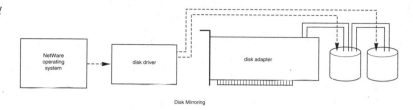

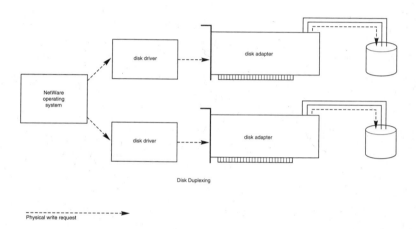

All that is required to mirror or duplex disks is that the two drives have exactly the same amount of disk space remaining after partitioning and configuring Hot Fix. The option to turn mirroring on is a menu selection in the server INSTALL utility. Once mirroring is installed, a low-priority background copy occurs, with no delay of user I/O requests.

System Fault Tolerant (SFT) Level III Features

Mirrored servers had been on the wish list for several years and finally shipped in 1992. A new SFT III server OS was designed to provide redundant servers. In case one server fails, the second server continues to service the network without interruption.

The current implementation of SFT III is a v3.11 OS. It is priced higher than normal NetWare, and of course it requires two complete servers, NICs, and subsystems. The two servers are physically connected with Mirrored Server Link (MSL) adapters (hardware) and drivers. A few varieties of MSL adapters are available, providing a physical link between the servers at very high data-transfer rates.

NetWare's Internal Router

An internal router was first incorporated into the NetWare server OS in version 2.0. The internal router can integrate two or more LANs into a single server. NetWare's internal routers move IPX packets from one server NIC to the other. Because this functionality occurs at the IPX packet level, after the LAN frame has been stripped off, it is not dependent upon the type of LAN. This provides integration of Ethernet, Token Ring, or any other type of LAN in the same network. Figure 3.5 illustrates how a NetWare internal router handles packets between two network addresses.

FIGURE 3.5.

A NetWare internal router.

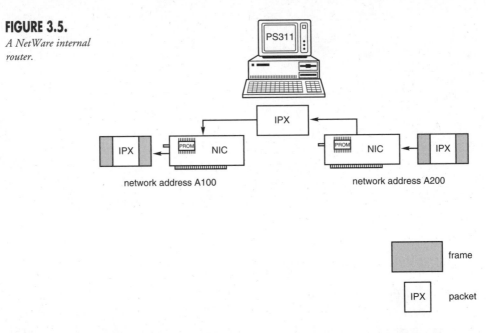

NetWare's IPX is a routable protocol that can be managed by both NetWare's internal routers and by third-party external routers. It is similar to TCP/IP, in which the network number in the packet header is used for routing services and does not require access to the proprietary portions of the protocol. The inherent capabilities of

Novell's IPX protocol and internal routers have encouraged extensive use of internetworking and placed NetWare in a different category from "nonroutable" protocols employed in LAN Manager, LAN Server, and NetBIOS-based, peer-to-peer networks.

Novell previously called the internal routing configuration an "internal bridge," which conflicted with standard industry terminology. The wording has been corrected in more recent documentation, but many references to "bridging" still linger in Novell and Novell-related literature. Many Novell-trained people still use the terms interchangeably, considering the difference to be insignificant (which is entirely untrue). Because IBM and Microsoft basically do not use routable protocols (relying on the use of bridges instead), and because so much of the industry is IBM- and Microsoft-oriented, many users are uncertain about the significance of this distinction.

NetWare Directory Services

NetWare naturally evolved as a workgroup networking solution. As networking has grown, NetWare has been used for integrating larger distributed organizations. The complexity of multiple departments, workgroups, and other enterprise-wide entities necessitated a more comprehensive method of organizing servers, file systems, and resources.

NetWare 4.x was introduced with NetWare Directory Services (NDS), an object-oriented resource-management system that links together network resources. NDS enables the management of *objects* (users, groups, servers, printers, volumes, directories, and other network resources) without the manager having to know where the resources are located. Object definition and security is stored in the Global Replicated Database, which is stored at the directory level and echoed throughout the network.

NetWare 4.x Special Features

Several enhancements were included in NetWare 4.x in addition to NDS. Some of the new features engineered by Novell set a new standard in file storage, memory management, and object management through graphical user interface (GUI) utilities. These enhancements include

- Block suballocation units
- Data compression

■ Data migration

■ OS_PROTECTED MODE DOMAIN

■ Flat memory allocation

■ Burst mode NCP

■ RIP/SAP filtering

Block Suballocation Units

One of the inefficiencies in any file system is the vast amount of disk storage space wasted on file blocks that are largely empty. NetWare's minimum 4K block-allocation unit size requires each file or portion of a file to occupy disk space in 4K increments. A file of only 1 to 4096 bytes takes up one block, 4097 through 8192 takes up two blocks, and so on. As a result, a substantial amount of disk space is normally empty but not usable.

However, NetWare 4.x's Block Suballocation Unit feature enables blocks that are not completely filled to be filled with remainders from other partial blocks. Blocks are broken into 512-byte *suballocation units* so that data can be stored more compactly on NetWare volumes. This results in fewer FAT entries and more data in less disk space.

Data Compression

Another challenge in providing efficient disk storage is the large number of files that are accessed occasionally or never accessed at all. Any file that is not accessed for an extended period (seven days by default, adjustable in the SERVMAN utility) is compressed in the background while file I/O is at a very low level. When the file is accessed, it is uncompressed with almost no noticeable delay.

Data Migration

Another new data-storage technique that extends file-system efficiency is NetWare 4.x's data-migration facility. This was designed for off-line storage on optical drives, CD-ROMs, and tape subsystems, in which retrieval could be accomplished transparently. When a device such as an optical jukebox is used, the appropriate storage medium can be retrieved, the volume mounted, and the data delivered without any user, administrator, or application intervention. This feature provides access to vast amounts of storage.

OS_PROTECTED MODE DOMAIN

As discussed previously in this chapter, NetWare executes all threads in ring 0 for improved performance under nonpreemptive processing conditions. The down-side to this strategy is that a poorly behaved driver or NLM can crash the server or dominate the processor.

To address this issue, Novell developed the OS_PROTECTED DOMAIN module with NetWare 4.x, so that untested NLMs or drivers can be loaded into any of the four rings. When a driver or NLM is executed in ring 3, memory protection restricts one thread from using a memory location in use by another thread, which can cause memory corruption and crash the server. Once the module has been tested, Novell recommends that the module be executed in normal mode (ring 0) so that full performance is available. Therefore, protection can be ensured without compromising performance or the security of the server OS. This feature will encourage more development and live testing of NLMs under production conditions.

Flat Memory Allocation

NetWare 3.x versions have five separate memory pools. In some cases, memory used by an NLM becomes fragmented and is not usable for cache buffers after the NLM is unloaded. Though this rarely causes problems, the new flat memory mapping in NetWare 4.x is an improvement. It is especially helpful in an NLM development environment, where this could be a problem.

Packet Burst Protocol

The normal connection-oriented service that NCP provides requires an acknowledgment packet for each packet sent. This effectively doubles the amount of traffic on a network, but it ensures the delivery of each packet—regardless of the reliability of the LAN or WAN upon which the packets are transported. The acknowledgments occupy only a negligible amount of bandwidth on an Ethernet or Token Ring LAN under normal conditions. However, the acknowledgment traffic on a WAN can be crippling, because most WANs have very limited bandwidth.

Packet Burst Protocol provides a single acknowledgment NCP packet for up to 64K of *packet fragments*. Each packet is batched into a burst of packet fragments, for which only one acknowledgment is necessary. Each fragment contains a sequence number, and the acknowledgment contains a listing of any packet fragments that may be missing from the sequence.

Packet Burst Protocol is a "sliding window" protocol that automatically adjusts the number of packet fragments in bursts according to the changing conditions encountered in a normal LAN/WAN environment. Configuration parameters at the workstation shell and at the server dynamically adjust to provide this service with little or no performance degradation.

Packet Burst Protocol is available for v3.11 servers and workstations with the addition of a new shell and an NLM at the server. It is integrated with NetWare 4.x at no additional cost.

RIP/SAP Filtering

RIP and SAP packets travel between servers to inform one another of their existence and routing information. Under normal conditions, these periodic broadcasts represent a negligible amount of traffic. However, on a large internetwork with many addresses and servers connected over a WAN, the RIP and SAP broadcast traffic can cause congestion. RIP and SAP packets and protocols are discussed in greater detail in Chapter 36, "Internetwork Performance."

NetWare 4.x's server-based SERVMAN utility enables an administrator to adjust the frequency of RIP and SAP broadcasts as well as the "keep-alive" time required between broadcasts before the server and routing information is lost. This feature can be added to a v3.11 server in the form of a pair of NLMs, but it is integrated with NetWare 4.x at no cost and easily managed through the server-based utility.

Summary

NetWare 3.11 and 4.x are the most powerful and most easily managed of any network operating systems available today. The feature-rich environment of NetWare is unsurpassed in performance and in fault tolerance. Though other network operating systems provide good service, anything other than NetWare constitutes a compromise in one, if not many, of the areas discussed in this chapter. Perhaps this is why Novell has garnered over 60 percent market share of all PC-based network operating systems.

File Server and LAN Interfaces

by Rick Sant'Angelo

IN THIS CHAPTER

4

A network can have many potential bottlenecks, but most potential bottlenecks are in the file server. The file server mainly provides disk storage and print services for user requests. The natural tendency of the consumer is to look for the fastest processor for file-server performance. Processor speed, however, is not the most critical factor in file-server performance. Only if you have server-based applications (for example, SQL Server or Oracle) is your file server's processor used for anything other than I/O processing. NetWare's nonpreemptive processing makes it quite different from other network operating systems. The I/O path is therefore the most significant area of concern.

The features discussed in this chapter were initially implemented by *superserver* developers. These designs were proprietary at one time and limited to a few vendors who had healthy research and development budgets.

Because these design features were standardized, many other developers followed the lead. Today, many choices are available at far lower prices without using proprietary hardware. It is no longer necessary to purchase a superserver to have superserver performance. A wide variety of hardware is available so you can assemble your own high-performance server; this has caused superserver prices to tumble. Today, the best reasons to purchase a superserver include brand loyalty, dependability, support, warranty, and fault-tolerant features.

CAUTION

Though "clone" computers are attractively priced, you should consider the advantage of having a major company supporting you if compatibility problems or defects arise with your server. Remember that a server's downtime can be very expensive, and this is not the place to cut corners.

In selecting a server, you should focus on four areas:

- Processor
- Bus design
- Disk subsystem
- Server NICs

Most importantly, your server should be designed to handle a specific job, and you should consider your future demands. Project your network's growth over the lifetime of the server and build the server to meet your highest projections.

TIP

For reliability, replace your server every two years. Most servers have a useful lifetime of several years; however, you should replace them more frequently. If you are in an environment where new user workstations are acquired on a regular basis, consider giving the old server to a user and replacing it with a new server.

By updating, your maintenance will be lower, and you can feel more secure knowing the new server is probably more dependable than an aging one. This also will enable you to project future demands more accurately, because the foreseeable server lifetime will be defined more accurately.

Processor

Increasingly powerful personal computers have two primary uses: as file servers or as GUI workstations. These two applications are the most technically demanding and therefore capture much of the attention of computer hardware designers. More importantly, they represent the largest market potential.

Both of these applications place the same kind of I/O demands on the computer, but GUI applications require a lot of math coprocessing. Most powerful personal computers make good servers, but the math-coprocessing features are wasted on a file server.

An appropriate processor for a file server should have a good clock speed, because this drives I/O demands faster, but does not necessarily have a fast internal clock speed or math-coprocessing abilities. The speed of a 486 processor is desirable, but the internal math coprocessor is not used. A DX2 (double internal clock speed) also is not used. A 66MHz 486 DX2 has an external clock speed of 33 MHz and a doubled internal clock speed. This will not help your server OS operate any faster. Only *external* clock speed is of concern. Most integrators select the best value in a server, so some of these extraneous features may be included; they certainly do not hurt.

TIP

Select a 486-33 or 486-50 MHz processor as the basis for your server. A 486 costs only a little more than a 386. Do not be swayed by 66MHz DX2 claims. The internal clock speed is not relevant to NetWare, nor is the internal math coprocessor. Though the internal math coprocessor feature of the DX (as opposed to the SX) is not used with NetWare, the internal cache is, which makes the DX a better deal. The Pentium processor is far more expensive at this time and does not measure up to the 486 in price-performance comparisons.

In summary, competitive factors have made 486-based servers so attractive that they makes a perfect platform for NetWare.

32-Bit Features of EISA, MCA, and Local Bus

For networking purposes, the most important design feature of your computer is the bus design. Microchannel Architecture (MCA), EISA, and local bus have been designed to overcome the limitations of the standard ISA bus architecture. A 16-bit ISA bus theoretically can accommodate 5M/sec. However, because every 16-bit word moved through the bus has an address byte, and because the bus can only accommodate a 16-bit data flow, your throughput will be limited to somewhat less than 1.5 million bytes per second. MCA has a current theoretical limit of 40M/sec, and EISA has a theoretical limit of 33M/sec when using a 32-bit OS with all the 32-bit hardware features discussed in this section.

Potential throughput is only part of the story. MCA and EISA were designed for *concurrent processing.* Concurrency enables more than one process to occur at the same time on different processors, sharing system memory and the interface bus. Factors that favor 32-bit bus and interface cards include

- The 32-bit data path
- Busmastering and concurrent processing
- Burst mode
- Streaming data mode

MCA and EISA enable multiple interface cards to move data at high rates with reduced conflict and restriction. ISA was not designed with this capability. An ISA bus only can service one device at a time. The interrupt controller stops (interrupts) each device to enable another device to control the bus. In ISA design, the CPU also must be interrupted to control the devices and move data. This is why a faster processor is so important in ISA design, whereas MCA and EISA devices can rely less on the CPU through a process called *busmastering*. Busmastering devices offload some of the processing to a processor on the interface card. Though some ISA devices feature busmastering design, the effectiveness is compromised by the limited bandwidth and interrupt-driven design of ISA.

Many MCA and EISA NICs and disk adapters have been designed to exploit the capabilities of these advanced computer architectures. Not all of them, however, fully exploit the advanced features mentioned previously. An MCA or EISA card can sport a 32-bit interface but not take advantage of busmastering. Many busmastering cards do not take advantage of the burst or streaming data modes. Tremendous differences exist in the sophistication—and therefore the performance—of 32-bit interface cards. It was not until Novell developed the NE3200 EISA and NE2/32 MCA NICs that these features moved from theoretical design into practical, nonproprietary technology. In 1992, a host of new 32-bit EISA and MCA busmastering interface products were introduced. Now many disk adapters and NICs are available, and prices are more reasonable.

MCA and EISA 32-bit busmastering devices can take advantage of all four features previously mentioned.

32-Bit Data Path

NetWare 3.x and 4.x versions use a 32-bit word. It takes a 32-bit operating system, such as NetWare, to take advantage of moving data in 32-bit words. Moving 32-bit words also requires 32-bit processor architecture—the requirement for a 386SX or higher processor for NetWare 3.x and 4.x versions.

It also takes a 32-bit OS to take full advantage of 32-bit hardware—an ISA (16-bit bus interface) bus must break down every 32-bit word into two 16-bit portions for a trip across the bus. Each word, in this case a 16-bit word, requires an address byte. Therefore, moving a 32-bit word across an ISA bus (or through an ISA interface card) requires four bus cycles. This is a tremendous restriction for a 32-bit OS.

ISA cards cannot access the burst or streaming data modes of MCA or EISA. Therefore, the use of 16-bit interface cards in an MCA or EISA bus can yield only a small portion of the benefits available from 32-bit bus design.

MCA

Many MCA cards are designed with a 16-bit interface. MCA was designed with no ISA compatibility, so conflicts with preexisting ISA designs is not a consideration. However, only two 16-bit cards of any type can be configured in an MCA bus. Other powerful features of MCA design cannot be used in these cards, because the other features (discussed in the following pages) require a 32-bit interface.

EISA

You can use 16-bit ISA cards in an EISA bus, but there are a few caveats that apply:

- Use of older-design ISA cards in an EISA bus can steal bus cycles and affect the performance of EISA cards.
- ISA cards are driven by the CPU and therefore have a tendency to increase CPU utilization.
- EISA configuration utilities are not able to detect hardware configurations of ISA cards used in EISA buses and therefore may result in physical configuration conflicts.

An ISA card installed in an EISA bus is not restricted by the limited bandwidth of an ISA bus and therefore can perform a little better. The problem with using ISA cards is the conflict between multiple cards installed in the bus.

Local Bus

The term *local bus* refers to a processor-direct interface bus separated from the standard I/O bus. Two separate local bus designs have emerged: Video Electronics Standards Association's (VESA) *VL-bus* and Intel's *Peripheral Computer Interface (PCI)*. These bus interfaces enable transfer speeds matched to processor speeds. These designs have the potential to interface disk adapters and NICs with even higher transfer rates and less conflict with devices residing on the ISA, MCA, or EISA bus. Computer designs currently incorporate local bus in addition to another I/O bus.

> **VL-bus** was developed to facilitate rapid video updates for better GUI performance. The VESA standard has evolved further, but it lacks busmastering capability. The number of devices on the local bus also are limited. Though many video cards have been developed for this bus, support for disk adapters is extremely limited, and as of mid-1993, no NICs have been announced supporting this standard.

PCI was developed by Intel to facilitate video, disk, and NIC interfaces. As soon as Intel announced the design, a standards committee was formed, and many vendors pledged to develop disk adapters and NICs based on this design. PCI includes support for up to 10 devices, 32-bit busmastering, burst mode, and streaming data mode. The most attractive feature of this local bus is the placing of the disk adapter and the NIC on separate buses. As of mid-1993, no actual products have shipped, so product testing is nonexistent. PCI promises even more efficient use of multiple disk adapters and NICs by combining local bus and other buses in one computer.

Busmastering and Concurrent Processing

Intelligent adapters can process I/O requests off-line and then use the arbitration controller for access to the bus. Caching on the intelligent adapter enables the flow of data to remain constant, even though access to the bus is in cycles. In many cases, data flow can be accomplished without any CPU intervention. A busmaster can take control of another busmaster as a slave. The master and the slave can flow data (through the bus), eliminating the wait for the CPU to process data transfers.

Busmastering not only reduces reliance on the CPU for I/O processing but makes more efficient use of the bus when combined with the burst and streaming data modes available to 32-bit busmastering devices (as discussed in the forthcoming section). Because I/O requests normally consist of transfers of many bytes from one device to another within the computer, these two features can enhance sequential data flow between devices.

Burst Mode

Normal I/O requests require one address byte for each data word to be moved through the bus. This costs two bus cycles, and causes latency in access to the processor for addressing and to the bus for movement of each word. Burst mode defines eight additional direct memory address paths for moving blocks of data. Each block of data is sent with one address byte. This increases the bandwidth available for data on the bus, reducing the percentage allocated for addressing. It also reduces the number of accesses to the CPU to address data transfers. Burst mode is designed for smaller blocks of random data.

Streaming Data Mode

Streaming data mode enables one address byte to be assigned to two words or blocks of words (if combined with burst mode). This effectively doubles data throughput. Streaming data mode is designed for extensive sequential transfers of data, which is the rule rather than the exception in a file server.

Conclusion: ISA versus MCA or EISA

Many NetWare servers manage only one disk drive, one server NIC, and fewer than 20 users. If this is your configuration, an ISA computer may be an ideal choice for you. For a few bucks more, you can have the added features of EISA or MCA. Both are comparable, and the performance differences between ISA and either EISA or MCA are tremendous.

Using an ISA device in an EISA server does not significantly improve the device's performance. Though the device may test slightly better under full capacity, you will probably never realize any improvement under normal circumstances. When using multiple NICs and disk adapters in your server, however, the difference is readily apparent in CPU utilization.

Finally, match your MCA or EISA server to well-engineered, 32-bit busmastering adapters. All 32-bit adapters are not created equal, so monitor your favorite LAN periodical for benchmark testing and reviews.

Using Multiple Adapters in a Server

One of the most important applications for busmastering products involves multiple interface cards being installed in the bus of a server. Normal traffic generated by one NIC and one disk adapter is usually not a problem. However, when multiple NICs and/or multiple disk adapters are used in a server, bus traffic can become bottlenecked and CPU utilization can run very high, causing an additional bottleneck at the CPU. MCA and EISA were designed specifically to alleviate this problem, but the computer and bus design provide only the *capability* for new performance levels. Your file server's performance relies heavily on the design and use of busmastering 32-bit interface in that bus.

EISA design is an ANSI standard that is well-defined and widely used. The EISA standard has led to the wide availability of EISA busmastering interface cards. Fewer MCA cards are available, but there is still a fair selection of MCA busmastering cards. It pays to shop carefully for 32-bit disk adapters and NICs.

Busmastering that is well engineered uses both the burst mode and the streaming data mode to increase the flow of sequential data and reduce CPU intervention. The effectiveness of busmastering varies widely, however. Most NIC test suites presented in periodicals treat CPU utilization as a major factor in choosing a 32-bit server disk adapter and/or NICs. Test results show that multiple cards working at full capacity affect CPU utilization in varying degrees.

> **CAUTION** ▶
>
> Recent tests have shown that some busmastering NICs are limited by CPU utilization when two or three NICs are used in the server and operating at full capacity, whereas others do not max out CPU utilization with four NICs at full capacity. These tests isolate LAN I/O, bypassing physical read and write requests. When normal disk adapter traffic is factored into these tests, you can expect that a single disk adapter and three NICs can max out an MCA or EISA server in any case. Disk duplexing and the use of 100-Mbps NICs can push CPU utilization to higher levels.

Disk Subsystems

The advent of MCA and EISA has enabled higher disk I/O speeds to be feasible. Normal ISA design did not enable sufficient data throughput for existing disk designs to be fully exploited. Development of powerful 32-bit SCSI adapters has expanded the performance envelope. Therefore, developers have now extended the capabilities of disk subsystems. More importantly, busmastering small computer system interface (SCSI) adapters enables NetWare's built-in split seek features to be activated, without taxing CPU utilization or interfering with concurrent NIC transfers (as long as all devices are well-designed busmasters).

The Power of SCSI

Older disk designs, including MFM, RLL, and ESDI, have become virtually obsolete. SCSI is actually a bus design—it combines a host adapter in the computer bus with intelligent embedded controllers on the disk. Each disk has the capability to read and write separately from the other bus devices.

As many as seven disk drives can be chained to a single SCSI host adapter. Other disk technologies rely on slave drives connected to a controller. Normally, controllers can run only two disk drives, with only one operating at a time. Though ESDI and IDE adapters that can drive up to four disk drives have been developed, performance is still limited to running only one drive at a time.

SCSI is an ANSI standard that allows more than one intelligent disk drive to read and write at the same time and to share the SCSI bus. Original SCSI standards specify up to a 5M/sec transfer rate through the SCSI bus. Many intelligent 32-bit busmastering adapters can effectively reach the theoretical transfer rate by transfering data from more than one drive at the same time, whereas ESDI and IDE drives are limited to the transfer rate of only one drive at any given time.

Several SCSI host adapters can be installed in a single ISA, MCA, or EISA bus. Though the limited number of available interrupts normally restricts an ISA bus to four or five SCSI adapters, many more can be used with MCA or EISA computers when using level-triggered (shared) interrupts.

SCSI adapters also affect CPU utilization less than MFM, RLL, IDE, and ESDI controllers, because those designs rely mainly on the CPU for many I/O operations.

SCSI-2

SCSI-2, a new ANSI standard, requires both an SCSI-2 host adapter and disk drive(s) to be implemented. SCSI-2 adapters are usually backward-compatible with original SCSI drives. SCSI-2 standards include two new features that make it a far better value:

Fast SCSI doubles the SCSI bus speed, effectively doubling the transfer rate ceiling to 10 Mbytes/sec. This feature requires nothing more than a SCSI-2 adapter and drive to be effective.

Command tag queuing enables up to 256 commands to be downloaded to the intelligent disk controller from the host adapter for processing off-line. The original SCSI design requires an acknowledgment after each request before another request can be sent. This feature requires the disk driver to be engineered to take advantage of the process.

SCSI-2 also enables multiple types of devices to be connected to the same adapter. Theoretically, you can connect disk drives, CD-ROMs, optical drives, and tape drives to the same adapter using multiple drivers. This option definitely would require drivers to use command tag queuing, or disk performance will suffer when slower devices are accessed. In current technology, this option is not practical.

32-Bit SCSI Adapters

Many SCSI adapters are available with excellent 32-bit busmaster design and performance. This is an essential device to use for configurations requiring

- Heavy I/O processing at the server
- Multiple NICs in the server
- Disk duplexing
- Any server configuration that spikes CPU utilization to 90 percent or higher (for example, server-based applications)

Using Integrated Disk Electronics (IDE) Drives in Servers

IDE drives are fast and quite inexpensive. They make excellent server disk drives when a server has only one disk drive and one NIC. The bad news is that there are several problems with integrating IDE disks under NetWare, including

- A variety of problems with integrating older IDE controllers
- Poor compatibility with older ROM BIOS versions
- Different adapter and controller transfer modes
- NetWare problems when using the ISADISK.DSK disk driver

The good news is that you can sidestep all of these issues as long as you know what to look for before buying.

An IDE drive works much like an MFM, RLL, or ESDI drive—it is a slave device of another controller. However, the adapter you put in your bus is a host adapter, whereas the controllers are embedded on the drive itself. IDEs became popular very rapidly and were not standardized until recently. As a result, not all adapters are compatible with the on-disk controllers. This is easily resolved by buying the adapter and drive together, or by making certain that the drive you buy will work with a built-in adapter.

> **NOTE** ▶
>
> If you are installing two IDE drives on one adapter, be certain to check the jumper settings for primary and secondary drives. Because the secondary drive must become a slave of the first drive's controller, there are normally jumper setting changes required to make them work together.

Newer computers are designed to work with just about any IDE drive, although this may not be the case with earlier model IDE drives and/or computers. With later model drives and computers, this is seldom a problem. You can therefore ignore horror stories you may have heard, especially if you buy the server with a pre-installed IDE drive.

Again, buying the adapter and disk together eliminates the problem of these devices using different transfer modes. In some cases, the setup or configuration utility enables you to choose the type of transfer mode used on your drive. In some cases, the drive itself has jumper settings for selecting the transfer mode. This may, however, make the drive more difficult to install and configure.

> **TIP** ▶
>
> In several aspects, IDE disk drive controllers are different from previous drives supported by Novell's ISADISK.DRV disk driver. Novell provides an IDE.DSK driver designed to alleviate many of the problems. Be certain to use this disk driver (not included with your v3.11 distribution diskettes), or suffer the consequences!
>
> If you have an IDE drive and are already using ISADISK.DSK, you cannot always successfully change to IDE.DSK without deleting and re-creating your NetWare partition. This is because ISADISK.DSK uses the configuration information stored in CMOS, whereas IDE.DSK uses information stored on the adaptor card's EEPROM. In some cases, they won't agree. The good news is that in those cases, the EEPROM information leads to a larger usable disk size, so switching yields additional "free" storage space.

Server NICs

There is a tremendous amount of confusion about which NIC is best for any given server. The answer is very simple if you decide to bite the bullet and buy the best you can find. Just study the magazine reviews.

If you are concerned about value, however, it may not be necessary to spend $500 to $1,000 or more for a server NIC. Many NetWare servers have only one NIC, one disk controller, and support fewer than 20 users. There is no reason under these circumstances to invest in an expensive server NIC when a 16-bit NIC will deliver the same level of performance. Several high-performance, 16-bit NICs are available for around $200 (retail) and can match 32-bit NIC performance under fully loaded conditions.

TIP ▶

If you use a 16-bit NIC in your server, watch the CPU utilization statistic on your server's monitor. If it frequently runs more than 50 percent, you may need to consider upgrading to 32-bit design.

NetWare's Protocol Stack

by Rick Sant'Angelo

5

Experience tells us that the key to effective troubleshooting is understanding the mechanics of what is to be fixed. Without an understanding of NetWare protocols and how they work, you are poorly equipped to understand what is happening when something goes wrong in your network.

Many integrators treat networks as "black boxes," regarding them as mysterious and frustrating systems. Actually, the workings of a network are quite simple to understand. Read this chapter carefully, and you will be able to understand NetWare—and the rest of this book—much better.

You will find it easier to read this chapter after you have read Chapter 2, "Local Area Networks," which covers LANs and their access protocols, and how terms are used in this book. Be sure to reference the glossary when you are uncertain about a term.

This chapter describes how data is transmitted over a LAN or WAN, how your workstation communicates with the server OS, and how each layer of protocol works. This is vital information for any integrator. You should know what goes on inside the wires in order to understand

- The mechanics of your network
- The source and meaning of network errors
- How you can optimize your system

The Overall Picture

Data does not travel over a network in a steady stream. If this were so, each user workstation would periodically dominate the network to the detriment of all other users.

Instead, data is broken into *packets*, or short segments of data, for transport over a LAN or WAN. Packets are formed, controlled, and read by *protocols*, which are various sets of functions and procedures.

Protocols are implemented in parallel layers on network nodes so that remotely located software applications and operating systems can function together—as if they were all contained within one computer. Packets are the vehicle for communicating between the corresponding protocol layers in each computer. Novell calls its implementation of protocols *Universal Network Architecture (UNA)*.

It is important to distinguish between the terms *packet* and *frame*, although many industry writers use them interchangeably. A packet of data is generated by higher-layer protocols in the NOS. Packets are encapsulated into LAN frames for transport through a LAN. Packets and frames operate at different layers of protocol, and each executes significantly different functions. The amount of data in each packet must be sized according to how much data can fit into the type of LAN frame being used. For example, Ethernet can accommodate no more than 1501 bytes in each frame. When used with Ethernet, NetWare sizes its packets for 1024 bytes, plus packet headers. Packets of data are encapsulated into LAN frames for LAN transmission, as illustrated in Figure 5.1.

FIGURE 5.1.

Packets are encapsulated into LAN frames.

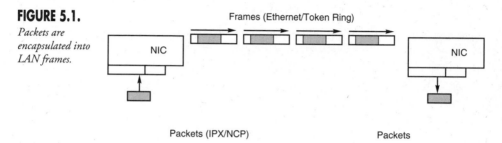

The basic benefit of network protocol functions is in enabling a workstation to use data located on the file server's disk, even if the file server is running a foreign operating system and the files are stored in a foreign format. Figure 5.2 illustrates the process of a workstation reading and writing files from both its local disks and the server's disks.

FIGURE 5.2.

Network protocols enable workstations to read and write from a server's disk.

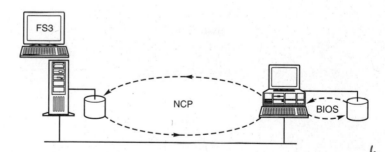

Networking and Layers of Protocol

LAN protocols are implemented in workstation software and in the NetWare server operating system. Protocols communicate between nodes with *packet header* information, which contains coded information fields that carry protocol information. Each layer of protocol physically communicates with the layer above and beneath it. Logical communications are established with the corresponding layer on the other computer, while the data transparently flows through the physical medium.

Only two types of packets are used in the vast majority of NetWare communications. Internetwork Packet eXchange (IPX) and NetWare Core Protocol (NCP) protocols and packets work together to handle the basic mechanics of communications between clients and servers. Other UNA protocols and packet formats include Sequenced Packet eXchange (SPX), Router Information Protocol (RIP), and Service Advertising Protocol (SAP). These protocols are discussed later in this chapter.

NetWare Core Protocol (NCP)

NCP is a connection-oriented protocol that provides transparent communications between two remote operating systems. Connection-oriented refers to communications that are confirmed in both directions; each NCP packet requires an acknowledgment NCP packet in return. NCP provides three levels of protocol functions, as follows:

- Establishes a connection between the workstation and server
- Forwards function calls between workstations and servers
- Acknowledges each packet sent, and resends each packet that is lost

NCP is part of the server OS, and its corresponding workstation software is the workstation shell or requester. The DOS shell, NETX.COM (or equivalent), remains Terminate Stay Resident in memory (TSR) and implements NCP at the workstation. In NetWare 4.x, the VLM workstation requester performs this function and is also a TSR. In an OS/2 workstation, the OS/2 Requester is the equivalent software module. To simplify discussion in this chapter, any of these software modules will be called the "workstation shell," or simply the "shell."

The workings of NCP are detailed in the following sections.

NCP Establishes a Connection Between the Workstation and the Server

When the workstation shell is executed, it sends out an NCP request that looks for an active file server. The function call that goes out is `Get Nearest Server`. A server responds with `Give Nearest Server` *server_name*. (The replying file server reports its name.) The workstation shell then requests routing information, and the server responds with its router login address. This becomes the interface point between this workstation and the rest of the network. At the same time, the server's OS allocates a "connection" for the workstation. Each workstation is granted a unique connection, that acts like a mailbox for incoming and outgoing NCP requests.

The connection request can be viewed from the file server. From a NetWare server console, type TRACK ON and you will see the server router tracking screen. Watch what happens when a workstation executes the workstation shell (NETX.COM or equivalent). Figure 5.3 shows a connection request and the subsequent handshake that occurs.

FIGURE 5.3.

An NCP

connection request.

```
Router Tracking Screen
IN  [0000E100:0000C06CC141]  2:49:22pm   Get Nearest Server
OUT [0000E100:0000C06CC141]  2:49:22pm   Give Nearest Server LANTECH
IN  [0000E100:0000C06CC141]  2:49:22pm   Route Request
OUT [0000E100:0000C06CC141]  2:49:22pm   AABBCCDD 1/2
<Use ALT-ESC or CTRL-ESC to switch screens, or any other key to pause>
```

Once a connection has been established, a user can log into the server (with NetWare 4.x, the user logs into an NDS context for a global network login instead of a server login). Regardless of whether the user has logged in, an NCP connection has established a vehicle for communications between the nodes that is transparent to any layers beneath it.

This process is similar to placing a telephone call. Once the phone call has been placed and the recipient picks up the phone, communication goes back and forth transparently. Neither the caller nor the recipient is overtly aware of the telephone equipment or lines between them. Likewise, an NCP connection is transparent to the user, the user's operating system, and the user's software. It is all managed by NCP and communicated with packet header information in combination with parameters stored in the workstation shell and server OS.

NCP Forwards Software and Operating System Function Calls Between the Workstation and Server

Software function calls and DOS operating system calls (redirected to the server) are echoed with NCP equivalents and forwarded to the server for processing. Figure 5.4 shows how a DOS function call is intercepted and how the corresponding NCP request is echoed to a server. The NCP function code effectively tells the server OS what to do with the packet. Figure 5.5 shows the NCP packet format, which includes the NCP function code field containing the NCP equivalent of the DOS (or OS/2) function call.

FIGURE 5.4.

The workstation shell intercepting a DOS function call.

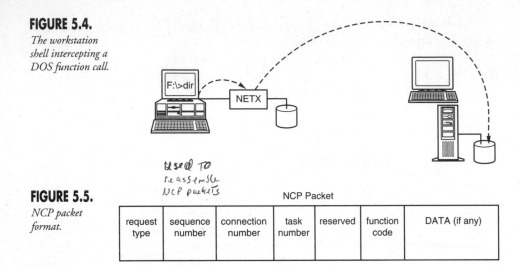

FIGURE 5.5.

NCP packet format.

used to reassemble NCP packets

NCP Packet

request type	sequence number	connection number	task number	reserved	function code	DATA (if any)

NCP also breaks down larger *messages* (transfers of data that exceed the length of one NCP packet) into multiple packets. The *sequence number* in the NCP packet header (see Figure 5.5) is used to reassemble the NCP packets back into messages at the receiving end. During an NCP connection request (discussed previously), the server and the shell negotiate a packet size, based on the workstation NIC drivers and the LAN(s) connecting the client and server.

Fewer than half of all NCP packets have any data at all in the data field. Many are exchanged to forward simple function codes to the server or to acknowledge receipt to the sending workstation. However, when executable files or data stored on the file server's disk are retrieved, a series of many packets may be required to load the data into workstation RAM.

Workstation requests may be directed to local devices, or they can be relayed to a server's OS through NCP. This is handled in one of two ways. If software sends a request to a network device, NCP is the forwarding mechanism. In applications using NetWare APIs, the software that NCP calls relays the network requests. Alternatively, if a request (such as a print capture or drive mapping) is sent to a redirected device, the workstation shell intercepts the request and redirects it to the network device. This is accomplished by monitoring just a few software interrupts.

NCP Confirms Receipt of Each NCP Packet with an Acknowledgment Packet

NCP is *connection-oriented*, which means that delivery of each NCP packet is guaranteed. If no acknowledgment is received, NCP resends the lost packet. (This is called a reexecuted request, or a retry.) After several retries, if no acknowledgment is returned from a workstation request, NCP times out and reports an error message.

> **NOTE** ▶
>
> A failed NCP request normally appears on-screen as `Network error: Abort, Retry?` This message does not indicate why the loss of connection has occurred, but it is an indication that connection between the server and the workstation has been lost.

NCP packets are handed off to the next layer of protocol—IPX—for encapsulation and transport to the ultimate destination.

Packet Burst NCP

NCP acknowledgments account for almost 50 percent of all traffic on a NetWare network. Novell developed *Packet Burst NCP* (sometimes called *Packet Burst Protocol* or *Burst Mode Protocol*) to reduce the impact of NCP acknowledgment traffic on a limited-bandwidth WAN. This variation of NCP reduces network traffic by eliminating the one-to-one ratio of NCP packets to NCP acknowledgments.

Up to 64K of "packet fragments" are grouped into a sliding window, with only one acknowledgment. The NCP packet shows the packet fragment sequence number, and the NCP acknowledgment confirms receipt of all packet fragments or lists which packet fragments are missing. The sliding window and shell buffers dynamically adjust themselves at the workstation shell for best performance under varying conditions on LANs and WANs in their path.

Packet Burst NCP is included in NetWare 3.12 and 4.x versions. It is an option that can be added to NetWare 3.11 by installing an NLM at the server (PBURST.NLM) and a burst mode shell at the workstation (BNETX.COM).

NETWARE 4 NOTE ▶

Packet Burst NCP is a standard feature of version 4.x.

Internetwork Packet eXchange (IPX)

IPX provides *connectionless* service between nodes. The purpose of IPX protocol is to transport higher layer packets (generally NCP packets) to their ultimate destinations—regardless of where they are located. *Connectionless* means that the communication is in one direction and does not require an acknowledgment. Similar to a mailed letter, each IPX packet goes to its destination with the assumption that it will make it to its final destination.

IPX is a *routable protocol*, which means that a nonproprietary router can read packet header information and route the packet without access to proprietary portions of the network protocol. This is, as opposed to NetBIOS, used in several other NOSs that cannot be routed without proprietary access to NetBIOS data and functions.

A *nonroutable protocol*, such as NetBIOS, generally relies on bridges (which work at the frame layer) to move data from one LAN to another. Routable protocols can be used with bridges and routers to form more sophisticated internetworks and to provide better interaction with the network protocols. Part V of this book discusses more about the implementation and management of internetworks and the use of both bridges and routers.

NOTE ▶

Use of the terms "bridge," "routable protocol," and "nonroutable protocol" in this book is consistent with industry standards, but the terms may be used differently elsewhere.

IPX protocol is implemented in a server OS and by the IPX packet-driver in a workstation. The IPX packet-driver must communicate with the NIC driver, and with NCP at a higher layer. The IPX packet-driver is one of the following files:

IPX.OBJ	Object code incorporated into an IPX.COM DOS workstation file
IPXODI.COM	Used with DOS ODI/MLID drivers
IPXODI.SYS	Used with the OS/2 Requester

In a server OS, the NIC driver is loaded, and the IPX protocol is bound to the NIC driver. Then, a network address is assigned to the LAN to which the NIC is attached. This network address is used by IPX to route IPX packets to the appropriate NIC drivers.

IPX protocol receives NCP packets, encapsulates them into IPX packets, and adds addressing. The addressing, as shown in the IPX packet format in Figure 5.6, provides the information needed to transport an IPX packet over one LAN, or to route it to another LAN or WAN to reach its ultimate destination-node address. The network address provides the information necessary to send the packet to the appropriate NIC (and therefore LAN). Information about LAN location is stored in routing tables in NetWare server operating systems and other routers.

Used for routing

FIGURE 5.6.

IPX packet format.

IPX Packet

chksum	length	trans ctrl	pkt type	dest net	dest node	dest socket	source net	source node	source socket	DATA (NCP, SPX, RIP, SAP Packet)

Sequenced Packet eXchange (SPX)

SPX is a connection-oriented protocol that can be used to guarantee both delivery and error control of NCP packets. SPX not only duplicates the simple connection service of NCP, it also adds error control in the form of a checksum and verification on the other end. SPX sends back either an acknowledgment (if the receiver's checksum agrees) or a negative acknowledgment (which indicates the packet was received but the checksum did not agree).

Unlike IPX or NCP, SPX is not used by default in NetWare communications. An application must specifically call to SPX to turn this connection-oriented service on, but because of the excessive overhead it creates, SPX is not employed most of the time. The only common NetWare application that employs SPX is the print server utility (PSERVER). When a print job is directed from the queue to the print server, and again from the print server to a remote printer, SPX is used to guarantee the accurate delivery of each packet. The Remote Console (RCONSOLE) utility also employs SPX.

SPX has been criticized for its excessive overhead, and Novell has responded with SPX II. This new variation of the SPX protocol may prove more efficient than traditional SPX and encourage more developers to use it.

> **NOTE** ▶
>
> Any type of LAN combined with NCP acknowledgment normally provides a high level of error control. SPX is used only in application procedures in which virtually 100 percent error-free delivery must be ensured.

Router Information Protocol (RIP)

RIP packets are exchanged among NetWare servers, indicating the availability of network addresses. NetWare servers broadcast RIP packets every 60 seconds. Each NetWare router must receive periodic RIP rebroadcasts to "keep-alive" the network's address availability.

RIP packets also indicate the number of *hops* between the source network address and the network address from which it is broadcast. Up to 50 sets of network address/hop counts can be included in one RIP packet. RIP packet format is shown in Figure 5.7.

FIGURE 5.7.
RIP and SAP packet formats.

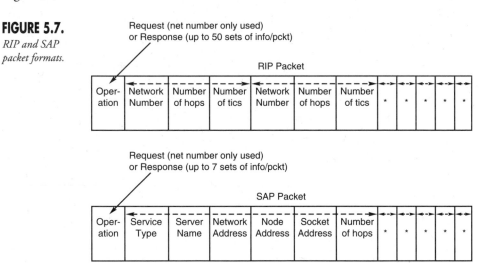

Service Advertising Protocol (SAP)

SAP packets are broadcast by all types of servers to inform file servers of their availability. Each SAP packet contains up to seven sets of server information showing the type of server and routing information, as shown in Figure 5.7. When a file server receives a SAP packet, it creates a temporary bindery object for the server. This makes the server available for user requests, and it contains the appropriate routing information so IPX packets can be addressed to the server.

SAP packets are broadcast on a frequent basis (depending upon several factors, including which version of NetWare is sending them).

NETWARE 4 NOTE ▶

The frequency and rebroadcasting of RIP and SAP packets are adjustable in 4.x servers to reduce the amount of broadcast traffic in large multiserver installations.

Putting It All Together

There are five different packet formats used in UNA. In a network, each layer of protocol must interact with the layer above it and the layer beneath it. The end result is logical transparent communication between equivalent layers. To bring UNA layers into perspective, Figure 5.8 shows the encapsulation of an NCP packet into an IPX packet and into a LAN frame. The software, firmware, and hardware layers that move data are illustrated in Figure 5.9.

FIGURE 5.8.

NCP, IPX, and LAN frame encapsulation.

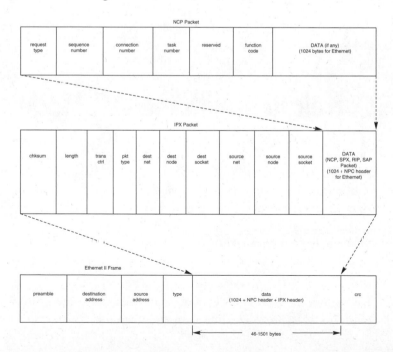

FIGURE 5.9.

Software, firmware, and hardware layers.

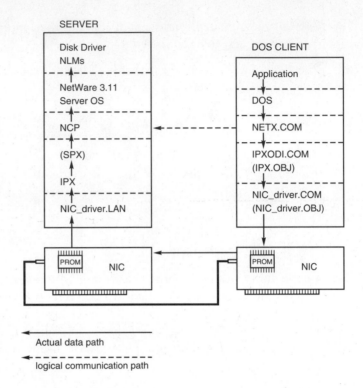

RIP and SAP packets also are encapsulated into IPX packets for delivery. The previous figures apply to these packets as well. A RIP or a SAP packet can be substituted for the NCP packet; the mechanics of delivery are the same.

Correlation with the OSI Model

In 1983, when Novell announced UNA, they also announced that they would follow the Open Systems Interconnection (OSI) model developed by the International Standards Organization (ISO). This model was designed to develop a common set of nonproprietary networking protocols that could be implemented in competing with vendors' products. The intention was to have truly open systems that could interoperate with higher-layer transparency. Though the actual OSI protocols have emerged, few American computer systems use them. UNA's close parallel to the OSI model, however, enables it to develop gateways and accomplish interconnectivity between systems.

The significance of the OSI model is not limited to the protocols that are used in common. OSI provides a model with which other systems can be compared and understood. Virtually all network architectures have corresponding protocols or functions. By comparing UNA to the OSI model, systems analysts can understand NetWare's UNA better.

There are important benefits to using a layered network architecture that corresponds to the OSI model, including

- Functional equivalence to other network architectures
- Hardware, software, and protocol independence
- Open architecture that lends itself to interoperability

Figure 5.10 shows the corresponding layers of protocol in OSI versus UNA versus TCP/IP at the server and various workstation operating systems. A brief description of each layer's function follows.

FIGURE 5.10.

UNA versus OSI versus TCP/IP.

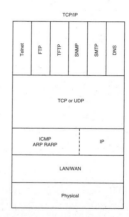

NOTE

IPX/SPX/NCP and TCP/IP/UDP are very closely related; they both use XNS packet formats. When using a protocol analyzer, packet types often are identified primarily as XNS packets.

The Network Layer

The OSI network layer provides routable packet delivery from source to destination nodes. IPX and Internet Protocol (IP) are functional equivalents of the OSI network layer. They both use network and node addressing for routing information.

The Transport Layer

The OSI transport layer provides error control and acknowledgment service. SPX, NCP, Transport Control Protocol (TCP), and User Datagram Protocol (UDP) are functional equivalents of the OSI transport layer. SPX, NCP and TCP provide connection-oriented transport services, whereas UDP is connectionless.

The Session Layer

The OSI session layer establishes connections between hosts. NCP, TCP and UDP provide the functional equivalents of the OSI session layer.

The Presentation Layer

The OSI presentation layer provides function call exchange between host operating systems and software layers. NCP, TCP, and UDP provide functional equivalents of this layer.

The Data-Link and Physical Layers

The OSI data-link and physical layers provide internode delivery within a logical LAN or WAN. The data-link layer is represented in LAN or WAN access protocols, which are implemented in firmware on LAN and WAN adapters. The physical layer consists of electrical and electronic mechanisms and media. This includes cabling, connectors, repeaters, and signal encoding, as well as other electrical vehicles. OSI specifications cite IEEE, ANSI, and other OSI protocols, such as 802.3, 802.5, and HDLC. These layers are represented in LANs and WANs used with NetWare or TCP/IP networks.

These two layers are key to the hardware independence of these protocol stacks, because they can use just about any LAN or WAN product, and all three architectures can share the very same data-link and physical layer products. This has encouraged development of standardized LAN and WAN products. The OSI model has altered the closed, proprietary nature of networking, wherein network customers were dependent upon single vendors and closed systems.

Summary

Largely because of ISO and the OSI model, TCP/IP vendors, and Novell, interoperability among systems is now a reality. Layered architecture has reduced dependence on proprietary hardware and software, and increased the availability of standardized LAN, WAN, and software products. In the future, we may see more consolidation of protocols. In a recent major announcement, Novell stated its intention to incorporate IP as a standard protocol that can be used in place of IPX at both servers and workstations.

Novell's support of open architecture and hardware independence has been a valuable contribution to the entire industry, and not incidentally it accounts for much of their market dominance. It has forced other vendors to adopt open policies and protocols to remain competitive. The industry enjoys flexible and cost-effective solutions to connectivity now more than ever, and the trend continues.

Downsizing and Migration Strategies

6

by Rick Sant'Angelo

This chapter discusses some obstacles you will need to overcome in order to expand your NetWare resources. Today's powerful PCs, LANs, and NetWare can satisfy very large demands, but typical networks grow quickly, and the job of adding nodes is a significant part of any system administrator's job. There are three basic areas that need to be dealt with to manage the growth of NetWare networks in any large organization. These are

- Downsizing
- Upgrading
- Centralization

There are many tools available to accomplish these tasks. We no longer need to wait for development to evolve our systems. Novell has made its reputation by introducing products when the market first develops a need for them. By the time competitors develop products, Novell's offering is mature and has established its stability. Because Novell has a keen sense of timing, it has developed a sizable market-share lead in networking software. The industry "vaporware" tradition—announcing products long before they are released—is no longer effective.

For most network administrators with a growing client base, an identifiable *strategy* is lacking in the evolution of their systems. Management has always looked to system vendors like IBM to provide strategy; now this job is in *your* hands. You need to develop strategies for downsizing, upgrading, and centralizing computing resources.

This chapter discusses the potential pitfalls, some helpful tools, and strategies that can accompany the growth of PC networks.

Downsizing from Mainframes and Minicomputers

Downsizing (or *rightsizing*) is the latest trend in information systems. Mainframe and minicomputer accounts have found that at least part of their computing workload can be handled less expensively with PCs.

Today's powerful computer hardware and software products have blurred the line between PCs and mainframes and lowered costs significantly. Though the mainframe and minicomputer communities have fought to remain competitive, almost all large accounts have moved a major part of their computing resources to PC-based networks.

Typically, larger firms, universities, and government agencies move through three distinct stages of NetWare implementation:

- Departmental networking
- Internetworking
- Consolidation and centralization of services and resources

Smaller companies may never need to move beyond the first step, but whenever more than one file server is installed in an organization, it is inevitable that the company will eventually enter stage two—internetworking. As internetworked LANs evolve, an eventual move to centralization is natural. Though many organizations have been downsizing for several years, many dyed-in-the-wool mainframe shops are just now including downsizing in their corporate strategy. These companies generally skip the natural progression and head straight to stage three—centralization.

Every organization is at some stage in the game of push-and-shove between centralization and decentralization/centralization. It often becomes a political hassle that must be resolved by management. Integrators and system administrators need to be sensitive to problems and aware of available solutions each step of the way.

Departmental Networking

The typical large organization that relies on vast computing resources first finds that departmental managers have brought in PC networks to handle smaller, departmentalized tasks or to consolidate personal-productivity software. DOS, Windows, and OS/2-based software are easier to learn and less expensive than mainframe and mini-computer applications. It is a natural progression to unite departmental or workgroup PCs and administer several users and applications from one console.

Problems

Once a departmental workgroup is established, a couple of issues eventually cause problems. A system administrator must be appointed to manage such workgroup-related issues as establishing user accounts, installing software, and creating a menu system. Other users look to the system administrator for help on all computer-related issues, so training and support are essential for both applications and network utility usage. Unfortunately, the system administrator is generally someone who has another full-time job and can spare little time for training. Unless the administrator finds time to learn the system and to refine its user environment, the problems can be overwhelming.

Tools

The system administrator is the glue that holds a workgroup together and enhances the productivity of the users. System administration is a demanding job that deserves priority attention. The chosen adminstrator should be someone who can devote time to support the network. Remember that several users' productivity depends on issues being managed properly. Because the server is located departmentally, and the configuration and applications are specific to a workgroup, the natural point of administration is within the department.

The best tools you can give an administrator are good training, support, and fewer duties that can conflict with his or her important job.

Solutions

The NetWare tools required to resolve these issues are discussed and clarified in this book. To effectively solve problems, a good system administrator needs to learn to use the tools at hand and must be able to respond to user demands on a timely basis. Support personnel, such as the system administrator, need reference materials, support, and time to deal with crisis situations. An administrator should also be skilled in DOS and any other workstation OSs that are used in the network.

Internetworking

In smaller companies, the trend stops with one (or just a few) workgroups and servers. Whenever more than one server is installed, however, demand for internetworking—coupled with NetWare's built-in routers—launches the company into the next stage of development. The second stage is a natural progression; linking departmental LANs happens almost by default.

The need to transfer data from one workgroup to another often is what leads departmental managers to employ the internetworking option. Sometimes a centralized Information Services (IS) group becomes involved. In shops where TCP/IP and UNIX are used, internetworking is already in place. Novell, often in conjunction with other developers, has marketed a line of off-the-shelf products that makes integrating NetWare with other systems possible.

Problems

Issues to consider in the conflict between departmental and centralized control of information resources include

- Determining responsibility for the installation, configuration, and maintenance of interdepartmental links
- Deciding the best tools and strategy for providing access
- Determining how the use of routers, bridges, and WANs affects performance
- Deciding how much access to allow, particularly to other computing systems

It is normal to become submerged in political considerations. Often, the IS department is reluctant to become involved, but PC networks generally grow to a level at which they cannot be ignored. Every company with large computing resources needs to establish an enterprise-wide strategy that includes both PC networks and internetworks — or suffer endless political rallying and conflict. This is the rightful turf of the IS department (or equivalent); it cannot avoid incorporating this area into its duties. Internetworking is a natural part of the normal mission of a central processing department.

Tools

Tools to resolve such issues include backbone LANs (or WANs), routers, gateways, and the central management of links. NetWare 4.x has new features that improve internetwork performance.

Solutions

In most cases, servers remain within the departments, with a departmental administrator and central control of routers and interdepartmental issues. Standardization of NOS and LAN/WAN hardware is essential for making internetworking easier.

Software is available that can monitor and troubleshoot areas of interdepartmental concern. Products to establish and manage these connections are discussed in Part V of this book. The point is that management needs to establish enterprise-wide strategies and standards for implementation and to take control of the interdepartmental links. Normally, it is more convenient for departmental administrators to administer their own hardware and software. In some cases, a centralized staff may be established to provide service and support.

Centralized service, support, and control of departmental resources should be dealt with separately. Part of the solution to resolving internetworking issues is to separate them from centralization issues. Management should segregate internetwork administration from other centralization issues and establish two committees (or individuals) to suggest solutions. Higher levels of management need to become involved and make firm decisions about where responsibility lines are drawn.

Generally, a large company calls in a consultant or hires an IS manager who is familiar with problems and who has experience with several options and successful solutions. A costlier alternative is trial and error, with subsequent damage-control measures. An ounce of advice is worth a ton of experience in your system evolution.

Consolidation and Centralization

At some point, it is inevitable that a large organization will decide to centralize management of distributed systems. In many cases, this involves selecting approved software and hardware and providing support. In other cases, IS takes control of servers, cabling, and system administration. If political conflicts have not been resolved, conflict resolution must be added to the mounting list of issues to address.

Generally, mission-critical applications have been moved to PC network platforms by this stage in the corporate evolution. Interaction between departments and the sharing of resources causes problems with accountability, and both productivity and revenue are threatened when systems become shared or internetworked. Undoubtedly, cost savings can be realized by consolidating resources, and the opportunities for improvement are too attractive to pass up; but along with these opportunities are increasingly more critical issues that need to be resolved.

Problems

The consolidation and centralization of computer resources and services raises the following issues:

- Departmental versus central system administration
- Departmental versus central support and maintenance
- Location and organization of servers
- Security and control of data

■ Management of software licensing

■ Optimizing server and LAN hardware and configurations

■ Reducing or eliminating downtime

Tools

Server Hardware

Server hardware can be consolidated, combining departmental servers into fewer, more powerful superservers. Workgroups still should have separate LANs, interfaced with separate server NICs. Departmental workgroups should retain separate directory tree structures, keeping their unique data and applications protected from other users' access.

System Administration

System administration is the politically charged issue in centralization. It usually is not feasible for a remotely located administrator to manage users' accounts. In large systems, from which hundreds of users exist, a central administrator is hard-pressed to manage the varying issues of so many departments and users. Departmental administrators should retain control of the user environment without having total system privileges. These issues can be resolved with standard NetWare tools.

NetWare 3.x can establish three levels of system administration to effectively handle the job of sharing control: *Supervisor, Workgroup Manager,* and *Account Manager.* For example, a departmental manager can be assigned as a Workgroup Manager and add user accounts, change login scripts, and assign access rights to departmental users and groups. A Supervisor can assign Workgroup Managers and delegate control of their users' environment. Workgroup Managers do not have access to many system-wide administrative functions. In this way, you can strike a healthy balance between system administration and control.

Support And Maintenance

Support and maintenance should be consolidated for maximum cost efficiency. It is not practical to duplicate tools that are used to manage larger networks in each department. A good example is the establishment of a help desk. Properly trained individuals and help-desk tools are valuable resources and often quite costly. They must therefore be centralized. However, support personnel should not be spread too thin or expected to handle a wide variety of software and networking issues. Each organization must establish divisional or centralized help-desk responsibilities, typically located in close proximity to the user. In larger companies, support personnel may specialize in given software applications and provide service to larger geographic areas.

Security and Control

Security and control tools are plentiful in NetWare and its third-party supplements. Security issues to consider include

- Establishment of company policies for security
- NetWare standard security and restrictions
- NetWare 4.x's advanced security and auditing
- Third-party administration utilities
- Virus monitoring and prevention utilities

Software-Licensing Control

Software-licensing control tools are available from various sources. Third-party vendors have products that control or monitor software usage. The Software Publishers Association has an audit kit that they furnish at no charge. Many managers are unaware of recent legal developments that place high costs, individually and corporate, on uncontrolled usage of software licenses.

Optimizing Performance

Tools for optimizing performance are specific to potential bottlenecks. Many tools exist, but each tool is specific to the different bottlenecks that develop. (Optimizing performance is addressed in detail in Part VI of this book.)

Reducing Downtime

Tools for reducing downtime also are specific to critical failure points. Many tools exist today to handle potential situations, so downtime should not be a significant issue. Without proper attention to this problem, however, this remains one of the most counterproductive aspects of downsizing. Reducing downtime is addressed in detail in Part VII of this book.

Solutions
System Administration

System administration should be handled by those closest to the objects to be managed. For example, departmental administrators for each workgroup can be appointed as workgroup managers with appropriate rights and assignments. These individuals can manage users, data, and software applications in their respective departments without similar access to other departmental users, groups, file system directories, and user security. IS can control shared network resources (servers and LANs).

Support and Maintenance Staff

Support and maintenance staff must be established at levels closest to the consolidation levels. For example, if a single server supports several departments, support and maintenance staff members must be thoroughly familiar with the unique configuration and demands of all connected users and groups. A remotely located IS staff may not be close enough to interdepartmental computing resources. Deciding what levels to consolidate is tied to the divisional level of consolidation. However, in larger companies, the opposite may be true. Specialists in each software or hardware category may be established to deal with several departments' or divisions' problems.

Security and Control

The establishment of security and the control of your environment should not be delegated or delayed. Though this issue is important, it does not appear urgent, so it is generally ignored until a costly disaster occurs that mandates control. You need to take action and establish policies and procedures that are formalized by top management. You are urged not to wait until disaster strikes.

Software Licensing

Software licensing is an issue that often is misunderstood. Corporate and individual civil and criminal liability for violations occurs with your tacit approval. Be aware of the penalties and that enforcement is very active today. Several software packages are available to police licensing, and the Software Publishers Association provides an audit kit at no cost. You may even find that your accounting firm includes a software license review in an audit. Learn about your liabilities on these issues; the awareness itself will motivate you to find solutions to software licensing abuses. Recent legal developments mandate that you can no longer turn your back on this issue.

Downsizing: Conclusions

During the past 10 years, Novell's foresight and timeliness have been astounding. Novell has provided the necessary tools to make networking grow, and the company has benefited handsomely. Novell has been awarded the highest honor in the computer industry: overwhelming market share.

Many tools exist to strike a balance between departmental and centralized computing goals. However, the development and evolution of distributed computing systems in a larger organization can be handled only with carefully developed strategies. Tools are not enough; management must decide which tools are best, how they will be implemented, and who controls the resources.

The most pressing problem you will encounter, however, is a lack of awareness of the relevant issues, tools, and solutions. These areas constitute the focus of this book.

Updating and Upgrading

A major strategy decision is whether to automatically upgrade when new products become available. Two opposing truisms are invoked here: *If it works, don't fix it* versus *Always use the latest and greatest.*

A basic issue that each organization must decide is whether to keep its NetWare version current or to enable servers to keep running until they no longer work. The latter is your *de facto* decision if you do not address this issue. On one side, you have costs that are not justified in the short run, whereas the alternative constitutes "management by crisis."

A study in 1989 by Infonetics Research revealed that Fortune 100 companies spent over ten times as much on performance upgrades for PC networks as they did on maintenance. Today, the situation is far more volatile, because mission-critical applications are increasingly being downsized.

You need to set a strategy on upgrading each of these elements of your networking system:

- Software applications
- LAN and server hardware
- NetWare versions

Software Application Upgrades

Software applications are no longer products that are purchased and remain productive for the useful life of the system. Most software applications are dynamically improving and evolving. Equate purchasing software with purchasing a subscription. You have almost no choice on this issue. As older versions age, support and interrelated software issues force you to upgrade. Upgrade procedures are time-consuming, so you should consider site-licensing as an alternative. Generally, software developers can keep your site licenses up to the most current versions with less hassle than it takes to upgrade each box.

Upgrading Server and LAN Hardware

Server hardware should be updated frequently. If you purchase user workstations on a regular basis, consider rotating new servers into use and retiring old servers to workstation duty. Rental car agencies learned this trick long ago: The reliability of a new piece of equipment is higher (and the cost of maintaining it is lower) in the first couple years of its life.

For the most part, LAN technology has been stable for quite some time now, and it hasn't changed rapidly. Ethernet workstation NICs can be used until they no longer work, but server NICs can be improved to EISA or MCA busmastering models. Because of new developments in Token Ring chip sets and design, you may want to evaluate new products for best efficiency. Chapter 4, "File Server and LAN Interfaces," discusses server NICs in greater detail.

Upgrading to faster 100-mbps LANs, such as FDDI/CDDI, Fast Ethernet, or TCNS, is normally not necessary for workgroups. Bandwidth and speed often are confused. A 100-mbps LAN has more bandwidth and the same speed and, for lightly loaded LANs, response time is not improved at all by upgrading. Heavily loaded LANs can adequately be managed by breaking them up into multiple LANs, interfaced to the same server. Chapter 4 discusses the conditions under which you should consider upgrades to higher-capacity LANs.

Upgrading NetWare

Upgrading NetWare is a strategy issue that deserves careful consideration. This actually involves two issues: *release updates* and new *version upgrades*. Release updates remain in the same number version; for example, version 3.0 was updated to 3.10, then 3.11, and then 3.12. It possibly will be updated to a 3.2 level, although Novell spokespersons have hinted that 3.12 may be the end of the line for the 3.x version. Version 2.15 was updated to 2.2, and Novell has stated that it will remain at that release. Upgrades, however, involve a change from one version number to a new version number (that is, version 3.12 versus 4.0). An upgrade to a new version number involves a change to a completely new OS.

Updating Releases

Minor releases constitute a normal maintenance improvement, such as incorporating bug fixes. For example, the upgrade from version 3.10 to version 3.11 was a minor release, which indicates the addition of a few features, and incorporation of bug fixes and small changes.

The update to 3.12 is also a maintenance release, incorporating bug fixes and newer versions of NetWare utilities. Although a few enhancements have been added, it is probably not worth the cost of the upgrade unless you have a pressing need for one of the new features, such as Packet Burst Protocol or BasicMHS electronic mail messaging.

Major releases retain the same OS but are more substantial. For example, the update from version 3.0 to version 3.10 included some major fixes and improvements to 3.0. For the most part, disk and LAN drivers need to be updated with the major release update.

It is highly recommended that you use the NetWare version in the most current release so you will have no unexpected problems under changing system conditions. An update normally does not involve any change of data structures or security, so it is a relatively benign procedure. Updating from 3.10 to 3.11, for instance, simply required replacing the SERVER.EXE OS executable, System, and Public files.

Novell has instituted a program called NetWare Update to keep users apprised of new releases. When a new release is to be shipped, Update subscribers receive notice, and merely agreeing to accept the upgrade yields a brand new set of books, disks, and so on. Minor patches, and new workstation and utility updates, are made available more frequently. Novell has an established track record of issuing new releases every couple of years. If you do not subscribe to the NetWare Update service, your cost of an update is set by Novell relative to how much Update users spend to stay current.

> **TIP** ▶
>
> You should seriously consider subscribing to Novell's NetWare Update service. It provides automatic upgrade within versions for a yearly subscription fee based upon the level of your version. You may also find it to be cost-effective, normally costing just a little more than paying for upgrades as they are released.

Upgrading NetWare Versions

Upgrades (as opposed to updates) are indicated by a change from one major version number to another, such as from 3.x to 4.x. A new release indicates major restructuring, generally effecting changes in file and organization structure. For example, upgrades from 2.x to 3.x require repartitioning of disks and conversion of data. Upgrading from 3.x to 4.x may require partitioning and does require conversion of data.

Generally, a new version also incorporates significant differences that may require extensive technical retraining. It also may require significant changes in the user environment and system administration.

> **NOTE** ▶
>
> NetWare Update service does not provide upgrades from one version number to another (for example, from 3.x to 4.x). Upgrades from one version number to another should be viewed no differently than buying an entirely different product, even though migration utilities can assist in the upgrade.

Novell charges upgrade fees based upon the difference in pricing between versions and then adds a little extra charge. An upgrade consists of the same documentation, disks, and related materials you receive when buying a new license.

TIP ▷

Always evaluate your cost of acquiring a new version versus the cost of an upgrade. In some cases, it may be more cost-effective to purchase a new license so you can use the old release for a hot online server, or you may want to move the old server OS to a smaller department.

An upgrade from one version number to another is a different matter, however. When you upgrade a 2.x server to 3.11 or 4.x, or when you upgrade a 3.x server to 4.x, you can expect to repartition your disk. Bindery files and 4.x Global Replicated Database have changed format in each of these versions. Conversion of data is required to move security data to the new server OS. 4.x also has significantly different procedures and utilities for system administration.

CAUTION ▷

The decision to upgrade to a new version should not be taken lightly or automated in any way. Each new version requires management review, and all options should be considered. Management review should not be based on reviews or statements gleaned from industry periodicals. You should establish a review board, and your organization's needs should be compared to actual features the new version contains. A path of prudent and conservative steps needs to be established before you make the move to a new version. The decision should be considered no more or less significant than a move to a competitive product.

When considering software upgrades, keep the following points in mind:

- First, it is not unusual for several announced features to be omitted in a final release. Generally, the pressure to meet delivery dates causes developers to put some features on the back burner until fixes and extensive use in production environments can be achieved.

- Second, an initial release of a version may not be stable or fully functional. Personal experiences with ".0" releases have caused many administrators and managers to become quite wary of first releases of new versions. Though Novell's reputation for stability is very good, it does not make sense to risk productivity and revenue on an unknown product, even if industry reviews have been good.

■ Third, formal training or in-house experimentation should be considered before committing to full conversion to a new version. In a production environment, it is not prudent to force administrators and users to handle changes on-the-job without the benefit of this step.

NETWARE 4 NOTE ▶

Upgrading to 4.x requires a shift to a new "object-oriented" system called NetWare Directory Services (NDS). Configuration decisions that are made concerning NDS are extremely difficult to undo. Implementing NDS should be preceded by substantial planning and experimentation.

Novell has discussed releasing utilities for reconfiguring NDS with less effort and downtime. See Chapter 8, "Planning a NetWare Directory Services Tree," for detailed discussion of implementing NDS.

PART

II

IN THIS PART

Planning and Installation

System Design

7

by Rick Sant'Angelo

This chapter addresses several aspects of system design:

- NetWare versions
- File servers
- LANs and server NICs and WAN interface cards
- Workstations
- Properly conditioning file server power

These issues are discussed in sufficient depth to assist you in planning your own network in a way that will serve you well into the future.

Planning a departmental network is a much bigger job than it used to be. Along with open system design comes the responsibility of selecting the very best components from several vendors' offerings. You may decide to have one brand of server, another brand of SCSI disk drive, a different brand of SCSI host adapter, several brands of workstations, and one or more brands of NICs, hubs, and so on. Getting all these items to work together is no simple task.

Designing a campus-wide or an enterprise-wide internetwork involves even greater complexity. The use of NetWare's internal and external routers, third-party external routers, plus the complexity of WANs, adds more layers of integration and planning to your task. Data-communication services add further complexity and additional vendors; both a long-distance company and a local telephone company are involved in bringing a leased line to you.

Generally, though, the biggest problems are political, and internetworks cross more organizational lines than departmental networks. They require more planning, and centralized or committee-oriented decision making is necessary unless mandates are received from a central authority.

This chapter outlines the decisions that need to be made when you integrate or upgrade a medium-to-large system with NetWare. If you are familiar with the complexity of all the components to be included in your system, skip this introductory chapter and go on to the more detailed, component-specific parts of this section. However, if you are not a networking expert, you will find that the material presented in the remaining sections of this book is based upon an understanding of material presented in this chapter.

As you read, keep in mind that campus-wide and enterprise-wide systems require the careful selection, configuration, and assembly of the following network components:

- A network operating system
- File servers
- LANs and WANs
- Workstations
- Power conditioning
- Routers (or bridges)
- Internetwork infrastructure

Network Operating System (NOS)

Choosing the appropriate network operating system (NOS) is the first decision you must make. Because all networking components are relative to the networking protocols to be used, you need to find the appropriate NOS. In this book, however, a decision to use NetWare is presupposed. You would not be reading this book right now if you were still shopping for a NOS.

"NetWare" alone is not the final answer; the next question is "Which version?" Each NetWare version limits the number of concurrent logins. You can purchase any version with a variety of choices for the number of users to be supported. Your basic NetWare choices are

- Version 2.2
- Version 3.12
- Version 4.01
- SFT III (version 3.11)

Version 2.2

Version 2.2 is based on 80286 processor architecture and is therefore quite limited in the amount of RAM and disk capacity per volume, the number of physical disk drives, and other operating system parameters. It is the basic NOS that has proven Novell's networking capability, but it is also quite outdated in this world of 386/486 PCs. With a 386 or 486 processor, 2.2 limits the processor's capability to that of an 80286. Version 2.2 is used in small businesses, limited departmental servers, and other small networks. Version 2.2 outshines such peer-to-peer NOSs as LANtastic and InvisibleNet, and it is very popular overseas; however, compared to NetWare version 3.11, it is quite limited, and thus seldom used anymore in larger American corporations. A detailed discussion of version 2.2 is not included in this book because its installed base is declining rapidly in the advanced networking market.

Version 3.12

Version 3.12 is the flagship product of the NetWare line. Introduced a few years ago, it is the fourth revision of this version, and it has proven its stability and the richness of its features. It is the most widely used version in the United States and the most trusted product in the category of NOSs.

In smaller networks, the most important design feature that sets 3.x apart from 2.2 is its dynamic allocation of resources. Server OS parameters are managed by an internal management agent. As conditions change, OS parameters fluctuate between minimum and maximum values, adjusting the OS for peak performance under widely varying conditions. A 3.x server can flex to perform at peak efficiency in small and large environments alike, with no administrator intervention.

Another major factor influencing the migration to 3.12 is its modular design. Server-based applications (NLMs) can be loaded on the server to provide many value-added services.

Unless your network consists of more than a few servers and access to multiple servers is a problem for users, NetWare 3.12 is the best choice for almost all systems. Most organizations opt for 3.12, even though it is more costly than 2.2, because of its superior capacity and performance, modular design, and internetworking enhancements. For now, many organizations have not upgraded from 3.12 to 4.0 for one of two reasons: 4.0 has not established its stability, or the organization does not have a pressing need for a directory-services configuration. Version 3.x established itself as the most powerful NOS on the market, and most users remain with it because nothing else has proven better.

Updating from 3.11 to 3.12

This new version is a maintenance release from 3.11. It contains bug fixes and utility revisions, plus a few new features, including

- Packet burst NCP
- BasicMHS/FirstMail electronic mail
- ElectroText online documentation
- VLM DOS requester
- Disk media manager

These features are discussed in greater detail in later chapters. The core OS is unchanged and differs from the 4.x OS. There is nothing radically different between it and 3.11.

Novell's policy is to freeze a release, so 3.11 was frozen with older utilities that had been revised and needed to be replaced after installation. Novell could not go on selling 3.11 as it was, so they replaced it with 3.12. There are few persuasive reasons to update 3.11 to 3.12. Unless you require one or more of these features, you may find that the high cost of upgrading from 3.11 to 3.12 has little justification.

> **TIP**
>
> If you plan to upgrade from 3.11 to 3.12, consider buying a new package instead of updating your 3.11. You may find the difference in cost to be very little. You can use the older version for another department, or to keep a hot online backup server ready for duty.

Version 4.01

Version 4.01 has several advantages over the basic 3.x operating system; however, its advanced directory-services internetworking design qualifies it as a completely new product. The OS has been reworked extensively from 3.x versions. Although the OS improvements are nice, NetWare Directory Services (NDS) is the essence of what makes 4.x so different. If your organization has more than a few servers, NDS may be for you. (NDS is discussed in greater detail in the following chapter of this book. See Chapter 3, "Advanced NetWare Operating System Features," for more details on both the 3.12 and 4.01 OS designs.)

> **NOTE**
>
> Version 4.0 was updated to 4.01. The only change made NDS updates more efficient, reducing the overhead between servers. All servers in a 4.x NDS must be the same level—that is, all 4.0 or all 4.01. The two versions will not link together into one root.

Many corporate integrators have resisted 4.x in production environments because of concerns about transition costs and stability. The product's stability is good, but any large system manager is always concerned about integrating a new product. The most conservative approach would be to pass on a ".0" release, opting to wait for a subsequent revision and associated real-world reviews. Despite these concerns, many large corporations have opted to integrate 4.x, due in part to widely favorable reviews and beta reports about its stability. Large, geographically dispersed organizations require directory services to simplify access to their data "jungles," and many NetWare shops have been begging for NDS. Those currently integrating 4.x are definitely guinea pigs, but they seem to be favorably impressed with NDS and 4.x's new OS features.

Novell has publicly recommended that 4.0 should not be put to the test in mission-critical situations. Most administrators like to live peaceful lives (if possible) and probably would not want to do more than test 4.01 at this time. However, top management and MIS departments in large companies are driving the migration to 4.01. These individuals want directory services from Novell and are willing to let *you* do whatever it takes to make it happen.

The current NetWare price structure for the available versions is shown in Table 7.1.

Table 7.1. NetWare version price comparison.

# of Users	v2.2($)	v3.12($)	v4.01($)
5	895	1095	1395
10	1995	2495	3195
20	n/a	3495	n/a
25	n/a	n/a	4695
50	3995	4995	6295
100	5995	6995	8795
250	n/a	12,495	15,695
500	n/a	n/a	26,395
1000	n/a	*	47,995

n/a = not available

* = available by arrangement only

System Fault-Tolerant Level III (SFT III), Version 3.11

SFT III enables the system to duplex servers. The need to have 100 percent up-time under all conditions has finally been met in a downsized product using current hardware resources. Though you may not think that the need for SFT III is pressing today, the fact that this option is available and stable is a tremendous breakthrough. Novell has proven that only when a product exists can true demand for its capabilities develop. SFT III places NetWare in a position to compete with a large base of far more expensive fault-tolerant systems. It also promises to improve reliability and confidence in NetWare. The use of SFT III in nonmission-critical situations also will increase.

SFT III entailed a special revision to the 3.11 OS. In order to provide the fullest degree of fault tolerance, the OS was split into two parts, one mirrored MS-engine to service requests and nonmirrored I/O engines that handle each server's identical I/O requests (as shown in Figure 7.1). If you separate the two functions, all requests can be processed concurrently, and physical I/O can occur as separate transactions that are managed by separate hardware.

FIGURE 7.1.

SFT III MS and I/O engines.

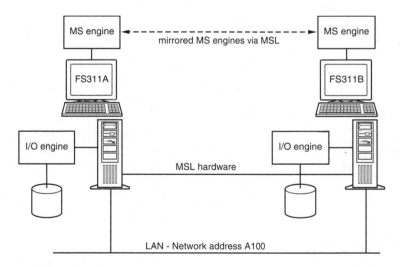

SFT III costs more than a single copy of NetWare but less than two copies. The Mirrored Server Link (MSL) interface cards required to provide exchange of requests between the mirrored servers are widely available and surprisingly low in cost. The cost of SFT III, as with other NetWare versions, is based on the potential number of concurrent logins, as shown in Table 7.2.

Table 7.2. Price structure of SFT III.

# of Users	Retail Price ($)
10	3995
20	5295
50	7495
100	10,495
250	18,995

For the most part, SFT III is a hybrid 3.11 product. All discussions of 3.11 in this book pertain equally to SFT III NetWare. Chapter 39, "Fault Tolerance with SFT III," discusses SFT III in more detail and discusses all considerations unique to the SFT III variety of version 3.11.

> **NOTE** ▶
>
> Novell has announced that SFT III will not be upgraded from 3.11 to another 3.x version. Instead, a new 4.x version will be available in the future.

Summary of Selecting a NetWare Version

Once you decide upon a version of NetWare, you can focus your attention on decisions that fit that product. Regardless of whether you select 3.11, 4.0, or SFT III, the rest of this chapter applies equally. For example, though you may use NetWare 4.0 and NDS to configure your internetwork, all the considerations of the physical infrastructure are the same. The same applies for building servers, selecting workstations, conditioning power, and segmenting your LANs and WANs.

Building an Optimized Server

You have two basic choices for selecting a server and its subsystems. You can purchase a fully assembled, NetWare-ready server; or you can purchase a server and select and install a disk subsystem from another vendor. The first choice simplifies installation and confines service and support on the server to a single vendor; however, this configuration often comes at a high cost and curtails some of the choices you might want to make.

A fully assembled server does not have to be of the *superserver* variety. Superservers are computers specially designed and built as network file servers. Some superservers have proprietary I/O buses, NICs, and disk adapters. Though the capabilities of such computers sound impressive, potential buyers should consider two factors: proprietary hardware and cost. High-performance server buses and subsystems are common, though this was not true just a couple of years ago. Any performance advantages that superservers enjoyed were temporary.

You should stay away from proprietary hardware. Because current standard hardware provides substantial capacity, the only possible benefits of a superserver would be the one-stop purchase and support, and fault tolerance. The integration of proprietary hardware currently affords no significant performance advantages and can actually penalize you with excessive replacement costs and limited availability of parts. For these reasons, the entire industry has turned towards equipment that is standards-based and nonproprietary. Figure 7.2. illustrates potential bandwidth characteristics of major server components.

FIGURE 7.2.

*Server components
and potential
bandwidths.*

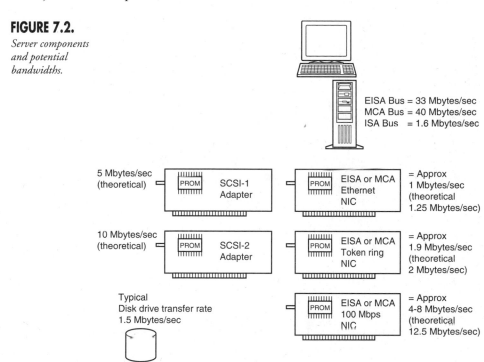

Generally, superservers used to carry a premium price for the advantage of having a factory-assembled, NetWare-ready system. Many computer developers now offer server or high-end workstation models with massive disk storage and RAM capabilities that are durable and standards-based. They do not need to limit their sales by designating them as file servers only. As a result, superserver prices have tumbled. You now have your choice of many brands of computers to use as a very powerful file server—without the price tag of a superserver.

Whether you choose to purchase such a unit or assemble your own from various vendor offerings, consider the advice offered earlier in this book. All servers should be EISA or MCA design. For most light-duty file servers, an IDE disk drive makes an ideal disk subsystem, but when multiple disks and NICs are used in a server, you should take advantage of 32-bit busmastering SCSI disk adapters and NICs. Chapter 4, "File Server and LAN Interfaces," provides significant details on why these choices make the most sense.

LANs and WANs

Which LAN to choose is not really a serious decision today. According to industry research, over 85 percent of all NetWare-related LANs are Ethernet or Token Ring. A 1993 study by International Data Corporation revealed that 54 percent of all PCs connected to LANs in 1992 were Ethernet nodes. That percentage is growing, and most of the latest technology for 100-mbps LANs is based on the same choices of cabling and access protocol. To decide between the Ethernet and Token Ring is normally simple, because someone at a higher level usually makes the decision, and the decision is often based on factors other than good, objective evaluation.

Most IBM shops seem to prefer IBM Token-Ring, whereas others opt for another brand of Token Ring. Most DEC, H-P, Sun, UNIX, and other shops that have minicomputers generally opt for Ethernet, because that is what they already know and use. Both of these choices are based on the use of unshielded, twisted-pair cabling as the most desirable medium.

Chapter 2, "Local Area Networks," goes into great detail on the advantages and disadvantages of each type of LAN, including the newer 100-mbps offerings. With NetWare, the choice does not matter. You can integrate any type of LAN into a NetWare internetwork because of the routable IPX protocol and NetWare's platform independence. Any NIC that is made today has a NetWare driver. Without compatibility in the NetWare market, an NIC would be relegated to a small segment of the user base because NetWare controls such a large majority of networks.

Choosing a WAN requires far more evaluation and extensive decision making than choosing a LAN. The complexity of internetworking local networks to remotely located LANs presents a host of issues that need to be resolved at the planning stage. Decisions made at this point incur fixed costs that can go on for years. Your investment in internetwork infrastructure can be likened to building a bridge: Once the material has been purchased and the foundation pylons have been poured, it is a little late to decide to change the basic design. That bridge is going to be there a long time—so it is with WAN decisions.

Fortunately, Novell and third-party WAN vendors are making it easier to build internetworks. Routers are the first choice for routable protocols such as IPX. In many cases, new-design routers are flexible and upgradable, and they are becoming less expensive and easier to configure and administer. Many routers can accommodate several ports and incorporate bridging functions and several networking protocols. The bridging function accommodates NetBIOS, LAT, and SNA traffic, whereas routing functions accommodate IPX, IP, AppleTalk, OSI, and other routable protocols. Today, *brouters* (bridging-routers) are truly all-purpose products that can link almost any LAN to any other LAN, regardless of the NOS, mainframe, or OS connected by them. In many cases, routers even offer protocol choices and upgradability to the various WAN protocols that are under development, such as Point-to-Point Protocol and Asynchronous Transfer Mode. Prices also are falling rapidly.

Communications vendors now offer high-bandwidth, reliable services in two categories.

1. Leased lines (analog or digital leased lines, T-1s, fractional T-1s, and T-3s), featuring

   - Fixed capacity
   - Point-to-point, fixed location
   - Fixed-cost, monthly recurring charges based on distance

2. Packet-switching networks (that is, frame relay, cell relay, and SMDS), featuring

   - Flexible bandwidth
   - Multipoint, anywhere-to-anywhere (to locations with a point-of-presence or that can be reached with a T-1 link to the POP)
   - Usage-based charges, not related to distance

Because of all these options, the extensive costs, and the magnitude of fixed expenditures, a separate study of WAN infrastructure is warranted before a decision is made. Bandwidth, stability, and cost are the factors that need to be judged. The hardware to interface is plentiful, upgradable, and cost-effective; however, the monthly recurring costs normally are in the thousands of dollars. The fact that these fixed costs become part of the corporate infrastructure means that a decision is similar to purchasing capital equipment or land—top levels of management usually need to get involved.

An entire section of this book is devoted to choosing a WAN. Before deciding on any product or service, you should read Part V of this book. It deals with various aspects of WANs in great detail.

Matching Workstations to the Job at Hand

When purchasing workstations, you need to consider the demands of user applications. This requires dividing demands into three categories:

- Simple, character-based applications
- Windows-based (or other GUI) applications
- Other types of processor-intensive applications

Though users can access more than one application on their desktop systems, they usually use only two or three applications on a regular basis. Sometimes PCs are designated for only one application. In a few cases, users demand the ability to access several applications, most of which are quite demanding. These users are called *power users*, and the selection of all network workstations should not be based on their demands. Selection should be based on what users need. In any case, the requirements must justify the costs.

The minimum configuration for a new workstation today requires a 386SX or higher processor. Most software today accesses XMS memory, and the 386 memory map provides significantly better management of extended memory than older processor models. The best and simplest advice is to buy the most processor, RAM, and video your budget can handle. Today's prices show that there is little difference between 386 and 486 workstations.

Equipping Workstations with Hard Drives

If you decide to exclude disk drives on the basis of historical costs, you'll miss new opportunities. With the low cost of disk drives, a single, centralized mass storage system in your server is the most cost-effective. Utilizing central storage can facilitate backup and maintenance of software. However, local drives can be warranted, especially with the very low costs of good, small storage devices. Small local hard drives (80-170M) generally cost less than $200 and afford the following advantages:

- Performance enhancement for Windows
- Storage for nonessential and nonshared files
- Simplicity in workstation training and operation
- The ability to operate on or off the network

Late-model local hard drives are good and inexpensive. They serve many purposes, simplify the user interface, and provide quick automated boot and local storage of OS files. All users are not forced to deal with centralized computing at all times, which provides good balance.

When choosing your hard-drive configuration, the most important factor to consider is the cost of centralized storage versus the potential cost of losing local files that the users have not backed up.

> **NOTE** ▷
>
> On the downside, local storage is rarely backed up. NetWare 3.12 and 4.x versions are shipped with the SBACKUP.NLM utility, which can back up workstation hard drives to a single, server-based storage device.

Character-Based Applications

Normal text-based applications typically require little power. Word processing, spreadsheets and shared databases account for the common applications used on a network. Unless large files, mail merges, and frequent switching of documents or applications are part of the workload, almost any 80286 or higher PC will do the job with just one megabyte of RAM.

Windows-Based Applications

Windows and other graphical user interfaces (GUIs) can be quite hardware-intensive, so processor, RAM, and video speed are important aspects to consider. You should buy the most workstation your budget can afford; Windows always can perform better on faster hardware.

You probably will find that access to the file server's disk is faster when the network is not heavily loaded, but the addition of a local hard drive can significantly reduce network traffic by locating the Windows swap file on local hard drives. The addition of a local hard drive is almost a necessity when you run Windows with a file server.

Video enhancements are an important part of the Windows workstation. Several designs, including local bus video cards and cards with accelerator chips, can make a tremendous difference in the perceived level of performance.

EISA or MCA bus design is not normally a factor to consider when buying a Windows workstation. EISA and MCA computers do not provide significantly better network I/O or video capabilities than ISA designs in DOS-based workstations. Compare product reviews in your favorite PC magazine; they usually compare workstations with Windows-oriented benchmark utilities. See Chapters 47, "Installing and Configuring Windows with NetWare," and 48, "Running Windows on a Network," for more information.

Workstation NICs

Workstation NICs do not demand the highest technology. A workstation NIC generally limits the workstation I/O throughput, and the differences between inexpensive and exotic workstation NICs are generally marginal. Compare brands, support, workstation performance, price, and warranties. Do not be misled by performance statistics obtained when the computer is used as a server NIC. Many NICs work two or three times faster as a server than they do as a workstation.

Another factor to consider with Ethernet is the the type of connector and cabling to use. Many new NIC models have both BNC and RJ-45 connectors for coaxial and 10BASE-T cabling. These features give you added flexibility and may reduce upgrade costs when you move computers or renew your cable plant.

> **TIP** ▶
>
> Unless a very high-bandwidth application demands high levels of I/O, your investment in NICs should be limited to inexpensive 8-bit and 16-bit models.
>
> Don't overlook warranty and support as important factors in decision making. Many NIC vendors now offer lifetime, free-replacement warranties and free, unlimited technical support.

If a workstation is a multitasking (OS/2 or UNIX) workstation, you may want to consider 32-bit busmastering NICs. DOS-based workstations either read or write, but do not do both at the same time. An 8-bit NIC can significantly restrict OS/2 and UNIX multitasking.

Upgrading Workstations

Another factor to consider in selecting workstations is *future demands*. A PC has a useful life of several years, but improvements and declining prices might mean that maintaining or upgrading a PC won't be sufficient. Many PCs are upgradable, but upgrading hardware has not proven to be cost effective. Sometimes the accumulated costs of an upgrade can be more than the cost of an entirely new PC.

You should select a workstation that will satisfy user requirements through the next several years. (The length of the period that you calculate is dependent on your ability to forecast demands.) Remember that purchasing insufficient resources costs more in the long run.

Accounting factors should be considered when calculating the cost of acquiring equipment. Equipment may be fully depreciated in five years and may be cost-effective to replace. Normally, however, hardware demands outstrip depreciation considerations and should be your primary concern.

The bottom line in workstation acquisition is a computer that will fit into the budget. Most users never have more power than they need. Conversely, buying an underpowered PC can result in lost opportunity over the few years of its useful life. If a single task that is repeated five times a day were to take an extra minute each time, the lost productivity would amount to more than 20 hours per year per employee. Multiply the lost productivity by the number of users affected, and you can see the immense cost of using underpowered PCs. Larger companies should consider the advantage of purchasing a little more power than might be needed, especially now that PC costs are so low.

Power Conditioning, Power Monitoring

An important factor to consider is the power you put through your file server. NetWare 3.x and 4.x versions can be hampered by poorly conditioned power. Most administrators are unaware that NetWare's nonpreemptive processing makes it especially susceptible to power defects. You have three basic considerations with file servers and power:

- Source interruption
- Conditioning
- Supply monitoring

Uninterruptible Power Sources

Your file server cannot handle an interruption of power from your AC source. If a momentary loss of power or drop in voltage causes your file server to go down, files can be damaged. Because active files are cached in RAM on the server, loss of power causes loss of updates and a loss of updated entries to volume DETs and FATs. (For a better understanding of why this occurs, refer to Chapter 3.)

Two types of power supplies are sold for file server protection: uninterruptible power supplies (UPSs) and switching power supplies. Both types generally are called UPSs; however, a true UPS provides battery power to your server, and AC power regenerates the battery. A switching power supply provides AC from your power receptacle and switches to battery power if the source is interrupted, as shown in Figure 7.3. A true UPS provides better protection and can also filter out power defects. A switching power supply is adequate if it can switch within four microseconds. A good UPS provides superior protection, and although it is more expensive, it can be more cost-effective when filtering out power defects, as discussed in the next section.

FIGURE 7.3.

A true UPS versus a switching power supply.

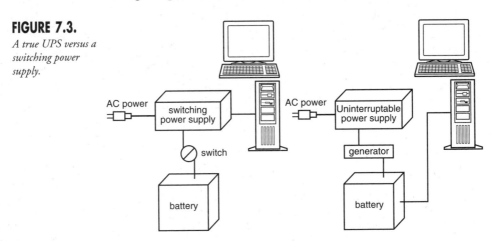

Power Conditioning

Many types of power defects can shorten the life of your file server's integrated circuits. Some power defects actually can cause your server to crash, depending upon what thread is in process on the file server. This is caused by NetWare's nonpreemptive processing (explained in detail in Chapter 2, "Local Area Networks"). Novell's Systems Research Department issued a research report in December 1991, "Power and Grounding for Distributed Computing," which explicitly detailed power problems and solutions for NetWare servers.

> **CAUTION** ▷
>
> UPS protection is not enough for a server. Many power defects can cause your server to crash, depending upon what thread may be running. Power in office complexes often is poorly conditioned.
>
> Special specifications for electrical installations do not always do the trick either, because electrical implementation is not governed by specifications alone. Very often, such installations do not accomplish what specifications say they should.

Surge protectors and suppressors do not do much (if anything at all) to protect your server. They are designed mainly for personal protection against large voltage or amperage surges and spikes, such as lightning strikes. Your computer power supply transforms all voltage to the lower voltages at which your computer's components operate anyway.

The problem with voltage or amperage surges or spikes is the *edge speed* of the transition—that is, how quickly the voltage or amperage change occurs. A power fluctuation may be small enough to slip past a surge protector but fast enough in edge speed to cause damage or crash your server.

> **CAUTION** ▷
>
> If a large spike is grounded to the common grounding wire on your electrical service, it can enter your computer's power supply through the ground—thereby escaping all protection. Such spikes also have been known to charge through an Ethernet cabling segment grounded in common. This can cause damage to multiple NICs and workstations. Always make certain that grounding is done to a good earth ground so that surges and spikes go directly to earth, and not back into other electrical equipment.

Another major problem many sites experience is poorly grounded power. Power differentials can exist between different parts of buildings. You may have a LAN segment connecting equipment that is powered from two different transformers, resulting in different voltage at one end than at the other. This is why Ethernet segments need to be grounded at one end only. A condition such as this can cause the higher-voltage end to leak electricity to the other equipment, resulting in data errors at high-bandwidth utilization levels.

Other grounding problems can cause excessive line noise and power defects. If electrical installations were performed in strict compliance with codes, these problems would not be so common. Even well-constructed buildings, however, suffer from various types of grounding deficiencies. The problem with electrical specifications is that they do not control how the installation is to be done, and often the method of installation cancels the expected benefits of the specifications.

> **TIP** ▶
>
> You can't detect some of these problems without a sophisticated power analyzer. If you have questions about your power protection, you should have your power line monitored with a Dranitz analyzer or a similar piece of equipment.

Many types of power transformers, power filters, and other devices are available, but the most comprehensive device to use is a good *power conditioner* that is grounded to a separate direct ground to earth. This device should be employed with your UPS—not in place of it.

UPS Monitoring

NetWare includes OS capability to automatically shut down the server OS when power is interrupted. A simple connection (via RS-232C or interface card and cable) between your power supply and server can notify the server OS that power has been shut off at the supply side of your UPS. This feature requires no special vendor server software but does require a UPS equipped for UPS monitoring.

Segmentation of LANs

When designing your system, planning sufficient bandwidth for the users on each LAN is a primary consideration. Users can be organized as workgroups, which have traditionally been assigned one LAN and one server. Today, NetWare design enables multiple LANs per server, so the most common way of providing workgroup performance is to configure a file server with an NIC for each workgroup, as shown in Figure 7.4.

FIGURE 7.4.

Workgroup LANs integrated into a single server.

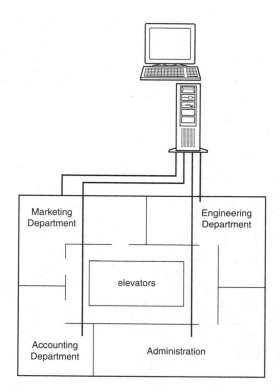

Monitoring bandwidth utilization and other LAN statistics is called *baselining*. Baselining is used to determine the amount of traffic and error levels on a LAN, which helps determine if the LAN should be broken down further into multiple smaller LANs.

NOTE ▶

When a single server has more than one NIC, you should consider the benefits of using 32-bit EISA or MCA busmastering NICs. Many tests have shown that a second ISA NIC can only marginally increase total LAN I/O traffic because of bus congestion and CPU saturation. Many tests also have shown that, depending upon the quality of the busmastering design, as many as four NICs can be installed in a single server without saturating the CPU.

Physical Infrastructure: The Topology of Your Internet

When multiple file servers are used with several LANs, a complex internetwork can result. Your internetwork's design can be described as its internetwork topology, which can consist of combinations of stars and linear buses. The network of LANs, servers, routers, and workstations forms a physical infrastructure that must efficiently route network traffic.

Many integrators see a network as a server-based infrastructure. Your first step in designing a physical infrastructure is to understand that the physical infrastructure and the logical configuration are two separate aspects of your internetwork, as illustrated in Figure 7.5. The user and system administrator see users, devices, and file systems as server-centric (or context-centric in a 4.0 NDS). However, the installer needs to configure a physical infrastructure that is LAN-centric (or WAN-centric). Similar to many other systems, the underlying hardware platform constitutes the infrastructure upon which NetWare is layered. System administration provides the logical configuration for the network (or internetwork) that masks the physical infrastructure.

If this resembles your network, pay particular attention to Part V of this book. As larger systems are downsized, administrators have difficulty with the incongruence of the physical-versus-logical aspects of their internetwork. Although Novell focuses on the logical design, you may need to learn far more than you expected about the physical infrastructure, including routers and IPX protocol, to be able to solve your problems and optimize internetwork performance.

FIGURE 7.5.

Physical infrastructure versus logical configuration of a network.

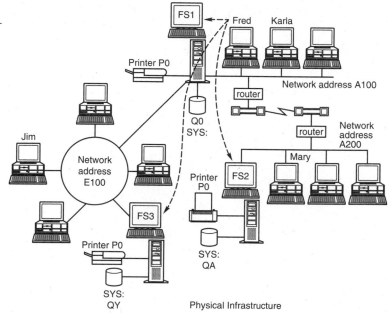

Physical Infrastructure

Logical Configuration:

FS1:
    Queue   = Q0
    Volume = FS1/SYS:
    User   = Fred
    User   = Karla

FS2:
    Queue   = QA
    Volume = FS2/SYS:
    User   = Fred
    User   = Mary

FS3:
    Queue   = QY
    Volume = FS3/SYS:
    User   = Fred
    User   = Jim

Summary

A well-designed network does not happen by default. Many factors must be properly planned and configured to create a system that works well. This chapter discussed many aspects that an integrator or administrator must consider in planning and installing NetWare in medium-to-large networks and internetworks.

Planning a NetWare Directory Services Tree

by Peter Kuo

8

IN THIS CHAPTER

In NetWare 4.x, the server-centric bindery used by NetWare 2.x and 3.x systems has been replaced by NetWare Directory Services (NDS), a global, distributed, replicated database of information that is *context-oriented*. The NDS includes information about network resources such as servers, printers, users, volumes, etc. Because of the complexity of NDS, it is important to plan your Directory tree before implementing it.

> **NOTE** ▶
>
> The term "Directory," with a capital D, refers specifically to the NDS database. It should not be confused with a file system's directory and its structure.

This chapter begins with a definition of NDS terms and an overview of NetWare Directory Services. It then discusses partitioning the NDS for performance considerations, replications for fault tolerance, and time-synchronization considerations. Finally, it puts all these pieces together by looking at some design and implementation issues for a hypothetical small company with multiple sites.

> **NOTE** ▶
>
> It is important to distinguish the physical infrastructure of your network or internetwork from the logical configuration created by system administration. In all IPX- and IP-based networks, the physical infrastructure contains actual hardware devices, which are *network addresses-centric*.
>
> In 3.x and 2.x versions, the logical user configuration is *server-centric*. In a 4.x environment, however, the logical view of the network as experienced by the user is *context-centric*, because objects represent physical devices and can be configured any way that suits administrative considerations.

Terminology of NetWare Directory Services

NetWare Directory Services is intended to be implemented in compliance with the Consultative Committee on International Telegraphy and Telephony's (CCITT)

X.500 naming requirements. CCITT's X.500 specification describes a global naming service. The objective of this specification is to have a common system in which the entire world could be networked. (Some of the other, more noted specifications from CCITT are X.25 for Public Data Networks (PDNs) and V.32 for modem standards.) It should be noted here that X.500 is still in the process of being finalized. Therefore, it is not yet a published standard.

Many of the terms and concepts, such as leaves, branches, and naming levels, have come from X.500. Novell has stated that once X.500 is standardized, NDS will be updated to be compliant. This section gives a brief definition of some of the NDS terms that you will encounter in this book.

Objects. An object in NDS is the data structure where information about a given physical entity is stored. It is not the physical entity itself, but a name for (or representation of) a physical entity. Currently, the following objects are defined within NDS.

User	Group	Profile	Organizational Role
NetWare Server	Volume	Directory Map	Print Queue
Print Server	Printer	AFP Server	Computer
Alias	Bindery Object	Bindery Queue	Unknown
[Root]	Organization	Organizational Unit	Country

Object Properties. Properties are different types of information associated with the NDS object. Depending on the given object, the list of associated properties differs. More than 100 separate properties are defined within the Directory Services Schema. For example, Login Name is one of 59 properties associated with a User object.

Property Values. The actual information. For example: "Peter" is the property value of the object property Login Name of an User object.

Object Rights. These define the permissible trustee actions on the object. These rights include the following: Browse, Create, Delete, Rename, and Supervisor.

Property Rights. These specify the possible action a trustee can perform on the information (property) associated with a given object. Each property can have a different set of rights. These rights include: Compare, Read, Write, Add Self/Delete Self, and Supervisor.

Context. This refers to one's current location in the NDS tree. It is similar to a "pointer" inside the database. It is sometimes also referred to as *Name Context.*

Overview of NetWare Directory Services

NetWare Directory Services uses a hierarchical tree structure to organize the various objects. Hence the structure is referred to as the NDS tree. The tree is made up of these three types of objects:

- The [Root] object
- Container objects
- Leaf objects

The [Root] object is the top of a given Directory tree. Branches are made up of Container objects and within them are Leaf objects. (See Figure 8.1.) A crude analogy is the directory tree of your hard disk: there is a backslash (\) or "root" at the top of a tree. Each container is a subdirectory; and leaf objects can be compared to files within a subdirectory.

FIGURE 8.1.

A schematic view of the NDS tree.

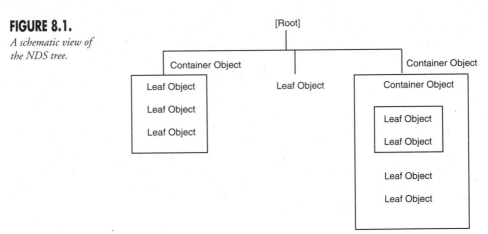

The [Root] object is created automatically when you first install NDS. It cannot be renamed or deleted. There can be only one [Root] object in a given NDS tree.

Container objects provide a way to logically organize other objects in the NDS tree. A container object can house other container objects within it. The top container is called the parent object or parent container. There are three types of containers: Organization (O=), Organizational Unit (OU=), and Country (C=).

There needs to be at least one Organization object within the NDS tree, and it must be placed one level below [Root]. This is usually used to denote a company, or a division within a company. Organizational Units are optional, and if you use them they must be placed one level below an Organization object or below another Organizational Unit. You can use OU to denote departments within a company, for example.

Because NDS is based on the CCITT X.500 specification, the use of Country container objects (C=) also is supported. It is to be located below [Root] and above Organization container objects. This is useful for a multinational company. (A list of country codes as defined by the International Standards Organization in 1992 is listed in Appendix D.)

WARNING ▷

Because of naming rules (which will be discussed later), it is recommended that you do not use Country objects in your NDS tree. It will make moving around within the NDS tree more difficult.

Leaf objects are single-entity objects. They do not contain other objects. They correspond to actual physical entities such as users, servers, and printers. A leaf object is denoted by CN= (Common Name). The following leaf objects have been defined in NDS.

User	*Group*	*Profile*	*Organizational Role*
NetWare Server	Volume	Directory Map	Print Queue
Print Server	Printer	AFP Server	Computer
Alias	Bindery Object	Bindery Queue	Unknown

As you can see, some of these objects are related to network users and groups, some are related to file servers, some are printer-related, and some are informational.

NOTE ▷

NetWare 2.x and 3.x servers are not automatically discovered and made part of the NDS. You need to manually define these resources within NDS using the NetWare Server objects.

Associated with each object is a set of rights. Depending on the object rights assignment, a user may or may not have access to certain parts of the tree. Specifically, he or she may or may not have access to network resources, such as printers, in those parts of the tree. These rights are NDS-based rights. When users are given access to a volume object, they still must be granted file system rights, which are separate from NDS rights.

Associated with each object is a set of properties. There are also rights associated with these properties, which are known as the *property rights*. These rights determine if and how certain properties (values) can be accessed. For example, in order to read a property, one must have the Browse property right. Object and property rights are discussed in more detail in Chapter 16, "Administering NetWare 4.01."

As with setting up a directory structure on a hard disk, there is no right way or wrong way of setting up an NDS tree. Most of it is a matter of company standard or personal preference. You can place container objects and leaf objects in different combinations as they best fit your needs. Figure 8.2 shows one possible configuration.

FIGURE 8.2.

A sample NDS tree.

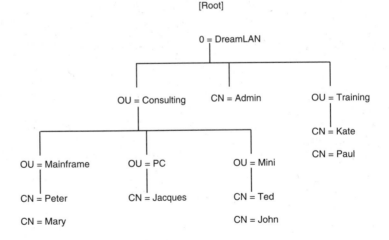

You can reference an object using either its complete name or a partial name. A complete name uses the full "path" to identify the object's location within the NDS tree. For example, in Figure 8.2 the complete name for the user object "Ted" is as follows:

```
.CN=Ted.OU=Mini.OU=Consulting.O=DreamLAN
```

Note the use of the leading period.

> **NOTE** ▶
>
> [Root] is implied in the reference.

> **TIP** ▶
>
> Most network operations require an object to be referenced by its complete name.

A partial name only lists part of the full name, relative to the current context within the NDS tree. For example, if your current context is OU=Consulting, the partial name for user object Ted is as follows:

```
CN=Ted.OU=Mini
```

Note that a leading period (.) is not required in partial naming.

These two NDS naming conventions are very similar to those of DOS directory naming conventions. If your current default directory is APPS, you can reference a directory using either the full directory path (e.g. \APPS\DB) or partial directory (DB) path.

There are three naming rules that NDS/X.500 uses for specifying complete or partial names, as follows:

The Path. The path begins from the left. The object is first, followed by its container, and so on up to their point of reference. For full names, it extends up to O= and for partial names, up to the current context.

Period Rules. Object names are separated by a period (.) which is the delimiter. A leading period causes the system to start the search from [Root]; no leading period starts the search at the leftmost field; a trailing period tells the system to start the search one level up. Multiple trailing periods are allowed.

Typeless Naming. In typeless naming, you can skip the attribute type of the object names. For example, .CN=Ted.OU=Mini.OU=Consulting.O=DreamLAN can be written as Ted.Mini.Consulting.DreamLAN.

> **NOTE** ▶
>
> NDS makes the following assumptions when interpreting typeless names:
>
> The rightmost name is of type O=.
>
> The leftmost name is of type CN=.
>
> Intervening names are of type OU=.
>
> Therefore, if you use a Country object in your tree, you cannot use typeless naming.

NetWare Directory Services is a globally distributed database that describes the location of your network resources, including users. Part of the NDS "data" is the access security to various portions of the tree. This is discussed in detail in Chapter 16.

Now that you have an understanding of the concepts and terminology of NDS, you can examine some of the issues related to protecting the NDS database as well as maintaining NDS data integrity.

Partitioning

Partitions in NDS are logical divisions (or "pieces") of the Directory's global database. Each partition is a distinct unit of the global database and can be stored in different locations on the network. Consider your NDS database as a large jigsaw puzzle, each piece corresponding to a partition. (See Figure 8.3.)

One or more partitions make up your NDS database. By default, a new partition is created when a NetWare 4.x server is installed in a new context in the Directory tree. The first such partition is called the Root partition. There is only one Root partition per NDS tree.

> **CAUTION** ▶
>
> NDS tree partitions should not be confused with file system partitions. NDS partitions do not contain information about the file system, only about NDS objects and their associated properties.

FIGURE 8.3.

This NDS Database is made up of four partitions.

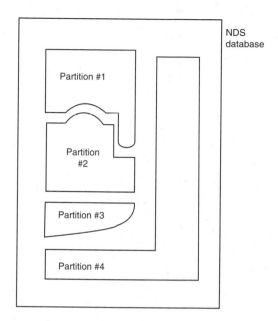

NDS
database

Partition #1

Partition #2

Partition #3

Partition #4

For lack of a better analogy, NDS partitions can be compared to the pieces in the aforementioned jigsaw puzzle. Every time a NetWare 4.x server is "installed" into a new context in the Directory tree, a new piece of the puzzle is created. Referring to the example of Figure 8.3, if a NetWare 4.x server is installed into a new container in, say, Partition #3, a fifth partition is created in this NDS database.

Consider a simple situation, as shown in Figure 8.4. The first 4.x server is installed in OU=Consulting. Because this is the first server in the NDS tree, a Root partition is created and a Master replica (a copy of this partition) is placed on server LAB_SERVER. When the second server is installed in OU=Training, a new partition is created as the server is placed in a different context. The CLASS_SERVER partition is created. A Master replica is stored on CLASS_SERVER.

By default, when a partition is created, a Read/Write copy (replica) of this partition is placed on the server containing the new server's parent context. In the example shown in Figure 8.4, a Read/Write replica of the CLASS_SERVER partition is placed on LAB_SERVER.

FIGURE 8.4.

Default partitions with two servers.

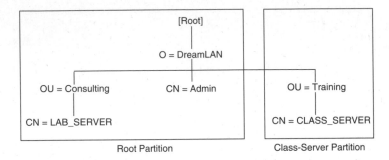

Root Partition

Class-Server Partition

CAUTION ▶

By default, no Read/Write replica of the Root partition is placed anywhere. You need to do that manually.

This default partition management is fine for sites that do not have a flat tree with multiple Organizational Units under the Organization container. Consider the NDS tree shown in Figure 8.5. With the default partition-management rules, the HQ_SERVER holds five Read/Write replicas of the partitions. Imagine more OUs branching off 0=, each with its own server. All their Read/Write replicas will be placed on the HQ_SERVER. The root server can quickly be overwhelmed by the extra management overhead because of all the replicas. The situation gets worse if WAN links are involved, because of the slower update traffics that the root server will have to deal with.

FIGURE 8.5.

Default partitions with multiple servers in a flat NDS tree.

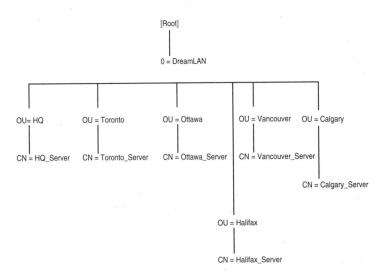

Study the flow of information in your NDS tree and make a decision on how many partitions are needed. Plan your tree to include as few partitions as needed to help reduce your partition-related network traffic. However, keep as many as are needed to provide the desired level of fault tolerance. When you are ready, use either PARTMGR or the "Partition Manager" function from NWAdmin to reorganize your partitions.

Replications

Replicas are copies of an NDS partition that can be distributed to remote NetWare 4.x servers. You use replicas to provide fault tolerance for the directory database by eliminating any NDS single point of failure *or* to provide faster access to NDS information for users across a WAN link.

CAUTION ▶

Replication of NDS partitions does not provide fault tolerance for your file system. Only the NDS information is replicated.

TIP ▶

If you want to provide fault tolerance to your file system, consider mirroring or duplexing your hard disks. For the ultimate in server fault tolerance, consider SFT-III. (These factors are the subject of Part VII, "Preventing Downtime.")

A replica of a partition is a mirror copy of the original partition. There are three types of replicas:

- Master
- Read/Write
- Read-Only

A master replica is the first copy (original) of a newly merged or split partition. There can be only one Master replica of each partition. If you want to change the Directory tree structure of a partition, you must work with a Master replica of that partition.

You use the Master replica to read and update the NDS database. To create and copy replicas, you need to have access to the Master replica. If you want to create a new partition, you have to work with the Master replica.

A Read/Write replica is the most common type of replica. It is simply a "copy" of the Master replica. When changes are made to a Read/Write replica, update traffic is sent to the Master replica and the Master updates other replicas of the partition. In essence, if you want to update the NDS database with a Read/Write replica, you do it indirectly through the Master replica. You can update a Read/Write replica, but cannot copy it to create another copy.

WARNING ▶

All servers containing a replica of a certain partition form what is called a *replica ring*. All servers in the replica ring must be online for a partition merge or split to complete successfully. If one of the servers in the replica ring is down when a partition merge or split is attempted, NDS will continue to try to update the replica on the missing server until it is successful. In these situations, NDS can flood the network with update requests and can seriously degrade your network performance.

A Read-Only replica is static. It changes only when update traffic is received from a Master replica. Because one cannot write to a Read-Only replica, one cannot use a Read-Only replica to support user login. However, it can be used to facilitate properties value lookup.

TIP ▶

It is recommended that to maintain good NDS performance, no more than eight replicas be placed on any one server.

When changes are made to either a Master or Read/Write replica, replica synchronization must take place in order to update the other replicas. Each NDS event is time-stamped. This is important, because updates need to be applied in the correct order. With a large network that has multiple routes and slow WAN links, time-stamping of NDS events becomes crucial. Therefore, it is very important that times are synchronized within your network.

NOTE ▶

If a change is made to a Read/Write replica when the Master replica is not available, it causes a conflict in versions. You must decide to use either the Read/Write replica to update the Master or the Master to update the Read/Write replica.

WARNING ▶

Because of some improvements made to the NDS-related NLMs in NetWare 4.01, NDS information stored on NetWare 4.0 servers will not be able to synchronize with those stored on NetWare 4.01 servers. Make sure you upgrade your NetWare 4.0 servers to 4.01.

Time Synchronization

As mentioned in the previous section, each NDS update event is time-stamped to ensure proper update order. Therefore, it is very important that network time be correctly synchronized.

There are four types of Time Servers:

1. **Secondary Time Server**. Obtains its time from other types of time servers. This is the default if it is not the first server installed.

2. **Primary Time Server**. Coordinates with others to establish a common time.

3. **Reference Time Server**. Gets its time from an external time source, such as an atomic clock.

4. **Single Reference Time Server**. Determines the time for all other servers on the network. This is the default for the first server installed.

Depending on your network layout and time-synchronization requirements, you need to pick one or more of the preceding time-server types.

A Secondary Time Server provides the time to clients, such as workstations. You should designate it to contact a Single Reference, Reference, or Primary server that is physically close (taking into account speed of link and number of routers) in order to cut down on network traffic between the time servers.

A Primary Time Server polls other Primary Time Servers or Reference Time Servers and then votes with them. An averaged time is used to synchronize the network time. Because Primary Time Servers adjust their clocks depending on the outcome of the vote, network time may drift slightly. Since the Reference Time Server does not change its time but Primary Time Servers do, eventually all Primary Time Servers will end up the same as the Reference Time Server.

> **TIP** ▶
>
> In general, Primary Time Servers are used on large networks to provide redundant paths for Secondary Time Servers. Novell suggests that a network should have at least one Primary Time Server for every 125 to 150 Secondary Time Servers.

A Reference Time Server gets its time from an external source. It provides a time to which all other time servers (Primary or other Reference) synchronize. You should use a Reference Time Server if it is important to have a central point to control network time.

> **NOTE** ▶
>
> 44Cadence, an NLM-based product from C-Note Software, P.O. Box 21556, St. Louis, MO, 63132 (Phone: 800-489-0090; Fax: 314-997-9666) can be used on a Reference Time Server to connect to an external time source.

The Single Reference Time Server provides time to Secondary Time Servers. It does not coexist with Reference and Primary Time Servers. In general, it is not recommended for a large network because it is the sole source of time on the network, and all other servers must contact it. The Single Reference Time Server is, however, perfectly fine for a small-to-medium-sized network.

> **WARNING** ▶
>
> The importance of proper time synchronization of the network cannot be emphasized enough. You also should *not* set the time of any of your servers to a "future" time. Consider this: if you set the time on a server "ahead" by 10

minutes, and an NDS event occurs (a user logs in, for example), this informa-tion will not propagate to other replicas until the network time catches up with the time-stamp associated with this event. This may take more than 10 minutes, depending on your time-server configurations.

Time servers discover each other using two methods: Service Advertising Protocol (SAP) information or manual configuration. By default, Primary, Reference, and Single Reference Time Servers use SAP to inform others of their presence on the network. Secondary Time Servers use this SAP information to find and choose a time server from which to obtain network time. Primary and Reference Time Servers use SAP information to find other servers in order to vote for an averaged network time.

You can quickly install your network using the SAP method because the discovery and reconfiguration process is automatic. However, for a large network you may have noticeable additional network traffic due to these SAPs. Another disadvantage of this method is if you constantly bring up and down "test" servers that are also configured as time servers. This can cause time disruptions on your network.

Using the custom manual-configuration method, you can avoid much of the prob-lems discussed herein and have complete control of your time-synchronization envi-ronment. However, you have to plan ahead for installation as well as any time-source changes. For example, if you are to remove a server that is also a Primary Time Server, you must manually update the approved time server list maintained on *each* file server on your network that this removal affects.

It is important to carefully consider your network layout before deciding on the type of time servers to implement.

Bindery Emulation

NetWare 4.x provides a feature called Bindery Emulation to support backward com-patibility with pre-NetWare 4.0 applications. This feature also enables NetWare 3.x and 2.x servers to coexist on the same network with NetWare 4.x servers running NDS.

Bindery emulation applies only to leaf objects in a specific container object. The container object to which bindery emulation points is called the "bindery context." By default, the bindery context of a given NetWare 4.x server is the container in which the server is installed. You must have on that server a Master or Read/Write replica of the partition in which the bindery context is located.

This is a very useful feature for sites slowly migrating from the older NETX client shells, as well as for products that do not yet support NDS. Examples are NetWare for NFS, NetWare for SAA, and NetWare for Macintosh.

Designing NDS Trees

When designing your NDS tree, you should consider the following:

■ **A naming convention**. It is important to have a naming convention so that you will not have duplicated object names. It also helps you and your users to locate a particular resource.

> **TIP** ►
>
> It is advised that you do not use the same name for a container and a file server. It can lead to confusion, especially when you are using typeless names (for example, `Toronto.Toronto.Novell`).

■ **Good design**. As with a database, a well-planned NDS tree is easy to manage and expand. Also, this helps to minimize network traffic. You also should build in NDS fault tolerance, including time synchronization.

■ **Good resource placement within the tree**. Consider how the various resources are to be utilized by your users. Place them in the same container whenever possible. This makes access much easier, and you will require less management work in setting up access rights.

■ **Logical grouping**. Whenever possible, set up user groups so access rights only need to be assigned once. This will also ease your management workload.

Following these rules, you will have a much easier time managing your NDS tree.

It may be worthwhile to use your company's organizational chart as a starting point for designing your NDS. The organizational chart shows you how user groups can be formed. Alternately, if your company has multiple sites, you may want to group by location instead. In many cases, one has to compromise between logical grouping and good resource placement by considering how people actually access the various network resources.

Generally, you do not have too many levels of Organizational Units. This increases the length of your user's context, which is a common source of confusion and problems. A rule of thumb is to use no more than about five levels of containers ([Root] is not considered as part of the level, because it does not appear anywhere in an object's context). Again, just as with a directory structure on your hard disk, it should not have too many levels of containers. Keep it simple.

To maintain good NDS performance, you shouldn't have more than 500 objects per container. Otherwise, you can experience problems with NDS-related NetWare utilities, such as CX.

The section that follows is a case study setting up a sample NDS directory tree for a hypothetical company, Universal Exports.

Case Study: NDS Tree for Universal Exports

Consider that the hypothetical company, Universal Exports, has two sites: the head office and a regional office. Each site has two NetWare 4.01 servers, and a 56K leased line links them together. Sales staff are located in both locations, and the engineering staff is only at the head office. What will the NDS tree look like? Figure 8.6 shows one possible layout.

FIGURE 8.6.

A Possible NDS tree for Universal Exports.

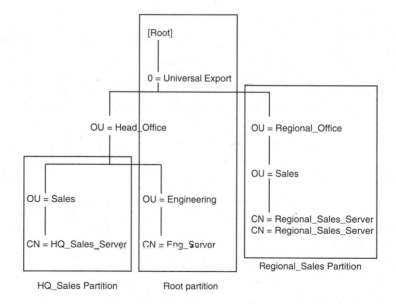

In this example, there is one OU for each location: OU=Head_Office and OU=Regional_Office. Under OU=Head_Office, there are two lower-level OUs, one for each department. Under OU=Regional_Office, you don't need a separate OU=Sales. However, when planning for future growth, having a separate OU=Sales makes it easier to add departments to OU=Regional_Office.

Three partitions have been created: the Root partition resides on the Engineering server Eng_Server; OU=Sales under OU=Head_Office has its own partition on server HQ_Sales_Server; and the Regional Office has its own partition on server Regional_Sales_Server1. Table 8.2 shows the location of various partition replicas, so there is NDS redundancy.

Table 8.2. Location of partition replicas.

Server	Partition	Replica type
Eng_Server	Root	Master
	HQ_Sales_Server	Read/Write
	Regional_Sales_Server1	Read/Write
HQ_Sales_Server	HQ_Sales_Server	Master
	Root	Read/Write
	Regional_Sales_Server1	Read/Write
Regional_Sales_Server1	Regional_Sales_Server1	Master
	Root	Read-Only
	HQ_Sales_Server	Read-Only
Regional_Sales_Server2	Regional_Sales_Server1	Read/Write
	Root	Read-Only
	HQ_Sales_Server	Read-Only

This configuration ensures that all partitions are replicated on at least one other server for backup purposes. Because the Engineering staff and HQ Sales people never travel to the regional office, there is no need to have a Read/Write replica. A Read-Only copy for lookup is sufficient. On the other hand, the regional-office sales staff travels often to HQ, so a Read/Write replica of their partition exists on the HQ_Sales_Server. If the HQ sales people also travel to the regional office, you can make the replica there Read/Write (instead of Read-Only).

Designate Eng_Server and Regional_Sales_Server1 as Primary Time Servers, and HQ_Sales_Server and Regional_Sales_Server2 as Secondary Time Servers. This way, on each side of the WAN link is a Primary Time Server. If the link goes down, the Secondary Time Servers still have their own local Primary Time Server. You use the default SAP method for time servers in order to discover each other and to perform time synchronization.

Remember, the NDS tree and network configuration is only one of many possible implementations. You need to properly understand your user needs and network resource layouts in order to design and implement a good NDS tree.

Summary

This chapter presented a brief introduction to NetWare Directory Services and some implementation considerations when designing an NDS tree, including partitions, replication, and time synchronization. A model NDS tree was presented for a hypothetical small company with multiple sites.

Installing the Server OS from CD-ROM

by Rick Sant'Angelo

9

Installing from CD-ROM can cut the time and labor involved in swapping diskettes. A CD-ROM install is necessary for 4.x versions because of the size of the installation—more than 79M of files arc installed for a full installation. NetWare 3.12 requires over 55M of disk space. The largest amount of disk space is consumed by on-line documentation. Because only electronic documentation is supplied, you should consider a full installation; and a CD-ROM makes your job simpler.

Resolving the Most Common Problems

You may install from a CD-ROM configured as either a DOS device or a NetWare device. Both methods are similar, but each initially requires the use of the CD-ROM as a DOS device. In the following chapters, installation instructions are provided for each method.

> **NOTE** ►
>
> Currently (because of disk driver availability), only SCSI CD-ROMs can be used as NetWare devices. In order to use a physical device as a NetWare disk drive, you must have a NetWare disk driver in addition to the CDROM.NLM that Novell provides with 3.12 and 4.x versions. Non-SCSI CD-ROMs do not have NetWare drivers and therefore can function only as DOS devices on your server.

Physically Installing a CD-ROM

CD-ROM setup procedures differ slightly from one brand to another; however, a driver with configuration switches is necessary in your CONFIG.SYS. Then you must load MSCDEX.EXE to convert the CD file system to a DOS format. When these two steps are done, your CD-ROM will have a DOS drive letter assignment—usually D:—that you can use to access the files on the CD-ROM.

If you have a CD-ROM that has its own non-SCSI type interface card or if your CD-ROM connects to a parallel port, your installation as a DOS device should be simple. You can install from your DOS CD-ROM very easily, but you will not be able to use the CD-ROM drive as a NetWare device, either during or after the installation.

If you are using a SCSI device, see your disk adapter installation guide for instructions on physically configuring the SCSI adapter and devices, and loading the DOS drivers to access DOS devices. Once you have set up your SCSI adapter to access disk drives with DOS, a second software layer—CDNSASPI or ASPICD—must be loaded to access the CD-ROM drive. Then MSCDEX can be loaded TSR to mount the file system as a DOS file system.

Installation is quite simple once you have set up the CD-ROM as a DOS device. Place your NetWare CD-ROM distribution disk into your DOS CD-ROM drive and execute the INSTALL batch file. To locate this file (and later during the installation when you copy the System and Public files), you can select the CD-ROM drive letter (normally drive D:) and identify the directory to install from. If your CD-ROM is drive D:, your pathname will be

```
D:\NETWARE.312\ENGLISH
```

or

```
D:\NETWARE.40\ENGLISH
```

From this point on, the installation procedures are discussed in the following chapters, depending upon which version you install.

Using the CD-ROM as a NetWare Device

Installation from your CD-ROM drive as a NetWare device is only a bit more involved. It requires that you load NetWare disk drivers to access the SCSI devices and then load the NetWare CDROM.NLM utility. The device driver enables NetWare to access the SCSI subsystem. ASPI is used for CD-ROM support, and the CDROM.NLM does the same that MSCDEX.EXE does in DOS—it enables the CD-ROM file system to look like a normal disk drive file system. Once you have loaded these drivers, you can access the device as if it were another NetWare volume.

Here is the procedure for loading NetWare System and Public files from a CD-ROM configured as a NetWare disk drive:

1. You must have a SCSI CD-ROM (installed properly), and it must be connected to its own SCSI adapter. It can't be connected to the same adapter as the disk drive that you intend to make a NetWare device.

> **NOTE** ▶
>
> When the SCSI device driver is loaded for an adapter, you can communicate with it either as a CD-ROM or a NetWare disk drive, but not both. Although it is possible to connect both types of devices on a SCSI-2 adapter, you will encounter conflicts during the NetWare installation. Therefore, your disk drive must be connected to one adapter, and your CD-ROM to another.

2. Bring up your CD-ROM drive and start your installation routine (similar to the installation from a DOS CD-ROM). Change to the CD-ROM drive and then change directories to the NETWARE.312\ENGLISH or the NETWARE.40\ENGLISH directory. Execute the INSTALL batch file and follow its instructions.

3. To copy the System and Public files, switch to the console screen and load the disk driver, the ASPI driver (usually called CDNSASPI or ASPICD), and the CDROM.NLM utility. If your adapter does not require the ASPI driver, ignore this step.

4. Mount the SYS: volume by typing `MOUNT SYS:`.

> **NOTE** ▶
>
> You will not be able to mount the CD-ROM volume unless the SYS: volume is mounted.

5. Mount the CD-ROM volume. First, type `CD DEVICE LIST`.

   You should see the CD-ROM volume name (for example, NETWARE_312).

   Mount the volume name you see listed. To mount the NetWare 3.12 CD-ROM, use the following command at the console prompt:

   `CD MOUNT NETWARE_312:`

6. Switch back (Alt+Esc) to the INSTALL utility and then continue your installation by copying the System and Public files from the pathname NETWARE_312:NETWARE.312/ENGLISH for NetWare 3.12 or from the root of the NETWARE_40 volume.

NOTE ▶

Although SCSI-2 standards enable different devices to be connected to a single adapter (that is, a disk drive and an CD-ROM), this is not possible during a NetWare server installation. When a NetWare driver is loaded for a SCSI adapter, that driver can function as either a disk driver or a CD-ROM driver, but not both at the same time.

Summary

Installing from CD-ROM is simpler than previous methods, after you have installed your CD-ROM drive as a DOS device. Novell provides the software to enable you to access your CD-ROM drive as a NetWare volume—provided you have drivers to access the device. This is normally possible only with SCSI CD-ROM devices, because other types do not have NetWare drivers.

Once you have mounted the CD-ROM as a NetWare device, users can access it like any other disk drive. You can leave your online documentation on the CD-ROM and save disk space if you like. You also can use your CD-ROM disk drive for other CD-ROM disks.

NOTE ▶

Whenever you would like to change the disk in your CD-ROM, you must first DISMOUNT the CD volume. After inserting an new CD-ROM disk, follow the preceding steps to MOUNT the new volume.

Installing and Configuring NetWare 3.12

by Rick Sant'Angelo

10

Any competent hardware/software technician can install NetWare 3.12. There have been, to be sure, horror stories about NetWare installation, but those stories are usually related to 2.x versions, which were more difficult to install. Those versions required the installer to select object code, configure it, link it into an executable OS file, install it, and then see if it would work.

Of course, it rarely worked the first time, and it was anyone's guess as to why. Another installation attempt meant starting all over again in the hopes that this would result in a functioning, executable OS file. To further complicate matters, compatibility used to be a horrendous problem, and disk drives often were not reliable.

NetWare 3.12's installation is simple. Hardware problems have been reduced to an occasional ISA NIC configuration conflict, and installation procedures have been reduced to loading drivers on top of an already-running operating system. Installing the OS is as simple as executing the standard unconfigured OS file from DOS and loading drivers just as you would execute any application on an OS. If a driver fails to load, the configuration is obviously not correct, or the device is simply not functioning. Fixing the problem does not mean starting a lengthy process all over again.

Loading the workstation shells also has become simpler. You must generate the DOS Requester installation diskettes from the CD-ROM and then execute the install application. You will be prompted to answer a few questions, such as what type of NIC you have installed. The process is similarly simple for OS/2 and Macintosh workstations. The hardest part of the installation is assembling the hardware, alleviating conflicting settings, and installing the Ethernet, Token Ring, or another type of LAN.

The purpose of this chapter is to guide you through the installation of NetWare 3.12's server OS.

Installing these products is similar to installing any other software product, except that physical hardware settings have to be identified when loading the software. This chapter does not go into detail about hardware, LANs, or other versions of NetWare. It is a simple "how to" guide for the installation of 3.12 servers and clients.

This chapter assumes the following:

1. You have selected and assembled a computer to be a file server.
2. Your LAN cabling has been installed.
3. Your NICs are installed and not conflicting with other hardware or software devices.
4. You have installed a CD-ROM drive as a DOS device.
5. You are installing a single server and just a few workstations.

The preceding assumptions are made in order to confine the discussion to the process of installing NetWare on servers and clients. Previous chapters dealt with the issues that precede these assumptions; later chapters deal with the complexity of internetworking and other related issues.

Installing a CD-ROM

NetWare 3.12 is best installed from a CD-ROM drive in the server. You can order 3.12 on floppy diskettes; however, the installation files weigh in at about 60 MB. This makes a floppy install quite impractical.

The CD-ROM drive may or may not be an SCSI device; however, if it is, it needs to be installed on a separate SCSI adapter from the disk drive that will be used for NetWare. (See the previous chapter for tips on installing and using a CD-ROM drive in your server.)

Installing the Server OS

The second step in installing your network is to install the NetWare 3.12 server operating system.

Overview of Server Installation

Installing the server OS comprises the following steps. These steps will be discussed in detail later.

1. Make a bootable floppy diskette for your server and copy a few files to the boot diskette, or make a minimum 5M bootable DOS partition on your disk.

2. Execute the INSTALL.BAT file from the CD-ROM. Follow the instructions.

3. Execute SERVER.EXE (the NetWare 3.12 OS).

4. Load INSTALL.NLM.

5. Partition the disk(s).

6. Create the volume(s).

7. Copy the SYSTEM and PUBLIC files.

8. Load and configure the disk driver.

9. Load and configure the NIC driver(s).

10. Bind IPX to the NIC driver(s).

11. Create the system startup files.

Make a Bootable Floppy Diskette or a 5M Bootable DOS Partition on Your Disk

If you prefer to boot your server from a floppy diskette, you must make a bootable diskette and copy the following files onto it:

1. SERVER.EXE

2. Your disk driver disk_driver.DSK (ISADISK.DSK or equivalent)

3. Your server NIC driver (*LAN_driver.LAN*)

4. INSTALL.NLM

If you prefer to boot your server from your server hard drive, you may make a 5M (or larger) DOS partition, make it bootable, format it with a DOS format, and put the DOS system files on it; or you can elect to have the CD-ROM-based Installation utility perform this step for you.

If you have made a DOS partition on your hard drive, copy your disk driver (*disk_driver.DSK*) and LAN driver (*LAN_driver.LAN*) to your DOS partition.

> **NOTE** ▶
>
> Your NetWare 3.12 SYSTEM-1 diskette contains Novell DOS system, FDISK.EXE, and FORMAT.EXE files. You can use this diskette to boot your server, create the bootable DOS partition, format it, and place the system files on it. You no longer need to purchase another copy of DOS for your file server.

> **NOTE** ▶
>
> Your SYSTEM-1 diskette contains your server OS serial number. You should use a diskcopy of this diskette for the installation procedure and store the original in a safe place. You will need the original if you ever decide to upgrade.

It is not necessary to diskcopy all of your original distribution diskettes. You will handle them only once during installation, and no changes will be written to them.

Once you have made your disk bootable, boot your server with DOS.

Execute the INSTALL.BAT file from the CD-ROM

You will find this file in the \NETWARE.312\ENGLISH directory. The screen shown in Figure 10.1 will appear.

FIGURE 10.1.

Select an Installation Option screen.

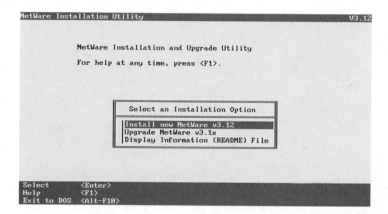

From this screen, select Display Information (README) File. This option provides a wealth of installation instructions, as shown in Figure 10.2.

FIGURE 10.2.

README listings.

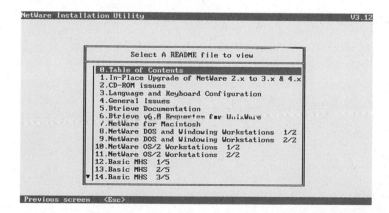

Next, select the option you want to use—either "Upgrade NetWare 3.1x" or "Install new NetWare 3.12." This chapter shows the "Install new NetWare 3.12" option. The procedures for the upgrade option are very similar.

When you proceed with the "Install new NetWare 3.12" option, you are given the choice of retaining your current partitioning or creating a new DOS partition as shown in Figure 10.3. If you already have made a DOS partition, select "Retain current disk partitions." Otherwise, follow the directions, which will create a bootable DOS partition and move you to the next step.

FIGURE 10.3.

Disk Partition options.

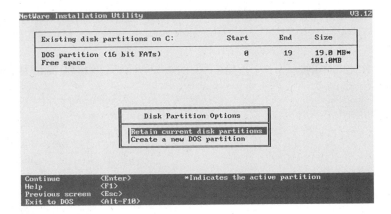

Name the Server and its Internal Network Address

The screen shown in Figure 10.4 will appear next. Assign a name per your requirements. You should make a name that is short (it will be part of the pathname) but descriptive of the server. You can't include illegal characters.

Next you will be prompted to assign an Internal Network Address, as shown in Figure 10.5. This address is a unique address to identify the location of the server's router. This address can be up to eight characters hexadecimal, and it must be unique from all other network addresses to be assigned to LANs, WANs, and other server internal network addresses.

FIGURE 10.4.

Enter server name.

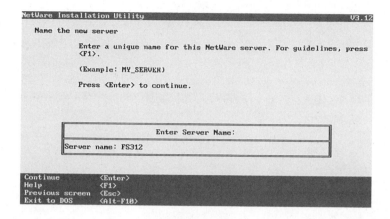

FIGURE 10.5.

Enter IPX Internal Network address.

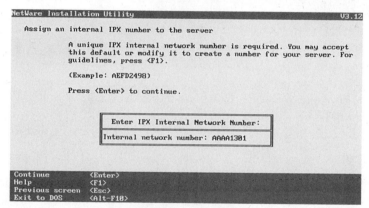

TIP ▶

It is a good idea to assign a numbering convention for network addresses. For example, internal addresses can all start with FFFF and can have some proprietary significance, such as the inclusion of a code signifying where the server is located.

Copy the Startup Files to your Server's DOS Partition

The INSTALL.BAT next prompts you to enter the path to copy your server boot files from and to, as shown in Figure 10.6. You can edit the path to copy from by pressing F2. If your CD-ROM drive is addressed as drive D:, enter the following path:

```
D:\NETWARE.312\ENGLISH
```

FIGURE 10.6.

Enter the path for your server boot files.

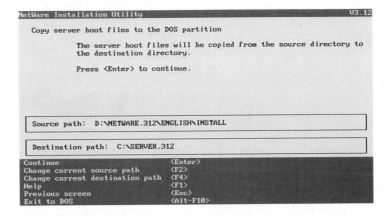

This copies SERVER.EXE, disk drivers, and other required files to the DOS partition. If you want to edit the destination directory on your hard drive, press F4. The directory you specify does not need to exist; INSTALL will make it for you.

When you press Enter, the screen shown in Figure 10.7 appears.

FIGURE 10.7.

The screen instructing you to insert the SYSTEM_1 diskette into drive A.

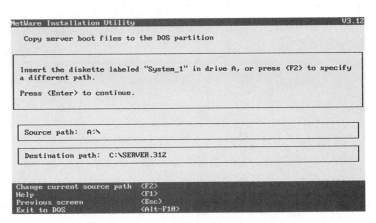

If you already have your SYSTEM_1 diskette in drive A:, you will not see this screen. The INSTALL.BAT utility will copy the appropriate files onto your DOS partition.

At this point, you may be notified of disk drivers and LAN drivers that need to be updated, as shown in Figure 10.8.

#### Chapter 10

FIGURE 10.8.

Instructions on updating disk and LAN drivers.

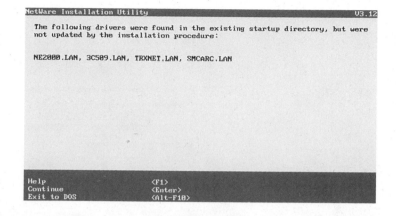

NetWare Installation Utility   V3.12

The following drivers were found in the existing startup directory, but were
not updated by the installation procedure:

NE2000.LAN, 3C509.LAN, TRXNET.LAN, SMCARC.LAN

Help   <F1>
Continue   <Enter>
Exit to DOS   <Alt-F10>

> **NOTE** ▶
>
> NetWare 3.12 includes LAN and disk drivers for an extensive selection of devices. However, your NICs and disk drivers may not be included, in which case, you will need to obtain new drivers from your vendor.
>
> Be certain to obtain the latest drivers for 3.12. Drivers for versions 3.11 and 4.0 often do not work properly with 3.12.
>
> Disk adapter vendors may require you to purchase a disk driver for NetWare separately. Drivers for SCSI disk subsystems come from the developer of the SCSI host adapter. Drivers for other types of drives normally accompany the disk controller.

Select the filename format to be used. Unless you intend to use keyboard support for a language other than English, select the DOS filename format, as shown in Figure 10.9.

> **NOTE** ▶
>
> The NetWare filename format option offers you two alternatives. Select the DOS filename format, or keyboard mapping might be case-sensitive.

FIGURE 10.9.

Selecting the filename format.

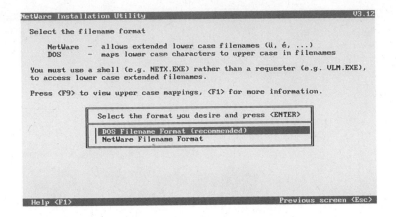

```
NetWare Installation Utility                                          V3.12
  Select the filename format

    NetWare  -  allows extended lower case filenames (ü, é, ...)
    DOS      -  maps lower case characters to upper case in filenames

  You must use a shell (e.g. NETX.EXE) rather than a requester (e.g. VLM.EXE),
  to access lower case extended filenames.

  Press <F9> to view upper case mappings, <F1> for more information.

          ┌─────────────────────────────────────────────────────┐
          │    Select the format you desire and press <ENTER>     │
          │  ┌─────────────────────────────────────────────────┐ │
          │  │ DOS Filename Format (recommended)                │ │
          │  │ NetWare Filename Format                          │ │
          │  └─────────────────────────────────────────────────┘ │
          └─────────────────────────────────────────────────────┘


  Help <F1>                                    Previous screen <Esc>
```

Make changes to your STARTUP.NCF and AUTOEXEC.NCF files, as shown in Figures 10.10 and 10.11.

FIGURE 10.10.

Edit the STARTUP.NCF.

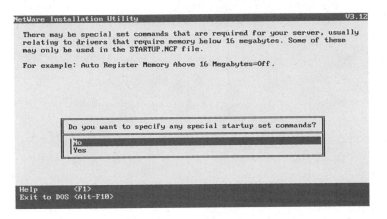

```
NetWare Installation Utility                                          V3.12
  There may be special set commands that are required for your server, usually
  relating to drivers that require memory below 16 megabytes. Some of these
  may only be used in the STARTUP.NCF file.

  For example: Auto Register Memory Above 16 Megabytes=Off.




          ┌─────────────────────────────────────────────────────┐
          │   Do you want to specify any special startup set commands? │
          │  ┌─────────────────────────────────────────────────┐ │
          │  │ No                                               │ │
          │  │ Yes                                              │ │
          │  └─────────────────────────────────────────────────┘ │
          └─────────────────────────────────────────────────────┘


  Help       <F1>
  Exit to DOS <Alt-F10>
```

FIGURE 10.11.

Edit the ATUTOEXEC.NCF.

```
NetWare Installation Utility                                          V3.12
  Copy server boot files to the DOS partition

     The ┌───────────────────────────────────────────┐e directory to
     the │ Do you want AUTOEXEC.BAT to load SERVER.EXE? │
         │  ┌─────────────────────────────────────────┐ │
     Pre │  │ No                                       │ │
         │  │ Yes                                      │ │
         │  └─────────────────────────────────────────┘ │
         └───────────────────────────────────────────┘


  ┌─────────────────────────────────────────────────────────────────┐
  │ Source path:  D:\NETWARE.312\ENGLISH\INSTALL                      │
  └─────────────────────────────────────────────────────────────────┘

  ┌─────────────────────────────────────────────────────────────────┐
  │ Destination path:  C:\SERVER.312                                  │
  └─────────────────────────────────────────────────────────────────┘


  Help        <F1>
  Exit to DOS <Alt-F10>
```

Make changes only as discussed in your LAN or disk driver manuals. Other changes for these files are not necessary. If you need to change them later, you will have an opportunity to edit them during installation and afterward.

The INSTALL.BAT will now start the server OS and leave you at a console (colon) prompt.

Load INSTALL.NLM. At the colon prompt, enter the following command:

```
LOAD INSTALL
```

You can abort the installation at this time and copy your latest 3.12 drivers onto your DOS partition. You may wait until the server OS is installed and then look for your LAN and disk drivers in the SYSTEM directory. Otherwise, you can load your drivers from floppy diskettes as discussed in the following step.

Continue or Execute SERVER.EXE

If you have exited to update your disk drivers, switch to your hard drive and execute SERVER.EXE. If you have elected to boot the server from a floppy disk, place your SYSTEM_1 diskette in any drive, switch to that drive, and type SERVER.

A colon prompt will be displayed, which indicates that the NetWare operating system is running and in the command mode. This screen is called the *console screen*. If you do not end up with a colon prompt, the OS has not started. Check the console for error messages. It is very rare that the OS will not load on any 386SX or higher processor.

Load INSTALL.NLM

Next, load the INSTALL.NLM module from a colon prompt in the same manner that you loaded the disk driver and LAN driver. This runs the installation program, which is entirely menu-driven. You will see the screen that is shown in Figure 10.12.

During this part of the program, disk partitioning, Hot Fixing, volume creation, creation of the automatic boot files, and copying of the system and public files occurs.

FIGURE 10.12.

The INSTALL.NLM Installation Options menu.

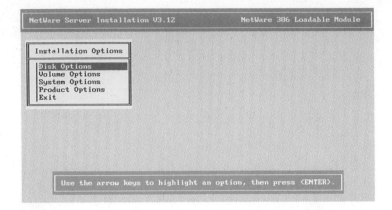

Partition Disk(s)

From the INSTALL main menu, select Disk Options. You will see the current disk partitioning information and the Create NetWare Partition menu, shown in Figure 10.13.

FIGURE 10.13.

Disk Options submenu.

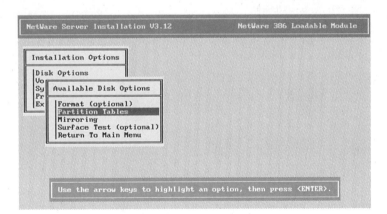

From this menu, select the Partition Tables option, as shown in Figure 10.14.

Partitioning Your Disk(s)

Select the option to Create NetWare Partition from this menu. If there are multiple disk drives, each physical drive should be listed in a menu.

FIGURE 10.14.

The Partition Options submenu.

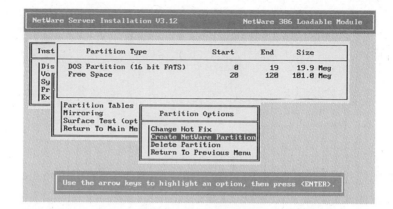

NOTE ▶

If a drive is not listed, check to see whether the driver was properly loaded. If it was, check to see whether the drive was low-level formatted. Some SCSI adapters require a setup program to be run before disk drives can be recognized.

Select a drive from the menu, and you will see the Partition Information screen, shown in Figure 10.15. If you have only one physical disk drive, proceed directly to this screen without an intermediate menu.

FIGURE 10.15.

The Partition Options screen.

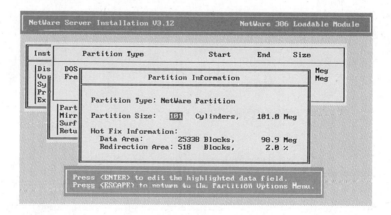

In this screen, the default partition size will be the available space remaining after the DOS partition on this disk (if one was created). You may edit the partition size, data area, and redirection area. Table 10.2 shows the meaning of each parameter:

Table 10.2. Parameters and their meanings.

Parameter	Meaning	Expressed in
Partition size	Size of NetWare partition	Cylinders
Data area	Area allocated to NetWare disk storage	Blocks
Redirection area	Hot fix volume	Blocks

The default value of two percent of disk space for the redirection area is far too much for large disk drives. You may reduce the size of the redirection area or increase the size of the data area. Either one adjusts the value of the other accordingly.

> **TIP** ▶
>
> For a 100M disk drive, an allocation of two percent for the redirection area is adequate; however, for a larger disk drive, it should be reduced. For a 1-gigabyte drive, one percent is more than sufficient. For disk drives between these sizes, calculate the amount of space that would be allocated to the redirection area and reconfigure the allocation according to your judgment.

> **NOTE** ▶
>
> If you have a fault-tolerant disk subsystem (for instance, RAID 5), enter 0 for the Hot Fix size. INSTALL will prompt you with the minimum and maximum ranges for Hot Fix. You should enter the minimum range, because it is not necessary to use Hot Fix at all. Even though it is not necessary, NetWare requires a minimum of one track for Hot Fix, which is what the minimum Hot Fix value is based upon.

When you exit this screen, a query asks if you want to save the configuration. If you answer Yes, the disk partition table will be altered immediately. You will be returned to the Disk Partition menu. You may select Return to Previous Menu or press Esc to return to the list of available disk drives. You can continue by partitioning other disk drives. Once you have finished, or if you have only one disk drive, you will return to the Available Disk Options menu.

Mirroring Your Disks

The advantages of mirroring are discussed in Chapter 3, "Advanced NetWare Operating System Features." You can mirror any two physical disk drives if the logical partition size is exactly the same on two disk drives. (The disk drives may differ physically, and they may be slightly different sizes, but after partitioning and allocating the redirection area, the remaining data area must be identical on the two physical disks.) You can mirror them according to the following procedure.

From the Available Disk Options menu, select Mirroring. You will see a Partition Mirror Status menu listing for each *logical partition* you have created. The term logical partition refers to the data area that remains after the partitioning and allocation of the redirection area, as shown previously in Figure 10.15.

> **NOTE** ▶
>
> Each logical partition is numbered in sequence, starting at "1." Physical device numbers identify physical disk drives and are numbered starting from "0."

FIGURE 10.16.

The Partition Mirroring Status and Mirrored NetWare Partitions screens.

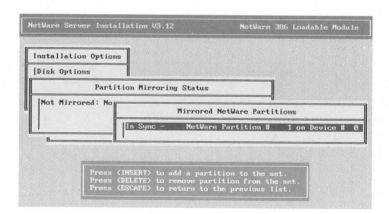

From the Partition Mirroring Status screen, select the logical partition to be designated as the primary disk in a mirrored pair. You will then see the Mirrored NetWare Partitions screen (that is also shown in Figure 10.16). You may press Insert to bring up a list of eligible logical partitions. An eligible partition would be any other logical partition where the data area size is identical. To mirror the two logical partitions, select the logical partition to be designated as the secondary disk in the mirrored pair. From this point on, the two logical partitions appear to be one.

> **NOTE** ▶
>
> Your disks are *duplexed* if the two data areas being mirrored reside on disks connected to separate adapters.
>
> Duplexing enables NetWare to split disk seeks, resulting in improved disk performance. It also provides better fault tolerance through redundant adapters. See Chapter 3 for more information about disk mirroring and duplexing.

Surface Testing Your Disks

You can perform a surface test of your disk for media defects by selecting the Surface Test option from the Disk Options menu. The test can be "destructive" or "nondestructive." A destructive test at this point cannot destroy any data and is more comprehensive. This process doesn't damage your disk; it uses your disk driver to write and read data to each track and sector. You can use this test to be certain that the drive is working properly and that no media defects are present.

> **TIP** ▶
>
> Your disk drive has been low-level formatted by the vendor or by a vendor-supplied utility and should be perfectly okay. Running the surface test is therefore not necessary. If you run the test anyway, expect it to take several hours. You can interrupt it at any time without damage to the disk.

You may abort the test at any time by selecting Stop Surface Test. This option does not damage your disk or its formatting. When done, select Return to Previous Menu or press Esc to return to the list of drives; then press Esc again to return to the Available Disk Options menu.

> **CAUTION** ▶
>
> Do not run the Format utility shown on this menu unless the disk drive instructions explicitly say to do so. This option performs a low-level disk format (initialization), which can destroy the format of your disk drive and render it unusable. Most disk drives are low-level formatted at the factory; others may require you to run a format utility from provided software under DOS, or from a BIOS chip on the adapter.
>
> A high-level format, such as a DOS format, is not required for NetWare.

Create Volumes

Escape to the Installation Options menu and select Volume Options. You will see a list of NetWare volumes, but it will have no volumes listed. Press Insert to create a new volume. The New Volume Information screen appears, as shown in Figure 10.17.

FIGURE 10.17.
The New Volume Information screen.

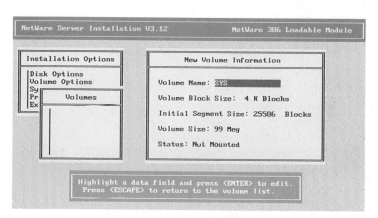

Your first volume must be named SYS:. You can then select the block size. For the SYS: volume, select 4K.

> **TIP** ▶
>
> If you would like to have larger block sizes, create a separate volume (or volumes) to contain large files only.

> **NOTE ▶**
>
> The block size can be regulated to provide for larger block sizes of 4K, 8K, 16K, 32K, or 64K. A larger block size is desirable when the volume contains large data files. With large files, a 64K block size volume has 1/16 (4/64) as many FAT entries as does a 4K block size. For smaller files, a larger block size will occupy more space, because each file—even if it is only one byte—will occupy an entire block.

Next, configure the size of the volume. You may skip the Initial Segment Size field if you would like the volume to fill the entire logical partition. If you want to create more than one volume on a logical partition, edit Initial Segment Size. Reduce the number of blocks allocated to the volume. When you press Esc, the volume gets created.

You can span a volume across two or more logical partitions and therefore across two or more physical disk drives. If you have more than one physical disk drive, when you select a volume you will see another list of Volume Segments of which the current volume is composed. If you press Insert, a menu appears listing Free Space Available for Volume Segments (if any are available). You can span the selected volume onto an additional logical partition by selecting an available logical partition from the list, selecting the block size, and confirming that you want to add the segment to the volume. If you have mirrored two disks, the volume(s) will be created on the mirrored pair.

> **NOTE ▶**
>
> A single volume can span up to 32 physical drives for a total of no more than 32 terabytes of disk storage for one (or for all) volumes.
>
> If you span volumes, when new data is added and free space on both logical partitions exists, file sectors will automatically be striped across the physical disk drives. When SCSI drives are used in this manner, striping results in improved disk I/O.

CAUTION ▶

When a volume is spanned across multiple disk drives, loss of a disk drive results in the loss of all data on all partition segments of the volume.

If you span volumes, you should also mirror (or duplex) the drives upon which the volume is spanned.

TIP ▶

The combination of spanning and duplexing is an excellent option for achieving the very best disk I/O performance.

Next, you must mount the volume that has just been created. To mount the volume, select it from the list of volumes, select the Status field, and press Enter. Select Mount Volume, and the volume will be mounted. Alternatively, you may press Alt+Esc (hold down Alt and press Esc) to change to the console screen, and then type mount all. If you would prefer to mount only a specific volume, enter the mount *volume_name*. You now have access to the mounted volume. SYS: must be mounted to proceed with the installation.

Copy System and Public files

Your next step is to copy the NetWare server working files to the server's SYS: volume. To do so, press Esc to reach the Installation Options menu, select System Options, select Copy System and Public Files, and follow the instructions shown on-screen. You will be prompted to insert each required disk, as shown in Figure 10.18. Each time a disk is read, INSTALL reads the disk label to be certain that the correct disk has been inserted.

You will be prompted to enter the path to copy the System and Public files, as shown in Figure 10.9.

FIGURE 10.18.

Press F6 to enter the path for System and Public files.

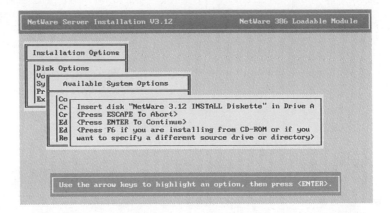

FIGURE 10.19.

Enter the path for copying System and Public files.

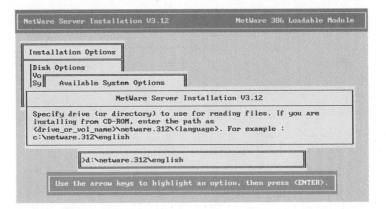

NOTE ▶

Enter the path of the CD-ROM drive as a DOS device. If the drive letter is D:, enter the path `D:\NETWARE.312\ENGLISH`.

You may mount the device as a NetWare volume. (See the previous chapter for more detail on how to mount your CD-ROM as a NetWare device.) If you have mounted your CD-ROM drive as a NetWare device, enter the path `NETWARE_312:NETWARE.312/ENGLISH`.

Load and Configure the Disk Drivers

At the colon prompt, type the command

```
LOAD disk_driver.DSK
```

NOTE ▶

Your current default drive is the SYS: volume after it has been mounted, so the preceding command loads the disk driver from the SYS:SYSTEM directory. Once SERVER is loaded, you can load drivers and NLMs from another drive by putting the drive letter into your load statement.

For example, if you loaded SERVER.EXE from C: but would like to load the ISADISK.DSK driver from A:, you can type

```
LOAD A:ISADISK
```

Substitute the name of your disk driver. You may type the driver name with the .DSK extension, or you may omit it. Novell provides a few disk drivers in the SYSTEM directory that are commonly used, but the developer of your disk adapter probably has written a driver that should be used instead. Many disk drives don't work with NetWare without a custom disk driver; others can use one of the standard drivers provided by Novell (such as ISADISK.DSK). In some cases, using a standard driver does not provide support for extended features or performance of a disk drive or adapter. You may need to purchase your disk driver separately for your disk adapter, because many developers do not automatically include it.

NOTE ▶

If you are using an IDE disk drive, make sure to use Novell's IDE.DSK. You may be able to use ISADISK.DSK, which is on your SYSTEM-1 diskette; however, IDE.DSK resolves several problems that have occurred with IDE disks, and it should be used.

Load the disk driver again for a second adapter, again for a third, and so on. Each disk adapter requires a disk driver in order to recognize the physical devices attached to it.

When you load the disk driver, the driver software normally asks for configuration information. At this point, if the driver loads properly and a colon prompt returns without errors, disks connected to that adapter will be recognized. The settings you enter must correspond with the physical settings on the adapter. If the driver fails to load, the adapter is not recognized for some reason. Your configuration settings may not correspond with the physical settings on the device, a physical conflict may exist between that device and another device, or the device may not be functioning properly.

Once you have loaded your disk driver, you should have access to all drives that are connected to the adapter for which the driver was loaded. Now you can partition the disk.

Load and Configure NIC Drivers

In the same manner that you loaded your disk driver, load the driver for your first server NIC. Novell provides drivers for IBM, 3Com, and Novell NICs. Other NICs are shipped with NetWare and other NOS drivers. Each vendor has a different way of structuring their driver disks, but normally somewhere on the disk that comes with your NIC will be a driver for one of the following:

- NetWare 3.x servers (with a .LAN extension)
- NetWare 2.x servers (two files—one with a .LAN, one with a .OBJ extension)
- Traditional IPX workstation (with an .OBJ extension)

The following example shows the loading of the TRXNET.LAN driver for ARCnet (bold indicates user input):

```
load trxnet
Loading module TRXNET.LAN
  Auto-loading module NMAGENT.NLM
Supported I/O port values are 2E0, 2F0, 300, 310, 350
I/O port: 2E0
Supported memory address values are D0000, C0000, E0000, CC000, DC000
Memory address: D0000
Supported interrupt number values are 2, 3, 4, 5, 7
Interrupt number: 2
:
```

When you load the driver, configuration information is queried again, and you should respond by inputting the physical settings on your NIC. Read the NIC driver installation instructions in the manual that came with your server NIC. Some NICs may require a couple more steps to properly load the driver per instructions from your NIC driver installation guide. Many new drivers require loading a few support modules before loading the driver. Other drivers automatically load support modules.

Repeat this process for each NIC installed in your server.

NOTE ▶

Though most NICs respond upon loading the driver, some NICs will not initialize until they are connected to a properly configured cabling system. Token Ring NICs generally need to be connected to an active ring. Connect your Token Ring NIC to a MSAU and configure the inactive ports per your installation instructions.

Some Ethernet NICs need to be connected to a cable with terminators or to a wiring concentrator; otherwise they will not initialize.

CAUTION ▶

Most Ethernet NICs can be configured with any one of four frame types. NetWare 3.12 drivers automatically select and load an Ethernet_802.2 frame type by default. The frame type loaded at your server must correspond with the frame types used by the workstations. When loading your workstation drivers, you may need to select the appropriate frame type to match your server's frame type.

CAUTION ▶

If an incorrect interrupt request is selected, or the interrupt request conflicts with another device, the driver may load, but the NIC will not work. Any other incorrect parameter will cause the driver to fail to load and produce an error.

If you cannot establish communications, check the interrupt configurations at both the server and the workstation to see if a conflict or incorrect interrupt request has been configured.

If you have installed another server NIC of a different type, repeat the same process for each different NIC. If you have more than one NIC of the same type in your server, you should load the same driver a second time. When you load the same driver a second time, the driver asks

```
Do you want to load another frame type for a previously loaded board?
```

If you want to load the driver for another NIC, answer N for No. The driver loads re-entrantly (more than one time) and asks for the physical settings for the second NIC.

A second frame type can be loaded to support another network protocol, such as TCP/IP. If you want to load a second frame type, answer Y for Yes. It will then query which frame type to load. In this manner, you can support all four frame types at the same time through one driver loaded into memory.

Bind IPX to NIC Driver(s)

Loading the driver enables communications at the data link layer (processes LAN frames). However, to enable NetWare IPX communications (processes network packets), you must bind the IPX protocol to the NIC driver. Type the following command at the colon prompt:

```
bind IPX to TRXNET
```

The IPX protocol engine responds with

```
Network number:
```

At this point, you should input the network address assigned to the LAN to which this NIC is connected. If no other servers are connected to this same LAN, this will become the network address for this LAN. If another server is directly connected to this same LAN, enter the same network address that was assigned to the other server's NIC. For further explanation of the term network address (or network number), see Chapter 5, "NetWare's Protocol Stack."

Create System Startup Files (NetWare Configuration Files)

Next, all the commands that were typed to load and configure drivers and to bind IPX must be automated so the server will boot without the user entering commands. Two files handle this: the STARTUP.NCF and the AUTOEXEC.NCF. STARTUP runs when SERVER.EXE is executed; it therefore must be stored on the DOS partition (or diskette) where SERVER.EXE is stored. AUTOEXEC.NCF is stored on the SYS: volume and is executed when the SYS: volume is mounted.

Creating the STARTUP.NCF file

From your Available System Options menu, select Create STARTUP.NCF. You will be prompted to edit the path where STARTUP.NCF should be stored. After editing or accepting the path, press Enter. You can edit the STARTUP.NCF file if necessary. You will see the commands for loading and configuring the disk driver with the appropriate syntax. Press the Esc key and confirm in order to save the file and continue.

> **NOTE** ▷
>
> You may need to add commands to this file. Check your disk driver and server NIC installation manuals for adjustments that need to be added to this file.

Creating the AUTOEXEC.NCF File

Next, from your Available System Options menu, select Create AUTOEXEC.NCF. You will see all the commands relative to bringing up the server, loading and configuring the NIC drivers, and binding the IPX protocol to the NIC drivers (including assigning network addresses). The appropriate syntax is used, so if you edit the file, be certain to retain the proper syntax.

> **NOTE** ▷
>
> NetWare assumes it will find the NIC drivers in the SYS:SYSTEM directory. Once you have connected a workstation, remember to log in as Supervisor, copy your third-party NIC drivers into the SYS:SYSTEM directory, and flag them as read-only.
>
> If you want to load the NIC drivers from the local hard drive or from a floppy, edit the AUTOEXEC.NCF to include the pathname (for example, `load C:\NE2000`).

Using an ISA Server with more than 16M of RAM

NetWare is not able to see more than 16M of RAM in an ISA server. The normal 16-bit bus in a server that is not an EISA or MCA server may only address 16M of linear memory. This is a limitation of the ISA bus because of its 24-bit addresses. To register memory over 16M, the following command should be placed into the AUTOEXEC.NCF:

`REGISTER MEMORY start_of_memory_segment length_of_memory_segment`

The first parameter, `start_of_memory_segment`, is the starting address for the segment of memory more than 16M. The second parameter, `length_of_memory_segment`, indicates the length of the segment of memory more than 16M. Both addresses are expressed in hexadecimal terms. The following example recognizes the 16M of RAM more than the 16M ISA limit:

`REGISTER MEMORY 1000000 1000000`

This command indicates that the additional memory the bus cannot recognize starts at 16M (1000000 hexadecimal) and continues for 16M (also 1000000).

> **NOTE** ▶
>
> This situation normally does not apply to EISA and MCA servers. Some EISA servers have an option to limit memory to 16M in the Setup or EISA Configuration Utility. This option should be set to normal EISA standards, which eliminates the 16M ISA ceiling. If the EISA server cannot be set without this limit, treat it similar to an ISA server—use the `REGISTER MEMORY` statement.

> **TIP** ▶
>
> To check how much memory your server recognizes, type `MEMORY` at the console screen.

Exiting INSTALL, Downing, and Rebooting the Server

Your server installation is now complete. You should exit the INSTALL module by escaping out of all menus and confirming your exit. As with all NLMs, you should exit from a menu selection rather than typing an unload statement from the console.

You should now down your file server OS by typing DOWN at the server console (colon) prompt. Next, boot your server to see if it will come up automatically. If it does not come up automatically, reload the disk driver manually, mount the volume (type MOUNT ALL at the colon prompt), load the INSTALL.NLM, and check out the STARTUP.NCF and AUTOEXEC.NCF files. If the disk driver was not loaded, make sure your STARTUP.NCF is in the same directory with SERVER.EXE and has the appropriate disk driver load statement(s).

> **TIP** ▶
>
> If the LAN drivers do not load and your drivers are not located in the SYS:SYSTEM directory, check the AUTOEXEC.NCF file to be sure that the drive letter is specified where your drivers are located. By default, it is assumed during creation of this file that you will copy the LAN and disk drivers into the SYSTEM directory.

Editing the AUTOEXEC.BAT

At the outset of running the INSTALL batch file from CD-ROM, you were asked if you would like the server to boot automatically. If you answered Yes, the AUTOEXEC.BAT will include the statement SERVER, which will load the NetWare file-server OS. If you did not, you can manually type the command SERVER from a DOS prompt. If the server comes up automatically and you wish to stop it, press Ctrl+C during boot. If you can catch the AUTOEXEC.BAT during execution, and if the DOS BREAK function was not set to "on" in the AUTOEXEC.BAT, the batch file will pause, and you can exit without running server.

To simplify the server boot, you can use the YESORNO.COM utility, which is included on the disk that accompanies this book. This will ask (during the DOS boot procedure) whether the server should be booted or not. The following server AUTOEXEC.BAT will ask for your input before bringing the server up. The following AUTOEXEC.BAT shows how you can ask whether to run SERVER.EXE.

```
@ECHO OFF
PROMPT $P$G
PATH C:\DOS;C:\UTIL
CLS
YESORNO Do you want to start the Server?
IF ERRORLEVEL 1 GOTO YES
GOTO END
:YES
SERVER.EXE
:END
```

Installing Other Server-Based Products

Other server-based modules can be installed by loading the INSTALL.NLM and accessing Product Options with your product installation diskette in any floppy drive. Several NLM products, such as BasicMHS, ElectroText, NetWare for Macintosh, and NetWare NFS, are loaded this way. For instructions on loading BasicMHS and ElectroText, see Chapter 13, "Installing and Using NetWare 3.12's Basic MHS/First Mail and ElectroText."

When loading other NLMs, be sure to watch your CPU utilization and some of your MONITOR statistics, such as Service Processes and Packet Receive Buffers. If they hit their default ceilings, you may need to adjust them upward.

Installing and Configuring NetWare 4.01

by Peter Kuo

11

IN THIS CHAPTER

The installation steps for NetWare 4.01 are very similar to those for NetWare 3.x. However, further "automation" has been added. This chapter presents the steps necessary for a successful NetWare 4.01 server installation. Installation of workstation clients also is covered. The end of the chapter presents a list of possible problems you may encounter during installation—and some suggested solutions. This information assumes that, as in the previous chapter, you have assembled your server hardware and resolved any hardware conflicts.

Installing the NetWare 4.01 Server

In earlier versions of NetWare, the user had to perform certain tedious preliminary tasks to prepare the server. In most cases, the hard drives needed to be partitioned and formatted. For those of you who remember pre-NetWare 2.2 installation, COMPSURF was a dreaded process. NetWare 3.x made life bearable. However, there were still a number of manual steps that you had to perform. The NetWare 4.01 installation process alleviates these problems.

> **NOTE** ▷
>
> English-language support module examples are used in this chapter; installation in Dutch, Spanish, French, and Italian also is supported.

Overview

As with NetWare 3.11, the installation of NetWare 4.01 comprises two parts: the DOS component and NetWare itself. Because NetWare 4.01 is shipped on a CD, one needs to have a DOS bootable diskette with CD-ROM device drivers installed to gain access to the CD. It is just as easy to have DOS installed on the server hard drive first. The steps presented in this section take that approach. Briefly, the necessary steps for a NetWare 4.01 server installation are as follows:

1. Install a DOS partition on your server hard drive (5-10M in size).

2. Set up a CD-ROM drive to be accessed under DOS.

3. Initiate the installation process by running INSTALL.BAT from the CD-ROM and picking the Install new NetWare 4.x option.

4. Assign a server name and an internal IPX network number.

5. Copy the server boot files from the CD to the DOS partition.

6. Configure the country code, code page, and keyboard for your server.

7. Select a filename format, either DOS or NetWare. (Choose the DOS format if you are unsure.)

8. Specify any special SET commands in STARTUP.NCF.

9. Enable INSTALL to modify your AUTOEXEC.BAT to auto-load SERVER.EXE.

10. Load and configure the correct disk driver(s).

11. Set up NetWare volumes as desired. Check the block size allocation, compression, and block suballocation options.

12. Install the license disk.

13. Copy the selected NetWare files to SYS: volume.

14. Load and bind the LAN drivers.

15. Install an NDS Tree if the server is the first server.

16. Select and verify time zone information.

17. Enter NDS information if the tree is new.

18. Create STARTUP.NCF.

19. Create AUTOEXEC.NCF.

20. Install optional programs and files as needed.

The following sections discuss each step in detail.

Installing the DOS partition

Although the 4.01 instructions call for a 5M DOS partition, you should create a 10-15M DOS partition. This will give you some working room in case you need to install other NetWare packages (such as NetWare for SAA).

NOTE ▶

It doesn't really matter which version of DOS you use. Most installations have been completed using DOS 5.0. If you encounter problems, try DOS 5.0.

Setting Up the CD-ROM Drive

Depending on the CD-ROM drive that you use, the CONFIG.SYS varies. Here is a sample file for an Adaptec 1542B SCSI controller:

```
DEVICE=C:\SCSI\ASPI4DOS.SYS /D
FILES=60
BUFFERS=40
DEVICE=C:\SCSI\ASPICD.SYS /D:ASPICD0
And the AUTOEXEC.BAT file looks like this:
@ECHO OFF
C:\SCSI\MSCDEX.EXE /D:ASPICD0 /M:12
PROMPT $P$G
```

> **NOTE** ▶
>
> Your CD-ROM drive must support the ISO 9660 CD-ROM specification to work with NetWare 4.01 install.

Novell has not published a list of tested CD-ROM drives. However, if your CD-ROM has a DOS driver, it is likely that it can be used for installation. This includes CD-ROM drives that connect to a parallel port.

> **TIP** ▶
>
> The author's experience suggests that the best SCSI controller and CD-ROM combination is an Adaptec SCSI controller and NEC CD-ROM drive. The faster the drive, the shorter the installation time.

> **CAUTION** ▶
>
> If you are using SCSI hard drives for the server, do not attach the CD-ROM drive to the same controller that will contain your SYS: volume during installation. Otherwise, the server will lock up when you attempt to copy NetWare files to SYS:. See the following section for a workaround.

Using CD-ROM on the Same Host Adapter as SYS:

The reason for the machine hanging when one has the CD-ROM on the same SCSI controller as the SYS: volume is a conflict between the DOS CD-ROM driver and the NetWare disk driver. Here is a suggested list of steps, originally provided by Adaptec technical support, to get around this problem (using an Adaptec 154x controller as an example):

1. Install your DOS driver for the CD-ROM. (Assume CD-ROM shows up as drive D:.)

2. Run INSTALL.BAT from the D:\NETWARE.40\ENGLISH directory off the CD.

3. At the LOAD DISK DRIVER screen, select ASPITRAN.DSK. (This is Step 10 in the preceding Overview section.)

4. Load another disk driver by selecting "Load another (different) driver" option. This time, choose AHA1540.DSK.

5. Continue with the installation as prompted by menu.

6. At the point of "Copy NetWare Files" (Step 13 in the Overview section), press ALT+F10 to abort the install.

7. Down the server and exit back to DOS.

8. Remove the DOS CD-ROM drivers from your CONFIG.SYS and AUTOEXEC.BAT.

9. Copy D:\NETWARE.40_____\C_03C\CDROM.NLM and D:\NETWARE.40_____\DISKDRV\ASPICD.DSK to C:\SERVER.40. (The directory name is composed of eight underscores.)

10. Reboot the machine.

11. Go to C:\SERVER.40 and execute SERVER.EXE with the -NA option.

12. After answering the questions for Server Name and Internal IPX Number, type LOAD C:AHA1540.

13. Mount SYS:.

14. Type LOAD C:ASPICD followed by LOAD C:CDROM.

15. Type CD MOUNT 1 at the console prompt.

16. Ignore the write error and wait for the CD to mount. It may take up to 10 minutes or more, depending on the speed of your server, hard drive, and CD-ROM drive.

17. Type LOAD C:INSTALL.

18. Select "Install A New 4.x Server."

19. Use NETWARE_40\NETWARE.40\ENGLISH as the source directory path. (If you are using different language, choose the appropriate directory.)

20. Continue with the installation as per standard.

These steps will be discussed in detail in this chapter.

TIP ▶

If you have another SCSI controller, it is best to install it temporarily and connect the CD-ROM to it.

Start the Installation Process

To start the automated installation process, invoke INSTALL.BAT from the \NETWARE.40\ENGLISH directory from the CD. From the menu, select "Install new NetWare 4.x." (See Figure 11.1.) If you are upgrading from NetWare 3.1x or a 4.0 server, choose "Upgrade NetWare v3.1x or v4.x."

FIGURE 11.1.

Selecting an installation option.

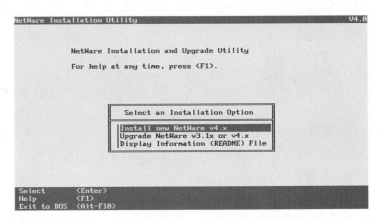

```
NetWare Installation Utility                                        V4.0

              NetWare Installation and Upgrade Utility

              For help at any time, press <F1>.



                    ┌─────────────────────────────────┐
                    │  Select an Installation Option   │
                    ├─────────────────────────────────┤
                    │ Install new NetWare v4.x         │
                    │ Upgrade NetWare v3.1x or v4.x    │
                    │ Display Information (README) File │
                    └─────────────────────────────────┘




Select        <Enter>
Help          <F1>
Exit to DOS   <Alt-F10>
```

NOTE ▶

Depending on the menu screen, the program alternates between Enter and F10 for selection.

Setup DOS Partition

On the next menu screen, you have the option to keep the current disk partition setup or create a new DOS partition. (See Figure 11.2.) Choose "Retain current disk partitions" if your current DOS partition is at least 5M in size.

FIGURE 11.2.

Disk partition options.

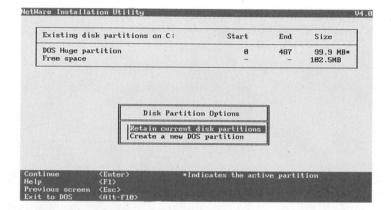

```
NetWare Installation Utility                                        V4.0

  ┌──────────────────────────────────────────────────────────────────┐
  │ Existing disk partitions on C:          Start      End      Size   │
  │                                                                    │
  │ DOS Huge partition                        0        487    99.9 MB* │
  │ Free space                                -         -     102.5MB  │
  └──────────────────────────────────────────────────────────────────┘


                    ┌──────────────────────────────────┐
                    │      Disk Partition Options        │
                    ├──────────────────────────────────┤
                    │ Retain current disk partitions     │
                    │ Create a new DOS partition         │
                    └──────────────────────────────────┘


  Continue        <Enter>            *Indicates the active partition
  Help            <F1>
  Previous screen <Esc>
  Exit to DOS     <Alt-F10>
```

> **NOTE** ▶
>
> If you use the INSTALL procedure to create a new DOS partition, DR DOS 6.0 will be used.

Define Server Name and Internal IPX Number

You will be prompted for a server name (Figure 11.3) and then an IPX internal network number (Figure 11.4). Make sure they are unique. The install program will randomly assign an internal IPX network number. If you have your own numbering convention, use it.

> **TIP** ▶
>
> As was mentioned in the previous chapter, it is best to have some kind of naming and numbering convention for your servers and IPX network addresses. They can help you quickly locate a given server on your internet.

In some cases, you can use a telephone number for the internal network number, because eight hexadecimal numbers are allowed. In cases where there are multiple servers, append A, B, C, and so on, to the end of the number.

FIGURE 11.3.

Server name prompt.

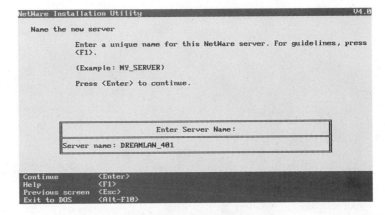

FIGURE 11.4.

IPX internal network number prompt.

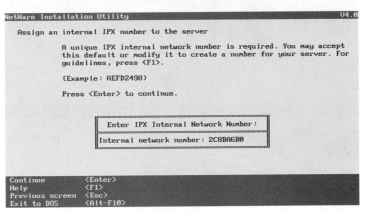

Copy Server Boot Files to DOS Partition

A number of server boot files are copied from the CD to the DOS partition. The default destination is C:\SERVER.40. If you want to use a different destination directory, press the F4 key. A progress bar graph (Figure 11.5) is shown when files are copied from the CD to the DOS partition.

FIGURE 11.5.

Server boot files progress bar graph.

```
NetWare Installation Utility                                        V4.0
    Copy server boot files to the DOS partition

   ┌──────────────────────────────────────────────────────────────┐
   │  Copying File: SERVER.EXE                                      │
   │                                                                │
   │  0%                                                        100% │
   └──────────────────────────────────────────────────────────────┘

   ┌──────────────────────────────────────────────────────────────┐
   │  Source path:  D:\NETWARE.40\ENGLISH_____                  │
   └──────────────────────────────────────────────────────────────┘
   ┌──────────────────────────────────────────────────────────────┐
   │  Destination path:  C:\SERVER.40                               │
   └──────────────────────────────────────────────────────────────┘
```

Configure Server for Correct Country Code, Code Page, and Keyboard Configuration

You need to specify the country code (Figure 11.6), code page, and keyboard mapping for your server. Similar to the Country Code drop-down menu, the Code Page and Keyboard Mapping menus enable you to make a selection. The DOS configuration is used as a default. (This step was not necessary for NetWare 4.0.)

FIGURE 11.6.

Country code selection.

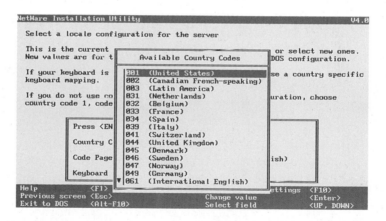

```
NetWare Installation Utility                                        V4.0
    Select a locale configuration for the server

    This is the current                                    or select new ones.
    New values are for t   ┌──── Available Country Codes ────┐  DOS configuration.

    If your keyboard is    │ 001  (United States)            │  se a country specific
    keyboard mapping.      │ 002  (Canadian French-speaking) │
                           │ 003  (Latin America)            │
    If you do not use co   │ 031  (Netherlands)              │  uration, choose
    country code 1, code   │ 032  (Belgium)                  │
                           │ 033  (France)                   │
                           │ 034  (Spain)                    │
        Press <EN          │ 039  (Italy)                    │
                           │ 041  (Switzerland)              │
        Country C          │ 044  (United Kingdom)           │
                           │ 045  (Denmark)                  │
        Code Page          │ 046  (Sweden)                   │  ish)
                           │ 047  (Norway)                   │
        Keyboard           │ 049  (Germany)                  │
                         ▼ │ 061  (International English)     │
                           └─────────────────────────────────┘
    Help            <F1>                                    ettings <F10>
    Previous screen <Esc>                  Change value             <Enter>
    Exit to DOS     <Alt-F10>              Select field       <UP, DOWN>
```

Select Filename Format

You need to tell the installation program which filename format to use when storing files on the NetWare volumes. (See Figure 11.7.) In most situations, you should use DOS naming conventions. If you are unsure, use DOS filename format. This step was not in NetWare 4.0.

FIGURE 11.7.

Filename format selection.

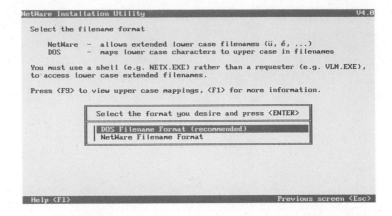

```
NetWare Installation Utility                                          V4.0
    Select the filename format

        NetWare  - allows extended lower case filenames (ü, é, ...)
        DOS      - maps lower case characters to upper case in filenames

    You must use a shell (e.g. NETX.EXE) rather than a requester (e.g. VLM.EXE),
    to access lower case extended filenames.

    Press <F9> to view upper case mappings, <F1> for more information.


        ┌─────────────────────────────────────────────────────┐
        │      Select the format you desire and press <ENTER>   │
        │  ┌─────────────────────────────────────────────────┐ │
        │  │ DOS Filename Format (recommended)                │ │
        │  │ NetWare Filename Format                          │ │
        │  └─────────────────────────────────────────────────┘ │
        └─────────────────────────────────────────────────────┘




    Help <F1>                                    Previous screen <Esc>
```

> **NOTE** ▶
>
> To maintain compatibility with DOS and future releases of NetWare, use DOS filename format. VLM DOS requesters use DOS filename format no matter what your choice is. However, NETX shells work either with DOS format or NetWare format.

Specify Special *SET* commands for STARTUP.NCF

If you have any special SET commands that must be included in the STARTUP.NCF file, you can specify them at this point in the installation process.

> **CAUTION** ▶
>
> If you have 16M or more RAM in your server, check your NIC and disk drivers to ensure that they can address more than 16M of RAM. Otherwise, you must disable the "auto-register memory more than 16MB" in your STARTUP.NCF and manually register the extra memory in your AUTOEXEC.NCF later. Failure to do this can cause the server to crash.

Modify AUTOEXEC.BAT File

Enable the installation procedure to modify your AUTOEXEC.BAT file so that the server is auto-loaded every time you turn on the machine. (See Figure 11.8.)

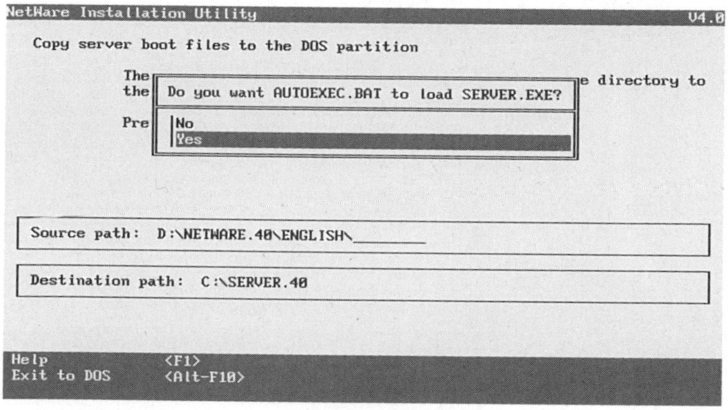

FIGURE 11.8.

Option to modify the AUTOEXEC.BAT file.

```
NetWare Installation Utility                                    V4.0
     Copy server boot files to the DOS partition

     The                                                  e directory to
     the │ Do you want AUTOEXEC.BAT to load SERVER.EXE?
     Pre │ No
         │ Yes



     Source path:  D:\NETWARE.40\ENGLISH_____

     Destination path:  C:\SERVER.40


Help          <F1>
Exit to DOS   <Alt-F10>
```

The following lines are appended to your AUTOEXEC.NCF file:

```
:BEGIN_SERVER
C:
cd C:\SERVER.40
SERVER
:END_SERVER
```

SERVER.EXE is executed so you can load the disk driver, create NetWare volumes, and copy files to SYS:.

Load and Configure Disk Driver(s)

CAUTION

If you have SYS: volume on the same SCSI adapter as your CD-ROM drive, see the section called "Using CD-ROM on the Same Host Adapter as SYS:" earlier in this chapter.

You receive a "Please wait" message while the installation process scans for drivers. Then you will be presented with a list of available drivers. (See Figure 11.9.) Select a disk driver that is most appropriate for your hard disk controller. If you are using IDE drives, choose the IDE.DSK driver. There have been cases in which the ISADISK driver works better than the IDE driver, however, it is suggested that you don't select this driver.

You need to configure the disk driver for the correct hardware settings. (See Figure 11.10.) After completion, you have the option of loading more drivers if needed.

FIGURE 11.9.

List of available disk drivers.

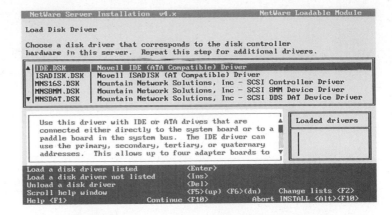

FIGURE 11.10.

Configure the disk driver.

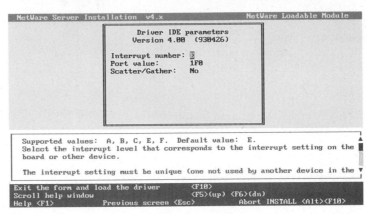

If you need to load the same driver many times for multiple controllers, the driver will be loaded re-entrantly.

Create NetWare Volumes

You have two ways of creating the NetWare partition: automatically or manually. (See Figure 11.11.) If you choose Automatically, all free disk space is allocated as NetWare partition, and no mirroring is established. (See Figure 11.12.)

If you select Manually, you can add or delete partitions. (See Figure 11.13.) When creating a new NetWare partition, you can specify the number of megabytes for the partition. Out of this, how much is data and how much is hot fix? (See Figure 11.14.) This is similar to NetWare 3.x.

FIGURE 11.11.

Options to create NetWare disk partitions.

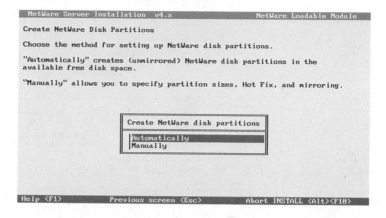

FIGURE 11.12.

Selecting automatic setup.

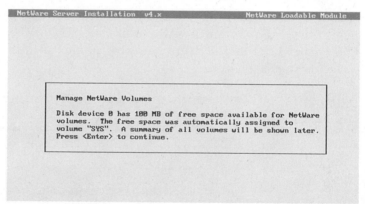

FIGURE 11.13.

Selecting manual setup.

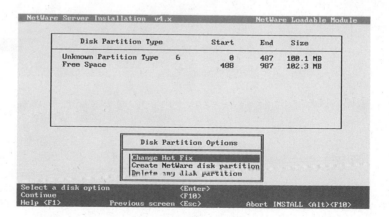

FIGURE 11.14.

Options for creating NetWare partitions.

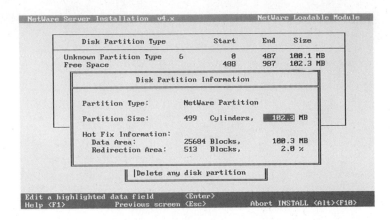

All free space is automatically assigned to volume SYS:. If you need multiple volumes, delete SYS:, re-create it with a smaller size, and then add your new volumes. (See Figures 11.15 and 11.16.) These steps are similar to those in NetWare 3.x, except the interface has changed.

FIGURE 11.15.

Options to manage NetWare volumes.

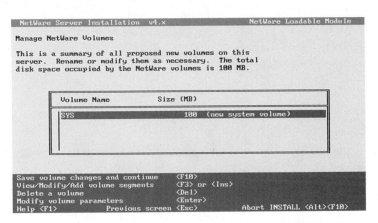

NOTE ▶

NetWare has a limit of eight volumes per physical hard drive.

FIGURE 11.16.

SYS: and DATA: volumes defined.

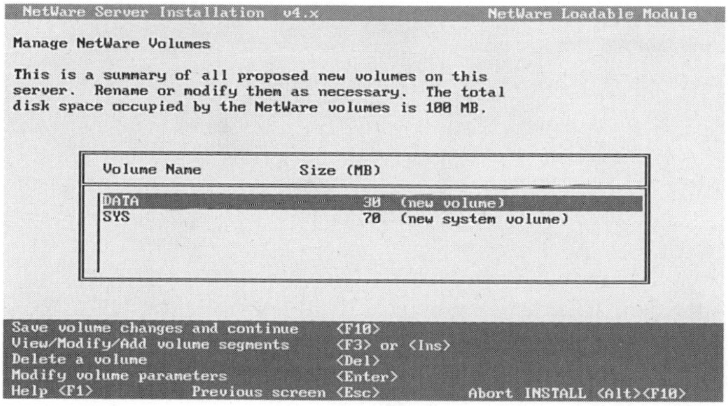

Before the volumes are actually created, you can change the following settings (see Figure 11.17):

Volume Block Size: Valid block size ranges from 4KB to 64KB. The default block size depends on actual volume size.

File Compression: You can enable files to be compressed if they are infrequently accessed. The default is ON.

Block Suballocation: Enables the server to use unfilled 512-byte blocks for storing files. The default is ON.

Data Migration: Permits the server to migrate data from a NetWare volume to secondary disk systems, tapes, or CD-ROM. The default is OFF.

FIGURE 11.17.

Volume options.

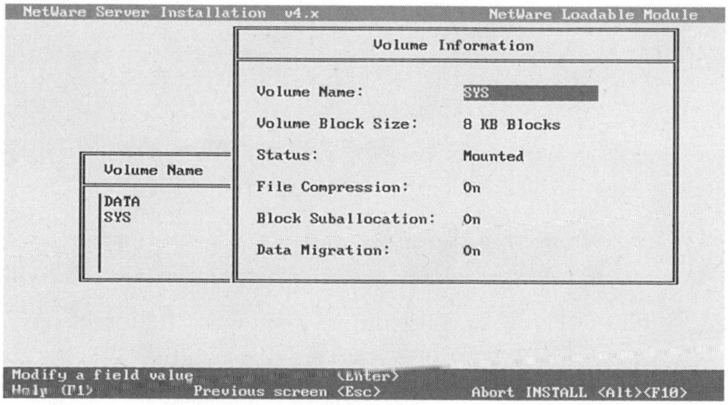

> **CAUTION** ▶
>
> Volume block size, file compression, and block suballocation are specified during volume creation. Once set, they cannot be changed. You must delete and re-create the volume to make any changes.
>
> Data migration may be turned on or off without re-creating the volume.

After you are satisfied with your volume configuration, press F10 to continue. Now you are ready to install the license diskette.

Install License Diskette

After the volumes are mounted, you are prompted to install the server license diskette. (See Figure 11.18.) If you have provided an invalid license, you will receive a "Not Valid" message. Following the successful installation of your license disk, you are ready to copy NetWare files from the CD onto your SYS: volume.

FIGURE 11.18.

License disk installation.

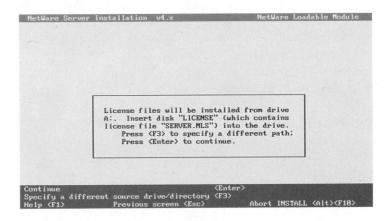

> **NOTE** ▶
>
> Similar to NetWare 3.1x and 2.x, NetWare 4.01 licensing is based on the number of connections per server. The number-of-connections information and serial number is now located on the license diskette, rather than in SERVER.EXE (such as was the case with 3.1x).

TIP

Because there is no license information on the CD, you can use the same CD for multiple installs.

CAUTION ▷

When you are installing multiple 4.x servers, keep track of which license diskettes have been installed.

TIP ▷

You can upgrade your license (for example, from 50-user to 100-user). At the server console, type LOAD INSTALL -R. Then select the "Maintenance/Selective Install" option, followed by "License Option." The -R flag (undocumented) enables you to overwrite the existing license with a new one.

Copy NetWare Files to SYS:

You will see a screen similar to Figure 11.19 just before NetWare files are copied from the CD to the SYS: volume. Before continuing, refer to the earlier section in this chapter called "Using CD-ROM on the Same Host Adapter as SYS:" (that is, if your CD-ROM drive is on the same controller as your SYS: volume).

FIGURE 11.19.

Ready to copy NetWare files to SYS:.

```
NetWare Server Installation   v4.x                    NetWare Loadable Module




     NetWare files will be installed from path
     D:\NETWARE.40\ENGLISH_____\.  If you are installing from CD-ROM or a
     network directory, make sure the above path corresponds to the directory
     where the NetWare server installation files are located.  On CD-ROM, this
     will be path <drive_or_vol_name>:\NETWARE.40\<language_dir>_____.
     (Press <F1> for help on CD-ROM installation.)

        Press <F3> to specify a different path;
        Press <F4> to specify a remote workstation path;
        Press <Enter> to continue.


Continue                                    <Enter>
Specify a different source drive/directory  <F3>
Specify a remote source drive/directory     <F4>
Help <F1>              Previous screen <Esc>          Abort INSTALL <Alt><F10>
```

You will be prompted to select the file groups to copy. (See Figure 11.20.) If you do not want to copy a certain group, highlight an entry and press Enter to deselect a group. Press F10 to start file copying. "File Copy Status" will update you of the copying in progress.

FIGURE 11.20.

Select file groups to install.

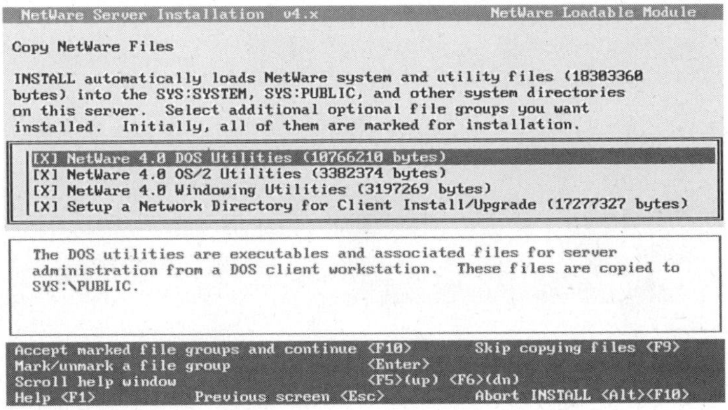

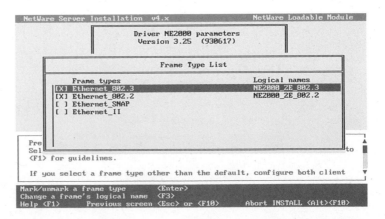

Depending on the file groups you selected and the speed of your CD-ROM drive, the file copying will take from 30 minutes to an hour.

Load and Bind LAN Drivers

You will be prompted to select LAN drivers. The process is very much like that of loading disk drivers, discussed previously. LAN drivers can be loaded re-entrantly. Configure LAN drivers with the correct hardware settings and frame types. (See Figure 11.21.)

FIGURE 11.21.

Configure LAN driver for correct frame types.

INSTALL will "search" the segment for an IPX network address in use. If it finds one, it will automatically be bound to the driver. Otherwise, a random network address will be generated. (See Figure 11.22.) You should double-check before accepting the value. This is done for each frame type specified for the NIC, and for each LAN driver loaded.

FIGURE 11.22.

Bind the LAN driver to IPX.

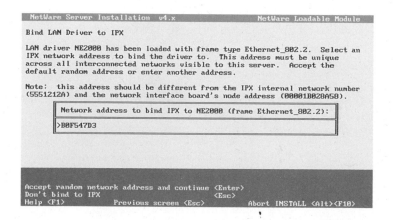

If this is the first server, you can install the NetWare Directory Services tree. If not, you should add this server to the existing NDS tree.

Install NDS

INSTALL searches your network to see whether an NDS tree exists. If it does not find one, you are given the option to search again, create a new one, or search a particular network/node.

> **CAUTION** ▶
>
> It is possible to have multiple trees on the same network. However, at this time, communication among different trees is not possible. Objects in one tree are not visible from another tree.

First Server in an NDS Tree

Select the "Yes" (this is the first Directory server" option) to create a new NDS tree. You are then asked to supply a tree name and time zone information. Because this is the first server in your tree, it is set to be a single reference time server by default.

> **CAUTION** ▶
>
> Do not change the time server defaults unless you understand the consequences. See the section "Time Synchronization" in Chapter 8.

You need to specify a context for which this server is to be installed along with your initial Organization (O=), Organizational Unit (OU=), as well as a password for user Admin. (See Figure 11.23.) NDS is then installed, and you are informed of the installation results.

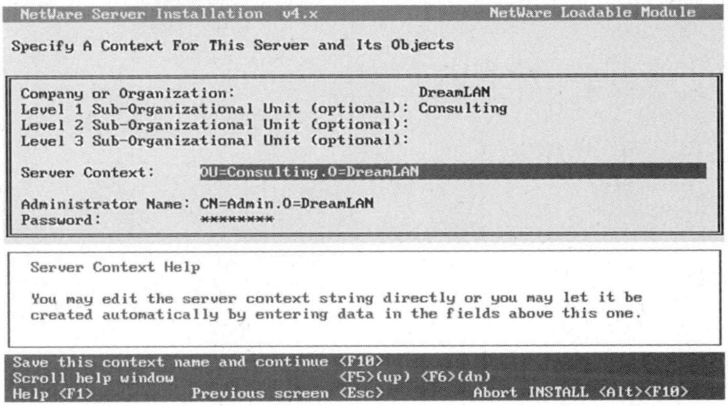

FIGURE 11.23.

Specify an NDS context.

```
NetWare Server Installation   v4.x                    NetWare Loadable Module

Specify A Context For This Server and Its Objects

┌─────────────────────────────────────────────────────────────────────────┐
│ Company or Organization:                        DreamLAN                   │
│ Level 1 Sub-Organizational Unit (optional): Consulting                     │
│ Level 2 Sub-Organizational Unit (optional):                               │
│ Level 3 Sub-Organizational Unit (optional):                               │
│                                                                            │
│ Server Context:      OU=Consulting.O=DreamLAN                             │
│                                                                            │
│ Administrator Name: CN=Admin.O=DreamLAN                                   │
│ Password:                ********                                          │
└─────────────────────────────────────────────────────────────────────────┘
┌─────────────────────────────────────────────────────────────────────────┐
│ Server Context Help                                                        │
│                                                                            │
│ You may edit the server context string directly or you may let it be       │
│ created automatically by entering data in the fields above this one.        │
└─────────────────────────────────────────────────────────────────────────┘
Save this context name and continue <F10>
Scroll help window                     <F5>(up) <F6>(dn)
Help <F1>              Previous screen <Esc>          Abort INSTALL <Alt><F10>
```

Adding to an Existing NDS Tree

If you are adding this server to an existing tree, select the listed tree name. If you have multiple trees on the network, make sure you choose the correct one. The rest of the steps are identical to those of "First Server in an NDS Tree," discussed in the preceding section.

You should note that, by default, the Time Server type for additional servers is set to Secondary.

Create STARTUP.NCF

You are prompted for STARTUP.NCF file information. (See Figure 11.24.) The disk driver is automatically filled in. Add any additional SET and LOAD commands as necessary.

FIGURE 11.24.

Create the STARTUP.NCF file.

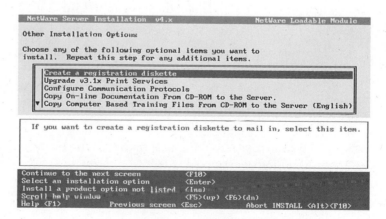

```
NetWare Server Installation  v4.x                    NetWare Loadable Module
Edit the STARTUP.NCF File As Necessary


┌──────────────────────────────────────────────────────────────────────────┐
│                            New STARTUP.NCF File                            │
├──────────────────────────────────────────────────────────────────────────┤
│ load IDE INT=E PORT=1F0                                                     │
│                                                                            │
│                                                                            │
│                                                                            │
│                                                                            │
└──────────────────────────────────────────────────────────────────────────┘

Save File <F10>
Help <F1>            Previous screen <Esc>          Abort INSTALL <Alt><F10>
```

Create AUTOEXEC.NCF

You are presented with the option to edit the AUTOEXEC.NCF file. In most cases, you do not need to do this unless you want to add extra SET commands or load additional NLMs.

Install Optional Files and NetWare Software

The last screen in the installation process enables you to create a registration disk, as well as to install optional Novell software—such as ElectroText online documentation. (See Figure 11.25.)

FIGURE 11.25.

Other installation options.

```
NetWare Server Installation  v4.x                    NetWare Loadable Module
Other Installation Options

Choose any of the following optional items you want to
install.  Repeat this step for any additional items.
┌────────────────────────────────────────────────────────────────────────┐
│ Create a registration diskette                                           │
│ Upgrade v3.1x Print Services                                             │
│ Configure Communication Protocols                                        │
│ Copy On-line Documentation From CD-ROM to the Server.                    │
│▼Copy Computer Based Training Files From CD-ROM to the Server (English)   │
└────────────────────────────────────────────────────────────────────────┘
┌────────────────────────────────────────────────────────────────────────┐
│  If you want to create a registration diskette to mail in, select this item. │
│                                                                          │
│                                                                          │
└────────────────────────────────────────────────────────────────────────┘

Continue to the next screen        <F10>
Select an installation option      <Enter>
Install a product option not listed  <Ins>
Scroll help window                 <F5><up> <F6><dn>
Help <F1>            Previous screen <Esc>          Abort INSTALL <Alt><F10>
```

Congratulations! You have just finished installing a NetWare 4.01 server and a NetWare Directory Services database. The next step is to install client software so the workstations can connect to your network.

Installing Workstation Clients

There are two ways to install workstation clients. You can boot up the workstation and log into the NetWare 4.01 server using the traditional IPX/NETX combination under bindery emulation. Then you install the new VLM drivers off the server. Or you can make a set of master diskettes from the CD and install the VLMs onto workstations as needed.

If you are installing OS/2 clients, the process is a little different. OS/2 requesters are OS/2-version specific. Therefore, if you have OS/2 v1.3, you cannot use the requester that comes with your NetWare 4.01 CD. For OS/2 v2.0 and v2.1, you can use either Requester v2.0 or v2.01. If you use Requester v2.0, make sure you also apply the patch, NSD202. This file can be obtained from the NOVLIB forum on CompuServe. Requester v2.01 is the version shipped on the NetWare 4.01 CD.

DOS Client Diskettes from CD

If this is your first NetWare server, you should create a set of installation disks from your NetWare 4.01 CD:

1. Change your current default directory to \CLIENT\DOSWIN on your CD.

2. Have three blank, formatted, high-density diskettes ready.

3. Make sure you have XCOPY and LABEL located somewhere along your DOS path.

4. Execute the MAKEDISK.BAT file in \CLIENT\DOSWIN. The syntax is makedisk *drive_letter*: *language*. (See Figure 11.26.) The colon after the drive letter is required.

5. Files will be copied to the appropriate diskettes by the batch file. (See Figure 11.27 for an example.)

FIGURE 11.26.
MAKEDISK.BAT command syntax.

```
D:\CLIENT\DOSWIN>makedisk
Usage:    MAKEDISK  drive_letter:  language

          drive_letter              = A - Z (including colon)
          language                  = ENGLISH
                                    = FRENCH
                                    = FRANCAIS
                                    = ITALIAN
                                    = ITALIANO
                                    = GERMAN
                                    = DEUTSCH
                                    = SPANISH
                                    = ESPANOL


Example: makedisk a: deutsch

D:\CLIENT\DOSWIN>
D:\CLIENT\DOSWIN>
```

FIGURE 11.27.
Create WSDOS_1 disk.

```
Please insert a formatted disk into drive b:
Press any key to continue . . .

Reading source file(s)...
..\.._____\WSDOS_1\AUTO.VLM
..\.._____\WSDOS_1\BIND.VLM
..\.._____\WSDOS_1\CONN.VLM
..\.._____\WSDOS_1\DOSNP.EXE
..\.._____\WSDOS_1\FIO.VLM
..\.._____\WSDOS_1\GENERAL.VLM
..\.._____\WSDOS_1\INSTALL.BAT
..\.._____\WSDOS_1\INSTALL.CFG
..\.._____\WSDOS_1\INSTALL.OVL
..\.._____\WSDOS_1\INST_DOS.EXE
..\.._____\WSDOS_1\IPXNCP.VLM
```

OS/2 Client Diskettes from CD

If this is your first NetWare server, create a set of installation disks from your NetWare 4.01 CD by following these instructions:

1. Change your current default directory to \CLIENT\OS2 on your CD.
2. Have three blank, formatted, high-density diskettes ready.
3. Make sure you have XCOPY and LABEL located somewhere on your DOS path.
4. Execute the MAKEDISK.BAT or MAKEDISK.CMD file in \CLIENT\OS2. The syntax is makedisk *drive_letter*: *language*. The colon after the drive letter is required.
5. Files will be copied onto the appropriate diskettes by the batch file.

DOS Client Disks from Server

If, during NetWare 4.01 installation, you choose to create a directory for client installation, a directory called CLIENT is created under SYS:PUBLIC. Under CLIENT, there is DOSWIN. A copy of MAKEDISK.BAT is located there as well. You create three installation disks using this batch file by following the steps outlined in the preceding section.

OS/2 Client Disks from Server

During installation, if you choose to create a directory for client installation, a directory called CLIENT is created under SYS:PUBLIC (as described in the preceding paragraph). Under CLIENT, there is OS2. A copy of MAKEDISK.BAT is located there as well. From your DOS workstation, create three installation disks using this batch file by following the steps outlined in the preceding OS/2 section. A corresponding .CMD file is available if you are using an OS/2 station.

DOS and Windows Clients

Installation of the DOS and Windows clients is very straightforward. The whole process is menu-driven. (See Figure 11.28.) You start by inserting the WSDOS_1 disk in the floppy drive and running INSTALL.BAT after you have changed your default working directory to that drive.

FIGURE 11.28.

NetWare Client Installation menu.

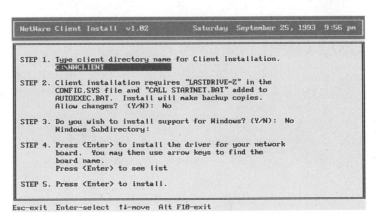

When you select an ODI driver, specify the settings to be used. (See Figure 11.29.) If you need to modify any of the settings, highlight the appropriate selection and press Enter. You will be presented with the available choices. (See Figure 11.30.)

FIGURE 11.29.

ODI Driver Setting selection menu.

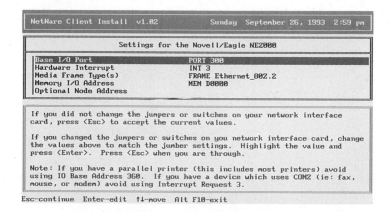

FIGURE 11.30.

Media Frame Type selection menu.

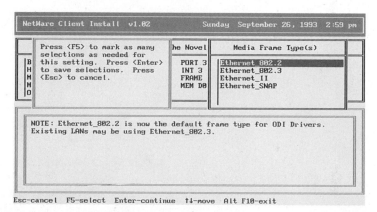

> **CAUTION** ▶
>
> The new Ethernet ODI drivers default to the frame type, Etherent_802.2. If you're also using this workstation to connect to NetWare 3.x and 2.x servers, make sure you select Ethernet_802.3 frame types. Failure to do so can render your workstation unable to communicate with the servers.

If your particular network card is not listed among the driver selections, choose Dedicated (Non-ODI) IPX driver to continue with the installation. You can edit the resulting STARTNET.BAT file to load your particular ODI driver. You cannot complete the installation without selecting an NIC driver. (See Figures 11.31 and 11.32.) Note that the message erroneously references the WSDRV_1 instead of the WSDRV_2 diskette.

FIGURE 11.31.

An NIC driver must be selected.

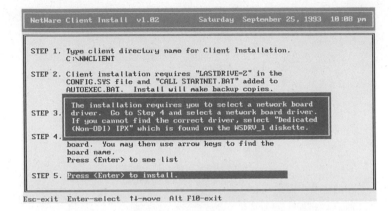

FIGURE 11.32.

Dedicated IPX driver selection.

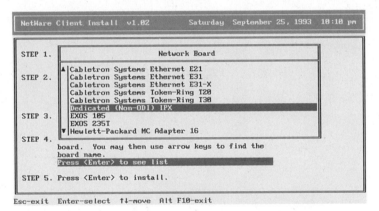

If you enable the installation process to modify your AUTOEXEC.BAT and CONFIG.SYS files, make sure you check these files afterwards, especially AUTOEXEC.BAT. The installation process inserts the calling of STARTNET.BAT (the batch file that loads the VLM drivers) as the first line of AUTOEXEC.BAT. (See Figure 11.33.) If you load any memory-resident programs (TSRs), such as DOSKEY, with your AUTOEXEC.BAT file, you will not be able to unload the VLM and ODI drivers.

CAUTION ►

The NET.CFG file created by the installation process is minimal. For version 1.02 of VLM driver (which is shipped on the 4.01 CD), you must include the following statement in your NET.CFG file, in the NetWare DOS Requester section:

LOAD CONN TABLE LOW = ON

If this isn't done, you will experience connection problems. Check the READVLM.TXT file in your C:\NWCLIENT\NLS\ENGLISH directory for more details. If you installed your VLM drivers elsewhere or used a different language, use the appropriate directory path.

You also should specify the proper Name Context for your workstation's user.

FIGURE 11.33.

Modified AUTOEXEC.BAT file. Note the location of `@CALL STARTNET.BAT`.

```
C:\NWCLIENT>type autoexec.bat
@CALL C:\NWCLIENT\STARTNET
C:\SCSI\MSCDEX.EXE /D:ASPICD0 /M:12
C:\WINDOWS\SMARTDRV.EXE
@echo off
cls
SET TZ=EST5EDT
SET path=C:\NMS\bin;C:\WINDOWS;C:\DOS
SET TEMP=C:\WINDOWS\TEMP
prompt $p$g
SET HELPFILES=C:\NMS\help\*.HLP
rem SHARE

C:\NWCLIENT>
```

OS/2 Clients

The installation of OS/2 clients is similar to that of DOS clients. Insert the WSOS2_1 diskette in the floppy drive, change your default working directory to the drive, and execute INSTALL.EXE. You must, however, do this from an OS/2 window or a full-screen box.

After selecting the language you want your prompts to be in, you will be presented with the main installation menu. (See Figure 11.34.) Select Requester on workstation from the Installation pull-down option. You will be prompted for the directory path in which to install the requester files. The default directory path is C:\NETWARE. In this book's example, the path has been changed to C:\NETWARE2. As with the DOS client installation, you can enable the installation program to modify your CONFIG.SYS file. For first-time installation, you should do so, because many lines are appended to the end of your existing CONFIG.SYS file. The NetWare requester section is clearly marked.

FIGURE 11.34.

OS/2 Client Installation main menu.

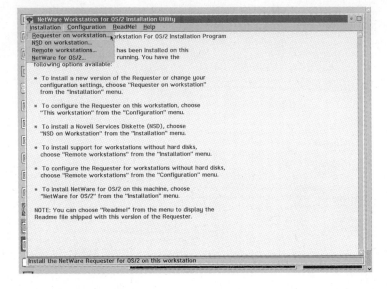

```
  NetWare Workstation for OS/2 Installation Utility
Installation  Configuration  ReadMe!  Help
Requester on workstation...  orkstation For OS/2 Installation Program
NSD on workstation...
Remote workstations...          has been installed on this
NetWare for OS/2...              running. You have the
following options available:

  ×  To install a new version of the Requester or change your
     configuration settings, choose "Requester on workstation"
     from the "Installation" menu.

  ×  To configure the Requester on this workstation, choose
     "This workstation" from the "Configuration" menu.

  ×  To install a Novell Services Diskette (NSD), choose
     "NSD on Workstation" from the "Installation" menu.

  ×  To install support for workstations without hard disks,
     choose "Remote workstations" from the "Installation" menu.

  ×  To configure the Requester for workstations without hard disks,
     choose "Remote workstations" from the "Configuration" menu.

  ×  To install NetWare for OS/2 on this machine, choose
     "NetWare for OS/2" from the "Installation" menu.

  NOTE: You can choose "Readme!" from the menu to display the
  Readme file shipped with this version of the Requester.



Install the NetWare Requester for OS/2 on this workstation
```

FIGURE 11.35.

OS/2 NetWare requester section in the CONFIG.SYS file.

```
REM ---- NetWare Requester statements BEGIN ----
SET NWLANGUAGE=ENGLISH
DEVICE=C:\NETWARE2\LSL.SYS
RUN=C:\NETWARE2\DDAEMON.EXE
REM -- ODI-Driver Files BEGIN --
DEVICE=C:\NETWARE2\TOKEN.SYS
DEVICE=C:\NETWARE2\ROUTE.SYS
REM -- ODI-Driver Files END --
DEVICE=C:\NETWARE2\IPX.SYS
DEVICE=C:\NETWARE2\SPX.SYS
RUN=C:\NETWARE2\SPDAEMON.EXE
rem DEVICE=C:\NETWARE2\NMPIPE.SYS
rem DEVICE=C:\NETWARE2\NPSERVER.SYS
rem RUN=C:\NETWARE2\NPDAEMON.EXE
DEVICE=C:\NETWARE2\NWREQ.SYS
IFS=C:\NETWARE2\NWIFS.IFS
RUN=C:\NETWARE2\NWDAEMON.EXE
DEVICE=C:\NETWARE2\NETBIOS.SYS
RUN=C:\NETWARE2\NBDAEMON.EXE
DEVICE=C:\NETWARE2\VIPX.SYS
DEVICE=C:\NETWARE2\VSHELL.SYS GLOBAL
REM ---- NetWare Requester statements END ----

C:\>
```

Next, you will be prompted for an ODI driver. Novell has supplied a set of drivers on the diskette labeled WSDRV_1. Choose the driver corresponding to the NIC you installed in the workstation. You are then prompted for NetWare support in the DOS and Windows applications. (See Figure 11.36.) There are three options, as follows:

Private NetWare Shell Support: In this mode, each DOS window will be independent from other windows and from the OS/2 sessions.

Global NetWare Shell Support: In this mode, the DOS windows share the same resources (for example, drive mappings) as the OS/2 sessions.

No NetWare Shell Support: This mode turns off network support.

FIGURE 11.36.

Choose NetWare support for DOS and Windows applications.

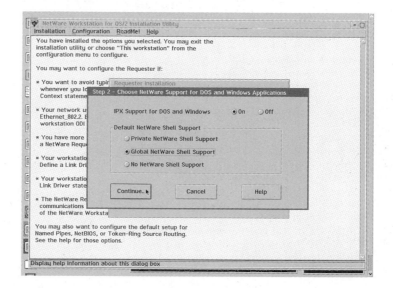

You are asked to select additional protocol support. Check the appropriate boxes. The unchecked options are commented out in the CONFIG.SYS file. Changes are then made to CONFIG.SYS. A backup copy of CONFIG.SYS is saved as CONFIG.BAK.

The installation program copies your ODI driver and requester files to the directory that you specified earlier. You can copy just the selected driver or all the drivers on disk. The status line at the bottom of the screen reflects the file currently being copied. The same is true when requester files are copied.

Finally, create a NET.CFG file. From the main menu, choose the Configuration pull-down menu and select This Workstation. The default location of NET.CFG is off the root of your boot drive. The exact syntax and an explanation of options are provided from the menu. (See Figure 11.37.) A sample NET.CFG file is shown in Figure 11.38.

FIGURE 11.37.
NET.CFG options.

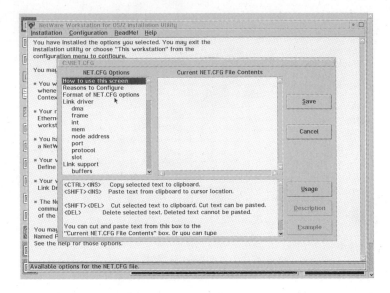

FIGURE 11.38.
Sample NET.CFG file.

```
Show dots=on

LINK SUPPORT
        BUFFERS 15 4202

PROTOCOL STACK IPX
        SOCKETS 64

PROTOCOL STACK SPX
        SOCKETS 32
        SESSIONS 32

NETWARE REQUESTER
        PREFERRED DREAMLAN
        DIRECTORY SERVICES OFF
        PACKET BURST OFF
        LARGE INTERNET PACKETS OFF

NETWARE SPOOLER
        NO BANNER
        COPIES 1
        NO FORM FEED
        NO TABS

C:\>
```

You need to reboot your OS/2 workstation in order for the changes to CONFIG.SYS to take effect.

CAUTION ▶

If you need to reinstall the requester, you must comment out or remove the NetWare requester lines from your CONFIG.SYS file and reboot the workstation. Otherwise, your reinstallation won't be complete because of opened requester driver files.

Summary

This chapter presented step-by-step installation procedures for the NetWare 4.01 server. It also provided the installations steps for DOS/Windows and OS/2 clients.

Installing Client Workstation Software

by Rick Sant'Angelo and Peter Kuo

12

IN THIS CHAPTER

NetWare documentation omits extensive instructions on installation of client workstations. Novell expects those who install NetWare to get training in order to become proficient. Any experienced computer professional can learn by doing with the proper assistance. This chapter is a comprehensive set of instructions, notes, and tips on how you can effectively integrate DOS and OS/2 workstations with NetWare. The chapter also includes notes and tips from highly experienced installers that you will certainly find valuable.

NetWare 3.12 and 4.x versions are shipped with new DOS and OS/2 Requester installation utilities. These installation utilities are the same for both 3.12 and 4.x versions. They can be run from your distribution CD-ROM drive, from a network drive, or from floppy diskettes. NetWare 3.11 was shipped with a WSGEN utility to install DOS clients, which has now been eliminated. This chapter discusses how to install DOS and OS/2 clients for 3.12 and 4.0 versions, as well as providing instructions for manually installing DOS clients with the DOS shell.

WSGEN is not discussed, because the use of traditional IPX drivers is obsolete. If you have been using WSGEN, it is time to switch to using ODI/MLID drivers. You can use the DOS Shell (NETX) or DOS Requester (VLM.EXE/NETX.VLM), but both run on top of the same ODI/MLID support files. Later NetWare versions require the use of ODI/MLID drivers to support newer features.

The DOS Requester is sometimes called the *universal client* because it can support all versions of NetWare, including Personal NetWare (NetWare Lite), 2.x, 3.x, and 4.x versions. The DOS Requester works a little differently from the older DOS Shell—NETX. The DOS Requester itself (NETX.VLM) is loaded as a Virtual Loadable Module, or VLM, (files with .VLM extensions). This enables your Requester to load into memory only what is needed at any given time, and to dynamically manage memory. The VLMs work similarly to overlaid files.

NetWare 3.12 can be accessed with the older DOS Shell (NETX), but it should be accessed with NETX.EXE version 3.32 or later. Some of the new features of 3.12 will not be available (for example, Packet Burst NCP). It cannot be used to access a NDS tree in a 4.x network.

The DOS and OS/2 Requester installation utilities can be run from

- Floppy diskettes
- CD-ROM
- A network drive

The recommended method is to install from floppy diskettes. It is the most straight-forward method, even though a few disk swaps are necessary. When installing dozens of workstations, another method may be preferred because of the amount of time involved in expanding and copying files from floppy disks.

How to Read this Chapter

This chapter includes instructions on several different methods of installing clients. It is organized according to the following steps:

1. Preparing and installing from each type of media. This portion is discussed in sections, categorized by installation media. There are separate sections on installing from floppy disks, CD-ROM, and network drive.

2. Running the Installation utility. This is discussed in a single section, because the procedure is virtually the same regardless of which medium is being used.

It is recommended that you scan through each method, select the a that suits you best, focus on that section, and ignore the others. You will find the instructions much less complex than they seem at first. Figure 12.1 shows a flow diagram that illustrates the flow of these instructions.

FIGURE 12.1.

Installation flow diagram.

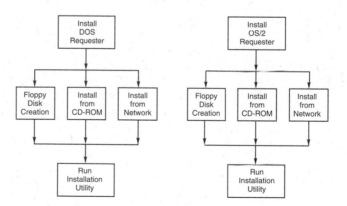

Before You Run the Installation Utility

In this chapter, it is assumed that the workstation NIC has been properly installed and is functioning. You must resolve any conflicts with other devices or memory managers, and you must record the NIC physical switch settings (for ISA NICs). For Micro Channel Architecture computers, you must run the IBM Reference diskette or the automatic setup for the NIC. For EISA NICs, you must have run your EISA configuration utility.

> **NOTE** ▶
>
> For ISA NICs, you should use test software to be certain that there are no conflicts between the NIC and other devices. When using ISA NICs in EISA computers, the very same advice applies. The EISA configuration utility normally does not detect conflicts with ISA devices.
>
> Several good utilities are available for testing hardware. See Chapter 34, "Workstation Performance," for more information on workstation testing utilities for this purpose.

> **NOTE** ▶
>
> You should check with your NIC developer for any updates that may be available for your NIC model before you begin. Drivers that are shipped with NICs are often out of date, because the product may have been packaged and shipped months before.
>
> There have been many changes to the NetWare NIC driver, support files, and shell/requesters. Some combinations will not work together. It is best to get the latest versions to avoid difficulty in connecting to the server.

Installing the DOS Requester

Choose the medium you will use to install your DOS Requester and client software: floppy diskette, CD-ROM, or network drive. Each method of installation is discussed in the following sections titled "Installation from Floppy Diskettes," "Installation from CD-ROM," and "Installation from a Network Drive," but each one will refer to a single section titled "Running the Installation Utility."

Installing from Floppy Diskettes

Installation from floppies requires three blank, formatted high-density diskettes. The CD-ROM must be installed as a DOS device—or if it is installed in the server as a SCSI device, it can be mounted as a NetWare volume. This Installation utility creates three floppy diskettes to be used to install DOS client workstations. Once the Installation utility is created on those diskettes, you proceed to the section on running the Installation utility later in this chapter.

To install from floppy diskettes, follow these steps:

1. Create your set of installation floppy diskettes. Run the MAKEDISK batch file from the CD-ROM drive specifying the destination drive as a switch. The batch file is located on the CD-ROM in the \CLIENT\DOSWIN directory (source). You must be in the source working directory for the application to work correctly. To make installation diskettes in drive A, type

```
MAKEDISK A:
```

> **NOTE** ▶
>
> Make sure you have a PATH set to your DOS directory. You will need to have the DOS external programs XCOPY and LABEL available to this batch file.

This program will create the following diskettes:

Volume Label	Description
WSDOS_1	NetWare Client for DOS
WSWIN_1	NetWare Client for MS Windows
WSDRV_2	NetWare Client Drivers

2. Execute INSTALL.BAT from the WSDOS_1 diskette.

3. Proceed to the section later in this chapter entitled "Running the INSTALL Batch File." Execute INSTALL.BAT from the WSDOS_1 diskette you have just created.

4. Reboot the workstation so changes to the CONFIG.SYS will take effect.

5. Execute the STARTNET.BAT that was created in the destination directory.

Installing from CD-ROM

You may execute the Installation utility directly from the CD-ROM. Client installation from a CD-ROM is the most direct procedure for generating the files for each workstation. The downside of this procedure is that a CD-ROM must be installed in each workstation in order to use install directly from it. It is possible to install a CD-ROM as a network device, and then install from a network drive letter. The latter option is explored under the section titled "Installing from a Network Drive."

It is feasible to use this option if you have an external CD-ROM that plugs into a parallel port. However, you may find that installing the drivers for the CD-ROM is more work than running the Installation utility from floppies.

You can execute the Installation utility directly from the CD-ROM if you generate the files onto a high-density floppy diskette. You can then copy the files from this diskette to your client workstation and manually edit your CONFIG.SYS, AUTOEXEC.BAT, and STARTNET.BAT files.

To install from a CD-ROM, follow these steps:

1. Switch to the CD-ROM drive.

2. Change directories to the \CLIENT\DOSWIN directory.

3. Type INSTALL.

4. Proceed to the section titled "Running the INSTALL Batch File," later in this chapter. If the destination is to be the current local workstation hard drive, the client directory name under step 2 should be C:. If the destination is to be another user's workstation hard drive, the client directory name in step 2 should be A:.

5. If the destination directory is the local hard drive, the installation will copy all appropriate files to your hard drive.

   If the destination drive is A:, a single high-density diskette can contain all the files in three directories. To re-create the directory structure with all files on the user's local C: drive, type

   ```
   XCOPY A:\*.* C:\client_directory /S /E
   ```

> **NOTE** ▶
>
> The DOS XCOPY command reproduces the same directory structure on the user's local hard drive, creating the subdirectories as it goes.

6. Edit your CONFIG.SYS on your local hard drive to include the command:

   `LASTDRIVE=Z`

7. Adjust your AUTOEXEC.BAT and STARTNET.BAT files on your local hard drive accordingly.

8. Reboot the workstation so that changes to the CONFIG.SYS will take effect.

9. Execute the STARTNET.BAT that was created in the destination directory.

Installing from a Network Drive

If you are upgrading clients who can already log in, installing from a network drive is the most convenient method. In some cases, you may want to manually install the DOS shell (NETX) and then upgrade to the DOS Requester, executing the Installation utility from a network drive. You can log in from any workstation and generate a new set of workstation files without switching a single diskette.

If your SCSI CD-ROM is installed as a NetWare device, you can mount the CD-ROM as a NetWare volume and use it as you would any other network drive. Once the volume is mounted, map root a drive letter to the NETWARE_312:CLIENT/DOSWIN directory and follow these instructions:

1. Copy the appropriate directories from your CD-ROM to a network volume. Use the DOS XCOPY or NetWare NCOPY command as follows:

   `NCOPY d:\CLIENT\DOSWIN\*.* volume:\destination_directory /S /C /E`

   where *d:* represents the CD-ROM drive letter, and *volume:* represents a network volume name.

> **NOTE** ▶
>
> If you are using a CD-ROM as a NetWare volume, skip the previous step.

2. Map root a drive letter to that directory and change to that drive.

3. Proceed to the section later in this chapter titled "Running the INSTALL Batch File." Execute INSTALL.BAT from the network drive letter you have just mapped. Specify your destination drive as the local hard drive.

4. Reboot the workstation so that changes to the CONFIG.SYS will take effect.

5. Execute the STARTNET.BAT that was created in the destination directory.

Running the INSTALL Batch File

When you execute the INSTALL batch file, the screen shown in Figure 12.2 will appear.

FIGURE 12.2.

The DOS Client Requester Installation utility.

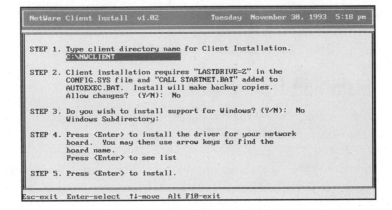

The following instructions are directly related to the steps displayed in the opening screen shown in Figure 12.2.

1. Enter the destination drive letter and directory to copy the workstation client files.

2. If you elect to enable the utility to make the changes for you, it adds the statement `LASTDRIVE=Z` to your CONFIG.SYS. This statement is required, or the DOS Requester will not be able to find a valid drive letter for drive mappings. It also adds the statement
   `CALL drive_letter:path_name\STARTNET.BAT`
   to your AUTOEXEC.BAT, which loads the drivers and DOS Requester during startup. (You can make these changes too, if you would like.)

3. If you answer Yes to "Do you wish to install support for Windows," IN-STALL copies the Windows files to your Windows directory. Enter the drive and path to your Windows subdirectory on your hard drive and press Enter.

> **NOTE** ▶
>
> The Installation utility assumes that Windows is installed on your local hard drive. If it is installed on your file server, make a directory for the user files on

your hard drive and copy the user files to that directory. Once the Installation utility has altered those files, you can copy them to the file server user directory.

The Installation utility creates a SYSTEM subdirectory under your Windows directory. Copy the files in that directory to the shared (main) Windows directory on your server. In order to do so, change the shared Windows files to read-write, copy the files, and then change them back to read-only.

4. Select your workstation NIC driver.

If this is a new installation, you will be prompted to insert a driver disk into any drive and specify the source path, as shown in Figure 12.3. Insert your WSDRV_2 disk in a floppy drive and press Enter to continue.

FIGURE 12.3.

Inserting driver disk WSDRV_2.

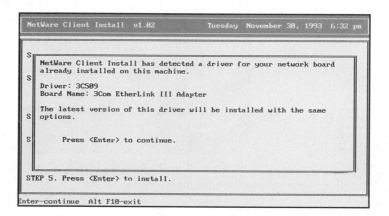

```
NetWare Client Install  v1.02              Tuesday  November 30, 1993  6:32 pm

S
   NetWare Client Install has detected a driver for your network board
   already installed on this machine.
S
   Driver: 3C509
   Board Name: 3Com EtherLink III Adapter

   The latest version of this driver will be installed with the same
S  options.

S      Press <Enter> to continue.



STEP 5. Press <Enter> to install.

Enter-continue  Alt F10-exit
```

If the workstation currently has an installed driver and this utility can detect it, the screen appears as the one shown in Figure 12.4. This indicates that the driver will be selected automatically, and the current configuration will be used. If the new driver has an older date than your existing driver, you will receive a warning before it is overwritten. Once you press Enter to continue, you will see a screen similar to that shown in Figure 12.3. Place your WSDRV_2 or vendor-supplied driver diskette into a floppy drive, and press Enter to continue.

You will see an extensive list of NIC drivers supplied on your WSDRV_2 distribution diskette, as shown in Figure 12.5.

FIGURE 12.4.

INSTALL detecting an existing driver.

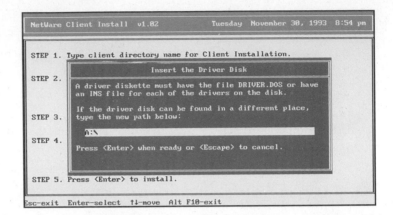

FIGURE 12.5.

List of Novell-supplied drivers on your distribution diskette.

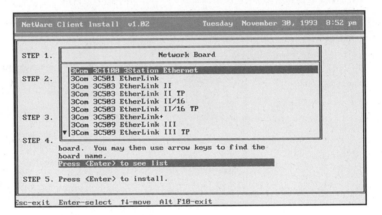

If the driver you want to install is not listed, or if you have a later revision of the driver, scroll to the end of the list and select OTHER DRIVERS; you will see the screen shown in Figure 12.3 again. You must locate the driver files (one with a .COM and one with an .INS extension), insert the driver diskette, and specify the path to find the files.

> **NOTE** ▶
>
> The Installation utility searches for the .INS file in the path you have specified. The .INS file must be present, or the Installation utility will not be able to use your driver. If you cannot load a vendor-supplied driver, check to see whether you have specified the correct directory name, or check with your NIC developer for a driver specifically written for use with 3.12 or 4.x.

Scroll through the list and select a driver. Once the driver has been read, another screen offers you hardware and driver configuration settings (see Figure 12.6). You may select each configuration parameter separately; each one has several options from which to choose.

Once you have configured the driver, press Esc to continue. All the files will be installed and updated. You will need to reboot your workstation so the CONFIG.SYS will be read. If you enabled the Installation utility to edit your AUTOEXEC.BAT, the STARTNET.BAT batch file created during installation will be automatically executed. If not, execute the STARTNET.BAT file in the network directory that you specified in the Installation utility opening screen (see Figure 12.2). The default directory is C:\NWCLIENT.

FIGURE 12.6.

Configuring the NIC driver.

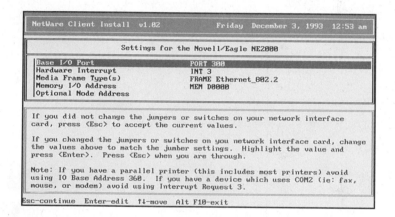

Important Notes

The following notes are not documented. Some are taken from README files, and others are accumulated from technical support and personal experience.

1. If your driver fails to load, check your NET.CFG file. In some cases, it will contain erroneous information concerning NIC configuration.

2. Ethernet users also should check the frame type. Later drivers default to Ethernet_802.2. Both the server and workstations need to use the same frame type in order to communicate. Check your server's frame type by looking at the MONITOR LAN Information menu selection.

3. The following files should be contained in a single directory, and that directory should be the current working directory when each is executed:

   LSL.COM
   Nic_driver.COM
   IPXODI.COM
   VLM.EXE
   *.VLM
   NET.CFG

NOTE ▶

You can locate VLMs in a separate directory using the VLM=*path_name* statement in your NET.CFG. See Appendix C for NET.CFG settings that you can adjust.

4. Windows users should add the following lines to their NET.CFGs:

```
SHOW DOTS = ON

SEARCH DIR FIRST = ON

ENVIRONMENT PAD = n
```

NOTE ▶

If you have expanded the size of the DOS environment in your CONFIG.SYS, it isn't necessary to specify the number of file handles when using the DOS Requester (VLM.EXE/NETX.VLM). It enables as many files to be opened as you have specified in your CONFIG.SYS.

5. 4.0 users must add the following command to the NET.CFG when using VLM.EXE 1.02 or later. (This does not apply to 4.01 users.)

   ```
   LOAD CONN TABLE = LOW
   ```

6. Do not mix older LSL.COM and IPXODI.COM files with later NIC driver files or vice versa; you may not be able to connect with your server. The files on your CD-ROM distribution disk are known to be stable and work together. You may need to obtain a later driver from your NIC developer. If you have difficulty connecting with your server, try installing the DOS Shell and older drivers (as discussed in the next section of this chapter).

7. The DOS Requester supports a pathname consisting of up to 64 characters.

8. If you use NDIS drivers, you also must load the ODINSUP.COM module. It must be loaded after LSL and before the NIC driver.

9. If you have hardware or software that requires NetBIOS, use the Novell NetBIOS emulator (NETBIOS.COM) supplied with NetWare. It works better with NetWare ODI/MLID drivers and is adjustable. In some cases, your software or hardware vendor requires the IBM NetBIOS interface to be used. NETBIOS.COM must be loaded after IPXODI.COM.

For additional tips on editing your NET.CFG, AUTOEXEC.BAT, or other files, see the section in this chapter titled "Loading the Workstation Files and Editing the AUTOEXEC.BAT and NET.CFG."

Manually Installing the DOS Shell and ODI/MLID Drivers

For NetWare 3.11, or whenever you have difficulty with the Installation utility provided with 3.12 or 4.x, you can manually install your drivers and DOS Shell.

> **NOTE** ▶
>
> 3.11 and 2.2 were shipped with the WSGEN utility, which generated a traditional IPX.COM driver. This older technology has been frozen from future revision, and it is recommended that you upgrade to the ODI/MLID drivers as discussed in this section.
>
> The files on the WSGEN distribution diskette are out of date and should be upgraded. You should obtain the latest workstation files from Novell.
>
> You can use later NetWare Shell/Requesters and drivers with earlier version servers, but not vice versa. It is a good policy to upgrade *all* workstations to the latest versions that are known to be stable.

> **NOTE** ▶
>
> You can download the latest files from Novell's NOVFILES forum on CompuServe. Unlike other forums, in which files are available in libraries,

NOVFILES is set up with a menu and downloads the file to you from menu selections. The latest workstation files (summer, 1993) were in the file DOSUP7.ZIP. This file has the following versions:

LSL.COM 2.01
IPXODI.COM 2.11
NETX.EXE 3.32

The files you need to install on your workstations include those in Table 12.1.

Table 12.1. ODI/MLID DOS workstation client files.

Filename	Name	DOSUP7.ZIP Version	Function
LSL.COM	Link Support Layer	2.01	Binds IPXODI and the NIC driver
NIC_Driver.COM	MLID Driver	various	NIC frame driver
IPXODI.COM	IPX/SPX Protocol	2.10	IPX packet driver
NETX.EXE	DOS Workstation Shell	3.32	DOS client shell
NET.CFG	Shell Configuration		Configures shell, IPX Protocol, and/ or MLID driver

Overview of Installation

The manual installation procedure for installing a DOS client with the DOS Shell is as follows:

1. Copy LSL.COM, IPXODI.COM, and NETX.EXE (or NETX.COM) into a working directory.

2. Copy the NIC driver executable file (with a .COM extension) from the disk that came with the NIC.

3. Create a NET.CFG file with the appropriate configuration entries (this is not necessary if all configuration parameters are set to the factory default settings).

4. Execute the workstation files in the following order:

   LSL.COM

   NIC_Driver.COM

   IPXODI.COM

   NETX.EXE (NETX.EXE, or VLM.EXE)

5. Change to the first available drive letter (usually F:).

6. Execute LOGIN.EXE.

NOTE ▶

Be sure to rename or delete NETX.COM from the working directory. If NETX.COM and NETX.EXE are in the same directory, NETX.COM will execute first. If you have NETX.EXE 3.32, you should use it.

Ethernet users should check both the workstation and the server to see that they are both configured for the same frame type.

Make sure that LASTDRIVE is not set to Z in your CONFIG.SYS; you will not be able to access the first network drive letter if it is.

Token Ring drivers may require ROUTE.EXE to be loaded for source-routing protocol driver support.

If you are running Microsoft Windows 3.1, you will find the following files on your Windows diskettes:

File	Version #
LSL.COM	1.21
IPXODI.COM	1.20
NETX.COM	3.26

Create NET.CFG

You can create your configuration file using an ASCII text editor, such as MS-DOS 5.0's or 6.0's Edit utility. The file designates the following information for the data link functions of your NIC driver:

Driver name
Base I/O address (port)
Interrupt request (int)
RAM buffer address (mem)
DMA Channel (dma)
Frame type (frame)

Other lines can be added to the NET.CFG to adjust the functioning of IPXODI.COM and NETX.COM. The following file is a typical example of a NET.CFG for an SMC EtherCard running under Windows. (The # statements are remarks that are ignored.)

```
#This part adjusts LSL.COM
Link Support
    Max Stacks 8

#This part configures the NIC driver SMC8000.COM
Link Driver SMC8000
    INT 10
    MEM C8000
    PORT 320
    Frame Ethernet_802.3

#This part adjusts NETX.EXE for Windows
show dots=on
file handles=80
environment pad=512
search dir first=on
#End of file
```

Many other parameters can be placed into the NET.CFG file. See Appendix C for complete details on configuration parameters that can be used. Parameters do not need to be included if the default parameters are okay. For example, if the driver in the preceding example needed to run an Ethernet_802.2 frame, you wouldn't have to include a line configuring the frame type, because this driver uses Ethernet_802.2 as its default frame type.

IBM PS/2 (MCA) and EISA NIC drivers normally require a simple NET.CFG that names the driver and the slot number it is in. The driver is able to read the configuration from the physical configuration that was software-selected on the board. A few ISA NICs also have switched to software configurable NICs and written drivers that read the settings from the board.

If the physical settings on the card are the default factory settings, and if the frame type works with your server driver, NIC drivers run without any NET.CFG file. For settings to be used with Windows, see the chapters in Part IX, "Windows and NetWare."

CAUTION ▷

Watch your NIC driver during load, or execute the driver re-entrantly to observe its messages to make certain that you are using the same frame type as your server.

The load message should specify the frame type it is using. You can specify the frame type for most MLID drives by including a frame statement in your NET.CFG file. If you cannot communicate with your server, check your NIC installation.

TIP ▷

You can unload ODI/MLID drivers by executing them with a /U switch in reverse order from which they were loaded.

Token Ring can use two different frame types—one for normal and one for source-routing bridges. Ethernet can use any one of four frame types. This currently appears to be a common problem with Ethernet drivers because Novell has recently changed the default frame type from Ethernet_802.3 to Ethernet_802.2. Many newer workstation drivers use Ethernet_802.2 as the default frame type, whereas the server NIC drivers, on older NetWare distribution diskettes, use an Ethernet_802.3 default.

NOTE ▷

Most server NICs can support more than one frame type, but workstations may or may not be capable of supporting multiple frame types.

Loading the Workstation Files and Editing the AUTOEXEC.BAT and NET.CFG

To connect with the server, execute the workstation files in the proper order. Though few TSRs conflict with NetWare workstation files, you should start with a stripped-down CONFIG.SYS and AUTOEXEC.BAT that only contains the most necessary commands. The files must be loaded in the correct order, as follows:

1. LSL.COM
2. *NIC_Driver*.COM
3. IPXODI.COM
4. NETX.COM (NETX.EXE or VLM.EXE)

NOTE ▶

Novell ODI/MLID drivers are designed to effectively load into upper memory blocks with little or no overhead in conventional memory. Use your DOS LOADHI (or HIGHLOAD) command to conserve conventional memory.

CAUTION ▶

Do not use the LOADHI command with VLM.EXE. It automatically detects extended or expanded memory and loads itself accordingly.

All these files and NET.CFG should reside in the same directory. If they do not, you may have problems recognizing various NET.CFG parameters.

Integrate loading these files into your AUTOEXEC.BAT or make up a network start batch file. A simple AUTOEXEC.BAT look similar to the following:

Batch command	Function
@echo off	Commands will not be shown on-screen.
prompt PG	Changes the DOS prompt to show the working directory.
set TEMP = c:\temp	Creates a DOS environment variable named TEMP.
path C:\DOS;c:\util	Sets the DOS path.

Batch command	*Function*
cd \net\smc	Changes to the \NET\SMC directory.
lsl	Executes LSL.COM.
smc8000	Executes SMC8000.COM.
ipxodi	Executes IPXODI.COM.
netx	Executes NETX.COM.
f:	Switches to drive F.
login rick	Logs in as user Rick.

The following file is an example of a workstation AUTOEXEC.BAT that enables the user to select whether to boot without loading the workstation files, or to load and log in. (The REMARK statements are ignored by DOS.)

```
REMARK Workstation local boot or network boot AUTOEXEC.BAT
@echo off
prompt $P$G
set temp = c:temp
path C:\DOS;c:\util

REMARK Load TSR utilities
doskey
fastkey a2
cls

REMARK Asks the question shown, and proceeds if "N" and branches if "Y"
yesorno Do you want to start NetWare?
if errorlevel 1 goto NW
goto END

REMARK Loads NetWare DOS workstation client software and logs in
:NW
cd \net\smc
lsl
smc8000
ipxodi
netx
f:
login rick
:END
```

The YESORNO.COM file referenced in this example is included on the diskette that accompanies this book. This AUTOEXEC.BAT file is also included.

> **TIP** ▶
>
> If you are using MS-DOS 6.0 or a memory manager with a memory optimizing utility, you should run the memory optimizing utility again after editing your AUTOEXEC.BAT and loading the NetWare workstation files.

Chapter 34, "Workstation Performance," discusses techniques in loading workstation files for maximum conservation of workstation memory.

Installing the OS/2 Requester

The installation of OS/2 clients is similar to that of DOS Client Requester, except it is an OS/2 Presentation Manager based application. Similar to the DOS Requester, you can install from

- CD-ROM
- A network drive
- Floppy diskettes

Choose the medium that you will use to install your DOS Requester and client software: floppy diskette, CD-ROM, or network drive. Each method of installation will be discussed, but each one will refer to a single section on running the Installation utility. First review each method for each type of media, decide which one you will use, follow the instructions in the appropriate section of this chapter, and ignore the other sections. The recommended method is installing from floppy diskettes.

Installing from Floppy Diskettes

Installation from floppies requires three formatted high-density diskettes before starting. The CD-ROM must be installed as a local device, or as a NetWare volume if installed in the server as a NetWare SCSI device.

1. Create the installation diskette set and run the MAKEDISK batch file or MAKEDISK.CMD from the CD-ROM drive. The Installation utility will create three floppy diskettes that can be used at each workstation. The batch file is located on the CD-ROM in the \CLIENT\OS2 directory. You must be in that working directory for the application to work correctly. You will be asked to have three formatted high-density diskettes ready.

NOTE ▶

Make sure you have a PATH set to your DOS directory. You will need to have the DOS external programs XCOPY and LABEL available to this batch file.

This program will create the following disks:

Volume Label	Description
WSOS2_1	NetWare Client for OS/2
WSWIN_1	NetWare Client for MS Windows
WSDRV_2	NetWare Client Drivers

NOTE ▶

If the driver for your NIC is not included on the WSDRV_2 disk, locate your vendor-supplied driver files (one with a .SYS extension and one with an .INS extension) and copy those files to a floppy diskette. The diskette does not need to have a label. The Installation application will read and copy your driver from that diskette.

2. Execute INSTALL.BAT from the WSOS2_1 diskette.
3. Proceed to the section later in this chapter entitled "Running the INSTALL Utility."
4. Reboot the workstation so changes to the CONFIG.SYS will take effect.

Installing from CD-ROM

Installation from a CD-ROM is the most direct procedure for generating the files for each workstation. The downside of this procedure is that a CD-ROM must be installed in each workstation. This can be an effective way to install if you have a CD-ROM that connects to a parallel port. It is the most efficient way to upgrade a workstation that may have an older driver loaded.

Follow these steps:

1. Locate the INSTALL.CMD application in the \CLIENT\OS2 directory. Launch the application from that directory. If the CD-ROM is installed as

a NetWare device and the volume is mounted, you will find it in the NETWARE_312:CLIENT/OS2 directory.

2. In Presentation Manager, launch the INSTALL.CMD utility from the CD-ROM drive. Proceed to the section titled "Running the OS/2 Installation Utility." Reboot the workstation so that changes to the CONFIG.SYS will take effect.

Installing from a Network Drive

Installing from a network drive is the most convenient method when you are upgrading the client workstation. If you can log in at a workstation from having installed a prior workstation shell or requester, you can launch the Installation utility from the network drive. You can log in from any workstation and generate a new set of workstation files without switching a single diskette.

1. Launch your Installation utility (INSTALL.CMD or INSTALL.BAT) from the SYS:PUBLIC/CLIENT/OS2 directory.

    During the 4.01 server OS installation, you were given a choice to "create a directory for client installation." The directory \PUBLIC\CLIENT\OS2 was created in volume SYS:. Proceed to the section titled "Running the OS/2 Installation Utility."

2. Proceed to the next section, "Running the OS/2 Installation Utility." Reboot the workstation so that changes to the CONFIG.SYS will take effect.

Running the OS/2 Installation Utility

Regardless of which medium you are using, once you launch the OS/2 Installation utility, the procedure is the same.

After selecting the language to be used, you will be presented with the main installation menu (see Figure 12.7). Select Requester on Workstation from the Installation pull-down option. You will be prompted for the directory path to which you'll install the requester files (see Figure 12.8). The default directory path is C:\NETWARE. In the example in Figure 12.8, the path is C:\NETWARE2. Similar to the DOS client install, you have the option of enabling the Install program to modify your CONFIG.SYS (see Figure 12.9).

For a first-time install, you should enable the Installation utility to edit your CONFIG.SYS. Check the last few lines to make sure that the lines appended to the end of the file are properly written. The NetWare Requester section is clearly marked (see Figure 12.10).

FIGURE 12.7.

OS/2 Client Installation main menu.

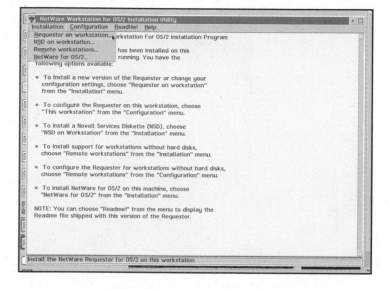

FIGURE 12.8.

Target directory path prompt.

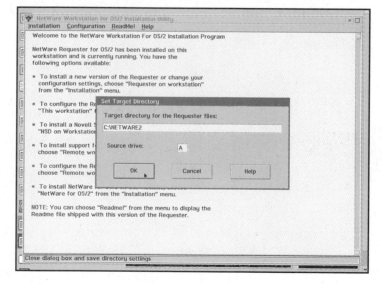

FIGURE 12.9.

Edit and File copy options.

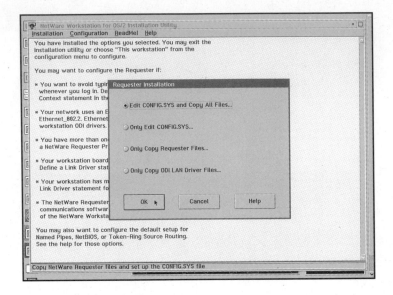

FIGURE 12.10.

OS/2 NetWare Requester section in the CONFIG.SYS file.

```
REM ---- NetWare Requester statements BEGIN ----
SET NWLANGUAGE=ENGLISH
DEVICE=C:\NETWARE2\LSL.SYS
RUN=C:\NETWARE2\DDAEMON.EXE
REM --- ODI-Driver Files BEGIN ---
DEVICE=C:\NETWARE2\TOKEN.SYS
DEVICE=C:\NETWARE2\ROUTE.SYS
REM --- ODI-Driver Files END ---
DEVICE=C:\NETWARE2\IPX.SYS
DEVICE=C:\NETWARE2\SPX.SYS
RUN=C:\NETWARE2\SPDAEMON.EXE
rem DEVICE=C:\NETWARE2\NMPIPE.SYS
rem DEVICE=C:\NETWARE2\NPSERVER.SYS
rem RUN=C:\NETWARE2\NPDAEMON.EXE
DEVICE=C:\NETWARE2\NWREQ.SYS
IFS=C:\NETWARE2\NWIFS.IFS
RUN=C:\NETWARE2\NWDAEMON.EXE
DEVICE=C:\NETWARE2\NETBIOS.SYS
RUN=C:\NETWARE2\NBDAEMON.EXE
DEVICE=C:\NETWARE2\VIPX.SYS
DEVICE=C:\NETWARE2\VSHELL.SYS GLOBAL
REM ---- NetWare Requester statements END ----

C:\>
```

You'll be prompted for an ODI driver. Novell supplied a set of drivers on the diskette labeled WSDRV_1 (see Figure 12.11). Pick the driver corresponding to the NIC you have installed in the workstation (see Figure 12.12). You are then prompted for NetWare support in the DOS and Windows applications (see Figure 12.13). There are three options:

> **Private NetWare Shell Support:** In this mode, each DOS window is independent of each other and from the OS/2 sessions.
>
> **Global NetWare Shell Support:** In this mode, the DOS windows share the same resources (for example, drive mappings) as the OS/2 sessions.
>
> **No NetWare Shell Support:** Turns off the network support.

FIGURE 12.11.

Diskette WSDRV_1 contains Novell-supplied ODI drivers.

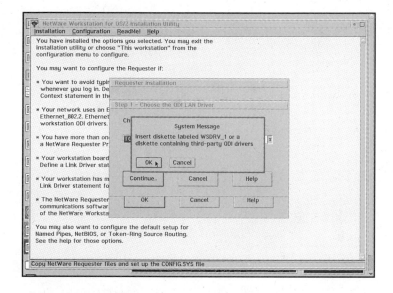

FIGURE 12.12.

Select an NIC driver.

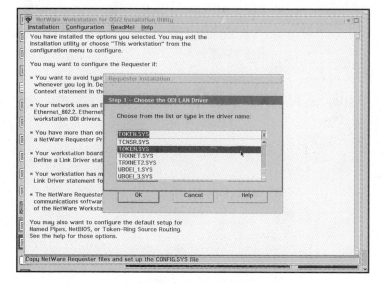

FIGURE 12.13.

Choose NetWare Support for DOS and Windows applications.

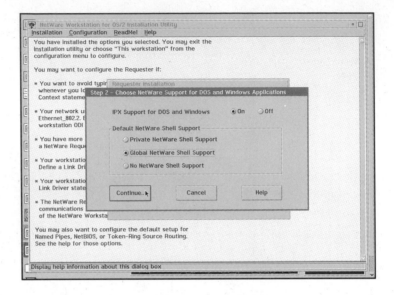

Next you are asked to select additional protocol support. Check the appropriate boxes (see Figure 12.14). The unchecked options are commented out in the CONFIG.SYS file. Changes are then made to CONFIG.SYS (see Figure 12.15). A backup copy of CONFIG.SYS is saved as CONFIG.BAK.

FIGURE 12.14.

Selecting additional protocol support.

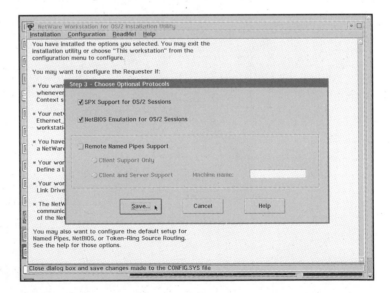

FIGURE 12.15.

Saving changes to CONFIG.SYS.

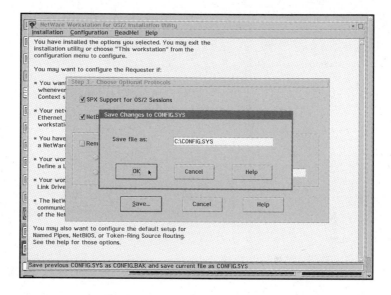

The Installation program copies your ODI driver and requester files to the directory you specified earlier. You have the option of just copying one selected driver or all the drivers on the disk (see Figure 12.16). The status line at the bottom of the screen reflects the file currently being copied (see Figure 12.17), and requester files are copied (see Figure 12.18).

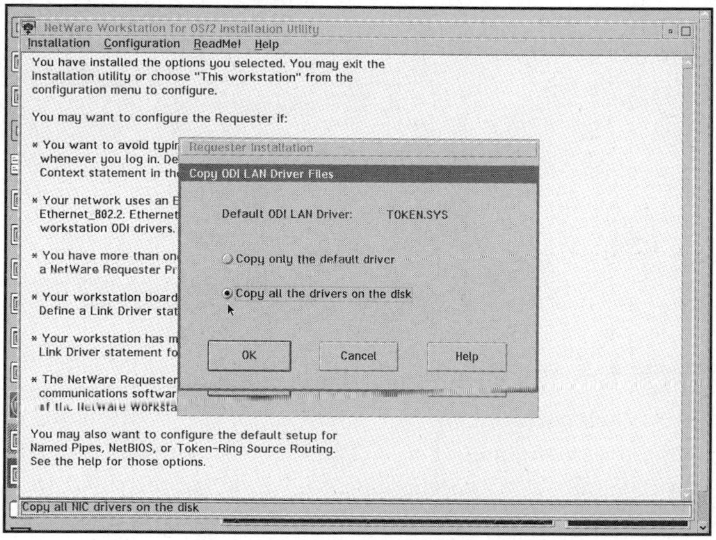

FIGURE 12.16.

Copy one or all driver files.

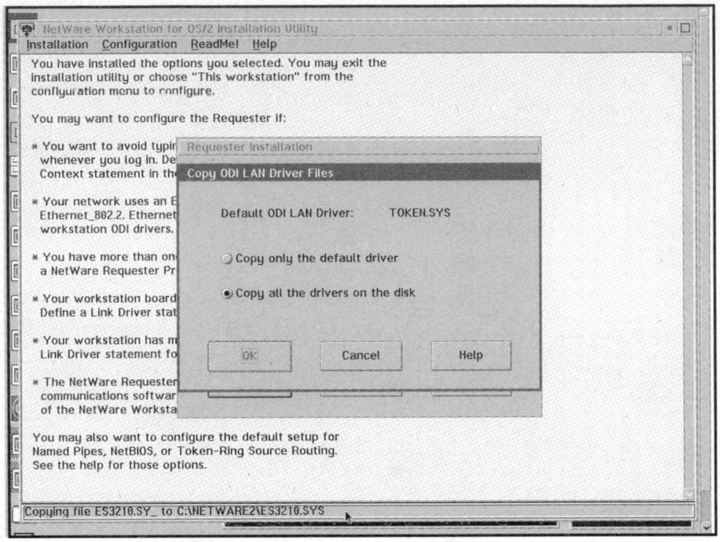

FIGURE 12.17.

The Status Line updates you of the driver-file copy.

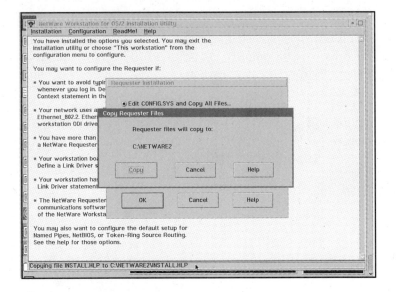

FIGURE 12.18.

The Status Line updates you of requester files copy.

Finally, you'll need to create a NET.CFG file. From the main menu, choose the Configuration pull-down menu and select This Workstation (see Figure 12.19). The default location of NET.CFG is off the root of your boot drive (see Figure 12.20). Exact syntax and explanation of options are provided from the menu (see Figure 12.21). A sample NET.CFG file is shown in Figure 12.22.

FIGURE 12.19.

Workstation configuration.

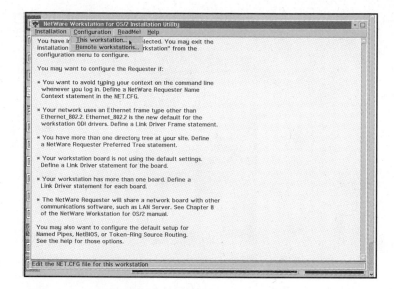

FIGURE 12.20.

Specifying the location of NET.CFG.

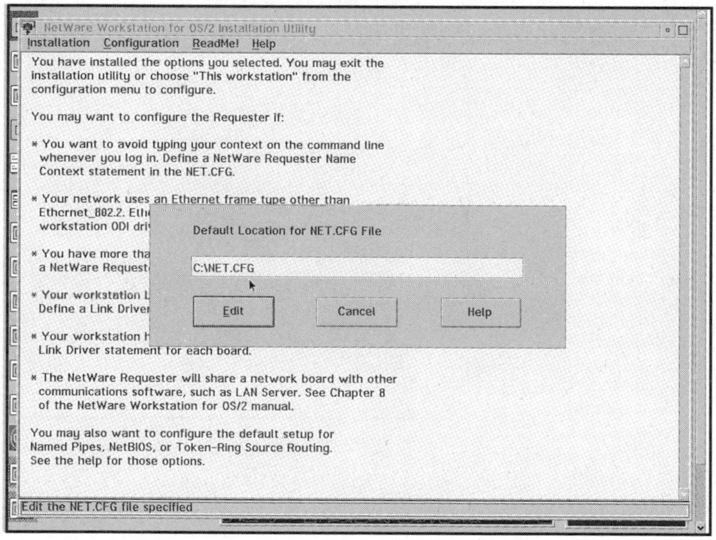

FIGURE 12.21.
NET.CFG options.

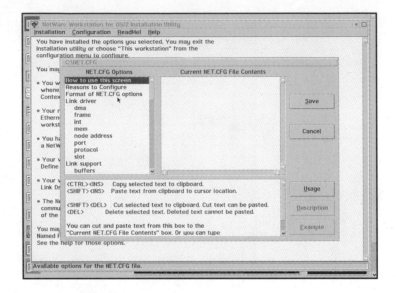

FIGURE 12.22.
Sample NET.CFG file.

```
Show dots=on

LINK SUPPORT
        BUFFERS 15 4202

PROTOCOL STACK IPX
        SOCKETS 64

PROTOCOL STACK SPX
        SOCKETS 32
        SESSIONS 32

NETWARE REQUESTER
        PREFERRED DREAMLAN
        DIRECTORY SERVICES OFF
        PACKET BURST OFF
        LARGE INTERNET PACKETS OFF

NETWARE SPOOLER
        NO BANNER
        COPIES 1
        NO FORM FEED
        NO TABS

C:\>
```

You need to reboot your OS/2 workstation in order for the new changes to CONFIG.SYS to take effect.

CAUTION

If you need to reinstall the requester, comment out or remove the NetWare Requester lines from your CONFIG.SYS and reboot the workstation. Otherwise, because of opened requester driver files, your reinstall will not be complete.

Troubleshooting Tips

When your Shell or Requester is executed, you should receive a message similar to this:

```
NetWare Workstation Shell V3.32 (930217)
(C) Copyright 1993, Novell, Inc. All Rights Reserved.
Patent Pending.

Running on DOS V5.00

Attached to server FS312
11-04-93     11:34:25 am
```

If you do not receive the message indicating you have attached to a server, see the following suggestions.

If you are using the OS/2 Requester, remark out the driver lines in your CONFIG.SYS and follow the same instructions from a DOS window using the DOS drivers and Shell/Requester. Once you resolve problems accessing a server from a DOS window, you can remove your remarks from the CONFIG.SYS and manually correct the problems that you found.

Check the File Server MONITOR Connection Information

See whether your workstation was given a connection. If a connection exists, check the first available drive letter. If using the DOS Shell (NETX.COM or NETX.EXE), check to see what your first available DOS drive letter is. It may be a drive letter other than F. If using the DOS Requester, you must have the LASTDRIVE=Z command in your CONFIG.SYS and the FIRST NETWORK DRIVE=F statement in your NET.CFG.

Execute Each Software Module Separately

Make sure (by watching screen messages) that each module executes properly *before* you execute the next. If you do get an error message, record it so you can thoroughly investigate it.

LSL, the NIC Driver, and IPXODI Load, But the Shell/ Requester Does Not

Check your cabling—the most likely cause. On a new installation, never attempt to hook up all nodes at once. Start with one workstation and the server. Use a single cable or the simplest connection possible between the two. Do whatever you can to make sure your cabling is right and the pinouts are correct.

Check all client workstation software modules. Review the notes (previously mentioned) about versions. If newer versions do not work, try older versions. Use older LSL and IPXODI versions with your NIC driver and then try newer versions. Try NETX.COM v3.26 (available on your Windows diskettes) and NETX.EXE v3.32 (other Shell versions are known to cause this problem). Newer drivers may not work with older support modules, and vice versa.

The NIC Driver Does Not Load

1. Check the NET.CFG configuration settings against your NIC hardware settings. Watch the screen message as the NIC driver attempts to load; make note of the hardware settings the driver recognizes.

2. Check to see if a memory manager or any hardware device is using the same memory address, interrupt, or base I/O address as the NIC. Observe the screen message when the driver attempts to load.

3. Run your NIC setup and diagnostics utilities. Make certain that your NIC is functioning properly.

4. Check all client workstation software modules. Review the notes mentioned previously about versions. If newer versions do not work, try older versions. Try older LSL and IPXODI with your NIC driver and then try newer versions.

5. Token Ring users normally must be connected to a valid ring before the NIC driver will load. Connect just one workstation and the server to a MSAU, and configure all the unused ports with your setup device or procedure.

6. Some Ethernet NICs must be connected to a terminated cabling segment (a tee with two terminators will do) or a wiring concentrator before the NIC will initialize.

You Still Don't Get Connected

At your server, type TRACK ON at the server console prompt. This brings up the router tracking screen. Watch this screen when DOS Shell (NETX), DOS Requester, (VLM.EXE), or OS/2 Requester is executed. You should see a connection occur between the server and the workstation, as shown in Figure 12.23.

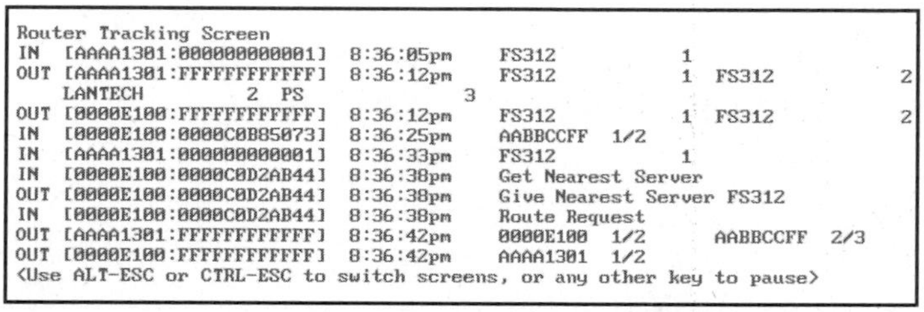

FIGURE 12.23.

A workstation connection request from the server TRACK ON router tracking screen.

```
Router Tracking Screen
IN  [AAAA1301:000000000001]  8:36:05pm   FS312          1
OUT [AAAA1301:FFFFFFFFFFFF]  8:36:12pm   FS312          1  FS312          2
    LANTECH        2  PS              3
OUT [0000E100:FFFFFFFFFFFF]  8:36:12pm   FS312          1  FS312          2
IN  [0000E100:0000C0B850073]  8:36:25pm   AABBCCFF   1/2
IN  [AAAA1301:000000000001]  8:36:33pm   FS312          1
IN  [0000E100:0000C0D2AB44]  8:36:38pm   Get Nearest Server
OUT [0000E100:0000C0D2AB44]  8:36:38pm   Give Nearest Server FS312
IN  [0000E100:0000C0D2AB44]  8:36:38pm   Route Request
OUT [AAAA1301:FFFFFFFFFFFF]  8:36:42pm   0000E100   1/2      AABBCCFF   2/3
OUT [0000E100:FFFFFFFFFFFF]  8:36:42pm   AAAA1301   1/2
<Use ALT-ESC or CTRL-ESC to switch screens, or any other key to pause>
```

Call Your NIC Developer for Technical Support

Only after you have tried the previous steps should you call for technical assistance. Don't forget to make notes recording what you have tried, exactly what the outcome was, and what screen messages were reported. Do not change more than one variable at a time; otherwise, you will not be able to determine what the cause was—and you will run into the problem on another workstation.

Your best (and least expensive) source of support is the NIC developer or manufacturer—not a distributor or retailer. Free unlimited phone support is one of the most important factors to check on before buying NICs. Some of the best NIC developers offer toll-free numbers with 24-hour support.

Be Persistent

Everything might not go perfectly the first time you try it. You must be persistent; methodically test all the possibilities mentioned in this section. If you do, given enough time and effort, you will find your problem and resolve it.

Summary

This chapter presented comprehensive installation instructions for installing the DOS Workstation Requester, the DOS Shell, and the OS/2 Workstation Requester. Once you have connected to the server, you should be able to log in as Supervisor and set up your system administration for groups and users.

Your installation is not complete, however, until you have installed ElectroText and BasicMHS. The following chapter discusses how to install and use these products (which are shipped with 3.12 and 4.x versions).

Installing and Using ElectroText and BasicMHS/FirstMail

by Rick Sant'Angelo

IN THIS CHAPTER

Your installation of NetWare 3.12 and 4.01 is not complete until you install two new products that were added to NetWare 3.12: ElectroText and BasicMHS. These two products add value to NetWare and are great additions. This chapter discusses installation, setup, and basic use of these two new products.

ElectroText

Novell has developed a good online help facility in ElectroText. This simple-to-use, Windows-based application gives a user easy access to all NetWare documentation. The opening screen shows a picture of each manual. All you need to do to find information is select the desired manual, look up the subject in the manual's outline or the index of all manuals, and then open the appropriate manual to that section. You also can search for text within each manual.

Documentation, including an entire manual or specific sections, can be printed out. Your text will print in the type styles and graphics as shown in the documentation. You also can print text with or without figures. A better online documentation system could not be designed.

ElectroText is provided with NetWare 3.12 and 4.0 in lieu of manuals. If you were to print all the manuals, the printout would total about 1,000 pages. You can purchase the full set of manuals from Novell's fulfillment company for $395. Your best option is to print only the manuals you need. A local printer can bind the printout in book form for less than two dollars per binding. Using ElectroText can reduce or eliminate your need for printed manuals.

You can install ElectroText on a NetWare volume, on a local hard drive, or access from a CD-ROM drive. ElectroText occupies about 40 MB of disk space. To conserve disk space, you may wish to access it from a CD-ROM. It can be accessed from a DOS workstation's CD-ROM drive or from a CD-ROM drive mounted on a NetWare server. An NLM to mount a CD-ROM drive on a NetWare file server is included with both NetWare 3.12 and 4.01 versions.

This chapter discusses a few basic tips on installing ElectroText, and how to find topics quickly and easily.

Installing ElectroText

ElectroText can be installed and accessed four ways:

- On a NetWare disk volume
- On a local DOS hard drive
- From a CD-ROM drive mounted on your server as a NetWare volume
- From a CD-ROM drive connected to a workstation as a DOS device

If you wish to install ElectroText on a NetWare volume, you can do so from the server-based INSTALL utility or by copying the DOC directory and all subdirectories to a NetWare volume.

Installing from a DOS CD-ROM Drive Connected to Your File Server

As discussed previously, you can install ElectroText much the same way you installed your server operating system—from a CD-ROM DOS device connected to your server. Follow these steps:

1. Install the CD-ROM drive as a DOS device on your file server (in this illustration, it is assumed the CD-ROM is DOS drive D:).

2. Load the INSTALL.NLM on the server. From the console prompt, type

   `LOAD INSTALL`

3. From the Installation Options screen shown in Figure 13.1, select Product Options.

FIGURE 13.1.

Product options.

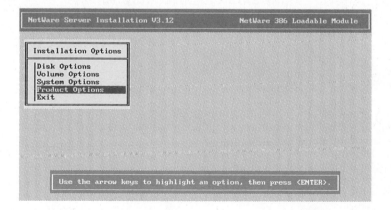

4. Enter the drive letter and path where the ElectroText PINSTALL.NLM application is stored. Enter the following path (as shown in Figure 13.2):

```
D:\NETWARE.312\ENGLISH\DOC or D:\NETWARE.40\ENGLISH\DOC
```

FIGURE 13.2.

Enter the drive letter and path for installing.

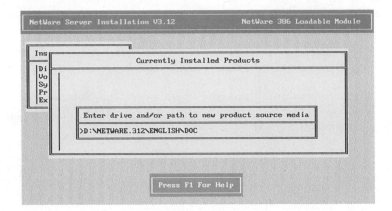

NOTE ▶

If your CD-ROM is not drive D, substitute the appropriate drive letter.

A PINSTALL.NLM file is located in that directory. As soon as the file is accessed, it begins copying the files from the CD to the server's SYS volume.

Running ElectroText from a NetWare Volume

To set up and run ElectroText:

1. Grant Read and File scan rights to the *volume_name*:DOC directory for all users who need to run ElectroText.

2. Add the ElectroText icon to your Windows Desktop. In your Windows Program Manager, select Files, New, Program Item. Point to the ET.EXE file located in your Public directory, as shown in Figure 13.3. This file has an icon associated with it and is automatically selected.

FIGURE 13.3.

*Adding the
ElectroText icon to
Program Manager.*

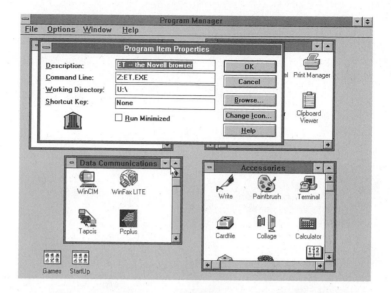

In the Command Line field (provided the PUBLIC directory is mapped as
drive Z:), use the path Z:ET.EXE without a backslash. This works regardless
of whether the drive letter is mapped as a ROOT.

3. Copy ET.INI from the server's *volume_name:*DOC\DATA\CONFIG
   directory into your Windows directory. This is the Windows directory on a
   local hard drive. It also may be the directory with unique user configuration
   files when Windows is installed on a file server (not the shared Windows
   directory).

You also may need to edit the ET.INI file to include all the necessary drive
pointers (mappings). In some installations, this information is erroneous and
may need to be corrected. In other cases, some entries will be omitted. The
file should include all the following entries:

```
[DYNATEXT]
DATA=z:/doc/data
AUTH=z:/doc/data/security/auth
```

```
PUBLIC_NOTES=z:/doc/pubnotes
PRIVATE_NOTES=e:/nonexist
[DOCSETS]
nw40=z:/doc/$NWLANGUAGE/nw40
ethelp=z:/doc/english/ethelp
nw312=z:/doc/english/nw312
[LIBRARIES]
PUBLIC_DIR=z:/doc/$NWLANGUAGE
OPEN=LIB1
LIB1=novell;public
ETLPATH=z:/doc/$NWLANGUAGE
[HELP]
LIBWIN=ethelp;libhelp
BOOKWIN=ethelp;bookhelp
[TABLES]
WVGA=1/1;12;12
WSVGA=1/1;12;12
WXGA=1/1;12;12
WLCDVGA=1/1;12;12
[PREFERENCES]
DEFAULT=QUERYLANG:simple
WVGA=OUTLINE:left;SEARCH:visible
WSVGA=OUTLINE:left;SEARCH:visible
WXGA=OUTLINE:left;SEARCH:visible
WLCDVGA=OUTLINE:left;SEARCH:visible
```

> **NOTE** ▶
>
> Depending on whether you have used a MAP ROOT or a simple MAP command, you may need to edit the entries in your ET.INI file. The preceding illustration works only if you have *not* used the ROOT switch with your MAP command.
>
> Also, be sure that changes made to your drive mappings do not change your drive letters. If drive letters change, the pathnames in your ET.INI file will not be correct.

Running ElectroText from a NetWare CD-ROM Volume

You can access ElectroText from a server-based CD-ROM drive if you have a NetWare driver to access the drive. NetWare drivers are available for virtually all SCSI disk adapters, but not for non-SCSI disk adapters. You normally have to purchase the NetWare driver as a separate software module, or in a kit with the adapter. Once you install this driver, the CDROM.NLM utility provided with NetWare 3.12 enables you to mount a CD file system as a NetWare volume.

Instructions for mounting your CD as a NetWare volume are provided in this book in Chapter 9, "Installing the Server OS from CD-ROM." Once you have installed the CD-ROM drive as a NetWare device, follow these steps to access ElectroText directly from the CD-ROM drive:

1. Load the CDROM.NLM after the disk drivers have been loaded.

2. Insert your NetWare 3.12 CD into the CD-ROM drive. Type the following command to mount the CD as a NetWare volume:

   ```
   CD MOUNT NETWARE_312: or CD MOUNT NETWARE_40
   ```

3. Copy the ET.INI file from the \DOC\DATA\CONFIG directory on your CD disk to your workstation Windows directory.

4. Map a drive letter to the CD-ROM volume.

5. Grant Read and File scan rights to the volume root for all users who are to access ElectroText.

6. Edit the pathnames in your ET.INI file to access the drive letter mapped to the CD-ROM volume.

7. Add the ElectroText icon to your Windows Desktop. In your Windows Program Manager, select Files, New, Program Item. Point to the ET.EXE file located in your server's PUBLIC directory.

NOTE ▶

Make certain the AUTOEXEC.BAT or STARTNET.BAT file that loads your workstation drivers/requester contains the following statement:

```
SET NWLANGUAGE=ENGLISH
```

(or whichever language is being used).

Without this statement, ElectroText cannot locate the appropriate directories.

Installing from a Workstation-Attached DOS CD-ROM

You may install ElectroText onto your local DOS hard drive or your NetWare volume by following these few simple steps:

1. Copy the \DOC and \PUBLIC directories from your CD-ROM, complete with all subdirectories and files onto your destination drive. The procedure is the same whether the destination is a NetWare volume or DOS disk drive. On a NetWare volume, however, you do not need to copy the \PUBLIC directory, because it already exists. Use the XCOPY or NCOPY command as follows:

   ```
   XCOPY D:\DOC\*.* C:\ /S /E
   XCOPY D:\PUBLIC\*.* C:\ /S /E
   ```

   or

   ```
   NCOPY D;\DOC\*.* C:\ /S /E
   NCOPY D:\PUBLIC\*.* C: /S /E
   ```

> **NOTE** ▶
>
> Be sure you have 40M or more of available disk space before installing.

2. Copy the ET.INI file from the \DOC\DATA\CONFIG directory on your CD disk to your workstation Windows directory.

3. Edit the pathnames in your ET.INI file to access the drive letter mapped to the CD-ROM volume.

4. Add the Electrotext icon to your Windows Desktop. In your Windows Program Manager, select Files, New, Program Item. Point to the ET.EXE file located in your server's PUBLIC directory.

Running from a Workstation-Attached DOS CD-ROM

The procedure is the same for installing a CD-ROM as a DOS workstation-based device as it is for a NetWare volume. While following the preceding instructions, substitute the drive letter for the workstation CD-ROM device in the ET.INI file.

Using ElectroText

When you select the ElectroText icon, the "Libraries" screen shows a "Bookshelf" of NetWare 3.12 manuals. Select this icon and you will see the screen shown in Figure 12.4, with icons for each manual.

FIGURE 13.4.

ElectroText manuals.

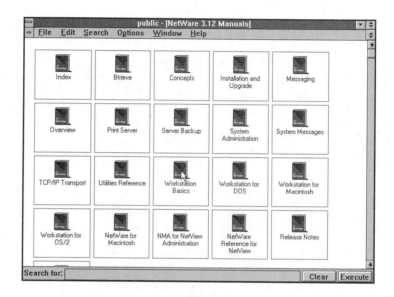

The material in the manuals is structured as follows:

Manual Name	Manual contents
Index	Index of all topics in all manuals
Btrieve	Manual for the Btrieve record manager (optional)
Concepts	Illustrated NetWare glossary
Installation and Upgrade	Instructions on installation
Messaging	Manual for BasicMHS (FirstMail)
Overview	Notes on new features of 3.12 and using the new DOS VLM Requester
Print Server	Manual for the Print Server utility
Server Backup	Manual for SBACKUP.NLM server-based backup utility

Manual Name	Manual contents
System Administration	Alphabetical Server utilities listings, a troubleshooting guide, and appendixes on some Server Monitor Custom LAN statistics
System Messages	Listing of NetWare error messages and their meanings
TCP/IP Transport	Manual for using loading TCP/IP support on your server
Utilities Reference	Alphabetical listing of all utilities
Workstation Basics	Comprehensive guide on workstation preparation, installation, and use
Workstation for DOS	Installation and usage guide for DOS VLM Requester
Workstation for Macintosh	Installation and usage guide for Macintosh workstations
Workstation for OS/2	Installation and usage guide for OS/2 workstations
NetWare for Macintosh	Installation and administrative guide for Macintosh server-based modules
NMA for NetView Administration	Installation and usage guide for the NetWare Management Agent for SAA services
Release Notes	Miscellaneous notes

When you open a manual, you have various options. You see a screen similar to the one shown in Figure 13.5, which shows the opening screen for the System Administration manual.

You may select an item from the outline on the left or scroll through the full text on the right. Through the View menu, you may expand the outline to greater detail, show outline only, text only, or split the screen horizontally instead of vertically. You can view graphics or tables within a text section by selecting the graphics icon in the text. You can open multiple books in multiple windows at the same time.

You also can search for text within this manual by using the Search field at the bottom of the screen. To do this, type in a word or phrase and select Next for the next occurrence of that item. You also can press F1 for help.

FIGURE 13.5.

A manual opening screen with outline and text.

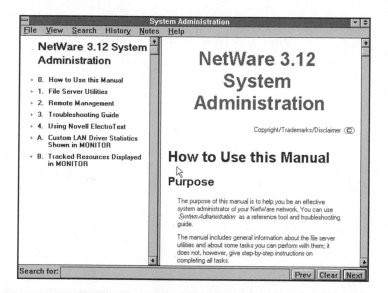

You usually can find any subject in the outline by expanding it to the second level. This provides enough detail to locate the section you are looking for, without excessive detail.

Once you find a subject, click it, and ElectroText takes you to that page.

ElectroText Conclusion

ElectroText is simple to use. Most users find this utility easier to use than paper manuals. You may order manuals from Novell's fulfillment company, but they cost $395 plus handling. You probably cannot operate without manuals, so you really should install and try ElectroText before you panic and buy or print all the manuals. You may just find that it suits your needs. You also might discover that you want to print out some manuals or just use others from disk.

BasicMHS/FirstMail

NetWare 3.12 and 4.x versions are shipped with an electronic mail package called BasicMHS. It actually consists of two parts, the BasicMHS server and the FirstMail user application. The following modules are included to enable you to install, set up, configure, administer, and use BasicMHS:

BasicMHS	(MHS.NLM)	Loads on the file server
FirstMail	(MAIL.EXE)	User application for sending and receiving
FirstMail Administrator	(ADMIN.EXE)	Administrator application
DirAdmin	(DIRADM.EXE)	For input or output to and from files
MHSUser	(MHSUSER.EXE)	Command-line administrator module

A server-based install procedure automates much of the installation and setup (modifications are necessary). You can install it manually, even with 3.11. This chapter is meant to prompt you through a simple installation, setup, configuration, and usage of this product.

> **NOTE** ▶
>
> You should print out all the documentation and then experiment with BasicMHS/FirstMail before putting it into production.

Finding and Printing All the Documentation

The documentation for this product is in the form of the Messaging manual provided in ElectroText. Unless you have purchased documentation separately, you must first install ElectroText and Windows to view and print out this manual. However, this manual does *not* have all the information you need for installing, configuring, administering, and using BasicMHS and FirstMail.

Text files, which also are supplied, supplement the Messaging manual and should be reviewed in addition to the ElectroText manual. These files are located on the CD-ROM disk, and upon installation, are copied onto a NetWare volume.

> **NOTE** ▶
>
> Not all the documentation you need is included in the ElectroText (or hard copy) Messaging manual. See the following README files for additional important information.

This chapter contains important information you need to know at each step of installing and setting up, but you need to read all the documentation for best results.

Table 13.1 lists the text files that you should locate, print out, and read. If you want to locate these files prior to installation, you will find them on your CD-ROM in the NETWARE.312\ENGLISH\BASICMHS or the NETWARE.40\ENGLISH\BASICMHS directory. In a server-based installation using default configuration, you will find the files listed in Table 13.1.

Table 13.1. BasicMHS/FirstMail documentation files.

File Name	Default path	Description
README.TXT	SYS:MHS/SYS	Short message and list of other documentation
ADMIN.DOC	SYS:MHS/SYS	Administering all the BasicMHS/FirstMail utilities
README.FM	SYS:MHS/SYS	FirstMail Install/Manage documentation
USER.TXT	SYS:PUBLIC	FirstMail user documentation
MESSAGES.DOC	SYS:MHS/SYS	BasicMHS/FirstMail error message listing/explanation

There are also several "gotchas" you may encounter, some of which are documented in the README text files referenced in Table 13.1. Look for notes and cautions in this chapter for additional details on what to do to make this package work right.

Installing BasicMHS

This product was designed to be installed from your 3.12 or 4.x distribution CD-ROM disk. An automated install utility that operates from within the INSTALL.NLM server-based application guides you through the process of installing the files, configuring the messaging server, creating user mail accounts, and editing files so they automatically load.

Requirements Prior to Installation

Check to be sure you have the following resources available on your server:

- 2.5M of disk space
- 250K of additional server RAM
- NetWare Btrieve v5.15 or higher
- NetWare C Runtime Library (CLIB.NLM) v3.11e or later

> **NOTE** ▶
>
> Check the version of Btrieve. From a DOS prompt, type BREQUTIL -VER.

Setup and Configuration of BasicMHS

BasicMHS is an electronic mail server module that runs as an NLM on your file server. It controls mail functions, such as forwarding messages to the appropriate user mail directory. You must install and configure BasicMHS on your server prior to using FirstMail. The install module provided on your 3.12 or 4.x CD-ROM automates the installation and configuration process for you by asking a few configuration questions.

The following steps discuss the installation process:

1. Load support for your server-based CD-ROM drive.

> **NOTE** ▶
>
> Follow the instructions provided in Chapter 9, "Installing the Server OS from CD-ROM," on installing and using a server-based CD-ROM drive. You can install BasicMHS from either a DOS or NetWare CD-ROM device.

2. Load the INSTALL.NLM from your file server's console screen with the following command:

    LOAD INSTALL

3. Run the BasicMHS installation module. From INSTALL.NLM's main menu, select Product Options. You see the screen shown in Figure 13.6.

FIGURE 13.6.
INSTALL.NLM's Main Menu.

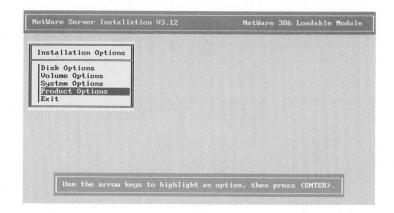

4. Press Insert to bring up the text window to locate the BasicMHS installation module. Type in the appropriate pathname where PINSTALL.NLM is located, as shown in Figure 13.7. For a DOS CD-ROM installed on your server as drive D:, enter the path D:\NETWARE.312\ENGLISH\BASICMHS or D:\NETWARE.40\ENGLISH\BASICMHS. If you have mounted your CD-ROM drive as a NetWare device, substitute the pathname NETWARE_312:NETWARE.312/ENGLISH/BASICMHS or NETWARE_40:NETWARE.40/ENGLISH/BASICMHS.

FIGURE 13.7.
Entering the pathname for the BasicMHS PINSTALL.NLM.

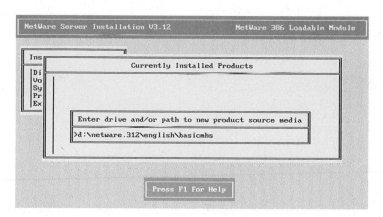

5. Answer the following configuration questions:

```
[Default] Workgroup long name : FS312
Accept Workgroup long name? [Yes¦No¦Quit]: >n
Enter Workgroup long name: >ALLMAIL
        Workgroup long name : ALLMAIL
```

```
Accept Workgroup long name? [Yes¦No¦Quit]: >y
[Default] Workgroup short name: ALLMAIL
Accept Workgroup short name? [Yes¦No¦Quit]: >y
[Default] Mail Volume Path: FS312/SYS:
Accept Mail Volume Path? [Yes¦No¦Quit]: >y
```

NOTE ▶

Assign your own short and long workgroup names. To simplify usage, keep them short and descriptive.

6. After the files have been copied to your NetWare volume, the following questions are asked:

```
Adding local messaging server information to database.
Adding Version Information to Database.
Adding The Administrative User
Special User added Successfully
Enable Messaging Services for Existing Users? [Yes¦No]: >y
Adding the users in group 'EVERYONE' to MHS.
User's Mail name is either the Full Name or Login Name
Use Full Name for user's mail name? [Yes¦No]: >n
     Adding: GUEST@wkgp (GUEST)
     Adding: RICK@wkgp (RICK)
     Adding: LINDA@wkgp (LINDA)
Update System Login? [Yes¦No]:  >y
Updating: NetWare System Login Script
REM - These lines added for Netware BASIC MHS:
MAP INS S16:=ADP1/SYS:MHS\EXE
DOS SET MV="ADP1/SYS:"
DOS SET MAIL=
Update Autoexec.ncf File? [Yes¦No]:  >y
Updating: NetWare System Autoexec.ncf File
; NETWARE BASIC MHS
SEARCH ADD SYS:MHS\EXE
LOAD BASICMHS
Full Installation: Successful.
<Press any key to close screen>
```

TIP ▶

You should say "no" to using user full names so that the users' login names will be used.

This NLM automatically copies the BasicMHS files to your server's SYS: volume, and updates your system login script and AUTOEXEC.NCF files so BasicMHS automatically loads. It also makes changes to user account information and the EVERYONE group.

> **NOTE** ▶
>
> This application grants appropriate rights to users during install and every time a new user is added.

7. Load BasicMHS. See the changes to your AUTOEXEC.BAT and execute those commands manually from your console prompt, or down the server and bring it up again. The preceding described setup requires the following commands:

```
SEARCH ADD SYS:MHS/EXE
LOAD BASICMHS
```

8. Check your server's Btrieve configuration. From your console prompt, type LOAD BSTART.

Select Set Btrieve Configuration. The following parameters should be set to these levels:

```
Number of transactions = 2 (or more)
Largest page size = 4096
```

> **NOTE** ▶
>
> Btrieve is a server-based record manager that controls file access for BasicMHS/FirstMail and often is used for other applications.

BasicMHS should be loaded and configured. To verify, check your INSTALL.NLM's Currently Installed Products screen. It should indicate that BasicMHS has been loaded.

TIP ▶

Check your System login script and AUTOEXEC.NCF files to see that the automatic update has not placed its updates in the wrong place.

For example, if you have installed Windows on your file server, the Windows/Windows applications directories should not change drive letters. If the search drive is added prior to your drive mappings (which the default installation does), you will need to alter all your Windows configuration files (that is, WIN.INI, ET.INI, and so on). Instead, move the section marked as the BasicMHS lines to the end of the login script.

Setup and Administration of FirstMail

The install procedure automatically sets up your FirstMail configuration. To manage this configuration, you must use the ADMIN.EXE utility. Before you run this utility, you must execute BREQUEST.

TIP ▶

BREQUEST stays resident in memory as a TSR. To automatically load and unload it, create the following batch file:

BREQUEST

ADMIN

BREQUTIL -STOP

The ADMIN User Login screen is displayed as shown in Figure 13.8. The default configuration appoints the Supervisor as the mail administrator. Enter the Supervisor password to continue. Any user can enter this application and view the configuration, but only the user Supervisor or Supervisor equivalent can make changes. Once you enter your password, you will see the Admin Functions menu shown in Figure 13.9.

FIGURE 13.8.

ADMIN User Login screen.

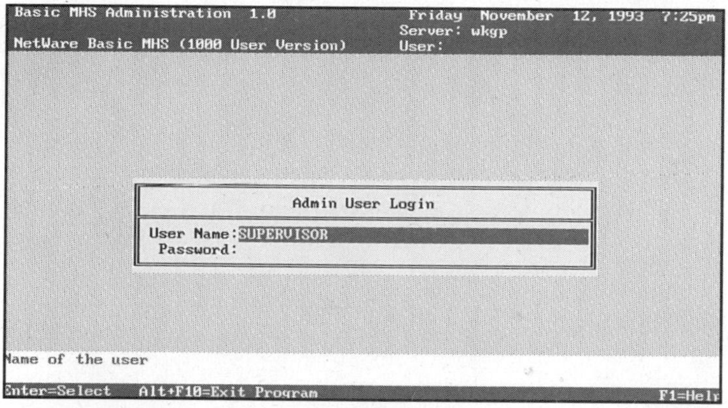

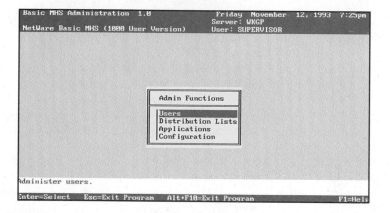

FIGURE 13.9.

Admin Functions menu.

Users

This menu selection shows all mail users (as illustrated in Figure 13.10). To create a user, press Insert when in the screen showing the list of users. When adding new user accounts to your system, you should add them from this screen instead of from SYSCON. A user account will be created as if you were using SYSCON, but not vice versa.

> **NOTE** ▶
>
> When adding users through ADMIN, a user account will be created, but the default Security Restrictions setup in SYSCON will be ignored. If you add a user in SYSCON, the user mail account is not automatically added in

ADMIN; therefore, you will need to add the user in both utilities if you start with SYSCON, and you will not if you start with ADMIN.

Deleting a user in ADMIN does not delete the user account, nor does deleting the user in SYSCON delete the user mail account from ADMIN. You need to delete the user in both utilities.

FIGURE 13.10.

Mail Options screen.

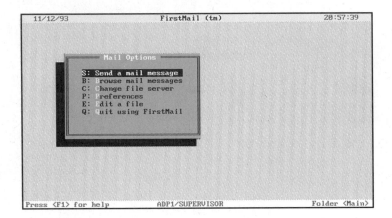

Distribution List

Distribution lists are created so a mail message can be addressed simultaneously to more than one user. When sending a mail message to a distribution list, the memo is duplicated and delivered to all users included in the distribution list.

You should add a distribution list called "Everyone" and put all members on this list. A *distribution list* is a group of users to whom a message can be addressed. The BasicMHS server replicates the message and delivers it to all members of the distribution list.

Applications

Several third-party electronic mail packages and software modules are compatible with MHS. In some cases, an application automatically sends files or messages between users or applications via MHS. If you have an MHS-compatible application, you can add it to this list to make BasicMHS and the application share mail messages. Check your third-party documentation for information on how to share messaging between MHS and your application.

Configuration

This enables you to change your BasicMHS configuration. Read the file ADMIN.DOC for detailed information on adjusting the BasicMHS default parameters.

> **NOTE** ▶
>
> Information about adjusting these parameters is only contained in the document ADMIN.DOC. Your ElectroText documentation references this text file, but it does not include any details on this option.

Using FirstMail

Almost all steps necessary to use FirstMail were done during the server-based installation from CD-ROM. In order for a user to use FirstMail, you need to have a search drive pointing to the SYS:MHS/EXE directory (or wherever you have installed BasicMHS) and the SYS:PUBLIC directory. A search drive was placed into your System login script by the server-based install module. The MAIL.EXE application used to access FirstMail is in the PUBLIC directory.

> **TIP** ▶
>
> If you have multiple servers, and some of the servers are earlier 2.x or 3.x NetWare versions, you should copy the PUBLIC files (including the MAIL.EXE application) to the older server. This will update the PUBLIC files to the latest versions.
>
> When copying the newer PUBLIC files to the older server version, you need to change all file flags in the older servers' PUBLIC directories to Read-write. After copying the files, flag all files in the PUBLIC directory to Read-only. You must use the NCOPY command so all attributes will be copied correctly.

Next you should create the following (optional) DOS environment variables in your AUTOEXEC.BAT, STARTNET.BAT, or login script:

```
SET USR=user_name
SET PWD=user_password
```

Executing FirstMail

To run FirstMail, execute the MAIL.EXE utility located in the PUBLIC directory. The screen shown in Figure 13.11 appears. If mail is waiting, an additional menu selection appears.

FIGURE 13.11.

The FirstMail Mail Options menu.

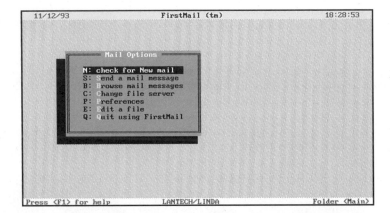

NOTE ▶

Help is available by pressing the F1 key from any screen. The most comprehensive Help menu is available when you press F1 while you are in the Send Message: Editing screen. Editor commands are basically WordStar-oriented, with some additions for simplicity.

TIP ▶

If you are using Windows, you will find the FirstMail icon in the PUBLIC directory under the name FIRST.ICO.

Sending Messages

To send a message, select Send a Message from the Mail Options menu. The message screen is self-explanatory, as shown in Figure 13.12. For a list of users or distribution lists, press F2. A list is displayed.

FIGURE 13.12.

The Send Message: Editing screen.

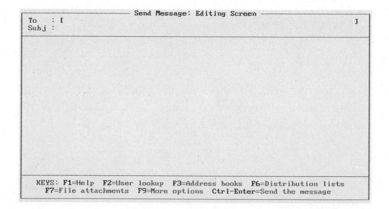

```
                          Send Message: Editing Screen
  To   : [                                                          ]
  Subj :




















  KEYS: F1=Help  F2=User lookup  F3=Address books  F6=Distribution lists
        F7=File attachments  F9=More options  Ctrl-Enter=Send the message
```

TIP ▶

To send the same message to several users, use the F5 key to mark users. An asterisk (*) shows the users to whom your message will be sent.

Receiving Messages

To check for mail, execute MAIL.EXE. It is located in the PUBLIC directory. You should be able to execute it from any directory or drive, because PUBLIC should be in your path.

If messages are waiting, include the option to Check for New Mail, as shown previously in Figure 13.11. Select this option and read your messages.

TIP ▶

You can check for new messages each time a user login occurs by entering the line #MAIL in the System login script.

Summary

BasicMHS and FirstMail are simple to install, configure, and use. This chapter has presented a quick-start guide to getting these modules up and running so users can send electronic mail. There are many more features you can use. Check your Messaging manual for full detail on using FirstMail. Don't forget to print out all the documentation included in various README files, discussed at the beginning of this chapter.

PART

III

System Administration

System Administration and Logical Configuration Strategies

by Rick Sant'Angelo

14

System administration is the essential factor in successful network implementation. A system administrator is the glue that holds the system together and the grease that makes it work efficiently. A system administrator balances control of user activity with the security of the system. A system administrator must possess superlative DOS skills and be a master software troubleshooter, very organized, and diplomatic. The system administrator, however, does not need to be a hardware technician. System administration does not usually deal with the physical infrastructure or hardware layers of the network.

To define a system administrator's role, one must first define what the users and network resources demand and how management has chosen to assign responsibility. In general, a system administrator is responsible for

- Providing access to shared resources
- Limiting access to shared resources
- Managing the users' environment

You should recognize that the physical infrastructure of the system is an entirely different schema from the administrative organization. The hardware platform is masked by the system administrator's configuration. A network or internetwork is based on the LAN itself (network addresses) as a central unit, of which servers and clients are ancillary devices; it is *LAN-centric*. However, the administrative configuration needs to provide users (who are normally organized into workgroups) access to physical resources that are related to servers. NetWare 3.11's administration is *server-centric*, meaning that access to network resources is provided by a login to a single server, and those resources are owned by one server or another.

NetWare 4.x goes further to mask the underlying physical infrastructure with object-oriented superstructure called NetWare Directory Services (NDS). NDS simplifies user access to network resources regardless of their location. It is a valuable tool for large, multiserver networks and internetworks, especially when those networks are geographically disbursed.

No matter which version of NetWare you are using, you should recognize that the physical infrastructure and the logical administrative organization are two completely different pictures of your network or internetwork. In previous sections of this book, the network system was discussed in terms of physical infrastructure. In this section of the book, the discussion assumes a logical configuration of system administration that masks the physical infrastructure, regardless of whether you are using 3.11 or 4.x.

The purpose of this chapter is to clarify the basic mechanics of system administration and to discuss administrative strategies that are common to both versions of NetWare. This chapter discusses

- System administrative strategies
- Mechanics and logical components of the NetWare file system
- Creating your file-system directory structure

System Administrative Strategies

Real-world administration does not consist of correct and incorrect procedures, only strategies and tools for implementation. To suggest that a certain strategy is the only correct way to manage NetWare servers is presumptuous. Some systems and their associated needs dictate simple open-door policies, whereas others require stringent restrictions. An administrator needs to implement policy that is consistent with the goals and policies of the organization in which the system exists.

Keep in mind that the system administrator often has no jurisdiction over users. As a system administrator, you generally have no line authority; usually only a staff relationship exists between users and the administrator. In some instances, when system administration is a side duty of a department manager, a user violation of the system administrator's rules may bring about disciplinary action from the manager; but even if a staff relationship exists, there are many sanctions that can be used to force users to conform. To enforce your rules, they need to be consistent with company policy, and you must have strong command of available NetWare tools and techniques. Unfortunately, unlike the usual case with mainframe installations, these considerations may not have been evaluated by management prior to your accepting this job.

The answer for applying system administration under varying conditions is in the proper use of NetWare tools. NetWare command-line and menu utilities can be applied in a variety of ways. There are also many ways to accomplish the same end results. For example, you may choose to use DOS environment variables to create different drive mappings for different users or groups. You may use login script variables with conditional statements in a system-wide login script. Or you may create different user login scripts and menus for each user. No one way of regulating access is right or wrong, but some strategies work better in some organizations, and other strategies work better in others. Any strategy that you choose must work to support your organization's goals.

You should note that this book is not defining your role as a system administrator—it is challenging you to research and define your role for the good of all concerned. It is advisable to have the system administrator's duties in writing and to have them formalized by management. It is impossible to do a good job when the job is not defined.

Before setting up an administrative organization, you (or management) should carefully consider the basic role of the system administrator for the network. In defining the role of administrator, answers to the pertinent questions are determined by the matrix of organizational responsibility.

Full Service System Administration versus Support Only

The first step in defining the job entails drawing the line between the users' responsibilities and the administrator's responsibilities in the maintenance of personal computing resources at the workstation.

In some organizations, the user is to install, configure, update, and maintain his or her own software, possibly even to install workstation hardware. In other cases, an administrator (or staff member) is responsible for installing, updating, and maintaining software. In the former case, the administrator becomes the first line of support, whereas in the latter case, the administrator is on the front line, giving direct service instead of mere support. Of course, someone needs to take control of centralized resources, such as a server or its disk storage, but the question to ask is what parts are to be centralized and what parts are left up to the user.

One of the big problems in downsizing is that many companies have not clearly defined these lines of responsibility. As a system administrator, you need to determine to what extent you become a "good Samaritan" in the services you extend to users. The good Samaritan approach is not effective when dealing with difficult situations (the kind that are usually resolved after hours). The most difficult support problems require enough effort and time that few people are willing to resolve such problems unless compelled to do so. The alternative to having the system administrator take this role entails the potential sacrifice of the individual users' productivity.

Perhaps the line should be drawn at the local hard drive. A typical balanced solution is for all software installed on a local hard drive to be the responsibility of the user, whereas the administrator can be responsible for all network startup files that reside on the hard drive and all files that reside on the server. In other cases, administrators are responsible for all applications, whether stored locally or on a server. In some cases, users have no hard drives and thus entrust all files to the administrator.

Another suggestion that works in larger companies is to dedicate some technicians to provide support for hardware, some for software, and others for system administration. By dividing duties up by specialty rather than by geographic location, the organization reduces the problems of networked versus non-networked resources. It is easier to train technicians when the scope of their responsibilities is drawn on resource-based lines. This, however, is not practical in smaller organizations where the system administrator is the kingpin (or scapegoat).

Wide Availability to Resources versus Tightly Controlled Security

Another factor to consider in your system administration is whether the system is to be open or restricted. Peer-to-peer networks are generally wide open, with little or no security, whereas mainframes are usually tightly controlled, with restricted access. PC-based networks fall somewhere in between these two extremes. Your job as "watchdog" may vary considerably.

It is a well-established fact that NetWare system resources need to be protected. For example, you cannot enable the user-at-large access to change print servers and their configurations. It could be disastrous if everyone had access to such sensitive data as personnel records. However, not every system has sensitive data. According to industry research, the vast majority of PC-based networks facilitate personal productivity software. Most NetWare servers are pushing around word-processing documents, spreadsheets, and e-mail messages. This, however, is a changing picture. More companies are downsizing mission-critical applications and data.

The job of a system administrator is to draw the line, to give users all the access they need to do their jobs, but not one bit more. On one level, system administration becomes a kind of game, with the administrator protecting and revoking privileges while the users attempt to find and destroy all the exposed resources. Though this may not be a gratifying application of the administrator's skill, it is an inevitable calling wherever resources are shared. In an unprotected system, it is simply a matter of time before someone deletes all the files in the wrong directory.

No outside expert or reference manual can tell you what restrictions are appropriate. It depends solely on your system's requirements. Unfortunately, the way this is normally determined is to experience a catastrophe of major proportions. When that happens, security restrictions are imposed upon the system by management. This is called *management by crisis*. Leaving administrative issues unresolved until this happens is not recommended unless you have well-established tenure within the company. Even then, it is a short-sighted and unplanned approach to system management.

Login to Network at all Times versus Occasional Access

Another factor to consider when defining a system administrator's job is whether users always log onto the network or whether they sometimes work off the network. If the latter is the case in your network, you have a bigger job in supporting the same software running under varying conditions. A related question is whether the system administrator is responsible for helping with situations that occur when users are not logged in.

Mechanics and Logical Components of the NetWare File System

NetWare's file system is not a DOS file system—it is a foreign file system that emulates a DOS file system. Like DOS, it utilizes a hierarchical tree structure. The file system is

- Based on volumes
- Divided into directories
- Accessed via drive mappings
- Restricted by trustee assignments

Your understanding of NetWare and your problem-solving ability are based upon your understanding of these basic conceptual ingredients. If you understand the material presented in this chapter, all other administration is a matter of learning the tools and procedures. Without this understanding, you can never master NetWare.

NetWare Volumes

The file system is divided into *volumes*. Though volumes are physically installed on a disk drive, they are not directly correlated in any defined ratio to hard drives. One volume can span multiple physical disk drives or can take up the entire data area on one disk drive, or there can be multiple volumes on a single disk drive. The discussion in this section focuses on the volume, regardless of where it physically resides. NetWare's first volume name is SYS:, but additional volumes can be created with almost any name.

Hierarchical Tree Structure—Directories

Volumes are further divided into *directories*, which can contain *subdirectories*. Each volume has a *root*, which is simply the base of the tree. Directories are used to organize the thousands of files into logical separations. Files are physically scattered all over the drive, but the file system configures them to look as if they are organized in separate areas. A file is therefore stored in a directory, and the entire hierarchy, called a *pathname*, becomes part of the filename. A NetWare directory pathname includes the following:

- File server name
- Volume name
- Directory name
- Subdirectory name
- Filename (with extension)

Though this is quite similar to DOS' hierarchical tree structure, NetWare's pathnaming conventions differ slightly from DOS. It includes the file server name and uses forward slashes (/) instead of backslashes (\). Pathnames in NetWare should be expressed in NetWare syntax when using the MAP command, especially in login scripts. An example of a NetWare directory name is the following:

FS311/SYS:APPS/LOTUS

Notice that the pathname includes the file server name. (This is usually omitted if only one file server is used, and MAP will default to the current file server if multiple servers are present.) It is followed by the volume name, a colon, and the main directory name (without a slash); subdirectory names are preceded by a forward slash.

> **TIP** ▶
>
> When using DOS commands, always use DOS pathname conventions; when using the NetWare MAP command, always use NetWare pathname conventions. This is especially important to remember in login scripts, but should be observed wherever the MAP command is used.

Drive Mappings

DOS is not able to access a volume named SYS:, so NetWare enables you to create *drive mappings* (sometimes called *drive pointers*) to access files on a NetWare volume. A drive mapping is established with the NetWare MAP command-line utility.

There are two types of drive mappings: *logical drive mappings* and *search drive mappings*. A logical drive mapping simply assigns a DOS drive letter to be substituted for a directory pathname. For example, the drive letter L: can be mapped to the SYS:APPS/LOTUS directory. A user can therefore switch to drive L: and be in the working directory SYS:APPS/LOTUS.

A search drive mapping not only assigns a drive letter, it puts the drive-letter mapping into the DOS Path. DOS Path statements can be supplemented or replaced by NetWare search drive mappings.

Logical and search drive mappings can be created by using the MAP command from a DOS prompt, in a login script, from within batch files, in menus, within Windows, or within the NetWare SESSION utility. A drive mapping is only valid during a user's current login. When the user logs out, the drive mappings are deleted. Drive mappings are individualized, and each user can have different drive mappings. Users can have the same drive letters mapped to different directories and can have different drive letters mapped to the same directory. No mechanics are in place to make certain that drive mappings make sense. It is up to the administrator to create drive mappings that provide users with appropriate access to NetWare directories and files.

> **TIP** ▶
>
> The use of the MAP ROOT command can help DOS applications locate the directory you want to use. If the ROOT switch is not used, many DOS applications look past the directory to the root of the volume. To mask the volume structure, use the MAP command with the ROOT switch. This is called a *fake root* and makes the directory look like a root directory.

User and Group Management

User accounts are created, with an assigned user name, so that users can log in to NetWare. Passwords can control user access. User accounts can be restricted or controlled in many ways, which is a large part of what system administration is all about. The administrator provides security and shields the user from having to learn anything about creating and controlling user accounts.

To simplify the management of user accounts, groups can be created in which users are organized according to what software and data they share. A group of users who share the same applications and data are called a *workgroup*. These groups may or may not correspond with the departmental groups into which your organization is divided. Some groups generally correspond with departments, whereas others span across departmental lines. The key consideration in organizing workgroups is group user access to applications and data.

Access Rights

User access to NetWare directories can be restricted according to various NetWare *access rights*. Access rights control what a user can do in a directory. NetWare access rights are superior to DOS attributes and file access—they cannot be overcome by any DOS command or access. The access rights shown in Table 14.1 are used in NetWare 3.11.

Table 14.1. NetWare access rights.

Right Description	Letter	Right Description
Read	(R)	Read from a file
Write	(W)	Write to a file
Create	(C)	Create files and subdirectories
Erase	(E)	Erase files and directories
Modify	(M)	Modify filenames and attributes
File Scan	(F)	Scan directory listings
Access control	(A)	Change access rights of other users
Supervisory	(S)	Ignores *all* access right restrictions

Each access right is independent of every other access right. A user can have the right to read from a file, but not necessarily have the right to write to the file. A user can have the right to write to a file, but not necessarily have the right to erase the file. However, in order for some rights to be available, the right to File Scan must also be assigned.

In version 3.12, Access Control and Supervisory rights are used in conjunction with the user's designation as an Account Manager or Workgroup Manager. (This is discussed in detail in Chapter 15, "Administering NetWare 3.x.") These rights grant limited Supervisory access to directories and subdirectories where assigned.

Trustee Assignments

Users and groups are called *trustees* when they possess NetWare properties or values (security restrictions). Access rights can be assigned to users or to groups, and when they are assigned, they are known as *trustee assignments*. Access rights that are assigned directly to a user or group are called *direct assignments*. When a user is assigned to a group, the user indirectly receives the trustee assignments that were directly assigned to the group, and the resulting rights are therefore called *indirect assignments*. Direct assignments assigned to a group become indirect assignments to the user assigned to the group.

Trustee assignments are additive: they only add to one another and cannot subtract rights that a user has been granted from another trustee assignment. For example, if a user has direct trustee assignments to his or her own HOME directory (the directory to be used exclusively by this user) and is a member of two groups, the user receives the direct trustee assignments to the HOME directory, the indirect trustee assignments that were directly assigned to the first group, plus the direct trustee assignments that were assigned to the second group. Trustee assignments may not be subtracted from any direct or indirect assignments from any source.

Trustee assignments are inherited; that is, they apply not only to the directory to which they are applied, but also to all subdirectories of that directory.

> **NOTE** ▶
>
> In NetWare 3.x and 4.x versions, you can apply NetWare trustee assignments to directories (as per the preceding discussion) and/or directly to files. In this book, the discussion of trustee assignments is only applied to directories; you can extend trustee assignments to further refine your system administration.

Inherited Rights Mask

Access rights also can be applied to directories and files in the same way as attributes. When they are implemented as such, they are called *directory rights* or the *inherited rights mask*. Directory rights are implemented through the FILER utility. The inherited rights mask can be applied to files or directories to make the files inaccessible to all users. When an access right is removed from the inherited rights mask, that right does not flow to the user, regardless of what trustee assignments have been granted.

When the inherited rights mask is applied to a directory, it also applies to all subdirectories of that directory. However, the inherited rights mask can be adjusted at the subdirectory level to either further restrict or lift the restriction of any access right.

> **NOTE** ▷
>
> Do not use the inherited rights mask unless you have a specific need for it that cannot be handled another way. Most experienced system administrators never use the inherited rights mask, because its application has very few purposes.

The inherited rights mask is rarely used, and you should not use it unless its use accomplishes a restriction that cannot otherwise be done with the combination of trustee assignments and directory structure. The inherited rights mask option often causes needless confusion for system administrators. In the upcoming chapters of this section, the inherited rights mask will not be considered as a normal system administrative tool. (Chapter 15 discusses this tool in greater depth in the context of the FILER menu utility.)

Effective Rights

Effective rights are what rights the user has in a directory at any given time. Effective rights are the result of adding together all trustee assignments (whether direct, indirect, directly assigned, or inherited) and subtracting the inherited rights mask. Because you probably will not be using the inherited rights mask, effective rights are normally the sum total of all trustee assignments.

Effective rights are the bottom line for what the user can do in any directory. The effective rights restrict user access and cannot be overridden by any client operating system or user software. The vast majority of software problems occur because of insufficient effective rights. You can very easily check a user's effective rights by using the NetWare RIGHTS command-line utility. Simply type RIGHTS at a prompt, and the user's effective rights will be displayed.

File and Directory Attributes

As with DOS or OS/2, NetWare has an extended set of file attributes, and some can even apply to entire directories. NetWare's attributes are sometimes called *file status flags,* and they can be adjusted using the NetWare FLAG command-line utility or the FILER menu utility. The DOS attributes have corresponding NetWare flags and actually apply to the very same attributes. The four DOS attributes can be adjusted using the DOS ATTRIB command or the NetWare FLAG command. The attributes shown in Table 14.2 apply to files and directories.

Table 14.2. NetWare/DOS attributes.

Attribute	flag	DOS	Directory
Read only versus Read write	Ro/Rw	Yes	No
Archive	A	Yes	No
System	S	Yes	Yes
Hidden	H	Yes	Yes
Shareable	S	No	No
Purge	P	No	Yes
Delete inhibit	Di	No	Yes
Rename inhibit	Ri	No	Yes
Copy inhibit	Ci		Applies to Macintosh only
Read audit	Ra		Not implemented in 3.x
Write audit	Wa		Not implemented in 3.x

Creating a File-System Directory Structure

You need to create a directory structure for NetWare volumes that differs from a normal DOS directory structure. In a DOS file system, users generally create directories from the root in order to house software applications, and then they create subdirectories for data. This, however, does not make a good strategy for any network; for NetWare, it is entirely unacceptable because NetWare's trustee directory assignments are inherited.

With NetWare systems, the same software applications often are shared by more than one workgroup. Giving a workgroup access to an application automatically grants it rights to that application's subdirectories. Even if one of those subdirectories is a data directory that should be restricted to one workgroup, all users who have access to the application also have access to all data. In such a configuration, NetWare trustee assignments cannot work as intended. Data files should be more closely controlled than software applications. Because the two file types require such different restriction requirements, it makes sense to use separate directory structures.

> **NOTE ▷**
>
> You may not realize that you have inadvertently granted excessive rights to users or groups because the picture of NetWare's trustee assignments is quite fragmented. You may have difficulty locating the source of user effective rights without extensive searching. See Chapter 18, "Creating and Using Menus," for information about third-party utilities such as Bindview Plus (LAN Support Group) that can help you find the whole picture and print reports detailing who has what rights from what sources.

From the perspective of good organization, it is better to divide your directories into as few directories off the root as possible. If you were to create all your directories off the root, you would have hundreds of directories, and no logical organization for them. You may even want to segregate your OS files into a completely separate volume. The general categories that you should use to divide your software and data are

- Applications
- Data
- Home
- Utilities

By logically parsing your software and data, you can create an organization similar to an office filing system, wherein you could find various files inside of hanging file folders (subdirectories) in a certain file drawer (directory) within a file cabinet (volume) within a particular room (file server). In such an arrangement, you can locate any application by locating the subdirectory under the APPS directory, any data file under the DATA directory, and any user private files under the HOME directory.

The following chart shows a typical DOS directory structure and the same directory organization for a NetWare file system.

```
C:\                              SYS:\
  | — DOS                          | — APPS
  | — EXCEL                        |   | — EXCEL
  |    ' — DATA |                  |   | — LOTUS
  | — LOTUS                        |   | — WINDOWS
  |    ' — DATA                    |   | — WORD
  | — NET                          |   ' — WP51
  | — TEMP                         ' — DATA
  | — UTIL                         |   | — ACCTG
  |    ' — TEMP                    |   | — ADMIN
  | — WINDOWS                      |   | — CLERICAL
  | — WORD                         |   | — ENG
  |    ' — DATA                    |   | — MKTG
  ' — WP51                         |   ' — SALES
       ' — DATA                    ' — HOME
                                       | — BSSMITH
                                       | — MLCROSS
                                       | — JWJOHNSO
                                       ' — JRMARKS
```

In the DOS part of this example, if a user has access to the WP51 directory, access is also granted to the \WP51\DATA directory. In the NetWare part of this example, the user has access to the SYS:APPS/WP51 directory from one source of trustee assignments, whereas access to data in the SYS:DATA/CLERICAL directory is from another source.

Create an Applications Directory Tree

With NetWare, you should install all applications into a subdirectory off the root designated for software applications, exclusive of data. In this book, the directory designated to contain applications is APPS. The following chart shows a typical APPS directory and subdirectory tree.

```
SYS:
     ' — APPS
           ' — EXCEL
                 ' — EXAMPLES
           ' — LOTUS
           ' — WINDOWS
                 ' — SYSTEM
           ' — WORD
                 ' — DLL
                 ' — CLIPART
                 ' — PCLFONTS
           ' — WP51
                 ' — TUTOR
```

The number of subdirectories housed in the APPS directory is the same as the number of unique software applications. This portion of the directory tree should be widely accessible to users, so it not a good idea to store data here. It is also impractical to store data here because it can get lost or buried in the thousands of application files located in these directories. Designating certain directories for data does not resolve the organizational complexity of the applications directories and subdirectories.

Create a Data Directory Tree

In order to restrict workgroup data access, it is necessary to create a data directory structure independent from application software directories. Workgroup data directories should be parallel to one another; they then can be used to confine usage to assigned workgroups. In almost all cases, every group should have its own group data directory in which to store data files shared among users in that group. Trustee assignments to that directory can be assigned to the whole group.

For example, in an organization assume you have marketing, engineering, and administrative departments, and therefore workgroups. The suggested structure for their data directories would be

```
SYS:
   \—DATA
          \——MKTG
          \——ENG
          \——ADMIN
```

In this example, each subdirectory, SYS:DATA/MKTG, SYS:DATA/ENG, and SYS:DATA/ADMIN are parallel to one another. When trustee directory rights are assigned to each one, the assignments will not affect the other directories because they are parallel. If one of these directories were to be a subdirectory of another, it would inherit the trustee assignments of the other.

> **TIP** ▶
>
> If you intend to restrict access to directories by workgroup, be sure to make your workgroup directories parallel to one another.

An important part of implementing trustee directory assignments is to make the workgroup directories parallel to one another (the same number of levels deep from the root), as in the following SYS:DATA directory structure example.

```
SYS:
      ' —DATA
             ' —ACCTG
             ' —AP
             ' —AR
             ' —GL
             ' —PAYROLL
             ' —SS
             ' —WP
      ' —ENG
             ' —DRAWINGS
             ' —ORGCHTS
             ' —PROJMGMT
      ' —SALES
             ' —PRJCTNS
             ' —REGION1
             ' —REGION2
             ' —REGION3
      ' —MKTG
             ' —PRODUCTA
             ' —PRODUCTB
             ' —PRODUCTC
```

TIP ▶

Make a data directory structure roughly parallel to the workgroup structure to reduce the need for system administrative intervention. If a directory is created under a group directory, the child directory inherits the same directory trustee assignments as the parent, with no administrator intervention. You also can assign an individual from the workgroup to be responsible for maintaining that portion of the tree. It is otherwise an impossible task to identify and eliminate dead files.

Create a User HOME Directory Tree

Each user should have an individual directory that is designated for private files. A user can use that directory as if it were a local hard drive. The directory is designated as a HOME directory and should be the default directory whenever the user exits to a DOS prompt. The user should have all trustee rights directly assigned to the user's home directory.

You should create a directory to house user HOME directories. The name of this directory in this book is HOME. Once the directory is created, all access rights, except Supervisory, should be assigned to that directory.

The UTILITY Directory

It does not make sense to store utility files, such as DOS files, in subdirectories of the system directories. DOS versions and utilities can be stored under the PUBLIC directory, or you can create a UTILITY directory. NetWare 3.x has a default group trustee assignment for all users to have Read and File Scan rights in the PUBLIC directory. Because this assignment already has been made, all files with similar functions, such as your DOS and utility files, can be stored in subdirectories of the PUBLIC directory and will enable Read and File Scan access to all users.

Managing Disk Space

No matter how much disk space is provided, users invariably will fill it up and demand more. A near-full disk can cause perplexing I/O errors. You will find that a large percentage of the files on a disk are files that are rarely or never used.

A system administrator must find a way to keep inactive files off the server's volume(s), while being careful not to eliminate files that are needed. Because users may scatter files all over the tree, an administrator must exercise particular oversight in two areas of file management. First, users must not have rights to create files just anywhere—the supervisor must restrict their file creation to departmental or user home directories. Second, the administrator must delegate responsibility for eliminating unused files to users who will know which files are expendable.

> **TIP** ▶
>
> An administrator should appoint a workgroup manager or representative to police each workgroup's data directory. Each user should be responsible for eliminating unused personal files. It is often necessary to restrict user and directory space allocations, which can be accomplished by using NetWare's DSPACE utility.

> **TIP**
>
> On a periodic basis, it is necessary to mandate the cleanup of unused files. Even though users do not work directly for you, you can force them to comply with your cleanup mandate. When users will not comply, simply back up all their personal files and then delete them. That will get their attention!
>
> Use the NetWare NDIR command to locate and sort all files larger than a certain size (for example 1M) as follows:
>
> ```
> NDIR \ /SIZE GR 1000000 /ACCESS BEFORE 01-01-93 /SUB
> ```
>
> This finds all files larger than 1M that haven't been accessed this year and searches the entire volume. The resulting file list will contain good candidates for archival.

Summary

The logical system administrative structure you design for your network or internetwork will mask the physical infrastructure, which includes LANs, WANs, file servers, volumes, files, and other network resources. The ideal structure should make user access as simple as possible, impose security restrictions as necessary, and be logical.

There are no correct or incorrect ways of administering a system. There are only different strategies that can be used with the many tools available to accomplish an objective. This chapter discussed some strategies you should consider based on your situation. Later chapters discuss version-specific tools and procedures to accomplish your goals and implement your strategies.

Structuring your file system is an important part of system administration. If you clearly understand the mechanics of your NetWare file system, including mappings, trustee assignments, and attributes, you can figure out how to do everything else. Without this basic understanding, no amount of "how-to" will train you to administer a system.

Your organizational structure will affect many users for a long period of time. The cumulative effect of inefficient administration can cost your organization hundreds of man-hours over a period of a year. Conversely, good system administration can make the system virtually transparent to users, so they can do what they were hired to do, instead of constantly wrestling with DOS and NetWare complications.

Administering NetWare 3.x

by Rick Sant'Angelo

IN THIS CHAPTER

15

NetWare has been managed with bindery-based security for a long time. Administering 3.x is not too different from earlier versions. Names of the access rights changed from 2.15 to later versions, and 3.x versions added the Supervisory access right, but system administration is much the same as it has been for several years. NetWare 4.x is not managed with a bindery, so what is discussed in this chapter is not relevant to 4.x. This chapter is specifically about system administration of NetWare 3.x.

This chapter gives a brief overview and provides explicit instructions for setting up your user environment, including

- Structuring directories
- Creating groups
- Creating user accounts
- Assigning trustee rights
- Imposing additional security restrictions on users

This process normally includes creating NetWare Login Scripts; however, an entire chapter follows this one that addresses login script programming in great detail.

For best results in learning this procedure, log in to your NetWare server as "Supervisor," execute SYSCON, and follow these instructions. You may create new groups and users without interfering with other groups or users. Once you have finished experimenting, delete the groups and users you have created. Be careful not to disturb the existing users and groups.

If you have time to experiment with a server before it is put into production, you should do so. You should familiarize yourself with all aspects of groups and users. When you actually set up a server from start to finish and administer the system you set up, you will understand NetWare security best. Real-world experiences are ultimately the only way to truly grasp the fine points of this subject.

You may wish to back up your bindery files and trustee directory assignments before attempting to experiment in SYSCON. You can quickly and easily back up security only by using NetWare's NBACKUP menu utility. Follow the instructions in Chapter 21, "Backup Strategies and Products," to make a backup of all NetWare security to a local hard drive. This provides an added degree of safety any time changes are made to the security configuration.

Default Configuration and Overview

NetWare 3.x versions store security information in three bindery files in the SYS:SYSTEM directory. Trustee assignments are stored in directory entries for directory names. The combination of these two references restricts access to the file system. This is why you need to use NetWare-enabled file utilities and tape backup systems. DOS utilities do not copy the trustee assignments of the NetWare directory listings because the bindery files are hidden system files. Because they are opened files and are set to non-shareable, they are not accessible to many utilities. In order to properly back up these files, the backup user must also be logged in with at least Read, File Scan, and Modify rights in all directories as Supervisor (or Supervisor Equivalent), because other users have no access to the SYSTEM directory.

Default Directories, Groups, Users, and Trustee Assignments

Your NetWare server OS installation yields a default configuration. Four directories, two users, and a group are created. A default login script is used in place of the user login script, which provides a few default drive mappings and access to the SYS: volume. This section of this chapter explores these defaults.

Directories

Your installation leaves four directories on the SYS: volume:

SYSTEM	OS drivers, NLMs, and bindery and system-related files
PUBLIC	NetWare command-line and menu utilities
LOGIN	Login, server location, and remote boot files
MAIL	System subdirectories for each user

Groups

The EVERYONE group is part of your default installation. Each user is automatically a member of this group. The EVERYONE group has the following trustee directory assignments:

SYSTEM	None
PUBLIC	Read, File Scan

| LOGIN | Read, File Scan (simulated when not logged in) |
| MAIL | Create |

This enables users to log in and use files in the PUBLIC directory.

Users

Upon installation, two default users were created:

    Supervisor
    Guest

Supervisor has full and unlimited use of the system, regardless of trustee assignments (or inherited rights masks). Guest only has indirect trustee assignments because it is a member of the EVERYONE group. Guest therefore has Read and File Scan access to the PUBLIC directory, and all rights have been granted to the Guest's MAIL subdirectory (except Supervisory and Access Control). This is the case for each user. As a user is added, an individual MAIL subdirectory is created (named with a hexadecimal value), and trustee directory assignments are created to enable full access to that directory. The user's login script and print job configuration files will be stored in this directory.

Default Login Script

The default login script executes only if no user login script has been created. It provides

- Drive mapping of the first available drive letter (normally drive F:) to SYS:
- A search drive to the SYS:PUBLIC directory

Without a default login script, you would not have access to the server's file system and would not be able to create a search drive mapping to obtain access. The default login script is shown in Appendix E of this book.

Overview of Setting Up

In order to provide access to any other users, you need to create user accounts, create directories, and assign trustee directory assignments to those directories. To do so, you should log in as Supervisor. Your first act as Supervisor should be to assign a password for this user. From this point on, Supervisor access must be severely restricted. You should not log in as Supervisor, except when performing tasks requiring supervisory access.

The following procedure lists the logical steps to be taken in setting up your system after you have initially logged in as Supervisor:

1. Create groups
2. Assign directory trustee assignments to groups
3. Create a user
4. Create a user home directory
5. Assign the user to a group
6. Create other users
7. Repeat steps 4 and 5 for each user
8. Assign additional user restrictions
9. Create login script(s)
10. Install and configure your printers
11. Install and configure your application software
12. Create user menus

This chapter discusses the first eight steps in the preceding list: creating groups, users, and trustee assignments. Login scripts would naturally fall into this process; however, login scripts are addressed in a separate chapter.

Creating Groups

Your first logical step in the process of setting up your system administration is to create *workgroups*. As discussed in the previous chapter, a workgroup is a group of users who perform the same functions and share the same data and applications. This normally coincides with a departmental configuration; however, these two group characteristics are not necessarily congruent.

Examples of Workgroups

Workgroups are assigned for the sole purpose of simplifying access to directories and files that are subject to NetWare trustee assignments. A workgroup can be a group of users within an organization that perform the same functions. The workgroups listed in Table 15.1 are representative of common workgroups you may find in a medium-to-large corporation:

Table 15.1. Sample workgroups.

Workgroup Full Name	Workgroup Name	Group Application	Group Data
Word-processing users	WP	Word processor	Various
Spreadsheet users	SS	Electronic spreadsheet	Various
Accounting department	ACCTG	A/P, A/R, G/L, Payroll	SYS:DATA/ ACCTG
Human Resources department	HRD	Personnel database	SYS:DATA/ HRD
Engineering department	ENG	CAD/CAM	SYS:DATA/ ENG
Marketing department	MKTG	Marketing database	SYS:DATA/ MKTG
Sales force	SALES	Contact-management database	SYS:DATA/ SALES
Administrative group	ADMIN	Various	Various

As you can see, the need for providing access to various software and data directories becomes apparent as we formulate groups based on what activities are part of users' jobs. Assume that users need access to the applications listed in Table 15.2:

Table 15.2. Applications.

Application	Directory Name	Trustee Rights Required
Windows	WINDOWS	RWCEMFA
WordPerfect 5.1	WP51	RWCEMFA
Word for Windows	WORD	RWCEMFA
Excel	EXCEL	RWCEMFA
FoxPro	FOX	RWCE F
FoxPro-based marketing database	MKTGDB	RWCE F

Application	Directory Name	Trustee Rights Required
FoxPro-based Personnel database	HRDB	RWCE F
XTree Net file management software	XTNET	R F

As the administrator, you need to consider three aspects of these software applications to properly create trustee directory assignments:

- To what applications does each group need access?

- What trustee assignments can be withheld from each application while still enabling it to work properly?

- What trustee assignments need to be granted to the data directories while still enabling the application to work properly?

Each of these issues will be discussed in detail in a forthcoming section of the chapter. Though many related issues may surface as you install your applications and give trustee assignments to access them, these three questions isolate the issues that determine the proper designation of workgroups. Members of a given workgroup, utilizing NetWare, would normally produce the same answers to these questions.

Groups can be created for other reasons, also. If all the users in the organization need access to a word processor, e-mail, or Windows, you may add the trustee assignments to the EVERYONE group. If access to one of these packages needs to be expressly assigned, you may create a WORDPROCESSING group or a WINDOWS_USER group. In these examples, there may not be a common data directory, or the data directory used to house data files may belong to another group. Since a user can be a member of multiple groups, a WINDOWS_USER group would have limited functions; in this case, it would be for the purpose of using the word-processing software or Windows if installed on the server.

> **TIP** ▶
>
> Another reason for creating a group might be to assign extra rights or privileges. The group ADMIN, for example, could be used to assign individuals as special user types, such as Console Operators, Queue Operators, and Print Server Operators.

Determining Which Applications Are Neccessary

Few people will know exactly which applications need to be accessed by group members. Probably the best person to consult about which applications the members of a department actually use is the department manager. In cases where users are not organized by departmental groupings, the system administrator may need to conduct an investigation or survey to find out all the software packages that the users need to access.

Determining Which Trustee Assignments to Withhold

You must get to know your applications before you can resolve this issue. In some cases, the manuals or technical support personnel will have a good explanation of what rights you should grant and which you may not withhold. In other cases, you need actual experience with the software, because support personnel may not be certain about what NetWare access rights can be withheld. When you revoke a right and the software does not work properly, you can assume the software needed that right. Of course, you should keep users from erasing files by mistake, but often an application needs to have the rights to create, update, and/or erase working files. Therefore, NetWare directory trustee assignments cannot do the job for you.

NOTE ▶

Software may fail during processing because of insufficient NetWare effective rights. Normally, error messages are not sufficiently explicit to pinpoint a missing NetWare access right. Very strange problems can occur that may not seem to pertain to the error message you receive. You must be cognizant of what effective rights are required for each application.

TIP ▶

You can protect specific files in a directory using Trustee File Assignments. Though this option is not explored in detail in this book, you can use Trustee File Assignments to protect application software from deletion, beyond whatever Directory Trustee Assignments have been implemented. You will find the option for assigning Trustee File Assignments in SYSCON, under both Group Options and User Information, just below the option for Trustee Directory Assignments.

Determining Which Data Directory Access to Grant

Protecting your data is the most important part of NetWare security. Just as with the preceding issue, however, your software manuals and their technical support personnel may not have the answer to this question. You may need to personally experiment with NetWare access rights to refine them to their lowest level. You should research and experiment to find what rights can be withheld for important data.

Certainly, you should not let one group have access to another group's data unless it's necessary. There is no reason to give access where not required; it simply broadens the exposure of the data to potential loss or security breaches. You must protect sensitive data, even though you may not be explicitly directed to do so. If you doubt this statement, just imagine who would be held responsible if important data were lost, destroyed, or violated when you have not taken steps to protect it. Your duty as a system administrator is to protect all data as much as possible.

Creating Groups and Trustee Directory Assignments

The administrator needs to create the groups and then assign the groups as trustees of the directories where access is required. To do this, log in as Supervisor and execute the SYSCON menu utility. The Available Topics menu will appear, as shown in Figure 15.1.

FIGURE 15.1.

The SYSCON Available Topics menu.

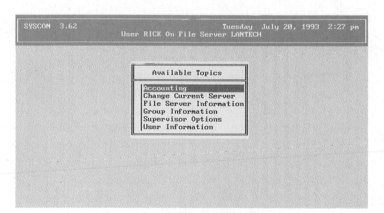

> **NOTE ▶**
>
> When using NetWare menu utilities, you can press F1 to see context-
> sensitive help. If you press F1 a second time, you will see key assignments.

From this menu, select Group Information. You will see a list with only one entry, the EVERYONE group. To create a group, press Insert and then type the name of the group to be assigned. The group is then added to the list. Then, select the group and select Trustee Directory Assignments from the submenu. You will see a box in which you should enter the pathname of the directory where you want to assign trustee rights, as shown in Figure 15.2.

FIGURE 15.2.

Entering the pathname to add trustee assignments.

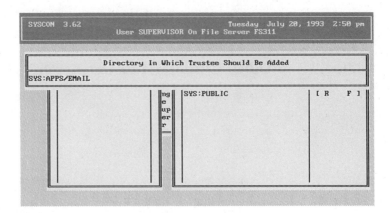

You may add to this list of rights by pressing Insert and entering the name of the directory to which you would like to grant trustee rights. Press Enter, and the directory will be added to the list of Trustee Directory Assignments with Read and File Scan access rights. To add more trustee assignments to this list, select the appropriate directory (by placing your cursor on the directory name) and press Enter. You will see a list of trustee rights that have been granted. You may press Insert to see a list of trustee rights that have not been granted, as shown in Figure 15.3. Select each right that needs to be added. You can use your F5 key and mark rights in the list to select more than one right at a time. You can create groups and add directory trustee assignments for each group the same way.

FIGURE 15.3.

Adding trustee directory assignments.

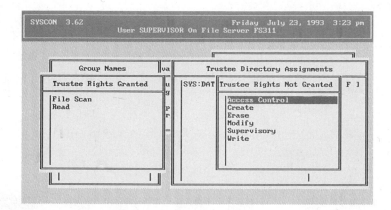

Creating Users

The next logical step in the process of setting up your system administration is to create user accounts, which enable each user to log in with his or her unique user name.

Creating the User and the User Home Directory

The administrator needs to create the users and then assign them to groups in order to grant indirect trustee assignments. To do this, log in as Supervisor and execute the SYSCON menu utility. From the Available Topics menu, select User Information. You will see a list of users, including Supervisor and Guest. You can add a user by pressing the Insert key. Enter the user name, as shown in Figure 15.4.

FIGURE 15.4.

Creating a user account.

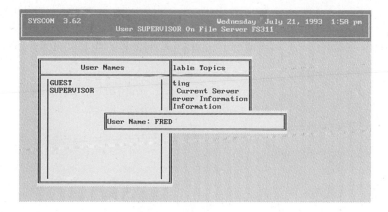

> **NOTE** ▶
>
> Restrict user names to eight characters or less so that you can make a user HOME directory that includes the user's login name. This enables you to use a variable in login scripts to locate the appropriate user HOME directory.

When you press Enter, you will be prompted to enter the pathname of the user HOME directory. Enter the appropriate directory path using NetWare pathname conventions, as shown in Figure 15.5.

FIGURE 15.5.

*Creating the user
HOME directory.*

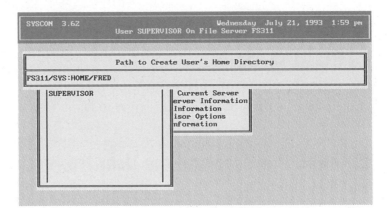

> **NOTE** ▶
>
> The first time you add a user, SYSCON will suggest placing the directory off the root of the SYS: volume. If you change the path, creating the user's HOME directory in a subdirectory off the root, SYSCON will suggest the same parent directory for subsequent user HOME directories.

Once the user account has been added, you will be returned to the User Information screen. Select the user account you have just created. You will see the submenu shown in Figure 15.6.

From the submenu, select Groups Belonged To and assign the user to whatever groups are necessary by pressing Insert from the list shown in Figure 15.7. You may select the groups individually, or you can use your F5 key to mark which groups to select.

FIGURE 15.6.
User Information submenu.

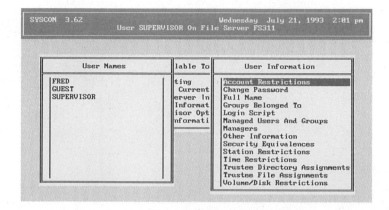

FIGURE 15.7.
Assigning the user to group(s).

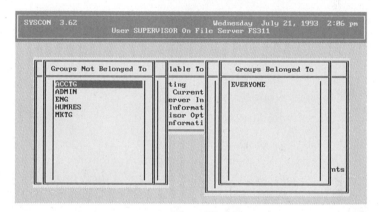

Your group selections grant indirect trustee assignments to the user. Those trustee assignments that were directly assigned to the group are indirectly assigned to the user.

Direct Trustee Assignments

You may also create direct trustee assignments for this specific user. An example of supplementing the group indirect trustee is to provide additional rights in a directory for a department manager or account manager. You can assign additional trustee directory assignments by selecting the user and then (from the User Information submenu) selecting Trustee Directory Assignments. You will see the assignments that SYSCON has created by default, including the user's HOME and MAIL directories, as shown in Figure 15.8. You can add more directory assignments by pressing Insert and adding the directory name, just as was done previously in adding assignments to groups.

FIGURE 15.8.

User trustee directory assignments.

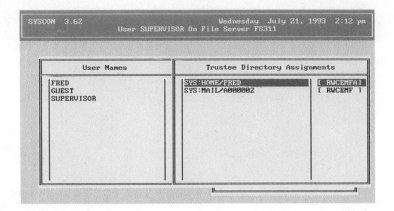

Supervisory User Types

There are three types of users, with varying degrees of user privileges:

- Workgroup Manager
- User Account Manager
- Security Equivalence

Each user type is designated in order to delegate supervisory tasks to other users. In very large networks, a single system administrator may not be able to manage so many groups and user accounts. You may think of these user types as being assistant system administrators. You will find a chart in Appendix D of this book that shows specific privileges of each user type.

Workgroup Manager

A Workgroup Manager can be a system administrator for one or more workgroups and users. Generally, this is a manager for one large workgroup, or for a department or division that has several workgroups. For most purposes, the Workgroup Manager can create and manage groups and user accounts. An entire group can be appointed as Workgroup Manager, in which case all the users who are members of that group are considered Workgroup Managers.

Normally, supervisory trustee assignments accompany an appointment as Workgroup Manager. This also gives the Workgroup Manager the capability to bypass all trustee assignments and inherited rights masks, install software, and change groups' and individual users' trustee assignments. The combination of these two factors makes the Workgroup Manager a very powerful user type.

To assign a user as a Workgroup Manager, log in as Supervisor, enter SYSCON, select Supervisor Options, Workgroup Managers, and then press Insert to select the groups and/or users to be managed. Then select the user from User Information and add the trustee assignment as necessary.

User Account Manager

A User Account Manager is generally appointed to manage a few coworkers. The User Account Manager can perform some of the same functions as the Workgroup Manager but cannot create new groups or users. A Supervisor, Supervisor Equivalent, or Workgroup Manager must assign the groups or users that the User Account Manager will manage.

Normally, access-control trustee assignments accompany an appointment as User Account Manager, which then enables this user type to change or create trustee assignments for managed groups or users. This user type is therefore more restricted than a Workgroup Manager but can nonetheless be of great assistance. A good candidate for User Account Manager is an accounts payable manager who has a few clerical coworkers responsible for processing vouchers and checks. The accounts payable manager can edit login scripts and change trustee assignments to closely control the coworkers' accounts.

To assign a user as the User Account Manager, log in as Supervisor or as Workgroup Manager, select the user or group of users to be appointed as User Account Manager, and press Insert to assign the groups and/or users that are to be managed.

Security Equivalence

You can assign a user to be a Security Equivalent to another user. This will enable the Security Equivalent to inherit the other primary user's direct trustee assignments. For example, you can make a user a Security Equivalent to the user Supervisor. The Security Equivalent will have all the same privileges as the user Supervisor. A Supervisor Equivalent can do anything a Supervisor can do, including changing the Supervisor's password.

This option should be used sparingly, because it is a very powerful option when equated to Supervisor. It is recommended that a Supervisor security equivalence be used for one purpose only: to create a user for backing up data.

To make a user Security Equivalent to another user, select the user from the user list; then from the User Information menu, select Security Equivalences, press Insert, and select the user to which you want this user to be equivalent, as shown in Figure 15.9.

FIGURE 15.9.

User Fred accessing SBT accounting software.

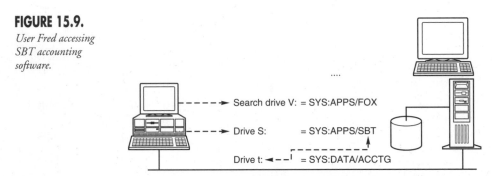

Search drive V: = SYS:APPS/FOX

Drive S: = SYS:APPS/SBT

Drive t: = SYS:DATA/ACCTG

> **NOTE**
>
> Security Equivalents do not receive indirect trustee assignments assigned to the primary user; they only receive direct trustee assignments. Therefore, a user who is a Security Equivalent to another user does not inherit the primary user's group trustee assignments.
>
> In the case of the user Supervisor, the Security Equivalent bypasses all trustee assignment restrictions.

Relating Group Assignments, Trustee Directory Assignments, and Drive Mappings: An Example

To illustrate a typical set of group trustee directory assignments, the example of using SBT Accounting software is provided. This set of accounting software modules is written in FoxPro and requires access to FoxPro runtime. To install this application and to implement the strategy of separating application and data files, you need to provide access to the following three directories:

SYS:APPS/FOX   (access to FoxPro runtime)
SYS:APPS/SBT   (access to SBT program files)
SYS:DATA/ACCTG   (access to data for SBT data files)

This example is somewhat complex because each of these directories requires trustee directory assignments and three drive mappings, and it varies from the software developer's recommended configuration. Each component, and the relationship among the three, is established in this example.

> **NOTE** ▶
>
> In many situations, you may decide that you would like to vary from the vendor's installation instructions to provide conformity with your system-administration strategies.

Table 15.3 shows the trustee directory assignments for the ACCTG group. This example shows a fictitious set of required trustee assignments, presumably learned through experience or from application documentation.

Table 15.3. Sample group trustee directory assignments.

Group Name	Group Full Name	Directory	Assignments Required
ACCTG	Accounting dept.	SYS:APPS/SBT	RWCEMFA
ACCTG	Accounting dept.	SYSSYS:DATA/ ACCTG	RWCEMFA
ACCTG	Accounting dept.	SYSSYS:APPS/FOX	RF

In order to execute the applications, a search drive mapping to the Foxbase directory must be created. This will enable the user to access FoxPro runtime even though the user's working directory is S:. A logical drive mapping to T: is provided, and SBT's setup was configured to search for data in drive T:. The following commands must be used to create the appropriate drive mappings:

MAP ROOT S3:=SYS:APPS/FOX   (search drive to FoxPro runtime)
MAP ROOT S:=SYS:APPS/SBT   (access application with drive S:)
MAP ROOT T:=SYS:DATA/ACCTG   (configure SBT setup for data
                                    located in drive T:)

Once you have assigned the trustee directory assignments to the group ACCTG, the user FRED can access the application with drive S:, as illustrated in Figure 15.9.

You should notice that the drive mappings enable the application to find the correct directories; however, user access is masked by the trustee directory assignments to the ACCTG group, of which FRED is a member.

Many illustrations can be given, but real-life implementation will assist you in creating a configuration that will work for your applications. Normally, an application's network installation instructions will let you know what drive mappings, search drive mappings, and trustee assignments need to be created. Most well-written applications are flexible with drive mappings and enable you the option of designating where data and applications are stored.

> **NOTE** ▶
>
> You should feel free to experiment with configuring your software in a different manner than described in your installation instructions. Experimentation, however, should be done when time for reconfiguration can be allotted that will not conflict with user demands. The way your software was developed may require "tricks" such as using the NetWare *fake root* (MAP ROOT).
>
> Software that is well-written for NetWare (using NetWare APIs) should be flexible with drive mappings and able to work regardless of where the directories are located. A NetWare drive mapping should be able to locate data and applications through a drive mapping and not require you to locate data and applications together or in the same part of the directory tree.
>
> The capability of the application to support flexible drive mapping with NetWare should be one of your software selection criteria.

Other Security Restrictions

Most users usually will not be bound by rules unless compelled to do so. It is therefore generally necessary to require a password, to restrict a user name to one concurrent log in, and to impose other security restrictions to control user access.

One should keep in mind that every restriction creates a potential for administrative support problems (that is, users receive error messages from their software that will not indicate that security violations have occurred). The administrator must weigh the potential for errors against the benefits of restricted access.

User Account Restrictions

In SYSCON, the administrator can control user account restrictions (security). This is done by adjusting the Account Restrictions within the user's account under User Information. Account restrictions enable the administrator to

- Restrict how many workstations can use the same login name at one time
- Restrict users to specific workstations
- Control minimum password length
- Control how often the password must be changed
- Restrict network disk storage by user

To apply any of these restrictions, select a user under User Information in SYSCON. Then select Account Restrictions. If you have installed Accounting, your selection will be Account Balance/Restrictions. You will see the screen shown in Figure 15.10.

FIGURE 15.10.

User account restrictions.

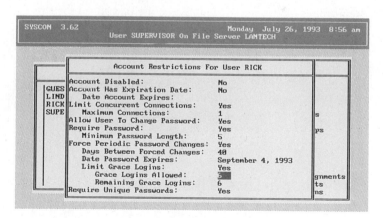

The available selections are explained in the following paragraphs.

Account Disabled

You may disable an account at any time, and the user will not be enabled to log in. The user account is not deleted, and it may be reactivated at any time.

TIP ▷

This is an effective sanction to use with users who will not follow your instructions. A system administrator may not have the authority to dismiss an employee who violates system rules, but this option prevents the user from using the system. It is an automatic enforcement device that will definitely get the user's attention.

Account Has Expiration Date/Date Account Expires

You may specify a date upon which this user account will become disabled. The option works the same way as the previous option.

Limit Concurrent Connections/Maximum Connections

A user should be restricted to logging in to only one workstation at a time. This restriction intends to prevent users from using other user accounts in order to obtain more rights or circumvent your security. The maximum number of connections is the number of concurrent logins that are permitted for this user account.

CAUTION ▷

You should restrict the user Supervisor to two or three concurrent logins in case the Supervisor's workstation gets locked up, or supervisory tasks need to be performed from two workstations at the same time.

Enable User To Change Password

You can assign passwords or enable users to change their own passwords. If you answer "no" to this question, users cannot change their own passwords. It would need to be done by the Supervisor or a Supervisor Equivalent.

Require Password

This option forces a password to be assigned for this user.

Minimum Password Length

You can select this option to require a password of a minimum length.

Force Periodic Password Changes/Days Between Forced Changes

You can specify how frequently the password must be changed.

Date Password Expires

This is the date that the user password will expire. You may specify a date.

Limit Grace Logins

You can limit the number of allowable logins with the old password after the system has suggested that the user change passwords.

Grace Logins Allowed/Remaining Grace Logins

This specifies the number of grace logins that will be allowed and states how many grace logins have been used.

Require Unique Passwords

You can require users to select a different password when a change is made. After approximately eight password changes, the user can reuse an earlier password.

Station Restrictions

Users can be restricted to logging in only at a given physical login address (workstation). You can specify several network addresses to enable users to log in from all the workstations on that LAN, or specify to which particular workstations the user can log in. The node address refers to the serial number of the NIC for Ethernet or Token Ring (where universal addresses are used) or the assigned local address. Figure 15.11 shows the station restriction screen.

FIGURE 15.11.

The Station Restrictions screen.

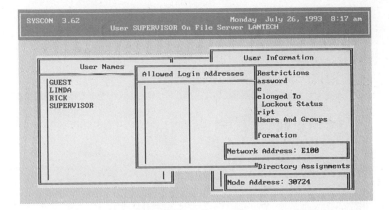

You should not restrict the user Supervisor to only one workstation. If the NIC is taken out of service, the Supervisor will not be able to log in. The Supervisor generally needs to log in at various workstations on different occasions and should not be restricted from doing so.

Time Restrictions

Users can be restricted to times that they may be connected, as shown in Figure 15.12. In order to restrict login times, mark the segment of time to disable by using the MARK key (F5), and press Delete. If a user is logged in during this time.

FIGURE 15.12.

The Time Restrictions screen.

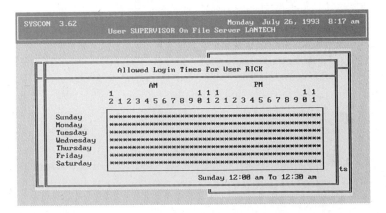

> **CAUTION** ▶
>
> If a user is updating a file when this restriction takes effect, the data files in process may become corrupted.

Users who are subject to this restriction receive a notice 30 minutes prior to the time the restriction will be enforced, and again at three minutes prior to the specified time.

Changing the Default Security Restrictions

You can change the default values for these user restrictions by selecting Supervisor Options from the SYSCON Available Topics menu, and selecting either Default Account Balances/Restrictions or Default Time Restrictions. From that point on, when you set up new user accounts, the default values will be accepted and can be individually adjusted.

Adjusting Existing User Accounts

You can select several user accounts and adjust their account balances, security restrictions, and time restrictions. From the User Information user account listings, mark the user accounts that you would like to adjust with the F5 key and then press Enter. The short menu will enable you to adjust Default Security Restrictions, Login Restrictions, and Time Restrictions for all marked users.

Intruder Detection

When users attempt to log in without authorization, a lockout can be imposed. Intruder detection is implemented by selecting Available Options, Supervisor Options, and Intruder Detection, as shown in Figure 15.13.

Once intruder detection is turned on, if an attempt to use a user login name fails, an attempt is recorded, and a notation is made at the server console (when the threshold is reached) in the Server Error Log and in the Accounting audit log file (if Accounting is installed). After the threshold is reached (the allowable number of attempts occur within the given time period), the user account becomes locked for the specified amount of time. This option makes it virtually impossible for a password to be guessed without detection.

FIGURE 15.13.

Intruder detection.

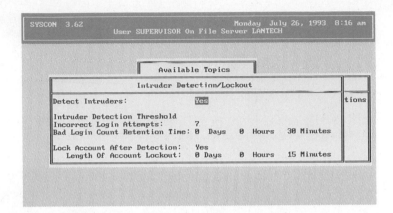

> **NOTE** ▶
>
> The Intruder Detection option is not turned on by default. It should be
> turned on in almost all cases to prevent the unauthorized use of user
> accounts.

Resource Accounting

This includes options that enable the System Administrator to charge users for
various file server services. Before using these options, it is necessary to install the
accounting features. This is done the first time you access Accounting from the Available Topics menu. When you access this menu selection, and if Accounting has not
been installed, it will ask "Install Accounting?" If you answer Yes, accounting audit
log files will be generated, and the file server will keep track of logins, intruder
attempts, and usage charges.

> **CAUTION** ▶
>
> Once Accounting has been installed, the audit log is created and will grow,
> with each login, logout, and charge creating an entry in the file. The audit log
> will grow larger and larger, occupying valuable disk space until it is manually
> deleted. To delete the audit log, log in as Supervisor and delete the file
> SYS:SYSTEM/NET$ACCT.DAT. The file may be deleted with no effect on
> the system, except to turn user balances back.

Accounting Charge Options

You can levy charges for the usage, as shown in the Accounting menu.

Accounting Servers

This option lists all servers to which this workstation is attached, if they are set up to use accounting services.

Blocks Read Charge Rates

Here, you can see the rates that are charged for data read. The system schedule that you will see enables the Supervisor to impose different rates for different times of the day.

Blocks Written Charge Rates

This is the same format and concept as the preceding menu selection, except these are charges for disk writes.

Connect Time Charge Rates

NetWare tracks the amount of time that the user has been logged in and charges accordingly. Again, differing rates can be charged for different time periods.

The user can see the time and charges that have accrued. Allotments can be regulated for reads, writes, connections, storage, and service requests. The system administrator can even have accounting force a logout for a user whose credit has expired. This can be used to pinpoint the usage to improve the system performance.

> **NOTE** ▶
>
> If users do not log out, connection time continues to run until the server terminates the connection. The server automatically will terminate a connection 15 minutes after the workstation shell has been taken out of memory,

Disk Storage

Users can be charged for each block-day of disk storage occupied by this user. To implement this option, charge only once a day for each block stored. Storage charges will be levied on the owner of the file.

> **NOTE**
>
> If you install the Disk Storage option, be sure that only the Supervisor installs applications, so that users will not be charged with the disk storage charges. Even then this is dangerous, because NetWare assigns ownership of a file to the one who updated it last. If dozens of users are manipulating a large database, the one charged will be the user who, by chance, happened to be the last one to update it that day.

Service Requests

This option charges the user for each packet the server receives from the workstation.

> **NOTE**
>
> Accounting charges for service requests are levied upon logout.

One unit of accounting charge is relative to the charge rate you have created. User charges can be allowed to accumulate (allow unlimited credit), or you can impose a limit. When the limit is reached, the user will not be allowed to log in until the system administrator expressly increases the limit or the audit log is deleted (which starts charges at zero).

> **CAUTION**
>
> When Accounting is first installed, the default account-balance restriction in each user account will not allow unlimited credit. If any charges are incurred, users will not be permitted to log in after incurring charges. The restriction won't take effect until after the user logs out; therefore, users will be locked out the second time they use the system.

Once Accounting is turned on, be sure to adjust all user account-balance restrictions to allow unlimited credit.

Supervisor Command-Line Utilities for Accounting

PAUDIT

The Supervisor can view the accounting audit log by executing the PAUDIT command line from the SYS:SYSTEM directory. The audit file is stored in binary format. To create an ASCII file for the current transactions, type

```
PAUDIT [> filename]
```

This enables you to pull the audit log into a spreadsheet or database for analysis and sorting.

ATOTAL

To view a daily and weekly summary of accounting charges, type

```
ATOTAL
```

This utility compiles the system accounting records and lists daily and weekly totals for each category of accounting charges.

For more analysis of your resource accounting audit log, third-party utilities, such as Bindview Plus and LT Auditor, are available.

Enhanced User Setup Utilities

There are two utilities that simplify the task of adding users: USERDEF and MAKEUSER.

USERDEF

This menu utility enables a Supervisor to simplify the addition of users. Each user generated will be assigned a home directory, a login script, a print job configuration data file, and a set of account restrictions from a chosen template.

The default template can be used, or the Supervisor may create a custom template. Templates are made up of two parts: parameters and login scripts. The default parameters template cannot be altered; instead, a new template needs to be made. The default login script, however, can be changed. This does not affect the default login script hard-coded into the operating system; it simply changes the default login script template to be used to create new users' login scripts. Care should be taken to match the user login script with the system login script, as discussed in the next chapter.

Once a template has been selected, the Supervisor adds users by pressing Insert and typing the user name to be added. USERDEF enables you to add only one user at a time and is limited in the options you may select.

MAKEUSER

This utility is more cryptic than USERDEF but more powerful for adding users. Many users can be added in one operation, and virtually all options for administration can be controlled through the use of MAKEUSER keywords. For administrators who manage large networks, and who add and delete many users at a time, this utility is indispensable.

MAKEUSER should be used instead of USERDEF when multiple users are to be added at one time, or when more control and flexibility over user parameters are desired. Script files with .USR extensions can be created that will enable MAKEUSER to create and delete users.

> **NOTE** ▶
>
> When employing MAKEUSER, default security restrictions that are set up in SYSCON will be ignored, but they can be created with commands in the USR file.

The USR file can be used to create new users, copy a default login script, assign a user to groups, assign passwords, add a user's home directory, set up account balances, and employ additional restrictions. Likewise, a USR file can delete users, and delete all files and directories in a user's home directory.

TIP ▶

When setting up a system for the first time, or when adding or deleting many users at once, MAKEUSER can create many users at the same time with perfect uniformity.

MAKEUSER is invaluable for situations in which new user accounts need to be added and deleted on a regular basis. For example, in a learning institution where dozens or hundreds of students need to be added and deleted each school term, MAKEUSER can do the job with just a few keystrokes. User account restrictions can be implemented, and at the end of the term, the user accounts and all home directory files can be deleted just as easily.

MAKEUSER Keywords

Each line in a USR file must be preceded by the character #. Like any programming language, this script file language requires a little experimentation until you get it right. Table 15.4 will help you learn what you can do in a MAKEUSER script file.

NOTE ▶

The syntax for USR files is a little difficult to learn. See the disk that accompanies this book for two files—NEWUSER.USR and DELUSER.USR—that are working examples of USR files you can modify.

Table 15.4. MAKEUSER keywords.

Keyword	Description
ACCOUNT_EXPIRATION *date*	Sets account expiration date
ACCOUNTING *balance*	Sets limit for accounting charges
CLEAR or RESET	New set of keywords
CONNECTIONS *Number*	Limits number of concurrent connections for a user
CREATE *UserName*	Creates user account(s)

continues

Table 15.4. continued

Keyword	Description
DELETE *UserName*	Deletes user account(s)
GROUPS *Group*	Assigns users to groups
HOME_DIRECTORY *dir_pathname*	Creates a home directory in a specified path
LOGIN_SCRIPT *FileSpec*	Copies an ASCII file as a user login script
MAX_DISK_SPACE *vol,KB;vol,KB;etc;*	Limits user disk storage per volume
NO_HOME-DIRECTORY	No home directory to be assigned
PASSWORD_LENGTH *length*	Requires minimum length password
PASSWORD_PERIOD *days*	Requires password change after *days*
PASSWORD_REQUIRED	Requires password
PURGE_USER-DIRECTORY *pathname*	Deletes user home directory/files
REM	Remark, ignored
RESTRICTED_TIME *day,start,end;day,start,end;and so on*	Time restrictions
STATIONS *net addr,node addr; net addr,node addr,and so on*	Station restrictions
UNIQUE_PASSWORD	Requires different password when changed

Some commands must precede others in order to be effective.

CREATE or DELETE can specify a single user login name, followed by four fields, delimited with a semicolon. Several users can be added, one per line, starting with CREATE, as follows:

```
;Full_Name; Password; Group1,Group2; direct_trustee_assignments
```

An example of adding the same three users at once is as follows:

```
#CREATE bill;Bill Williams;willie;acctg,ss,wp;
#CREATE fred;Fred Fredrick;freddy;ss,wp;
#CREATE mary;Mary L. Lamb;marymary;acctg,admin;
```

These lines would do the following:

1. Create the user "Bill"
2. Assign the full name "Bill Williams"
3. Assign the password "willie"
4. Assign Bill to the ACCTG, SS, and WP groups
5. Create the user "Fred"
6. Assign the full name "Fred Fredricks"
7. Assign the password "freddy"
8. Assign Fred to the SS and WP groups
9. Create the user "Mary"
10. Assign the full name "Mary L. Lamb"
11. Assign the password "marymary"
12. Assign Mary to the ACCTG and ADMIN groups

In the preceding example, all other lines, such as password restrictions, apply to all the users being created. Here is a simple example of a typical USR to add users:

```
#CONNECTIONS 1
#HOME_DIRECTORY SYS:HOME
#LOGIN_SCRIPT SYS:PUBLIC/UTIL/LOGIN.GEN
#CREATE BOZO;Bozo the Clown;HONK!;ACCTG,WORDPROC;
#CREATE JOHN;John Smith;SMITTY;FINANCE,WORDPROC;
```

In the previous example, all four delimiters (;) must be present, but if one is filled in, all lines must have that field filled in. Here is a simple example of a typical USR file to delete users:

```
#PURGE_USER_DIRECTORY
#HOME_DIRECTORY SYS:HOME
#DELETE BOZO,JOHN^
```

As you can see, one file uses the CREATE command delimited with four fields, and the other uses the DELETE equivalent with multiple names in one line. MAKEUSER is one of those programs that can save advanced administrators dozens of hours.

Advanced Administrative Utilities

There are several system administrative tools of which you should be aware. This section briefly describes these tools and their uses.

BINDFIX/BINDREST Command-Line Utilities

On rare occasions, you may encounter a damaged bindery. There are three bindery files:

```
NET$OBJ.SYS
NET$PROP.SYS
NET$BVAL.SYS
```

These are key files in making NetWare work properly. They are protected by the Transaction Tracking System, so they will not be rendered unusable if the disk becomes full during use or if the files are not updated. However, they can become damaged. Two situations that can cause damage to these critical files are a media defect that appears after the files have been stored, or a restore that overwrites one or more of the files but not the others.

When these rare occurrences are encountered, you can experience strange problems, such as user accounts disappearing, old users appearing, passwords being lost, print servers rendered unlocatable, and other problems.

To repair your bindery files, log in as Supervisor, change directories to the SYS:SYSTEM directory, and execute BINDFIX. The procedure is rather simple and does not require the system to be removed from use. It will pack and reindex the bindery, check all objects and properties for consistency, and give you a *warm fuzzy* feeling that the bindery is okay.

If you need to restore the old bindery, execute BINDREST in the same manner. BINDFIX builds new bindery files, backs up the old bindery files with .OLD extensions, and removes the file attributes. BINDREST restores the backup bindery files.

FCONSOLE Menu Utility

This utility, shown in Figure 15.14, enables you to broadcast a message to all nodes, check active connections, down a file server remotely, change the server's data and time, disable logins, and view the NetWare OS version and release date. For many of the options, you must be a Supervisor, Supervisor Equivalent, or Console Operator (assigned in SYSCON).

FIGURE 15.14.

FCONSOLE.

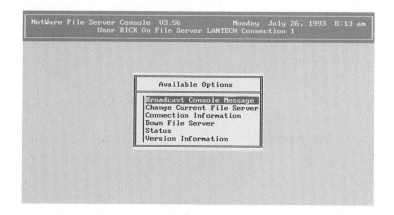

The Remote Console Utility, RCONSOLE

This utility enables a user to access the file server console from any workstation, provided a couple of NLMs are loaded at the server. You must first load REMOTE.NLM and then RSPX.NLM at your server. You will be prompted for a password that is used to protect console access. If no password is assigned, the Supervisor password is required to use RCONSOLE. RCONSOLE.EXE, the workstation software that communicates with the server NLMs, is in the SYS:SYSTEM directory. That directory is set up by default with no access allowed to any users except the Supervisor (or Supervisor Equivalent).

Access to the remote console is reported on the server console and saved to the System Error Log file and the Accounting audit log file.

Console Commands

In addition to NetWare 3.11's standard NLMs, several commands can be entered at the console to facilitate management or give information. Table 15.5 lists console commands that may be of assistance to you.

Table 15.5. NetWare 3.11 console commands.

Command	Purpose
BROADCAST *message*	Sends a message to all logged-in users
CLEAR MESSAGE	Clears messages from the console screen

continues

Table 15.5. continued

Command	Purpose
CLEAR STATION *connection_number*	Clears a connection
CONFIG	Shows configuration of OS, including LAN and NIC drivers
DISABLE LOGIN	Prevents server OS from responding to login requests
ENABLES LOGIN	Toggles login requests back to ON
DISABLE TRANSACTIONS	Turns off TTS
ENABLE TRANSACTIONS	Reverses DISABLE TRANSACTIONS
DOWN	Shuts down the server OS
DISMOUNT/MOUNT *volume*	Dismounts volume, removing it from use
DISPLAY NETWORKS	Lists network addresses available
DISPLAY SERVERS	Lists all servers
DISK	Shows active disks, mirroring, and operating status
DOWN	Shuts down the file server OS
NAME	Displays the file server name
OFF (or CLS)	Clears the console screen
PURGE	Globally purges all salvageable files
RESET ROUTER	Blanks router tables, enabling reconfiguration
SEND "*message*" to user or group	Sends a message to a user or group
SET *set command*	Changes OS operating parameters
SET TIME *hour.minute:sec*	Sets the server time and date
SPOOL	Enables v2.0 server printers to be directed to queues and sets a system-wide default
TIME	Displays server time
TRACK ON	Opens router tracking screen that shows messages sent from and to routers

Command	Purpose
TRACK OFF	Closes router tracking screen
UPS	Displays status of UPS monitoring

SET commands are discussed in greater detail in Chapter 33, "Monitoring and Adjusting Server Performance," and in the *System Admininstration Manual* that is provided with NetWare 3.11. You also can type SET at the server console and select from a list the OS operating parameters that are currently set. You can change those parameters by typing the SET command, followed by the entire command with the switch at the end. For example, you can tell the server not to reply to user connection requests by typing

```
SET REPLY TO GET NEAREST SERVER = OFF
```

Some SET commands must be placed in the STARTUP.NCF file (on your DOS startup partition) in order to take effect. You can automate them by putting them into your AUTOEXEC.BAT or STARTUP.NCF files.

Summary

This chapter described and demonstrated the means of providing access to applications and data restricted with the NetWare trustee directory assignments and drive mappings. The procedure is as simple as possible; there are only a couple of steps necessary to add users once you have created your groups.

To overcome obstacles associated with running DOS applications in a NetWare environment, a system administrator should have superlative DOS skills. The best you can hope is for NetWare to be transparent while still providing restricted access. (You should never accept unrestricted access as the only solution to accessing an application on NetWare.)

Applications that are well-written for NetWare should be simple to install and configure using the suggestions in this chapter. If you have difficulty making applications work properly under NetWare, you should rely on the combination of your DOS skills, NetWare knowledge, and experimentation to resolve problems.

Even the largest software vendors may not have written their applications specifically for NetWare, so you can expect that you will be required to refine your configuration quite often. It is very important for a good system administrator to be resourceful and flexible.

Another important step that is required in setting up your system is the creation of login scripts. Login scripts can be quite complex and are a common tool used in both v3.11 and 4.x.

Administering NetWare 4.x

by Peter Kuo

16

In most ways, administering a NetWare 4.01 server is the same as administering a 3.x server. There are users, groups, trustees, and trustee rights. However, there is the added layer of NetWare Directory Services security. To a user, there is no difference in accessing a 2.x, 3.x, or 4.01 server. But as a system administrator, you no longer administer a single NetWare 4.01 server. You now administer a NetWare 4.01 *network.*

> **NOTE**
>
> Although this chapter explicitly refers to NetWare 4.01, the management of NetWare 4.0 is the same. However, because a number of problems in version 4.0 which have been corrected in version 4.01, it is strongly suggested that you upgrade to version 4.01 as soon as possible.

Depending on how your NetWare Directory Services tree is set up, you may be able to manage only one portion of the tree. However, the underlying concepts are the same, no matter if you only manage a container or the whole tree. This chapter discusses the management issues behind NDS in some detail but only touches lightly upon the file-system management (the same as with NetWare 3.x, which has been discussed in a previous chapter).

NetWare Security

NetWare 4.01 implements network security in "layers," as follows:

- **Login Security**. This controls initial access to the network.
- **NDS Security**. This controls access to various network resources.
- **File System Security**. This controls access to directories and files on a given file server.

Under NetWare 2.x and 3.x, there is only login and file system security.

> **NOTE**
>
> This chapter does not discuss the physical security of the file server; however, this is probably the most important security consideration. Physical access to your file server should be a top security concern.

Login Security

Login controls the initial access to the network. Similar to NetWare 3.x security structure, login security for NetWare 4.x has the following features:

- Username/password verification
- Account restrictions
- Password restriction
- Station restrictions
- Time restrictions
- Intruder limits

> **NOTE** ▶
>
> Intruder limits under NetWare 4.x are set at the container level and apply to all the user objects in that container. This is different from NetWare 3.x, where intruder limits are set on a per-file-server basis.

You should keep in mind that under NetWare 4.x, you are authenticated to the network rather than to a given file server (as is the case under NetWare 2.x and 3.x).

NetWare Directory Services Security

NetWare Directory Services security controls access to objects (network resources) and their properties within the NDS database. One must have rights to an object in order to see that object. To view or modify any information associated with that object (properties), one also must have the appropriate property rights.

In a sense, this is very similar to the file-system security from the NetWare 2.x and 3.x environment. In order to see a directory, one must have rights to the directory. In order to modify any files within that directory, one also must have the appropriate rights to that file. When a user is given rights to a directory, the user becomes a trustee of the directory. Similarly, there are trustees in NDS.

Rights within NDS flow down the tree, just as rights within a file system flow down the directory structure. Filters can be set up to block rights. Effective rights are then determined using the rights assignments and the rights filter. This concept is the same for both NDS and file-system security.

The following sections examine each of these concepts in some detail.

Object Rights

Object rights are used to manage and view objects within the NDS. There are five types of object rights, as follows:

1. **Browse**. This is the right to see an object in the NDS tree. This does not enable the property values of the object to be viewed. You need to have the appropriate property rights to do this.

2. **Create**. This right enables the creation of a new object below this object in the NDS tree. This right applies only to container objects.

3. **Delete**. This is the right required to remove an object from the NDS tree. You can delete only leaf objects and empty containers.

4. **Rename**. This right enables the name of an object to be changed. Only a leaf object's name can be modified.

5. **Supervisor**. This enables full rights to an object and its properties.

In most cases, users would require only the Browse rights to an object in order to use the object and the resource it represents. For example, for a user to see and use a server volume, the Browse right to the volume object is required. Other object rights are used to manage objects and need not be granted to users.

By default, when a user object is created in the NDS, a Browse right is given to the user object itself. This is so the user can see itself in the NDS tree.

Property Rights

Each object in the NDS tree has a set of properties. Each property has rights associated with it. These rights control what users or other objects can do to the property. There are five property rights:

1. **Compare**. Gives the right to compare any value to a value of the property. An operation can return True or False, but the user will not be allowed to see the property value.

2. **Read**. Enables the user to read the value of the property. Having the Read right, Compare is implied.

3. **Add or Delete Self**. Gives the right to add or remove itself as a value of property. With this right, the user cannot affect any other values of the property.

4. **Write**. The right to add, remove, or change the values of the given property. Having the Write right, Add or Delete Self right is implied.

5. **Supervisor**. Grants all rights to the property.

As an example, having the Compare right, you will be able to determine if a login script exists for a given user. However, you will not be able to read it because Compare does not grant you read permission. If you have Add or Delete Self right to a group object, you can add or remove yourself as a member of that group.

> **NOTE** ▶
>
> Property rights can be assigned to all properties of an object or only to specific properties of an object.

When a user object is created in the NDS, the user object itself is given Read rights to all properties of that object. In addition, the user is given Read and Write rights to its login script and Print Job Configuration properties. This is consistent with the 2.x and 3.x environments in that a user can manage his or her own User login script and Print Job Configuration.

> **NOTE** ▶
>
> You will see in the NWAdmin or NETADMIN program that there is an entry in the property listing called [All Property Rights]. This is a shortcut in referring to all the properties of the object.

Access Control List (ACL)

Associated with each object is a property known as the Access Control List (ACL). It lists and controls who has rights and what those rights are to the object. If an object has the Write right to the ACL, that object can then modify any of the rights of the object. For example, if user object "Peter" is given only the Browse right to the volume object Server_SYS: but has the Write right to the ACL of this volume object, Peter can modify the ACL and grant himself more rights to the volume object.

Inheriting Rights

In NDS, object and property rights flow down the tree, just like file system rights do. When a right flows down the tree, this is known as an *inherited* right. Consider the NDS structure shown in Figure 16.1. If John is granted Browse, Create, and Delete rights to the container called Consulting, John inherits those rights for every object in OU=Consulting and below. Unless John gets a new set of rights assignment for OU=Mainframe or if OU=Mainframe has an Inherited Rights Filter (IRF), John will have the same set of rights for OU=Mainframe, CN=Peter, and CN=Mary. The same applies to OU=PC and OU=Mini. However, John will have no rights to CN=Admin and OU=Training and anything below OU=Training. (See Figure 16.2.)

FIGURE 16.1.

Sample NDS tree.

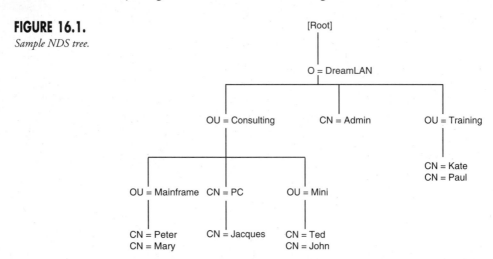

NOTE ▶

Only one specific set of rights assignments can be active at a time. If a user is given multiple sets of rights assignments at different points in the Directory tree, the lower set is the inherited one. For example, if John is given Browse,

Create, and Delete object rights at OU=Consulting, and the Browse object right at OU=PC, then when John's context is OU=PC, he only has the Browse right to CN=Jacques. (See Figure 16.3.)

FIGURE 16.2.

Rights inheritance example.

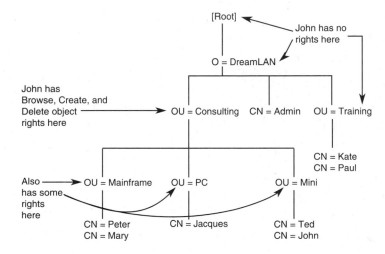

FIGURE 16.3.

Multiple rights assignments example.

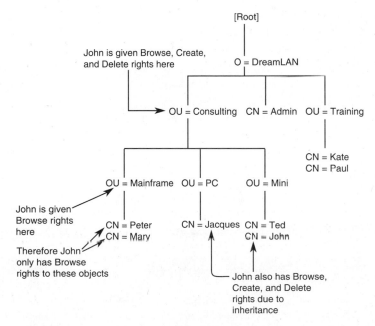

Property rights are handled differently. Because in most cases, the specific properties of objects differ from each other (for example, Organizational Unit versus User), property rights are not inherited. However, there is one exception. The special [All Property Rights] is inherited. Thus, using the example in Figure 16.1 again, if John is given the Compare and Read property rights to the address property for OU=Training, John does not inherit these rights for CN=Kate and CN=Paul. However, if John is given the Compare and Read property rights to [All Property Rights] for OU=Training, he inherits these rights for CN=Kate and CN=Paul.

Inherited Rights Filter (IRF)

There may be situations when you need to ensure that certain rights are not inherited into a particular branch of your NDS tree. This can be easily done with the Inherited Rights Filter (IRF). This is very similar to the file-system rights filtering concept. Rights can only be taken away and not gained. Using the filter, you specify which rights *can* be inherited. Therefore, if a given right appears in the list, it can be inherited.

Shown in Figure 16.4 is an example of the operation of IRF. Peter is given a set of trustee object rights of Browse, Create, and Delete for O=DreamLAN. OU=Consulting has an IRF of Browse, Delete, Rename, and Supervisor (B_DRS), meaning no Create right is to be inherited. Therefore, Peter has only Browse and Delete rights in OU=Consulting. Now, OU=PC has an IRF of Browse (B____), therefore Peter can inherit only the Browse right in OU=PC. However, because Peter also has a trustee assignment of Browse, Create, Delete, and Rename (BCDR_) for OU=PC, the IRF does not come into effect. Peter can exercise Browse, Create, Delete, and Rename object rights on CN=Jacques. This is consistent with the file system security most people are familiar with in the NetWare 3.x environment. IRF in NetWare 4.x can be directly compared to NetWare 3.x's IRM (Inherited Rights Mask) feature.

IRF is also available for property rights. It works in exactly the same manner as IRF for object rights. An exception exists when Supervisor rights are being filtered with IRF. If you filter out a Supervisor *property* right but not a Supervisor *object* right, an object inheriting a Supervisor object right from above will not be affected by the property IRF. This is because a Supervisor object right grants all property rights.

> **NOTE** ▶
>
> IRF is part of the ACL property. In order to modify the IRF of an object or property, you need to have either a Write or Supervisor property right to the ACL property.

FIGURE 16.4.

Inherited Rights Filter example.

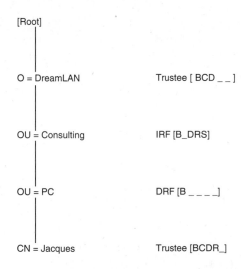

[Root]	
O = DreamLAN	Trustee [BCD _ _]
OU = Consulting	IRF [B_DRS]
OU = PC	DRF [B _ _ _ _]
CN = Jacques	Trustee [BCDR_]

> **WARNING** ▶
>
> Within NDS, it is possible to use IRF to filter out a Supervisor object and property right. If you are not careful, you can find portions of your NDS tree unmanageable.
>
> There is no safeguard built into NDS to prevent this from happening. This is part of the requirement for C2 security certification. If you need to filter out the Supervisor right using IRF, make sure you assigned the Supervisor right to an object for this container. The NetWare utilities will warn you if you try to remove the Supervisor right using IRF when no trustee assignment is present.
>
> If you are using IRFs to block a Supervisor right, be extra careful when deleting objects from your NDS. If you delete the object with the explicit trustee assignment, you can lose access to the container with IRF blocking a Supervisor right.

Security Equivalence and Trustee Status

The concept of security equivalence and trustee status in NDS is very similar to those same features in NetWare 2.x and 3.x. However, there are some system defaults for security equivalences and trustee assignments that cannot be changed or revoked.

NOTE

Within NDS, *any* object can be made a trustee of another object. For example, a container object can be granted rights to a volume object.

However, in NDS, Security Equivalences is a property of user objects. It is not available for all objects.

CAUTION

One must be careful when granting rights to the Security Equivalences property. If a user is given the Write or Supervisor property right to his or her Security Equivalences property, he or she could possibly add a user with Supervisor rights to the list who would then have access to the whole network.

There are three system default security equivalences, as follows:

- Automatic security equivalent to [Root]. All objects are automatically made security equivalent to [Root].
- Automatic security equivalent to [Public] trustee.
- Automatic security equivalent to all containers that are part of its complete name.

When an object is created in your NDS, it is automatically made security equivalent to [Root]. This enables you to grant [Root] a trustee assignment to a file, directory, or another object, and every object in your NDS will have those rights. For example, you can grant [Root] access to your e-mail directory so that everyone in the NDS would have rights to that directory.

[Public] is a special trustee that can be added to any objects, including directories and files. By default, [Public] is given the Browse right to [Root]. For each server installed into your NDS tree, [Public] is given Read and File Scan rights to the SYS:LOGIN directory. Each object is automatically made security equivalent to [Public]; therefore, it will have automatic access to the SYS:LOGIN directory of every server in your NDS.

NOTE ▷

[Public] is not a real object. You will not find it listed in your NDS tree.

WARNING ▷

Users need not be logged in (authenticated) to your NDS in order to have all the rights that are granted to [Public]. This feature enables users to "walk around" your tree to find their context before logging in. However, the down side of this is if you give excessive rights to [Public], it can become a potential security hole.

When an object is created in a container, it automatically is security equivalent to the container it is in. You can consider, to a degree, that containers are groups in the traditional sense. When an object is defined within that container, it is automatically made to be a "member of the group." This simplifies your NDS management. You assign all the trustee assignments that you want the container to have at the OU level, and all users will be given the same rights. When a user is moved from one container to another, the user will immediately get all the rights assigned for that new OU and lose all rights from the old OU.

When a server is installed into a container, the container is given Read and File Scan rights to SYS:PUBLIC. Because of default security equivalence, you want to create your users in the same container as where you define your file servers. That way, they will automatically have access to the utilities and information in SYS:PUBLIC. (This feature can be compared to the function of the EVERYONE group in the NetWare 2.x and 3.x environments.)

CAUTION ▷

Be careful when assigning rights to the containers in your NDS tree. Unless IRFs are used at the lower portion of your tree, your users may have more rights than you would want them to have.

Consider the example in Figure 16.1. User Peter is security equivalent to OU=Mainframe, OU=Consulting, and O=DreamLAN. If any of these containers have trustee rights to other portions of the NDS tree, Peter also will have the same type of rights. For example, if OU=Consulting has Create and Delete object rights to OU=Training, Peter can create and delete objects in OU=Training, even though he "belongs" to the Consulting division.

Any user can browse any portion of the NDS tree because they are security equivalent to [Public], which has a Browse object right to [Root]. This flows down to all branches of your NDS tree unless it is blocked by an explicit trustee assignment or IRF.

NOTE ▶

These three default security equivalences cannot be changed, nor can they be viewed using NETADMIN or NWAdmin utilities.

File System Security

NetWare 4.x file-system security works the same as in NetWare 3.x, with a few minor differences. You still make trustee assignments to users and groups. You also can make file-system trustee assignments to containers. With the exception of the user's home directory, you need to grant explicit trustee assignments manually. The easiest way is to use Group and Container objects.

In order to have a Supervisor file right to the root of all volumes of a given server, you need to have only the Write property right to the ACL property of that server object (or have a Supervisor object right and a Supervisor property right to the server object).

CAUTION ▶

Because Supervisor rights (both object and property) in NDS can be blocked by IRF, you should consider assigning explicit Supervisor trustee assignments to server objects.

Some new file and directory attributes have been added because of the file-compression and data-migration features in NetWare 4.x. They include the following:

- **Cannot Compress (CC)**. Status attribute to indicate the file cannot be compressed because of limited space savings.
- **Compress (CO)**. Status attribute to indicate the file is a compressed file.
- **Don't Compress (DC)**. If assigned to a directory, none of the files within that directory will be compressed. Also can be assigned to a specific file.
- **Don't Migrate (DM)**. If assigned to a directory, none of the files within that directory will be migrated to secondary storage. Also can be assigned to a specific file.
- **Immediate Compress (IC)**. If assigned to a directory, all files within that directory will be considered for compression as soon as the operating system can handle the action. Also can be assigned to a specific file.
- **Migrated (M)**. Status attribute to indicate the file has been migrated to a secondary storage device.

NOTE

File compression and data migration is enabled or disabled during volume installation. These can be set differently for individual volumes.

Data migration can be turned on or off "on the fly," but file compression cannot.

File compression and data migration thresholds can be adjusted using SET commands at the file server console or by using the SERVMAN.NLM.

Summary

This chapter discussed the various considerations in managing a NetWare 4.x network. Login Security and File System Security in NetWare 4.x have changed very little as compared to NetWare 2.x and 3.x. The additional layer of NetWare Directory Services Security is the hurdle that most migrating administrators will have to cross.

In many respects, NDS security works in the same manner as file-system security: there are trustee rights assignments, and rights flow within the NDS tree. It is important to remember, however, that there are separate object and property rights from file-system rights. Most important of all, Supervisor rights within NDS can be filtered out by Inherited Rights Filters. Supervisor rights within file systems are not affected by any IRF of the file system.

Login Scripts

17

by Rick Sant'Angelo

IN THIS CHAPTER

Login scripts configure the user environment as a login occurs. NetWare's login script language has many commands; it supports conditional statements and identifier variables, and any executable file can be executed during the login script. This makes for a very powerful language that can accommodate virtually any requirement without requiring DOS variables or a series of batch files.

For NetWare 3.x, when a login occurs, the system login script executes first, followed by the user login script. For 4.x, when a user logs in, an organizational login script runs, and then the user login script executes. If no user login script exists, a hard-coded default login script executes. Once both login scripts execute, the user exits to the workstation operating system.

> **NOTE** ▶
>
> A user profile login script can be created with version 4.0, which can execute instead of (or in addition to) an organizational login script. The user profile can be relative to the context, group, or any other basis.

Login scripts perform necessary functions to configure the DOS or OS/2 environment to work properly with NetWare. They are used to

1. Map logical drive letters
2. Map search drives
3. Capture printers
4. Set DOS environment variables and configurations
5. Execute applications

In this chapter, login scripts are discussed as a single topic. Whether you implement the commands in a system/organization login script or in a user login script does not change the way the commands execute. This chapter discusses

- Login script strategies
- Login script commands
- Mapping in the login script
- Using identifier variables
- Using conditional statements
- Executing applications from within a login script
- Combining all tools to provide a single login script for all users

Login Script Strategies

Like many other parts of NetWare system administration, there is no right or wrong way to do login scripts; there are only differing strategies. Some strategies are very labor-intensive and provide the opportunity for many problems to occur, whereas other strategies can simplify administration and reduce the need for support. Each of the following subjects can be handled in a way that is effective for all users and can reduce complexity and effort.

Default Mapping and Printer Captures

One strategy used in login scripts is to provide a default or set of drive mappings, search drive mappings, and printer captures. If the user never changes them, or no changes are made in menus or batch files, these effectively are a permanent set of drive mappings. Alternatively, some administrators elect to provide basic system defaults and enable the user to create drive mappings and printer captures.

> **TIP** ▶
>
> To reduce and simplify the administrative workload, always use as few drive mappings as necessary. You should not create drive mappings unless they are required by an application or they reduce user effort.

Another good piece of advice is to use the same basic drive mappings for each user. It often increases your support burden to have users whose drive mappings vary when they are accessing the same directories.

Choosing Between System/Organizational and User Login Scripts

There are two types of login scripts and three possible combinations of them. You can employ the following:

- Both a system (or organizational) login script and user login scripts
- Only a system (or organizational) login script
- Only user login scripts

Because both types of login scripts exist, administrators naturally place commands that are common to all users in the system or organizational login script. However, commands that are unique to each user are placed in the user login script. This strategy works well for small networks, but for systems with dozens or hundreds of users, this strategy becomes quite labor-intensive. If an additional drive mapping is added for many users, the administrator may need to edit dozens or hundreds of user login scripts.

Though all login script commands that are unique to a user can be placed in the user login script, other ways of handling unique configurations include the use of NetWare *identifier variables* and *conditional statements* in the system or organizational login script. These options are discussed in greater detail later in this chapter.

The simple solution to this dilemma is to use conditional statements in the system or an organizational login script to isolate the users that need to have the custom drive mapping.

Allowing Users to Edit Login Scripts

Another decision you should make is whether to allow users to edit their own login scripts. Ordinarily, an individual user cannot edit a system or organizational login script (unless the user is Security Equivalent to the Supervisor or Admin), but can edit his or her own login script. To protect the login script from user edits, the system or organizational login script is the logical choice.

 TIP ▶

You can prevent the user from editing the user login script by changing the trustee assignments in the user's MAIL subdirectory, revoking the rights to write to files.

Using DOS Environment Variables versus NetWare Identifier Variables

When administrators are well-versed in DOS (or OS/2) and are accustomed to using variables to handle all sorts of unique situations, their use of environment variables can become a way of life. Applying the same techniques to the NetWare environment can work, but it may not be as good an option as using NetWare variables, for two reasons:

1. Insufficient environment space
2. The ability of other administrators to edit the configuration

First, the DOS environment space is limited to 160 bytes by default and therefore may not accommodate numerous and lengthy entries. Many network applications use the DOS environment to store variables for future use. Normally, the DOS environment space should be expanded or your variables may not work. NetWare variables (used in the login script) do not need to be set into the workstation environment space, which exempts them from some problems typically encountered in the DOS environment.

> **TIP** ▶
>
> You may need to expand your DOS environment space from the default value of 160 bytes because many network applications write to the DOS environment space. This can be done by placing the following command into your CONFIG.SYS:
>
> `SHELL=d:\COMMAND.COM /P /E:size`
>
> (*d* = boot drive letter, and `E:size` specifies the new size of the environment space)

Second, many users have difficulty learning to use DOS variables. Variables don't work the same in the different versions of DOS and can be affected by problems such as insufficient environment space or a change to a batch file. NetWare login script identifier variables are simpler to use, cause fewer problems, and are fully documented.

When another administrator takes over for you, he or she may have difficulty following your DOS variables, especially if the variables differ for various users and if workstation batch files have been deleted. NetWare identifier variables are more consistently stable and rely on user account or NET.CFG (or SHELL.CFG) file statements for their input.

Login Script Commands

NetWare's login script language is simple but powerful. It has very few commands, but these commands cover almost any situation that needs to be addressed within a login script. Login script commands are listed in Table 17.1.

Table 17.1. Login script commands.

Command	Description
ATTACH	Logs a user into a file server without log out from current file server
BEGIN/END	Conditional statement for multiple commands
BREAK	Enables user to use Ctrl+C or Break during login script
COMSPEC	Inserts location of COMMAND.COM into DOS environment
DOS SET	Sets into DOS environment (same as SET from DOS)
DOS VERIFY	Turns on DOS verify for local drives
DRIVE *d:*	Makes stated drive letter the default network drive letter
EXIT	Terminates execution of login script
#	Shells out to DOS and executes a program
DISPLAY	Displays contents of an ASCII text file
FDISPLAY	Same as DISPLAY, but suppresses control characters
FIRE PHASERS *n*	Produces audible "phaser" sound *n* times
IF...THEN	Enables the use of programming logic
INCLUDE *pathname/filename*	Includes contents of ASCII file as part of login script
MAP	Assigns drive letters and search drives to directory pathnames
MAP DISPLAY	Prevents messages from printing to screen
MAP ERRORS	Prevents login script errors from printing to screen

Command	Description
PAUSE	Pauses and displays "strike any key to continue"
PCCOMPATIBLE	Resolves problems when %MACHINE is other than default
REMARK (*or ;)	Instruction to ignore this line
WRITE	Prints text delimited with quotes to screen

NOTE ▶

Batch files and internal DOS commands cannot be executed from login scripts unless you call the applications within another copy of COMMAND.COM.

You can execute DOS batch files or internal commands as follows:

```
#COMMAND /C batch file or internal command
```

For example, to execute a clear screen (which is a DOS internal command), type

```
#COMMAND /C CLS
```

Provided that COMMAND.COM is in the path, this line shells to DOS, executes another copy of COMMAND.COM, executes the CLS command, and then is removed from memory.

Mapping in the Login Script

The main function of a login script is to map drive letters.

Logical Drive Letter Mappings

Only one drive letter mapping is required to access each NetWare volume. Without a mapping to a volume, DOS has no access. If you have no login script, the default login script maps the first available drive letter (after the last drive that DOS has configured) to the SYS: volume. Normally, this is drive F:. However, the first available letter can vary depending upon your last DOS drive letter. Some exceptions are

- `CONFIG.SYS LASTDRIVE` statement (first after the `LASTDRIVE`)
- A large, local hard drive with more than three logical DOS volumes
- A diskless workstation (first drive letter can be A:)

The `MAP` command, used as a command-line utility, works the same way, but with one exception: NetWare syntax must be used within login scripts, because the login script version of the `MAP` command recognizes backslashes as a switch delimiter and causes difficulty. You should not use a slash after the volume name colon; you should use a forward slash (/) instead of a backslash (\).

You should map drive letters for the following basic configuration requirements:

- Any volumes to which the user must have access
- The user home directory
- The workgroup shared directory

Other drive letter mappings should be created to accommodate applications that may require a drive letter to access a data directory separate from the application directory. Drive letter mappings may be created to simplify user access. You may want to use the `MAP ROOT` command to make the directory appear to be a root directory. The following command is an example of a proper NetWare drive mapping for a user home directory:

```
MAP ROOT U:=SYS:HOME/RBSMITH
```

Search Drive Mappings

Search drive mappings are added to the DOS path and should follow logical drive letter mappings. A search drive pointing to the SYS:PUBLIC directory should be mapped at all times. You can map a search drive to the PUBLIC directory with the `ROOT` switch, as follows:

```
MAP ROOT INSERT S1:=SYS:PUBLIC
```

The `MAP` command makes search drive mappings out of existing DOS paths, and the `INSERT` command inserts this search drive, pushing others back, to make this one the first (S1:).

> **NOTE** ▶
>
> Search drive mappings should be created after logical drive mappings. If a drive letter is already in use, the search drive mapping will select the next available drive letter. If a logical drive mapping specifies a drive letter already in use by a search drive, the search drive will be lost.

Examples of Login Script Drive Mappings

The following commands create drive letters:

```
F:
L:
G:
U:
Search Drive 1:
Search Drive 2:
Search Drive 3:
```

```
MAP F:=FS311/SYS:
MAP G:=FS311/VOL1:
MAP L:=FS311/VOL1:APPS/LOTUS
MAP M:=FS311/VOL1:DATA/ACCTG
MAP U:=FS311/SYS:HOME/GEORGE
MAP S1:=FS311/SYS:PUBLIC
MAP S2:=FS311/SYS:PUBLIC/MSDOS/V5.00
MAP S3:=FS311/SYS:APPS/FOX
```

Using Identifier Variables

NetWare identifier variables can be used in pathnames, in text strings, and for conditional statements. This enables the same type of flexibility as other types of programming, except NetWare identifier variables are specifically for the business of login scripts, and new identifier variables cannot be defined. Table 17.2 describes valid identifier variables and their meanings. Table 17.3 shows user/workstation variables, values, defaults, and uses.

Table 17.2. Identifier variables for date and time.

Variable	Values	Use
YEAR	Year in four-number format	
SHORT_YEAR	Year in two-number format	
HOUR	(1-12)	Time of day, hour of the day
HOUR24	(00-23)	Time of day, hour of the day (military)
MINUTE	(00-59)	Time of day, minute
SECOND	(00-59)	Time of day, second
AM_PM	AM or PM	Time of day, AM or PM
GREETING_TIME	(Morning, Afternoon, Evening)	Time of day
MONTH	(01-12)	Month of year (numeric)
MONTH_NAME	(January-December)	Month of year (ASCII)
DAY	(1-31)	Day of month (numeric)
DAY_OF_WEEK	(Sunday-Saturday)	Day of week (ASCII)
NDAY_OF_WEEK	(1-7)	Day of week (numeric)

Table 17.3. User/workstation variables.

Variable	Values	Default	Use
LOGIN_NAME		none	User account login name
FILE_SERVER		this one	File server name
FULL_NAME		none	User full name

Variable	Values	Default	Use
USER_ID		none	User's MAIL directory name
STATION		none	Connection number
P_STATION	(12 hex digits)	none	Physical node address
SHELL_TYPE			Workstation shell version
OS		MSDOS	Workstation OS
DOS NAME	user-defined (5 char)	none	(MSDOS or OS2) to force assignment of "OS" value
OS_VERSION	V*x.xx*	none	DOS version number
MACHINE NAME	user-defined		Variable used to identify workstation
MACHINE user-defined	IBM_PC	LONG MACHINE TYPE (in NET.CFG)	
SMACHINE user-defined	IBM_PC	SHORT MACHINE TYPE (limited to 4 characters)	
NETWORK_ADDRESS	(8 digits hex)	none	Network address/ number
<dos_variable>			Inserts the value or string of a DOS variable

Identifier variables can be used to define a pathname according to a user name or physical workstation node address. For example, one statement in the system or organizational login script can define each unique user's home directory, as follows:

```
MAP U:=FS311/SYS:HOME/%LOGIN_NAME
```

NOTE ▶

When identifier variables are used inside of an ASCII string or a pathname, the percent (%) character must precede the variable.

The following line can map a drive letter to a unique directory for workstation-specific files:

```
MAP P:=FS311/PUBLIC/WKSTN/%P_STATION
```

The following example shows how an identifier variable is used in a WRITE statement to be displayed to the screen:

```
WRITE "It is %DAY_OF_WEEK, Do you know where your backups are?"
```

NOTE ▶

Some identifier variables are case-sensitive; however, if you always use capital letters, they always work.

For further detail on login script conditional statements, see Appendix E of this book, or Appendix A in your NetWare installation manual.

Using Conditional Statements

Conditional statements are used to introduce logic to your login scripts. A conditional statement specifies that if a condition is true, one action is taken; if not, another action is taken. This is very helpful for providing one login script that can handle many conditions that may exist. For example, on a certain day of the week you may want to display a message, or perhaps you would like to provide different drive mappings for each group.

Conditional statements are statements such as

```
IF...THEN
IF...THEN[el]ELSE
IF...BEGIN[el]END
```

An example of a simple login script command to find the Supervisor's home directory is as follows:

```
IF LOGIN_NAME = "SUPERVISOR" THEN MAP ROOT U:=FS311/SYS:HOME/SU
```

The preceding example is an exception to the statement shown previously in which the user home directory was locatable according to the user's login name. You can solve this problem in one of two ways. You can show the following two lines:

```
IF LOGIN_NAME = "SUPERVISOR" THEN MAP ROOT U:=FS311/SYS:HOME/SU
IF LOGIN_NAME <> "SUPERVISOR" THEN MAP ROOT U:=FS311/SYS:HOME/
%LOGIN_NAME
```

or you can solve it with one conditional grouping as follows:

```
IF LOGIN_NAME = "SUPERVISOR" THEN
    MAP ROOT U:=FS311/SYS:HOME/SU
    ELSE
    MAP ROOT U:=FS311/SYS:HOME/%LOGIN_NAME
    END
```

NOTE

"Equal to" can be signified with

=

==

IS

EQUALS

and "not equal to" can be signified with

<>

!=

IS NOT

DOES NOT EQUAL

NOT EQUAL TO

The symbols shown in the Note box can be combined with identifier variables to provide solutions to almost any condition. A simple conditional statement to display a message on Fridays would appear as follows:

```
IF DAY_OF_WEEK = "Friday" THEN WRITE "TGIF!"
```

NOTE ▶

When an identifier variable is used as a condition in a conditional statement, the percent (%) character is omitted.

Other identifier variables assist in the use of conditional statements, as shown in Table 17.4.

Table 17.4. Identifier variables used in conditional statements.

Variable	Values	Description
ERROR_LEVEL	(0, 1)	0 if no error occurs, 1 if error occurs
MEMBER OF "*group*"		Workgroup identifier
ACCESS_SERVER	(True, False)	Returns True if access server is functional

Following is an example of using the MEMBER OF identifier variable to have a whole different set of drive mappings for various groups:

```
IF MEMBER OF "ACCTG" THEN BEGIN
     MAP F:=FS311/SYS:
     MAP G:=FS311/VOL1:
     MAP L:=FS311/VOL1:APPS/LOTUS
     MAP M:=FS311/VOL1:DATA/ACCTG
     MAP U:=FS311/SYS:HOME/%LOGIN_NAME
     END

IF MEMBER OF "MKTG" THEN BEGIN
     MAP F:=FS311/SYS:
     MAP G:=FS311/VOL1:
     MAP H:=FS311/VOL1:APPS/HG
     MAP M:=FS311/VOL1:DATA/MKTG
     MAP U:=FS311/SYS:HOME/%LOGIN_NAME
     END
```

As you can see, between conditional statements and identifier variables, you can do just about anything with your login scripts. For more detail on conditional statements, see Appendix E of this book or Appendix A in your NetWare installation manual.

Executing Applications from Within a Login Script

You may execute a DOS application in a login script by preceding the command with the External Program Execution (#) character. This is an appropriate method for executing NetWare command-line utilities or external DOS commands.

> **NOTE** ▶
>
> As a rule, you should not execute TSR applications during the login script or EXIT to a TSR. This can cause memory conflicts.

Summary

This chapter discussed how to use login script commands, identifier variables, and conditional statements. The following example demonstrates how these three tools can resolve several situations:

```
REMARK This file is saved on the disk that accompanies this book:
NET$LOG.DAT
MAP DISPLAY OFF

REMARK Map Drive letters, assign DOS logical drive letters to
directories
MAP F:=SYS:
MAP ROOT G:=FS311/VOL1:DATA
MAP ROOT Q:=FS311/VOL1:DATA\QWIN
MAP ROOT T:FS311/VOL1:DATA\TOSHARE

REMARK Map Search Drives, assign DOS letter and add to DOS PATH
MAP ROOT S1:=FS311/SYS:PUBLIC
IF P_STATION = "00001B37597E"
     MAP S2:=D:\DOS
     ELSE
     MAP S2:=C:\DOS
     END
MAP ROOT S3:=FS311/SYS:PUBLIC/UTIL
MAP ROOT S4:=FS311/SYS:PUBLIC/XTG
MAP ROOT S5:=FS311/VOL1:APPS/WIN31
```

```
IF LOGIN_NAME = "SUPERVISOR" THEN BEGIN
     MAP ROOT U:=FS311/SYS:HOME/SU
     MAP ROOT S6:=FS311/SYS:HOME/SU/WIN
     ELSE
     MAP INS ROOT S6:=FS311/SYS:HOME/%LOGIN_NAME/WIN
     MAP ROOT U:=FS311/SYS:HOME/%LOGIN_NAME
     END
MAP INS ROOT S7:=FS311/VOL1:APPS/PM4
MAP INS ROOT S8:=FS311/VOL1:APPS/ALDUS
MAP INS ROOT S9:=FS311/VOL1:APPS/MGXWORKS/MGXLIBS

REMARK User LINDA gets drive D: assignment and special search drives
IF LOGIN_NAME = "LINDA" THEN BEGIN
     MAP ROOT D:=FS311/VOL1:DATA/PERSONNEL
     MAP INS ROOT S16:=FS311/VOL1:APPS/FOX
     MAP INS ROOT S16:=FS311/VOL1:APPS/BRIEF
     MAP INS ROOT S16:=FS311/VOL1:APPS/WP51
     END

REMARK Capture print output, clear screen, write greeting
#CAPTURE NT
#COMMAND /C CLS
WRITE "Good %GREETING_TIME, %FULL_NAME."
#WHOAMI
IF DAY_OF_WEEK = "Friday" THEN WRITE "TGIF!"

REMARK Switch to drive U:, exit, execute menu system
DRIVE U:
PCCOMPATIBLE
EXIT "menu sample"
```

Creating and Using Menus

18

by Rick Sant'Angelo

The menu system that ships with NetWare 3.12 and 4.x has changed significantly from that of earlier versions. This menu system was developed by Saber for Novell and is included at no additional cost. Among the improvements in functionality and manageability are the following:

■ True 0K overhead when executing menu selections

■ Compiled menu scripts

■ Syntax errors discovered and corrected at compile time, not runtime

■ Enhanced user prompting

■ The capability to control where temporary files are placed

■ The capability to enable (or prevent) users to shell out to DOS

Setting up this menu system is slightly more complex than the old menu system (and understandably so). This section discusses how to use the menu system, gives examples, and then briefly summarizes the steps you need to take. The end of the chapter discusses how to convert your existing Novell menu file to the new format using the MENUCNVT utility.

This menu system is not the same as the full Saber Menu System. You may purchase the full Saber Menu System without reworking the menus used with this menu utility.

Menu System Setup

Setting up the menu system requires a couple of steps that are not readily apparent. You need to create a directory or two to house the menu and working files, and then you need to create some DOS environment variables.

Setting Up the Directories

The NetWare menu system requires a bit of setup before it can be used. First, you must decide where you want to place your menu script files. The menu system executables reside in the SYS:PUBLIC directory and should not be moved because they rely on the SYS:PUBLIC\NLS directory.

NOTE ▶

You may place your menu script files in the SYS:PUBLIC directory for simplicity's sake. The only requirement for the menu script files is that they are placed in a search drive.

All who use the menu system must have at least Read and File Scan rights to directories containing menu script files. It is a good idea to limit users to Read-only access to the menu script files to prevent tampering.

Next, decide where you want the temporary files to go. The menu system creates temporary batch and data files in the user's working directory for each item the user executes. You may opt to have all temporary files placed in one directory, or the temporary files may be placed in each user's home directory. The menu system deletes the temporary files when it is done, but it can leave some behind if the user's system locks or is rebooted. For this reason, it is recommended that the temporary files be placed in a single public directory so that they are easily identified and can be deleted easily. All menu system users must have Read, File Scan, Write, Create, Erase, and Modify rights in any directory that is a destination for temporary files.

TIP ▶

If you create a separate directory for menu working files as discussed previously, use the NetWare 3.x's FLAGDIR (FLAG /DO for 4.x) command or FILER (ADMIN for 4.x) to set the directory attribute to Purge. When files are deleted, they will not be salvageable and therefore will not tie up disk space reserved for salvageable files.

Setting the Environment Variables

The next step is to tell the menu system where to put the temporary files and what to name them. This is done by setting two environment variables: S_FILEDIR and S_FILE. The S_FILEDIR environment variable should be set to the fully qualified path where the temporary files are to be placed. It should contain a drive letter, a path, and a trailing backslash (\). Set the S_FILEDIR variable to a subdirectory of the PUBLIC directory in the system login script with the following command:

```
SET S_FILEDIR="F:\PUBLIC\TEMP\"
```

NOTE ▶

This example assumes that F: is mapped to the SYS: volume without the ROOT switch and that the users have the proper rights to that directory.

The S_FILE environment variable contains the template filename for the temporary files. It may be from one to seven characters in length, and it may contain any legal DOS filename character. If you are placing all temporary files in one directory, it is crucial that S_FILE be set to a unique value for each user.

TIP ▶

To ensure each user has a unique value, you can set the S_FILE environment variable to the logical station number in the system login script as follows:

```
SET S_FILE="%station"
```

CAUTION ▶

If you receive the DOS error "Out of environment space," add the following line to your CONFIG.SYS:

```
SHELL=C:\COMMAND.COM /P /E:size
```

or substitute the boot drive for C:.

Menu Building Blocks

A menu script actually requires the creation of two files. The source file is an ASCII file that you create to define the menu; it must have an extension of .SRC. You must then compile the source file into binary using the MENUMAKE utility. This creates a file with a .DAT extension, which will be the actual file used by the menu system.

The source file contains three types of statements:

Menus	Defines the menus and submenus that exist in the source file
Items	Defines the items under each menu
Commands	Tells each item what to do

MENU Statements

A MENU statement defines a menu and its title. The statement consists of three parts: the word Menu, a menu number, and a menu title. Each menu in a menu script file must be given a unique number between 1 and 255. This is merely a reference number and has no bearing on the order of menu items. The menu statement has the following syntax:

```
MENU menu_number,menu_title
```

Here is an example of a menu statement:

```
MENU 10,Administrator Utilities
```

ITEM Statements

ITEM statements define the title of each item in a menu. Up to twelve ITEM statements may be placed after each MENU statement in the menu source file. At least one item command must follow each ITEM statement. An ITEM statement consists of the word item, an item title, and some optional switches that affect the behavior of the item. The syntax of the ITEM statement is

```
ITEM item_title { switches }
```

The *item_title* may be up to 40 characters in length and contain any printable characters. If switches are specified, they must be enclosed in curly braces ({}). The following list shows the allowed switches and their purposes.

Switch	*Purpose*
BATCH	Instructs the menu system to execute the item with 0K overhead. This causes the menu system to completely unload itself from memory before the item's commands are executed.
CHDIR	Instructs the menu system to save the current drive and directory and restore it after the item executes. This switch is automatically turned on if the BATCH switch is specified.
PAUSE	Instructs the menu system to wait for a user keypress after the item has executed.
SHOW	Displays the item commands on-screen before the item is executed.

Specify the BATCH switch only if your application is memory-intensive or if you are loading a TSR. The menu system reloads faster if the BATCH switch is not specified.

Here is an example of ITEM statement that will display the menu option to execute 4.0's NETADMIN utility. When the command is executed (requiring an EXEC command statement to follow) it will execute it with 0K overhead:

```
ITEM Network Administrator Console { BATCH }
```

Command Statements

Command statements provide a course of action for each ITEM statement. There are six different command statements, each of which is outlined in the following sections.

EXEC

The EXEC statement executes a DOS command. You may specify as many EXEC statements as you wish per ITEM statement. Each EXEC statement is added to the list, and all of the EXEC statements are executed as a single batch file. The EXEC statement has the following syntax:

```
EXEC command
```

Command may be any valid DOS command up to 250 characters in length. Environment variables will be properly expanded, and they are not counted in the 250 characters.

Here is an example of an EXEC command that will execute the FILER utility:

```
EXEC FILER
```

Three special versions of the EXEC statement instruct the menu system to perform a special function:

Statement	Function
EXEC DOS	Runs a DOS shell, enabling the user access to a DOS prompt. The user must type EXIT to return to the menu system.

EXEC EXIT   Exits the user from the menu system to a DOS prompt. Users cannot exit the menu system unless this command is included somewhere in the menu.

EXEC LOGOUT Ends the session and logs the user out of the network.

> **NOTE** ▶
>
> For each of the preceding EXEC commands, you must use uppercase. For example, EXEC Dos will not work, but EXEC DOS will.

SHOW

The SHOW statement is used to show another menu. The syntax of the SHOW statement is

SHOW *menu_number*

When a SHOW statement is placed under an ITEM statement, the menu specified by *menu_number* is activated when the user selects the item. The user may press the Esc key to return to the previous menu. Menus may be nested up to eleven levels deep using the SHOW statement. If you place the SHOW statement under an ITEM, it may be the only statement under that ITEM.

Here is an example of a menu item, which was labelled as menu 10 in a previous MENU statement, that brings up the Administrator Utilities menu:

MENU 10

LOAD

The LOAD statement is used to chain to another menu file. The syntax of the LOAD statement is

LOAD *menu_filename*

When the LOAD statement is specified under an ITEM, the menu file specified by *menu_filename* is loaded, and the first menu in that file is activated. As with the SHOW statement, menus may be nested up to eleven levels deep. You may specify a fully qualified path, or just the filename for *menu_filename*. The LOAD statement is useful if you have very large menus, or if you would like to group your menus by function or department.

GETO, GETR, and GETP

GETO, GETR, and GETP enable you to prompt the user to enter information and use this information along with the EXEC statements in the menu script. GETO and GETR gather the information the user enters and append it to the end of the next EXEC statement that occurs in the menu script. You may place as many GETO and GETR statements as you need before each EXEC statement. The difference between GETO and GETR is that GETR requires the user to enter text in its entry field, while GETO enables the user to leave the field blank.

The GETP statement functions a bit differently. You may have only nine GETP statements per ITEM statement. The GETP statement stores the user input from each statement into a replaceable parameter, accessible by using the tokens %1 through %9. The first GETP statement in an item becomes %1, the second %2, and so on. If you use a token that has not been defined, it is simply removed when the item is executed. The GETP statement, as with the GETR statement, requires the user to enter at least one character in its entry field. The syntax for GETx statements is

GETx *user_prompt {prepend_text} length,prefill_text, {append_text}*

Here are some examples of GETx statements:

```
GETR Enter your user ID {} 128,, {}
GETP Enter the destination drive {} 1,F, {:}
GETO Enter the volume label {/V:} 11,, {}
```

Following are the parameters for GETx statements.

Parameter	Description and usage
user_prompt	The text displayed along with the entry field.
prepend_text	Literal text to precede the text the user will enter. Leading and trailing spaces are significant between the curly braces.
length	Specifies the maximum length of the text the user can enter. This may be between 0 and 255. The entry field will scroll horizontally if necessary.
prefill_text	The initial contents of the entry field. You may use an environment variable here by placing it between percent signs (%)—for example, %PATH%.
append_text	Literal text to be appended to the text the user enters. Leading and trailing spaces are significant between the curly braces.

The *prepend_text* and *append_text* parameters are optional, but even if you do not use a parameter, you still must place the curly braces in the GETx statement. The *prefill_text* parameter is also optional, but its comma must be placed in the statement as a placeholder.

The menu system automatically formats the entry fields on the screen for you, placing up to 10 entry fields per dialog box. If an item has more than 10 GETx statements, more than one dialog box is presented to the user.

When the item is executed, the menu system gathers the user's input and stores it. GETx statements, where the user did not place at least one character in the entry field, will be discarded; of course, the only GETx statements that the user can leave blank are GETO statements. All nonblank GETx statements are then processed. The actual text that a GETx statement will produce consists of the *prepend_text*, the text entered by the user, and the *append_text*.

GETx statements may seem a little confusing at first, but after some practice you will find them to be a powerful tool.

> **NOTE**
>
> All GETx statements are processed first, and then the EXEC statements are executed. The menu system takes the user input from the GETx statements and the EXEC statements, builds a batch file, and then runs it.
>
> The output of one GETx statement *cannot* be used as the input for another or as the *prefill_text* field for another.

Building Your First Menu

Now that all the menu script commands and their syntax have been covered, you can begin to build a menu. At the end of this section, you will have a working and functional menu from which to build.

> **NOTE**
>
> The example that is given in this section is saved in a file named SIMPLE.SRC. You will find that file compressed into the file MNUSAMPL.ZIP included on the disk that accompanies this book.

First, name your main menu and assign it a number. For simplicity, the following example uses Main Menu as the title and 1 as the menu number. You may assign any menu number you want as the first menu, but remember that the first MENU statement in a menu script is always the main menu and the first one a user will see.

Next, add the items on the main menu. In the example, each item uses the SHOW command to display a submenu. The last item enables the user to exit to DOS using the EXEC EXIT command. The example shows the MENU line followed by the ITEMs that appear on Main Menu:

```
MENU 1,Main Menu
     ITEM Administrator Utilities...
          SHOW 10
     ITEM User Utilities...
          SHOW 20
     ITEM Printer Utilities...
          SHOW 30
     ITEM Diskette/Directory Utilities...
          SHOW 40
     ITEM Exit to DOS
          EXEC EXIT
```

The result of the preceding example is shown in Figure 18.1.

FIGURE 18.1.

The Main Menu screen.

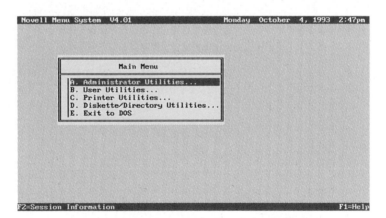

The indentation of the ITEMs and their commands is not required, but it does make the menu script much more readable. Also, using the ellipsis (...) after menu items that display another menu is a good idea. Users know that items with an ellipsis display a submenu, and items without it invoke an immediate action.

Next, use the previous example to define the Administrator Utilities menu and its items:

```
MENU 10,Administrator Utilities
     ITEM NetAdmin { BATCH }
          EXEC NETADMIN
     ITEM NetWare Audit Console { BATCH }
          EXEC AUDITCON
```

The screen shown in Figure 18.2 is generated by the previous lines of code.

FIGURE 18.2.

The Administrator Utilities screen.

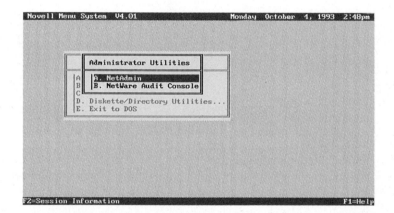

Both NETADMIN and AUDITCON in NetWare 4.x are large, memory-intensive applications, so the BATCH switch is specified for both of these items. This will cause the menu system to completely unload itself, leaving the maximum amount of free memory for these applications.

Next, define the User Utilities menu:

```
MENU 20,User Utilities
     ITEM NetUser { BATCH }
          EXEC NETUSER
     ITEM View Users Logged On { PAUSE }
          EXEC NLIST User /A
     ITEM View User Information { PAUSE }
          EXEC WHOAMI
     ITEM Send a Broadcast Message { PAUSE }
          GETR Message { "} 40,, {"}
          GETR To { TO } 00,, {}
          EXEC SEND
```

The screen shown in Figure 18.3 is generated by the preceding lines of code.

FIGURE 18.3.

The User Utilities screen.

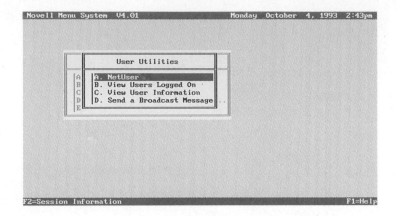

Note the use of the PAUSE switch on the last three items. The menu system pauses after each of these items has been executed and waits for a user keypress. This is useful because it keeps the screen from clearing immediately and going back into the menu system without enabling the user to view the information presented.

The last item makes use of the GETR command to prompt the user for the broadcast message and destination. Note the use of a space in the *prepend_text* parameter of the first GETR. Without this leading space, the quote character (") is placed directly after the SEND from the EXEC SEND statement, resulting in a DOS error when the item is executed.

If the menu item Send a Broadcast Message were selected in the preceding example, and the user were to type HELLO JOE in the Message entry field and JOE in the To entry field, the resulting command sent to DOS would be

```
SEND "HELLO JOE" TO JOE
```

The next menu to be defined is the Printer Utilities menu. Here are its commands:

```
MENU 30,Printer Utilities
    ITEM NetWare Print Console (PCONSOLE) { BATCH }
        EXEC PCONSOLE
    ITEM Printer Definition (PRINTDEF) { BATCH }
        EXEC PRINTDEF
    ITEM Configure Print Jobs (PRINTCON) { BATCH }
        EXEC PRINTCON
    ITEM Control a Remote Printer...
        SHOW 35
```

The screen shown in Figure 18.4 is generated by the preceding lines of code.

FIGURE 18.4.

*The Printer
Utilities screen.*

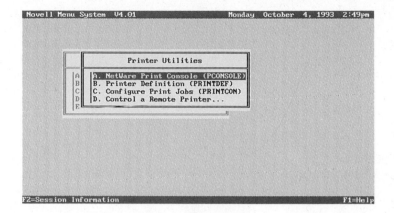

The BATCH switch is used for the first three items to give the applications extra memory. The last item displays a submenu dedicated to the Print Server Control (PSC) program, enabling the user to manipulate a remote printer. Here is the Control a Remote Printer menu:

```
MENU 35,Control a Remote Printer
    ITEM Get Status of a Remote Printer { BATCH PAUSE }
        GETP Print Server {PS=} 80,, {}
        GETP Printer Number {P=} 10,, {}
        EXEC PSC %1 %2 STAT
    ITEM Pause a Remote Printer { BATCH }
        GETP Print Server {PS=} 80,, {}
        GETP Printer Number {P=} 10,, {}
        EXEC PSC %1 %2 PAU
    ITEM Start a Remote Printer { BATCH }
        GETP Print Server {PS=} 80,, {}
        GETP Printer Number {P=} 10,, {}
        EXEC PSC %1 %2 STAR
    ITEM Stop a Remote Printer { BATCH }
        GETP Print Server {PS=} 80,, {}
        GETP Printer Number {P=} 10,, {}
        EXEC PSC %1 %2 STOP
    ITEM Abort a Remote Printer { BATCH }
        GETP Print Server {PS=} 80,, {}
        GETP Printer Number {P=} 10,, {}
        EXEC PSC %1 %2 AB
    ITEM Mark Top Of Form on a Remote Printer { BATCH }
        GETP Print Server {PS=} 80,, {}
        GETP Printer Number {P=} 10,, {}
        EXEC PSC %1 %2 MARK
    ITEM Mount a Form on a Remote Printer { BATCH }
        GETP Print Server {PS=} 80,, {}
```

```
     GETP Printer Number {P=} 10,, {}
     GETP Form Number {MO F=} 10,, {}
     EXEC PSC %1 %2 %3
ITEM Make a Remote Printer Private { BATCH }
     GETP Print Server {PS=} 80,, {}
     GETP Printer Number {P=} 10,, {}
     EXEC PSC %1 %2 PRI
ITEM Make a Remote Printer Shared { BATCH }
     GETP Print Server {PS=} 80,, {}
     GETP Printer Number {P=} 10,, {}
     EXEC PSC %1 %2 SHA
```

These lines generate the menu shown in Figure 18.5.

FIGURE 18.5.

The Control a Remote Printer menu.

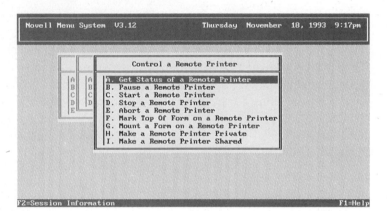

This menu utilizes all PSC parameters except one, the Down Print Server command. Each item prompts the user for the print server name and the printer number using the GETP statement, and passes the parameters, along with the PSC command for that remote printer, to the PSC program.

Last to be defined is the Diskette/Directory Utilities menu as follows:

```
MENU 40,Diskette/Directory Utilities
     ITEM Filer { BATCH }
          EXEC FILER
     ITEM Format a Diskette { SHOW PAUSE }
          GETR Select Drive to Format { } 1,A, {:}
          GETO Volume Label { /V:} 11,, {}
          GETO Other Options { } 30,, {}
          EXEC FORMAT
     ITEM Copy a Diskette { SHOW PAUSE }
          GETR Source Drive { } 1,A, {:}
          GETR Destination Drive { } 1,B, {:}
          EXEC DISKCOPY
```

The Format a Diskette item demonstrates how useful the GETO statement can be. Here, the user is required to specify the drive to format, but the volume label and other options are optional. If the user leaves the Volume Label entry field blank, the entire GETO statement will be ignored, including the /V: in the *prepend_text* parameter. The same is true for the Other Options entry field. This makes the GETO statement ideal for specifying optional parameters to a program. The Format a Diskette screen generated from the preceding lines is shown in Figure 18.6.

FIGURE 18.6.

The Format a Diskette option screen.

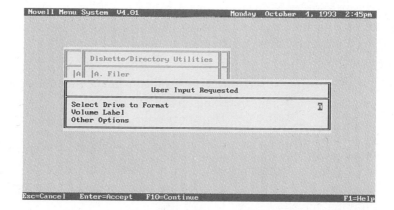

This menu provides a good starting point for building a working menu system for your users. The next section describes how to compile and execute menus. If you are upgrading from NetWare 3.11 or earlier and you have some of the old Novell menu files you would like to convert, see "Converting Your Novell Menu Definition File to a Saber Source File" at the end of this chapter.

Compiling and Running Menus

As mentioned previously, each menu consists of two files: the source file and the compiled menu file. Suppose you have typed in the previous menu script and saved it as MAINMENU.SRC. The NetWare menu compiler is called MENUMAKE, and it takes a single parameter: the name of the menu source file. To compile MAINMENU.SRC, type MENUMAKE MAINMENU.

> **NOTE** ▶
>
> MENUMAKE assumes the extension of the filename you give it to be .SRC. You may override this default by specifying the extension of the file, if necessary. If MENUMAKE detects no errors, it tells you that MAINMENU.DAT has been written. Otherwise, the errors are listed on-screen.

If your source file does contain errors, MENUMAKE displays an error message for each error it encounters. Each error message consists of the filename containing the error, the line number at which the error occurred, and a descriptive error message. At this point you should examine the source file, correct the errors, and run MENUMAKE again.

Once the menu has compiled successfully, you are now ready to run the menu. To run the menu system and bring up MAINMENU.DAT, type the following:

```
NMENU MAINMENU
```

Voilà! Your first menu is up and running. Keep in mind that if you haven't set the S_FILE and S_FILEDIR variables, the temporary files are being stored in the current directory. Follow the few simple steps in the next section to get your users up and running quickly.

Quick Setup Steps

Following is a summary of the steps for creating a menu system:

1. **Create the temporary directory**. Create a TEMP directory to house your working files. A good place to create it is in a subdirectory of the SYS:PUBLIC directory.

2. **Give users rights to the temporary directory**. Use SYSCON for 3.12 or NETADMIN (NWADMIN for Windows) for 4.x and grant the menu users Read, File Scan, Write, Create, Erase, and Modify rights to the temporary directory.

3. **Create and compile your menu scripts**. Create your main menu and compile it. Create a simple one at first. You can go back and add to it later. Be sure to add an item with the EXEC EXIT statement, or you won't be able to exit the menu system.

4. **Map a drive to the temporary directory**. Map a drive to the temporary directory in either the system or user login script. This drive should be the same for all users to make setting the environment variables simpler.

5. **Set the** S_FILE **and** S_FILEDIR **variables**. It is recommended to set these DOS variables in your system login script; however, if you prefer, it can be done in your AUTOEXEC.BAT or user login script.

6. **Execute the menu from the login script**. This step is optional, but it makes users more functional from the get-go. The simplest way to do this is to use the EXIT login script command followed by the statement in quotes to execute the menu:

```
EXIT "MENUEXE menu_name"
```

Converting Your Novell Menu Definition File to a Saber Source File

If you have previously used Novell's MENU.EXE runtime with a Menu Definition File (an ASCII file with an .MNU extension), you can convert that file to a new .SRC file. This is an extremely simple procedure.

1. Execute MENUCNVT.EXE to convert your old menu definition file. This creates a .SRC file. Here is an example for a menu definition file named SAMPLE.MNU:

```
MENUCNVT SAMPLE.MNU SAMPLE.SRC
```

2. Execute MENUMAKE.EXE to compile your source file into binary. Following the same example, here is the command you would use:

```
MENUMAKE SAMPLE.SRC
```

3. Execute your menu with the following command for this example:

```
MENUEXE SAMPLE
```

NOTE ▶

Your menu will work just as it did with the previous menu system, but in order to execute an application with 0K overhead you need to add the {BATCH} switch as discussed previously.

If you would like to use the added functionality of GETR and GETP statements, you will need to add a few GETx statements.

Printing Services

19

by Rick Sant'Angelo

NetWare printing services provide robust printing capabilities that are very flexible. The NetWare printing environment is made up of the following components:

- Queues
- Command-line utilities
- Menu utilities
- Print servers
- Remote printers

Starting at the user workstation, a print job follows a path from the user's software output to the network printer (with perhaps a few passing points on the way). This chapter discusses that printing path, including

- A brief overview of printing
- Setting up the Print Server utility
- Using and controlling output
- Creating print job configurations
- Using third-party utilities and devices

A Brief Overview of Printing

Every print job must be redirected to a NetWare *queue*. A queue is a file where the print job is staged, to be subsequently dispatched to a network printer, as shown in Figure 19.1.

Print Redirection and Spooling to a Queue

This process is accomplished through the NetWare CAPTURE command-line utility. CAPTURE redirects print output, that was sent to a parallel port, to a queue. Alternatively, an application can redirect print output by using NetWare APIs, which accomplishes the same result as a CAPTURE command. Whichever method is used, the workstation shell monitors memory, intercepting and redirecting the print output to the NIC, and then across the LAN where a file server spools the printing to a binary file. The CAPTURE command is usually automated in a login script, or it can be issued in a menu or batch file when the application is executed.

FIGURE 19.1.

*Redirection to
a queue.*

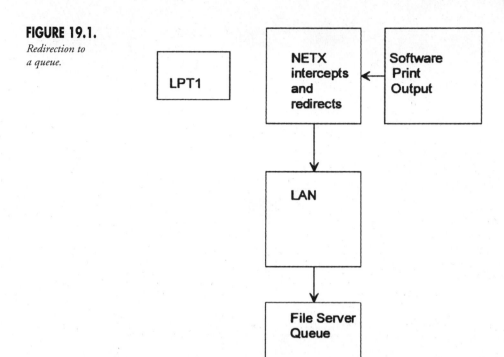

Spooling Output to a Network Printer

After the print job is redirected to a queue, the NetWare Print Server utility takes over to direct the print job as configured in the PCONSOLE menu utility. In PCONSOLE, the system administrator creates a print server, selects printer configurations, and configures the connection between the queues and the network printers. Once the print server software is loaded on a file server or a stand-alone print server, the print server polls the queues (every 15 seconds) that are waiting for print jobs to arrive so it can send them to their final destination, as shown in Figure 19.2.

FIGURE 19.2.

*Print server
spooling print
output to a network
printer.*

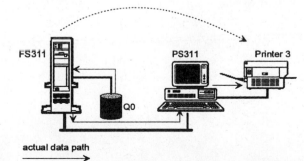

If the network printer is a *remote printer*, that is, one connected to a workstation and designated as a network printer, the print job takes another trip to the remote printer, as shown in Figure 19.3. The client software that receives the print job and utilizes the parallel port on the workstation is RPRINTER (NPRINTER for version 4.x).

FIGURE 19.3.

Spooling output to a remote printer.

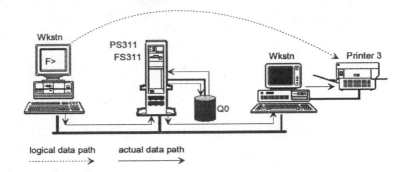

The mechanics of every print job are the same. There is no way to circumvent this process except to print to a local printer thus bypassing all network printing.

Setting Up the NetWare Print Server Utility

During installation, no printer or print server configurations were created for you, and no printing services exist until you create them with the following procedure. You must set up and then load the NetWare Print Server. This utility consists of the following:

PSERVER.NLM   On a 3.x/4.x server, PSERVER.NLM is loaded from the console. Loading can be automated within the AUTOEXEC.NCF. The file server also doubles as a print server.

PSERVER.EXE   As an executable file, this application makes a DOS workstation a dedicated print server and cannot be used as a workstation. (This is not available with 4.x).

RPRINTER (3.x)	This TSR is executed at a workstation that will share its printer on the network as a remote printer. It is the client of PSERVER. When RPRINTER is executed (and the print server and printer number is specified), it accepts print output from a PSERVER.
NPRINTER (4.x)	NPRINTER is the 4.x equivalent utility of RPRINTER. It also must be loaded as an NLM when file server printer ports are to be used. It is loaded as an .EXE file when a print server port or remote printer is used on a workstation.
PCONSOLE	This menu utility is where the print server, network printers, and their configurations are created.
PSC	This utility is used to control printers. It can check the status of printers, stop or start them, and specify a form that is loaded in the printer (among other functions).

NETWARE 4 NOTE

If you have a very simple printing setup, you can save time and effort in setting up your printers with 4.x by executing the PSETUP utility. Log in as Admin and execute PSETUP.EXE.

PCONSOLE has a Quick Setup option that you can select to set up one printer, one print server, and one queue.

Create Queues

First, execute PCONSOLE. You will see the Available Options menu, as shown in Figure 19.4.

In order to separate print traffic intended for different printers, a separate queue is created for each printer. Although multiple queues can be directed to a single printer and a single queue can be directed to multiple printers, NetWare normally sets up printing by creating a queue, which is equivalent to a printer. Although the other options can enable additional functionality, you should create one queue for each network printer.

To create queues, select Print Queue Information from your PCONSOLE Available Options menu. Then, press Insert and specify a queue name.

FIGURE 19.4.

*PCONSOLE
available options.*

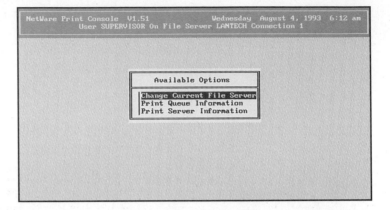

```
NetWare Print Console  V1.51                Wednesday  August 4, 1993  6:12 am
                User SUPERVISOR On File Server LANTECH Connection 1



                        ┌────── Available Options ──────┐
                        │Change Current File Server     │
                        │Print Queue Information         │
                        │Print Server Information        │
                        └───────────────────────────────┘
```

> **TIP** ▶
>
> Queue names should be short, because they will be used in capture com-
> mands. A queue name also should be unique from that of other objects.
> Queue names should not be the same as a server, user, group, or any other
> NetWare object. The queue should not be named after a printer, because the
> printer also will have a name. Keep in mind that the queue is only indirectly
> related to the printer; it is not equivalent to the printer itself.

Once you have created a queue for each printer, press Esc until you reach the Available Options menu.

Create the Print Server

Your next step is to create a print server. This is done in much the same manner as
creating a queue. From the Available Options menu, select Print Server Information.
You can press Insert and enter the name of the print server.

> **TIP** ▶
>
> Print server names should be short, because they will need to be typed at
> times. A print server name also should be unique from other objects. They
> should not be the same as a server, user, group, or any other NetWare object.

Create and Configure Network Printers

Once you have created the print server, select it from the list of print servers. Then select Print Server Configuration and Printer Configuration. You will see a list of printers, each marked Not Installed. Select a printer number from the list, and you will see the screen shown in Figure 19.5.

FIGURE 19.5.

The Printer Configuration screen.

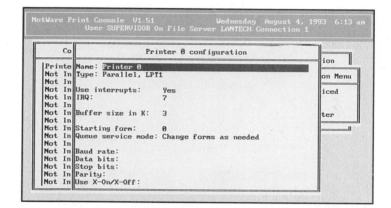

You may enter configuration information for the network printer that corresponds to this printer selection. The fields you see have the following significance:

Name. You may specify the name of the printer or leave the printer named with the default value of "Printer 0," "Printer 1," and so on.

Type. When you press Enter, you will see a list of printer types, as shown in Figure 19.6.

FIGURE 19.6.

List of printer types.

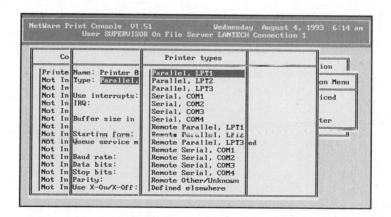

Select the type of printer. If the printer is connected directly to the print server, you should select Parallel LPT1 or one of the first seven selections corresponding to which parallel or serial port the printer will be connected.

If a printer is to be a remote printer connected to a workstation printer port, select Remote Parallel LPT1 or the appropriate remote printer port to be used.

> **NOTE** ▶
>
> Don't select Remote Other/Unknown or Defined Elsewhere unless you are using a third-party printing utility or device, and the instructions specifically say to select one of these options.

Use Interrupts. You always should use interrupts and specify the appropriate printer-port interrupt in use.

> **NOTE** ▶
>
> When a printer is connected to a server and the wrong interrupt or no interrupt is selected, you may experience several types of printing problems. You should answer No to the query Use Interrupts if you are unable to make your printer work any other way.

The proper physical configuration of interrupts is the key to sending data through the server bus without conflict, and the configuration option must be correctly addressed for the printers to work efficiently (or even to work at all).

> **TIP** ▶
>
> Make certain you do not have any conflicting physical interrupt settings between printer ports and other devices in your server. Novell has fixed PSERVER.NLM, so conflicting interrupts should not crash the file server; however, they can. If not, you will experience very slow printing and other printing problems until the interrupt conflict is resolved.

IRQ. Specify the physical interrupt setting on this printer port.

Starting Form. Forms may be designated for various types of paper. Forms are configured in the PRINTDEF utility and are discussed later in this chapter. If you have not set up forms in PRINTDEF, do not edit this option. When forms are subsequently created, it will automatically select the default form.

Queue Service Mode. When multiple forms are serviced in a queue, this option selects the basis on which messages are sent that indicate a forms change is required. You may select this option to see a submenu.

Configuration Information for Serial Printers. See the following configuration:

baud rate	(bits-per-second communication rate)
data bits	(7 or 8 bits)
stop bits	(1 or 0)
parity	(even, odd, or none)
use X-on/X-off	yes or no

NOTE ▶

Always physically set serial printers the way their instructions indicate, and then select the configuration options to conform to those physical settings.

Many serial printers have switch settings or menu selections for their physical settings. If you set the printer to conform to the default configuration in PCONSOLE, you may have serious problems making the printer work right.

If you encounter problems making a serial printer work, first set it up and make it work under DOS, then re-create your MODE configuration in these menu options.

Once you have created each printer, press Esc twice to return to the Print Server Configuration Menu.

NOTE ▶

If you press Enter from a configuration screen, your configuration will be saved. If you press Esc before saving, the configuration changes will be abandoned. After making a change, select the option again and check to see whether your changes were saved.

Direct Queues to Network Printers

After you have created and configured the printers, you must tell the print server which queues should spool to which printers. From the Print Server Configuration Menu, select Queues Serviced by Printer. You will see a list of printers. Select a printer and press Insert to see a list of queues. Select a queue. You will be prompted to input the priority level. Priorities can be assigned if more than one queue is directed to the same printer. If you accept the default, print jobs sent to that queue will be forwarded to the printer you have just configured.

Load PSERVER

You can load PSERVER.NLM on a file server. When this option is selected, printers configured for Parallel LPT1 will be sent to the server's LPT1 port. To load the PSERVER NLM from the console prompt, type

```
LOAD PSERVER print_server_name
```

TIP ►

If you have v 3.11, obtain the latest Print Server utility files from Novell. Your distribution diskettes contain an older version of PSERVER and RPRINTER that are known to have bugs. You can download the latest files from NetWire's NOVLIB forum. The most recent file is named PSERVx.ZIP. x is a number that increments upward every time a new release is put out.

NOTE ►

PSERVER.NLM should load properly. If the next screen requests a password and no password has been assigned in PCONSOLE, you have not entered a valid print server name.

Loading PSERVER.EXE

You may designate a DOS or OS/2 workstation as a print server by loading PSERVER.EXE at a workstation. A DOS workstation becomes a dedicated print server if you do so.

> **NOTE ▶**
>
> Before loading PSERVER.EXE, you need to alter your NET.CFG (or SHELL.CFG) file to configure the workstation for more SPX connections. You must include the following line in your NET.CFG, or your print server will fail to load:
>
> ```
> SPX CONNECTIONS = 60
> ```

Load RPRINTER (for NetWare 3.11)

To bring a remote printer online, you need to load RPRINTER as a TSR at the workstation to which the network printer is connected. You may designate one or more printer ports on a DOS or OS/2 workstation by executing the RPRINTER software, with switches indicating which print server and printer number this copy of RPRINTER is using.

> **NOTE ▶**
>
> Before loading RPRINTER.EXE, you need to alter your NET.CFG (or SHELL.CFG) file to configure the workstation for more SPX connections. You must include the following line in your NET.CFG, or you will encounter errors at the remote printer workstation:
>
> ```
> SPX CONNECTIONS = 50
> ```

Enter the command as follows:

```
RPRINTER Print_server_name Printer_number
```

If you have changed the default printer number to a printer name, you can enter the name instead. Your remote printer is now capable of accepting output from the print server.

Load NPRINTER (for NetWare 4.x)

To bring a remote printer (called a *network printer* in your 4.x documentation) online with NetWare 4.x versions, you need to load NPRINTER as a TSR at the workstation to which the network printer is connected. You may designate one or more printer ports on a DOS or OS/2 workstation by executing the NPRINTER software with switches indicating which print server and printer number this copy of NPRINTER is using.

> **NOTE** ▶
>
> Before loading NPRINTER.EXE, you need to alter your NET.CFG (or SHELL.CFG) file to configure the workstation for more SPX connections. You must include the following line in your NET.CFG, or you will encounter errors at the remote printer workstation:
>
> ```
> SPX CONNECTIONS = 50
> ```

Enter the command as follows:

```
NPRINTER Print_server_name Printer_name
```

You do not need to specify the print server name if only one print server exists on the network. Your remote printer is now able to accept output from the print server.

To use one or more 4.x server's ports as network printers when a PSERVER is located elsewhere on the network, load NPRINTER.NLM on the server. This is not necessary when PSERVER.NLM is loaded on the file server, because PSERVER.NLM autoloads NPRINTER.NLM.

Your print services are now installed, and you may CAPTURE output to a queue for printing to a print server's client printer.

Using and Controlling Output

Once your printers are properly set up and working, you need to know how to manage print output. There are four NetWare printing commands that need to be used:

```
CAPTURE
ENDCAP
NPRINT
PSC
```

Capturing Print Output

Print jobs must be redirected to a NetWare queue, as previously discussed. Any time the CAPTURE command is executed at a DOS prompt, print output is redirected. A CAPTURE statement must at least designate which local printer port will be captured and to which queue the print output will be directed. For example, to simply redirect output intended for LPT1 to a queue named "Q0," type the following command:

```
CAPTURE L=1 Q=Q0
```

If no switches are specified, LPT1 print output will be spooled to the default queue (if one exists). Several switches can be added to manage options (see the following sections). You can type the entire switch or just the portion that is underlined and capitalized.

The following switches are used with the Capture command.

SHow

This option shows current CAPTURE status of LPT ports. This option cannot be used with other Capture options.

AUtoendcap

This option enables data to be sent to a network printer or a network file when you exit or enter an application. Autoendcap does not end the capture. "Autoendcap enabled" is the default setting.

Timeout=n (default = timeout disabled)

NoAUtoendcap

This option prevents data from being sent to a network printer or a network file when you enter or exit an application.

TImeout=n (default = timeout disabled)

This option defines the wait period before the print spool file is closed. The delay n is entered in seconds from 0 to 1000. A timeout interval is used to keep a print job active when pauses occur in the application's output. The timeout interval needs to be sufficient to bridge any gaps in print output.

> **TIP** ▶
>
> Always set your timeout interval to at least 5 seconds (TI=5).
>
> A print job cannot be accepted by the print server for output until the spool file closes, indicating that the print job is finished. In some cases, a pause may occur during a print job, which may result in a form feed or two print jobs getting mixed together.

> **TIP** ▶
>
> You may experience a long delay before print jobs start, or they may seem to get "stuck" and then begin to print some time later.
>
> Because CAPTURE defaults to "timeout disabled," your print job will not start to print if your spool file does not close.
>
> If you experience this problem, set a timeout interval to force the file to close at the end of the specified interval.

Local=n (default = 1)

This option defines the LPT port (1, 2, or 3) output to be captured.

Server=server_name

This option indicates to which file server the data should be sent for printing. The default is your current server.

Job=job

This option specifies the name of the print job configuration to be used. Print job configurations are defined in the PRINTCON menu utility.

Queue=queue_name

This option indicates the queue name for this print job.

Form=form_name

This option specifies the form that is required for this print job to print. The PRINTDEF menu utility is used by the supervisor to define forms on the file server.

Copies=n (default n=1)

This option specifies the number of copies requested for this print job, from 1-256.

Tabs=n (default = 8 spaces)

This option replaces all tab characters in the print job with the number of spaces specified (0-18). This is required only if the application program does not have a print formatter.

NoTabs

This option forwards all tab characters in your print job to the network printer unchanged.

> **TIP** ▶
>
> If you are experiencing garbage characters in your print jobs or a failure to interpret fonts or graphics properly, try using the No Tabs switch in your CAPTURE command.

NAMe=name (default=user login name)

This option specifies the name to be printed in the upper half of your banner page (*name*).

Banner=banner_name (default = LST)

This option specifies the banner name (up to 12 characters) you want to appear in the lower half of the banner page. An underscore will print as a space.

NoBanner

This option suppresses the banner page.

FormFeed (default)

This option causes the printer to eject the page at the end of the print job.

NoFormFeed

This option suppresses the form feed at the end of the print job. If your software ejects the page at the end of the print job, this switch suppresses the extra page that is ejected at the end of each print job.

CReate=pathname/filespec

This option prints to a file in ASCII format instead of to a network printer. The filespec is the filename that will be created.

KEEP

This option saves your print job in a queue if it is interrupted for any reason (for example, if a workstation hangs). This option should be used when print jobs have pauses longer than can be regulated by the timeout interval (1000 seconds).

> **TIP** ▶
>
> When a CAPTURE command is issued for a parallel port, the KEEP command overrides previous options.

ENDCAP (default L=1)

This command ends the capture of one or more of your workstation's LPT ports. Switches and options used with ENDCAP are as follows.

Local=n (default is 1)

This option ends the capture of the specified port, *n* (1, 2, or 3 for LPT1, LPT2, or LPT3.)

ALL

This option ends capture of all LPT ports, but enables the data already scheduled to be printed to complete.

Cancel

This option ends the capture of LPT1 and discards the data prior to printing.

CnclLocal=n (default = 1)

This option ends the capture of the specified LPT port and discards the data prior to printing.

Cancel ALL

This option ends the capture of all LPT ports and discards the data prior to printing.

NPRINT

This utility prints the contents of an ASCII file to a network printer. Option switches employed with this utility are the same as the CAPTURE utility, with just a few exceptions.

PSC Command-Line Utility (Print Server Command)

PSC is used to control print servers and their printers. When using this command, you must specify the print server and printer number that you would like to affect.

The syntax is as follows:

```
PSC [PS=print_server] [P=printer_number] switch
```

The following sections are the switches.

STATus

This option gives the status of the network printer. Status messages are

> Waiting for job
> Mark/Form feed
> Mount form n
> Not connected
> Printing job
> Not installed
> Paused
> In private mode
> Ready to go down
> Off line
> Stopped
> Out of paper

FormFeed

This option ejects a page.

PAUse

This option stops printing and is reversed with the STARt command.

MOunt form=n

This option tells the print server that form number n is installed. Print jobs in the queue that need form n can then print.

ABort

This option kills the job currently printing.

STOp [Keep]

This option stops the current print job and deletes it from the queue. The Keep switch does not delete the job from the queue; instead it restarts the print job from the beginning when the PSC STARt command is issued.

STARt

This option restarts the printer after a stop or pause.

PRIvate

This option temporarily suspends network printing and enables use of the local parallel port.

SHared

This option resumes network printing.

CancelDown

This option halts a down command issued from PCONSOLE.

Mark [character]

This option marks top of form.

> **NOTE** ▶
>
> To down a print server, the user must be the Supervisor or a Print Server Operator. To down a print server, access PCONSOLE, select Print Server, and then select Print Server Status. (This option appears only if a print server is running.)

This is the only place in NetWare where a supervisor equivalent cannot automatically do the same as Supervisor. SE cannot down or otherwise manage a print server unless first made a print server operator. Fortunately, an SE has the power to make him or herself a PSO and thus easily correct the problem.

RPRINTER

This utility can be loaded into memory to share a local printer as a network printer, and it can be removed from memory, returning the printer to local print. To load it, type

```
RPRINTER print_server printer_number
```

To unload it, type

```
RPRINTER print_server printer_number -r
```

Alternatively, a shared printer can be toggled between PRIvate and SHared using the PSC command.

Using PCONSOLE to Manage Queues and Print Servers

You can manage queues, manage print jobs while they are in the queues, and monitor print servers with PCONSOLE for NetWare 3.11. Several functions are available, two of which are discussed on the following pages:

    Managing print jobs in the queues
    Managing print servers

Managing Print Jobs in the Queues

To manage jobs that are queued up for printing, enter PCONSOLE. Then select Print Queue Information, the queue to manage, and Current Print Job Entries. You will see a screen with print jobs stacked for printing, as shown in Figure 19.7.

FIGURE 19.7.

Print queue list.

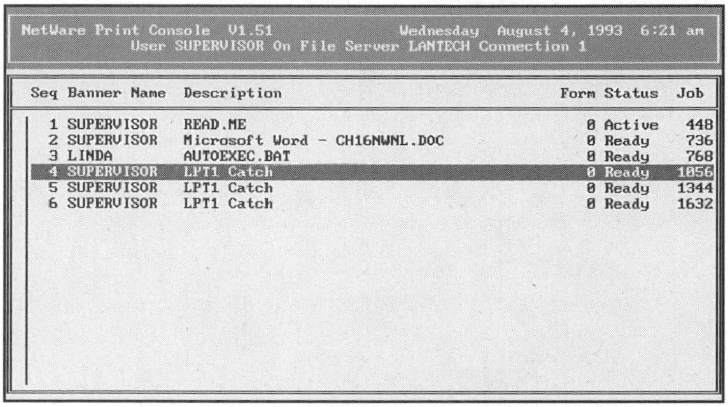

```
NetWare Print Console  V1.51            Wednesday  August 4, 1993  6:21 am
                    User SUPERVISOR On File Server LANTECH Connection 1


  Seq Banner Name  Description                        Form Status  Job

    1 SUPERVISOR   READ.ME                              0 Active   448
    2 SUPERVISOR   Microsoft Word - CH16NWNL.DOC        0 Ready    736
    3 LINDA        AUTOEXEC.BAT                         0 Ready    768
    4 SUPERVISOR   LPT1 Catch                           0 Ready   1056
    5 SUPERVISOR   LPT1 Catch                           0 Ready   1344
    6 SUPERVISOR   LPT1 Catch                           0 Ready   1632
```

You can delete a job from the queue, even the current job. If you select a job, you will see the Print Queue Entry Information screen, as shown in Figure 19.8.

FIGURE 19.8.

Print Queue entry information.

```
NetWare Print Console  V1.51            Wednesday  August 4, 1993  6:21 am
                    User SUPERVISOR On File Server LANTECH Connection 1


                    Print Queue Entry Information

  Print job:        1056           File size:       30135
  Client:           RICK[1]
  Description:      LPT1 Catch
  Status:           Ready To Be Serviced, Waiting For Print Server

  User Hold:        No             Job Entry Date:  August 4, 1993
  Operator Hold:    No             Job Entry Time:  6:19:48 am
  Service Sequence: 4

  Number of copies: 1              Form:            def
  File contents:    Byte stream    Print banner:    No
  Tab size:                        Name:
  Suppress form feed: Yes          Banner name:
  Notify when done:  No
                                   Defer printing:  No
  Target server:    (Any Server)   Target date:
                                   Target time:
```

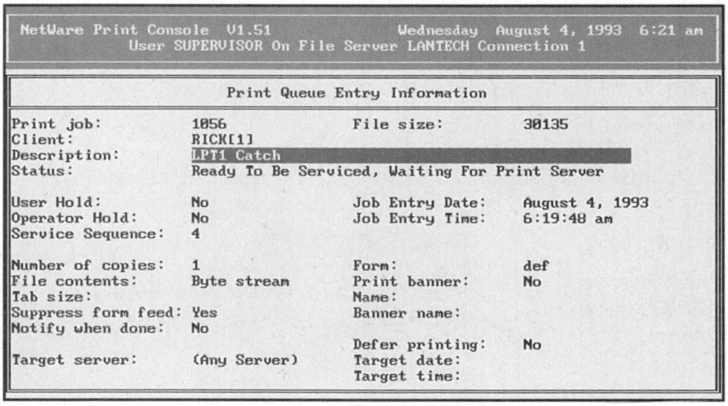

Any field that has a cursor can be edited. You can perform tasks such as moving jobs ahead of other jobs, putting a hold on a job, changing the print output from text to byte stream, and so on.

> **NOTE** ▶
>
> You can only delete, hold, or move print jobs ahead of other print jobs if you are a Print Queue Operator (the Supervisor is the default Print Queue Operator).

To assign a user or group as a Print Queue Operator, select the option from the Print Queue Information menu that appears after a queue is selected.

TIP ▶

You can delete any job, even the active one, from here. However, deleting the active job from the print queue's current entries screen can hang the print server. To properly delete the active print job, use PSC, or delete the job through the print server status and control screen.

Managing Print Servers

You can manage a print server from PCONSOLE's Print Server Information submenu options. Execute PCONSOLE, select Print Server Information, and then select the print server you would like to manage. You will see the Print Server Information submenu, as shown in Figure 19.9.

To adjust this option, you must be a system administrator.

FIGURE 19.9.

The Print Server Information submenu.

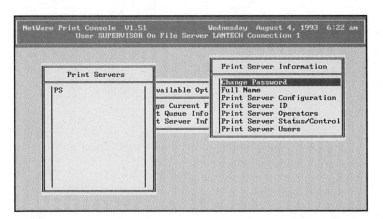

Assigning a Print Server Operator

To manage your print server, you need to be a Print Server Operator. By default, only a Supervisor or equivalent is assigned as such. You can assign a Print Server Operator from the Print Server Operators menu selections, shown in Figure 19.9.

Checking Status and Downing a Print Server

To check the status of a print server, or to down it, select Print Server Status/Control from the Print Server Information submenu. You will see the Print Server Status and Control submenu, shown in Figure 19.10.

Select the Server Info option to check the current status of the print server or to down it. All the selections are menu-driven and simple to follow. Several other functions are contained in these submenus. Spend a little time becoming familiar with this submenu system.

FIGURE 19.10.

Print Server Status and Control submenu.

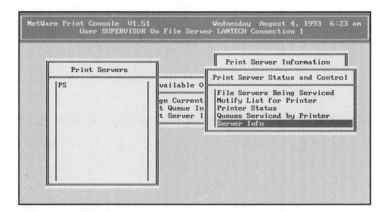

Creating Print Job Configurations

Print job configurations automate capture options plus additional printer features. At least one default configuration should be set up that will clear all print codes out of the printer's memory and eliminate the need to type all the switches with the CAPTURE command. Once you create a default configuration, the command CAPTURE will include the default configuration options.

Print job configurations are created using both PRINTCON and PRINTDEF menu utilities, but you must define print devices in the PRINTDEF utility before you can create print job configurations. This section guides you through the task of creating print job configurations. You will wonder how you ever got along without them.

Define Print Devices and Options in PRINTDEF

PRINTDEF is used to

- Define *printer drivers* for specific models of printers that activate the printer features, including *printer modes*, which identify the features to be used, and *functions*, which are the ASCII escape sequences executed to activate the modes

- Define *forms*, which identify different paper types and enable the print jobs to be held until the appropriate form is mounted

You can further define any functions (and therefore modes) of which your printer is capable. You also can combine modes to make your printer perform any combination of modes.

To execute the procedure for adding print devices, the user must have Supervisor or Print Server Operator privileges. Type PRINTDEF at a DOS prompt, and the menu shown in Figure 19.11 will appear.

FIGURE 19.11.

PrintDef Options menu.

```
Printer Definition Utility  V1.51            Tuesday  August 3, 1993  2:04 pm
                        User RICK On File Server LANTECH


                              PrintDef Options
                             ┌──────────────────┐
                             │ Print Devices    │
                             │ Forms            │
                             └──────────────────┘
```

From this menu, select Print Devices and Import Print Device. You will see the Defined Printer Device list, as shown in Figure 19.12. Press Insert to view the available Printer Definition Files (PDFs). You will find your PDFs in the SYS:PUBLIC directory.

NOTE ▶

You will not be able to access the Print Device Options menu unless you are Supervisor or equivalent.

FIGURE 19.12.
*Defined Print
Device list.*

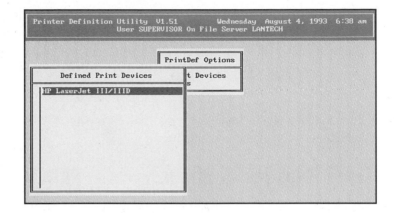

When you have selected the appropriate device, you will return to the Print Device
Options menu. Look at Edit Print Devices to see a list of installed PDFs.

Define Additional Printer Functions (Optional)

From the Print Device menu selection, select Edit Print Devices, and then select a
printer from the list of Edit Print Devices. You will see Edit Device Options menu
with two options:

1. Modes   Names assigned to represent the functions that are activates
   (such as condensed and letter quality)
2. Functions   Functions can be defined (in ASCII sequence) that are not
   listed

You can select modes from a preprogrammed list to activate many options that your
printer can perform.

Create Forms

You can create, delete, or modify unique forms (types of paper) from PRINTDEF.
Select Forms from the PrintDef Options menu, and then define the forms. They
must be numbered, and form number 0 is the default form that is used unless otherwise specified.

When a form other than the default form is specified in the CAPTURE command or in
a print job configuration, the print job will be held in the queue or handled as specified in PCONSOLE's Print Server Status/Control options. Normally, the forms will

need to be physically mounted in the printer, and then a Print Server Operator must issue the PSC command with the MO switch, specifying which form is to be mounted, as follows:

PSC PS=*print_server_name* P=*printer_name* MO *form_number*

Forms are used to control the flow of print jobs intended for different paper types. This is the best way of handling paper changes in your printer, and forms changes can be part of a print job configuration.

Setup Print Job Configurations in PRINTCON

Now that the ground work has been done, you can set up your print job configurations in PRINTCON. This menu utility sets up a database of configurations that can be invoked from the CAPTURE and NPRINT command-line utilities, from within PCONSOLE or any other utility that will enable a print job to be sent. Forms, devices, and modes are selected that were previously set up in PRINTDEF.

To create your print job configurations, execute PRINTCON and select Edit Print Job Configuration. When you press Insert, you will see the screen shown in Figure 19.13.

FIGURE 19.13.

PRINTCON Print Job Configuration creation.

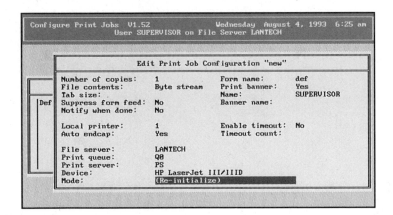

The selections are obvious; you can select most of the options that would normally be switches with the CAPTURE command. You also can select items that cannot be activated with capture switches which can be quite helpful. In addition to capture options, you can select

Byte stream versus text output

Notification to the print job owner when the job is done

Any of the printer modes configured in PRINTDEF

Once the Print Job Configuration is saved and you exit PRINTCON (saving the configurations), you can execute a capture, specifying the print job configuration to be used. The following command selects a configuration:

```
CAPTURE J=print_job_configuration_name
```

If the CAPTURE command is issued with no switches, the default print job configuration applies. The first configuration to be created becomes the default. The default configuration can be changed from the Available Topics Menu.

> **TIP** ►
>
> You should use a simple default print job configuration that reinitializes your printer.
>
> Many applications do not clear formatting out of your printer (such as compressed print), so other users have their print job formatted according to the codes left in the printer from the last print job.

The PRINTCON database, PRINTCON.DAT, is stored in the user's MAIL directory (which can be located by selecting Other Information from the User Information selection within SYSCON). To delete the configuration database, delete this file from the user's MAIL directory.

Print job configurations apply only to the user who created them, unless they are copied to other users. If you have logged in as Supervisor or equivalent, you will have a third menu selection, which enables this option.

> **TIP** ►
>
> If you have dozens of users, you can streamline the process of copying configuration files by copying the PRINTCON.DAT file using DOS COPY, NetWare's NCOPY, or your favorite file management utility.
>
> Unless you are logged in as Supervisor or equivalent, you do not have sufficient trustee rights to copy files to other users' MAIL directories.

To print from within PRINTCON, select a queue from the Print Queue Information Menu and then press Insert. The user will be prompted to select or type in a directory path and filename to print. A menu will appear with the print job configuration selections.

Using Third-Party Print Servers and Utilities

Several third-party products enhance NetWare printing services. They fall into one of three categories:

- Third-party print server software
- Printer NICs
- Stand-alone print server devices

Each software and device has its own features and selling points. These products continually evolve, providing more options for less money. Information for products that are mentioned in this sections may be outdated by the time you read this book.

Third-Party Print Server Software

A few third-party software developers built print server software before Novell did. Some of their products perform better, have simpler menu systems and TSR menus, or provide better support for unique print job configurations. For example, if you have PostScript printers, you may be disappointed with the rudimentary features supported by NetWare's Print Server utility. If you have a PostScript cartridge in an HP LaserJet, you can switch back and forth between PostScript and PCL modes, which is not supported by NetWare but is supported by other vendors.

A few utilities that you may want to investigate are listed in Table 19.1. Their top features are listed along with them.

Table 19.1. Third-party print server software packages.

Product	Developer	Outstanding Features
LANSpool	Intel	Windows-based utilities TSR DOS menus
Printer Assist	Fresh Technology Group	Windows-based utilities More PostScript support
PS Print	Brightworks	Windows-based utilities More PostScript support
Mosaic	Insight Development Resource Accounting	Enterprise printer management Expanded font downloading More PostScript support

Printer NICs

Several fine board products are made that plug into the I/O Port of HP LaserJet printers. Some of these can function as a remote printer, and others can be configured as a print server, eliminating the superfluous step of spooling through the print server in the printing process. The board interfaces the LaserJet directly to a cabling segment of your LAN. Products are available in Ethernet (BNC, AUI, and 10BASE-T) and Token Ring varieties.

Normally, print jobs are paced by the output device port. A printer NIC reduces the parallel or serial port bottleneck. Some printers, such as the HP IIIsi and HP 4 LaserJets have Modular I/O ports that can accept print output at full LAN throughput speeds. The HP products (see following list) come with their own software for setup, configuration, and management.

The following list includes a few products that are available:

> *Network Printer Interface Card*, Hewlett-Packard, for LJ I, II, III, and personal LaserJets
> *JetDirect*, Hewlett-Packard, for IIIsi and HP 4 LaserJets
> *JetPress*, Castelle
> *PacificPage*, Pacific Data

Stand-Alone Print Server Devices

Several products have been developed that incorporate a LAN interface with a complete print server on a ROM (or flash RAM) chip with one to four printer ports. The first product developed like this was the Microtest *NETport*, which has been acquired and further developed by Intel. This product has two parallel ports, hooks up to a LAN cabling segment, and can be configured as a remote printer or as a print server. It comes with its own configuration and management software and comes in Ethernet (BNC, AUI, and 10BASE-T) and Token Ring models.

Several products feature parallel port throughput that is several times faster than traditional parallel ports. Another feature that is helpful is support for both NetWare and TCP/IP printing where the network environment is integrated. You should check each product carefully to find features that meet your needs now and in the future. The products listed in Table 19.2 are well established.

Table 19.2. Print server device listing.

Product	Developer	# ports	LAN options
NetPort II	Intel	2	Ethernet AUI, BNC, or 10BASE-T Token Ring
LAN Press	Castelle	4	Ethernet AUI, BNC, or 10BASE-T, Token Ring
Pocket Print Server	Xircom	1	Ethernet AUI, BNC, or 10BASE-T, Token Ring Plugs into printer parallel port
JetLAN	ASP Computer	1	Ethernet AUI, BNC, or 10BASE-T, Token Ring
Products	NETSprint		Digital Products, Inc.

Summary

An integrator or system administrator who deals with NetWare is pressed to use all the material that was covered in this section. Chapter 35, "Printing Performance," goes into more detail about print performance and optimization.

Third-Party System Administration Utilities

by Rick Sant' Angelo

IN THIS CHAPTER

20

Managing a network is a big job, and as PC networks have evolved into multivendor systems that are integrated in-house, the complexity of managing a network has been magnified. Since networking products have evolved on a component-oriented basis, administrators have often managed by crisis, responding to problems as they occur.

Organizations demand that their systems be reliable. Management by crisis is no longer acceptable in most situations. What can be done to improve reliability and more effectively manage network systems? The answer lies in a new breed of products, designed to detect problems before they disable your network. These products can move an administrator from reactionary mode to a pro-active mode, finding problems in their early stages and giving positive diagnostic indications when disabilities do occur.

Though Novell developed MONITOR.NLM as part of the version 3.x and 4.x operating systems, far more can be done to monitor a file server's activity. However, management of other layers of the network has been notoriously haphazard. Now some third-party developers have stepped in to fill the gap.

Several fine tools have been developed to assist administrators in managing NetWare. The chapter discusses the following types of products:

- System administration aids
- File server monitoring tools
- Centralized workstation management tools
- Metering applications
- Security and anti-virus protection tools

Toward the end of the chapter, the following utilities are discussed:

> *Frye Utilities for Networks,* Frye Computer Systems, Inc.
> *Intel LANDesk Manager,* Intel Corp.
> *Saber LAN Workstation,* Saber Software Corp.
> *Xtree Tools for Networks,* Xtree Company
> Various products from Brightworks, Inc.
> *Bindview NCS,* LAN Support Group
> Shareware, copyrighted, and public-domain packages

This chapter omits any discussion of one very important part of managing your network: managing and monitoring the LAN itself. LAN management and monitoring is an issue of such magnitude that an entire section, Part IV of this book, is devoted to addressing it in greater detail.

> **NOTE** ►
>
> Because NetWare 4.x is relatively new, software developers have not yet introduced many packages supporting version 4.x. Watch your favorite LAN periodical for reviews of new product introductions.

System Administration Aids

Though NetWare's menu and command-line utilities can accomplish almost everything you need to do with NetWare, some third-party packages improve upon the existing user interface and provide extended functionality. For example, it would be nice to have more information about a user account available at the time you are assigning user trustee assignments. Some utilities combine more information into a user configuration screen to assist you.

NetWare 3.11's direct trustee assignments, indirect trustee assignments, and inherited rights mask complicate the issue of who has what rights and where. No NetWare utility gives you a listing of what users have rights in each directory. Actually, Novell has almost totally ignored the report-output requirement. This is information every secure environment should have readily available. Some products produce reports on such matters so you can check for "hackers" who gain access with Supervisory privileges, or to control the inadvertent assignment of rights the user should not have. Other packages have free-form report-writing capabilities that enable you to create reports on any aspect of user account security, privileges, and rights.

File Server Monitoring

As an administrator, you need to keep an eye on several server operating system factors as discussed in Chapter 30, "Dial-in, Dial-Out Services." Many of these statistics are shown in MONITOR, and Novell offers its NetWare Services Manager, which does a good job in covering what MONITOR lacks. Other packages monitor basically the same parameters but usually add a few more features, such as graphing and recording CPU utilization over a period of time.

Most of these packages are server-based NLMs that monitor and collect data while a workstation-based executable module views the statistics that have been collected. Workstation modules normally poll databases to find and report the statistics.

Centralized Workstation Support versus Control

Your role as a system administrator, and therefore your requirements for support tools, can vary widely. In some companies the administrator is concerned only with the network, while the user is responsible for the workstation and all its software.

In such a case, the only task for which the system administrator is responsible is to update the workstation drivers and shells, and perhaps to provide front-line technical phone support to the user in matters regarding the network. Here a system administrator needs simple tools that can extend support to all users quickly and efficiently.

In other cases, management does not want users to install and configure their own workstations and software. Instead, centralized support people are hired to do this, so the users can spend all their time doing the job for which they were hired. In this scenario, a system administrator may need more robust tools that enable full management of workstations from his or her desk.

Many workstation support packages load a TSR at the workstation to simply report some of this LAN information. Others use host-remote software that enables an administrator remote access to a user workstation. Other functions include keeping track of workstations, internal hardware components, and software.

Centralized Support of User Workstations

For those system administrators who only support network-related workstation issues, their job is restricted to supporting user workstations, only dealing with users' configuration and network batch files. Installing and maintaining files physically located on the user workstation is a job that can be handled in a decentralized manner. Novell's WSUPDATE utility is included in your NetWare to provide updates of workstation files during login. Particular utilities that offer these capabilities are discussed later in this chapter.

An administrator may wish to employ the available tools to

- Edit user workstation files
- Replace user workstation files automatically
- Intelligently select appropriate files for update

NOTE ▶

If you are using 3.11 and plan to use WSUPDATE, you will need to download the latest version from NetWire or from your distributor. The WSUPDATE on your distribution diskettes has bugs that complicate its use.

The features provided with many workstation management packages make this much easier than physically attending to each workstation. If you have hundreds of users, some located remotely, you should have tools to perform these functions remotely.

Centralized Control and Management of User Workstations

When users are not to spend their time installing software and maintaining the complexities of a personal computer, these tasks must be delegated to the administrator and/or a support staff. In this case, you should have an arsenal of tools to reduce your workload and increase your efficiency. The detailed description of available utilities presented later in this chapter will give you some idea where you might find the particular tools you need.

Ideally, an administrator would like to have tools to

- Edit user workstation files
- Replace user workstation files remotely
- Intelligently select appropriate files for update
- Remotely control a user workstation
- Inventory and control hardware
- Inventory and control software

Metering and Locking Applications

Avoiding copyright violations should be a serious concern for system administrators. In the past few years, two major trade organizations have been founded to protect software developers' interests, and a new federal law increases the penalties for software violations that exceed a value of $2,500. Trade organizations have become very active in prosecuting offenders, and ignorance of the law is not a valid defense. An administrator who observes (or should have been aware of) copyright violations, and does not take action to prevent them, can be held personally liable. Therefore, you are well-advised to police software usage on your network and to be certain that employees do not abuse license agreements.

The user community has objected to most forms of copyright violation control. It adds needless complication to the difficult task of installing and maintaining software, especially in a networked environment. Though some software packages attempt to control usage through techniques such as semaphore locking and controlling the number of installations that can be done from original diskettes, the vast majority of packages rely on fines and prosecution as a deterrent. Therefore, it is often up to the system administrator to monitor and/or control license agreements.

You may pay a license fee based on the number of concurrent users accessing an application. Often, it is quite difficult to determine just how many users concurrently access the application; therefore your license fees may be overestimated. At any given time, only a fraction of the users may access the application. By metering usage, you may be able to reduce the user licenses you need to purchase. Maintaining a record of who has accessed which applications and how long they have used them can assist in planning for system utilization. Several software packages meter application usage, and some even control them.

A couple of products are available to lock out additional users when the maximum number of concurrent users has been reached. Whether you meter or lock, you can protect yourself and your company from liability if you use some form of sanction and control.

Security

Though NetWare's security functions can greatly control access, in many cases, more control is demanded. Some menu systems add passwords to menu selections, and/or administrators can specify which menu selections each user can access.

A gaping hole in security occurs when a user walks away from a logged-in workstation. If this is a concern, look for a package that has a screen saver that requires a password to get the screen back. Other packages log the user out if the workstation has been unused for an extended period. Another restriction you may want to impose is to lock the user into a menu system. One problem with this is software that enables the user to shell out to DOS. Some menu systems are designed to prevent users from shelling out.

Some of these functions can be handled by a menu software package. Some of the packages (listed in the section titled "Third-Party Utilities") control this, although they do not make menus.

Virus Protection

Many network utilities include protection for viruses. Virus infections on networks can cause extensive loss of productivity, because one user's infection can affect hundreds of users. Few of the utilities discussed here monitor and scan for viruses. Many good stand-alone virus utilities are available. You should select one and use it to monitor, scan, and remove viruses.

You should not be without virus protection. If you have not had a previous incident or if you are not convinced about the necessity to protect your system, you should at least have one such product on hand, along with information about where you can obtain relief 24-hours-a-day. This is why Viruscan from McAfee Associates is provided on the disk that accompanies this book. You should have it on hand like a fire extinguisher. If you use it, you must pay for it, but it costs you nothing to have it available just in case. The files that accompany Virus also can have plenty of virus information and the number of a 24-hour BBS to contact if needed.

Third-Party Utilities

Though the utilities discussed in this chapter are not the only ones on the market, this brief review covers several of the more prominent ones. The products discussed in this chapter are examples that demonstrate the most outstanding features that you should have.

Frye Utilities

This product has several modules, so you can get one or all of the capabilities discussed in the following modules:

Frye Utility for NetWare (FUN)

This module

- Monitors file server utilization
- Collects server statistics
- Manages server configuration
- Has remote-control server functionality
- Meters application usage

- Manages server SET parameters
- Works with multiple servers

Note Tracker (NT)

This module

- Collects workstation statistics
- Collects network statistics

Early Warning System (EWS)

This module sets thresholds and alarms to notify you when problems may be developing.

Software Update and Distribution System (SUDS)

This module is designed to automatically distribute software.

LAN Directory (LAND)

This module is customizable, and can

- Inventory software
- Inventory hardware

NetWare Console Commander (NCC)

This product

- Watches the clock and calendar
- Automates scheduled execution of NLMs and console commands
- Sends messages to users and groups

XTree Tools for Networks

This product includes Net Track and Server Monitor. XTree has always had a good user interface, which is true of this product also. It uses Novell-type bounce menus and shows files in a tree format, but it adds information and functionality. Net Track can sample and accumulate statistics to determine what might constitute normal versus heavy activity. It can execute applications or batch files when thresholds are reached. It can notify you by e-mail or pager if critical levels are reached.

Intel LANDesk Manager

This product is a Windows-based application, so it is easy to use. It makes use of Window's Dynamic Data Exchange to share data among modules. It also enables you to create custom scripts for automating common system administrative tasks. It enables you to

- Monitor server utilization
- Manage multiple server configurations
- Collect workstation and server statistics
- Set thresholds and alarms
- Remotely control workstation software
- Inventory hardware and software
- Monitor application usage
- Protect against viruses

It is also very helpful for monitoring. The Traffic Monitor tool can spot traffic patterns that isolate the bottlenecks and determine how to alleviate them. It notifies you through NetWare messages or cc:Mail. It has features for monitoring IPX and IP statistics and monitors print queues.

Saber Menu System and LAN Workstation

Saber Menu is a product that controls and meters software usage. You can customize each user's menu and assign passwords for each menu selection. It also creates a database to log user access and the amount of time an application is used. A slimmed-down version of this utility is shipped with NetWare 4.x versions. Saber Menu can work with Windows.

Saber's LAN Workstation can lock further access to an application when the maximum number of concurrent users has been reached. It is a Windows-based utility that inventories all detectable hardware and enables manual entries for asset management. It tracks hardware changes, and records who logs in from what workstations.

The software inventory function maintains a database of applications. It identifies many applications that it can detect, according to information supplied by software developers.

Brightworks

Brightworks makes several products for help desks. Their products provide

- Server monitoring
- Workstation inventory software
- Applications metering
- Virus protection
- Remote control workstation software
- A help desk database

Bindview NCS

Bindview is an application that has several functions, and it includes one that other applications discussed in this chapter do not have—bindery security reporting. It can produce reports on who has what rights in each directory, and can determine from where those rights came. This is a recommended tool for almost every network. Its report writer can report on almost any information that pertains to user and file security.

The company's latest product, Bindview NCS, also has extensive file server and network monitoring. It is modular and can support multiple servers from one console. The products comes in separate parts: the NCS Console, Server Information Module, and the Workstation Auditing Module. Additional Server Information Modules can be added for each server. Combined modules handle the following:

- Software license management
- Configuration file management meter
- Disk space auditing
- Security auditing
- Hardware configuration management
- Inventory/asset management

There are quite a few features in this product that have earned it and its earlier versions many awards.

Shareware, Copyrighted, and Public-Domain Packages

Many private software developers have uploaded so much software to NetWire that Novell added a new forum, NOVUSER, just for non-Novell uploads. Check it out and see what new arrivals can be found.

The disk that accompanies this book has several software packages for various functions that NetWare and the other commercial packages lack. Most of these utilities add new functions to administrative tasks that can extend your productivity.

The following utilities are provided:

NUTIL5	More than 30 utilities to help you in your management and troubleshooting duties
SUPER	Switches Supervisor equivalences on and off
NOVBAT	For enhanced batch-file programming that recognizes groups and versions of DOS
TOOLBOX	A collection of tools for many additional administrative functions
TSRCOM	A set of utilities for loading, unloading and managing TSRs
BVCHOW	For changing file ownership in bulk
DSUM23	More information about disk drives, local and network
CASTAW	Notifies when e-mail or messages arrive
CREATQ	For creating a print queue on other than the SYS: volume
LOGRUN	Fixes some of LOGIN.EXE's memory management problems
TTLOGIN	Lets you know why you cannot log in
LOGOFF	Logs you out more gracefully than LOGOUT

Many users have found these utilities to be indispensable. See Appendix F for more information about what is on the disk that accompanies this book.

Summary

Though NetWare has many great features, you may want to supplement your arsenal of tools with a few software packages. This area of software development is growing rapidly, and you may find that the previously discussed products have added new features by the time you read this book. Though several packages and functions are discussed in this chapter, you should monitor your favorite LAN-oriented periodical for reviews and evaluations of products. You can check Appendix F of this book for complete details on what is on the disk that accompanies this book.

Backup Strategies and Products

21

by Rick Sant'Angelo

IN THIS CHAPTER

Today, some of the most sophisticated backup devices are available for NetWare. However, sophisticated backup devices are not enough. You need to establish strategies and policies for backing up data. You also need to perform backups religiously. No job is more important than saving and protecting your data. This chapter explores several aspects of backing up data.

Media

Streaming tape drives have been used for backing up large amounts of data for many years. Magnetic tape has proven to be the preferred storage medium for mainframes, minicomputers, and PCs alike. However, it is no longer the only logical choice. New media become popular as technology improves.

Magnetic Tape

Magnetic tape has several advantages and disadvantages. In the past, tape streamers were the fastest, most cost-effective way to back up and restore data. The wide availability of media and the reliability of tape made it a good choice.

A couple of problems have soured administrators' opinions of tape backups, however. Tapes develop media defects much easier than disks or other media. When selective files are to be restored, the amount of time that is spent rewinding to retrieve the directory listings and then to advance to the area where the files are stored often is considerable. Verifying tapes after a backup session is almost as time-consuming as backing up in the first place. Formatting new tapes, and reformatting and retensioning tapes are all maintenance activities that are time-consuming.

Another potential problem develops when a tape has been exposed to temperature fluctuations or excessive heat or cold. It does not take much to expand or contract the tape sufficiently to require retensioning, or to render the tape altogether unreadable.

All these problems cast a shadow over the secure feeling you would like to have about your backups. Tapes are more dependable than ever, but new technologies and cost factors provide other choices in backup devices and media.

Hard Drives

Hard drives have become less expensive and more dependable than before; therefore, storing data on a hard drive is now feasible. Store your data on a hard drive if you may need to access it on a frequent basis. You may archive data to either network drives or local drives using a simple data compression utility, such as PKZIP.

Keep in mind, however, that large-capacity disk drives are not easily removed from the premises for storage, so this factor limits their effectiveness as backup devices.

Write-Once, Read-Many (WORM) Drives

Full-sized WORM (write-once, read-many) drives have very large capacities and can be loaded and unloaded easily. They store more compactly than tape drives and are also faster. Though the access rate is not on a par with a hard drive, it is certainly faster than tape. The transfer rates are also very fast, because a spinning disk can move faster than a streaming tape.

This kind of optical storage is also more dependable than tape. Optical disks are less susceptible to damage from magnetic sources and temperature fluctuations. They are not susceptible to magnetic damage, and are even less susceptible to other damage that tapes are subject to, such as damage from tempurature extremes.

Floppy Optical Disks (Flopticals)

These disks are almost indistinguishable from normal 3 1/2-inch floppy disks but contain up to 20 MB of disk storage.

They are used in situations in which smaller amounts of storage or backup of specific data only is required. Because they must be swapped, they are more labor-intensive to use than tapes for backing up large amounts of data.

Digital Audio Tapes (DATs)

These tapes are ideal for backing up because of their high-density and low-error properties. They are also compact, about the size of an audio cassette tape. Though they are more expensive, they are more durable than normal magnetic tape.

Backup Strategies

Your choices in backup media should be part of a strategy to archive data in the most efficient and effective manner. There are many other decisions to be made to ensure the safety of your data.

Several selections are at your disposal to integrate a comprehensive backup strategy. You need to decide whether your backup device is installed in the server or in a workstation. You also need to make several decisions to ensure that backed-up data is secure. In addition to the hardware and software you choose for your backup device, you need to decide the following:

- Whether to perform the backup yourself or to delegate the task
- How many generations of backups must be kept
- Whether you will back up only those files that have changed
- Where to store backups

Server-Based versus Workstation-Based Tape Drives

Workstation-based backup devices have been the standard for many years. Any file on your server's disks can be backed up over the network. One advantage of a workstation-based backup device is the flexibility to back up any server's data.

When backing up with a workstation-based device, you must have at least Read, File Scan, and Modify rights to all volume root directories. None of the files in the SYSTEM directory are accessible to anyone other than a Supervisor or equivalent. NetWare security is stored in the SYSTEM directory and with each directory listing.

Server-based tape backup units enable unattended backup of any files on a server without login as Supervisor. These devices use software developed as NLMs, installed and executed on the server OS. A backup NLM can be programmed to provide unattended backup without the need for the user to physically log in.

Delegating Backup Duties

One of the big mistakes that system administrators make is to personally retain the duty of backing up the system. Because pressing support issues often dominate an administrator's schedule, the chore of backing up can be neglected in favor of more urgent issues. Backing up data is not a procedure that should ever be overlooked or preempted. By assigning the duty of backing up to a clerical employee, it can be given a high priority.

When delegating backup to another employee, you should provide adequate training and supervision to ensure that backups are done reliably and on a regular basis. The employee must be highly dependable but does not have to be highly skilled. Backup software can be automated to eliminate the need to make decisions.

Keeping a Backup Log

A backup log book should be kept, indicating the date and time of the backup and the initials of the person who performed the backup. This is especially important when backup responsibilities have been delegated. A manager should periodically check the backup log and personally verify that the tapes are restorable and contain the data they are supposed to contain.

Rotating Backup Schedule

Backups tapes should be rotated at least three generations. When attempting to restore a backup, it may be determined that the backup is not restorable, or that a file may have been damaged at the time of the last backup. In either case, a previous backup can be restored if it exists. Tapes can be reused on a rotating schedule, such as every three days or weekly.

Backing Up Only Files That Change

You can choose to back up only those files that have changed since the last backup. DOS attributes include the archive (A) attribute. When a file is backed up, this attribute is removed. When a file is changed, it is added again. Tape backup software can select files to back up based on this attribute.

When backing up only those files that have changed, it is important to perform a full backup every few days or every week. When restoring files from a backup of only files that have changed, you need to restore a full backup and then each subsequent backup of only changed files.

Storing Backups Off-Site

Backups should be removed from the premises as soon as feasible and stored in a safe location. Fire, theft, and environmental damage can occur, so off-site storage should be selected on the basis of security from these dangers.

Many armored-car service companies provide data storage facilities and can pick up your tapes. Be careful about using courier services whose employees have not been adequately trained to properly handle magnetic media. Your tapes can be damaged from resting in a sunny place inside a vehicle or can be exposed to theft and other hazards. Security of your data is vitally important.

You should never depend upon "fire-safe" file cabinets to store tapes. Though contents may be protected from burning, the temperatures inside a fire-safe storage cabinet can damage tapes during an intense fire. When tapes are subjected to extreme temperature fluctuations, tape can become stretched or otherwise damaged. Retensioning can sometimes help, but often it does not restore the readability of a tape.

Backing Up NetWare Security for 3.11

Though your tape drive may back up NetWare security, you should have an alternative backup of only security. If you must restore older backups, you can restore your latest security backup on top of it, thereby restoring security to current levels, even though you have restored older data.

It is quite simple to back up only security. You can use NetWare's NBACKUP utility, backing up to a local hard or floppy drive. You must back up the bindery files and all directory listings. Because the bindery files are hidden system files and are stored in the SYSTEM directory, you must log in as Supervisor or Supervisor equivalent in order to back up security. You also must back up all directories, because the directory listings contain trustee assignments. You may, however, exclude all other files.

NBACKUP is no longer available with NetWare 3.12 or 4.x.

> **NOTE ▶**
>
> This procedure is used to back up directory file listings, trustee assignments, and bindery files only. If you have assigned trustee rights at the file level, this procedure will not back up all security.

To perform a security-only backup for NetWare, follow these steps:

1. Log in as Supervisor or Supervisor equivalent
2. Execute NBACKUP, select DOS Device, and then select Backup Options
3. Select and enter the working directory to be used
4. Select Backup by Directory
5. Answer the backup configuration questions (displayed in Figure 21.1) as follows:

Backup directories?	Yes
Backup trustees?	Yes

Modified files only?	No
Clear modify bit?	No
Files to include?	All
Files to exclude?	Select and press Insert (exclude *.*)
Directories to include?	All
Directories to exclude?	None
Backup Hidden files?	Yes
Source Directory?	SYS:
Destination Directory? (local pathname)	Same as pathname specified for working files

6. Press Enter to continue. Follow prompts as displayed.

CAUTION

The working directory and the directory receiving the backup must be on a local device. If your server's drive goes down, you will not be able to restore backups that have been made to it.

Figure 21.1 shows an NBACKUP security archive.

FIGURE 21.1.

Making an NBACKUP security archive.

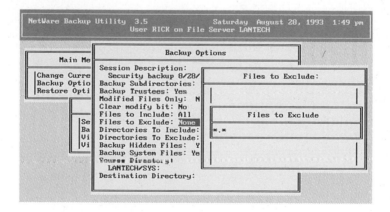

This procedure will back up all directories and their associated trustee assignments, and the hidden system bindery files. All nonessential files, however, will be ignored. Trustee assignments are normally assigned at the directory level. If you have assigned trustee privileges at the file level, they will not be backed up unless the specific files assigned are also backed up.

The backup is very quick, and the data is compressed. The destination device can be a floppy drive, if desired, and will contain all data necessary to restore security (users, groups, passwords, trustee assignments) by simply using the restore option.

You may be able to duplicate these options in your tape backup software. Whether you do is not as important as having two backups of the same information created with two different tools. If a tape is lost or not usable, you may find this backup to be invaluable. Because it is security only, no thought is involved in determining which backup has the current state of security. Every time you change security, you should back up again, so you will never have to reconstruct your balance of security.

Backup Products

A few backup products have distinguished themselves from all others.

ARCserve by Cheyenne Software

ARCserve comes with drivers for most of the popular backup devices. It is a server-based product that installs as an NLM on the server for direct backup to a server-installed device. It is designed for access from any node and can back up any server that is internetworked. The server-based NLM can perform unattended backups without a login as Supervisor while the system is in use. The workstation-based management software comes in DOS and Windows varieties with several features, including the following.

Auto Pilot Tape Management

This feature guides the operator with tape management, rotation, and labeling. It has procedures for formatting, tensioning, and otherwise grooming tapes, as well as disaster-recovery capabilities.

Tape Usage Database

This feature keeps track of tape usage, errors, and other information to assist in determining when tapes should be retired.

Quick Start

This feature simplifies backup and restoration by automatically creating backup scripts without forcing you to learn all about using the software.

File Tracking System and Quick File Access

This feature makes locating files for selective restoration simple and fast.

The Windows version runs backup tasks in a background mode, freeing up your workstation for other tasks. The Windows version also provides Parallel Streaming to enable backup and restore operations with as many as seven SCSI backup devices simultaneously. It also provides messaging when errors or problems occur.

It can integrate with Cheyenne's FAXserve to send messages and alerts through FAX, and with InocuLAN for virus detection during backup. It also supports Novell's Storage Management Services script files for backup from the command line.

Connor Hierarchical Storage Management (HSM)

Connor Peripherals, Inc., has developed a product that automatically migrates data that is seldom used off your file server to a special HSM server. The HSM server features mirrored hard drives, optical disks, and DAT backup devices. When files become aged, they automatically migrate to the HSM hard drive. After another aging period, they migrate to the optical jukebox and then to storage on DAT. Any time files that are archived on the hard drive or the optical jukebox are requested, the files are placed back into service. Once they are moved to the DAT, they need to be manually retrieved.

This approach to managing disk storage has been used for several years in the mainframe community, but no other product does this with PC networks. It relieves the system administrator from the time-consuming evaluation of which files can be archived and which should be left on primary hard disks.

Summary

No matter how fail-safe and fault-tolerant your system is, you still need to provide backups. Any system administrator who has had a serious incident of data loss knows how valuable backups are.

It is essential to establish adequate backup policies and procedures to ensure the availability of backups. Off-site storage is one of the most important considerations. It is recommended that the system administrator delegate backup duties to a clerical or administrative employee who can reliably allocate daily time for backing up without being preempted by more urgent tasks.

With so many choices of backup devices and software, you should select a system that provides the capacity and features you need and can fit in your budget.

Network Management

IV

Monitoring LANs

by Peter Kuo

22

LANs are like people—sometimes they're healthy, sometimes they're not. Without the aid of monitoring products, it is not always easy to recognize the symptoms of a faulty LAN before it's too late. Because it is an important part of your function as a system administrator to monitor the health of your LANs, it is useful to have specific value-added products to help you detect and report the kinds of LAN error conditions that are not immediately obvious.

LAN monitoring increases the stability and even the productivity of your network by warning you of conditions that can reduce performance or bring your LAN down. Over 70 percent of network problems are related to the physical layer of your LAN, while about 25 percent are in the data link layer and the rest are related to higher layers.

This chapter discusses the following issues with regard to the physical and data-link layers of the LAN:

- Common error conditions
- Reasons for the errors
- Acceptable levels of these error conditions

Error conditions are very specific to the access protocol of your LAN. For example, Ethernet has very different problems and error conditions from Token Ring. Therefore, this chapter is divided into two sections, one for Ethernet and one for Token Ring.

Ethernet-specific issues that will be discussed include

- Collisions and bandwidth utilization
- Local and remote collisions
- Late collisions and CRC/alignment errors
- Fragmented frames
- Illegal length frames and jabbers

The second half of the chapter deals with issues more specific to Token Ring, including

- Ring poll
- Ring reconfiguration
- Ring purges
- Ring recovery (loss of active monitor)
- Beaconing

- Soft errors
- Congestion
- Token rotation time

Token Ring error conditions do not normally appear as messages on workstation or file server screens. The only way to detect them is to use hardware and software designed to capture these errors and report them.

This chapter discusses statistics that can be monitored to prevent problems from reaching the stage where they can disable your network, along with ways to determine and locate the fault should your LAN go down. The following two chapters discuss specific Novell and third-party products that can be used for this purpose.

Ethernet Monitoring

The media access protocol used by Ethernet, CSMA/CD, is very dependent on cabling for error control. As discussed in Chapter 2, "Local Area Networks,"collision detection depends upon the length of cable, characteristics of the cabling, configuration of cable segments, and many other factors that control access to the bus. Even minor cabling or connector damage can cause reflections, which transceivers may perceive as (false) collisions, causing further problems. Many Ethernet vendors produce "smart" LAN devices that can detect these conditions and report them to the management software modules for your information. These are sometimes called "managed" devices.

Several conditions can be monitored to assist you in determining what types of errors may be reducing performance or interrupting communications on your Ethernet LAN. Each one is discussed in the following section.

Collisions and Bandwidth Utilization

On a busy Ethernet LAN, it is common to experience collisions when two or more NICs attempt to transmit at the same time. Collisions cannot be avoided on Ethernet LANs because CSMA/CD is a demand-based contention access protocol. Although collisions are considered normal for Ethernet LANs, excessive collisions reduce the overall throughput of the network. So how much is too much?

The number of collisions is directly related to bandwidth utilization, as shown in Figure 22.1. Bandwidth utilization is expressed as a percentage of theoretical capacity (10 Mbps for Ethernet). At less than 25-percent bandwidth utilization, the probability of a collision is low. As bandwidth utilization increases, or as long cable plants are used, the likelihood of generating collisions increases exponentially. Depending on cabling conditions, collisions can make the network unusable at somewhere between 60 to 90 percent of theoretical bandwidth utilization. Even the best and shortest cable plant cannot handle levels higher than about 90 percent of theoretical bandwidth utilization.

FIGURE 22.1.

Number of collisions as a function of bandwidth utilization.

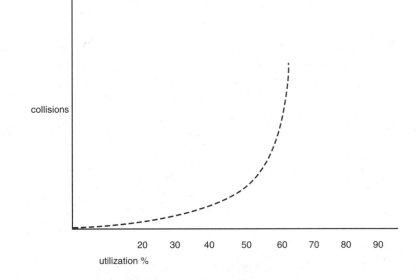

> **NOTE** ▶
>
> Because not every cable plant is capable of reaching the theoretical high bandwidth utilization of 90 percent, you should not expect your LAN to perform as well as some benchmark tests you may have seen in magazines, which are run under ideal conditions. Normal conditions generally limit Ethernet LANs to between 60 and 75 percent utilization.

It is important to realize that LAN utilization is not a constant factor. It is by nature very "bursty," since users may decide at any time to retrieve information from or save data to the server. Because this activity is unpredictable, it makes it difficult for you to determine if excessive traffic is causing a problem. To compensate for this possibility, a figure of 25- to 30-percent bandwidth utilization is considered an acceptable level. At about 70- to 80-percent bandwidth utilization, your LAN generally becomes fully saturated.

Usually you can tell when the LAN is extremely busy based on the response time observed at a workstation. However, this does not identify the source of excessive network load. Also, under normal conditions, global collisions on a LAN cannot be detected at any single NIC. Each NIC's firmware is designed to only listen to frames addressed specifically to it, or to those that are addressed as a broadcast. Some wiring concentrators have collision-indicator LEDs, whereas some simply have no indication of collision counts.

> **NOTE** ▶
>
> A wiring concentrator is an excellent listening device for collisions, because NICs can only detect collisions in which they are involved. A wiring concentrator can detect collisions anywhere on a physical LAN to which it is attached.

Many "smart" wiring concentrators contain an "agent" that listens for collisions. It then reports them to a software-management module running at a console located somewhere on the LAN. Many use an out-of-bandwidth serial port on the wiring concentrator to enable communications even if the LAN goes down.

> **CAUTION** ▶
>
> To determine if a condition is unusual, it is necessary to understand what the "normal" condition is. All LANs are unique in their configurations. What is normal for one network may not be considered normal for another.

You need to *baseline* the normal activity for your network. Baseline information relates to bandwidth utilization and should contain data to help you answer the following questions:

- What is the bandwidth utilization as a function of time over a normal working day and throughout the week?
- What types of protocols are using the bandwidth?
- Which users are taking up most of the bandwidth?

One of the standard baselining recommendations is to monitor your LAN over a long period of time to gather statistically significant information. For best results, perform this over a period of at least one month, so you can gather information on processes that happen only once a week or once a month. This information also can help you in planning for network growth.

Bandwidth utilization is, therefore, a good indicator of collision likelihood. When monitoring an Ethernet LAN, 30-percent bandwidth utilization is a level at which you should become concerned. This level indicates too much traffic on the LAN, which can lead to excessive collisions and throughput degradation. It is recommended to "segment" your LAN. This can be done by breaking it into separate physical LANs connected to multiple NICs in the file server, or by the use of bridges or routers.

> **TIP** ▶
>
> When doing baselining or examining bandwidth utilization, you should take into account how your particular business operates. For example, if yours is an accounting firm, high utilization can be expected during month ends and tax-return time. You should have a number of different "baselines" for different periods of your business year.

Local and Remote Collisions

When looking at the statistics from Ethernet LAN monitors, you will see counters for local collisions and remote collisions. Local collisions are collisions that occur on the local cabling segment. These collisions are detected by the collision-detection circuitry in the transceiver or in the NIC. As a result of a collision, collision fragments appear on the cable. A collision fragment is less than 64 bytes in length and has an invalid CRC.

> **NOTE** ▶
>
> There is some confusion in the networking industry when referring to a "frame." Some experts just consider the data field as the frame, whereas others take into account the MAC header and trailer as part of the frame. In this book, the term "frame" includes the MAC header and trailer but excludes the preamble, unless otherwise specified.

Remote collisions occur on the other side of a repeater (or other cabling segments connected to the wiring concentrator). A remote collision is assumed when a collision fragment is detected without triggering the collision-detection circuitry. Repeaters only repeat bits, and therefore pass on collision fragments to all connected cabling segments, whereas bridges and routers do not. Table 22.1 compares local and remote collisions.

Table 22.1. Comparison of local and remote collisions.

Collision type	Frame size	Bad CRC?	CD pair triggered?
Local	Less than 64 bytes	yes	yes
Remote	Less than 64 bytes	yes	no

Ethernet NICs recover from those collisions that are detected by resending frames that were involved in collisions. What is an acceptable collision level? Depending on the type of work being done on the network, various collision levels can be reached before noticeable performance degradation occurs. An unacceptable threshold level is reached whenever user complaints arise. The general rule of thumb for an acceptable level is that your collision count is no more than 5 percent of the total transmitted packets.

When you are troubleshooting excessive collision problems, it is important also to look at the bandwidth utilization. This information will help you to determine whether the excessive collisions are due to an overloaded LAN or a faulty component. If bandwidth utilization and collision counts are both high, then it is likely the collisions are a result of higher traffic volume on the LAN. One possible solution is to segment traffic using bridges or routers.

If collisions counts are high while bandwidth utilization remains normal, then it may be possible that your cable segment exceeds the maximum allowed by specifications, there are faults in your cabling, or there are violations of the 5-4-3 rule (as discussed in Chapter 2). Under these conditions, devices at the far end of the cable may consider the cable to be free, when in fact a frame is on the wire. Since the frame on the wire may not have propagated throughout the cabling system, devices at the far end may continue to transmit, thus causing a collision. If the cabling length is past specifications, or too many repeaters are used, the collision may even go undetected. This results in the loss of frames, requiring a higher-level network protocol (normally NCP) to detect the loss of data and resend it.

TIP ▶

If you are observing a high number of remote collisions, it is an indication that the cabling segment on the other side of the repeater is experiencing high local collisions. To reduce the amount of remote collisions that reach your local cabling segment, isolate your cabling segment from the remote and then troubleshoot for the cause of high collision counts on that remote cabling segment.

> **NOTE** ▷
>
> A LAN with multiple cabling segments connected by repeaters should have about the same amount of traffic on all cabling segments, since all traffic is "repeated" and not filtered. If one cabling segment is showing more collisions than others, it may be the result of faulty hardware on that particular cabling segment.

Signal Quality Error (SQE)

Sometimes false collisions can be caused by the presence of a Signal Quality Error (SQE—also known as "heartbeat") signal when it is not required. Ethernet version 2.0 transceivers send an SQE signal through the collision-detection pair back to the NIC right after each frame is sent to verify that the collision-detection circuitry is working. Ethernet version 1.0 transceivers do not do this. Most NICs in use today do not support this feature. Thus, using SQE with such an NIC will cause the NIC to think there is a collision when there is none.

A repeater is not designed to recognize SQE; therefore, the transceivers to which the repeater is attached must have SQE disabled. This is usually done through a dip switch or a jumper. If SQE is not disabled, the repeater will interpret this signal as a collision, and according to the specifications, it will generate a jam (62 bits on the wire to guarantee devices on that segment recognize a collision). Jamming is used for *jabber control*, which prevents a busy node from dominating the LAN. With SQE enabled, the jam sequence is sent after each frame transmitted on the LAN.

> **CAUTION** ▷
>
> When using external transceivers, disable SQE.

Late Collisions, CRC, and Alignment Errors

When a frame of size between 64 and 1518 bytes with an invalid CRC is detected, the condition is known as a *late collision*. This collision also fires the collision-detection circuitry in the NIC if it happens on the local segment and usually cannot be distinguished from a normal collision. If a bad CRC is detected without the NIC's collision-detection circuitry firing, then the condition is called a CRC error, and it is assumed to have occurred on a remote segment.

Normally, a frame ends on an 8-bit (or byte) boundary. For example, one does not usually get a frame that is 75 bytes and 2 bits long. If a frame does not end on an 8-bit boundary, an alignment error has occurred. By convention, both CRC errors and alignments are grouped together as CRC/alignment errors during reporting.

Unlike local and remote collisions, which are normal for Ethernet LANs, bad CRCs, alignment errors and late collisions are not healthy symptoms. They are usually caused by hardware problems, such as faulty cabling or NICs. Some of the most common causes are:

- A cable segment that is too long.
- Improper termination.
- Spacing between taps that is less than the recommended minimum (a common error in 10BASE-2 and 10BASE-5 environments).
- Noisy cable due to induced electromagnetic interference from nearby sources, such as florescent lights and the motors in ceiling fans.
- Improper grounding of the cabling segment, resulting in ground-loop.
- NIC failure to detect a collision or frame on the wire. Such a node is sometimes known as a *deaf node*.

TIP ▶

When running cables, do not exceed the maximum allowable distance. A Rule of thumb is to use about 80 percent of recommended maximum distance. This will allow for signal loss because of noise on the wire.

CAUTION ▶

For long coaxial cable runs, make sure only one end of the cable is grounded. Grounding both ends, especially to different grounds, may cause ground-loops (and thus data corruption).

Fragmented Frames

Frame fragments are less than 64 bytes in size with an invalid CRC. They are normally a result of local or remote collisions. There is always some amount of fragment frames on your LAN, since collision is unavoidable in Ethernet. However, the number of fragmented frames should be less than 10 percent of your overall frames. Otherwise, your LAN is approaching saturation and needs to be segmented into separate LANs.

Illegal Length Frames and Jabbers

A legal Ethernet frame must be between 64 bytes and 1518 bytes in length. If a frame is less than 64 bytes in length and contains a valid CRC, it is known as a short frame or a "runt." A frame that is longer than 1518 bytes and has a valid CRC is known as a long frame. These illegal frames are usually caused by faulty drivers. Updating to the latest version of the driver should cure these problems.

A jabber is a frame that is over 1518 bytes in length with an invalid CRC. This is usually caused by a faulty transceiver. By design, a transceiver can only transmit for 150 milliseconds, long enough to transmit 1518 bytes. If the transceiver does not stop after transmitting 1518 bytes, a jabber condition has occurred.

TIP ▶

If you suspect a jabbering node, check the transmit light on the NIC or transceiver to see if it's lit continuously.

Opposite to a deaf node, there can exist a "chatty node," which was discussed in a previous section. This is when a transceiver or NIC goes on and on generating any one of several types of signals, which then get interpreted as collisions. This could bring the whole LAN to a grinding halt, since no other device can transmit.

This section defined various Ethernet frame errors, as summarized in Table 22.2. Understanding how they occur will help you to better monitor your LAN and set alarm thresholds to manage these errors before they degrade your network communications.

Table 22.2. Various Ethernet error types and their conditions.

Error type	Error condition
Local collision	Less than 64 bytes
	Bad CRC
	Collision-Detection (CD) pair triggered
Remote collision	Less then 64 bytes
	Bad CRC
	CD pair *not* triggered
Late collision	Between 64 and 1518 bytes
	Bad CRC
	CD pair *may* be triggered
CRC error	Between 64 and 1518 bytes
	Bad CRC
	CD pair not triggered
Alignment error	Between 64 and 1518 bytes
	Bad CRC
	Does not end on 8-bit boundary
Short frame (runt)	Less than 64 bytes
	Good CRC
Long frame	More than 1518 bytes
	Good CRC
Jabber	More than 1518 bytes
	Bad CRC

Token Ring Monitoring

Token Ring protocol has many built-in self-management features. These are affected through the Media Control MAC frames. They provide recovery from ring troubles such as the loss of Active Monitor, the loss or corruption of frames or tokens, and intermittent hardware faults. They also provide constant updating of upstream neighbors' addresses, which is essential in the isolation of a fault domain during troubleshooting processes.

To facilitate self-management, Token Ring architecture specifies five *functional stations*:

- Active Monitor
- Standby Monitor
- Ring Parameter Server
- Ring Error Monitor
- Configuration Report Server (also known as Network Manager)

Functional stations are special "software" devices that take on specific station functions. Active and Standby Monitor functions are built into each NIC as part of the chip set functions. The remaining three are all enabled through special software (such as the IBM LAN Manager software). These three stations do not have to "exist" on a ring in order for the ring to function. The following is a brief description of their functions:

> **Active Monitor** provides master clocking for the ring and ensures the presence of a token. Usually it is the first active device on the ring.
> **Standby Monitor** is any device that is not an Active Monitor. They are to ensure that there is an Active Monitor on the ring.
> **Ring Parameter Server** provides parameter settings for devices at the time of insertion into the ring.
> **Ring Error Monitor** is a central "console" for collecting errors from other ring devices.
> **Configuration Report Server (Network Manager)** keeps track of the current ring configuration and controls individual NIC parameters such as various timers.

There are two types of errors in the Token Ring protocol: soft errors and hard errors. Soft errors are intermittent errors from which the ring can generally recover without disrupting ring functionality. Some hard errors may be resolved by the use of Media Control MAC frames, whereas some may require manual intervention.

In this section we will examine some of the most important Media Control MAC frames in Token Ring. We will also look at the most common causes of soft errors. You will learn how they can help you diagnose the health of your rings and how they can help you find a cure for a problem.

Ring Poll

Every 7 seconds, the Active Monitor initiates a ring poll process to

1. Inform all Standby Monitors that an Active Monitor is present
2. Inform all ring devices that the ring is functioning properly
3. Enable ring devices to update the address of their Nearest Active Upstream Neighbor (NAUN)

This process happens regardless of whether there is any traffic on the ring (except when the ring is beaconing). In IBM terminology, this is known as the Neighbor Notification process.

CAUTION ▶

If you cannot detect the ring poll process occurring every 7 seconds, you have a serious Token Ring protocol problem. If this is happening on your ring, locate the Active Monitor, as it is likely that it has a faulty NIC or that its "Active Monitor Timer" has been changed. If you do not correct this, you may notice many MAC frames of the "Active Monitor Present" and "Neighbor Notification Incomplete" type, and possibly a nonfunctioning ring. This, however, is *very* rare.

TIP ▶

You can determine the physical order (as connected into the MSAU) of the Token Ring devices based on the ring poll frames. This is useful information to have when troubleshooting (see the forthcoming section on beaconing) and for documentation purposes.

Ring Reconfiguration

Each Token Ring device keeps track of the hardware MAC address of its nearest active upstream neighbor (NAUN). This is normally learned from the ring poll MAC frames. However, when a new device is inserted into or removed from the ring, a "Ring Change" frame is sent by its immediate downstream neighbor to the ring error monitor. Normally, the number of such frames are small. They usually occur in the morning when users turn on their workstations, over lunch period when people power off/on their machines, and when workstations are powered off at the end of the working day.

> **TIP** ▶
>
> If you notice a large number of ring change MAC frames outside of these "normal" hours, it is likely that you have one or more Token Ring devices constantly inserting and de-inserting from the ring. Check for possible faulty wiring, hardware, or LAN drivers. Use a protocol analyzer, such as the ones described in the next chapter, to isolate the faulty device(s).

Ring Purges

When the Active Monitor detects a lost token or frame, it must determine if the ring is functioning properly before releasing a new token. The way the Active Monitor checks the general health of the LAN is by transmitting purge frames. They are transmitted in 4-millisecond intervals for up to one second. As soon as the Active Monitor receives back just one uncorrupted purge frame, it assumes the ring is healthy and releases a free token. This is the first step taken by the token-passing ring access protocol in trying to recover from a hard error.

> **TIP** ▶
>
> There will always be a small amount of purge frames on your ring. They are usually caused by stations entering and leaving the ring. If you detect a constant stream of purge frames on your ring, you are having an intermittent physical problem with cables, connections, MSAUs, or NICs. You will also notice the performance of your LAN grinds to a halt.

If the Active Monitor does not receive an uncorrupted purge frame within one second, the ring goes into ring recovery.

Ring Recovery (Loss of Active Monitor)

In most Token Ring protocol monitors, there is a ring recovery counter. This counter is incremented every time a monitor contention process occurs to elect a new Active Monitor. In IBM terminology, this is also known as the Claim Token process, and it happens under the following conditions:

1. The Active Monitor does not detect an error-free purge frame within 1 second after it started transmitting purge frames.

2. The Active Monitor does not detect the completion of the ring poll process within a given time.

3. A Standby Monitor detects the lack of a ring poll process within a given length of time (about 12 seconds).

As with ring purges, it is normal to have a few ring recoveries, but as with purge frames, they should be few and far between. This is the second stage in the Token-Ring physical error recovery scheme.

> **CAUTION** ▶
>
> If you detect a constant level of purge frames, your ring is ill, and you are suffering a performance hit. If the ring recovery counter is steadily increasing, your LAN is in serious trouble, and you should take immediate action.

When the ring cannot complete a monitor-contention process within one second, it goes into the third and final stage of hard-error recovery, a process called beaconing. If the error is resolved by monitor contention, a ring purge follows and the ring is back to normal operation status.

Beaconing

Beaconing is the last desperate attempt by the Token Ring protocol to recover from a hard error. While the ring is beaconing, the ring is nonfunctional; no new device can insert into the ring, and no user data will be transmitted by the stations.

If the hard error is due to a faulty Token Ring adapter or cable lobe, the beaconing process can usually recover the ring. However, most problems that cause beaconing require manual intervention to resolve. Fortunately, the beacon MAC frame contains information indicating the cause of the error, as well as an indication of a fault domain. A fault domain is the area between the station reporting the beaconing and its active upstream neighbor.

> **TIP** ▶
>
> Having a list of MAC addresses of Token Ring NICs and their location on your ring will greatly help you in locating the physical device that is causing the beaconing. This list can be generated by examining ring poll frames.

> **CAUTION** ▷
>
> One of the most common causes of NetWare file server beaconing is a loose cable at the NIC end of the connection.
>
> Probably the most common cause of beaconing on a ring is the mixing of Token Ring NICs that are set for different speeds. You cannot have even one NIC set at 4 Mbps on a 16 Mbps ring, or vice versa. And most Token Ring NICs are shipped with 4 Mbps as the default speed setting. Check this before installation.
>
> If you run the IBM PS/2 Reference Disk to "auto-configure" your cards, the Token Ring card will be set to 4 Mbps.

Once the cause of the beaconing is resolved, the ring performs a monitor contention, followed by a ring purge, and then the ring is back to normal. Figure 22.2 illustrates the flow of hard-error recovery processes.

FIGURE 22.2.

Hard-error recovery flow chart.

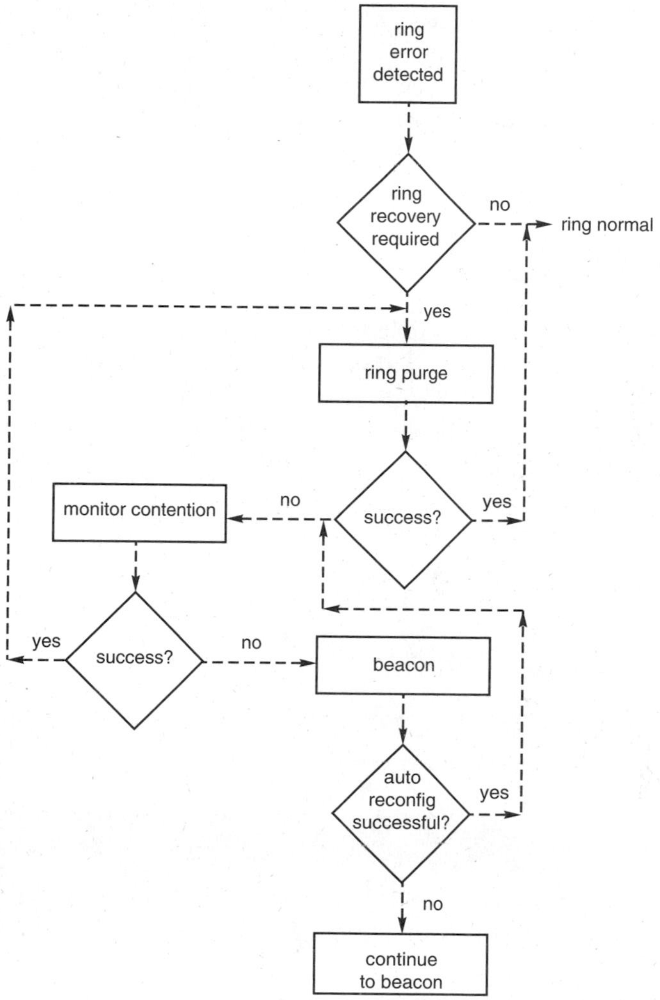

Soft Errors

Soft errors are intermittent errors from which the ring can recover easily and automatically. Sometimes it is difficult to classify what is a hard error and what is a soft error. Some experts consider beaconing a hard error while everything else is a soft error. Token Ring protocol defines four types of errors:

Type 1 Errors that require no recovery procedure by the ring
Type 2 Errors that are corrected by a ring purge process
Type 3 Errors that are resolved by a monitor contention
Type 4 Errors that require beaconing

Each of these errors is generated by specific conditions.

Type 1 Errors

Typical Type 1 errors are "Receiving Congestion" and "Frame Copied" errors. Congestion errors are discussed in greater detail in the next section of this chapter. Recall from Chapter 2 the discussion of how Token Ring works: When a data frame reaches the destination node, the receiving node changes two bits in the trailer (the Addresses Recognized Indicator, ARI, and the Frame Copied Indicator, FCI). If a station detects a frame addressed to its specified address and either or both of the ARI and FCI bits are *already* set, this condition is known as a Frame Copied error. This is normally caused by line noise that corrupts the frame.

Type 2 Errors

The most common Type 2 soft error is the "Burst 5" error. It constitutes over 90 percent of all observed soft-error counts.

> **NOTE ▶**
>
> A Burst 5 error occurs when a station detects five half-bits of the differential Manchester signal without a phase change. In other words, in five half-bit times, no data was detected. (A "bit time" is how long it takes to transmit a bit on the ring.)

Whenever a station is inserted into or removed from the ring, the integrity of the ring is temporarily broken. This causes a Burst 5 error (more commonly referred to as Burst error). There are always a small amount of Burst errors on your ring. This is because of users turning their workstations on and off. However, the errors should normally occur only in the early morning, around noon, and in the late afternoon. If you observe a large number of Burst errors during other hours of the day, you should investigate the cause. This is because Burst errors cause ring purges, and ring purges use up a ring's bandwidth. If there is a constant level of Burst errors, there will be a constant level of ring purges, and this causes performance degradation.

TIP ▶

Burst errors are isolating errors. When a device reports a Burst error, it includes the address of its upstream neighbor. Therefore, from the address of the station reporting the Burst error and its upstream neighbor's address, you now have a fault domain to troubleshoot.

A constant level of Burst error is usually due to faulty cabling or connectors.

WARNING ▶

If you observe Burst errors from *all* devices on your ring, it is very likely that your cabling system is out of specification (for example, using "Type 3" cables instead of "Type 1" for 16 Mbps operation).

You will also observe Lost Token and Lost Frame errors (both are Type 2 soft errors) when you detect Burst errors.

Type 3 Errors

"Lost Monitor" is a Type 3 error. This is reported by a Standby Monitor when it detects that the Active Monitor has left the ring. A monitor contention process is initiated to elect a new Active Monitor.

Type 4 Errors

Type 4 errors are any errors that cannot be resolved by a monitor contention and therefore lead to beaconing. It is generally agreed that a Type 4 soft error is the same as a hard error.

Congestion

Congestion error is one of the more common Type 1 errors. It occurs when a station detects a frame that is addressed to its specific location but has insufficient buffer or time to copy it. In most cases, it is due to a slow NIC in the station.

The NIC in the file server and any bridge or router should be the fastest on the ring. Otherwise, they would be the cause of Congestion errors.

In some cases, congestion can be caused by a memory conflict in the workstation. For example, when a RAM buffer or ROM address used by the Token Ring NIC overlaps with an expanded or extended memory address in use, the NIC's buffer space can be reduced, which in turn leads to insufficient buffer for copying frames.

Token Rotation Time

Token rotation time is one of three basic "vital sign" statistics to be monitored periodically on every Token Ring. The three "vital signs" are

1. Token-rotation time
2. The number of purge frames
3. The number of ring recoveries

Token rotation time is a measure (in microseconds) of how often a Token Ring device detects a free token. For example, a token-rotation time of 30 microseconds means that, on average, a station can capture a free token every 30 microseconds.

There is no "typical" token-rotation time. Every ring is different. However, from experience, it is observed that for a 16-Mbps ring, with 386-type workstations, a token-rotation time of 1 microsecond per active device on the ring can be expected. That is to say, if there are 20 active devices on at the time, one can expect a token-rotation time of about 20 microseconds.

As the bandwidth utilization increases, token-rotation time also increases. This is very similar to the principle that the amount of collision in Ethernet is a function of utilization. You will observe that token-rotation time increases when ring purge, monitor contention, and (especially) beaconing processes are happening. This is because no free token is available when these processes are going on.

TIP ▶

You should baseline your token-rotation time when you think your ring is performing well. And keep an eye on this timing information to determine if your LAN usage is increasing or if you are having a ring problem.

The two other two vital signs, ring purges and ring recoveries, were discussed in detail earlier in this chapter.

WARNING ▶

As these three vital-sign counters increase, it is an indication that your ring is having problems. Resolve them before your ring beacons.

The rest of the chapters in this section explore how some of the Novell and third-party products can help us in detecting and managing the various errors and statistics discussed in this chapter.

Novell Products for
LAN Monitoring

by Rick Sant'Angelo

Now that you know what kind of errors can happen to your Ethernet and Token Ring LANs, what can you employ to detect these conditions and provide an early warning of potential problems before they cripple the LAN? In response to the LAN-management needs of the user community, a number of products are now available to assist you. This chapter examines some of the Novell products that can help you detect and correct problems on your network. These products include the following:

1. LANalyzer for NetWare 2.0
2. LANtern Network Monitor and LANtern Services Manager 1.3x
3. NetWare Management System v1.1x
4. NetWare Hub Services 2.0 and Hub Services Manager 1.0
5. NetWare Management System v2.0

Screen shots of actual product screens are presented whenever possible to illustrate how you can extract information for your troubleshooting and management needs. Emphasis is placed on how these products can be applied to LAN monitoring and management, which is the focus of Part IV. For each product, this chapter also discusses any installation and operational "gotcha's." NetWare Management System v2.0 has changed dramatically from NMS 1.1x, so it warrants its own section. Note, however, that this chapter is not intended to be an operations manual on how to use the products.

LANalyzer for Windows 2.0

Formerly known as LANalyzer for NetWare 1.0 (LZFN), LANalyzer for Windows 2.0 (LZFW) is a Windows-based, software-only, network-management tool for monitoring and analyzing both Ethernet and Token Ring networks. This product enables you to monitor and capture data frames sent across Ethernet and Token Ring wires. It can decode all NetWare, AppleTalk, and TCP/IP protocol suites; for protocols it does not support, you will be presented with the hex dump of the contents. More importantly, it can detect and report the various Ethernet-specific and Token Ring-specific errors discussed in the previous chapter.

LZFW uses an easy-to-understand graphical user interface (GUI). The main screen is divided into three areas. The top portion is called *Dashboard*, which presents an easily understood view of your LAN condition (see Figure 23.1). The Dashboard contains three real-time gauges to show packets per second, bandwidth utilization percentage, and errors per second.

FIGURE 23.1.

LANalyzer for Windows (Ethernet configuration) desktop.

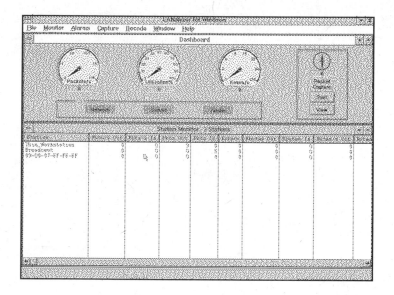

Notice that in each gauge, a needle indicates the current rate or percentage. Because this is a real-time display, the needles move according to rate and percentage changes. The rate gauges are based on a logarithmic scale, and the utilization percentage gauge is based on a linear scale. The "red arc" around the gauge indicates the alarm threshold level.

The three (rectangular) "lights" below the gauges are warning lights that alert you of network, server, or router alarms; they are normally green, but when an alarm is detected, the corresponding light turns red. Also, the alarm icon (yellow in color) will appear at the alarm status bar to indicate an alarm has been set off.

The *Station Monitor* shows a table listing all the active devices on the LAN and their related statistics. Figure 23.1 shows an Ethernet configuration. The Station Monitor for the Token Ring configuration is very similar to that of Ethernet, except for an extra column titled "Order." (See Figure 23.2.) This identifies the logical order of the devices on your ring. This list is updated every seven seconds (using information from the ring poll process).

FIGURE 23.2.

LANalyzer for Windows (Token Ring configuration) desktop.

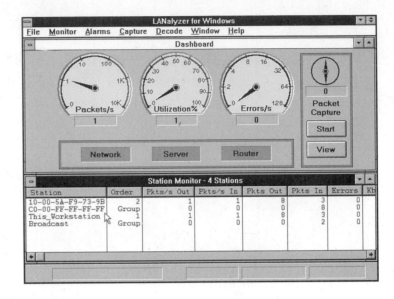

At the bottom of the screen is the alarm status bar, where an alarm icon and any alarm messages (in ticker-tape format) are displayed. It is used to notify you of error conditions. (See Figures 23.1 and 23.2.) Included with the software is a *NetWare Expert* option. Other than being a computer-based training (CBT) tool, it also can be used to help explain the cause of an alarm and suggests possible solutions. (See Figure 23.3 for an example.)

FIGURE 23.3.

The Server Alarms Log window.

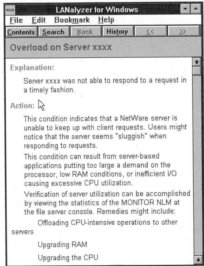

LZFW enables you to monitor the performance and characteristics of your local Ethernet segment of the LAN and your local ring of a multiring LAN. You can monitor the following information:

Real-time traffic information
Performance of active devices, including servers and routers
Trend data
Various alarm conditions

> **NOTE** ▶
>
> LZFW only "sees" the traffic on the segment to which it is attached. It cannot capture frames that are across a bridge or a router. To troubleshoot a multisegment network, you need to move the LZFW station from segment to segment or have multiple LZFWs running.

Real-Time Traffic Information

The software tracks statistics about packet rates, utilization, error rates, and data throughput rates. This information is displayed on the Dashboard, various monitor tables, and in the Detail graphs and tables.

Values in the Dashboard gauges and Monitor tables are updated every second. The Detail graphs display information for the preceding 15 minutes of operation. A point is plotted on the graph every 5 seconds. The point indicates the current value averaged over 5-second intervals.

Shown in Figures 23.4 through 23.8 are the screens depicting Detail-Packets/s, Detail-Utilization%, Detail-Errors/s for Ethernet, Detail-Errors/s for Token Ring, and Detail-Kilobyte/s, respectively. Associated with each graph is a table displaying the values of the current rate/percentage and other related statistics. The statistics displayed by these graphs and tables can be used for troubleshooting, planning, and setting alarm thresholds.

FIGURE 23.4.

*Detail-Packets/s
screen.*

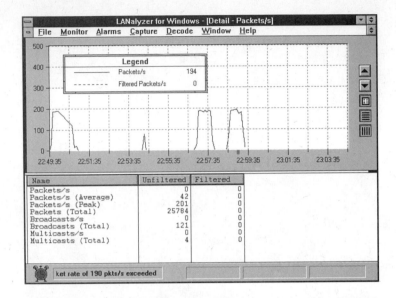

FIGURE 23.5.

*Detail-
Utilization%
screen.*

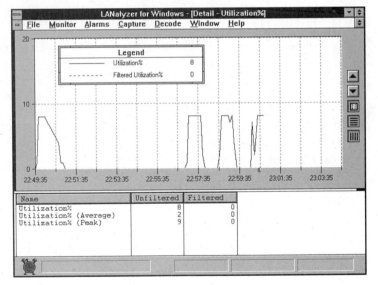

FIGURE 23.6.

Detail-Errors/s screen for Ethernet.

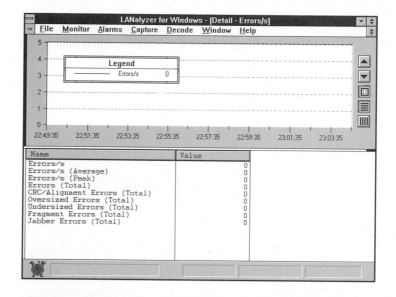

FIGURE 23.7.

Detail-Errors/s screen for Token Ring.

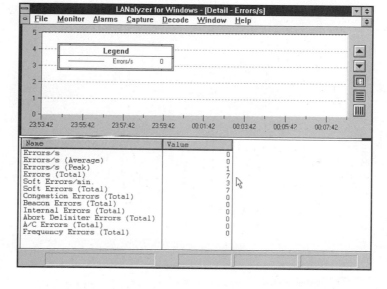

FIGURE 23.8.

Detail-Kilobyte/s screen.

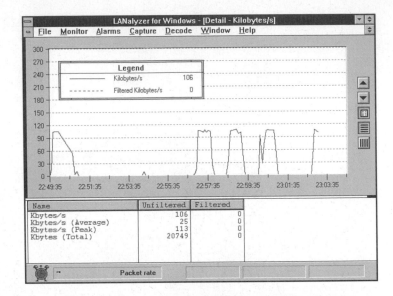

> **NOTE** ▶
>
> The information presented in the tables of the Detail-Packets/s, Detail-Utilization%, and Detail-Kilobyte/s windows is identical for Ethernet and Token Ring. The information presented in the table of the Detail-Errors/s window for Token Ring differs from the one for Ethernet because the types of errors for these two configurations are very different.

Because Ethernet is much more susceptible to bandwidth utilization problems than Token Ring, the statistics provided by the Detail-Packets/s, Detail-Utilization%, and Detail-Kilobyte/s windows are very useful troubleshooting information for Ethernet LANs.

> **TIP** ▶
>
> When you observe high collisions (more than 5 percent), check the Detail-Utilization% window to see what the utilization is like during the same time period. If the utilization percentage is low, chances are that you are either seeing remote collisions or you have a faulty NIC on your local segment.

> **CAUTION** ▶
>
> It is normal to have some errors on an Ethernet LAN because of its CSMA/CD access method. However, if you observe an error rate that is consistently more than five to seven errors per second, there is a problem on your LAN. Use the Capture feature to capture some of these error events and see if you can locate the source of the error by examining the source address.

Table 23.1 lists some appropriate uses for the statistics presented in the various Detail screens.

Table 23.1. Statistics summary.

Statistics	When to Use
Long Term Average	Set alarm threshold
Peak Packets/s	Set alarm threshold
Peak Utilization%	Set alarm threshold
	Plan for network growth
Peak Error/s	Set alarm threshold
Average Error/s	Set alarm threshold
	Troubleshooting
Errors/s	Troubleshooting

Sometimes it is useful to monitor only the traffic between certain stations. This can be accomplished using the Capture Filter option to "key" on two stations. (See Figure 23.9.) Unfortunately, you can monitor only traffic either between two stations or between one device and "any" other device. LANtern Services Manager/LANtern Network Monitor, discussed later in this chapter, can monitor traffic between all devices in a "Conversation Table."

FIGURE 23.9.

*LZFW Capture
Filter setup.*

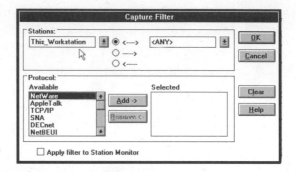

Performance of Active Devices

The Station Monitor table displays the activity of all active stations on your local segment, including workstations, servers, and routers. The displayed information is updated every second. If the Gather Station Names utility has not been run, the MAC addresses of the active devices will be displayed with their current statistics (see Figure 23.10); otherwise, server and login names will be displayed instead. (See Figure 23.11.)

FIGURE 23.10.

*Station Monitor
table with MAC
addresses
(Ethernet).*

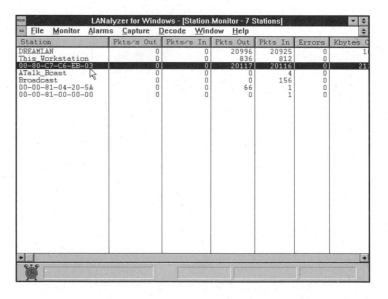

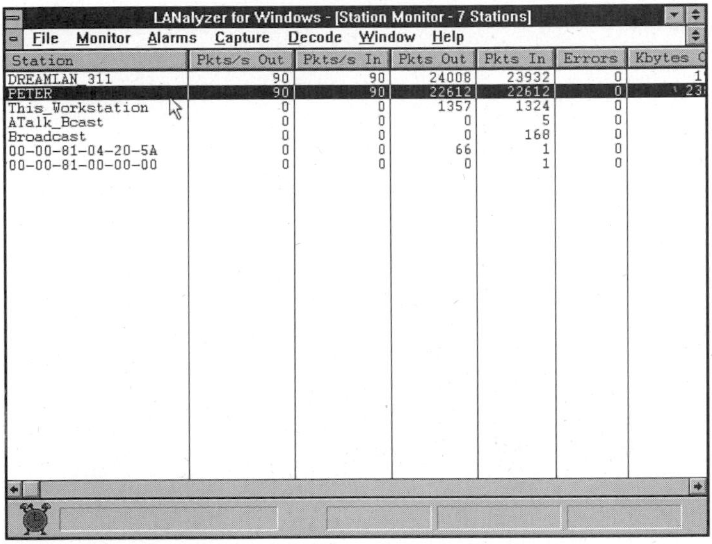

FIGURE 23.11.

Station Monitor table with server and login names (Ethernet).

Station	Pkts/s Out	Pkts/s In	Pkts Out	Pkts In	Errors	Kbytes O
DREAMLAN_311	90	90	24008	23932	0	1
PETER	90	90	22612	22612	0	23
This_Workstation	0	0	1357	1324	0	
ATalk_Bcast	0	0	0	5	0	
Broadcast	0	0	0	168	0	
00-00-81-04-20-5A	0	0	66	1	0	
00-00-81-00-00-00	0	0	0	1	0	

NOTE

You activate the Gather Station Names utility by accessing the Capture pull-down menu option, and then choosing Station Names from the selection.

By monitoring the various statistics columns in the table, you can find out which is the busiest device. For the purpose of error monitoring, the column of interest is the Errors column. Unfortunately, this is a "global error" counter. It does not give you a breakdown of the different types of errors. However, you can find out the different types of errors you have by double-clicking the Network "light box" on the Dashboard. To obtain an explanation of the error, as well as possible causes and solutions, highlight the error entry and select the NetWare Expert icon. (See Figure 23.12.)

From the table, you can get a detailed screen of a given device and print out the associated statistics. (See Figure 23.13.) For Token Ring devices, you also can get the associated ring information. (See Figure 23.14.)

TIP

Using the Upstream and Downstream "buttons" available in the Ring Information window, you can "walk" up or down the ring to view the ring-monitor statistics of the next known station. You do not have to go back to the table.

FIGURE 23.12.

Network Error screen for Token Ring.

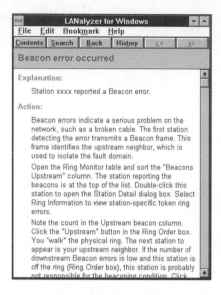

FIGURE 23.13.

Station Detail screen for a Token Ring device.

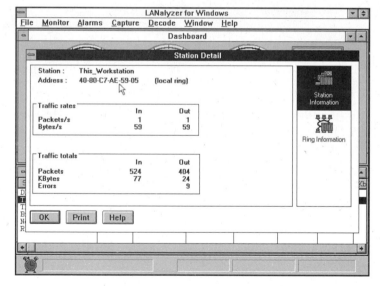

FIGURE 23.14.

Ring Information screen for a Token Ring device.

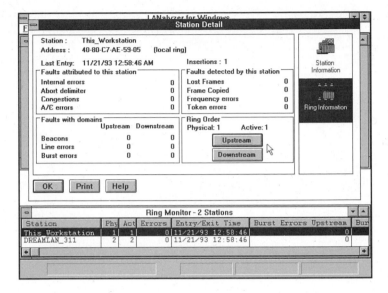

If you are interested only in looking at server or router devices, select the appropriate monitor option from the Monitor pull-down menu option. The Server Monitor window provides a list of known NetWare and AppleTalk file servers and their status. (See Figure 23.15.) Router Monitor provides information about known NetWare and AppleTalk routers, their statuses, and which protocols are supported. (See Figure 23.16.) Ring Monitor presents information about all local Token Ring devices (whether they are active or not), errors, and the last entry and exit times. (See Figure 23.14.)

FIGURE 23.15.

Server Monitor window.

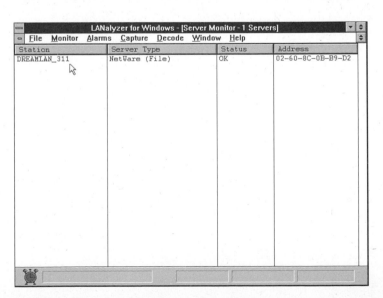

FIGURE 23.16.

*Router Monitor
window.*

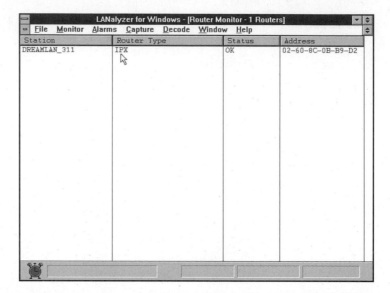

NOTE ▷

The current version of LANalyzer for Windows (2.0) does not identify IP routers.

Four different trend graphs are available:

1. Packets/s
2. Utilization percentage
3. Errors/s
4. Kilobyte/s

In a trend graph, the statistic is plotted every 15 minutes, and the value is an average over this 15-minute time period. The trend data is saved automatically by LZFW in binary files. At the beginning of each calendar month, a new binary trend data file is generated. The naming convention of the files have the form *mmmddyy.TRD*—for example, JUL0193.TRD. The binary trend data can be exported as a comma-delimited ASCII text file so it can be easily imported into spreadsheet and database applications. A sample Utilization% trend graph is shown in Figure 23.17.

FIGURE 23.17.

Utilization% trend graph window.

As discussed in the previous chapter, it is important for you to baseline your network so you know the level of "normal" activity. This helps you plan for network growth and troubleshooting. The trend information is also helpful in setting alarm thresholds.

> **TIP** ▶
>
> It is a good idea to print out your trend graphs on a monthly basis as part of your long-term baseline record. This will give you an idea if your network needs segmenting, for example. This is especially useful after you have reorganized your network (to see if your new design is working out).

Various Alarm Conditions

LZFW tracks different alarm conditions and reports them to you with the following means:

An alarm indicator (which turns from green to red)
An alarm-clock icon
A ticker-tape message

> **CAUTION** ▶
>
> Alarms and messages logged by LZFW are not saved on a permanent basis. When you exit LZFW, all that information is lost. You should print out the Alarm Log when you are troubleshooting.

TIP ►

Liberal use of the NetWare Expert option should be exercised whenever possible during troubleshooting.

You can configure LZFW to alert you to any of the following unusual conditions:

Excessive packet rate
Excessive error rate
Excessive utilization
Overloaded servers
Servers that go down
Routers that go down
Ethernet-specific errors
Token-Ring-specific errors

LZFW differentiates between network, server, and router errors. They are reflected by the three rectangular alarm indicators on the Dashboard turning from green to red. (Refer back to Figure 23.1.) At the same time, a yellow alarm clock icon appears at the bottom of your screen in the alarm status bar area. A ticker-tape message describing the problem will scroll by, next to the alarm clock. This same message is logged in the appropriate Alarm Log. A beeping sound will be sounded through your PC speaker.

You can view the alarm messages by double-clicking the appropriate network, server, or router alarm indicator. Or you can select the Alarm pull-down menu, and then select View Network, View Server, or View Router option.

LZFW comes preset with certain alarm thresholds. However, they may not be appropriate for your particular network. You should modify the thresholds after you have the chance to baseline your network activity. This is important because you want to be alerted to problems before they get out of hand; but you don't want to get too many false alarms.

CAUTION ►

Remember, no two network segments are the same. Therefore, the alarm threshold settings for one network segment may not be appropriate for another.

NOTE ▷

The threshold settings are indicated by a red arc on top of the Packets/s and Utilization% gauges on the Dashboard. The Errors/s gauge does not show a red arc for its threshold setting.

You can configure additional types of errors that will trigger an alarm (through the Advanced Alarm Settings feature). These are listed in Table 23.2.

Table 23.2. Advanced alarm settings.

Ethernet	Token Ring
Short Packet error	Congestion error
Long Packet error	Internal error
Jabber error	Beacon error
	Abort Delimiter error
	ARI/FCI error
	Frequency error

One of the most important features in LZFW enables you to specify an application to execute when a predefined alarm happens. For example, you can have LZFW execute a communication program to call your pager when a server goes down. You configure this through the Alarm -> Execute on Alarm pull-down menu option.

TIP ▷

You can pass alarm information to your application by using the following command line parameters:

%t—Time

%d—Date

%a—Alarm type

%m—Message

For example, if the command line you specified is `PAGER %t, %d, %a, %m`, and a Server Down alarm occurs, the PAGER program sends you the following message:

```
13:02:43, 07/31/93, Server, server_name no longer responds
```

Some Tips in Troubleshooting Using LZFW

Depending on the experts, some say Ethernet is easier to troubleshoot while others argue Token Ring is easier because of the built-in MAC control frames. This section discusses some tips that can help you troubleshoot your LAN.

First, consider Ethernet collisions. You may notice frames with a source address of "AA-AA-AA." These are collision fragments or jam patterns resulting from collisions. It is very likely that the station that transmits right after a collision is the cause of the collision. Of course, given the first-come, first-served nature of Ethernet, this is not always the case.

When trying to locate Ethernet errors, it is best to use the Station Monitor table (see Figure 23.1) and check the Errors counter. Double-clicking this heading will sort the table, placing the station with the most errors reported at the top. This also works for Token Ring errors.

It is a little easier to track down Token Ring errors than Ethernet errors. For example, in most cases when a burst error is detected, only the downstream station would report it. It has been observed that in certain situations, multiple downstream stations will report burst errors. In such cases, the station that reported the most is closest to the source of the error. You can easily determine the location of the station that is causing the error by using the Upstream and Downstream buttons in the Ring Information windows to "walk" around the ring and view statistics for all ring stations that LZFW has observed. (Refer back to Figure 23.14.)

Because LZFW has post-capturing capability, it is best to capture all frames during the troubleshooting process. With the original trace file saved, you can then apply different filter options to examine the events from different angles. Without post-filtering, one either captures too much data or not enough. The more RAM you have in the LZFW station, the bigger the capture buffer.

You can increase the number of frames captured by reducing the "packet slice" to be saved. By default, the whole frame is saved. You can change it with the Capture Options dialog box.

TIP ▶

The capture buffer can be as large as the virtual memory available to Windows. However, performance is best when the capture buffer fits within the available physical (extended) memory of your LZFW station.

Installing LANalyzer for Windows

Installing LZFW is no different from installing any Windows-based packages. From the Windows Program Manger, click the File menu, select Run, and type A:\SETUP or B:\SETUP, as appropriate.

CAUTION ▶

In order to use LZFW with your particular NIC, you must have an ODI-compliant driver that supports *promiscuous* mode operation (the capability of an NIC to make a copy of the frames that are not addressed to it). If the driver you need is not supplied with LZFW, you need to contact the manufacturer.

If DI.COM fails to load and gives you an error message indicating it cannot find a support card, you need to update your driver.

NOTE ▶

Normally, NICs only accept frames addressed to them, as indicated in the destination-address field in the MAC header. As previously defined, the promiscuous mode is the capability of an NIC to make a copy of the frames that are not addressed to it. In the case of Token Ring, it also does not set the bits in the MAC trailer to indicate this frame has been "recognized" and copied.

CAUTION ▶

Note that not all Token Ring cards can be put into the promiscuous mode. For example, the IBM 16/4 Token-Ring card and *any* card that uses the TROPIC chipset cannot be used with LZFW. This is a limitation of the chipset.

Only the Madge cards have been certified by Novell. However, as of this writing, you also can use Xircom, Thomas-Conrad, Olicom, Intel TokenExpress, and Proteon Token Ring adapters. Check with the vendors for their latest ODI driver.

Because of a bug in the shipping version of DI.COM, most Token Ring drivers have problems seeing NCP packets. A new DI.COM (v2.01) can be downloaded from CompuServe or found on NSEPro. The filename is LZFWDI.EXE.

CAUTION ▶

There have been some reports that some Ethernet cards, such as 3COM's EtherLink III (3C509), do not correctly report errors to the drivers; in such a case, LZFW could not notify you of possible problems. When in doubt, double-check with a *real* NE2000 card. Sometimes, compatible cards are not 100-percent compatible at the driver level.

TIP ▶

LZFW might not run correctly on some PCs if you are using an EXOS205 NIC or an Ethernet LANalyzer adapter in a 16-bit slot in the 16-bit mode. The solution is to force the adapter to work in the 8-bit mode.

If you do not have AppleTalk traffic, you can comment out the APPLE.EXE line from your LZTSR.BAT file and the VTXRX.386 line from Window's SYSTEM.INI file. However, upon starting LZFW, you will be warned that VTXRX.386 is not loaded and that AppleTalk server-checking cannot be started, but the application will otherwise function normally.

LZFW is shipped with a number of drivers. If the driver for your particular NIC is not listed, the installation procedure does allow for an "unknown" card. Pick Other from the list. The installation program will prompt you for the driver name as well as related information.

These days, it is very common for Windows to be installed on a network drive to simplify file management. However, you should not MAP ROOT the drive that points to the Windows directory; in such a case, LZFW will not be able to find its files. Also, running LZFW off the server can cause extra traffic that may confuse your troubleshooting efforts.

TIP ▶

To simplify your troubleshooting efforts, run your LZFW off a local hard disk. Save captured data to local hard disk as well.

CAUTION ▶

LZFW 2.0 does not work under Win/OS2 in OS/2 2.1.

Name Gathering in LANalyzer for Windows

LZFW can use station names instead of MAC addresses in its tables. This is highly desirable because one can identify a station much more readily when it has a distinctive name. LZFW must log into a NetWare server in order to obtain the login names and server names.

TIP ▶

You should run the Name Gathering utility during your prime network usage hours in order to capture as complete a name file as possible. Names you have missed can be added manually.

CAUTION ▶

Every time you run the Name Gathering utility, LZFW overwrites the old name file entries. Ethernet station names are stored in NAMES_ET.CSV and Token Ring station names are stored in NAMES_TR.CSV.

> **TIP** ▶
>
> If you want to save the names permanently, put them in *LZFW.INI* under the section [Predefined Addresses-Ethernet] or [Predefined Addresses-Token Ring].

If LZFW discovers multiple station addresses with the same name, it gives each station a unique name. This is done by appending a tilde (~) character and a number at the end of the name. For example, if LZFW found the name Peter on two stations, the second station will be assigned the name Peter~2.

> **NOTE** ▶
>
> Names are not shown for stations logged in under GUEST and SUPERVISOR. Also, the station running LZFW software will show up as This_Workstation.

LZFW has two ways of handling AppleTalk names. If the AppleTalk stack is running on a NetWare server, the name of the server is displayed for the AppleTalk router. For non-NetWare AppleTalk routers, such as FastPath or Gatorbox, the name of the form consists of the notation RTR, followed by the number of the local AppleTalk network, followed by the number of any other AppleTalk network to which the router routes. For example, if you have a Gatorbox on AppleTalk Network 1 and routes to AppleTalk Network 2, the router name displayed by LZFW 2.0 is of the form RTR-1-2.

Known Limitations and Bugs

The following is a list of some known bugs and limitations in LZFW version 2.0:

1. The Token Ring source-routing decode function does not decode the ring numbers correctly. The solution is to use the hex dump information.

2. Checksum error on IP frames reports false checksum error on ICMP (ping) frames. The solution is to ignore these false errors.

3. Out of the box, LZFW 2.0 does not decode certain new NCP function calls in NetWare 4.x. The solution is to use a patch, available from the NetWire forum on CompuServe, called LZW40.EXE (18-Jun-93; 149296 bytes) which addresses this limitation. This file is also available on NSEPro (Network Support Encyclopedia, Novell Professional Volume).

4. If you are using a Compaq 386/33L or Compaq Deskpro 386/20e with the LANalyzer Ethernet adapter, LZFW might crash at high network loads.

5. Sometimes the EXOS205 or LANalyzer Ethernet adapters might erroneously report good events as Undersize Errors.

6. When using a shared memory Ethernet adapter, you must ensure that the adapter interrupt level is set lower than that of the mouse.

LANtern Network Monitor and LANtern Services Manager 1.3x

LANtern Network Monitor

Novell's LANtern Network Monitor is a rack-mountable device that can help you manage and monitor your multivendor Ethernet networks from a central source. It is a dedicated listening device that gathers statistics and detects events on the network segment to which it is attached. For smaller networks, LANtern LTD can monitor up to 32 stations on a single Ethernet segment and can be upgraded to a standard LANtern.

> **NOTE** ▶
>
> A "standard" LANtern comes with 1 MB of RAM and is capable of tracking up to 3,000 devices. An upgrade to 2 MB of RAM enables up to 6,000 devices.

> **CAUTION** ▶
>
> You need a LANtern Network Monitor for *every* Ethernet segment you want monitored.

As with LANalyzer for Windows (discussed in the previous section), LANtern Network Monitor gathers both real-time data and long-term trend data. Real-time data sampling intervals are user-selectable, and long-term trend data is acquired over 15-minute intervals. Because LANtern is a stand-alone device, you do not need to have a dedicated console as you do with LZFW.

With specialized hardware built in, LANtern is able to detect various Ethernet-specific error conditions such as jabber and CRC/Alignment errors. Separate counters are kept for each error condition. It can keep statistics on the frame-size distribution that LZFW cannot. LANtern has five "bins" for the size histogram (see Figure 23.18), as follows:

1. 64- to 127-byte packets

2. 128- to 255-byte packets

3. 256- to 511-byte packets

4. 512- to1023-byte packets

5. 1024- to 1518-byte packets

FIGURE 23.18.

LANtern real-time counters.

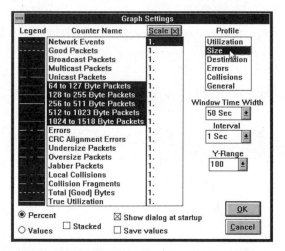

driver or your application may not be making full use of the "1K" frame size offered by Ethernet. However, sometimes this cannot be avoided, such as with terminal emulation.

Here are some of the notification alarms (Figure 23.19) and thresholds (Figure 23.20) you can configure LANtern to provide:

New Station: A station is transmitting for the first time. This is useful in detecting intruders.

Station Inactive: A station has not transmitted for a specific period of time. This is useful in tracking servers and routers.

Station Active: A station starts transmitting again after it has been classified as "inactive." This is useful in tracking servers and routers.

Duplicate IP Address: More than one station has the same IP address. This helps in troubleshooting and network management.

Cable Failure: Periodically checks the cable to which LANtern is attached. This helps cable management.

Utilization: Monitors bandwidth-utilization percentage. This helps network growth planning.

Error: Monitors overall error frames as a percentage of total events on the wire. This helps in troubleshooting.

Collisions: Monitors overall collisions as a percentage of total network events. This helps in troubleshooting.

FIGURE 23.19.

LANtern Alarm Notification Settings.

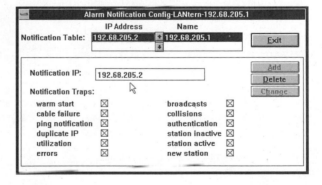

FIGURE 23.20.

*LANtern Alarm
Threshold settings.*

```
┌─────────────────────────────────────────────────────────────┐
│ ─        Alarm Thresholds Config-LANtern-192.68.205.1        │
│ ┌─Configure Alarm Type────────────────────────┐  ┌─────────┐ │
│ │ ⦿ Utilization  ○ Broadcasts  ○ Collisions  ○ Errors │  │  Exit   │ │
│ └─────────────────────────────────────────────┘  └─────────┘ │
│ ┌─Alarm Gauges────────────────────────────────────────────┐  │
│ │  State:  ⦿ Enabled     ○ Disabled           ┌─────────┐  │  │
│ │                                             │ Change  │  │  │
│ │  Interval (sec):        1        High Threshold:  030.0 %  │  │
│ │  [←──────────────────→]          [←──────────────────→]  │  │
│ │                                                          │  │
│ │  Min Traffic (packets)  50       High Threshold Delta:  005.0 %  │  │
│ │  [←──────────────────→]          [←──────────────────→]  │  │
│ └──────────────────────────────────────────────────────────┘  │
│ ┌─Alarm Data──────────────────────────────────────────────┐  │
│ │  Last Sampled Value:      009.1%                          │  │
│ │    Peaks           Current    Date Last Reset   Time Last Reset │  │
│ │  Low Water Mark    000.0%       11/21/93          3:08:26 │  │
│ │  High Water Mark   009.1%       11/21/93          3:08:50 │  │
│ └──────────────────────────────────────────────────────────┘  │
│ Alarms are generated for each alarm type when monitored parameters cross │
│ either the high or low threshold.  Alarms may be enabled or disabled.  The │
│ interval over which a particular gauge is to be sampled is specified in │
│ seconds.  The Minimum Traffic setting indicates the number of packets that │
│ must arrive during the sample time before the gauge value is updated.  The │
│ High Threshold Delta indicates the value of the gauge that rearms alarm │
│ generation, and is specified relative to the threshold. │
└─────────────────────────────────────────────────────────────┘
```

> **CAUTION** ▶
>
> The Cable Test option is useful only if you are using 10Base2 or 10Base5 cabling. You will not be able to detect cable failure in a 10BaseT environment, except for the cable segment to which LANtern is attached.

LANtern uses the industry-standard Simple Network Management Protocol (SNMP) to communicate with a central management console. You can use third-party network-management consoles to communicate with LANtern as long as they use SNMP. LANtern Services Manager (LSM), Novell's own central-management console software, is designed to take full advantage of LANtern. It uses Novell's Btrieve database to collect and organize data polled from different LANtern Network Monitors that you have installed on different segments.

> **CAUTION** ▶
>
> One disadvantage of LANtern is that it needs to communicate over TCP/IP. Therefore, if you have IPX-only routers, you cannot use LANtern to report back to your management console through your network. You can, however, communicate with LANtern with a modem.

LANtern Services Manager

LANtern Services Manager (LSM) is a Windows-based management console software. Similar to LZFW, it has a simple-to-use and easy-to-understand graphical user interface. You can easily search, sort, and rearrange the Btrieve database to set up a convenient, informative view of your network.

> **NOTE** ▶
>
> LSM will automatically discover LANtern Network Monitors installed on your whole network if the intervening routers pass BOOTP frames. If the intervening routers do not pass BOOTP frames, you need to manually provide LSM information about those "blocked" LANtern Network Monitors.

The LSM desktop consists of a menu bar across the top of the screen and three windows: a Background Activities window, a World window, and an Alarms window. (See Figure 23.21.) The World window displays an icon for each network segment that has a LANtern Network Monitor attached. When a problem occurs on such a segment, LSM may display one or more alarm icons next to the segment icon. (See Figure 23.22.)

FIGURE 23.21.

LANtern Services Manager desktop.

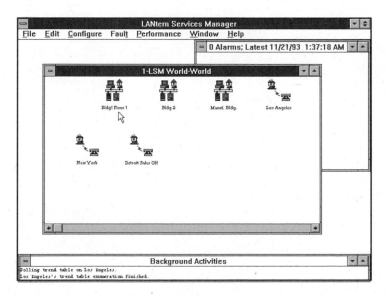

The Background Activities window displays a short description of each LSM activity as it happens. (See Figure 23.23.) The Alarm window displays a short description of each alarm condition, the name of the LANtern Network Monitor that reported it, and the time and date stamp. (See Figure 23.24.)

FIGURE 23.22.

Segment with an alarm condition.

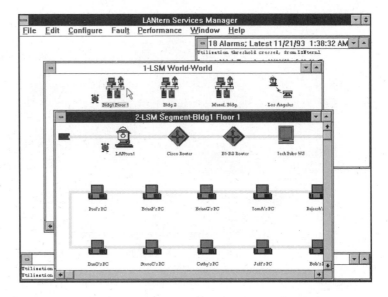

FIGURE 23.23.

LSM Background Activity window.

FIGURE 23.24.

LSM Alarm window.

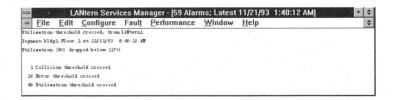

Using the various performance gauges and graphs, you can monitor the health of your Ethernet segments. The following sections will examine how you can apply these tools.

Real-Time Performance Gauges and Counters

There are four performance gauges available in LSM (see Figure 23.25), as follows:

1. **Utilization**: A measure of the average percentage of bandwidth utilization used by all traffic in the current polling interval

2. **Broadcasts**: A measure of broadcast frames as a percentage of good frames

3. **Collisions**: A measure of collisions as a percentage of all events on the local Ethernet segment

4. **Errors**: A measure of error events as a percentage of all frames (good and bad)

FIGURE 23.25.

LSM Performance Gauges.

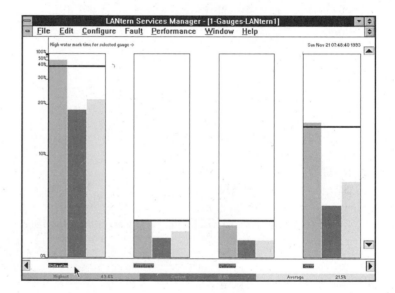

Each LANtern Network Monitor has its own set of four performance gauges. Each gauge consists of three bar graphs showing the highest value in red, the current value in green, and the average value in blue.

> **TIP** ▶
>
> When you click a gauge name, its highest, current, and average numeric values are displayed across the bottom of the window.

It is important to properly set the alarm thresholds of these gauges to provide you with early warning. You can set the threshold of a gauge by either clicking the left edge of the gauge box and moving the resulting line up and down to the desired threshold level, or with the pull-down menu: Configure -> Active Window.

> **TIP** ▷
>
> You can use the F3 hot key to bring up the gauge threshold configuration dialog box.

Table 23.3 shows some Novell recommended gauge-threshold settings.

Table 23.3. Novell recommended LSM gauge settings.

Gauge	Interval	Min. Traffic	High Threshold (percent)
Utilization	1	0	25
Broadcasts	2	250	90
Collisions	1	100	2
Errors	1	100	2

A total of 19 real-time counters are available to measure different events or traffic on the monitored segment. (Refer back to Figure 23.18.) They are expressed either as percentages or numbers. All percentages are calculated in terms of network events, except for bytes per second, for which 100 percent is 10 Mbps.

You can separately select the sampling intervals for the gauges and counters. The gauges' time interval can range between 1 and 60 seconds. The counters' range is between 1 second and 5 minutes.

> **TIP** ▷
>
> It is strongly advised that you set the time interval for longer values so your polling traffic is not impacting the overall network traffic. However, for troubleshooting purposes you should use a small time interval so you get a better sampling of your traffic condition. Otherwise, any anomalies may get "averaged" out.

One of the nice real-time monitoring features in LSM is its Conversation table. (See Figure 23.26.) The table lists the source and destination MAC address of each frame, among other information. This can help you identify servers, routers, and power-users on your network. Also, this is useful in determining the possible sources of high bandwidth-utilization.

FIGURE 23.26.

LSM conversation table.

LANtern Services Manager - [1-Conversations-192.68.205.1]

File	Edit	Configure	Fault	Performance	Window	Help

Source	Destination	Protocols	Bytes / Se	Packets /	Errors / S	First transmit	Last transmit	S
192.68.205.1	00-00-1b-02-82-58	IP	0	0	0	11/21/93 3:04:24	11/21/93 3:08:50	00
192.68.205.1	Broadcast	IP	0	0	0	11/21/93 3:04:24	11/21/93 3:04:24	00

Long-Term Trend Data

LSM provides only long-term trend data in terms of counters. No gauges are available; the same 19 counters are available. However, the information presented is in percentages only. (See Figure 23.27; compare it with Figure 23.18.) Recall that trend data is averaged over a 15-minute interval and is not an configurable option.

FIGURE 23.27.

LSM trend information counters.

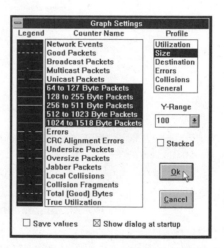

CAUTION ▶

Remember that LANtern Network Monitors can store only 25 hours worth of trend data. If your LSM station does not poll the monitors at least once a day, you risk having gaps in your trend database.

Long-term trend data can be used to set alarm thresholds as well as for network growth planning.

LANtern Alarms

LANtern Network Monitors send both gauge alarms and problem alarms. Gauge thresholds are configured with LSM. (See Figure 23.20.) Various alarms can be logged into the Alarm Log database as per your specification. (See Figure 23.28.) This is done through a pull-down menu option, Configure -> Alarm Disposition. Separate Alarm Log tables are kept for each monitored segment.

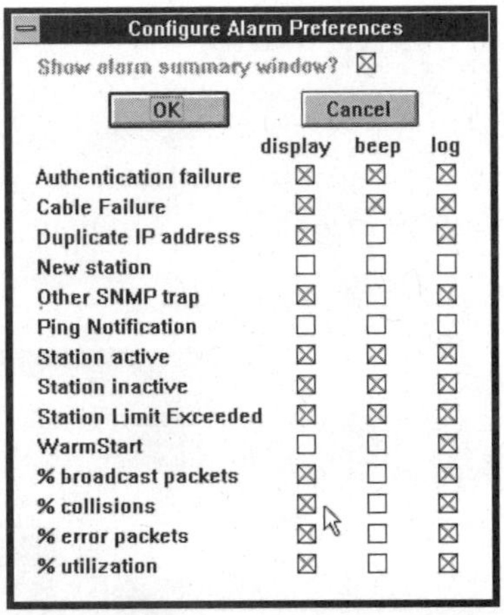

FIGURE 23.28.

Alarm disposition.

TIP ▶

In order to view the "All Segments" Alarm Log table, you must first close the World View window. Then, access the pull-down menu, Fault-> Alarm Log. Otherwise, you will see only the Alarm Log table for the particular LANtern segment you have opened or selected in the World View window.

Because LANtern Network Monitors send their alarms as SNMP traps, you can configure each LANtern to send its alarms to different management consoles. These consoles do not have to be LSMs. They can be third-party SNMP-based management consoles.

Cable Testing

You can configure LSM to periodically test the cable segment to which it is attached. (See Figure 23.29.) Whenever a scheduled cable test is performed by a given LANtern Network Monitor, an entry is displayed in the Background Activity window.

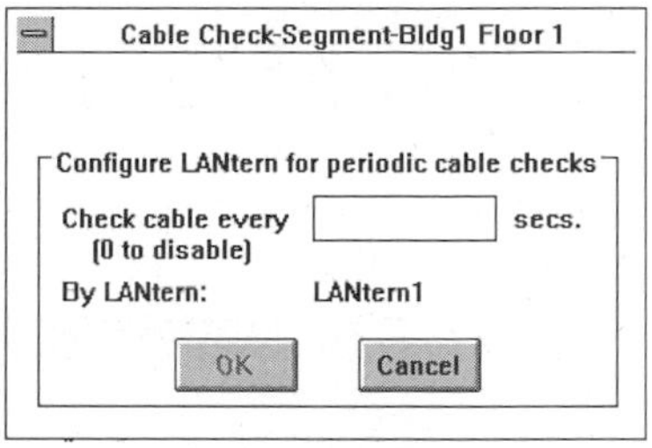

FIGURE 23.29.

Cable Check configuration window.

```
┌─────────────────────────────────────────┐
│ ⊟   Cable Check-Segment-Bldg1 Floor 1    │
│                                          │
│  ┌ Configure LANtern for periodic cable checks ┐
│  │                                        │
│  │  Check cable every  [_____]  secs.  │
│  │  (0 to disable)                        │
│  │  By LANtern:        LANtern1           │
│  │                                        │
│  │       [   OK   ]    [ Cancel ]         │
│  └────────────────────────────────────────┘
│                                          │
└──────────────────────────────────────────┘
```

CAUTION ▶

In certain situations, the Cable Test function fails to detect an "open segment." This is possibly because the transceiver thinks the wire is busy. Therefore, do not rely too heavily on this feature.

Installing LANtern Network Monitor

LANtern Network Monitor is shipped with the following factory default settings:

LANtern network IP address	192.68.205.1
Network subnet mask	255.255.255.128
LANtern serial IP address	192.68.205.129
Serial subnet mask	255.255.255.128
Gateway address	0.0.0.0

Although LANtern is suppose to be a "plug-and-play" monitor, you may want to change some of its default settings, especially if you have IP traffic on your network. You need to connect a terminal or a workstation that is running terminal emulation to the monitor. The communication setting is 9600 baud, 8 data bits, no parity, and 1 stop bit.

TIP ▶

To get into the built-in setup program, you need to hold the reset switch down (one in the back and one in the front of LANtern) *while* turning the power on. You have to supply a break character to initiate the setup program. Some terminal emulators are not capable of generating a proper break character for this purpose.

It is possible to field-upgrade the firmware in LANtern Network Monitors. This is easily done by using a TFTP (Trivial File Transfer Protocol) server. A TFTP daemon program is included with the LANtern Services Manager software. (See Figure 23.30.)

FIGURE 23.30.

Download Settings dialog window.

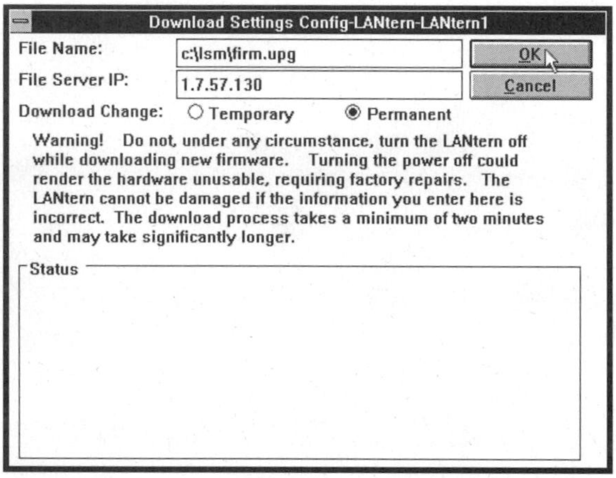

CAUTION

It is *very* important that you do not turn off the LANtern Network Monitor or leave the Download Settings dialog box in LSM until the download process is complete. You risk destroying the EPROM in the LANtern Network Monitor.

Installing LANtern Services Manager v1.3

Although LSM is a Windows-based product, the install program is called INSTALL.EXE rather than the more traditional SETUP.EXE. It is a DOS program, thus you do not need to run it from Windows. It uses the old C-worthy style interface. You don't have a choice of directories into which the software will be installed. It has to be installed to \XLN; you can, however, pick the drive to which it is installed.

As with the LANalyzer for Windows installation, if your NIC is not listed in the LSM list of drivers, you can either manually install it by choosing Skip Adapter Install, or choose Other and specify the name and path of your driver.

CAUTION ▷

If you have to rerun the installation program or reinstall LSM, the installation program does not warn you before deleting your existing LSM software and database.

NOTE ▷

The installation program requires about 500K of conventional memory to run. If you have your NIC drivers loaded low, you may not have sufficient conventional memory to perform the install.

TIP ▷

The TCPIP.EXE file that comes with LSM is from LAN WorkPlace for DOS v4.0, and the VTCPIP.386 file is the older version that does not work well with NIC set at interrupt 2. If you do not have LAN WorkPlace for DOS 4.1 or newer, change your NIC's interrupt. If you have LAN WorkPlace for DOS 4.1, you may need the newer VTCPIP.386 file from Novell. This file can be downloaded from NetWire or from NSE.Pro. At the time of this writing, the file is part of WINUP7.ZIP. This VTCPIP.386 is dated 11-13-92, 4:10am, and is 10,556 bytes in size.

For more technical information regarding the functionality of LANtern Network Monitors, download LANTRN.TXT from NetWire or NSEPro. The file size is 262,188 bytes, dated for 30-Nov-92.

NOTE ▷

LANTRN.TXT also contained LANtern MIB information, so you can compile a LANtern schema file for communication with LANtern from a third-party management console.

TIP ▶

In some situations when TrueType fonts are used in Windows, LSM may display in unreadable fonts. Get LSM119.EXE (297,153 bytes; 02-Jul-93) from NetWire or NSEPro.

CAUTION ▶

You may want to install LSM and Windows swap file on different partitions (if you have the choice). LSM might report "Out of Disk Space" after collecting data for a number of weeks, while there is still much free disk space. This is caused by the *permanent* Windows swap file on the same partition. A temporary swap file does not present this problem.

NetWare Management System v1.1x

Novell's NetWare Management System (NMS) is really a suite of products. The core of NMS is known as NMS Runtime, formerly referred to as NetWare Management Map (NMM). This software provides a common platform of basic services necessary for managing a multivendor network. (See Figure 23.31.)

NMS Runtime supports "snap-in" modules so that end users and third-party developers can support their own devices by sending information to the NetWare Management System. By using a common management console interface, you eliminate the need to switch between various network management applications to manage your network. NMS enables you to have an integrated network management system with a graphical user interface by adding in the appropriate snap-in modules.

FIGURE 23.31.

NetWare Management System screen.

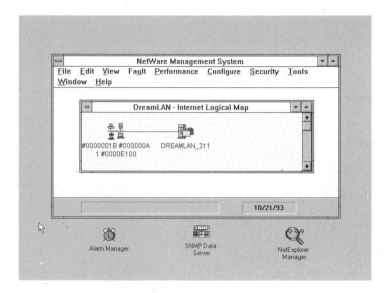

Among the various built-in monitoring and error-logging options, the NMS Runtime management console will also accept and log any SNMP traps. That means you can set up the LANtern Network Monitors to send their alerts to NMS instead of to LANtern Services Manager. Unfortunately, the current version of NMS (v1.1x) does not enable you to configure the LANtern Network Monitors. You will still need LSM for this purpose. A future version of NSM should address this shortcoming.

NMS Runtime is composed of three parts: a management station, the NetExplorer server, and the NetExplorer Plus "agents." The NetExplorer server discovers and gathers information about IPX and IP networks. It also gathers network topology information from servers and routers and transmits this information to the management station. NetExplorer Plus software can be installed on all your NetWare servers to send back extra discovery information, such as user names for workstations and segment media information, to NetExplorer.

You will find that the main desktop window layout of the NMS Runtime console is very similar to that of LANalyzer for Windows: there is a pull-down menu at the top and an alarm status bar at the bottom with a ticker-tape window. Alarms are handled differently in NMS when compared to LZFW and LSM. In NMS, once an alarm is logged in its Btrieve database, it needs to be "acknowledged." Otherwise, this alarm condition will always be displayed on the map. (See Figure 23.32.) This very useful feature ensures that error reports are not easily overlooked.

FIGURE 23.32.

NMS Runtime internet map with outstanding alarms.

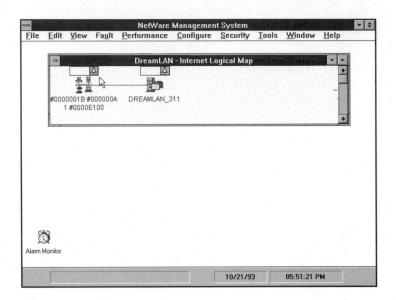

Keep in mind that NMS v1.1x is designed to merely provide a common platform into which specialized snap-in modules will plug, thus creating a custom centralized management and monitoring console. The inherent LAN monitoring and management features are minimal. You may wonder, then, why we are discussing this product here?

NMS is relevant because many third-party vendors are either writing their hardware monitoring and management software to use NMS or are building hardware that can be managed by NMS-snap-ins. Novell's Hub Services Manager, Intel's EtherExpress TPE Hubs (discussed in a forthcoming section), and SynOptics' Optivity for NMS (discussed in the next chapter) are examples. Novell recently started shipping a snap-in management module, NetWare for SAA Services Manager v2.0 (formerly known as Communications Services Manager v1.1), for its very popular communications product, NetWare for SAA. It is expected that NMS will become popular among mid-size to large NetWare sites. Therefore, some mention of how one can take advantage of its built-in features (for the sake of LAN monitoring and management) is warranted.

The following two sections look at how you can utilize some of the available information from NMS Runtime itself, as well as NetWare Services Manager (NSM), a Novell snap-in module, to help troubleshoot and manage your network. NSM is shipped with NMS Runtime.

NOTE ▶

For OS/2-oriented network managers, Novell offers NetWare Services Manager (for LAN NetView) v1.5. It is an OS/2-based NetWare-management application that "snaps" *unmodified* into IBM's LAN NetView product. NSM (for LAN NetView) v1.5 replaces NetWare Services Manager (OS/2 Option) 1.0.

Network Alarms

NMS Runtime deals with alarms in the following three ways:

- It gives a visual notification of alarm detection and its severity.
- It categorizes and describes the alarm.
- It logs the alarm in a permanent Btrieve database

TIP ▶

Depending on the severity of the alarm, the color and position of the alarm bell icon differ, as follows:

Severity	Color	Position
Minor alarm	Yellow	Left
Major alarm	Magenta	Center
Critical alarm	Red	Right

When an alarm is received, NMS Runtime displays a ringing alarm-clock icon in the bottom-left corner of the desktop. Optionally, a ticker-tape message is available, describing the problem, its severity, and the object that generated the alarm. (See Figure 23.33.)

TIP ▶

The alarm clock rings for only 20 seconds and then disappears. The same is true for the ticker-tape message. However, because an alarm-bell icon will be displayed over the LAN segment that originated the alarm, you can use either the Alarm Monitor or Alarm Report to find out the alarm details.

FIGURE 23.33.

NMS alarm notification.

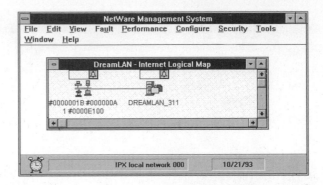

You probably would not want to log every single alarm into the database because it can get very large very quickly. You can use the Alarm Disposition option (accessed through the Fault pull-down menu option) to configure if a given alarm is to be logged.

CAUTION ▷

If you configured NMS Runtime so that no alarm is logged into the database, the alarm-bell icon will not appear on the map.

The information presented in the Alarm Monitor screen is not permanent. This window is opened automatically when you start up NMS. When this window is closed and reopened, it will be cleared of alarm information.

NOTE ▷

To reopen the Alarm Monitor screen, use the pull-down menu option, Fault-> Alarm Monitor.

Alarm Report entries are permanent. This is where you "acknowledge" the alarms. Notes can be made for each alarm in the table. If you are unsure where a particular alarm originates, use the LAN icon. (See Figure 23.34.) You also can get some help on the cause and possible solution to a given alarm by first selecting an alarm and then selecting the question mark icon. (See Figure 23.35.)

FIGURE 23.34.

Alarm Report window. The mouse pointer indicates the LAN icon.

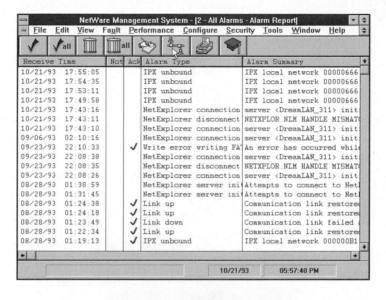

FIGURE 23.35.

Online alarm help.

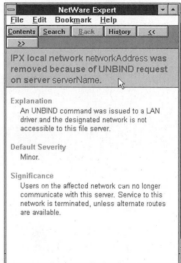

As with LANalyzer for Windows, you can configure NMS to execute programs upon receipt of alarms. However, you can configure NMS to execute *different* procedures, depending on the alarm. (This is not possible with LZFW v2.0.) Using this feature in conjunction with the "early warning" capability of LANtern Network Monitors or other SNMP-based network monitoring devices, you can receive customized alert messages in a variety of ways.

This discussion of alarm-handling also serves as a basic building block for when this book discuss snap-in modules such as Novell's Hub Services Manager and SynOptics' Optivity for NMS.

NetWare Services Manager

Because NMS v1.1x was not designed to be a LAN-monitoring or a management tool, it has no built-in features to detect errors on your LAN. However, with the help of Novell's NetWare Services Manager snap-in module, you can baseline your LAN traffic. For example, by monitoring the amount of traffic going in and coming out of each of your servers, you can obtain a fair, but not necessarily 100-percent accurate, bandwidth-utilization profile of your LAN segments.

> **CAUTION** ▶
>
> If you have multiple servers on a LAN segment, you need to sum the traffic statistics from all your servers to get a feel for the overall utilization. Note that utilization due to broadcasts is not included. Therefore, the number you get will be an underestimate of the actual traffic.

You can monitor the traffic by the following protocol types (See Figure 23.36):

IPX traffic
IP traffic
ARP traffic
RARP traffic
CLNP traffic
AppleTalk traffic

You should be careful when setting the polling interval. Choose a short time interval if you are troubleshooting server problems. Use a longer interval when you are baselining your server for historical trend information.

> **CAUTION** ▶
>
> You should be aware when analyzing your data that each collection interval may not be the exact same length. Delays introduced by Windows, NMS, or the network itself may shorten or lengthen the real time period during which data is collected.

FIGURE 23.36.

*Protocol Graph
Settings.*

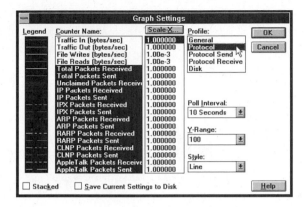

Constant monitoring of the amount of traffic going in or out of your servers will give you a good handle on your segment bandwidth-utilization. This is especially true if you track the bytes per second, Traffic In and Traffic Out statistics. Couple this information with other tools, such as LANalyzer for NetWare, and you can easily determine which server is responsible for the majority of your LAN traffic. You also can determine which protocol is responsible for the high bandwidth-utilization

Installing NetWare Management System Runtime

NMS Runtime installation entails configuring the management station and installing NMS and TCP/IP transport services. NMS Runtime software installation also installs the NetExplorer software on one of your 3.11 servers and NetExplorer Plus agent software on all your 3.11 servers. For the most part, the installation is very straightforward. However, you should have the following information on hand *before* you start the install program (*SETUP.EXE*) from Windows:

1. Supervisor passwords of NetWare servers to which you will install NetExplorer and NetExplorer Plus. You cannot use Supervisor Equivalent here. (This is fixed in v2.0.)

2. NIC information for the management station (that is, type of NIC, name of ODI driver, settings).

3. IP information, if necessary.

CAUTION ▷

There is a "limitation" in the install program; you cannot install or upgrade NetExplorer or NetExplorer Plus servers if you are logged into them. (This is fixed in NMS 2.0.)

TIP ▷

For the optimal performance of your management console, use a workstation with a high-performance CPU (80486) and at least 12MB of RAM. Minimize the number of programs running concurrently with NMS in Windows.

Use a dedicated 3.11 Runtime server as your NetExplorer server and set it as the preferred server for your NMS console. This will prevent your console from hanging when you take down one of your normal servers for maintenance.

NOTE ▷

Your workstation must be attached, but not logged in, to a file server (that is, NETX loaded) before you can successfully run SETUP.

The installation program also modifies your AUTOEXEC.BAT and CONFIG.SYS files. The AUTOEXEC.BAT file loads the DOS SHARE program. Make sure you have a path to where SHARE.EXE is located on your system.

CAUTION ▷

If SHARE.EXE is not loaded before starting NMS, you will get a "share violation" error.

TIP ▷

The installation program creates a SHELL.CFG file in the root of your drive. You should copy the contents of this file into your NET.CFG file if you have one. Otherwise, rename it from SHELL.CFG to NET.CFG and place it in the same directory as your ODI drivers.

CAUTION ▶

Ensure that you update the SNMP files on your NetWare 3.11 servers by checking the last option on the installation menu, "Install NetWare 3.11 SNMP Update software (NetWare Server)."

If you do not update the SNMP.NLM file and use the TCP/IP MIB browser function of NMS Runtime to query the NetWare SNMP agent, the server will abend.

You can have a number of NMS consoles located throughout your network, each configured differently. For example, you can have three different NMS consoles, wherein one logs only LAN traffic-related errors, one logs only server-related errors, and one logs all errors (so you can cross-check and cross-reference with the other two consoles). You can then assign two different support staffs to be in charge of each console and to respond to the alarms.

CAUTION ▶

You should have only one NetExplorer server on the entire network. If you have more than one NetExplorer server, they will not function correctly. However, you can have many NMS management stations communicating with the same NetExplorer server.

CAUTION ▶

Older versions of "Sidewinder" NLM (SIDEWIND.NLM; prior to v1.5) of NetExplorer Plus peaks the CPU utilization to about 80 percent every five seconds. It does not readily release the CPU when other processes need it. Therefore, loading the old SIDEWIND.NLM on a heavily utilized server may cause occasional abends.

SIDEWIND.NLM v1.5 addresses this problem by yielding more readily when other NLMs need CPU time. However, it still peaks your server CPU utilization at five-second intervals.

The installation steps modify each of your servers' AUTOEXEC.NCF files to include some calls to NCF files. You need to uncomment these lines:

NCF File	Function
NMSBASE.NCF	Loads NLMs required for NMS
NETXPLOR.NCF	NetExplorer-related NLMs
NXPPLUS.NCF	NetExplorer Plus-related NLMs

Installing NetWare Services Manager

After installing NMS Runtime, you can install NetWare Services Manager. You follow an installation procedure similar to NMS Runtime. The install program (SETUP.EXE) integrates the NSM function into your NMS Runtime console. Optionally, you can install the NetWare Management Agent onto your servers ("instrument" your servers).

NOTE

NetWare Services Manager comes with *one* license for your NetWare server. You need to purchase additional licenses to "instrument" other NetWare servers on your network.

The NetWare Management Agents (NMAs) enable you to manage and monitor NetWare server resources. For example, you can set thresholds on file cache buffers (see Figure 23.37) and track your server's CPU utilization as a function of time. (See Figure 23.38.)

CAUTION

NetWare Management Agents v1.1x is *not* compatible with NetWare 4.x servers. You need NetWare Management Agents v1.5 or higher to support NetWare 4.x servers.

NetWare 2.x and NetWare 3.11 SFT-III servers are not supported.

FIGURE 23.37.

Server threshold settings.

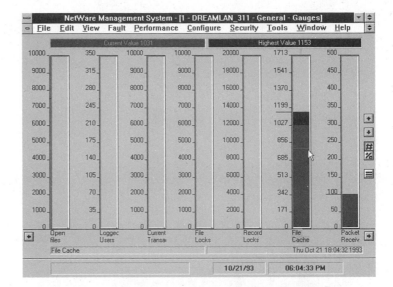

FIGURE 23.38.

CPU utilization graph.

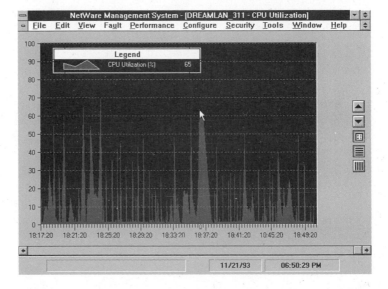

A special user, NETMAN, is created by the NSM installation program. This user name is used to log into your "instrumented" servers. In order to protect the security of the information collected by NMA, you should assign a password to NETMAN on each server and "register" this password in NSM. (Use the pull-down menu Security -> Register NETMAN Password.)

Make sure you edit the instrumented servers' AUTOEXEC.NCF to uncomment the NMA.NCF line so the agents will load automatically when your servers reboot.

NetWare Hub Services 2.0 and Hub Services Manager 1.0

In 1991, Novell introduced Hub Management Interface (HMI), an extension to its Open Data Interface (ODI), as a standard way of communicating with drivers that is capable of network management. In early 1992, Intel introduced EtherExpress 10BaseT twisted-pair Ethernet (TPE) hub adapters, the first NetWare-managed hub adapters conforming to Novell's HMI. In mid-1993, Eagle Technology introduced its own HMI-compliant hub adapters. These are targeted at small- to medium-size networks. For large networks, you can use a traditional hub chassis that has built-in NetWare management services, such as NetWare Hub Services. NetWorth's Series 3000 TriSegment Stackable Hubs are such an example.

NetWare Hub Services, a set of 3 NLMs, can be used to manage these HMI-compliant hub adapters from the file server. HUBCON.NLM provides you with a familiar C-worthy interface from the file server console. (See Figure 23.39.) You can access HUBCON either from the server console or with NetWare's Remote Management Facility (RMF—more commonly known as the RCONSOLE utility). HUBSNMP.NLM is an SNMP agent that enables communication with remote SNMP consoles, such as NSM Runtime, either with TCP/IP or IPX/SPX.

FIGURE 23.39.

HUBCON screen.

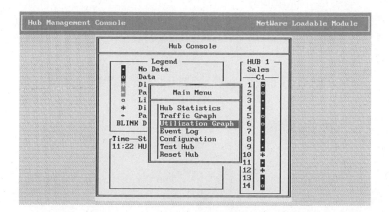

If you have XCONSOLE from either NetWare NFS or NetWare FLeX/IP installed on the server, you can access HUBCON from workstations running X-Windows. You need to tell HUBCON not to use some special characters that X-Windows cannot handle:

```
LOAD HUBCON SIMPLEASCII
```

NetWare Hub Services provide real-time information about HMI-compliant hubs. It can show you the number of ports per hub adapter, the status of each of these ports, the traffic volume on each port, and error statistics on each port. Information is displayed as graphs, tables, and by colors to indicate specific conditions. (See Figures 23.40 through 23.43.)

FIGURE 23.40.

Ethernet hub statistics screen from HUBCON.

```
Hub Management Console                          NetWare Loadable Module

Hub # 1              Sales   EtherExpress(tm) TPE Hub Intel Corporation
Version                1.0   Intel ISA TPE Hub V1.0
Health State        HUB OK   (Health state is OK)
Cards Installed          1   Collisions/s        36    Total KBytes/s      737
Total Ports             14   Very Long Events     0    Total Utilization   61%

  Card Port Name          Login     State Link    Errors Packets  Bytes Coll'ns
    1    1  Mike R.        SUPERVIS  Enab  Up          0       2    158        0
    1    2  Vijay          N/A       Enab  Up          0      69   4680        7
    1    3  Glenn          N/A       Enab  Up          0      82   5707        4
    1    4  Suzanne        N/A       Enab  Up          0      43   3215        5
    1    5  Dave           N/A       Enab  Up          0     255  17424        1
    1    6  Mike P         N/A       Enab  Up          0      40   2758        4
    1    7  Ravi           N/A       Enab  Up          0       0      0        0
    1    8  Ramanan        N/A       Enab  Up          0       0      0        0
    1    9  Bill B.        N/A       Enab  Up          0       0      0        0
    1   10  N/A            N/A       Enab  Down        0       0      0        0
    1   11  Nita           N/A       Enab  Up          7       0      0        0
```

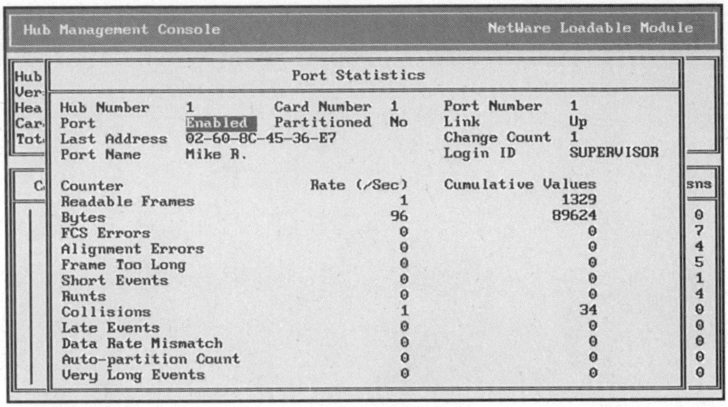

FIGURE 23.41.

Ethernet port statistics screen from HUBCON.

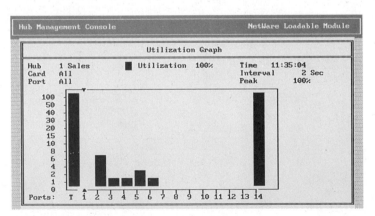

FIGURE 23.42.

Ethernet port traffic graph from HUBCON.

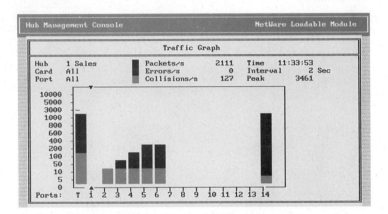

FIGURE 23.43.

Port utilization graph from HUBCON.

If you have a large number of hub adapters distributed across your network, managing them with HUBCON is an inefficient process—you need to access each server or PC workstation in turn to detect and isolate problems. With help from Hub Services Manager, a Novell snap-in module for NMS Runtime, you can manage multiple hubs from one single location with a few simple keystrokes. Using Hub Services Manager, you can obtain the same information as HUBCON, but it is presented in a much more user-friendly fashion. (Sec Figures 23.44 through 23.48.)

FIGURE 23.44.

Hub backpanel window from Hub Services Manager.

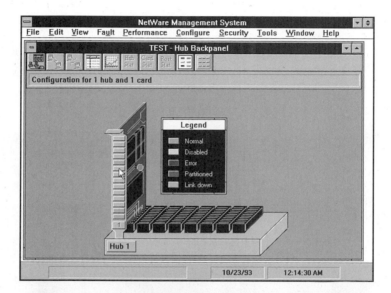

FIGURE 23.45.

Hub port map.

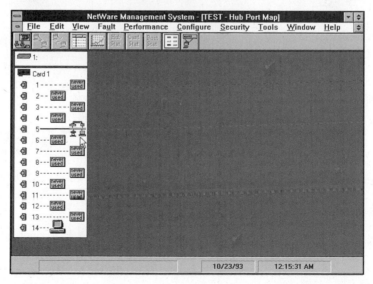

FIGURE 23.46.

Hub port details.

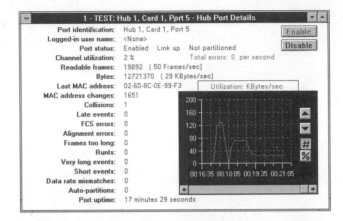

FIGURE 23.47.

Hub port utilization graph.

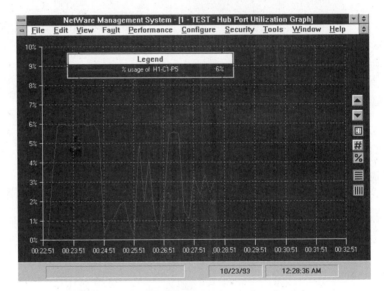

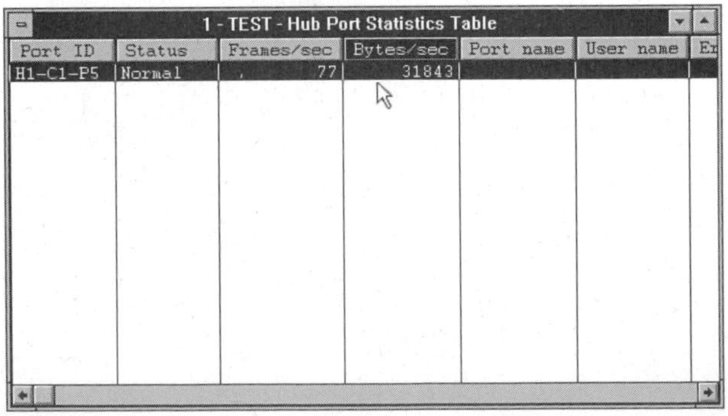

FIGURE 23.48.

Hub port statistics table.

Some Usage Tips and Techniques

There are a few situations in which you may want to consider disabling ports on your hub cards:

1. To remove a faulty NIC from your network.

2. To isolate your segment or hub from other hubs or segments for troubleshooting or security reasons.

3. To prevent an unauthorized station from attaching to your network from your unused ports.

Take full advantage of the error indicators provided by Hub Services Manager. A change in icon color indicates error detection. Use the Hub Port Details window to obtain more detailed information about the type of error that has occurred. If the error occurs continuously, disable the port and then troubleshoot.

Among the statistics provided by the Hub Port Details window (see Figure 23.46) are the "Last MAC address" and "MAC address changes." "Last MAC address" shows the source node address of the last frame that was detected on that port. This should be a constant address. The "MAC address changes" counter increases every time a new node address is observed transmitting on the port. In most cases, this value should be one; if no frame has ever been sent, the counter is set at zero. By keeping track of the address and this counter, you can easily tell if users are moving equipment around on their own, which is one of the most common source of problems.

> **TIP** ▶
>
> If the "MAC address changes" counter increases frequently, the port is most likely connected to another hub, a coaxial Ethernet cable, or a bridge.
>
> If the port is *not* connected to one of these devices, if the counter is not changing frequently, and you know equipment is not being moved, you have either a cable or an NIC driver problem (because the source address field in the frame is getting corrupted).

The Port Status information from the Hub Port Details window can tell you if the wiring between your hub and workstation is okay. For example, with proper wiring on a 10BaseT connection, the port should show a Link Up status when the attached device is powered on. If Port Status shows Link Down, the port is not connected, and the attached device is powered off (or you have a wiring problem).

TIP ▶

If Port Status shows Link Down when the attached device is powered on, there is either an NIC or wiring problem.

When a port detects more than 30 consecutive collisions, it is automatically isolated from the network while the condition persists. This is known as *autopartitioning*. Port Status will show "partitioned," and the "Autopartitions" counter is incremented.

TIP ▶

If the autopartition rate and bandwidth-utilization rate are high (more than 30 percent), consider segmenting your network using bridges or routers to reduce the amount of traffic on each segment.

Installing Hub Services

To install NetWare Hub Services, do the following:

1. Copy the NLMs from the NetWare Hub Services diskette into SYS:SYSTEM directory on your server.

2. Edit AUTOEXEC.NCF on that server. Load hub driver, bind IPX to it, and load HSL. If you want SNMP management, load SNMP and HUBSNMP. If you want SNMP over TCP/IP, load the TCP/IP protocol stack and bind IP to the hub card.

NOTE ▶

If you want SNMP management but not over TCP/IP, specify an IP address of 0.0.0.0 when loading HUBSNMP. For example:

```
LOAD HUBSNMP ADDR=0.0.0.0
```

You can install NetWare Hub Services as part of the Hub Services Manager installation, as described in the following section.

Installing Hub Services Manager

You need to have NMS Runtime installed on your management station before you can install Hub Services Manager. You follow an installation procedure similar to NMS Runtime. The install program (SETUP.EXE) integrates the Hub Services Manager function into your NMS Runtime console. Optionally, you can install NetWare Hub Services onto your servers with hub cards.

NetWare Management System v2.0

NetWare Management System v2.0 incorporates NetWare Services Manager (NSM) as well as Hub Services Manager, which was sold separately. Some new features also have been added, making NMS 2.0 a serious contender in the network monitoring and management arena. The following features have been added since NMS v1.1x:

> NetWare Services Manager (NSM)
> Hub Services Manager
> NetWare LANalyzer Agents
> Router Monitoring
> New LANtern Network Monitor firmware

This chapter previously discussed NSM, Hub Services Manager, and LANtern Network Monitors. The new LANtern Network Monitor firmware available with NMS 2.0 implements the Internet RMON standard (see the following section) over IP.

The following sections concentrate on the new NetWare LANalyzer agents and router monitoring function.

NetWare LANalyzer Agents

NetWare LANalyzer Agents are a set of NLMs that provides a distributed version of the same features found in the LANalyzer for Windows interface. They are fully compliant with all nine groups of the Internet Remote Network Monitoring Management Information Base (RMON MIB) standard over IP and IPX protocols, on either Ethernet or Token Ring.

NOTE ▶

The nine object groups of RMON are as follows:

■ **The Statistics Group**. Features a table that tracks about 20 different traffic characteristics, including total frames and errors.

■ **The History Group**. Enables you to specify frequency and intervals for traffic sampling.

■ **The Alarm Group**. Permits you to establish thresholds and criteria under which the agents will issue alarms.

■ **The Host Group**. Presents a table containing each LAN node listed by traffic statistics.

■ **The HostTopN Group**. Enables you to set up sorted lists and reports based on the highest statistics generated by the Host Group.

■ **The Matrix Group**. Keeps two tables of traffic statistics based on pairs of communicating nodes. One table is based on sending node addresses, the other is based on receiving node addresses.

■ **The Filter Group**. Permits you to define, by channel, particular characteristics of frames. For example, a filter may be applied to just capture IPX traffic.

■ **The Packet Capture Group**. Works in conjunction with the Filter Group. Enables you to specify the amount of memory resources to be used for storing captured frames that meet the filter criteria.

■ **The Event Group**. Enables you to specify a set of parameters or conditions to be tracked by the agent. Whenever these conditions or parameters are met, an event log will be recorded.

You need to install LANZ Agents only on one server in each segment of your network. For example, if you have a server with two NICs, one copy of the Agents can monitor both segments. Figure 23.49 illustrates that for a four-segment network, you need the LANZ Agents only installed on two servers. With these agents installed, you can do the following:

- Remotely collect real-time and long-term segment traffic information.
- Obtain real-time Network Dashboard displays of a segment's packet rate, broadcast rate, error rate, and utilization percentage.
- Perform remote frame captures into multiple buffers.
- Decode IPX, IP, and AppleTalk frames.
- Determine ring order identification on Token Rings.
- Set alarm thresholds on certain segment performance parameters.
- Detect network events such as errors.

FIGURE 23.49.

Placement of LANZ Agents on a four-segment network.

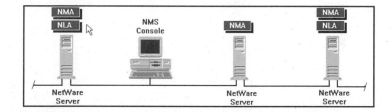

> **NOTE** ▶
>
> The advantage of LANZ Agents over other options is that you have a distributed LAN monitoring system without having to invest in extra hardware. Consider this: with the distributed nature of LANZ Agents, you can monitor and capture frames from different network segments at the same time. This lets you track the flow of a problem right to the source, even across routers. You can do this without having to leave your desk. You also can use this multicapture buffer feature to monitor traffic between a specific server and multiple client workstations, regardless of where they are located.
>
> LANZ Agents have the same functionality as LANalyzer for Windows v2.0, and more. For example, using LANZ Agents you can obtain an overall segment traffic table (see Figure 23.50) and obtain a Network Dashboard display with real-time statistics on packet rate, broadcast rate, error rate, and utilization percentage. (See Figure 23.51.) Double-clicking a "speed gauge" brings up a real-time performance graph for the past hour as well as an averaged look for the past day. (See Figure 23.52.)

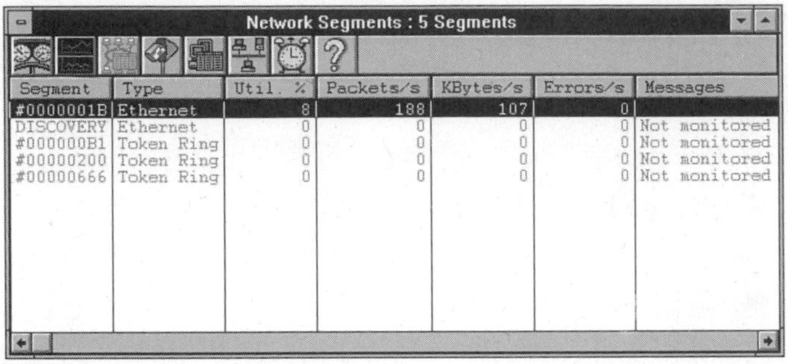

FIGURE 23.50.

Network Summary window.

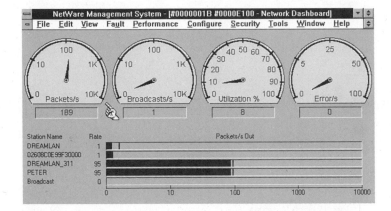

FIGURE 23.51.

Network Dashboard window.

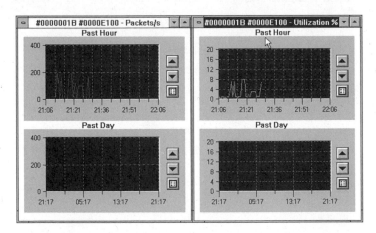

FIGURE 23.52.

Segment graph for packet rate and utilization percentage.

NOTE ▶

Segments without LANZ Agents installed have the entry "Not Monitored" in the Message column.

TIP ▶

You can "tile" multiple Network Dashboards on your screen to monitor several segments at once.

You can easily get a table of the top 20 "talkers" on each segment by looking at the Stations table (see Figure 23.53); the lower half of the Network Dashboard—the Top Stations graph—displays the top eight stations.

FIGURE 23.53.

Top Stations table window.

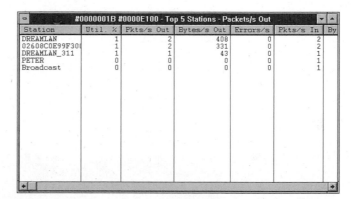

Station	Util. %	Pkts/s Out	Bytes/s Out	Errors/s	Pkts/s In	By
DREAMLAN	1	2	408	0	2	
02608C0E99F30(	1	2	331	0	2	
DREAMLAN_311	1	1	43	0	1	
PETER	0	0	0	0	1	
Broadcast	0	0	0	0	1	

#0000001B #0000E100 - Top 5 Stations - Packets/s Out

NOTE ▶

By default, the Stations table is sorted by Packets/s Out, with the most active station at the top of the column. You can sort the listing by any of the statistics simply by double-clicking the desired column heading.

You can configure the Top Stations graph to be based on different statistics. With the desired Network Dashboard window displayed, use the pull-down menu, Configure->Active Window. Save your selection as "default."

The same also can apply to the Top Stations table.

Based on traffic information collected by LANZ Agents, you can, for example, obtain a picture of how heavily a router or server is being used. This is provided by the Conversations table. (See Figure 23.54.) It lists all other stations that converse with the selected station.

FIGURE 23.54.

Conversations table.

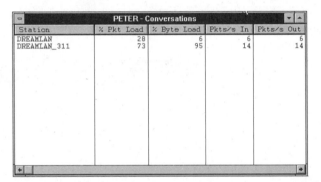

The Conversations table lists the percentage of traffic that each station contributes to one station's load. However, because not all samples are taken at the same time and statistics are rounded, the numbers in the columns do not always add up to 100 percent.

Although the Segment Network Summary table gives you error rate, the Segment graph can be used to obtain a breakdown of specific error types. Figure 23.55 shows a list of specific Ethernet error statistics that can be graphed. A similar set is available for Token Ring. Combining this information and the diagnostic information discussed in the previous chapter, you can have a good sense of the general health of your network.

FIGURE 23.55.

Ethernet Segment Graph and configuration window.

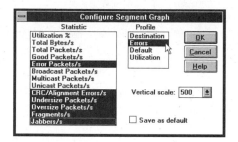

You can configure the LANZ Agents to monitor a number of error statistics and send alarms to your NMS console. With the alarm-logging feature of NMS, you can keep a health record for your network.

CAUTION ▷

By default, LANZ Agent alarms are disabled. You must manually enable them for each monitored segment.

As mentioned in the previous chapter, it is important to have a baseline of various traffic statistics. That can be done by using the Segment Graph. Then, set your alarm thresholds according to the average and peak traffic levels you recorded. (See Figure 23.56.)

FIGURE 23.56.

Segment alarm settings.

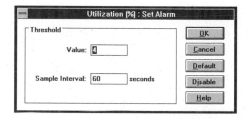

TIP ▷

You should set your threshold levels so they are high enough for your normal traffic volume, yet low enough that no significant network problems go undetected.

You also should adjust the sampling intervals so the LANZ Agents do not consume too much CPU cycles on the servers.

NOTE ▶

To prevent the same condition from generating multiple alarms, NMS requires network performance to fall at least 10 percent below the threshold setting and then rise above the threshold once more before this alarm will be recorded again.

One of the most valued capabilities of LANZ Agents is its capability to capture frames off the network segments, regardless of whether they are good or error packets. These captured frames are stored in a buffer in the RAM of the server. A copy of them is sent to the NMS console when requested.

CAUTION ▶

The performance of a server can be affected when the LANZ Agent is capturing data. Therefore, you should capture frames only for as long as necessary. Do not perform unnecessary captures, because CPU cycles are taken away from other server processes.

LANZ Agents recognize the following protocols:

NetWare
AppleTalk
TCP/IP
SNA
DECnet
NETBEUI
XNS
Banyan Vines
MAC (Token Ring)
(Full decode is available for NetWare, AppleTalk, and TCP/IP.)

The Packet Capture Setup window (Figure 23.57) looks very similar to that of LANalyzer for Windows (Refer back to Figure 23.9)— with one exception. For LANZ Agents, you can specify the Capture Buffer size, whereas for LZFW it uses all the available RAM in your workstation.

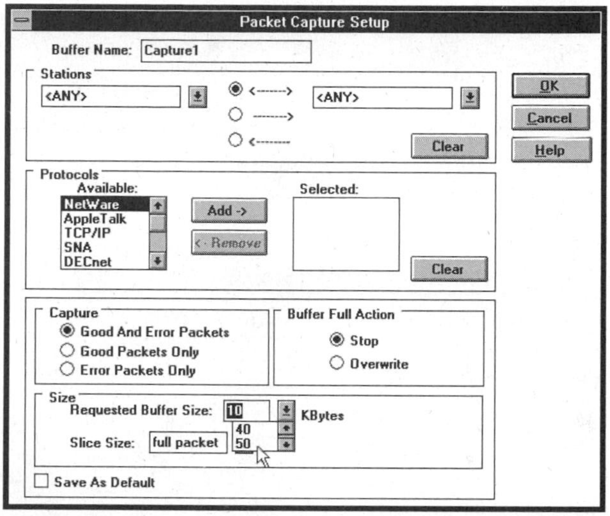

FIGURE 23.57.

*LANZ Agent
Packet Capture
Setup window.*

> **CAUTION** ▶
>
> Do not specify too large of a size for LANZ Agent's Capture Buffer. This will take memory away from Cache Buffers for the server. When Cache Buffers drops to 30 percent or less, the server may become unstable.

As with LZFW, a Capture Filter may be applied to the Capture Buffer to capture traffic *to* a device, traffic *from* a device, traffic *between* two devices, or traffic caused by a specific protocol or protocols.

> **NOTE** ▶
>
> If you select more than one protocol for the filter, frames can meet either protocol criterion to be captured.

A maximum of 20 separate Capture Buffers can be defined for each LANZ Agent. Each buffer can be assigned a name for easy reference.

CAUTION

The Capture Buffer is *deleted* when you close the Capture Status dialog box. However, LANZ Agent capture continues if you minimize the Capture Status dialog box and shut down the NMS console.

You can view the captured frames by clicking the View button in the Capture Status dialog box. (See Figure 23.58.) NMS retrieves data from the LANZ Agent only as necessary to display the frames as you view them. This reduces the amount of traffic between NMS and the LANZ Agent.

FIGURE 23.58.

Capture Status dialog box.

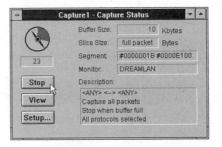

TIP

You can view only one Capture Buffer at a time. If you need to compare capture data from different segments, save the buffers into packet files first. You can view multiple packet files simultaneously.

The Packet Display window of NMS looks exactly like that of LZFW. (See Figure 23.59.) As a matter of fact, the packet-file format saved by LANZ Agent is the same as that of LZFW and the earlier, hardware-based LANalyzer (now sold by Network Communications Corporation).

NetWare LANalyzer Agents are not meant to be a replacement for LANalyzer for Windows 2.0. They complement each other. LANZ Agents are for day-to-day monitoring functions and remote problem-solving. You also can use the Agents' frame-capture function to do some preliminary troubleshooting ground work. If the problem is one that requires a visit to the segment's physical location, LANalyzer for Windows is the portable tool you can bring along with you. One drawback of the LANZ Agents is that they are only useful in conjunction with a network management console, such as NMS.

FIGURE 23.59.

Packet Display window.

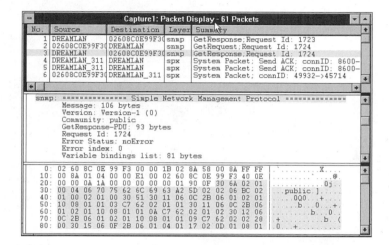

Router Monitoring

Using the new Router Monitoring function in NMS 2.0, you can get a global display of all routers on your network. (See Figure 23.60.) From the System Details window, you can find out the protocol, frame type, and hardware and software address information for each of the NICs installed in the router. This provides the same information as the CONFIG console command on NetWare servers.

FIGURE 23.60.

Router Information and System Details windows.

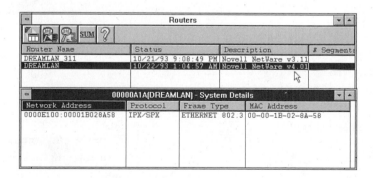

You also can obtain detailed interface statistics for one or more routers. (See Figure 23.61.) By examining the graphs, you can determine your busy segments.

FIGURE 23.61.

*Router Interface
Statistics graphs.*

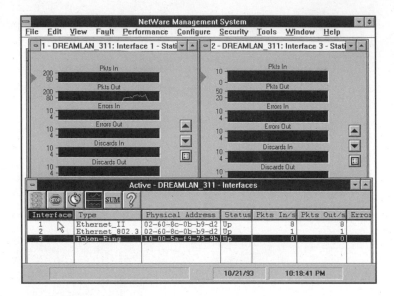

A Simple Case Study

Using NMS 2.0, you can simultaneously monitor CPU utilization and network traffic for a variety of servers. This enables you to see if the CPU overload on your servers is caused by a sudden rise in use of the network. You can then use the top "talkers list" in the LANalyzer Agent Dashboard to determine who is generating all the traffic. There may be a problem that needs to be addressed; or, for example, someone just happened to be accessing some large files for a while. The following describes a simple case study.

In this configuration, you have one NetWare 4.01 server (DREAMLAN), one NetWare 3.11 server (DREAMLAN_311), and two workstations on the same Ethernet segment. (See Figure 23.62.) Figure 23.63 shows that there is a sudden rise in packet rates and that high utilization percentage has triggered an alarm condition. (See Figure 23.64.) By looking at the time scales of CPU utilization and traffic statistics, it seems the traffic is directed at DREAMLAN_311. By examining the Conversations table (Figure 23.65), you notice that user Peter is communicating with this server constantly. After doing a remote capture and going over the frames (Figure 23.66), you find that Peter is doing a lot of copying from the workstation to the server. Possibly, he is backing up his workstation onto the server.

FIGURE 23.62.

Internet Map for case study.

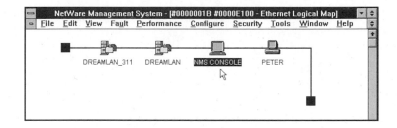

FIGURE 23.63.

Traffic Statistics and CPU Utilization graphs.

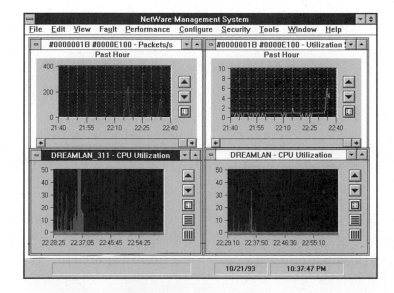

FIGURE 23.64.

Alarm Report for case study.

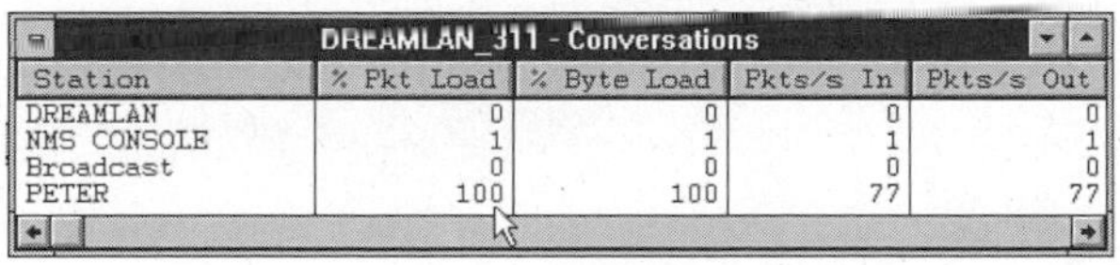

FIGURE 23.65.

Conversations table for case study.

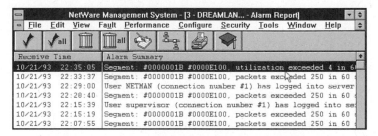

FIGURE 23.66.

Packet Display for case study.

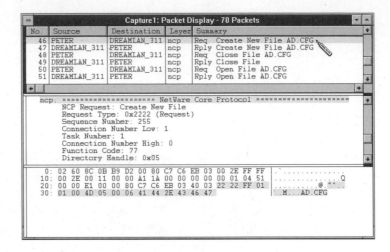

Using NMS 2.0 and LANZ Agents, the whole troubleshooting exercise took less than 10 minutes to complete.

Installing NMS 2.0

The installation steps for NMS 2.0 have not changed much from NMS 1.1x. You run the SETUP.EXE program from within Windows. However, you now have an option to install and run through an installation tutorial. (See Figure 23.67.)

FIGURE 23.67.

NMS 2.0 installation main screen.

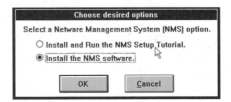

Unlike previous versions, NMS 2.0 also supports NetWare 4.x, which means you need to use VLM drivers. If you do not have VLM drivers installed, the installation program will abort.

> **NOTE** ▶
>
> You can install NetWare Management Agents from a PC running the older shell software (NETX.EXE).

When installing NetWare Management Agents (NMAs) onto your servers, the SETUP.EXE program will transparently detect if it is a 3.x server or a 4.x server, and it will copy the correct NLMs across.

> **CAUTION** ▶
>
> At the time of this writing, NetWare 3.x SFT-III was not supported. NetWare 2.x also was not supported.

Installing LANalyzer Agents

You need to install the LANZ Agents from the server. Use INSTALL.NLM and select Product Options from the menu. You will be prompted for the adapter board to monitor. Use the F5 key to select the proper adapter (that is, LAN segment). After you have installed the LANZ Agents, edit your AUTOEXEC.NCF file to uncomment the following two lines:

```
SEARCH ADD SYS:LANZ
LANZ.NCF
```

FIGURE 23.68.

LANalyzer Agent installation screen.

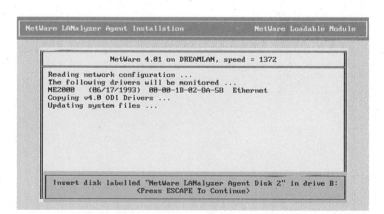

> **CAUTION** ▶
>
> It may be difficult to see the prompt for the adapter boards that you want to monitor on a monochrome screen. You *must* select at least one adapter board and then press the F5 key to have the LANZ Agents monitor that board. F5 acts like a toggle switch.

If you don't have NetExplorer or NetExplorer Plus installed on this server, you should also uncomment NMSBASE.NCF from the AUTOEXEC.NCF file.

Summary

This chapter reviewed a number of Novell network management products that can assist you in your day-to-day LAN monitoring and troubleshooting needs. The next chapter examines some third-party LAN management and monitoring products.

Third-Party LAN-Monitoring and Management Products

24

by Peter Kuo

IN THIS CHAPTER

This chapter examines third-party LAN-monitoring and management products. The products to be discussed include

- Thomas-Conrad Sectra Token Ring Server for DOS v1.10
- SynOptics LattisNet Management System for DOS 4.2
- SynOptics Optivity for NMS v1.0
- Triticom EtherVision v2.20
- Triticom TokenVision v2.15
- Intel NetSight Analyst v1.1
- Intel LANDesk Manager v1.01
- XTree Tools for Networks v1.02

Not all of the products discussed here were designed as LAN-monitoring or management tools. However, some of the statistics they provide can be used for these purposes. Also, some of these products are popular tools (for example, XTree Tools) that most NetWare sites have. This chapter discusses how these tools can be used as rudimentary LAN-monitoring and management tools.

Thomas-Conrad Sectra Token Ring Server for DOS v1.10

Sectra Token Ring Server for DOS (or Sectra Server for DOS) is a network management tool from Thomas-Conrad Corporation. It enables you to monitor, control, and troubleshoot *any* IEEE 802.5 Token Ring network. Sectra Server for DOS can monitor and control up to two rings simultaneously. (See Figure 24.1.)

FIGURE 24.1.

Sectra Server for DOS startup screen.

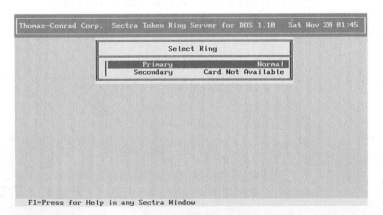

After selecting the ring you wish to view statistics on, you are presented with the menu shown in Figure 24.2. You can customize Sectra Server for DOS to your personal requirements, such as the types of errors to log (Figure 24.3) and the alarm thresholds (Figure 24.4).

FIGURE 24.2.

View/Manage Ring menu.

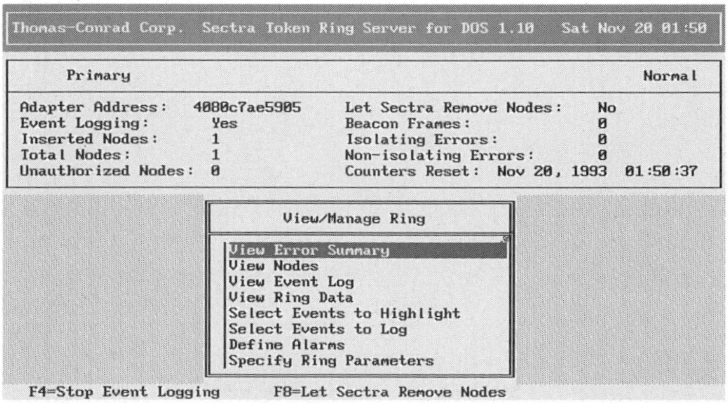

```
Thomas-Conrad Corp.  Sectra Token Ring Server for DOS 1.10   Sat Nov 20 01:50

   Primary                                              Normal

   Adapter Address:     4080c7ae5905    Let Sectra Remove Nodes:    No
   Event Logging:       Yes             Beacon Frames:              0
   Inserted Nodes:      1               Isolating Errors:           0
   Total Nodes:         1               Non-isolating Errors:       0
   Unauthorized Nodes:  0               Counters Reset:  Nov 20, 1993  01:50:37


                            View/Manage Ring

                        View Error Summary
                        View Nodes
                        View Event Log
                        View Ring Data
                        Select Events to Highlight
                        Select Events to Log
                        Define Alarms
                        Specify Ring Parameters


     F4=Stop Event Logging       F8=Let Sectra Remove Nodes
```

FIGURE 24.3.

Selecting events to log.

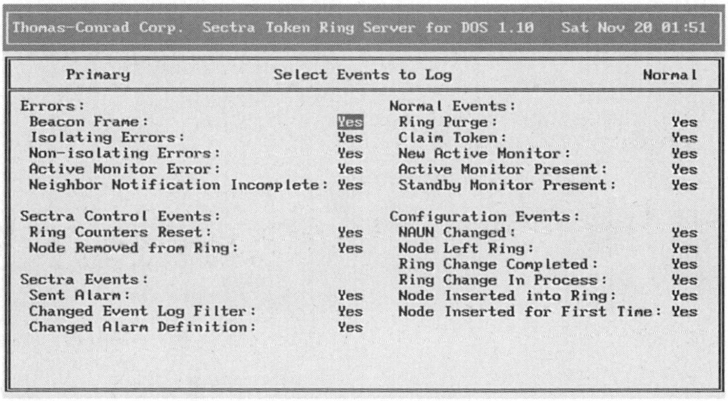

```
Thomas-Conrad Corp.  Sectra Token Ring Server for DOS 1.10   Sat Nov 20 01:51

   Primary              Select Events to Log              Normal

   Errors:                            Normal Events:
     Beacon Frame:              Yes     Ring Purge:                 Yes
     Isolating Errors:          Yes     Claim Token:                Yes
     Non-isolating Errors:      Yes     New Active Monitor:         Yes
     Active Monitor Error:      Yes     Active Monitor Present:      Yes
     Neighbor Notification Incomplete: Yes  Standby Monitor Present:  Yes

   Sectra Control Events:             Configuration Events:
     Ring Counters Reset:       Yes     NAUN Changed:               Yes
     Node Removed from Ring:    Yes     Node Left Ring:             Yes
                                        Ring Change Completed:      Yes
   Sectra Events:                       Ring Change In Process:     Yes
     Sent Alarm:                Yes     Node Inserted into Ring:    Yes
     Changed Event Log Filter:  Yes     Node Inserted for First Time: Yes
     Changed Alarm Definition:  Yes
```

If you are security conscious, you can use Sectra Server for DOS to define which nodes (by MAC address) are allowed on your rings and the days and times during which these devices are allowed on your ring. (See Figure 24.5.) Optionally, you can prevent unauthorized nodes from inserting into your rings. (See Figure 24.6.)

Sectra Server for NetWare enables you to monitor up to eight rings simultaneously using Thomas-Conrad Token Ring adapters. Because it is implemented as a NetWare Loadable Module (NLM), you can run it on your 3.1x servers without having to dedicate a separate machine. With this version, you also can define a selected list of users to be notified of error conditions.

FIGURE 24.4.

Defining alarm thresholds.

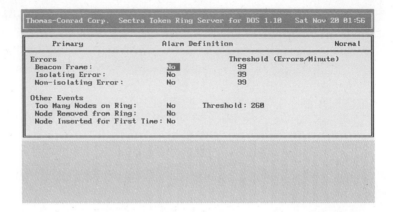

FIGURE 24.5.

Node information.

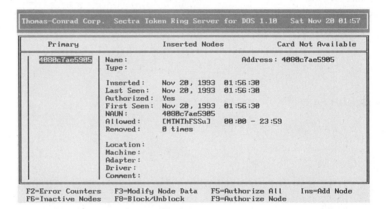

FIGURE 24.6.

Ring parameter.

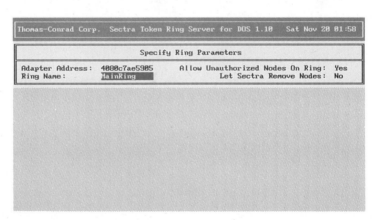

Installing Sectra Server for DOS

Sectra Server for DOS requires an 80286 machine or better, with a minimum of 1M of memory. Depending on how much error-logging you specify, 2-5M of free disk space is recommended. One Token Ring adapter is required for each ring to be monitored. Sectra Server for DOS can operate using either (IEEE 802.2) LLC drivers, such as IBM's LAN Support Program, or promiscuous ODI drivers.

NOTE ▶

You need at least `FILES=20` in your CONFIG.SYS for Sectra Server to operate properly.

The software installation involves the copying of program files from the distribution diskette to your workstation's hard disk. Here is a sample CONFIG.SYS for IBM Token-Ring cards:

```
FILES=50
BUFFERS=30
DEVICE=C:\LSP\DXMA0MOD.SYS
DEVICE=C:\LSP\DXMC0MOD.SYS
```

And here is a sample AUTOEXEC.BAT:

```
@Echo Off
Path C:\DOS;C:\SECTRA
CD \SECTRA
SECTLLC
SECTRA
```

SECTLLC.EXE is the LLC initialization module for Sectra Server for DOS. It can be loaded as a device driver. This should be loaded after the LLC drivers of your NIC. SECTRA is a batch file that loads Btrieve and starts Sectra Server for DOS. Btrieve is unloaded by this batch file upon your normal exit from Sectra.

Following is a sample NET.CFG file for Thomas-Conrad Token Ring cards:

```
Link Driver TCTOKSH
     Port 2A0
     DMA  5
     INT  2
     REINSERT
```

The corresponding AUTOEXEC.BAT looks like this:

```
@Echo Off
Path C:\DOS;C:\SECTRA;C:\NET
```

```
CD \SECTRA
LSL
TCTOKSH
SECTODI
SECTRA
```

For the preceding, SECTODI.COM is the ODI initialization module.

> **CAUTION** ▶
>
> When a Thomas-Conrad Token Ring adapter is blocked from the ring, the TCTOKSH driver will not reinsert the NIC into the ring. This conforms with the IEEE 802.5 specification. With the REINSERT keyword in NET.CFG, the driver will reinsert the NIC into the ring immediately after it is blocked. This is recommended for stations running Sectra Server for DOS. Without it, once the station receives a "Remove from Ring" MAC frame, Sectra terminates abnormally and corrupts its database.

SynOptics LattisNet Management System for DOS v4.2

LattisNet Management System from SynOptics enables you to centrally monitor and manage SynOptics hubs and concentrators. Versions are available for the DOS platform as well as for UNIX. Following is a brief look at the DOS implementation.

In many respects, LNMS is similar to Hub Services Manager from Novell. You can use it to monitor and control each hub and concentrator out on your network. Unlike Hub Services Manager, LNMS uses IP as transport. Therefore, if you have routers in your network, they must route IP information in order for you to manage all your SynOpitcs devices from a central location.

Depending on the type or level of monitoring agent loaded in each hub, you may only perform certain tasks from LNMS console. With only the Basic Agent, you can monitor the overall traffic flow through a hub.

Installing LNMS

Because LNMS is a Windows application, you run SETUP off the diskette from within Windows. You start with the OpenView 1 of 2 diskettes. (See Figure 24.7.)

You are first prompted for the directory in which OpenView is to be installed. (See Figure 24.8.) The default is C:\OV. A status bar on-screen informs you of file copy status. (See Figure 24.9.) You are then prompted for the various diskettes as needed. When the OpenView application has been installed, a group icon is automatically created. (See Figure 24.10.)

FIGURE 24.7.

Setup screen of OpenView.

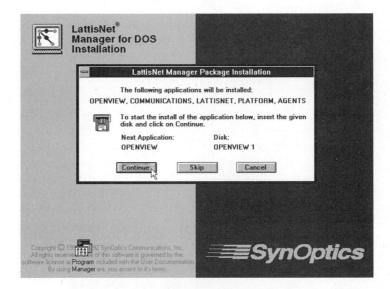

FIGURE 24.8.

Specify directory for OpenView files.

FIGURE 24.9.

File Copy status bar.

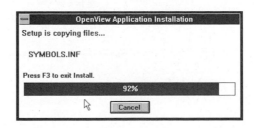

FIGURE 24.10.

*Creation of
OpenView group
icon.*

Communications related files are installed next. (See Figure 24.11.) The default directory for this is C:\COMM. (See Figure 24.12.) A file copy status bar updates you of its progress, just as with OpenView installation. An icon is created automatically. You then need to tell the configuration program (CUSTOM) what type of NIC you are using. (See Figure 24.13.) The supported interfaces are: Ethernet, Token Ring, FDDI, and SLIP (Serial Line IP). You then need to configure the NIC. (See Figure 24.14.) Drivers for 3COM, Intel, Novell/Excelan, Racal InterLan, Western Digital, and Xircom NICs are supplied. The next step is IP address (Figure 24.15) and subnet mask (Figure 24.16) assignment. Finally, you need to provide a Host Name (Figure 24.17) and a Domain Name (Figure 24.18). You must exit CUSTOM before you can click OK on the Application Installation screen (Figure 24.19).

FIGURE 24.11.

*Communications
file install.*

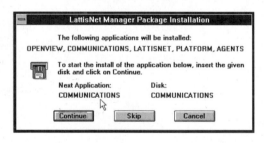

FIGURE 24.12.

*Specify directory for
communications
files.*

FIGURE 24.13.

Select network interface.

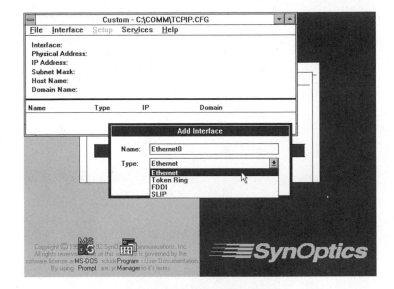

FIGURE 24.14.

Hardware configuration.

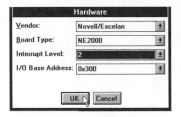

FIGURE 24.15.

Assign IP number.

FIGURE 24.16.

Assign subnet mask.

FIGURE 24.17.

Assign host name.

FIGURE 24.18.

Assign domain name.

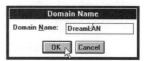

FIGURE 24.19.

Close custom application before clicking OK.

CAUTION ▶

LNMS uses NDIS drivers—not ODI drivers. Make sure you have an NDIS driver for your NIC. Check your driver diskette that came with the NIC, check with the NIC's vendor, or check the 3COM library forums on CompuServe.

The next phase is the installation of LattisNet applications, such as Concentrator Manager (Figure 24.20) and TELNET software. The default directory for LattisNet software is C:\LNM. (See Figure 24.21.) Following the LattisNet applications installation is the Platform applications installation (Figure 24.22), such as object database files. These files must be installed in C:\LNM (Figure 24.23) as the "Copy to" field is grayed out.

FIGURE 24.20.

Installation of Concentrator Manager application.

FIGURE 24.21.

Specify directory for ConMgr.

FIGURE 24.22.

Installation of Platform software.

FIGURE 24.23.

Platform files must be installed to the same directory as LattisNet files (C:\LNM in this case).

Finally, the various agent files are installed. First, copy the Advanced Agents (Figure 24.24) into the same directory as the Communications files (C:\COMM in this example). Then copy the Basic Agent files into the same directory. Click Done to exit the installation program. (See Figure 24.25.) Figure 24.26 shows the icons that are created for LattisNet Manager for DOS.

FIGURE 24.24.

Installing Agent files.

FIGURE 24.25.

End of installation.

FIGURE 24.26.

LNMS icons.

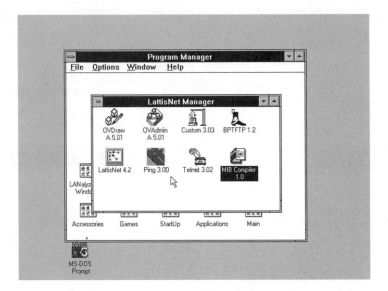

Modifications are made to CONFIG.SYS and AUTOEXEC.BAT files to include the necessary drivers. Shown in Figures 24.27 and 24.28 are sample AUTOEXEC.BAT and CONFIG.SYS files, respectively.

> **NOTE**
>
> A number of backup AUTOEXEC.BAT and CONFIG.SYS files are made during the installation. The final "working" set is AUTOEXEC.LNM and CONFIG.LNM.

FIGURE 24.27.

Sample AUTOEXEC.BAT file.

```
C:\>type autoexec.bat
@echo off
cls
SET TZ=EST5EDT
SET path=C:\NMS\bin;C:\WINDOWS;C:\DOS
SET TEMP=C:\WINDOWS\TEMP
prompt $p$g
SET HELPFILES=C:\NMS\help\*.HLP
C:\WINDOWS\SMARTDRV.EXE

path = C:\OV;%path%
path = C:\COMM;%path%
C:\COMM\NETBIND
path = C:\LNM;%path%
share.exe

C:\>
```

FIGURE 24.28.

Sample CONFIG.SYS file.

```
C:\>type config.sys
FILES= 80
BUFFERS= 40
DEVICE=C:\WINDOWS\HIMEM.SYS
dos=high,umb
STACKS=9,256

DEVICE=C:\COMM\PROTMAN.DOS /I:C:\COMM
DEVICE=C:\COMM\NE2000.DOS
DEVICE=C:\COMM\NETMANAG.DOS

C:\>
```

CAUTION ▶

The installation software does not check to see if you are already loading SHARE.EXE in your AUTOEXEC.BAT. It will add a call to it, even if you already have one.

Check your final AUTOEXEC.BAT and CONFIG.SYS before rebooting your workstation.

NOTE ▶

You need a user name and password to access the LattisNet console. The default user name and password is MANAGER. It is not case-sensitive.

Configuring BOOTP Server

You do not have to have a BOOTP server to configure the hubs. However, having a BOOTP server will make your management task much easier. With it, you do not need to manually configure each hub through the service port—all the configuration information can be automatically downloaded to the hub upon its boot up. Presented here is a brief summary on how a BOOTP server can be set up.

Before you start configuring, obtain the following information:

1. Obtain the MAC address of your Network Management Module (NMM) if you are using a System 3000 concentrator. If you are using a workgroup concentrator, it is the MAC address of the concentrator itself. This is given as a 6-character hexadecimal number on a label on the front of the unit.

2. If you are using an Advanced Agent, obtain the Agent Key. You may have to purchase this separately from SynOptics.

3. Check in the COMM directory to make sure you have the appropriate .CFG file that matches your NMM. For example, for LNMS 4.2 and Ethernet NMMs, use EN42.CFG. For 3314 NMM with Advanced Agent, use A351X41.CFG.

4. Check in the COMM directory to make sure there is an image file (.IMG) that matches your NMM. The same rule from the preceding instruction applies.

5. Obtain the IP address for your NMM.

Once you have all this information, you need to edit the BOOTPTAB.TXT file. This is an ASCII text file; therefore, you can edit it using any text editor that can save an ASCII text file, including Notepad from Windows.

Find the line that describes your NMM and Agent License level. For example, if you are using Ethernet and Advanced Agent, locate the line that says, `This is a sample entry for advanced ethernet NMM`. (See Figure 24.29.) Copy this line (less the # sign) and paste it under the original line. Make the following changes and save the file with its original name (see Figure 24.30).

1. Change the six x characters in the hardware address (`HA=`) to your MAC address (from Step 1 in the preceding instructions).

2. Change the IP address from the sample number to your NMM's IP address.

3. Change the .CFG filename at the end of the line to the MAC address of your NMM. (Just use the six characters; leave .CFG as the extension.)

TIP

The .CFG filename must be unique for every NMM loaded over the network. You don't have to use MAC address as a naming convention, but it is strongly recommended.

FIGURE 24.29.

Location of Ethernet entry in BOOTPTAB.TXT file.

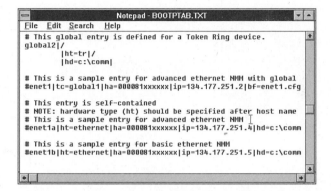

```
                    Notepad - BOOTPTAB.TXT
 File   Edit   Search   Help
# This global entry is defined for a Token Ring device.
global2|/
          |ht=tr|/
          |hd=c:\comm|

# This is a sample entry for advanced ethernet NMM with global
#enet1|tc=global1|ha=000081xxxxxx|ip=134.177.251.2|bf=enet1.cfg

# This entry is self-contained
# NOTE: hardware type (ht) should be specified after host name
# This is a sample entry for advanced ethernet NMM
#enet1a|ht=ethernet|ha=000081xxxxxx|ip=134.177.251.4|hd=c:\comm

# This is a sample entry for basic ethernet NMM
#enet1b|ht=ethernet|ha=000081xxxxxx|ip=134.177.251.5|hd=c:\comm
```

Next, copy the .CFG file for your NMM to its new filename. In this example, the hub is a Model 2813, and the MAC address is 00-00-81-04-20-5A. Therefore, EN42.CFG was copied to 04205A.CFG. Now edit this ASCII file with a text editor. At the very first uncommented line, enter the name of your image file. Next, you need to enter the Agent Key if you are using Advanced Agent. Following that, you need to specify a subnet mask. This must be the same as the one you specified in the CUSTOM program when installing your management console.

Now you can start your BOOTP server from within Windows.

FIGURE 24.30.

*Entry corresponding
to a hub.*

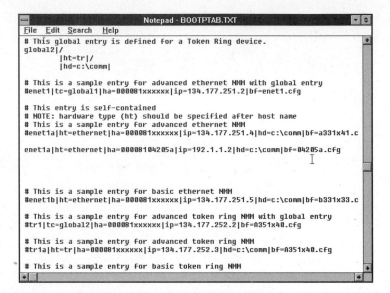

```
                    Notepad - BOOTPTAB.TXT
 File  Edit  Search  Help
# This global entry is defined for a Token Ring device.
global2|/
          |ht=tr|/
          |hd=c:\comm|

# This is a sample entry for advanced ethernet NMM with global entry
#enet1|tc=global1|ha=000081xxxxxx|ip=134.177.251.2|bf=enet1.cfg

# This entry is self-contained
# NOTE: hardware type (ht) should be specified after host name
# This is a sample entry for advanced ethernet NMM
#enet1a|ht=ethernet|ha=000081xxxxxx|ip=134.177.251.4|hd=c:\comm|bf=a331x41.c

enet1a|ht=ethernet|ha=00008104205a|ip=192.1.1.2|hd=c:\comm|bf=04205a.cfg



# This is a sample entry for basic ethernet NMM
#enet1b|ht=ethernet|ha=000081xxxxxx|ip=134.177.251.5|hd=c:\comm|bf=b331x33.c

# This is a sample entry for advanced token ring NMM with global entry
#tr1|tc=global2|ha=000081xxxxxx|ip=134.177.252.2|bf=A351x40.cfg

# This is a sample entry for advanced token ring NMM
#tr1a|ht=tr|ha=000081xxxxxx|ip=134.177.252.3|hd=c:\comm|bf=A351x40.cfg

# This is a sample entry for basic token ring NMM
```

SynOptics Optivity for NMS v1.0

Optivity for NMS from SynOptics is a snap-in module for Novell's NetWare Management System. It enables NMS to discover SynOptics hubs and to monitor and manage them from within the NMS console in lieu of the user accessing LattisNet Management System from a different console.

When NMS auto-discovers devices on your NetWare network and locates SynOptics hubs, it assigns hub icons to them. (See Figure 24.31.) When you double-click a hub icon, it brings up the front panel view of the hub. (See Figure 24.32.) If Advanced Agent is loaded on the hub, you can obtained detailed traffic statistics on a per-port basis. (See Figure 24.33.) You also can enable or disable a port remotely, similar to Hub Services Manager.

FIGURE 24.31.

*NMS segment map
with SynOptics hub
icons.*

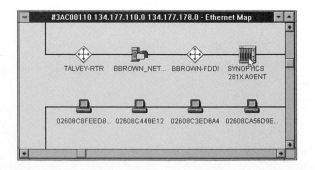

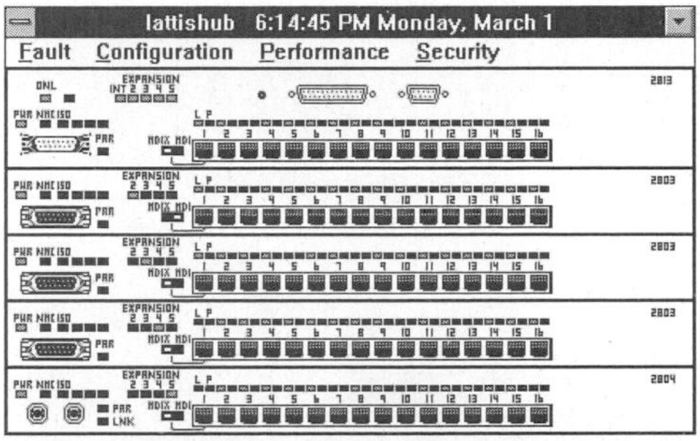

FIGURE 24.32.

Front panel view of hub.

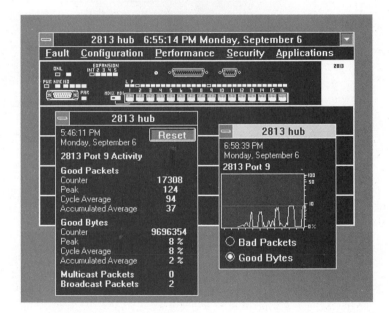

FIGURE 24.33.

Detailed port statistics.

If you are running NMS and have SynOptics concentrators on your network, Optivity for NMS is a snap-in tool that will help you manage your network much more effectively and easily.

Installing Optivity for NMS

Optivity for NMS is shipped with a copy of NMS Runtime v1.15B. If you have already installed NMS with a version prior to v1.15B, upgrade your NMS Runtime with the copy shipped with Optivity for NMS.

To install Optivity for NMS, start Windows, select Run from the File pull-down menu, and enter A:SETUP or B:SETUP. (See Figure 24.34.)

FIGURE 24.34.
*Setup screen for
Optivity for NMS.*

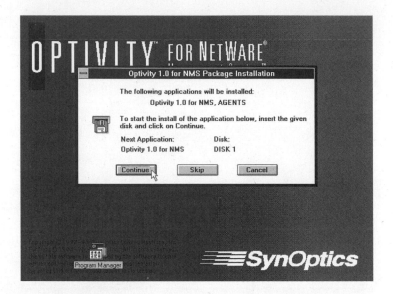

NOTE

During the installation process, there is a lot of disk activity. This is normal.
Because Optivity for NMS is to be integrated with NMS itself, many additions and changes to the NMS console are made.

After Optivity for NMS has been installed, you will not find much difference with
your NMS console. However, when you start up NMS, an extra process is spawned
in the background—the Optivity Hub Poller. (See Figure 24.35.)

Triticom EtherVision v2.20

EtherVision from Triticom monitors and displays activity on the Ethernet/IEEE 802.3
LAN. It monitors and maintains statistics on all network traffic, regardless of protocols. You can monitor the traffic either by source or by destination address. (See Figure 24.36.)

FIGURE 24.35.

Optivity Hub Poller background process.

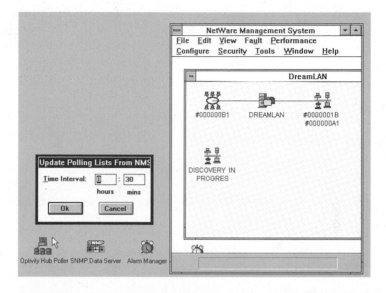

FIGURE 24.36.

Traffic monitoring can be based on either the source or destination address.

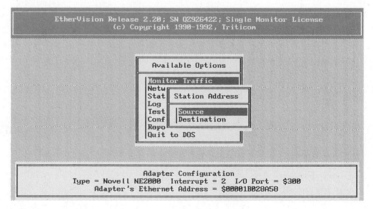

These three real-time displays are available:

Station. Gives you a sorted list of the number of frames, bytes, and errors sent or received by each station. (See Figure 24.37.)

Skyline. Gives you a view of your segment utilization for the past 60 seconds or 60 minutes. (See Figures 24.38 and 24.39.)

Statistics. Gives you information such as frame size distribution, utilization percentage, bytes per second, frames per second, and identification of station errors. (See Figure 24.40.)

FIGURE 24.37.

*Real-time segment
Station display
from EtherVision.*

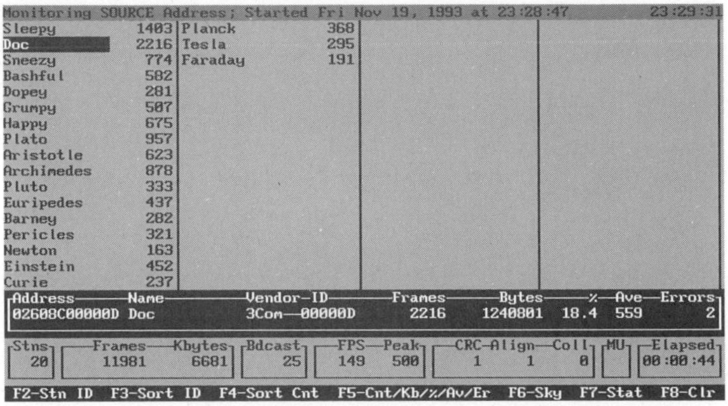

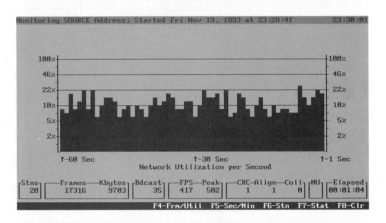

FIGURE 24.38.

*Real-time segment
utilization Skyline
display for the past
60 seconds from
EtherVision.*

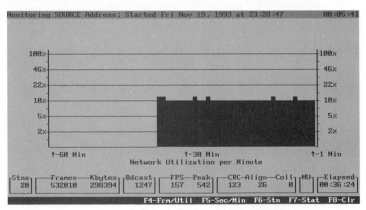

FIGURE 24.39.

*Real-time segment
utilization Skyline
display for the past
60 minutes from
EtherVision.*

FIGURE 24.40.

Real-time segment Statistics display from EtherVision.

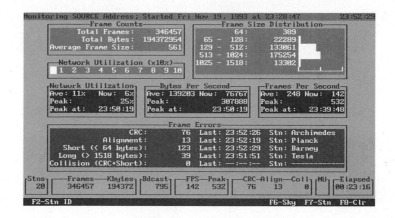

One nice feature of EtherVision is its Test Cable function. It tests for

- Cable shorts
- Bad cable termination
- Bad cable connections

Failed tests are logged and a check mark indicates which error has occurred. (See Figure 24.41.) This function is not found in all LAN-monitoring software.

FIGURE 24.41.

Cable Test function in EtherVision.

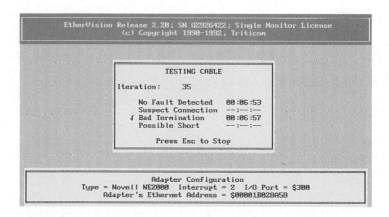

As with many LAN-monitoring software products, you need to dedicate a workstation to running EtherVision. Because it uses its own built-in device driver, you are limited to the choice of NIC. On the other hand, you do not need to load extra drivers to use this software, which is a distinct advantage.

Installation

The installation procedure for EtherVision could not be easier—you simply copy the files from the software diskette onto your hard disk. You can run EtherVision off the diskette if you like; however, if you enable error logging, a hard disk is preferable.

PC/MS-DOS 3.1 or higher and a minimum of 384K of free RAM is required for EtherVision. Built-in Ethernet adapter drivers are used. Supported adapters for v2.20 are shown in Table 24.1.

Table 24.1. Supported Ethernet adapters for EtherVision v2.20.

Vendor	Adapters
Novell/Eagle	NE1000, NE2000, NE/2 (microchannel)
SMC/Western Digital	EtherCard Plus (WD8003), EtherCard Plus16 (WD8013)
Gateway Communications	G/Ethernet-8, G/Ethernet-16
Intel	EtherExpress 16
PureData	PDI8023, PDI8023-16, PDuC8023 (microchannel)
3COM	EtherLink II (3C503), EtherLink III (3C509)

Because EtherVision is a DOS application, you can run it on an 8088 machine. However, for best performance and to avoid missing frames, an 80386 (or better) processor and a fast NIC are recommended.

Triticom TokenVision v2.15

TokenVision provides real-time Token Ring traffic monitoring for any 4- or 16-Mbps IBM/IEEE 802.5 Token Ring LAN. It also acts as Ring Error Monitor. Its capabilities are very similar to those of EtherVision. Along with the real-time Station, Skyline, and Statistics displays (see Figures 24.42 through 24.44), it has the following two additional real-time displays:

MAC Statistics. You can monitor the various types of MAC frames on your ring—for example, Active Monitor Present frames, Ring Recovery MAC frames, and Soft Error Report MAC frames. (See Figure 24.45.)

Topology Map. From this map, you can obtain a list of all active nodes and their physical relationship. You can "walk around the ring" using the cursor keys. Detailed statistics about the highlighted node are displayed in the lower portion of the display. (See Figure 24.46.) Fault domains are displayed on this map, along with the station-reporting beaconing, shown as a blinking square.

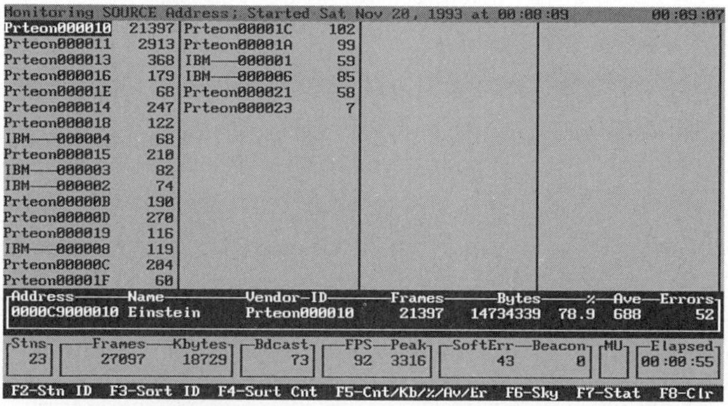

FIGURE 24.42.

Real-time ring station display from TokenVision.

FIGURE 24.43.

Real-time ring-utilization display from TokenVision.

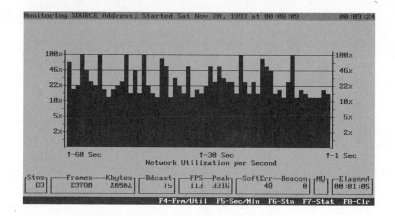

FIGURE 24.44.

Real-time ring statistics display from TokenVision.

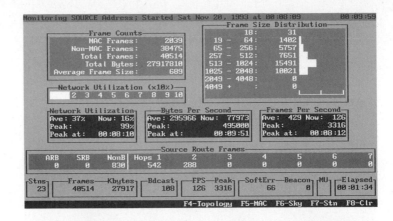

FIGURE 24.45.

Real-time MAC frame display from TokenVision.

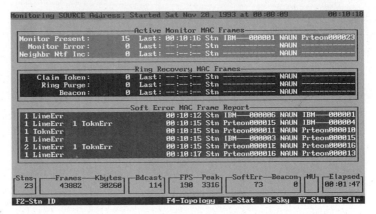

FIGURE 24.46.

Real-time topology map display from TokenVision.

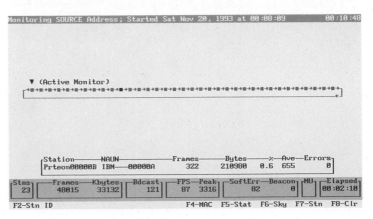

TokenVision features an Intruder Detection Alarm. It triggers an alarm if a new station enters the ring that has not been predefined by assigning it a name. This alarm can be used to detect unauthorized address changes.

Although TokenVision does not decode actual Token Ring frames, it keeps track of source-routing frames and gives you a breakdown of hop counts. (See Figure 24.44.)

Installation

Installing TokenVision is just like installing EtherVision. Simply copy all the files from the software distribution disk to your hard disk. Make sure you use XCOPY /S because there are subdirectories.

TokenVision supports more than 50 different Token Ring adapters, including the following:

Proteon	Madge	Olicom
Thomas-Conrad	Andrew	Black Box
Everex	General Technology	Inmac
Intel	MegaHertz	Optical Data Systems
PureData	Startek	Ungermann-Bass

For a complete list of vendors and adapter model numbers, contact Triticom.

MS/PC-DOS 3.1 or higher and a minimum of 512K of free RAM are required to use TokenVision. Although TokenVision will run on an 8088 machine, for best performance, use an 80386 (or better) processor.

Intel NetSight Analyst v1.1

Similar to LANalyzer for Windows from Novell and Tritcom's EtherVision and TokenVision, Intel's NetSight Analyst is a software-based network protocol analysis tool. It can capture and decode IPX/SPX, SMB (Microsoft LAN Manager, IBM LANServer), TCP/IP, and AppleTalk frames on Ethernet and Token Ring networks. Token Ring MAC frames also are decoded.

If you have an Ethernet NIC with Extended Packet Monitoring capability, you will be able to capture on bad Ethernet frames, such as fragments. Intel's EtherExpress NIC is an example. You should check the READ.ME file on your distribution diskette for packet drivers that support this mode.

As a LAN-monitoring tool, NetSight offers three real-time display modes:

- Full Packet mode
- Address Pairs mode
- Sky Line mode

In the Full Packet mode (see Figure 24.47), a frame summary on a single line is displayed. Partial decoding of each frame is done, making it easy to interpret the type of frame being displayed. In the Address Pairs mode (see Figure 24.48), a table is displayed. It shows pairs of addresses and a count of the total number of frames sent from each address to the adjacent address. In the Sky Line mode (see Figure 24.49), you get a histogram of total frames per second and total Kbytes per second over time. Filters can be applied to Address Pairs mode and Sky Line mode displays. All three modes display frame information across the top section of the screen, such as the number of errors and their type.

FIGURE 24.47.

Full Packet display mode.

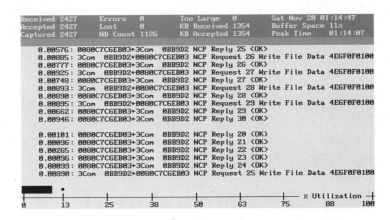

FIGURE 24.48.

Address Pairs display mode.

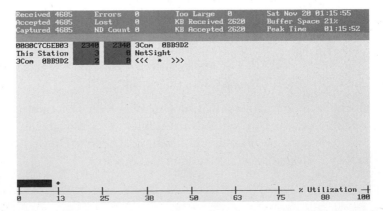

FIGURE 24.49.

Sky Line display mode.

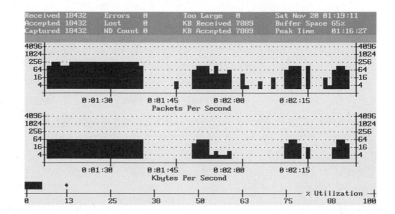

From a LAN protocol troubleshooting perspective, NetSight has one advantage over Novell's LANalyzer for Windows and Tritcom's products: the Traffic Generation feature. (See Figure 24.50.) This is very useful in stress-testing your network as well as for capacity-growth planning. You can generate the same frame over and over again at a constant rate or play back your capture buffer at the same rate at which it was received.

FIGURE 24.50.

Traffic Generation menu.

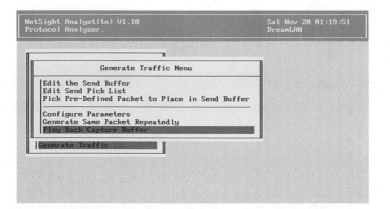

CAUTION ▶

Be very careful when replaying your capture buffer, especially onto a live network. Depending on the information carried in the frames, you could cause file corruption.

Installation and Configuration

You must first configure the software on the diskette before you can copy the resulting files to your hard drive. The installation program is menu-driven. It will prompt you for all the necessary information. You start by placing the NetSight Analyst diskette in a disk drive and then typing A: INSTALL or B: INSTALL. You are first asked for your name or company name (see Figure 24.51), and then a permanent supervisor password (Figure 24.52). You are then prompted to select and configure your NIC. (See Figure 24.53.)

FIGURE 24.51.

Name prompt for NetSight install.

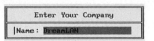

```
        Enter Your Company
  |Name: DreamLAN
```

FIGURE 24.52.

Permanent Supervisor password prompt.

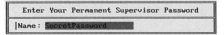

```
    Enter Your Permanent Supervisor Password
  |Name: SecretPassword
```

FIGURE 24.53.

Main installation menu.

```
            Main Menu
  Configure Driver
  Install on Hard Drive
  Reboot Computer
```

CAUTION ▶

Once set, the Permanent Supervisor Password cannot be changed. This, and a secondary password that you can assign later, controls access to the System Commands menu. This prevents unauthorized use of the more advanced features, such as Traffic Generation.

NetSight cannot use IPX drivers. However, if you have one loaded when running the install program, it will read the hardware configuration from the IPX driver and present it in the Driver Configuration screen. This assists you in configuring the packet driver. (See Figure 24.54.) Select a driver from the list and configure the various settings as necessary. (See Figures 24.55 and 24.56.) Press Esc when done.

FIGURE 24.54.

Driver configuration screen.

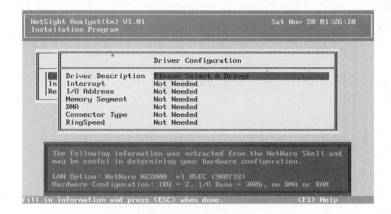

FIGURE 24.55.

Available packet driver listing.

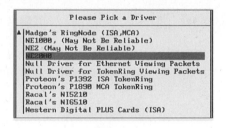

FIGURE 24.56.

I/O address selection.

To copy NetSight to a hard disk, select the Install on Hard Drive option from the menu. You will be prompted for a directory path (see Figure 24.57). Make sure to include that directory path in your PATH= command in AUTOEXEC.BAT.

NetSight can be started by using the GO.BAT file created during installation. It is placed in the directory into which you installed the software.

It is best to have as much base memory as possible for NetSight. This is especially true if you are capturing data frames on a busy network. NetSight processes captured frames in base memory and then stores them in an EMS-based capture buffer. Therefore, the larger the base memory, the bigger the burst of traffic NetSight can capture.

FIGURE 24.57.

Installing NetSight onto the hard drive.

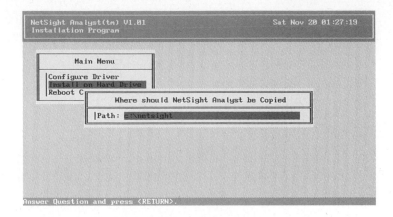

Intel LANDesk Manager v1.01

LANDesk Manager is an integrated set of Windows-based, LAN-management tools. Among its various features, the one of interest here is its capability to monitor packet rates, utilization, and error levels.

There are three default windows within the Traffic Monitor module: Active Filters, History Window, and Rate Windows. You also can add a Station Log display to it. (See Figure 24.58.) This table tracks the active devices on your network and displays some traffic statistics associated with each.

FIGURE 24.58.

Traffic Monitor window.

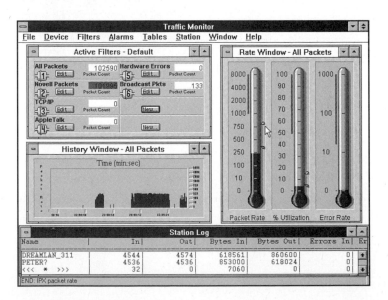

You can set up to eight active filters and threshold settings using the Active Filters window. By default it keeps count of the following:

- Total number of frames on the network
- Number of NetWare frames on the network
- Number of TCP/IP frames on the network
- Number of AppleTalk frames on the network
- Number of error frames on the network
- Number of broadcast frames on the network

These counters can give you an idea of the relative amount of traffic caused by the various protocols you have on your network.

For each counter, you can set a threshold value. (See Figure 24.59.) You can set both a minimum and a maximum value, if applicable. You also can define a duration for which the threshold must be exceeded before the alarm triggers. This is very useful in avoiding traffic "spikes." This also can be configured with the Alarm pull-down menu. (See Figure 24.60.)

FIGURE 24.59.

Alarm configuration.

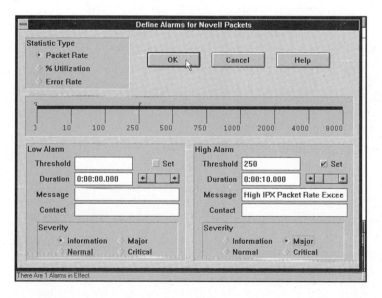

The History window gives you a real-time look at your traffic in terms of frames per second on your network segment. (See Figure 24.61.) You can control the type of frames tracked by this window, statistics type, sampling rate, and time scale along the x-axis. (See Figure 24.62.)

FIGURE 24.60.

Alarm pull-down menu.

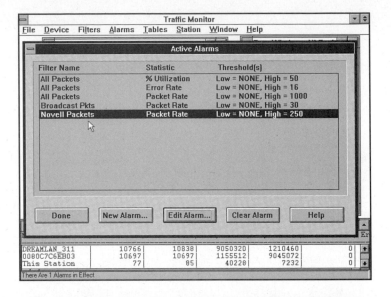

FIGURE 24.61.

History window.

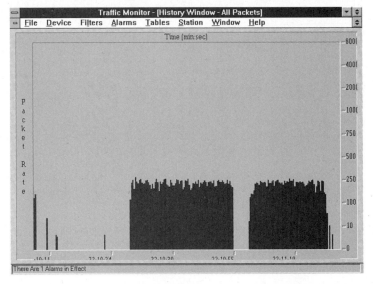

The Rate window gives a "thermometer" reading of the current data rate on your segment. Similar to the History window, you get a real-time report of data rate, utilization percentage, and error rate. (See Figure 24.63.) Just as with the History window, you can configure this to give you rates depending on protocol and different sampling frequency. (See Figure 24.64.) Two "markers" are shown: a high-water mark (peak rate) and a current rate. On a color monitor, the peak rate marker is yellow, and the current rate marker is green. The vertical bar (red) is the "danger" zone or your threshold region.

FIGURE 24.62.

History window configuration.

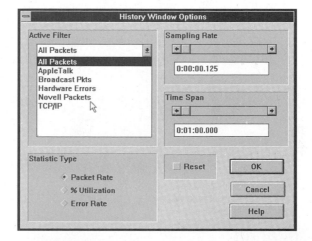

FIGURE 24.63.

Rate window.

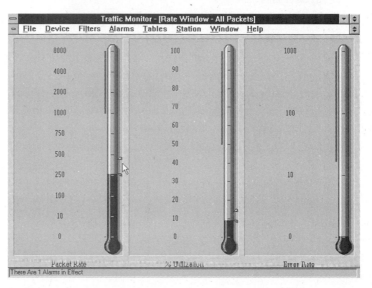

Overall, LANDesk Manager is similar in nature to LANalyzer for Windows in that it provides traffic information. However, it does not have the data-capture and de-code capabilities of LZFW or NetSight. Therefore, it is a good monitoring package, but is somewhat limited as a troubleshooting tool.

FIGURE 24.64.

*Rate window
configuration.*

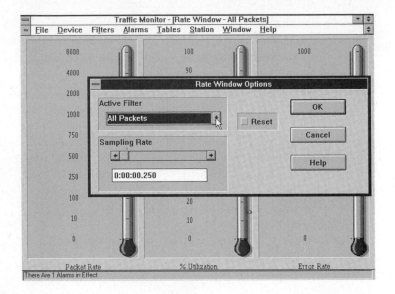

Installation

Because LANDesk Manager is a Windows-based application, you install it from Windows. You must log into a server before you can perform the installation. As with any Windows product's installation, you execute the SETUP.EXE program from the distribution diskette. There are two installation modes: Default and Custom. The Default setup installs all LANDesk Manager features, and the Custom setup enables you to select the feature(s) you need. (See Figures 24.65 and 24.66.) Files are copied both to your server and to your workstation.

FIGURE 24.65.

*LANDesk setup
selection.*

FIGURE 24.66.

Feature selection.

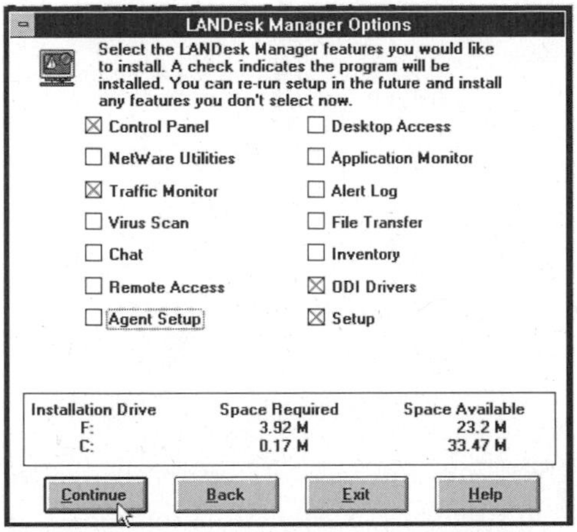

By default, most of the LANDesk Manager modules are installed on the server. However, the traffic caused by the loading of different LANDesk DLL files off the server can mask the real amount of traffic on your network. Consider installing at least the Traffic Monitor application on your local drive.

The same reasoning applies when using a server-based Windows installation for traffic monitoring.

For the Traffic Monitor function to perform properly, your ODI driver must support promiscuous mode. A number of such drivers are supplied with LANDesk Manager and are located in the F:\LANDESK\ODI directory (if you used the defaults). If you are not sure whether your current ODI driver supports promiscuous mode, you can use a program called TESTPRO.EXE to test your driver. (See Figure 24.67.)

If you have more than one frame type defined in your NET.CFG file, TESTPRO will report once for every frame type defined. Because three frame types were defined for NE2000 in Figure 24.28, TESTPRO reported the result three times.

FIGURE 24.67.

Test the ODI driver for promiscuous mode support.

```
F:\LANDESK\ODI>testpro

LANDesk Promiscuous Mode Test Program Version 1.0.
Copyright (c) Intel 1992-1993

Mlid: NE2000     Port: 300  Int: 2    Mem: N/A ,
        Will Support Promiscuous Mode

Mlid: NE2000     Port: 300  Int: 2    Mem: N/A ,
        Will Support Promiscuous Mode

Mlid: NE2000     Port: 300  Int: 2    Mem: N/A ,
        Will Support Promiscuous Mode


F:\LANDESK\ODI>
```

If your driver does not pass the test, you can check to see whether a new one is available in the ETHERNET or TOKEN directory. If not, contact your vendor or consider using packet driver. A set of packet drivers is located in F:\LANDESK\PACKET.DRV directory. For detailed information on using packet drivers or getting ones that are not provided in the package, consult pages 24 through 27 in the LANDesk Manager Setup manual.

XTree Tools for Networks v1.02

XTree Tools for Networks is a set of eight modules that are designed to provide the means of changing, monitoring, alerting, testing, and backing up of your NetWare server's data and its configuration. The module of interest here is NetTrack. It enables you to monitor real-time performance statistics of your NetWare server. The statistics of interest to us here are the LAN I/O statistics. It gives you information on the following:

- Total number of packets
- Packets routed
- Packets received
- Packets sent
- KB received
- KB sent

When you let NetTrack run for an extended period of time, you can get a sense of the traffic load on your server by looking at the Average and Maximum values under your LAN I/O statistics. (See Figure 24.68.)

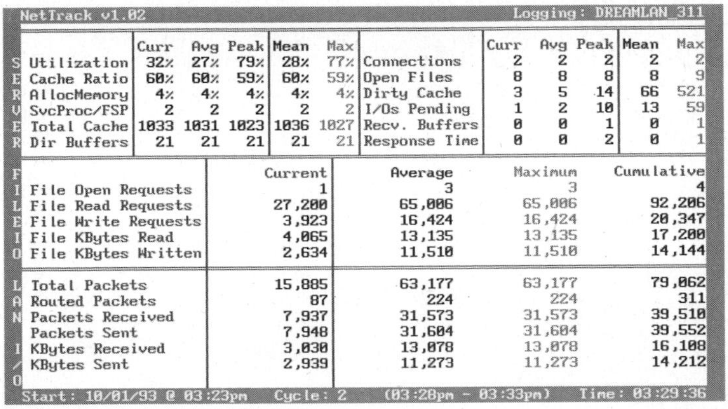

FIGURE 24.68.

NetTrack report screen.

```
NetTrack v1.02                                          Logging : DREAMLAN_311
        ┌────┬────┬────┬────┬────┐                    ┌────┬────┬────┬────┬────┐
        │Curr│Avg │Peak│Mean│Max │                    │Curr│Avg │Peak│Mean│Max │
S Utilization│32%│27%│79%│28%│77%│Connections      │ 2 │ 2 │ 2 │ 2 │ 2 │
E Cache Ratio│60%│60%│59%│60%│59%│Open Files       │ 8 │ 8 │ 8 │ 8 │ 9 │
R AllocMemory│ 4%│ 4%│ 4%│ 4%│ 4%│Dirty Cache      │ 3 │ 5 │ 14│ 66│521│
V SvcProc/FSP│ 2 │ 2 │ 2 │ 2 │ 2 │I/Os Pending     │ 1 │ 2 │ 10│ 13│ 59│
E Total Cache│1033│1031│1023│1036│1027│Recv. Buffers   │ 0 │ 0 │ 1 │ 0 │ 1 │
R Dir Buffers│ 21│ 21│ 21│ 21│ 21│Response Time    │ 0 │ 0 │ 2 │ 0 │ 1 │

                        Current      Average      Maximum     Cumulative
F File Open Requests         1           3            3             4
I File Read Requests     27,200      65,006       65,006        92,206
L File Write Requests     3,923      16,424       16,424        20,347
E File KBytes Read        4,065      13,135       13,135        17,200
I File KBytes Written     2,634      11,510       11,510        14,144
O
L Total Packets          15,885      63,177       63,177        79,062
A Routed Packets             87         224          224           311
N Packets Received        7,937      31,573       31,573        39,510
  Packets Sent            7,948      31,604       31,604        39,552
I KBytes Received         3,030      13,078       13,078        16,108
/ KBytes Sent             2,939      11,273       11,273        14,212
O
Start: 10/01/93 @ 03:23pm    Cycle: 2    (03:28pm - 03:33pm)    Time: 03:29:36
```

For a LAN-monitoring tool, XTree Tools for Networks is not a great package. However, it provides extensive information on file-server statistics. It is also useful in server management and configuration reporting.

Installation

Log into your server as Supervisor or equivalent before you can install XTree Tools for Networks. To install the software on your server, run INSTALL.EXE from disk 1 of the XTree Tools diskette set. First you need to enable the license for the server to which you are installing the product. (See Figure 24.69.) You then specify where on the server or workstation you want the software to be installed. (See Figure 24.70.) The files are then extracted into the specified directory. (See Figure 24.71.)

> **NOTE** ▶
>
> You need to manually copy XTREE.NLM from your software directory to SYS:SYSTEM. It is not copied automatically. Include LOAD XTREE in your AUTOEXEC.NCF if you want it to be loaded every time your server is booted.

FIGURE 24.69.
Enable license for server.

XTree Tools for Networks TestDrive Version 1.02
Select Server to Enable
DREAMLAN_311
[Enter] Select Server [Esc]

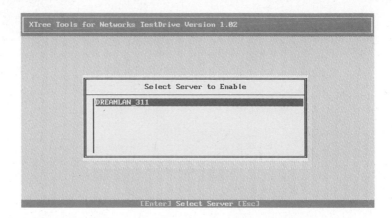

FIGURE 24.70.
Specify directory path for software install.

XTree Tools for Networks TestDrive Version 1.02
Install XTree Tools for Networks
Enter the path where you would like to store the
XTree Tools for Networks program files.
Path : c:\xtree
Enter path. Examples : C:\XTOOLS, C:\TOOLS, F:\TOOLS

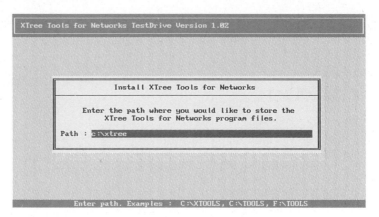

FIGURE 24.71.
Extracting files into specified directory.

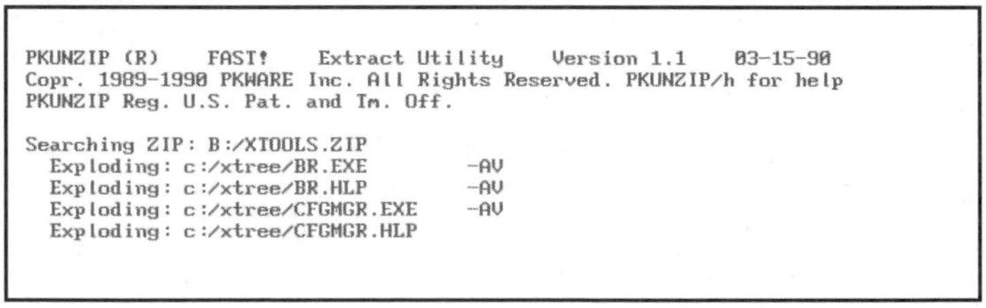

PKUNZIP (R) FAST! Extract Utility Version 1.1 03-15-90
Copr. 1989-1990 PKWARE Inc. All Rights Reserved. PKUNZIP/h for help
PKUNZIP Reg. U.S. Pat. and Tm. Off.
Searching ZIP: B:/XTOOLS.ZIP
Exploding: c:/xtree/BR.EXE -AV
Exploding: c:/xtree/BR.HLP -AV
Exploding: c:/xtree/CFGMGR.EXE -AV
Exploding: c:/xtree/CFGMGR.HLP

You can execute NetTrack either as a stand-alone program or from the XTree Tools menu. In order to use XTOOLS.EXE, you must first log into a server. To run NETTRACK.EXE as a stand-alone program, you need to be attached only to a server—not necessarily the server you are monitoring. However, the server being monitored must have XTREE.NLM loaded.

PART

V

Internetworks and WANs

Basics of Internetwork Data Communications

by Rick Sant'Angelo

IN THIS CHAPTER

25

Internetworking used to require special expertise to implement. However, products are now being marketed that enable integrators to remotely connect NetWare without extensive training and experience. Some caveats apply, but today it is easier than ever to integrate your network with users who are geographically disbursed.

On the topic of internetworking, you will find that the industry uses terms inconsistently. The purpose of this chapter is to define the terms and mechanics used throughout this section of the book and to provide an overview of how various aspects of internetworking are covered within the section.

This chapter divides basics of internetworking into two categories: *communications servers* and *transmission media.*

NetWare's client/server design includes more than file servers. The two types of communications servers that are discussed in this chapter are

■ Asynchronous communications servers

■ Routers

Because longer distances preclude the possibility of owning the links between connection points, three types of services are commonly available:

■ Switched dial-up

■ Leased lines

■ Switched data networks

The types of media used with these servers are

■ Public switched telephone networks (PSTNs)

■ Analog leased lines

■ Digital leased lines

■ Switched data network services

■ Unbounded media

Products are marketed and reviewed in industry publications on the basis of what they *do*; but the needs of information managers are not structured the same way as the product features. Therefore, the information manager needs to match his or her needs with product offerings. This chapter helps you make the transition from what you require to choosing what products and services can fulfill those requirements.

Standards Organizations

Two industry standards organizations play big roles in determining how products and services work and what they are called: the Consultative Committee for International Telegraph and Telephone (CCITT) and the International Standards Organization (ISO). In the past, large system vendors could set their own standards for connecting remote users with their proprietary mainframes and minicomputers. Today—thanks to these standards organizations—many nonproprietary systems can connect to each other and move data with transparency. Without standards organizations, we might be stuck with dedicating separate communications links and equipment for each system. For example, we might need one WAN for an IBM SNA mainframe and remote cluster controllers, plus a second link for NetWare. Standards organizations are working towards combining traffic on the same link—as they now do with NetWare and TCP/IP traffic.

Consultative Committee for International Telegraph and Telephone (CCITT)

This organization internationally standardizes communication links. Largely because of the efforts of this group, telephone and data communications between continents can occur. Telecom services in the U.S., Europe, and the Orient are different; however, because of CCITT telephony standards, data can be transferred across international boundaries. For example, CCITT standards implemented in telephone switching equipment enables a U.S. T-1 line (1.544 MBps) to interface with European E-1 lines (2.048 MBps).

CCITT has gone further in extending telecommunications standards to include the following:

- Packet switching networks (X.25, X.3, and so on)
- Modem standards (V.35, V.32, V.32bis, V.42, and so on)
- Directory services (X.500)
- Electronic mail (X.400)

International Standards Organization (ISO)

ISO was previously discussed in this book as the organization that developed the OSI Model for networking protocols (see Chapter 5, "Novell's Protocol Stack"). ISO works with CCITT, IEEE, ANSI, and other standards organizations to take standards internationally. Because many of these standards are influenced heavily by governments, ISO standards are added to international treaties to establish international consistency and compliance. The end result is functionality among data communications equipment, links, and protocols—whether used domestically or internationally.

Telecommunications Terms

The following sections explain some basic terms that form the foundation for wide area networking. The software and hardware components that are used depend on these telecom services and mechanics.

Binary Data

Data sent over a telecommunications line is converted to the binary numbering system; each character is represented by a combination of 1s and 0s. The ASCII character set, which is represented in seven or eight bits per character, is normally used. IBM uses its own standard numbering system in mainframe communications (EBCDIC), which may require translation when the two types of systems are interfaced.

Analog

Analog data communications are used to send data over normal voice telephone lines at actual transmission rates of up to 19.2 kbps. Data compression potentially can increase throughput up to four times this rate. In all practicality, throughput rates do not normally exceed 38.8 kbps when using analog data transmission (V.42*bis* standard).

Binary data is signaled by modulating amplitude, phase, or a combination of both, in nondiscreet variations. Modems are used to transmit binary analog data.

Digital

Digital service requires special lines and equipment that support digital—instead of analog—service. Digital services are available at rates beginning at 24 kbps. LANs use digital data transmission, but long distance carriers normally offer lines with up to 1,544 kbps transmission rates (T-1s).

Digital transmission uses various encoding methods, such as Manchester, Differential Manchester, 4B/5B, and Robbed-Bit Signaling (RBS) encoding. Regardless of which type is used, bits are relayed by signaling current on and off in discrete variations (that is, on=+5 volts, and off=0 volts).

Data Terminal Equipment (DTE) and Data Communication Equipment (DCE)

To establish communications, a DTE prepares and controls data for transmittal, and the DCE actually transmits the data. A DTE may be a PC or a communications server in a WAN, whereas a DCE consists of two types: modems for analog data and Digital Service Unit/Channel Service Unit (DSU/CSU) for digital data.

Asynchronous

In asynchronous communications, each byte is framed with a start and a stop bit for alignment. The characters can use seven or eight bits and may use the eighth bit for a parity check. Asynchronous communications are generally analog and are relegated to use for dial-in and dial-out services. Asynchronous communications normally are not used in transmissions of more than 9.6 kbps. At higher rates, modems usually switch to synchronous transmission—regardless of what is sent by your communications software.

Synchronous

In synchronous communications, blocks of data are encapsulated into a data frame. The frame includes a starting delimiter, an ending delimiter, and a checksum (or cyclic redundancy check) preceding the ending delimiter for error control. Synchronous transmissions have less overhead, and they more fully utilize available bandwidth of transmission media. They also have better error control than asynchronous transmissions. Synchronous transmission is used in both analog and digital communications.

Telecommunications Services

The following telecommunications products are available for almost every point in North America.

Public Switched Telephone Networks (PSTNs) ("Dial-Up" or "Switched")

Normal telephone lines are called PSTNs and are designed to provide analog data rates of up to 9.6 kbps (though your local telephone company will not guarantee error-free transmission at this rate). When your call is placed, switching equipment finds a route and makes a connection. Your charges are relative to both the amount of time the connection is active and the point-to-point distance. Sometimes a PSTN is referred to as Plain Old Telephone Service (POTS).

Modems are used with analog asynchronous protocols over dial-up lines at transmission rates of up to 9.6 kbps. Most modems that claim higher data rates switch into synchronous mode and use data compression to achieve better transfer rates. A modem working at higher transfer rates needs to be matched to a receiving modem that uses the same protocols and mechanics. CCITT has established standards such as V.32*bis* for modems at speeds exceeding 9.6 kbps, but many modems use standards set by Hayes, US Robotics, or other modem developers.

Because many fast modems were produced prior to standards being firmly set and stabilized, you should make certain that modems on both ends of a link are the same type of modem, or you may find that the modems might not be able to communicate at rates of over 2.4 kbps. Use of dial-up switched lines is simple and inexpensive, but slow and not very dependable for sustained data transfers. They are, however, very practical for dial-in/dial-out services.

Dial-up lines provide only point-to-point connectivity between two locations and cannot provide multiple point connectivity like a LAN.

Leased Lines

Leased lines are available at various limited bandwidth capacities and are charged on a basis of time and distance, not usage. The line may be established through switching equipment, but once the connection is established, your connection is available for your exclusive use 24 hours per day. This works better than dial-up lines for sustaining low error rates.

Leased lines provide only point-to-point connectivity between two locations. Connecting more than two points requires multiple leased lines and a mesh topology, as shown in Figure 25.1.

FIGURE 25.1.

A point-to-point leased line mesh topology.

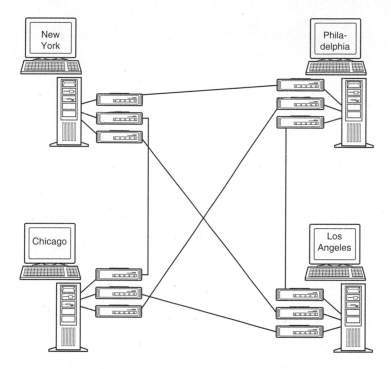

Analog Leased Lines

An analog leased line is a straight connection with no dial tone. Analog leased lines support data rates up to 14.2 kbps (56.8 kbps with data compression). Previously, analog leased lines were the most popular WAN media; however, lower digital rates have reduced their attractiveness. Leased lines are available from local telcos within their service areas, and long distance carriers for inter-LATA service (between telcos).

Digital Leased Lines

Digital lines are available in many different forms (depending on which carrier and service you choose). Digital service is generally provided from 24 kbps up to gigabit-per-second rates (SONET). Digital services are rapidly expanding, and they are becoming less expensive. The trend to faster, less expensive digital services is escalating in speed, availability, and ease of use. Digital service at 56 kbps is often just as inexpensive as analog leased lines and has lower error rates. Most digital services are offered in 64 kbps increments (channels).

> **NOTE** ▶
>
> In digital transmissions, you use only 56 kbps out of a 64 kbps channel.
>
> In North America, call-processing functions are handled through Robbed-Bit-Signaling (RBS) to deliver error-controlled services. RBS removes the least significant bit from each 8-bit sample in every sixth frame. Usable bandwidth is limited to only 7 of each 8 bits, resulting in a 56 kbps effective transfer rate on a 64 kbps line.

The following sections explain a few variations of digital services, such as T-carrier lines, and digital data service and fractional T-1s.

T-Carrier Lines

In North America, T-carrier services are offered by four major providers: AT&T, MCI, Sprint, and Wiltel. These companies have acquired right-of-ways to most major cities. Service to a carrier's closest Point of Presence (POP) can be provided by local telcos or a competing carrier. When communicating over international boundaries, European E-1 lines (2.048 mbps) interface with T-1s.

T-carrier services are available in various forms:

- T-1 at 1.544 mbps (1.536 mbps plus 8 kbps for framing)
- Fractional T-1 at 64 kbps (56 kbps plus 8 kbps for framing)
- T-3 at 44.736 mbps

T-1s can be used as 24 separate 64 kbps channels. Fractional T-1s can be combined for multiples of 64 kbps, such as 128, 256, and 512 kbps data service. Each channel can carry different communications, such as voice, data, and video.

Because of deregulation and the highly competitive nature of the telecommunications industry, rates have drastically dropped. A few miles can cost a few hundred dollars a month, and a typical coast-to-coast T-1 can cost more than $10,000 per month. Because of competitive POPs and supply versus demand, costs can radically vary from city to city.

T-1 service is available in all but remote areas of North America. In other countries, standards may differ; for example, the standard service in Europe is 2.048 mbps. Thanks to CCITT standards, telecommunications between different systems is available.

T-3 service, which is equivalent to 28 T-1s, is provided on the same basis as T-1 service. T-3 service is available almost anywhere T-1 service is offered.

Digital Data Service (DDS) and Fractional T-1s

Digital lines are available in most metropolitan areas that accommodate digital traffic at up to 56 kbps. This service is called *Accunet* by AT&T and is offered all over North America. AT&T, Sprint, and MCI have fiber-optic networks stretching across North America and offer the same services at competitive rates. These companies and other carriers offer digital services under a wide variety of names. Quite often, a 64 kbps or 56 kbps line is actually a fractional T-1, but is not called by the same name.

Switched Services

This type of medium provides charge rates based on usage—as opposed to time and distance. In many cases, usage is restricted to certain times of the day, or capacity demands fluctuate wildly. A switched service can provide more economical rates under such conditions.

Integrated Services Digital Network (ISDN)

ISDN is scheduled to provide switched digital service through local telcos. In November, 1992, the first commercial ISDN telephone call was completed, heralding this much-awaited service. ISDN was designed to enable local telcos to offer inter-LATA data rates of up to 1.544 mbps, as well as digital and analog voice, PBX, video, alarm, and telemetry services. Currently, transmission rates of up to 64 and 128 kbps are offered in many major cities around the U.S.

If ISDN service is accessible, you can have an on-demand digital link. ISDN circuits and switches are not as compatible as originally planned. You need to check for availability between your originating and destination telcos. You also must have the appropriate lines between your location and the telco's local loop. Local telcos are currently improving local loops to offer this service. Availability varies in all locations; contact your local telephone company for information.

Digital telephones are increasing in popularity as ISDN services are installed. New products are available that incorporate a DSU/CSU and communications board in one product. ISDN will probably become the most commonly used data service as soon as the links are put together.

Public Data Networks (PDNs)

Often referred to as packet-switching networks or X.25 networks, these services provide asynchronous and synchronous point-to-point service at data rates of up to 56 kbps. Service is offered at the provider's Packet Assembler/Disassembler (PAD). To access a PDN, you normally use X.25 protocol, which is processed at the PAD with the following:

- HDLC synchronous protocol over a leased line (analog or digital) at 56 kbps
- Dial-up asynchronous service with X.3 Packet Assembler/Disassembler (PAD)

PDNs typically use X.25 protocol internally (some use their own proprietary protocol). X.25 packet format is the same as HDLC frame format, with a routing field added. Each packet is routed internally through the provider's network of nodes with PADs in many locations. HDLC is the frame (OSI Data Link Layer), and X.25 the routing protocol (OSI Network Layer). X.25 is a CCITT standard protocol, and HDLC is an ISO standard.

Once connected, the service provides the same type of connection as those listed previously (up to 56 kbps) on demand. Charges are based on a monthly connection fee plus a traffic charge per packet (or kilopacket).

Frame Relay

Frame Relay networks have recently come on the scene providing virtually any data rate. A frame relay network consists of T-carrier lines, but it is offered on a demand-usage basis in any combination of channels. Frame relay networks are operated by providers who own or lease fiber-optic lines all over North America. Frame relay networks switch digital communications packets at very high speeds. Because frame relay providers use their own internal protocols transparently, they provide compatibility with almost any type of bridge or router.

Several frame relay providers are currently offering service—including AT&T and Wiltel. Providers generally bundle local access to their POP and sometimes even bundle routers and DTE/DCE equipment. Not only do these services give high data rates, the carriers also generally take full responsibility for the reliability of the link.

Frame relay network services are charged on contract rates based upon either usage or capacity. When excess capacity is available, they can enable higher data transmission rates. If contracted rates are exceeded, the charge basis can be revised.

Major advantages of frame relays are that they provide high-bandwidth communications for limited time periods and long distances at lower costs than comparable leased lines. Providers also offer load balancing and redundant lines for better fault tolerance and less bottlenecking. Frame relay has become almost an overnight sensation. The best part of using frame relay is the service offered by the vendor. A company will provide all the products and services necessary to get you connected and keep up your link.

Cell Relay

With speeds up to 150 mbps, Cell Relay is expected to be the next generation of communication service. Cell relay works similar to frame relay, except very high-speed switching equipment and protocols are used. Service is severely limited and expensive now, because few alternatives exist at these data rates. Although not currently defined as a specification, work is progressing toward a standard.

Unbounded Media

Magnetic waves (radio, microwave, and other bands) and light emissions provide excellent media for transmitting data. There are a few limitations, however, because each form is still under development as a data communication carrier.

Microwave

Microwave links can be owned or leased. They can be used for repeaters, bridges, or routers for line-of-sight distances (distance depends on visibility, but is typically good for up to 50 miles). A single microwave link provides up to 45 mbps bandwidth over a line of sight. Implementing a microwave link can be expensive, but it may be more cost effective than a T-carrier line because it is a one-time cost. A microwave medium can be used as an Ethernet LAN for distances up to 8.6 miles. Both ends of a microwave link typically can be established for less than $25,000.

Satellite

Services are provided by carriers in much the same manner as T-1 lines or PDNs. Satellite carriers provide local access with dial-up, ISDN, fractional, and T-1 links. Communications satellites can carry large data rates in steady streams; however, propagation delays (usually about one-half per second) cause problems in half-duplex protocols (such as IPS/SPX) and two-way communications.

Laser and Magnetic Media

Laser, infrared, and radio wave systems are now appearing. Generally, a system using unbounded media (magnetic radiation) is purchased. Some systems require FCC permits for frequencies to be used. Although radio waves provide multipoint communications, some media (such as laser and infrared) provide only point-to-point capabilities.

Products based on these technologies are new and not yet as low in cost and high in reliability and performance as many wire-based competitors. However, these alternatives do exist when circumstances preclude the use of more common media.

WAN Protocols

WAN access protocols, similar to LAN access protocols, operate between nodes on the WAN. They are typically designed to be used across communications links that span long distances and use telecommunications links that exist today. Most WAN protocols are point-to-point oriented—they only operate between a sender and a receiver.

Basic communications protocols are used for synchronous communications over WANs. A few protocols have become standardized and have been in use for many years.

WAN protocols are full-duplex (can transmit in both directions concurrently) and are generally connection-oriented (require acknowledgment for each block or group of blocks sent).

Novell's IPX/SPX protocol is not well-suited for WANs because each packet must receive an acknowledgment. IPX/SPX must be encapsulated in a WAN frame or packet for transmission over telecommunications lines.

NOTE ▶

Novell has a new Packet Burst Protocol that can be implemented in servers and workstations that reduces acknowledgment packet traffic. See Chapter 5, "Novell's Protocol Stack," and Chapter 26, "Routers and Bridges," for more detail on Packet Burst Protocol.

High-Level Data Link Control (HDLC)

HDLC is a bit-oriented, full-duplex ISO standard. This protocol is widely used and is an OSI layer two (data link layer) frame format. Packets or frames can be encapsulated into HDLC frames for analog or digital transmissions.

Most proprietary synchronous protocols either use or are based on HDLC. Many vendors have improved HDLC to refine protocols used in their own equipment. This, of course, means that their equipment is not interoperable with other vendors' equipment, which is generally the case.

Synchronous Data Link Control (SDLC)

IBM's development of SDLC is based on HDLC. SDLC is a subset of HDLC and is 100-percent compatible with HDLC. The reverse is not true, however, because SDLC does not use some of the advanced functions of HDLC. IBM uses SDLC in WAN terminal-to-mainframe connections.

Digital Data Communications Message Protocol (DD-CMP)

DEC uses a DLC-type protocol very similar to SDLC, except that SDLC is bit-oriented, and DD-CMP is character count-oriented. The difference does not make it better, only different. DD-CMP is proprietary to DEC and used only in DEC equipment. For this reason, DEC equipment is not interoperable with other DLC protocols.

X.25

This protocol is a routing protocol, operating at layer three of the OSI model. X.25 is a CCITT standard and is identical to HDLC, with the exception of a routing field that is placed just before the data. The routing field is used to route each packet from node to node within a network that may have numerous redundant routes. This places X.25 at layer 3—the network layer of the OSI model. X.25 enables this protocol to be routed through nodes instead of being strictly a point-to-point protocol like HDLC.

Transmission Control Protocol /Internet Protocol (TCP/IP)

TCP/IP is used in both LANs and WANs. Unlike other WAN protocols, TCP/IP is not point-to-point oriented and is used to tie many hosts into internetworks. These two protocols are equivalent to OSI network and transport protocols; however, higher layer protocols also are defined in these specifications. IP is routable and provides the routing capability for this multiple host internetworking.

TCP/IP is extensively used to tie together thousands of computers over various types of links to form the Internet across T-1 links. Internet provides workstation access to thousands of host computers in the Department of Defense, governmental agencies, universities, and government contractors.

TCP/IP was originally developed by Defense Advanced Research and Projects Agency (DARPA) within the Department of Defense. It was developed to connect DOD computers and became a military standard in 1978. DOD required its use for many agencies and contractors. Today, TCP/IP is widely used because it is free from royalties and works well for all types of network connections.

TCP/IP is widely used in many networked systems so that interoperability is accomplished. TCP/IP is used as the transport/network protocol in many routers. TCP/IP network and transport protocols are equivalent to layers 3 and 4 of the OSI model.

Point to Point Protocol (PPP)

PPP is part of a new generation of synchronous protocol designed to be used with great flexibility. PPP has been developed by several vendors who are working together to define a standard so that their products will work with one another.

Novell and other vendors use PPP in several of their communications products. PPP shows great promise if vendors are able to develop a standard that will enable interoperability. Novell and other vendors have formed a consortium to unite emerging variations of PPP development projects for future compatibility. PPP is not restricted by speed and can operate at very high rates through modern digital switches. Therefore, it should not become obsolete as new types of media become available.

Asynchronous Transmission Mode (ATM)

ATM is one of the newest WAN protocols that promises future gigabit-per-second data throughput rates. ATM currently is being developed as a LAN access protocol at bandwidths of 100 mbps and 143 mbps to compete with FDDI. One advantage of ATM is the promise of merging LAN and WAN access protocols into one single standard, which will alleviate the need for encapsulation into another frame or packet in bridges and routers.

Summary

No longer do you need to rely on data communications experts or integrators to link LANs with remote users or remote LANs. If you are familiar with a few basic terms, products, and services discussed in this chapter, you can put together your own WAN. The subsequent chapters in this section of the book more clearly define the hardware and software products that you can purchase to assemble your WAN.

> **TIP** ▶
>
> Most hardware distributors, vendors, and data carriers have evaluation programs that enable you to try a product with the right to return it or void your contract for any reason during a limited period. When integrating WAN products, it may be prudent to arrange an evaluation; so you can be assured that the product will provide the functionality that you expect.

Routers and Bridges

26

by Rick Sant'Angelo

Routers and bridges constitute boundaries between networks to form internetworks. This chapter focuses on these devices that link LANs and WANs into an internetwork to configure the physical infrastructure upon which your system is based. When dealing with an internetwork, your knowledge of the IPX protocol and how it relates to these devices is essential for an efficient and trouble-free internetwork.

> **TIP** ▶
>
> By reading this section, you will better understand the complexities of bridges and routers if you consider a NetWare internetwork to be based on network addresses, not based on servers.
>
> The paradigm of a server-based network confuses your understanding of how NetWare's IPX and its internal routers work. Most of the information you may have read about configuring internetworks has probably missed this subtle distinction, which makes all the difference in clarifying this subject.
>
> For more explanation of conceptualizing networks and internetworks, see the Introduction and Chapter 5, "NetWare's Protocol Stack."

To Route or to Bridge, that is the Question

A continuing argument haunts us to this day: whether to use bridges or routers to grow our networks into larger systems. There is really a simple answer to this question: it is better to use routers with IPX, IP, and OSI protocols, while it is necessary to use bridges with NetBIOS and SNA protocols. This simple conclusion is an obvious and simple result of understanding routable protocols and how they work. The reason so many writers in our industry confuse readers is due to the inconsistent use of terminology. This causes less technical people to become confused about what these devices do and how they work with various protocols.

Routable versus Nonroutable Protocols

NetWare is based on a routable protocol, IPX, and internal server routers. Since 1985, Novell has incorporated a router into its server operating system. With the introduction of NetWare v2.0, the internal router gave NetWare the capability to support multiple NICs in the server.

> ⊕ Packet header contains all information to route packets to their ultimate destination, regardless of whether the destination node is located on the same LAN or a different LAN

IPX protocol is a *routable* protocol. Routable means that the packet header contains all the information necessary to route packets to their ultimate destination, regardless of whether the destination node is located on the same LAN or a different LAN. The internal router enables each NIC to be connected to a separate LAN, and the internal router moves packets from one NIC to the other (that is, it routes them) if they need to be moved.

To better understand routable protocols, you need to take a look at protocols that are nonroutable. A good example of a widely used nonroutable protocol is NetBIOS. Originally developed by IBM and Sytek, NetBIOS is used in many peer-to-peer LANs, such as LANtastic, Windows for Workgroups, and NetWare Lite. It is also used in Microsoft LAN Manager and IBM LAN Server.

In a NetBIOS network, when a device is to be shared with other users on a network, the computer to which the device is connected must be initialized as a server. Then a command is issued to share the device and a name is assigned to the device. From that point on, a user can attach to that server and use any device that is shared by calling it by name.

The NetBIOS packet is directed to a server and has the name of the device that is to be used. A NetBIOS packet contains information necessary to move the packet to a server and to look for the named device in the location table of the server, which in turn points at the device. It is assumed that the user and the server exist on the same LAN and that the device exists within the server to which the user has attached.

In this system, separate physical LANs must be connected with a bridge (not a router), because the bridge makes the two physical LANs appear to be one logical LAN. Bridges can connect LANs and WANs, but the entire physical infrastructure of the internetwork looks like one single LAN. Routers cannot be used, because there is no information in the NetBIOS packet header that provides routing information to identify separate logical LANs, and it is therefore impossible to route the packet.

NetWare's approach differs from this scheme. Instead, each separate physical LAN is identified with a *network address* (sometimes called a network number). The combination of the network address and the node address identifies each node's location, regardless of where it is located. It can be located on any one of thousands of separate physical LANs or WANs connected with routers. The network address and node address—the combination is called a *login address*—are placed into the IPX packet header. A router can read the login address and forward the packet to its ultimate destination.

> ⌐ Combination of network address and node address identifies each node's location.

In this system, a router is substituted for the bridge. The routers learn all the available routes to any server and can forward packets to anywhere on the internetwork regardless of whether the user is attached to the server that contains that device.

Routers are firm separations between LANs and have methods of calculating the *least-cost route* to send packets to their ultimate destinations. An internetwork based on routers can be quite extensive yet simple to configure. As long as the network addresses are labeled properly, the routers learn of all the available routes and route packets on the least-cost route according to the routing protocol used in the router.

Routable protocols have the network and node addresses in the packet header. This information is available to any device that can receive the packet—it does not require any proprietary knowledge of the protocol. Therefore, any third party can build a router to work with the protocol. All routable protocols work somewhat the same way. Table 26.1 lists the most commonly used network protocols.

Table 26.1. Commonly used network protocols.

Protocols	Routable
IPX	Yes
NetBIOS/NetBEUI	No
SNA	No
OSI	Yes
AppleTalk	Yes
TCP/IP	Yes

Novell's IPX protocol and internal routers work similar to TCP/IP and OSI protocols and routers. Many larger accounts have been using TCP/IP protocols and routers for years. And as a result, they understand the mechanics, issues, and considerations involved with these other protocols; therefore, it has not been difficult for larger accounts to capitalize on NetWare routing features. This explains much of the large market share that NetWare enjoys and why it is a favorite in large, internetworked accounts, particularly those already using TCP/IP and UNIX.

Which is Better?

Bridging is not necessarily a better or worse choice than routing. Whichever method is chosen for an internetwork, however, should be consistent. Bridges disguise two

Routers = clear and definite boundaries between multiple LANs. [handwritten]

separate LANs to look like one LAN, whereas routers constitute clear and definite boundaries between multiple LANs. Both link LANs together and isolate traffic, but the level of protocol and the manner in which they work are completely different.

If bridges and routers are mixed in an internetwork, routers cannot calculate the best routes. Routers take into consideration the number of *hops* (processing through a router) that an IPX packet must take in order to get to the ultimate destination as part of the method of determining the least-cost route. However, because a router works at the IPX protocol layer and a bridge works at the LAN MAC or LLC layer (part of the OSI Data Link Layer), a router cannot perceive a hop that occurs in a bridge.

Routers take into consideration the number of hops. [handwritten]

The difference is easy to understand if you draw a distinction between a *physical hop* and a *logical hop.* In order for an IPX packet to make it from one LAN to another, it must be moved across a bridge or router. A physical hop is an actual move across a bridge or router. A logical hop is one that is detected by a router. A bridged hop is not detected by a router but still incurs the latency of a physical hop. The two can be quite different, as shown in the following examples, which illustrate why NetWare and routers work best together.

Physical hop is an actual move across a bridge or router. [handwritten]

Logical hop is detected by a router. [handwritten]

Bridged hop is not detected by a router. [handwritten]

Problem #1: Inefficient Routing and Router Configuration Errors

Figure 26.1 shows a path from A to B where no hops exist, because the two servers and the workstation are connected on the same LAN (network address). An alternate path from A to B contains one hop across a bridge. Because the bridge works at the frame layer using the IEEE MAC or LLC layer to move the frame, the IPX protocol in the server's router cannot detect the hop across the bridge. This results in a physical hop, but no logical hop is detected.

Path B costs one physical hop (but no logical hops), but path A is more direct, requiring no hops at all. Both paths require the same number of logical hops (0), but the NetWare routers (based on IPX) cannot see the hop across the bridge, and therefore calculate that both routes are equally cost-effective, when in fact they are not. In this case, the workstation packets going to file server FS4 may take either path. Choosing path B, with one physical hop, results in some delay in handling the movement of data from one LAN to the other. The degree of delay is predicated on the efficiency of the bridge and its congestion, but path B will not be equal to the more direct and efficient path A. Study Figure 26.1 and really pay attention, because if you can see the difference, you will understand why a bridge is not the best device to use with NetWare.

FIGURE 26.1.

A bridged internetwork.

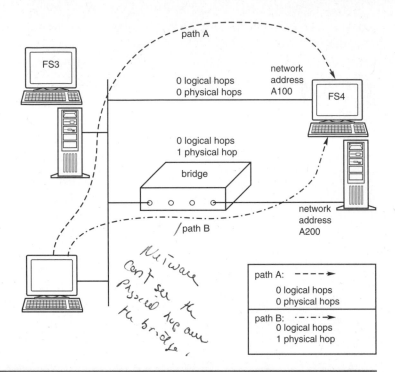

CAUTION ▶

This configuration *will* result in router configuration errors and *may* result in frames traveling in infinite loops over both physical LANs.

NetWare 3.x and 4.x server operating systems require that each NIC in a server must be assigned a unique network address. It is impossible to make this configuration work properly with NetWare, even though you can configure your internetwork as in this example.

In this example, the benefit to be derived from a bridge is reduced by its lack of communication with NetWare's server OS routers, which can determine which network address to use for forwarding the workstation's packets.

Problem #2: Mixing Bridges and Routers

Another problem occurs when mixing bridges and routers, as shown in Figure 26.2. If two paths exist between a source and a destination, and one is bridged while the other is routed, inefficient routing decisions can be made and router configuration errors will result. This is because the routers identify network addresses and broadcast routing information to one another. When both bridged and routed paths exist, at least one LAN will be identified with conflicting network addresses, as shown in Figure 26.2.

FIGURE 26.2.

Bridged and routed redundant paths.

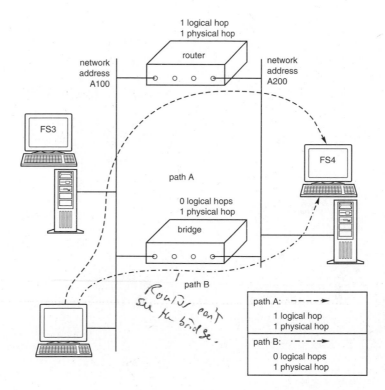

When one path contains a bridge, a physical hop is hidden from the router, and it therefore cannot equitably distinguish this factor as part of its routing decision. Worse, when duplicate paths exist, one routed and one bridged, conflicting information will be distributed to the routers. They will identify the two physical LANs that are bridged as being one LAN and also identify the same two physical LANs as being two separate logical LANs.

NOTE ▶

NetWare routing decisions are made at the server OS on the basis of the number of logical hops. When two paths exist and the number of logical hops are the same, the server's internal router makes a routing decision based on other information. It is virtually impossible to tell which path the routers will select, and the decision may vary for each login.

Problem #3: Inefficient Routing and No Router Configuration Errors

Figure 26.3 contains a configuration that will not result in router-configuration errors, but will result in inefficient routing decisions. In this illustration, two paths exist—path B is connected through two bridges, and path A is connected with a single router.

FIGURE 26.3.

Path B connected through two bridges and Path A connected with a single router.

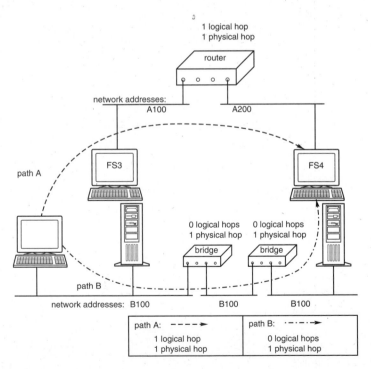

Path A is more efficient and it is recorded as one logical hop, whereas path B is recorded as no logical hops. Path B actually has two physical hops, yet it will be the primary route established by the NetWare server routers. As far as NetWare is concerned, however, the NICs installed in the servers can be configured properly and will not cause router-configuration errors.

Packets versus Frames

One of the most common causes of confusion over bridging and routing is easily cleared up if you recognize different names for the units of data that are being processed. A bridge processes frames, which are generated by the access protocol (such as, CSMA/CD—Ethernet). A router processes packets, which are generated by the network protocol (such as, IPX). Each packet is encapsulated into a frame. A bridge is not aware of routing information contained in the packet header, whereas a router is. Conversely, a router never sees the frame; it has been stripped off by the NIC driver.

Those who write about Novell-related products do the entire industry an injustice by swapping the terms "frame" and "packet." Generally, Novell material describes both of these data units as packets, leaving us unsure at times about which layer of protocol is being discussed. Furthermore, previous NetWare documentation discussed internal routers as "bridges," and even to this date, some of the NetWare learning materials do not clearly draw the distinctions that you need in order to understand this simple issue. Swapping the terms frame and packet simply compounds the error and makes it more difficult to understand this subject.

Though this discussion may seem trivial to some, integrators without clear information can find it difficult to choose between bridges or routers and to assign network addresses.

> **NOTE** ▶
>
> Two bridged LANs need to be identified with the same network address, while two routed LANs need to be identified with different network addresses. When binding the IPX protocol to a NIC driver in your server, you need to know whether your LANs are bridged or routed so you can configure the operating systems accordingly.

Conclusions About Bridging with NetWare

The preceding illustrations give you good reasons to avoid bridges with NetWare. You may have heard conflicting recommendations at times, due to industry confusion with regard to the terms and mechanics of bridges, routers, and the IPX protocol. Generic recommendations about bridging or routing internetworks are complicated by the fact that many network operating systems use nonroutable protocols and therefore must rely on bridges to connect them.

It is a clear and simple conclusion that bridging with NetWare is not a good choice, even though you may be able to resolve router-configuration errors and inefficient routing. As previously discussed, one reason for this conclusion is the complexity of network addressing; another is the reduced capability of the NetWare routers to distinguish the least-cost path. Future flexibility is a third factor that should be seriously considered.

When an integrator installs bridges, resolves all difficulties, and gets everything to work properly, he or she may consider that this constitutes an acceptable method of internetworking. However, because internetworks have a tendency to grow and because integrators and administrators move on to other responsibilities, the possibility of a bridged internetwork hampering future expansion is very real. The simplest way to lessen the risk of reintroducing configuration and routing problems to a growing internetwork is to use routers *exclusively*.

> **NOTE** ▶
>
> Although the author is recommending that you choose routers for your internetwork configuration, you may decide that the potential problems of using a bridge are offset by the integration expertise that you and your organization possess.

Bridging

Although it is suggested that bridges may not be the most effective way to internetwork with NetWare, it is necessary to continue a discussion of bridging in greater detail. In some cases, the decision has already been made or the bridges are already in place, and in those cases the integrator's job is to resolve router-configuration errors and find inefficient routes that may be affecting performance.

The following section discusses these four types of bridges:

- MAC layer bridges
- Spanning-tree bridges

- Source-routing bridges
- Brouters (bridging routers or routing bridges)

MAC Layer (Transparent, Learning) Bridges

This type of bridge is the simplest, most economical type of bridge or router in use. MAC layer bridges rely on simple MAC layer addressing that is present in a LAN frame to forward LAN frames from one LAN to another. This is a very simple process, because the source and destination node addresses in the LAN frame header are all that is needed to connect two or more LANs. These are sometimes called *transparent bridges*, because they are transparent to routable network protocols and routers; in other words, they disguise the two separate physical LANs as one logical LAN. They are also at times called *learning bridges*, because they need to learn which node addresses exist on each side of the bridge.

A MAC layer bridge simply reads the frame header to determine the destination. It also reads source addresses from frames that are circulating around each LAN in order to build a table of node addresses. Though different models use different procedures and algorithms for building these tables, a MAC layer bridge relies exclusively on these two fields in the frame header for its decision.

Figure 26.4 shows a simple MAC layer bridge configuration, connecting two LANs, each with its own file server. In this illustration, the bridge operates by isolating traffic on each LAN unless it needs to be copied onto the other LAN. Notice that both LANs are identified with the same network address for both servers' interfaces.

Figure 26.4 illustrates that when user Mary logs in to server FS4 and uses its disk, the traffic that is generated stays on LAN B. When user Bill logs in to server FS3 and uses its disk, the traffic stays on LAN A. The source and destination node addresses in each frame header from Mary to server FS4 will show 30886 as the source node address and 30769 as the destination node address. Frames addressed *to* Mary from FS4 will show just the opposite. In this case, the bridge views the frames, looks up the destination address in its table, and makes the decision to ignore (filter) the frame. The frame is therefore never propagated on LAN A.

If Mary decides to log in to server FS3, however, frames from her workstation will be addressed from node 30886 to node 30724. When the bridge sees one of these frames, it looks up the destination address in its tables, recognizes that the destination node address is located on LAN A, and therefore copies the frame (that is, forwards it) to LAN A. In this case, the frame is propagated on both LANs.

FIGURE 26.4.

Two LANs and servers inter-networked with a MAC layer bridge.

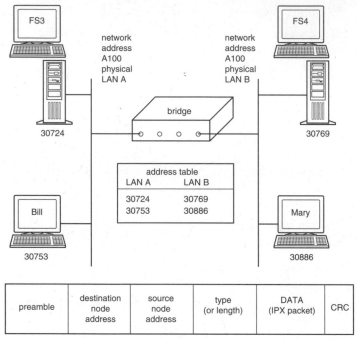

Ethernet frame header

NOTE ▶

When evaluating traffic patterns on LANs, the important factor to consider is which nodes propagate traffic on which LANs. This knowledge must include bridged and routed traffic.

Spanning-Tree Bridges

MAC layer bridges work well when a few physical LANs are linked together. However, when complex internetworks contain multiple routes, MAC layer bridges may generate frames that are propagated from one LAN to another and back again, resulting in an infinite loop. This problem is demonstrated in Figure 26.5. Pay close attention to the bridge's table. Because the bridge is transparent, it sees all node addresses on both sides and *may* forward frames back and forth endlessly.

FIGURE 26.5.

Two MAC layer bridges connecting two LANs.

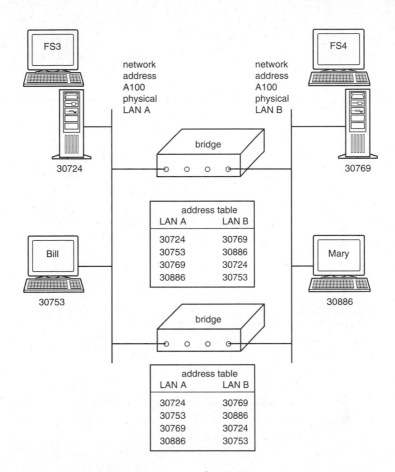

Though some MAC layer bridges have methods of dealing with this scenario, as internetworks become more complex, more problems are introduced. For example, if three or more LANs are bridged and some of the bridges are in series, bridges may receive configuration errors as a result of nodes appearing on various LANs, depending on whether traffic is being forwarded to that LAN. Configurations can be created that normal MAC layer bridges cannot handle.

This situation is handled by adding another layer of protocol to the bridging process and to the LAN frames. IEEE's 802.2 specification defines frame formats for spanning-tree protocol, which enables a route to be selected and placed into the frame header for use by the bridges. An Ethernet_802.2 frame header, as shown in Figure 26.6, includes a Destination Service Access Point (DSAP) field and a Source Service Access Point (SSAP) field. These two fields designate which bridge will handle the frame to be forwarded (SSAP) and which will deliver the frame to the destination

LAN (DSAP). The spanning-tree protocol, implemented in the workstation NIC and in the bridge, controls the flow of frames through bridges so they will take the most efficient path and will not be duplicated needlessly.

FIGURE 26.6.

An Ethernet_802.2 frame.

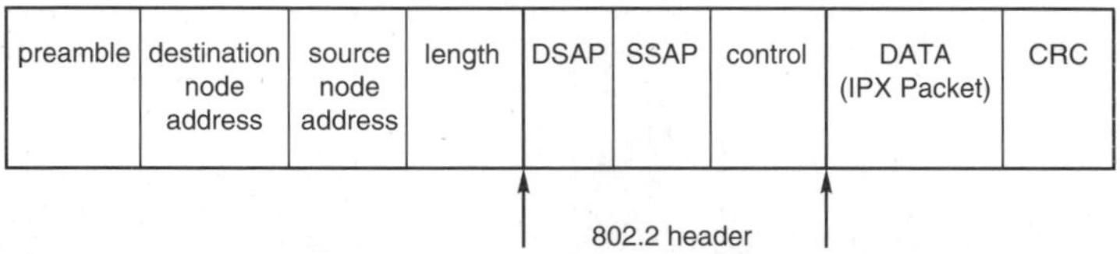

preamble	destination node address	source node address	length	DSAP	SSAP	control	DATA (IPX Packet)	CRC

802.2 header

> **NOTE** ▶
>
> Because of the widespread use of spanning-tree bridges among other types of networks, Novell decided to change to the Ethernet_802.2 frame as its default. You do not have to have spanning-tree bridges to use this frame type. The decision was made to make NetWare's default compatible with TCP/IP products, where this was already the default frame type.
>
> The same frame type needs to be supported at your workstations and at the server; otherwise, the two will not communicate.

Source-Routing Bridges

IBM's SNA and NetBIOS protocols are nonroutable. They require another way to connect Token Ring LANs together. IEEE's 802.2 protocols include a method of bridging Token Ring at the LAN frame layer, even if complex internetworks are configured. Source-routing protocol is implemented in a similar manner to the spanning-tree protocol, as discussed previously.

Like spanning-tree, source-routing uses DSAP and SSAP fields to designate the bridges that the frame will use to traverse the system of bridges. A routing-information field is added, which lists each segment that the frame must travel across.

The scheme used in source-routing involves a method of configuring the path that the frame will travel. The reason it is called source-routing is that the source node determines the path that will be taken. When source-routing drivers are used, each time a node powers up, it sends out a *discovery frame*. This frame is propagated onto every ring by every bridge. Each frame can therefore be duplicated, triplicated, and so on, until all routes are explored. The destination node responds to each discovery frame, and the first and second reply frames to reach the sender become the primary and secondary paths to be used. If the primary path fails, the secondary path is used, and if the secondary path fails, a new discovery frame is issued.

Though this scheme has some drawbacks, it has worked well for IBM. It enables coexistence with all network protocols, because it is nonprotocol specific. It is rudimentary in its method of determining the least-cost route, and sometimes it is foiled by a congested bridge during the discovery process, but for the most part, it works well. Source-routing bridging is implemented at the LAN frame LLC layer, so protocols contained in the frame are not used to forward the data from one ring to another. A token ring, source-routing frame is shown in Figure 26.7.

FIGURE 26.7.

A source-routing Token Ring data frame.

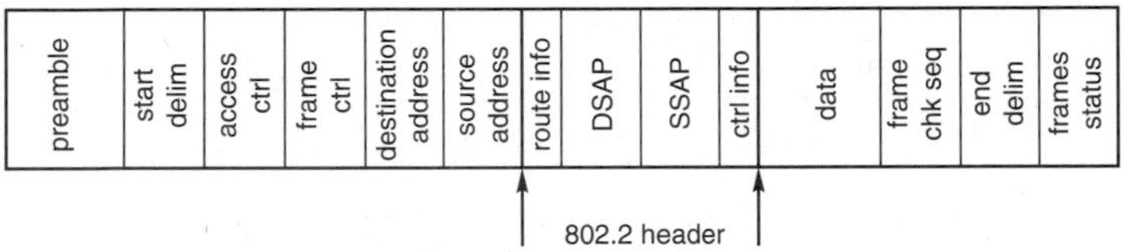

data frame fields: preamble | start delim | access ctrl | frame ctrl | destination address | source address | route info | DSAP | SSAP | ctrl info | data | frame chk seq | end delim | frames status

802.2 header

Routing

NetWare and other industry routing works at a completely different layer of protocol from a bridge. Bridges operate at the IEEE MAC or LLC layers, which together are exactly equivalent to the OSI data-link layer. Routers act at the OSI network layer and not the LAN frame layers of protocol. A bridge never sees the network-layer protocol, whereas a router acts upon the network-layer routing information.

> **NOTE** ▶
>
> A router must be capable of routing all of the packet types used on your networks. Be sure the product you purchase can support all of the routable protocols you use—that is, IPX, IP, AppleTalk, and/or OSI protocols.

NetWare's Internal Routers and Protocols (3.x versus 4.x)

When an IPX packet enters a router, the LAN frame is stripped off by the NIC driver before the router examines the packet. The packet has routing information in the header, as shown in Figure 26.8. The IPX packet header contains the network address and node address of both the source and destination nodes.

FIGURE 26.8.

IPX packet header routing fields.

chksum	length	trans ctrl	pkt type	dest net	dest node	dest socket	source net	source node	source socket	DATA (NCP, SPX, RIP, SAP packet)

Routers build routing tables from the Router Information Protocol (RIP) packets that are broadcasted among servers. The router uses the combination of the packet header, the internal protocol, and RIP packet information to determine where to send the packet. Because each NIC driver is labeled with a network address, when IPX protocol is bound to the NIC driver, the router can send the packet to the appropriate NIC driver for forwarding to the appropriate LAN (as shown in Figure 26.9).

FIGURE 26.9.

A router forwarding a packet.

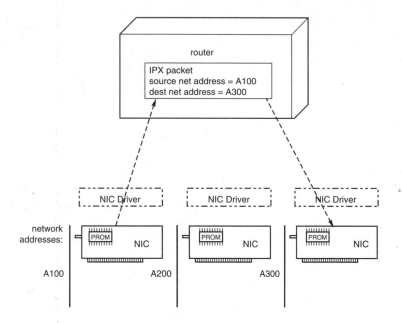

NetWare routers communicate with one another by broadcasting RIP packets on a frequent basis. RIP packets must be sent occasionally to keep the other routers informed of the available network addresses and their proximities (number of hops) from the current router. Each router in turn relays the RIP packets to other network addresses, adding a hop to the hop count in the packet headers. (For specific information about RIP packets, see Chapter 5, "Novell's Protocol Stack.")

NETWARE 4 NOTE ▶

NetWare 4.0's SERVMAN console utility enables regulation of RIP and SAP packets. The frequency of required transmissions to keep-alive and the time between transmissions can be regulated in order to reduce unnecessary broadcasts on WANs.

Shortcomings of Novell's RIP versus Other Routing Protocols

RIP has a basic shortcoming. The method used to determine the most cost-effective route is based solely on the number of logical hops. Earlier in this chapter, it was discussed how routers based on RIP can mistake the number of physical hops when bridges are involved in an internetwork.

Another condition exists that often affects the efficiency of NetWare routing. When two or more paths exist and both are detected with the same number of logical hops, nothing can determine whether one path may be more cost-effective than another. One path may include a WAN link, whereas another is a LAN-to-LAN connection. If both paths have the same hop count, NetWare's routing decision is made on the basis of other nonessential factors, instead of using a secondary method of determining the least-cost route. A user can unexpectedly become attached to a remote file server in another city rather than one located locally, because of their equal hop counts.

To resolve this issue, other routers use different methods, such as Open Shortest Path First (OSPF), to determine the least-cost path. OSPF determines cost-efficient paths based on more explicit information.

NetWare Link Services Protocol (NLSP)

Novell's Multiprotocol Router uses a new routing protocol developed to overcome some of the deficiencies of RIP. Novell's NLSP determines the least-cost route, based on the time it takes to receive an acknowledgment. Another factor of NLSP is that it does not require redundant broadcasts on a frequent basis to keep paths open in the router configuration tables. Instead, NLSP packets are only sent when a route is altered. This can reduce traffic on a WAN substantially when several servers are linked together.

Novell's Multiprotocol Router (MPR)

This product can be installed on a file server or on any 386-based computer. It runs as an NLM on a server or a dedicated router platform. A runtime of the NetWare 3.x OS is provided, so MPR can be installed on a computer that is external to the file server. It is a better router than the internal router in a NetWare OS.

MPR has proven that the highest levels of performance can be derived from building your own router. It features limited filtering of RIP and SAP packets, multiprotocol support for IPX, IP, AppleTalk, and OSI protocols, and Packet Burst NCP.

MPR is licensed to other vendors for inclusion in their routers. When you purchase MPR, you also must purchase the communications boards and WAN Links, which contain the drivers for the communications boards.

> **TIP** ▶
>
> For maximum efficiency when building a router, you should use 32-bit EISA or MCA bus-mastering NICs. For more detail, see Chapter 4, "File Server and LAN Interfaces."

Newport Systems LAN2LAN/MPR

Newport Systems bundles Novell's MPR with synchronous communications boards, but it adds a couple of features that Novell does not offer in its software-only MPR solution. Newport Systems believes that you should receive added value from intelligent communications boards with on-board processors, whereas Novell's strategy is to use software-only solutions whenever possible.

Communications Board Options

Newport Systems' intelligent synchronous communications boards can be configured for

- Asynchronous analog communications at rates of up to 19.2 Kbps
- Synchronous analog communications at rates of up to 56 Kbps
- Synchronous digital communications at rates of up to 2.048 Mbps

These boards also can be purchased with RS232C, RS422, or V.35 ports. Each board is available in four-port models.

RIP and SAP Filtering

Newport Systems' boards filter out redundant RIP and SAP packets, only forwarding the packets that have changed. A copy of each RIP and SAP is kept at the receiving end and broadcast on the local LAN without the need for sending redundant packets across a potentially limited-bandwidth WAN.

Data Compression

An optional data-compression daughterboard can be added to these boards, compressing data to one-fourth its original size (on average). This gives you an effective throughput of 256 Kbps on a 64 Kbps line. Data compression is only effective at rates of up to 128 Kbps. One 128-Kbps line can therefore move 512 Kbps worth of data before compression across a 128-Kbps line. Data compression daughterboards are now available from Newport Systems that can work at T-1/E-1 bandwidths.

Novell has not yet developed this capability, although it is working on building data compression into MPR software. Newport Systems believes that its boards provide better value by offloading this function to the on-board processor. This feature can reduce CPU utilization on your server-based router when compared with a purely software-based solution.

Load Balancing

A single board can accommodate up to four lines. These lines can connect the same source and destination locations to effectively increase throughput. More importantly, the board automatically balances the load, spreading it equally among lines that are connected. If one line goes down, all the traffic will shift to the lines that are still up.

Load balancing, as implemented in these boards, also reduces downtime. If a line goes down, the load is automatically distributed to other lines. When using both load balancing and data compression, only two ports can be used on one board.

Third-Party Turnkey Routers

Several companies have improved upon the design of NetWare's internal router. Cisco, Ungermann-Bass, 3Com, Proteon, NetWorth, Synoptics, and many other vendors have developed routers to be used with NetWare. Most of these third-party routers are hardware-based turnkey solutions with fast RISC processors. Many are programmable, so you can upgrade them and include more protocols on an as-needed basis.

Many also are managed, sending out SNMP alerts when problems are detected. Most products support NetWare's IPX protocol as well as IP and AppleTalk network-layer protocols.

Because routers work at the network layer, any type of NIC can usually be installed to support Ethernet, Token Ring, FDDI, or any other type of LAN. (In some cases, proprietary busses severely limit the selection of NICs.)

Some of these products enable the administrator to filter out traffic based on several criteria. For example, you may want to filter out all AppleTalk traffic, thereby restricting Mac users to the local LAN. In some cases, specific network and node addresses can be restricted.

Novell's MPR is so reasonably priced that it has driven router prices down. For example, Cisco has introduced a very powerful router for just a little more than $3,000.

Brouters

Brouters, sometimes called bridging routers or routing bridges, incorporate both bridging and routing functions into one box. This is useful when routable and nonroutable protocols are used with the same device.

> **TIP** ▶
>
> Though this definition describes most vendors' brouters, some vendors use the term "brouter" to describe their LLC bridges.
>
> When purchasing a bridge, router, or brouter, you should not rely on the terminology, because some vendors take the liberty of calling these devices whatever names they choose. Find out what the products really do before you buy one.

Summary

As you might surmise from reading this chapter, there are more considerations involved in building the physical infrastructure of an internetwork than Novell has discussed in its manuals.

With NetWare, routers make better internetworking devices than do bridges. Whatever solution you choose, make sure you understand the complexities of NetWare's IPX protocol before you start buying bridges, routers, and other internetworking devices.

Many third-party internetworking solutions offer more functionality, better price, better support, and a number of extra features that Novell does not have. Keep in mind, however, that terminology is sometimes used differently by different vendors. Compare what the products actually do before you make a purchasing decision.

If you are combining routable and nonroutable protocols on an internetwork, you might want to consider a brouter. A brouter, as defined here, can be used to bridge the nonroutable protocols and route the routable protocols.

TCP/IP and NetWare

27

by Rick Sant'Angelo

The use of the Transmission Control Protocol/Internet Protocol (TCP/IP) is becoming more common. TCP/IP is now the common denominator for connecting unlike systems. Since TCP/IP is in the public domain, and since the Department of Defense required its use in defense agencies and their affiliated contractors, research facilities, and universities, virtually all major computer system vendors now offer TCP/IP; many use it as their native networking protocol stack. It provides a common set of protocols for communicating among various systems, including NetWare 3.1x and 4.x servers, and workstations running TCP/IP software.

This chapter investigates the options available when interconnecting NetWare and TCP/IP. TCP/IP and NetWare fit together well, and integration of the two networking protocol stacks is available in software solutions, since TCP/IP and NetWare will coexist on the same LANs and WANs. This chapter discusses the following:

- The basics of TCP/IP
- TCP/IP implementation
- Implementation with NetWare
- Workstation-based TCP/IP software products

The Basics of TCP/IP

TCP/IP was developed in the 1970s by the U.S. Department of Defense's *Defense Advanced Research Projects Agency (DARPA)* for the purpose of linking together military agencies, defense contractors, universities, and research contractors into a WAN. The protocol stack could be implemented in computer systems, and later it was a prerequisite to winning contracts with various military agencies, contractors, and universities. It was given in grants and was introduced into the public domain. Since the Internet grew from this simple idea to the vast network it is today, many enhancements and further developments occurred, as received by the Internet community in the form of Request for Comments (RFCs).

In 1988, Congress mandated that various agencies use TCP/IP as an intermediate step to the eventual implementation of Government Open System Interconnection Profile (GOSIP), where the OSI protocols would be used within two years. The GOSIP part of this mandate never occurred, for many reasons. However, this general movement toward interoperability spurred TCP/IP to new acceptance. TCP/IP has also enjoyed new acceptance since the Internet was opened to commercial use.

Today, TCP/IP is implemented in virtually every major computer system, and there are hundreds of software products that provide support. Its use continues to grow.

What Is TCP/IP?

TCP/IP is a set of networking protocols that was developed by the DARPA to enable better communication among government, research and industry. Research grants and procurement contracts required the use of this protocol stack in network architectures used by DOD and just about anyone working with them. This forced many computer vendors to build TCP/IP support into their systems or else forgo sales to these organizations and companies.

TCP/IP provided connection to the Department of Defense Network (DDN), which is now called *Milnet*, and the broad network of university and government-contractor computer systems. This entire system is now called the *Internet*. It has thousands of host computers linked over WAN and LAN links, and it has now been open for commercial use. Access to the Internet is granted by petition to a contractor designated for assigning Internet addresses (much like network addresses in NetWare). These addresses allow TCP/IP routers and workstation software to find and route IP packets all over the Internet without router-configuration errors.

TCP/IP is a protocol stack that consists of several layers of protocol. TCP and IP can be used as LAN and WAN network and transport-layer protocols. Because of the popularity of TCP/IP and its wide acceptance, TCP/IP is used as a native protocol stack by many computer vendors, including:

- Digital Equipment Corporation
- Sun Microsystems
- Hewlett Packard
- Data General
- Prime
- Santa Cruz Operation UNIX Systems
- Unisys
- NCR
- IBM RS/6000 Systems
- AT&T

TCP/IP currently provides intra-enterprise connections of dissimilar operating systems within a corporation. DEC, NetWare, HP, IBM, Sun, and other systems can be internetworked with simple functionality between systems. TCP/IP provides a common networking scheme for the exchange of files and electronic mail, but it does not provide real-time sharing of data located on hosts.

The TCP/IP Protocol Stack

The TCP/IP protocol stack compares with the OSI Model as shown in Figure 27.1. Each protocol mentioned in this diagram is discussed briefly herein.

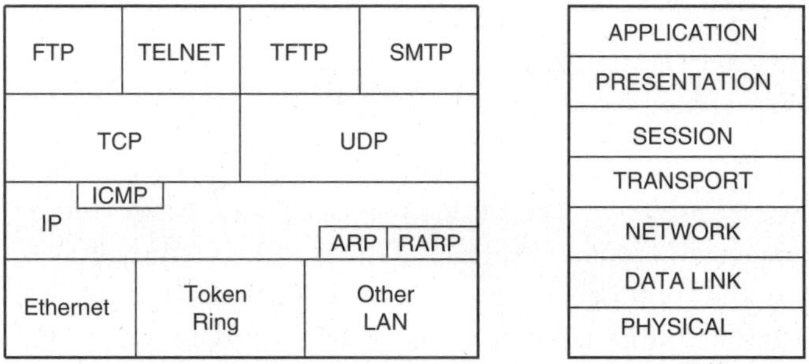

FIGURE 27.1.

The TCP/IP protocol stack versus OSI.

FTP	TELNET	TFTP	SMTP
TCP		UDP	
ICMP			
IP		ARP	RARP
Ethernet	Token Ring	Other LAN	

APPLICATION
PRESENTATION
SESSION
TRANSPORT
NETWORK
DATA LINK
PHYSICAL

Internet Protocol (IP)

IP is a routable packet protocol, similar in function, design, and packet structure to Novell's IPX protocol. IP and IPX were both derived from XNS, and both use network and node addresses to locate destination hosts. IP provides the header information for IP addresses (network numbers and host addresses) to facilitate routing across the many hops in a TCP/IP network such as the Internet.

Internet Control Message Protocol (ICMP)

ICMP is an aid to IP, and provides basic control messages and error reporting. It can detect error conditions and malfunctions for reporting back to the sender. ICMP allows diagnostic messages to reach individuals involved in malfunctions at the network layer (such as an unavailable host).

Address Resolution Protocol/Revised ARP (APR/RARP)

ARP or RARP is used to discover hosts and network numbers.

Transmission Control Protocol (TCP)

TCP is the connection-oriented error-recovery mechanism and connection agent for linking a workstation to a host. It functions similarly to Novell's SPX protocol. Like Novell's SPX, this protocol is not often used, because it consumes network resources because of its connection-oriented mechanisms.

User Datagram Protocol (UDP)

UDP is normally used in place of TCP for connectionless datagram service (no end-to-end error control). It is a one-way mechanism for sending data.

File Transfer Protocol (FTP) and Trivial File Transfer Protocol (TFTP)

FTP provides workstation and server software modules for file transfers across TCP/IP networks.

Simple Mail Transfer Protocol (SMTP)

This protocol provides a common medium for electronic mail.

Telnet

Telnet provides a common protocol for terminal-emulation software on various operating-system platforms.

Simple Network Management Protocol (SNMP)

This protocol was developed to report problems detected in networking devices. Though this protocol is part of the TCP/IP stack, it is also used with NetWare. It carries messages detected by a networking device and reports them to a centralized database for evaluation and/or warnings.

This protocol provides network management for network devices with an *SNMP agent*. The SNMP agent is the hardware or software that implements the SNMP protocol. Each SNMP agent sends data concerning its status to a collector database.

> **NOTE ▶**
>
> Each SNMP agent has a predefined *Management Information Base* (MIB). The MIB is a set of objects on which the agent provides status information. At present, the specifications for MIB I and MIB II are published standards. MIB I is a subset of MIB II, and vendors may elect to provide information on additional objects, called *MIB Extensions.*

The collector database is consulted by the SNMP manager workstation (a workstation that is used to monitor and administer the network). This workstation can request additional information from the agent or modify the devices' configuration via the agent. In addition, an SNMP agent may send *SNMP traps* (or alerts) to the collector database. An SNMP trap is a predefined error or alarm condition. For example, a trap may be sent if network utilization reaches a high level. Figure 27.2 shows a diagram of how SNMP operates.

FIGURE 27.2.

SNMP diagram.

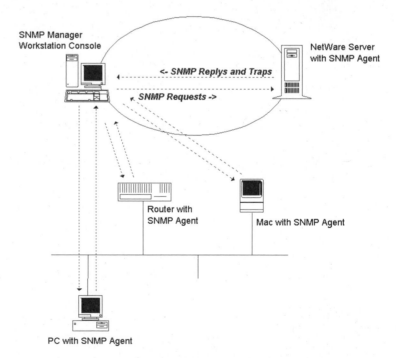

SNMP is supported by virtually all network components, including: servers, hubs, bridges, routers, workstations, power supplies, and more. The original SNMP specification called for SNMP to be transmitted over the IP protocol. Therefore, often times IP is required to run on an internetwork to facilitate SNMP management. On a large IPX network, this can mean providing IP routers to support access to all SNMP devices.

> **NOTE** ▶
>
> Some intelligent hubs that have SNMP communicate with IP packets. This requires TCP/IP routing to be enabled on the file servers in order to provide a complete path through the network for the SNMP data traffic. If IP routing is not provided, some of the hubs may not be managed via the SNMP manager workstation.

IP Addressing

Like IPX, IP workstations and hosts must be assigned addresses to be used as sources and destinations for IP packets. You can assign your own addresses internally, but if you intend to connect to the Internet, you must apply for host address assignments. Addresses are assigned in three classes: Class A, B, and C.

IP host addresses are generally expressed in decimal notation and are masked with decimal points into four sets of threes (i.e., XXX.XXX.XXX.XXX). They are divided into two parts: a network address, and a local address according to the classes. Each class of address yields a different number of potential network and node addresses, to be used as required by the organization. The network number is a mask that is used in the same way as a NetWare network address; the local address can be used the same way as a NetWare node address. The combination of these two tell the routers where to forward the packets. The big distinction between IP and IPX addressing is that the network address portion can be different for classes of host address assignments.

Class A Addresses

In a Class A address, the first byte of the IP header is a value between 0 and 127. Two address values (0 and 125) are reserved for Global Broadcasts. This leaves a total of 126 potential assignees. The first set of three decimal numbers are assigned as the network address. Since the entire length of the address is constant, this leaves a very large number of addresses (16,777,214) available for local addresses per network address.

These addresses are only assigned to major network participants, such as IBM, ARPANET, MILNET, DEC, and AT&T. Each of these few participants can have a large number of hosts.

Class B Addresses

In this classification of address, the first byte has a value of between 128 to 191. Two values are also reserved for Global Broadcasts (000.000 and 192.255). The first two sets of three decimal numbers are reserved for the network address. This provides more potential network address combinations (16,384), and fewer local address combinations (65,024) for each network address. Class B addresses are assigned to large companies with needs for many local addresses.

Class C Addresses

These addresses are assigned to the vast majority of applicants. The first byte has a value of between 192 and 223. The first three sets of decimal numbers are reserved for the network address, leaving 2,097,152 network addresses, each one with 254 potential node addresses. Rather than assign a Class B address to a company with a few hundred nodes, two or three Class C addresses are assigned.

Through this numbering convention, Internet IP addresses can be assigned in a manner wherein thousands upon thousands of nodes can have addresses, neatly organized by network address.

IP routers each operate independently, reading IP addresses and forwarding packets to known paths that are discovered on-the-fly. The orderly process of assigning addresses is important to allow a very large number of workstations within various organizations.

If you do not intend to connect to the Internet, you must configure each TCP/IP node with a valid host address that conforms to this numbering system. As long as you assign valid numbers in your organization, you will be able to exchange IP packets. To exchange IP packets with maximum performance, you need to organize your network addresses with the same quality of organization that is required in an IPX network.

TCP/IP Implementation Strategies

Access to TCP/IP workstations, including UNIX workstations, minicomputers, and mainframes with TCP/IP support, can be accomplished in three ways: by workstation-based TCP/IP support, a TCP/IP gateway, or by substituting IP for NetWare's native IPX protocol.

Workstation-Based Support

Workstation-based TCP/IP products load IP support locally, as depicted in Figure 27.3. Each NetWare workstation loads IP and IPX protocol stacks concurrently. Novell's LAN Workplace is an example of a workstation-based TCP/IP product.

FIGURE 27.3.
Workstation-based TCP/IP.

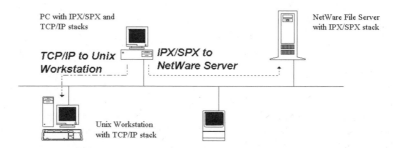

TCP/IP Gateways

The TCP/IP gateway solution eliminates the need to load the IP protocol stack at each workstation, as depicted in Figure 27.4. Using this method, the workstations communicate via IPX with the gateway, which then converts (or translates) IPX packets into IP packets.

FIGURE 27.4.

Server or gateway-based TCP/IP.

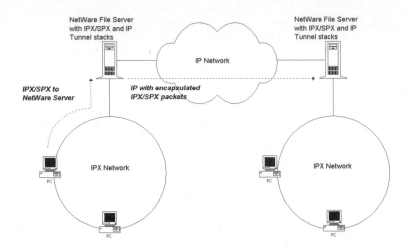

Running TCP/IP Instead of IPX with NetWare

Novell has introduced a product called *NetWare-IP* that allows the server to use IP instead of IPX. NetWare-IP allows workstations to communicate with the file server using the IP protocol in lieu of IPX.

NetWare-IP is a big step in the direction of simplifying and standardizing network communications. Though you may choose to use IPX because of its familiarity or simplicity, you may wish to fully integrate all your systems with one common network protocol, and this product does it.

> **NOTE** ►
>
> NetWare-IP's performance is not as good as native IPX performance. This is currently an add-on module that must be purchased. Since the product is in its first release stages, it may be prudent to weight the relative costs and benefits of integrating IPX with IP or replacing IPX with IP.

Tunneling IPX

Some internetworks only support TCP/IP protocol. Internetworking NetWare across IP-only networks can be accomplished with *tunneling*. Using this method, IPX packets are encapsulated (or tunneled) into IP packets for transmission across the IP-only network. (See Figure 27.5.) Once IP packets arrive at the remote side of the connection, the IP packet header is stripped, and the IPX packet is transmitted to the destination. IP tunneling can function on a NetWare 3.11 or 4.x server, as well as a workstation running a TCP/IP product that supports IP tunneling (such as LAN Workplace).

FIGURE 27.5.
PX packets encapsulated for transmission across an IP network.

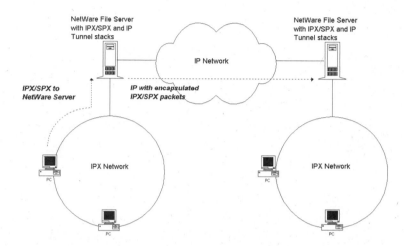

TCP/IP Implementations with NetWare

As discussed previously, TCP/IP can be implemented one of two ways with NetWare:

- Via server-based IP support
- Via workstation-based TCP/IP

Server-based support enables the NetWare server to be used as a single IP host connection point to a TCP/IP network, whereas workstation-based products provide a more robust bundle of higher-layer TCP/IP support.

Server-Based IP Support

NetWare supports *IP routing* on 3.1x and 4.x platforms only. IP routing enables the system to route IP traffic across LANs and WANs, but it does not give workstations native access to NetWare file servers via TCP/IP.

If you have multiple IP networks within your internetwork, and you activate IP routing, the server can route IP packets in addition to IPX packets. Also, the file server supports an SNMP agent. NetWare 3.1x provides an MIB I SNMP agent. However, with NetWare 4.x, an MIB II agent is provided. The IP support in NetWare 3.1x and 4.x provides the following:

- Support for all IP classes and subnet masks
- Support for TCP/IP Routing Information Protocol (RIP)
- Support for IP gateway ("the router of last resort")
- SNMP trap forwarding

NOTE ▶

At present, IP routing support is provided concurrently with IPX support. All 3.1x and 4.x server LAN drivers are compliant with the Open Datalink Interface (ODI) specifications and thus can support multiple protocols concurrently.

NetWare 3.1x and 4.x IP Routing

Enabling IP routing support on a NetWare server is quite painless. Essentially, the IP protocol engine is an NLM. Once loaded, IP is then bound to the appropriate network board driver and the job is done. (See Figure 27.6.)

FIGURE 27.6.

Enabling IP routing on a NetWare file server.

```
:load ne2000 port=340 int=5 frame=ETHERNET_II name=ip_board
Loading module NE2000.LAN
   Previously loaded module was used re-entrantly
:load tcpip forward=yes
Loading module TCPIP.NLM
   TCP/IP for MPR
   Version 2.10w   April 29, 1993
   Copyright 1992, Novell, Inc.  All rights reserved.
IP: Configured for gateway operations.
:bind ip to ip_board addr=192.2.3.4 mask=255.255.255.0
IP: Bound to board 2.  IP address 192.2.3.4, net mask FF.FF.FF.0
IP LAN protocol bound to NetWare NE2000  v3.14 (910726)
   :
```

Parameters can be defined when loading the TCPIP NLM as follows:

```
LOAD TCPIP [FORWARD=YES¦NO] [RIP=YES¦NO] [TRAP=IP ADDRESS]
```

FORWARD= YES or NO	(Default is NO)
	YES enables IP routing, NO disables IP routing
RIP= YES or NO	(Default is YES)
	YES enables IP Routing Information Protocol (RIP), NO disables RIP
TRAP= X.X.X.X	Specifies the IP address to which SNMP traps will be forwarded

NOTE ▶

The TCPIP module automatically loads the SNMP support module. Thus, the TCPIP module is manually unloaded, and it may be necessary to also unload the SNMP module.

In the following expression, the bind command has several TCP/IP-related optional parameters:

```
BIND IP TO driver_name addr=X.X.X.X [mask=X.X.X.X] [bcast=X.X.X.X]
[gate=X.X.X.X] [defroute=yes¦no] [arp=yes¦no] [cost=hop_#]
[poison=yes¦no]
```

Considered individually, the parameters are as follows:

MASK= *X.X.X.X*

> Specifies the IP address subnet mask. If none is specified, the default is used. Figure 27.7 shows the default subnet masks for all IP address classes.

BCAST= *X.X.X.X*

> Specifies the default address to use for IP broadcasting on this network. The default value is all ones in binary (255.255.255.255 in decimal). This should only be changed to maintain compatibility with older TCP/IP systems that use other forms of broadcast addressing.

GATE= *X.X.X.X*

> Specifies the IP address of the gateway. The gateway will be used if the server does not know to which router the packet should be forwarded.

DEFROUTE= *YES¦NO*

> Enables the broadcasting of this node as the default gateway via the RIP protocol. This is only enabled if the TCPIP.NLM was loaded with routing enabled (FORWARD=YES). The default is NO.

ARP= *YES¦NO*

> Indicates whether the Address Resolution Protocol (ARP) should be used on this network. ARP maps MAC-layer addresses to IP addresses. The default is YES.

```
COST= integer from 1 to 15
```

> Number of hops to assign as the cost for this interface. Each packet is incremented by this cost value when routed across this interface. The default is 1.

```
POISON= YES¦NO
```

> Enables the use of RIP poison reverse for routing updates sent on this interface. Poison reverse is used to prevent routing loops caused with networks that contain multiple paths. The default is NO.

Once the TCPIP module is loaded, the bind command is issued with the appropriate IP address and subnet mask. (See Figure 27.7.) To verify that the IP protocol is bound and running, use the CONFIG command at the server console prompt. (See Figure 27.8.) The CONFIG command displays the network configuration information for each instance of the board driver.

FIGURE 27.7.

Default subnet mask table.

Class	IP Address Range	Default Subnet Mask
Class A	1 to 127	255.0.0.0
Class B	128 to 191	255.255.0.0
Class C	192 to 223	255.255.255.0

FIGURE 27.8.

Results from executing the CONFIG *command with TCP/IP routing enabled.*

```
:config
File server name: NETWARE-UNLEASHED
IPX internal network number: 00002342

NetWare NE2000  v3.14 (910726)
        Hardware setting: I/O Port 340h to 35Fh, Interrupt 5h
        Node address: 00001B1D0D1E
        Frame type: ETHERNET_802.3
        Board name: IPX_BOARD
        LAN protocol: IPX network 33334340

NetWare NE2000  v3.14 (910726)
        Hardware setting: I/O Port 340h to 35Fh, Interrupt 5h
        Node address: 00001B1D0D1E
        Frame type: ETHERNET_II
        Board name: IP_BOARD
        LAN protocol: ARP
        LAN protocol: IP  address 192.2.3.4  mask FF.FF.FF.0  interfaces 1
:
```

NOTE ▶

An instance is defined each time the driver is loaded. Thus, if you load the NE2000.LAN driver three times, there are three instances of that driver in use. However, the driver code is only resident in memory once.

Frame Types

By default, most Ethernet and Token Ring TCP/IP implementations use the Ethernet_II and Token Ring_SNAP framing formats, respectively. This is because TCP/IP specifications call for their use. Thus, when enabling IP routing support, the LAN driver should be loaded with the correct frame type. This is accomplished by specifying the 'frame' parameter when loading the driver, as follows:

```
LOAD NE2000 frame=Ethernet_II
```

or

```
LOAD TOKEN frame=Token-Ring_SNAP
```

This will load an instance of the driver with the Ethernet_II or Token Ring_SNAP frame type. This can be confirmed by using the CONFIG command at the server console prompt. (See Figure 27.8.) By contrast, Ethernet and Token Ring IPX implementations use the Ethernet_802.3 and Token Ring framing formats, respectively. It is possible to use other framing formats and mix frame formats; however, these are most normally used.

NOTE ▶

In order for two nodes to communicate with one another, they must have the same frame format loaded. If your workstations are "talking" Ethernet_802.3, and your server is "listening" Ethernet_802.2, they will not be able to communicate.

TCP/IP requires the use of Ethernet_II or Ethernet_802.2 frame formats, while most NetWare workstation NIC drivers and the 3.1x server defaults to Ethernet_802.3. Be sure to load all frame types on your server's NIC driver that you wish to support.

Ethernet IPX generally defaults to Ethernet_802.3. The Ethernet_802.3 uses the IPX raw format, an Ethernet header without Logical Link Control (LLC) data. Novell uses the Ethernet_802.2 frame format for true 802.2 Logical Link comparibility. The NetWare 4.x server defaults to running both the Ethernet_802.2 and Ethernet_802.3 frame formats.

NOTE

Novell recently changed their default frame type for Ethernet drivers. Drivers used to default to Ethernet_802.3, but later 3.1x drivers should default to Ethernet_802.2, and 4.x drivers default to loading support for both Ethernet_802.2 and Ethernet_802.3.

NetWare 3.1x and 4.x IP Tunneling

Tunneling IPX within IP frames will allow for transmission across IP-only networks. The IPX frames are encapsulated (or enveloped) into an IP frame. Once the packet reaches the remote side of the IP-only network, the IP envelope is removed. Figure 27.9 shows two IPX networks interconnected via an IP-only network. The file servers on each of the IPX networks have tunneling enabled, thus creating a single logical IPX network.

FIGURE 27.9.

IP Tunneling across an IP-only network.

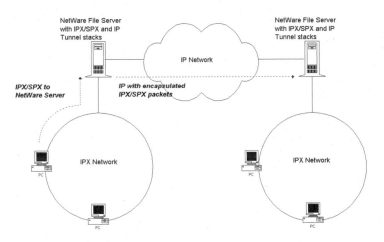

Enabling IP tunneling is a very straightforward process. Figure 27.10 shows the commands that are used to enable tunneling on a network interface.

FIGURE 27.10.

Enabling IP Tunneling on a NetWare file server.

```
:load iptunnel peer=192.10.11.12
Loading module IPTUNNEL.LAN
  IP Tunnel for IPX
  Version 2.02   April 29, 1993
  Copyright 1991 Novell, Inc.  All rights reserved.
IPTunnel: Using 192.2.3.4 as the local IP address for tunneling
IPTunnel: Added 192.10.11.12 to the list of peers
:
```

An IP Tunnel consists of internetwork IPX routers that have an intermediate IP network. The IPX routers are known as *IP Tunnel peers*. It is important to carefully select peers, as well as IP addresses to prevent a network configuration error.

The LOAD IPTUNNEL command has several options, as follows:

LOAD IPTUNNEL [peer=*X.X.X.X*] [chksum=*yes¦no*] [local=*X.X.X.X*] [port=*UDP port number*] [show=*yes¦no*]

Considered individually, these parameters are as follows:

PEER= *X.X.X.X*

> Specifies an IP address to add to the *peer list*. The peer list is a list of servers in the tunnel. (Remember that each IPX broadcast is transmitted to each router in the peer list.)

CHKSUM= *YES¦NO*

> Enables or disables UDP checksums on transmitted packets. Default is YES.

LOCAL= *X.X.X.X*

> Specifies a single IP address for the tunnel. The default value is the IP address of the first TCP/IP bound interface.

PORT= *UDP port number*

> Sets the UDP port for the tunnel to use. Valid entries are from 1 to 65535. The default is 213.

SHOW= *YES¦NO*

> Requests a detailed configuration report. The default is YES.

IP tunneling configuration can be verified by using the CONFIG command. Figure 27.11 shows the results of the command on a file server with tunneling enabled.

FIGURE 27.11.

Results from executing the CONFIG *command with IP tunneling enabled.*

```
File server name: NETWARE-UNLEASHED
IPX internal network number: 00002342

NetWare NE2000  v3.14 (910726)
        Hardware setting: I/O Port 340h to 35Fh, Interrupt 5h
        Node address: 00001B1D0D1E
        Frame type: ETHERNET_802.3
        Board name: IPX_BOARD
        LAN protocol: IPX network 33334340

NetWare NE2000  v3.14 (910726)
        Hardware setting: I/O Port 340h to 35Fh, Interrupt 5h
        Node address: 00001B1D0D1E
        Frame type: ETHERNET_II
        Board name: IP_BOARD
        LAN protocol: ARP
        LAN protocol: IP  address 192.2.3.4  mask FF.FF.FF.0  interfaces 1

IP Tunnel for IPX
        Hardware setting: I/O Port D5h
        Node address: 0000C0020304
        Frame type: IP
        No board name defined
        No LAN protocols are bound to this LAN board
:
```

NetWare's TCPCON Utility

Netware 3.1x and 4.x includes the TCPCON.NLM, which is an SNMP-based, menu-driven console interface to various MIBs via TCP/IP. By default, TCPCON.NLM accesses the local server TCP/IP stack, but it can access any workstation or server running the SNMP stack over TCP/IP. This utility monitors the TCP/IP stack, providing detailed statistics on IP, ICMP, TCP, and UDP. In addition, it provides access to the routing tables, SNMP trap log, interface tables, and more.

TCPCON.NLM can be loaded with an *SNMP community name,* if required. An SNMP community name is used to provide security for SNMP, by default the community name is set to "public." The community name is set when loading the SNMP agent. To monitor or access an agent via TCPCON with a community name set to *password,* load TCPCON.NLM as follows:

```
LOAD TCPCON community name=password
```

Once loaded, all SNMP request messages will use *password* as the community name. Therefore, the SNMP community name should be consistent throughout the managed network.

Workstation-Based TCP/IP Software Products

With the increasing need for communication and access to TCP/IP-based hosts, there has been a demand for workstation-based IP higher-layer protocols, such as the following:

- File Transfer Protocol (FTP)
- Terminal Emulation (TELNET)
- Remote Execution (RSH)
- Simple Mail Transfer Protocol (SMTP)

These protocols are not the only protocols that you will need to use, but to implement these functions you will need to use TCP/IP workstation software running with an IP stack in lieu of IPX. TCP/IP workstation software, combined with ODI drives, allows a workstation to talk IPX with NetWare servers and to talk IP with TCP/IP hosts without unloading and reloading drivers.

> **NOTE** ▶
>
> TCP is a connection-oriented protocol and is used when guaranteed delivery is required. For example, TCP is used by terminal-emulation and file-transfer programs to ensure accurate delivery of data.
>
> User Data Protocol (UDP) is a connectionless protocol. Thus, the overhead for using the UDP services is lower than for TCP. UDP is used by the ECHO program.

There are a number of products available for workstations that provide TCP/IP services while concurrently providing access to NetWare servers via IPX. These include products for DOS, Windows, OS/2, and the Apple Macintosh. All of them provide a varying degree of support for additional services, such as Reverse Address Resolution Protocol (RARP), BOOTP, FINGER, COOKIE, and PING, to name a few. Some of the available products include:

LAN Workplace (Novell, Inc.)
PCNFS (SunConnect, Inc.)
PC/TCP (FTP Software, Inc.)
Chameleon (Netmanage, Inc.)
Pathway Access (Wollongong, Inc.)

NOTE ▶

There are probably more than 75 different software products for workstation-based TCP/IP services. Some, including NCSA, are available in the public domain. This list is just a sample of the products that are available.

All of these products require some configuration; at minimum, an IP address must be specified. If your network has a RARP or BOOTP server, these facilities can also be utilized by the workstation software. Additionally, some products give you the software to make a workstation act as a RARP or BOOTP server.

LAN Workplace for DOS/Windows

To provide an example of how workstation software is configured, this section discusses Novell's LAN Workplace for DOS/Windows, version 4.1. This product was originally developed by Excelan in 1985 and became a Novell product when Novell acquired Excelan in 1986.

Configuring LAN Workplace requires two steps: setting up the configuration files and loading the TCP/IP stack.

The LAN Workplace TCPIP module is compliant with ODI specifications and thus utilizes a NET.CFG configuration file. This file contains the parameters for ODI driver layers, including TCPIP. A sample NET.CFG file is shown in Figure 27.12. This file is consulted when the appropriate ODI layers are loaded. For workstation-based TCP/IP support, focus on the following three sections of the file:

- Link Driver
- Link Support
- Protocol TCP/IP

The *Link Driver* section is consulted by the network interface card driver. The TCP/IP-specific settings include the frame type and protocol id. For more information, see Chapter 2, "TCP/IP" of this book. Figure 27.12 shows a sample NET.CFG configuration file.

FIGURE 27.12.

Sample NET.CFG configuration file.

Link Support

    Buffers 8 1500

    MemPool 4096

Link Driver NE2000

    Int 5

    Port 320

    Frame Ethernet_802.3

    Frame Ethernet_II

    Protocol IPX 0 Ethernet_802.3

Protocol TCPIP

Path Script	c:\net\script
Path Profile	c:\net\profile
Path LWP_CFG	c:\net\hstacc
Path TCP_CFG	c:\net\tcp
ip_address	192.3.2.1
ip_router	192.3.2.253
ip_netmask	255.255.255.0
tcp_sockets	8
udp_sockets	8
raw_sockets	1
nb_sessions	4
nb_commands	8
nb_adapter	0
nb_domain	

The *Link Support* section is consulted by LSL.COM to determine the amount of workstation resources to keep available for usage. The *buffers* and *mempool* settings are important when using TCP/IP. The buffers setting determines the number and size of receive buffers that will be maintained. Modifying this parameter will increase the number of packets that can be received before the workstation will reject additional incoming packets. The mempool parameter is used to configure the size of the memory pool that will be retained for outgoing transmissions.

The *Protocol TCPIP* section is consulted by the TCPIP.EXE module to determine the IP address information as well as the location of the additional configuration files.

These configuration parameters are typical of TCP/IP software and ODI drivers. For more information, consult the LAN Workplace or your TCP/IP workstation software documentation.

Once the NET.CFG file has been modified, the ODI stack needs to be loaded (or unloaded and reloaded if already resident in workstation memory). When the TCPIP.EXE file is loaded, the address for the workstation is set, except if the address is being determined from a network resource using RARP or BOOTP.

> **TIP**
>
> It is possible to use multiple NET.CFG files by specifying the file to use with the `-c` option. For example: `TCPIP.EXE -c=path\filename`. Where path denotes the location, and filename is the name of the file (normally NET.CFG).

To verify network communication, execute the PING command with the address of a known, working IP station. Once communication is verified, you are then able to communicate with remote TCP/IP hosts.

LAN Workgroup

Novell LAN Workgroup is a server-based edition of LAN Workplace. With this product, all configuration and program files are located on a NetWare server. A BOOTP NLM and an unlimited license BOOTP relay agent are provided. Workstation TCP/IP software can be centrally administered and software-licensing control is enhanced. Thus, all IP addressing and configuration files (including NET.CFG) can be managed via the file server.

Third-Party Solutions

In addition to the aforementioned Novell solutions for TCP/IP support, a number of third-party companies provide TCP/IP solutions for NetWare. These solutions are divided into two categories: NetWare server-based solutions (NLMs) and dedicated gateway solutions.

The NetWare server solutions consist of NLMs that run on the NetWare server to provide TCP/IP gateway functionality. The dedicated gateway solutions require a workstation dedicated to providing gateway functionality. Some also require an OS/2 or UNIX operating system to be running on the dedicated gateway.

These products allow workstations connected to the IPX network to communicate with the gateway (dedicated or server-based NLMs). The gateway then converts (or translates) the request into an IP transmission and sends it to the destination. Inbound communications (to the workstation) are addressed to the gateway, which then translates the packet into IPX format for transmission to the workstation. Thus, a TCP/IP host appears to be communicating with another IP host, and all translation is handled by the gateway.

The UNIX Connection

28

by Peter Kuo

With the increasing popularity of UNIX systems, the need for interconnecting UNIX machines and NetWare networks has become greater. This chapter examines a number of NetWare products that will help you to achieve this objective. It then uses specific case studies to illustrate how each product meets a particular set of requirements. (However, it is beyond the scope of this book to go into details on installing and configuring these products.)

> **NOTE** ▶
>
> The products discussed in this chapter are not limited to connecting UNIX systems with NetWare. They can be applied to any TCP/IP-based machines. The TCP/IP protocol stack is available for a wide variety of platforms, ranging from Digital VAXes to Data General machines to IBM mainframes and AS/400.

The ideal connectivity apparatus would address the following needs:

1. NetWare users need to access printers attached to UNIX machines.
2. NetWare users need to be able to log onto the UNIX machines from their desktop. Users do not want dumb terminals on their desk.
3. NetWare users need to *transparently* access files on UNIX machines.
4. UNIX users need to access printers attached on NetWare LANs.
5. UNIX users need to run some DOS applications. They do not want both a terminal and a PC on their desk.
6. UNIX users need to *transparently* access files on NetWare servers.
7. UNIX users want simple file-transfer capability between UNIX and NetWare servers.

This chapter examines the features available in various NetWare UNIX connectivity products that will help you in achieving these objectives.

NetWare NFS and FLeX/IP

NetWare NFS is a collection of NLMs designed to provide a comprehensive set of services for UNIX systems. TCP/IP is the transport protocol most commonly used within the UNIX environment. The services provided by NetWare NFS include the following:

- **Network File System (NFS) Server.** This enables NFS client machines (typically) fully-transparent access to files residing on the NetWare server.
- **Lock Manager Daemon (LOCKD).** A UNIX-compatible lock manager that supports advisory file and record locking.
- **Status Daemon (STATD).** A UNIX-compatible status monitor that supports the file and record locking in the stateless NFS environment.
- **UNIX-to-NetWare Print Service (LPD).** A Line Printer Daemon that enables UNIX clients to spool print jobs directly to NetWare print queues.
- **NetWare-to-UNIX Print Gateway (LPR).** A Line Printer client that spools print jobs from NetWare servers to UNIX printers.
- **File Transfer Protocol (FTP) Server.** Enables UNIX clients to have nontransparent file access to a NetWare file server.
- **XConsole.** An X-client that enables any X-server access to the NetWare server console.

> **NOTE** ▶
>
> In discussing TCP/IP protocols, the term "server" and "daemon" are used interchangeably.

Network File System Protocol

The Network File System protocol (NFS: RFC1094) was developed in the early 1980s by Sun Microsystems, Inc., and has been licensed by a large number of vendors. The NFS protocol provides transparent remote access to files across networks. The NFS protocol is designed to be portable between different machines, operating systems, and network architectures. Novell implemented the NFS server with a set of NLMs so that, through NFS, UNIX-based workstations, minicomputers, and mainframes can access files that reside on the NetWare server.

> **NOTE** ▶
>
> The Internet protocol gets "defined" through Request For Comments (RFCs). Generally when a protocol is proposed, an RFC describing the specification is made available on the Internet. Interested parties can then comment on it (hence the name RFC). Each RFC is numbered, such as RFC1094 in the preceding paragraph.

In order for a volume or file system to be available to remote NFS clients, it must be "exported." Remote NFS clients then "mount" this exported volume or file system onto their system, and it will appear as a local file system to them. (See Figure 28.1.) This is very similar to the NetWare environment in that the server's hard drive appears as an extension to your workstation.

FIGURE 28.1.

A UNIX client sees NetWare volume as a local file system.

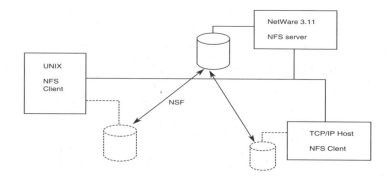

File and Record Locking

NFS is a *stateless* protocol, meaning that the server maintains no record of previous actions it has performed on behalf of a client. This is a useful feature when a server fails. If an NFS server crashes while a client is making a request, the client simply repeats the request until the server is available.

Although a stateless server is helpful in the event of a server crash, it is important to keep track of file and record locks. These are *stateful* operations and cannot be implemented using the NFS protocol. Additional services are required to provide these functions. The locking procedure is provided by a server program called Lock Manager Daemon (LOCKD). The LOCKD implementation in NetWare NFS uses the underlying file- and record-locking features of the NetWare server. Therefore, locks applied by NFS clients are enforced upon all NetWare clients.

CAUTION ►

UNIX systems typically use "advisory" file and record locking. This means that applications use special library routines. Novell's LOCKD.NLM conforms to this. However, if an application does not use advisory locks, it does not work with files on the NetWare NFS file system.

The Status Monitor (STATD) is used to reestablish file locks after an NFS server crash.

Line Printer Daemon

The most commonly used remote-printing protocol between UNIX systems is the Line Printer Daemon (LPD: RFC1179). It can be compared to the CAPTURE command in the NetWare environment. LPD was first designed and implemented on machines running versions of UNIX based on the Berkeley Source Distribution (BSD). Since then, LPD has been implemented widely on other versions of UNIX and other computer systems supporting the TCP/IP protocols.

The LPD service enables UNIX clients to print transparently to any NetWare-attached printers. (See Figure 28.2.) UNIX print jobs are spooled into NetWare print queues, which are then serviced by NetWare print servers. As with NFS, in order for a NetWare print queue to be available to LPD clients, it must first be exported.

FIGURE 28.2.

UNIX to NetWare printing.

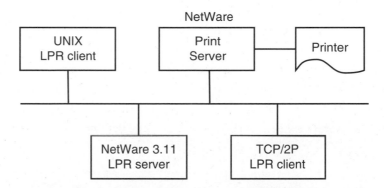

CAUTION ▶

Besides exporting the print queues, you also must define which UNIX clients can send print jobs to your server. These clients are called *trusted hosts*.

To satisfy NetWare print-queue security, you also must set up the UNIX user ID (uid) to NetWare user name mapping. Otherwise, your UNIX users may not be able to print to your NetWare server.

If AppleTalk support is loaded on your NetWare server, UNIX users can send print jobs to printers on the AppleTalk network.

Line Printer Client

Novell also implemented the client portion of the LPD protocol, the LPR protocol. Using this gateway, you can print from a DOS client, Macintosh workstation, or an OS/2 machine to a UNIX printer. (See Figure 28.3.)

FIGURE 28.3.
NetWare to UNIX printing.

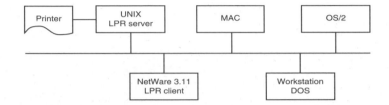

> **NOTE** ▶
>
> After configuring your NetWare server, you also need to configure the UNIX host by making sure of the following:
>
> 1. The IP address and NetWare server name is listed in the /ETC/HOSTS table.
> 2. The printer is defined in /ETC/PRINTCAP (or equivalent, depending on your flavor of UNIX).
> 3. The name of your NetWare server (as defined in /ETC/HOSTS) is included in the /ETC/HOSTS.lPD FILE (depending on your flavor of UNIX).

> **TIP** ▶
>
> For detailed information on setting up bidirectional printing using UNIX Systems Laboratory (USL) and other UNIX systems, download USLPRT.TXT and NFSPRT.TXT from the NetWire forum on CompuServe. You also can find these files on the NSEPro CD. NFSPRT.TXT is a reprint of the December 1992 AppNote.

File Transfer Protocol

Most Internet Protocol implementation comes complete with a File Transfer Protocol (FTP: RFC959), which enables you to transfer files between TCP/IP hosts in a nontransparent manner. FTP client is typically implemented as a user program with a simple command-line interface. The FTP server included as part of NetWare NFS is fully RFC959 compliant. Therefore, you can transfer files to and from a NetWare NFS server from any TCP/IP host that has an FTP client. Using FTP, you can transfer both text and binary files.

When an FTP client accesses an FTP host, one must have a valid user ID and password on the host. All file-system security associated with that user ID is enforced during the FTP session. Generally, FTP clients can access only files on a host that has an FTP daemon running. However, Novell's FTP daemon enables you to access other NetWare servers that do not have the FTP server running. To accomplish this, the FTP client must first log onto a NetWare NFS server and a corresponding user name and password must exist on the remote NetWare server. (See Figure 28.4.) Other than this requirement, no extra NLM or VAP is required on the remote NetWare server.

FIGURE 28.4.

FTP file access to remote NetWare server.

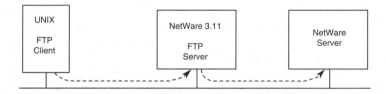

CAUTION ▶

FTP clients do not take up licensed connections on your NetWare FTP server. However, if they hop to a remote NetWare server, a licensed connection is taken up on the remote server.

Anonymous FTP access is supported by the NetWare FTP server. However, you need to manually create the ANONYMOUS NetWare account using SYSCON. It is not created automatically.

NOTE ▶

Anonymous users are requested to provide a password when logging onto the FTP server. By convention, anonymous users supply their e-mail address. However, *any* password will work.

The password for the ANONYMOUS NetWare account is not used when an anonymous user logs onto the NetWare FTP server.

If you have implemented Station Restriction or other NetWare-based user security for your NetWare users, it is not enforced during an FTP session with the NetWare server. This is because FTP connection is made with TCP/IP and not with IPX. Therefore, NetWare user security cannot be enforced.

If you want to prevent certain users from using the FTP services, list their NetWare user names in the SYS:ETC/FTPUSERS file.

XConsole

The XCONSOLE.NLM is a remote console program for X-Window servers. Therefore, it gives TCP/IP-based systems access to your NetWare server console in the same manner as RCONSOLE and ACONSOLE.

Although the X-Window System is based on a networked client/server environment, the terminology used in the X-Window environment is the reverse of what you might be used to. In X-terminology, the *client* is an application that runs on the remote host. The *server* is the software running on the workstation that is controlling the window display. See the example presented in Figure 28.5. The X-Window server (TCP/IP host in this case) sends a movement request to the X-Window client (NetWare server running XCONSOLE.NLM) such as "cursor down;" the X-client then sends back the corresponding graphics commands to tell the server how to draw the screen.

FIGURE 28.5.

X-Window client/
server environment.

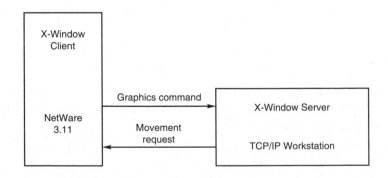

NOTE ▶

To enable XCONSOLE, properly configure your NetWare server to support TCP/IP. After loading REMOTE.NLM, load XCONSOLE.NLM. You can have RSPX.NLM loaded at the same time. This way, you can manage the console using either RCONSOLE or X-Window.

The NetWare FLeX/IP software contains the same set of software as NetWare NFS except for the NFS server NLMs.

```
FLeX/IP = FTP, LPR/LPD, XCONSOLE over TCP/IP protocol
```

This is a less-expensive solution for sites that require only the bidirectional printing between NetWare and UNIX machines and only need occasional (nontransparent) file-transfer capability.

NOTE ▶

The standard NetWare NFS software is not limited to the number of NFS clients who may mount the NetWare exported volumes. However, there is a less expensive "five-user" version, also known as Starter Pak, that enables only five NFS clients to simultaneously mount the exported volumes.

TIP

The latest version of XCONSOLE supports Telnet connection with VT100/220 emulation.

At the time of writing, the latest patch for NetWare NFS 1.2B is NFS153.EXE and for FLeX/IP 1.2B is FLX146.EXE. These files contain the new XCONSOLE as well as new NLMs that enable you to install these products on a NetWare 4.01 server or NetWare 3.12 server (but not a 4.0 server). These files can be found in the NetWire forum on CompuServe and NSEPro CD.

NetWare NFS Gateway

NetWare NFS Gateway implements the following three services:

1. NFS Client
2. Domain Name Service server
3. Network Information Service server

The NFS Client NLM enables you to mount UNIX file systems as a volume on your NetWare server. Your users can then transparently access these files using DOS and NetWare commands. The remote file system will appear as a regular NetWare volume to your users.

NetWare and UNIX file-system security are enforced when users access a mounted file system. First, the NetWare access right is checked. If this passes, the request passes to the remote NFS server and the remote server does another check. This enables the NetWare supervisor to have greater control over the access security than those set on NFS.

Before NetWare file-access rights can be translated to NFS file-access permissions, or vice versa, the NetWare user must have an account on the remote NFS server and both accounts must be mapped together. The mapping of NetWare username and group to NFS user ID and group ID is done by using the Network Information Service (NIS).

NIS is a TCP/IP industry standard technique that is used for looking up UNIX user and group information (such as username and password). NetWare's implementation expanded it to include UNIX-to-NetWare user and group mappings.

Domain Name Service (DNS) is another TCP/IP industry standard technique that NetWare NFS Gateway uses to locate remote TCP/IP hosts. Traditionally, a /ETC/HOSTS table (the file is SYS:ETC\HOSTS on a NetWare server) is used to keep track of the IP address for each hostname you access. However, this can be very inconvenient if you have many such files to track and update. DNS enables centralized management of IP address-to-hostname mapping.

You can configure your NFS Gateway either as an NIS/DNS server or client, depending on your environment and needs.

NOTE ▶

The installation of these products (NetWare NFS, FLeX/IP, and NFS Gateway) does *not* enable your TCP/IP hosts to log onto a NetWare server with Telnet. There currently is no TELNETD, a Telnet daemon for NetWare servers.

TIP ▶

At the time of writing, NetWare NFS Gateway version 1.1 does not support NetWare 4.01. To install NFS Gateway on NetWare 3.12 servers, you need to apply GWY160.EXE (available from NetWire and NSEPro CD).

UnixWare

UnixWare is Novell's implementation of UNIX. It is based on one of the industry standards, System V Release 4 (SVR4). UnixWare is available in two versions: Personal Edition and Application Server. The Personal Edition (PE) does not come with TCP/IP, but IPX support is built in. Therefore, you can use PE as a regular IPX workstation and log onto a NetWare server. Included as part of the operating system is a Graphical User Interface (GUI) that you can configure to look like the industry standard Motif OpenLook or HP OpenView interface.

NOTE ▶

It does not matter which GUI interface you choose; the only difference is in the windowing features. All other functions are unchanged.

UnixWare comes with the following features:

- ▪ DOS session support
- ▪ Message Handling System (MHS) for electronic mail
- ▪ IPX client stack

- Novell Virtual Terminal (NVT) support
- Remote application sharing
- Bidirectional printing
- TCP/IP and NFS support
- X-Window support

(The last two items listed are not standard features of the PE version but are available for the Application Server version.)

Worth mentioning here is the Novell Virtual Terminal (NVT) support by UnixWare. This enables users to "telnet" into UnixWare or any NVT servers (such as NetWare for UNIX servers) over IPX. No TCP/IP is necessary. One product that supports NVT is Pop/Term from Rational Data Systems.

UnixWare is binary compatible with System 5; therefore, software for System 5 on an Intel platform will work under UnixWare. An example of such software is Lotus 1-2-3 for UNIX.

TIP ▶

The current version of UnixWare is 1.0, and you should download and apply the latest set of patches (Patch4) from the CompuServe UnixWare forum. These files are also available on the NSEPro CD.

UnixWare is not a connectivity solution, but if you are considering UNIX for your NetWare environment, it could be a useful accessory.

NetWare for UNIX

Novell licensed the source code for NetWare 3.11 to a number of vendors, including HP, Data General, and IBM. These vendors ported NetWare to run under their own UNIX environment, and the resulting product is known as NetWare for UNIX. As far as the users are concerned, it is a NetWare server. All the "standard" DOS and NetWare commands can be used with it. The only difference is that you cannot load NLMs on a NetWare for UNIX server. Also, the typical performance is comparable to that of a 386/33 machine. UNIX and NetWare users can share files that reside on the same UNIX machine transparently. NetWare for UNIX is also known as Portable NetWare.

Most, if not all, NetWare for UNIX servers support NVT. Therefore, IPX worksta-tions can connect to these UNIX machines without having to run TCP/IP; there-fore, you should cut down on the RAM overhead requirement on the workstations.

Currently, Novell is working on a new version of Portable NetWare known as Processor Independent NetWare (PIN). Novell will separate out the code that is processor-independent, and the various vendors will write the drivers specific to their hardware. In such cases, NetWare runs as a native operating system on the different platform, rather than another process under UNIX. This way, one can take advantage of the hardware's speed. Some of the vendors involved in this project are Hewlett Packard, IBM, Data General, and DEC.

Putting it all Together

Now that this chapter has described the specific attributes of the various NetWare UNIX connectivity products, you can compare them to the seven attributes of an ideal configuration that were listed at the beginning of this chapter. The following list will give you an idea of which product meets which need.

1. *NetWare users need to access printers attached to UNIX machines:*

   NetWare NFS (LPR client)

   NetWare FLeX/IP (LPR client)

2. *NetWare users need to be able to log onto the UNIX machines from their desktop. Users do not want dumb terminals on their desk:*

   NetWare for UNIX (NVT).

   (Although not discussed in this chapter, Novell's LAN WorkPlace and LAN WorkGroup provide this functionality through TCP/IP in both DOS and Windows environment.)

3. *NetWare users need to transparently access files on UNIX machines:*

   NetWare NFS Gateway (NFS client)

4. *UNIX users need to access printers attached on NetWare LAN:*

   NetWare NFS (LPD server)

   NetWare FLeX/IP (LPD server)

5. *UNIX users need to run some DOS applications. They do not want both a terminal and a PC on their desk:*

   UnixWare (Personal Edition or Application Server)

6. *UNIX users need to transparently access files on NetWare servers:*

    NetWare NFS (NFS server)

7. *UNIX users want simple file-transfer capability between UNIX and NetWare servers:*

    NetWare NFS (FTP server)

    NetWare FLeX/IP (FTP server)

Summary

This chapter reviewed some of the Novell UNIX connectivity solutions and applied them to specific connectivity requirements. However, this chapter discussed only server integration options (not workstation options).

Gateways to IBM Hosts

29

by Jeffrey Wade

There are a number of Novell and third-party products available for connecting your NetWare network to an IBM host system. In the late 1980s, Novell acquired Systems Network Architecture (SNA) connectivity talent through the acquisition of niche firms specializing in gateway and emulator products, and the company was very successful in selling its NetWare SNA gateway solution in the marketplace. There were limitations to this product set, however, and customer demands, combined with the desire to produce a "best-of-breed" product, fueled the evolution of Novell's current gateway solution: NetWare for SAA.

This chapter discusses

- Why you would want to consider NetWare for SAA
- Features SAA provides to network users, and system requirements
- Installation, configuration, and considerations
- Optional products that can be used to extend functionality in your environment

Why NetWare for SAA?

NetWare for SAA is a flagship product for integrating traditional IBM Systems Network Architecture (SNA) environments with NetWare environments. It provides users of DOS, Microsoft Windows, Macintosh, OS/2, and UNIX workstations with comprehensive access to IBM mainframe resources. NetWare for SAA also provides seamless integration support for installations employing IBM AS/400 minicomputers. It is supported by a wide variety of Novell and third-party products, which enhance functionality and provide the integrator with flexibility.

Packaging Options

NetWare for SAA is implemented as an extension of the NetWare Communication Executive, a series of NetWare loadable modules (NLMs) that enable the NetWare operating system to support communication activities. Because it is implemented using the NLM architecture, it can be integrated into existing NetWare 3.x or 4.x servers that already provide file and print services to network workstations. This can be a perfect solution for departments or small offices where the cost of dedicated SNA gateway hardware cannot be justified. This reduction in network hardware also eases administration duties and helps to reduce support costs.

For those installations desiring a dedicated arrangement, NetWare for SAA ships with the Netware 3.1x Runtime product, which, acting as an NLM platform, enables an administrator to deploy NetWare for SAA as a single service on a dedicated server. In this manner, all server processing capacity can be devoted to gateway operations, thereby providing optimal performance.

NetWare for SAA is licensed according to the number of user sessions it provides and it is currently available in the following configurations:

- 16 sessions
- 64 sessions
- 128 sessions
- 254 sessions

It is possible to run two copies of the software on a single system, thereby increasing the maximum number of supported sessions to 508 on any one gateway server. You are free to mix and match session counts, so it's possible to have a 144-session configuration by combining a 16-session version with a 128-session version, or a 32-session configuration by combining two 16-session versions.

> **NOTE** ▶
>
> This capability to combine versions is unique to the NetWare for SAA environment. Many competing products cannot provide the same maximum session density per gateway. This potential hidden cost should be taken into consideration when evaluating other products against NetWare for SAA.

Host Connectivity Options

NetWare for SAA provides you with a full complement of upstream host and peer system connectivity options, as depicted in Figure 29.1.

FIGURE 29.1.

NetWare for SAA connectivity options.

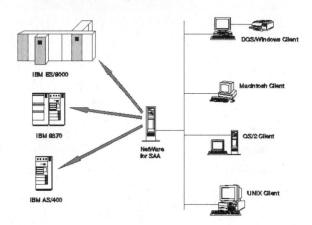

NetWare for SAA Connectivity Options

You may select from any of the following connectivity options:

■ An IBM 3725/3745 front-end processor (FEP) that has been equipped with a Token Ring Interface Coupler (TIC) or Ethernet Attachment Feature, or an IBM 3172/3174 controller similarly equipped with LAN attachment features

■ Directly to a System/3X0 channel using specialized hardware adapters from third-party developers

■ Directly to an IBM 9370 equipped with a Token Ring Communication Subsystem

■ Directly to an IBM OS/2 SNA Gateway

■ Directly to an IBM AS/400 minicomputer as an upstream host, or using a peer-to-peer interface

Physical connectivity can be accomplished using any of the following:

■ Any Novell Open DataLink Interface (ODI) v4.0 compliant adapter for Ethernet or Token Ring

■ Any Synchronous Data Link Control (SDLC) or Qualified Logical Link Control/X.25 (QLLC/X.25) adapter supported by an ODI driver

■ Custom third-party channel interface adapters developed specifically for NetWare for SAA and certified with Novell's Independent Manufacturer Support Program (IMSP)

PU Support

NetWare for SAA provides support for SNA Physical Unit types 2.0 and 2.1 (PU 2.0 and PU 2.1) connections. PU 2.0 connections are specified on links to upstream hosts. Devices that emulate PU 2.0 depend on the presence of an IBM host configured as a System Services Control Point (SSCP) to establish communication sessions on their behalf. PU 2.1 devices support a peer connection convention, which enables them to establish communication sessions with other PU 2.1 devices without the services of an SSCP host.

Not all SNA connection options support PU 2.1. If you are planning to use your SNA network as a transport for non-SNA data, be certain to verify your configuration with the appropriate host support personnel. Often, configuration and software revision levels must be adjusted in order to accommodate PU 2.1 features.

NetWare for SAA enables two PU connections per server. These connections can be over the same or different interfaces, and you may communicate with up to two hosts (each interface can be connected to different hosts, or both may be connected to the same host). This provides the ultimate in configuration flexibility. Each PU is capable of supporting up to 254 SNA Logical Units (LUs).

> **NOTE** ▶
>
> NetWare for SAA reserves one LU for its own use; therefore, the maximum number of available sessions on a 254-session PU would be 253.

New to NetWare for SAA v1.3 is support for Downstream PUs (DSPU), also known as a PU Concentrator feature. This enables NetWare for SAA to provide a host connection and LU support on behalf of a downstream system such as the following:

- ■ An IBM AS/400 system
- ■ An OS/2 SNA Gateway
- ■ An OS/2 Communication Manager/2 client
- ■ A 317X controller
- ■ Another NetWare for SAA gateway server
- ■ Any downstream device supporting a full SNA protocol stack

Support is provided for a maximum of 253 downstream PUs when using a Token Ring or Ethernet interface. If you are using a QLLC/X.25, this support is limited to 32.

LU Support

NetWare for SAA supports the following LU types as defined by SNA specifications:

LU Type 0	Used for specialized, user-definable purposes
LU Type 1 or 3	IBM 3287 Workstation printer support
LU Type 2	IBM 3270 Display station
LU Type 6.2	Application-to-application communication support

See Figure 29.2 for additional detail.

FIGURE 29.2.

NetWare for SAA supported LU types.

NetWare for SAA Supported LU Types

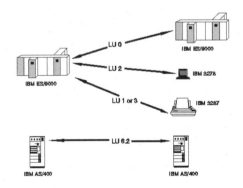

Workstation Client Support

NetWare for SAA is positioned to provide support for many different client workstation platforms. Most popular 3270 emulation software packages on the market today include support for this gateway.

> **TIP** ▶
>
> Even if your emulator does not explicitly provide NetWare for SAA support, you still may be able to accommodate it with the DSPU feature. IBM's Personal Communications/3270 is an example emulator. Check your emulator specifications to be certain.

The flexibility to support varied client platforms is a distinguishing feature of NetWare for SAA and is a natural extension provided by the ODI protocol support built into NetWare 3.1x and 4.0x. This enables clients to communicate with NetWare for SAA using Novell SPX, Apple's Appletalk, TCP/IP, and IEEE 802.2 Logical Link Control (LLC) protocols. DOS, Windows, and OS/2 clients will generally use SPX or 802.2. Macintosh systems are supported by the Appletalk protocol stack, and UNIX clients accomplish their emulation with the native TCP/IP protocol.

Emulation Software

Emulation software is a workstation application that provides the 3270 terminal "look and feel" to the user. You are not limited to a single emulator when you install NetWare for SAA as your gateway product. In fact, more than a dozen emulation products are supported for the DOS environment alone. With all these products on the market, how do you choose one? Nothing beats an in-house evaluation in your own environment, but here are a couple of key features to look for. Most vendors license their product on a single workstation basis. Some vendors also give you a choice of server-based licensing. Server-based licensing allows you to install the emulator once as a network-based application rather than individually on each workstation. This can be of great benefit in large installations.

TIP ▶

Not only is server-based licensing easy from an implementation and administration standpoint, but you'll almost always save money because the overall cost per workstation is lower. You also save time when it becomes necessary to install updates to the software, because you only have one copy on your network server to maintain.

Novell maintains a list of supported emulation products. You'll find Novell, IBM, Wall Data, DCA, and NetSoft on this list, among others.

Why Routing (IPX/SPX) versus LLC Bridging (IEEE 802.2)?

As discussed earlier, one of the key features of NetWare for SAA is its capability to enable clients to communicate using their native protocols. In many cases, workstations are already equipped with support for the IPX/SPX protocol stack and can provide simultaneous access to NetWare file/print servers, as well as NetWare for SAA. SNA's traditional strategy for internetworking SNA protocols (which are not routable) uses source-route bridging at the data link layer (IEEE Logical Link Control—802.2). All SNA protocol processing is performed at the SAA gateway on behalf of the client station. This is sometimes referred to as a *split-protocol stack* or *skinny client*. This arrangement conserves client memory resources and obviates the need for multiple client protocol stacks. For more information about IPX/SPX versus LLC bridging, see Chapter 26, "Routers and Bridges."

Many 3270 emulators, particularly those from IBM, require each client to support a full SNA protocol stack using the IEEE 802.2 protocol for communication. As mentioned in the discussion of DSPUs, it is possible to support such workstations with NetWare for SAA, but you should be prepared for extra configuration and support headaches.

NOTE ▶

802.2 clients present two primary problems. First, you must purchase a separate software product to provide the IEEE 802.2 driver support (IBM LAN Support Program) for each client that requires it, and learn how to install it alongside the IPX/SPX protocol so that both will harmoniously share a single NIC. This is not a trivial task. Second, the combination of IEEE 802.2, IPX/SPX, and SNA protocols requires an extraordinary amount of conventional memory in a DOS workstation. Usually, much tuning and meddling is required to produce an acceptable configuration.

AS/400 and IBM PC/Support 400

For a long time, customers wanting to connect their workstations to an IBM AS/400 for file sharing, printing, and emulation support had no choice but to purchase and install IBM's PC/Support 400 product. While very functional, the product requires IEEE 802.2 support at each client, thereby limiting your connectivity options and also requiring a healthy portion of available memory. NetWare for SAA addresses these problems by providing replacement modules for some of the IBM modules found in PC/Support 400. These basically replace the IEEE 802.2 protocol interface with an IPX/SPX interface. The PC/Support 400 client can then be placed on any type of LAN supported by NetWare (as opposed to only those supporting IEEE 802.2), and the memory requirements are also reduced. See Figure 29.3 for more detail.

FIGURE 29.3.

AS/400 integration.

NetWare for SAA-AS/400 Integration

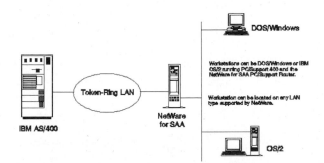

> **NOTE ▶**
>
> This eliminates the requirement to purchase the IBM LAN Support Program
> for each workstation because NetWare for SAA provides all necessary proto-
> col driver modules. This can represent a significant cost savings.

There is no loss of function when PC/Support 400 clients are connected in this
manner.

NetWare Communication Services

NetWare Communication Services (NWCS) is a set of NLMs that extend the
NetWare operating system, giving it the capability to support communication-based
activities. It can be thought of as a platform (see Figure 29.4) upon which communication applications such as NetWare for SAA can be built. This platform also can
support activities such as WAN routing and dial-out model pooling.

FIGURE 29.4.

*NetWare
Communication
Services.*

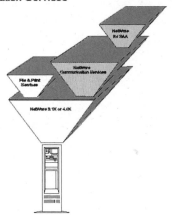

NetWare Communication Services

Eight NLMs constitute NWCS. They work together to provide configuration support, connection management, service management, network management, security,
and trace services. Each specific NLM is listed here with a brief description of its
function:

- CNSMX.NLM: Connection multiplexer. Acts as a message-passing agent
  and handles communication between all other NLMs in NWCS.
- COMMEXEC.NLM: Communications Executive. Provides a console
  interface to NWCS for operator interaction and control.

- CM.NLM: Connection Manager. Processes incoming requests from client workstations needing access to NWCS resources.

- CSSECUR.NLM: Security Agent. Verifies user access to NWCS resources by checking the NetWare bindery and other security definitions.

- SMA.NLM: Service Mapping Agent. Provides resolution between user-defined service names and actual services.

- NMA.NLM: Network Management Agent. Provides a management interface capability to external management systems such as Novell's Communication Services Manager or IBM's NetView product.

- DBA.NLM: Stores NWCS configuration information using NetWare's BTRIEVE record management services.

- TRACE.NLM: Tracing Agent. Provides a facility for tracing communication activity within NWCS. Assists operators in the diagnosis of problems.

Features, Functions, and System Requirements

Before you begin planning the connectivity details for your installation, you'll need to choose an operating configuration. NetWare for SAA supports integrated and dedicated configurations, as shown in Figure 29.5. Integrated configurations enable you to install and operate NetWare for SAA along with traditional NetWare 3.1x or 4.0 functions on the same hardware platform. Although there is a cost/performance tradeoff with this configuration, it provides an excellent fit for many installations.

FIGURE 29.5.

Dedicated versus integrated configurations.

NetWare for SAA - Dedicated vs. Integrated Configuration

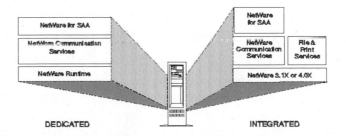

> **TIP** ▶
>
> Study the *Rules of Thumb* publication that comes with NetWare for SAA carefully if you are considering an integrated configuration. Make certain that the hardware components you choose will provide the desired level of performance.

An alternative configuration is to run NetWare for SAA on a separate hardware platform. This type of configuration is known as dedicated and is installed using a copy of NetWare Runtime. NetWare Runtime was created to provide a stand-alone platform upon which additional Novell NLM-based services can be installed. It enables only a single client connection and is therefore unsuitable for file/print services. It does, however, make an excellent platform for dedicated communication services.

> **NOTE** ▶
>
> NetWare Runtime is included free with most Novell products that have large resource requirements. This provides you with configuration flexibility as your environment changes and grows. You may initially configure an integrated setup but discover at some later date that a dedicated configuration will better serve your needs. No additional software (other than maybe a copy of MS-DOS) is required to migrate your configuration.

> **TIP** ▶
>
> In general, you can choose an integrated configuration for small installations or where cost is of primary concern. For performance-oriented installations, you should opt for dedicated configurations.

Platform Choices

One of the biggest factors that will influence the performance of NetWare for SAA is your choice of hardware components. Because the product is based on NetWare 3.1x, you will need at least an 80386 system operating at 20MHz or greater. This would be sufficient for small configurations; however, larger configurations will perform best with an 80486 system in the 33-50MHz range. Normally, internal processor speed is not the first performance factor to consider when planning a NetWare-based system, but because NetWare for SAA is a server-based application, all of its processing occurs at the server. Internal processor speed, in this case, plays a major role in determining overall performance.

Bus Architecture

As a rule of thumb, you should avoid using Industry Standard Architecture (ISA)-based systems in all but the very smallest servers and/or gateway configurations. The limited throughput capabilities imposed by the ISA bus specifications can lead to poor performance and throughput problems as the number of client workstations increases. A much better choice, especially when good performance is a primary goal, is to use an Extended Industry Standard Architecture (EISA) or MicroChannel (MCA) system. The throughput capabilities of these systems is many times greater than ISA, and they are much less likely to suffer bottleneck conditions due to bus performance.

> **NOTE** ▶
>
> Just because a system is EISA- or MCA-based does not automatically guarantee a high level of overall performance. You should always strive to purchase adapter cards that are of 32-bit design and that feature bus-mastering capability. These adapters are generally more expensive, but they are designed to exploit the capabilities of the EISA or MCA bus and provide superior throughput as compared with standard adapters.

Estimating Memory Requirements

In order to understand its memory requirements, it is important to understand the role that NetWare for SAA plays in enabling clients to communicate with a host system. That role is primarily to perform a translation between the client's native protocol and presentation environment and that of an IBM SNA network. If the NetWare for SAA system is speedy at processing this translation, minimal buffering (and therefore minimal memory) is required to handle each client connection. If the translation process is affected by performance bottlenecks (for example, a slow NetWare for SAA system, slow throughput to or from the SNA network, or slow NIC throughput), more memory is required to buffer each client connection, as information must wait to be translated and forwarded. In short, a fixed amount of memory is required to load and initiate NetWare for SAA, and a variable amount is required based on the throughput and the number of client connections. The amount of memory required also is affected by your choice of an integrated or dedicated configuration.

> **NOTE** ▶
>
> NetWare 3.1x and NetWare 4.0x manage and dispense memory in very different manners. You should have an understanding of the particulars of your version in order to effectively tune and support your installation.

For dedicated configurations, the following minimums are in effect:

- 16 sessions   8M
- 64 sessions   10M
- 128 sessions   12M
- 254 sessions   16M
- 508 sessions   20M

For integrated configurations, you must first calculate the memory requirements for your NetWare 3.1x or 4.0x environment and then calculate the following:

1. Start with 4M for NetWare for SAA.
2. Multiply the number of client sessions by 20K and round the result to the nearest megabyte.
3. Add the results from steps 1 and 2 to your original NetWare memory requirements.

> **TIP** ▶
>
> More information on calculating memory requirements can be found in the NetWare manuals and *Rules of Thumb* flyers that accompany NetWare and NetWare for SAA.

NetWare 3.1x Memory Pool Considerations

NetWare for SAA makes use of NetWare's Alloc Short Term Memory Pool for storing connection information and data buffers. Under default conditions, this memory pool can dynamically expand up to the maximum of 2M, which is usually sufficient.

As NetWare for SAA activates additional communication sessions, it draws on the resources of this pool. You should monitor pool memory usage and adjust the ceiling parameter upward if indicated. This parameter is adjusted using the console SET command. It can be adjusted dynamically, but you will need to make your changes permanent by editing the server's AUTOEXEC.NCF file. For more information about using SET commands to tune your NetWare OS, see Chapter 33, "Monitoring and Adjusting Server Performance."

> **NOTE** ▶
>
> The Alloc Short Term Memory Pool can grow in size up to a maximum of 16M. The maximum size parameter is usually adjusted upward in 1M increments until NetWare is satisfied. If the pool reaches maximum size and cannot expand, NetWare generates console error messages. NetWare for SAA may become unpredictable when this situation occurs, or the NetWare kernel may abend with an error message. You should keep a very close eye on the memory pools until you are satisfied with the accuracy of your tuning efforts.

Another point to be aware of is the interaction between memory pools. You may negatively affect other pools when you make adjustments to the Alloc Short Term Memory Pool. This usually occurs when total system memory is insufficient to meet the overall requirements of the server environment. Again, this will manifest itself in the form of console error messages, erratic performance (including ABENDs), or both. If you find yourself in this situation, the only remedy is to add additional physical memory to your configuration.

Host Interface Choices

NetWare for SAA provides you with several choices for interfacing to host systems. Each of these choices has different performance characteristics; therefore, it is in your best interest to choose the best performing interface for your particular environment. Figure 29.6 depicts the various connectivity options that are available. For local connections where NetWare for SAA and the SNA resources are within the same facility, host channel interfaces will provide the best throughput. This is a relatively new connectivity option in the NetWare for SAA product, and it would be a good choice for environments with heavy file-transfer requirements and large numbers of concurrent users. Of course, it is also the most expensive of the host interface choices. Most installations in this situation choose instead to use a LAN host interface, which provides excellent performance without the expense of a host channel connection.

FIGURE 29.6.

Local/remote host interface options.

NetWare for SAA Local/Remote Host Interface Options

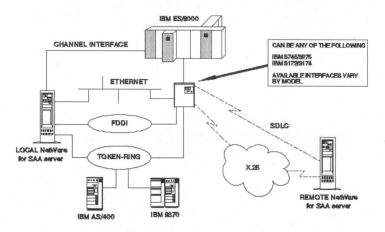

> **TIP**
>
> If you're considering a host channel connection, make sure you understand the cabling issues involved. Traditional IBM host channel interfaces use a Bus-and-Tag cabling scheme that is extremely bulky. This type of connection doesn't lend itself to frequent moves and changes, and you must faithfully respect cable length and termination specifications. If your facility employs IBM ESCON technology, cabling restrictions are considerably relaxed because ESCON enables fiber-optic connections between components. If you're unfamiliar with this scenario, spend some quality time with your host support personnel.

For LAN host interfaces, NetWare for SAA enables you to choose from any NIC that is supported by an ODI v4.0 compliant driver. Several NICs fit into this category, but from an SNA perspective your choices will usually be Token Ring or Ethernet, and possibly Fiber Distributed Data Interface (FDDI). In most cases, Token Ring or Ethernet will provide plenty of throughput. The determining factor between the two is usually which option is available on the SNA host side of the connection. Again, spend some planning time with your host support personnel to arrive at the most applicable alternative.

Installation, Configuration, and Other Considerations

Integrating NetWare for SAA requires experience with NetWare and with SNA configuration. Many of your NetWare for SAA choices are predicated on SNA/3270 hardware and configuration options. This section guides the integrator or system administrator through several configuration options that are available in the integration stage of SAA.

Installation and Customization Issues

Beginning with version 1.3, NetWare for SAA is installed using the standard INSTALL.NLM utility included in NetWare 3.1x and 4.0. The basic steps for installing NetWare for SAA and its associated components are as follows:

1. Decide on the interface to be used in attaching to your host system.

2. Install any hardware required to support your interface choices on your host system and NetWare for SAA server.

3. Decide on the PU and LU configurations required to serve your workstation community, and coordinate with your host support personnel for the necessary Virtual Telecommunications Access Method/Network Control Program (VTAM/NCP) definitions.

4. Install NetWare for SAA.

5. Install 3270 emulation software either on each workstation or as a network application on your file server, as appropriate.

6. Create customized service profiles for each logical host connection.

7. Modify the AUTOEXEC.NCF and COMMEXEC.NCF files as necessary in order to automate the loading and activation of NetWare for SAA.

8. Perform customization for each workstation session as required by your 3270 emulation software.

9. Monitor performance and perform tuning steps as required.

LU Configuration Possibilities

NetWare for SAA is shipped with fairly complete and straightforward planning and installation manuals. It is recommended that you read these publications prior to attempting an installation, because many choices and decisions (particularly in the area of LU configuration) should be made beforehand. Before you begin creating the service profiles for your installation, you should ask yourself a couple of questions: Will all my 3270 workstation sessions be identical, or are there workstations with unique requirements? Do I have more workstations than total gateway sessions? Will everyone need access to 3270 applications at all times? The answers will help you decide between the following possible LU configurations:

■ **Dedicated**. A dedicated LU is always reserved for a particular user or workstation. Each time the workstation requests access to the gateway, it receives the same dedicated LU. During periods when the workstation is not accessing the gateway, the LU remains idle and cannot be accessed by another workstation.

NOTE ▶

Many installations prefer this type of configuration because it provides a consistent workstation-to-host relationship. This makes for easier problem diagnosis and simplifies usage tracking on a workstation basis. The disadvantage is that you must purchase enough sessions to support every workstation concurrently, even though 100 percent usage is most likely unrealistic.

■ **Public**. Public LUs can be set up for use by any user. The Public LU concept is analogous to a public phone. These LU sessions are available to anyone on a first-come, first-served basis.

■ **Pooled**. Pooling is typically used to share a set of LUs between a specified group of workstations. You may want to allocate LUs on a departmental or workgroup level to ensure equal access, or to control access to selected host applications on a workgroup basis. Pooling also is useful if you have a group of workstations that require only occasional host access. A pool with a 1:2 or 1:3 session-to-workstation ratio might adequately meet the access requirement while conserving LU usage. Pool sizes can be adjusted as needed, to meet changing demands. One disadvantage of pooling is the lack of a consistent workstation-to-host relationship. Each time a workstation requests gateway access, the first available session in the pool will be allocated for use. This may present problems for your installation.

TIP ▶

Don't try to use pooling with host printer sessions. Although it may seem like a good idea on the surface, you should resist the temptation. In general, network printing is the nemesis of most installations. Pooling host printer sessions only serves to escalate confusion; the host IDs will change depending on the LU session to which you connect.

NOTE ▶

When pooling terminal sessions, do not mix different model types in the same pool. For example, do not combine 3278 Model 2 LU sessions with 3278 Model 5 LU sessions. Doing so will cause unpredictable results if the connecting workstation does not exactly match the defined LU. If you have a requirement for mixed model types, create a separate pool for each type.

Enhancing NetWare for SAA

NetWare for SAA is not only a robust gateway for accessing IBM SNA resources, it is also a platform for implementing additional SNA integration products. Several add-on products produced by Novell fit this category.

NetView Support

If your host installation depends upon NetView for management of the SNA network components, you may want to consider adding NetView support to NetWare for SAA. NetView support enables NetWare for SAA to act as an entry point into the NetView environment; error and warning conditions detected at the NetWare OS or NetWare for SAA level can be forwarded as alerts to an operator at a NetView console. NetView also provides a facility known as the RUNCMD interface. This facility enables a NetView operator to send commands from the NetView console to a NetWare for SAA server, thus providing a way to centralize control of NetWare-based servers. Command filtering is also provided, enabling you to define the scope of control over the NetWare environment. NetView support is installed as an additional service under NetWare 3.1x or 4.0x and includes files to assist in the customization of the NetView environment.

NetWare HostPrint

NetWare HostPrint is designed to simplify network printing from the host environment. Without NetWare HostPrint, host printer LU sessions configured in NetWare for SAA must direct any received print data to a workstation running a suitably configured 3270 emulation session in order to direct the print data to a physical printer. The physical printer can be one attached to the workstation running the emulation software or any network printer that can be accessed with the NetWare CAPTURE command. This arrangement presents a potential problem in that no host printing to network printers can occur unless a workstation is powered up and has the appropriate software configured and loaded.

NetWare HostPrint removes that workstation requirement from this scenario by redirecting host print data received at the gateway directly into a defined NetWare print queue. HostPrint is loaded as an additional NLM service on the NetWare for SAA server and provides a control panel interface at the server for each configured printer session. Print data can be redirected to any defined queue on any available NetWare server. NetWare HostPrint is available in 8-, 16-, 64-, and 128- session versions and is licensed as a separate product.

> **NOTE** ▶
>
> NetWare HostPrint *must* be installed on the same physical platform as the NetWare for SAA software. It will not function correctly if installed on another server platform.

NetWare SNA Links

NetWare SNA Links is another add-on product to NetWare for SAA that enables two or more LANs to be connected together over an SNA network. To be connected, each LAN must have a NetWare for SAA server with SNA Links installed and a supported connection to the SNA network, as shown in Figure 29.7. SNA Links operates by establishing the SNA network as a virtual LAN between the NetWare servers. Each server sees the SNA network as a LAN interface and binds to it using the standard IPX/SPX protocols. SNA links then encapsulates the IPX/SPX traffic into SNA Path Information Units (PIUs) for transport across the SNA network. You must configure NetWare for SAA to support PU Type 2.1 because SNA Links uses the LU 6.2 Peer Protocol across the SNA network to establish logical connections between servers. After the server connections are established, workstations on each LAN can access the NetWare resources of any other connected LAN.

FIGURE 29.7.

NetWare for SAA enhanced with SNA Links.

NetWare for SAA Enhanced with NetWare SNA Links

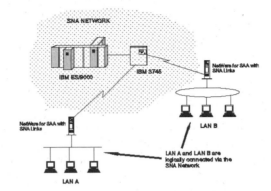

Summary

NetWare for SAA is a thoughtfully designed and powerful platform for integrating your NetWare environment with IBM host systems. The software goes beyond the standard 3270 terminal and printer session support offered by most products, giving you the flexibility to fully exploit the services available on an SNA network.

More information on NetWare for SAA and associated products is available by fax 24 hours a day through Novell's FaxBack service. This service can be accessed from any touch-tone telephone by calling 800-NETWARE. You'll be presented with a menu of options, which includes a FaxBack selection. Once in FaxBack, you should request a catalog of available documents, which lists all available documents on the service.

You can receive plenty of great support and advice by accessing NetWire over CompuServe—currently a separate section of the NCONNECT forum, sections 3, 4, and 5. You pay only for CompuServe connections charges. SysOps and other third parties like you monitor this section and exchange information and support for NetWare for SAA and related issues. Expert independent SysOps (as well as SysOps employed by Novell) will answer any support questions within 24 hours if addressed to "SysOps" or "All." Questions addressed to "All" are open for discussion among all reviewing this section.

Additional information also can be found in the NetWare Buyer's Guide and the NetWare for SAA 1.3 Information Guide, which are also available by calling 800-NETWARE or on the NetWare Support Encyclopedia, Professional version (NSE Pro).

Dial-In, Dial-Out Services

30

By Rick Sant 'Angelo

Several products for dial-in and dial-out services exist for PCs—specifically for NetWare networks — at many levels of usefulness. This chapter discusses several methods of providing remote dial-in and dial-out services, from the most basic to the most full-featured options.

Dial-in and dial-out services for remote users can be provided by one or more modems to which all users on the LAN have access. Simple remote-modem software can be used to share a single modem, or you can build a modem server that will provide LAN connections for as many as 32 users per server, which can be used to dial-in or dial-out. Many products exist, providing various levels of functionality.

It is important to know your user and usage requirements before you decide on a product. Many of the solutions presented in this book have features or limitations that may not conform to your user requirements. It is good to keep in mind that in many organizations, the availability of new services spawns new requirements. For example, perhaps your company does not currently use remote access for electronic mail, but as soon as this capability is available, the demand for dial-in remote electronic mail may become very high. It does not make sense to spend tens of thousands of dollars for a current solution that limits your future options. Some of the costly products have severe limitations, of which you should be aware.

Many products use the Network Communications Services Interface/Network Asynchronous Services Interface (NCSI /NASI) APIs, developed by Network Products Corporation. The APIs provide a method for creating an Asynchronous Communications Server (ACS) with serial ports shared across networks utilizing IPX. This provides network connections to the file server for dial-in purposes to access serial ports via IPX. It also enables access from any internetworked node.

An alternate method of accessing serial ports on a LAN is through the use of NetBIOS. This method, however, enables only users located on the same logical LAN (network address) to access the shared device. Because NetBIOS is not routable, it cannot use NetWare routers to access devices on the other side of a router. The NASI interface is preferable for enabling users access across NetWare routers.

The tools that can be used to provide remote access on a NetWare network include the following:

- Remote-host software
- Modem-sharing software
- Modem-sharing devices and shared modems
- Asynchronous communications servers

■ Dedicated processor boards

■ Remote node bridges and routers

Each type of product is suited for distinct levels of service and has distinct limitations. You should select the simplest and most economical solution to meet your needs. If you have very low levels of current needs, you should provide the simplest capabilities and watch demand grow before purchasing solutions that may become inadequate.

Remote-Host Software

Remote-host software, such as Carbon Copy or pcAnywhere, enables a network workstation with a modem to become a host computer for a remote terminal. A PC with a modem can dial up and connect to the host, thus emulating a terminal. The remote user can access any applications and services, just as if he or she were sitting at the host PC. (See Figure 30.1.)

FIGURE 30.1.

Remote-host
dial-in.

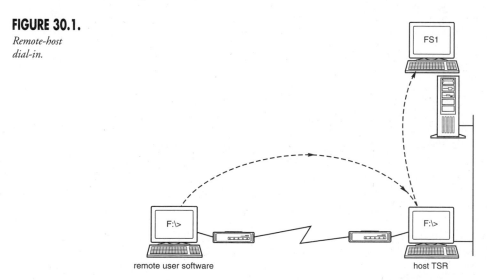

remote user software   host TSR

In Figure 30.1, the remote user dials in and takes control of the host, which in this case is also a network node. The remote user can now log in, execute any applications, and perform file transfers between the host and the remote storage devices (and virtually any functions that could be done on-site).

Available Products

- *pcAnywhere*, Symantec Corp.
- *Close-Up Remote*, Norton-Lambert Corp.
- *Carbon Copy*, Microcom Inc.
- *Crosstalk*, DCA
- *CO/Session LAN II*, Triton Technologies
- *Commute*, Central Point Software
- *NetRemote*, Brightworks

Common Features of Remote-Host Software

- The PC can function as a host, operating as terminate-and-stay-resident (TSR) in memory, using standard dial-up voice telephone lines.
- The remote user can function as a terminal, controlling the processing resources of the host workstation.
- Only video and keyboard transmissions are sent across the modem. (2400 bps is acceptable for text-based applications.)
- The remote user can use the DOS prompt, run executable programs, log onto the file server, and basically do anything that could be done on-site.
- The user can print at the host site or at the remote site.

Limitations of Remote-Host Software

- Remote-host software packages are very slow with GUIs such as Windows. New versions use Windows API calls to enhance performance. Mouse support is sometimes limited or erratic.

> **NOTE** ▷
>
> Improvements have been made for Windows with several of these packages, but you should carefully evaluate these products to be certain that they suit your purposes.

- If a problem causes the host to lock up, the remote user may have problems gaining access unless someone reboots and reruns the host software. Some software packages are better than others at clearing dead connections.

- When using an ACS (discussed later in this chapter), the network user must use special network communication software version to share interrupt 14H.

Modem-Sharing Software

Software for sharing a modem installed in a workstation may be the simplest solution to providing dial-out access on your network. A few products (such as Modem Assist and LANSight) are designed with NetBIOS peer-to-peer software specifically for the purpose of sharing a modem. The other packages in the following list enable a remote user to take control of the host. Once the remote user is in control of the host, the modem can be used, just as if the user were at that workstation.

To use either type of software, a TSR is loaded at the host workstation where the modem is to be shared, and communication software is loaded at the remote user workstation. The remote user can access the host and dial out, as shown in Figure 30.2.

FIGURE 30.2.

Modem sharing for dial-out access.

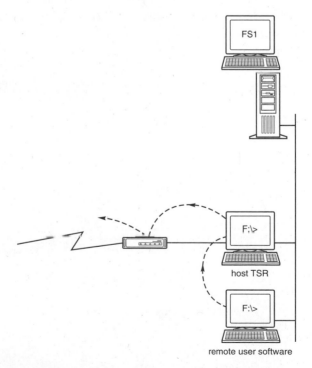

Available Products

- *Modem Assist*, Fresh Technologies
- *LANSight*, Intel
- *Sparkle*, Triton Technologies
- *Close-Up LAN*, Norton-Lambert

Common Features of Modem-Sharing Software

- Shares a modem (or any local device) in a network node PC with other LAN users.

- Modem Assist (Fresh Technologies) enables any user to access the modem as if it were a modem server with several remote-host products (as mentioned previously). This requires the use of special network versions that can utilize interrupt 14H for dial-out.

- Close Up LAN and LANSight enable any user on the network to control the computer with the modem. This works the same way as remote-host communications software, except the connection is through a LAN instead of telco lines. In such cases, the LAN remote user can execute the LAN host user's communications software and dial-out. Close Up Remote enables a user to dial in, taking control of the host connected to the LAN, and accessing the LAN server located elsewhere on the LAN.

Limitations of Modem-Sharing Software

- Generally limited to access of devices located only on the same network address (cannot cross a router).

- Some products limit host-computer user activity while the remote user has the modem.

- Designed for light modem usage—not suited for heavy shared-modem access.

> **NOTE** ▶
>
> Most LAN remote-host software packages enable access only to host computers if they are located on the same logical LAN (network address). This restricted access is caused by the limitation of NetBIOS.

Modem-Sharing Devices

A few devices enable NetWare users to access a modem or a device to which a modem (or multiple modems) can be attached. The device or modem can be attached directly to a LAN cable, and the ports are shared for all network users. These devices integrate ACS software in a ROM or flash RAM chip in the device.

These products are versatile and very simple to install; just connect them to a LAN cable. Several remote-host communications software packages have LAN versions that can provide dial-out as well as dial-in service.

Available Products

- *Net Port II,* Microtest
- *Asynchronous Communication Server 2/Standalone (ACS2/SA),* Network Products Corp.

Common Features of Modem-Sharing Devices

- Shares serial ports as an ACS
- Enables remote users to dial in with a direct connection to the network
- With network version of remote-host software, enables users to dial in and take control of any workstation on the network
- With network version of remote-host software, enables users to dial out

Limitations of Modem-Sharing Devices

- Enables only two modems to be shared
- Enables only dial-in with direct connection to network; requires remote-host software packages for full functionality

Shared Modems

These products work the same way as the Net Port II and ACS2/SA, except that a modem is built into the ACS device.

Available Products

- *NetModem/E*, Shiva Corp.

Features of a Shared Modem

- Enables remote node to access both local and network drives, which enables the execution of local applications with data located on a file server
- Enables remote users to dial in with a direct connection to the network
- With network version of remote-host software, enables users to dial in and take control of any workstation on the network
- With network version of remote-host software, enables users to dial out

Limitations of a Shared Modem

- Enables only two modems to be shared
- Enables only dial-in with direct connection to network; requires remote-host software packages for full functionality

Asynchronous Communications Servers (ACS)

This software is used to create modem servers that are able to connect many remote users to a LAN—with speeds of up to 38.4 kbps—if the multichannel communications boards enable that bandwidth. ACSs use the NASI interface to enable true client/server services using IPX. Dial-out services can be provided by using communications software that captures software-interrupt 14H BIOS calls and re-direct requests to the shared serial ports on the ACS.

Through the use of multichannel communications boards, such as Novell's Wide Area Network Interface Module (WNIM) board, several products enable as many as 16 modems located on the ACS to be shared among networked users. Other companies make multichannel communications boards that are better and less expensive than WNIM boards. DigiBoard has a 16-port model that can replace four 4-port WNIM boards.

Turnkey solutions of hardware and software also have become very popular because of the common-place difficulties in configuring hardware and software for communications.

Figure 30.3 shows an ACS with several modems.

FIGURE 30.3.

An Asynchronous Communication Server.

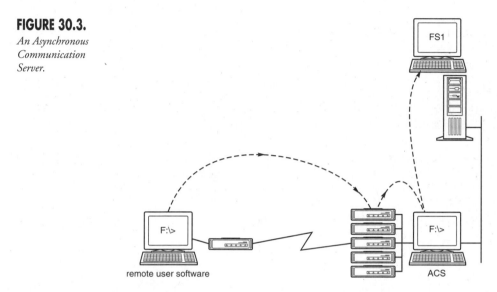

remote user software · ACS

Available Products

- *NetWare Asynchronous Communication Services (NACS)*, Novell (software only)

- *NetWare Asynchronous Communication Services (NACS)*, Microdyne (turnkey hardware and software)

- *Asynchronous Communication Server 2 (ACS2)*, Network Products Corp. (software kit with multichannel communications board)

- *NetWare Access Services (NAS)*, Novell (software only)

- *NetWare Access Services (NAS)*, Microdyne (turnkey hardware and software)

Features of ACS Products

Each of these products have different features, requirements, and limitations, as detailed in the following sections.

NetWare Connect

This product replaces NetWare Asynchronous Communication Server (NACS), which has been available for many years as an ACS version. It is now available only as an NLM to be installed on a 3.x or 4.x server, or a 3.x OS runtime. OS is provided to make a standalone communications server. NACS provides access for up to 32 serial ports located on the NACS using Novell's WNIM+ boards or any one of several choices of multichannel communication boards. It is now sold in various user increments, from 5-user to 32-user versions.

NetWare Connect is designed primarily to function as a modem server affording dial-in service to a network. It can be used for dial-out with the use of several LAN-version communications software applications that redirect interrupt 14H. Remote-host communications software can be used when loaded at both the remote site and at a dedicated workstation on the LAN to act as a host. When used this way, NACS becomes the gateway to the LAN between the user and the host computer.

NACS' NLM is menu-driven and has many options for monitoring, controlling, and managing communications ports and port activity.

Features

- Enables up to 32 modems to be shared
- Offers dial-out to all users (general port or specific port)
- Enables access over NetWare routers using IPX
- Can be used with remote-host communications software for dial-out and remote program execution
- Clears lines reliably if a disconnect or lockup occurs

Limitations

- Dial-out requires network version communication software that redirects interrupt 14H.
- Dial-in requires remote-host software in order to execute application software that is loaded on the server. This also requires a separate PC on the network dedicated to host each session.
- Once a port is used for dial-out, it cannot be used for dial-in (or vice versa), without rebooting the NACS.

Asynchronous Communication Server 2 (ACS2)

The company that developed the original NACS version, Network Products Corp., still produces their ACS2 product, which includes their ACS software and their own multichannel communications board. It is an excellent product, and in a few ways it is better than Novell's NACS standalone product. When using their communications boards, up to 32 modems can be used in one server, and modem speeds of up to 38.4 kbps are supported.

Features

■ Enables up to 32 modems to be shared.

■ Dial-out is available to all users (general port or specific port).

■ Enables access over NetWare routers using IPX.

■ Can be used with remote-host communications software for dial-out and remote program execution.

■ Clears lines reliably if a disconnect or lockup occurs.

Limitations

■ Dial-out requires network version communication software that redirects interrupt 14H.

■ Dial-in requires remote-host software in order to execute application software loaded on the server. This also requires a separate PC on the network dedicated to host each session.

■ Once a port is used for dial-out, it cannot be used for dial-in (or vice versa) without rebooting the NACS.

NetWare Access Server (NAS)

NAS was developed as a solution to some of the limitations of NACS. NAS is also an ACS-type server, using the NASI interface; however, NAS functions as a multiuser host for up to 16 remote users. Processing occurs at the NAS server.

NAS enables remote users with DOS, Windows, OS/2, Macintosh, and ASCII terminals to dial in and use the processing power of the host NAS. This implementation enables a 386- or 486-based computer to become an applications server for sites requiring remote access capabilities. NAS utilizes the 386 or 486 processor's capability to create virtual machines, enabling up to 16 users access to a single machine while providing remote job processing. Remote-host software is included with the server software as one complete package.

Though there are many good points about NAS, the product is limited in RAM availability and processing power. By using the virtual machine features of 386 or 486 architecture, a remote user gets a limited amount of available RAM, the processing power of an 8086 (at best), and no facilities to use expanded or extended memory. Windows runs in the real mode — and is slow when there are just a few users — and even slower when several users access the system.

NetWare Access Server (NAS)

This is the same version of NAS, as discussed in the preceding section, but it is installed in a turnkey hardware and software system. It comes in four- and eight-port models.

Limitations

- Enables dial-in use only
- Has limited processing and RAM
- Cannot use third-party communication software

Dedicated Communications Controllers

This type of device is placed in the bus of a server or router and becomes a node on the network. The device is a PC on a card, and the LAN is the bus of the server or router in which it resides. When such a device is used as a remote modem server, normal LAN communications software that uses interrupt 14H for shared access can be used to provide dial-in and dial-out service. Many controllers can be placed in one server or router, and they appear as one LAN, with one network address and driver.

When users dial in, they take control of the on-board processor using remote-host software. They can execute any software as a local user, and only screen output is sent to them as a remote terminal. Their keyboard input drives the remote device. The boards have built-in video devices as well as a serial port. They boot automatically, just as a diskless workstation does, and some even have built-in IDE adapters to add a hard drive. Communications controllers come in a variety of models, some with multiple processors on one card, some with 286, 386, or 486 on-board processors and several megabytes of RAM.

As an added bonus, any LAN user can off-load processing onto an inactive processor card. Close Up LAN, or a comparable product, can be loaded TSR on the communication controller processor so it can be accessed by another network user. This provides access to LAN users, even if bridged or routed on any LAN. Normal dial-up lines can accommodate up to 38.4 kbps, which provides very fast access to host processes.

These products constitute an ideal solution for full-featured LAN remote access. There are no restrictions in processing power except the limitations of the physical controller card itself, and models are available with 486 power and 16 MB of RAM. The only limitation a remote user needs to consider is the inherent slowness with GUI applications, such as Windows. With the proper remote-host software, however, GUI access is acceptable.

Available Products

- *QL Series Boards*, Cubix Corporation
- *Chatterbox*, J&L Information Systems

Common Features of Dedicated Communications Controllers

- Installs in a server or router as LAN cards
- Serves as host for remote user
- Can accommodate up to 32 cards per server/router using expansion bus
- Boots as diskless workstation, or it can have dedicated hard drives
- Shares a single floppy-disk drive in multiplexed mode
- Monitoring software clears locked or inactive lines
- Communication software is included, or it can use third-party software

Limitations of Dedicated Communications Controllers

- None. This is the optimum product for dial-in, dial-out.

Remote Node Bridges and Routers

These products connect remote PCs as LAN nodes. LAN2PC/Mega uses a workstation shell and routes IPX packets, whereas RLN bridges Ethernet frames addressed only to the remote PC. Performance is better than a direct connection over a modem using normal communications software, but it requires a higher speed line for adequate performance.

These products enable a user to access both local and remote drives. Applications can be located on a local drive, and data can be accessed remotely for best performance. Unlike other communications software, these products can be used with T-1 or fractional T-1 lines.

Available Products

- *LAN2PC/Mega*, Newport Systems Solutions, Inc.
- *Remote LAN Node (RLN)*, DCA

Common Features of Remote Node Bridges and Routers

- Connects remote PCs at the data link layer
- Uses high-speed digital lines for access
- Enables use of both local and network volumes

Limitations of Remote Node Bridges and Routers

- Can be slow, even with T-1 lines, if applications are accessed remotely
- A high-cost solution for remote user access

Summary

Many types of products are available to provide NetWare users remote access to their LANs. You should find the product type that fulfills your user needs and evaluate the available options accordingly.

VI
PART

Performance Optimization

Benchmark and Workload Testing

31

by Rick Sant'Angelo

You should always question the validity of conclusions drawn from benchmark tests. Benchmark tests are conducted by magazines and testing laboratories and are designed to fully saturate a component to expose its maximum level of performance for the purpose of product comparison. But do they really accomplish this goal? Do the statistics generated characterize performance factors that are relevant? And are the conclusions drawn valid and applicable to your production workload?

Isolating a component or subsystem in a network is not truly possible. A network is a system comprised of many subsystems, each of which is made up of many components. Each subsystem operates in concert with others, and each component relies on others for its performance. A change in one component causes other components and subsystems to work differently. If you switch a disk drive, NICs may perform better or worse; if you replace an NIC, disk performance may change. Other components, like system memory, may operate more or less efficiently based upon many other components in the server. Bus transfer rates can never be accurately recorded because of the many other components between the tester and the bus. As tests proceed, bottlenecks shift and flow from one subsystem to the next.

So how can benchmark testing be used to gather useful information about servers, NICs, disk subsystems, and other parts of a network? How can you compare subsystems or components in order to select the best? How can you test a fully configured system, and what will the benchmark testing tell us?

This chapter explores these issues and directs you to use benchmark testing to assist you in answering some of these questions. It also discusses how to run various tests that can help you compare system components and test your system under heavy loads.

You should conduct tests to isolate bottlenecks in your system and compare system performance before and after making changes. However, you should accept product comparison tests with skepticism. The statistics upon which conclusions are made may not be relevant to your environment or production workload. The numbers can be used for comparisons, but should not be interpreted literally.

Interpreting Test Conclusions

Prior to running tests you should clarify what needs to be learned from the tests. During the selection or design of the test, and during the test itself, you need to stay focused on this purpose. Test results may be inconclusive, and you should not become trapped into projecting or correlating results.

Testing is valuable for three reasons:

- Benchmark testing components for selection
- Workload testing a system for bottlenecks
- Stress-testing your system to know how it withstands heavy usage

Characteristics of testing must be explored before you can select or design a test to fulfill your requirements. These characteristics pertain to all types of testing. How to select or design tests for each of these purposes is addressed later in this chapter.

Testing versus Workload Characteristics

Software requirements and user access vary in each system. Some software products are disk-intensive, others are processor-intensive, and still others are both processor- and disk-intensive. Usage factors that can add many times the level of system performance variation change from one system to another. Factors that vary from one system to another include the following:

- Number of active users at any given moment
- Types of software
- Software access requirements
- Activity of users
- Delays between user activities
- Software delays

If you consider the many preceding variables, it becomes evident that designing a test to duplicate or approximate your real working conditions would be tremendously difficult. Therefore, tests need to be designed and selected on a basis of what they can tell us, not whether they actually duplicate real circumstances. Tests need to be designed with extensive engineering knowledge to pinpoint various aspects of system performance. Conclusions drawn from tests must be evaluated with careful study of the correlation among the testing apparatus, the engineering know-how, and the purpose of the test itself.

AppNotes, published by Novell's System Research department, has discussed testing benchmarks on several occasions. It is Novell's belief that production workload characteristics and tests cannot be correlated directly. However, Novell has decided to develop and use a new test utility known as Ghardenstone to simulate various working conditions—with the caveat that the test results are not to be construed literally.

If you want to know whether one product outperforms another, the best test is to actually use the product in the heaviest circumstances of normal production workloads. You can arrange product evaluations with your vendors, test competing products, and elect to return those which do not meet your expectations. When comparing several well-engineered products, you might not find perceivable differences under normal conditions.

How Hardware, Software, and Protocols Conspire to Mask Bottlenecks

As with almost every aspect of networking, large gaps in understanding are revealed each time you approach a subject. It is therefore best to start with a brief discussion of testing characteristics. If you understand the characteristics of various tests, you can select those which can accomplish your testing purpose.

Testing always is related to system performance. A system is a complex assembly of many hardware components and subsystems, and protocol and software layers. All these items are combined so each system is uniquely assembled and configured, regardless of how outwardly similar they appear. NetWare Core Protocol (NCP), which is at the center of almost all file server requests, affects how these components relate to one another.

NCP is a connection-oriented protocol, which means each request packet must be acknowledged and each reply packet containing data must be acknowledged. If any packets are missing, they must be re-sent. NCP paces how your hardware and software works together.

For example, a typical file read request works as follows:

1. Workstation software requests a file read of 4096 bytes

2. NETX intercepts the request and requests a file handle

3. NCP at the server searches file listings, replies with information about the file, and checks the user trustee assignments

4. NETX acknowledges the attributes and initiates the file read

5. NCP at the server reads the file and sends the first of four packets, because the LAN frame (Ethernet) only accommodates a 1024-data-portion-packet size

6. NETX acknowledges receipt of packet one

7. NCP at the server reads the file at the offset and sends the second of four packets

8. NETX acknowledges receipt of packet two

9. NCP at the server reads the file at the offset and sends the third of four packets

10. NETX acknowledges receipt of packet three

11. NCP at the server reads the file at the offset and sends the last of four packets

12. NETX acknowledges receipt of packet four

Packet Burst NCP works a little differently. A Packet Burst NCP works as follows:

1. Workstation software requests a file read of 4096 bytes

2. NETX intercepts the request and requests a file handle

3. NCP at the server searches file listings and replies with information about the file location, attributes, and user trustee assignments

4. NETX acknowledges the attributes and initiates the file read

5. NCP at the server reads the file and sends the first of four packets, because the LAN frame (Ethernet) only accommodates a 1024-data-portion-packet size

6. NCP at the server reads the file at the offset and sends the second of four packets

7. NCP at the server reads the file at the offset and sends the third packet

8. NCP at the server reads the file at the offset and sends the last packet

9. NETX acknowledges receipt of all four packet fragments, listing any missing ones

As you can imagine, each hardware component between the disk file and the workstation's memory is being turned on and off, servicing this request and requests from other workstations. Packet Burst works better to reduce pauses between file reads and acknowledgments and any latency that occurs during the trips between server and workstation. However, no matter the method employed, NCP paces the movements of the hardware and the movement of the software through the system.

Each request or reply must wait for its counterpart. If you attempt to locate a bottleneck in the server's disk subsystem, your efforts are clouded by the sequence previously discussed. Perhaps by the time the third file read occurs, the server is busy servicing another request, or write requests have become aged, so file write requests are now a high priority. This may cause delay in the file server's response, or it may respond with a Request Being Processed reply packet, which indicates the server is too busy to handle the request at this time. This causes NETX to re-try the request. In this case, the disk is not allowed to operate at its full capacity, and the throughput at the NIC is reduced, because it also has to handle error recovery.

This situation, and the resulting latency, worsens as your LAN cabling system causes more errors. Most test beds are performed under perfect laboratory conditions to prevent problems that cause error recovery and its subsequent effect on performance. In real life, error recovery is unavoidable because the world is imperfect.

Therefore, it is impossible to isolate any hardware component and say that any file read or write test can isolate a NIC or disk drive. Each of these components can only respond as fast as NCP and the other components feed packets. Faster or slower hardware at the workstation or server can enhance or reduce NCP's performance. Though a single component can form a bottleneck that affects this sequence, it only affects—not controls—NCP's request and reply pacing.

Benchmark Testing Components for Selection

Benchmarking involves running a test and timing it. This measures the performance of a component or subsystem in relation to the system in which it is installed. Benchmarking is only helpful in determining the effectiveness of a component in facilitating better overall system performance.

A benchmark test should be designed to isolate a component, subassembly, or system for the net throughput available in a given context. However, it is virtually impossible to totally isolate a component. For example, an NIC test can benchmark how much data flows during a test, but the conclusion needs to be carefully qualified. One NIC may perform better under one set of circumstances and worse under a different set of circumstances. Most testers have experienced quite a bit of difficulty in drawing a direct correlation between test results and the effectiveness of a component.

Benchmark testing for the purpose of testing a component or subassembly should be conducted under identical circumstances. The test should be run identically with only one difference: the component switch. Only then can a tester say whether one product worked better under test circumstances than the other. It is often not possible to say that a product that performed better under testing will perform better under normal production workloads. The reviewer should be careful about projecting the results to other workload conditions.

Workload Testing the System for Bottlenecks

Novell's Systems Research department has evaluated testing extensively and has concluded that it is virtually impossible to develop a test bed that duplicates a real-world workload. The best that can be done is to characterize a workload, create a similar set of conditions, then exaggerate characteristics in a system performance test. Novell developed a test suite for this type of testing.

The test bed Novell developed is called Ghardenstone. With it, Novell is able to simulate and manipulate near real-world conditions. Ghardenstone enables the tester to configure a test bed that simulates activity generated by a certain number of users using a particular software package. Running this test can assist in the ability to draw more specific conclusions (for example, determining how effective a certain type of disk drive is when several users are running Microsoft Word for Windows). Stating results from Ghardenstone also requires qualification. It is impossible to re-create the random operations generated by users thinking and working while performing software operations that vary in cycle, or delay between cycles, duration, and intensity. IBM has developed a similar test, which it calls Claire. Claire is used in IBM lab tests, and to benchmark client systems.

Tests that run with Ghardenstone simulate various numbers of users running given software applications. These tests reveal how various aspects of network performance are affected under specific conditions. For example, users can watch CPU utilization under a simulated workload of 100 versus 200 users running Microsoft Word for Windows during a mail merge. Watch for tests conducted with Ghardenstone, and expect that the number of users it simulates is just that—a simulation.

These tests are purely speculative and not meant to be interpreted literally. The point to be made by using Ghardenstone or any other system test is to get an idea of how light or heavy traffic may affect various performance statistics in a system. The number of users indicated in tests should be recognized for what they are: an approximation generated under unrealistic conditions.

Stress Testing the System

Several testing utilities can be used to stress a system beyond normal workloads. This may help determine whether a server, LAN, cabling system, disk subsystem, router, or any other part of the network can stand up to the highest traffic that may occur. If this type of testing is not done, you may find that a system, which apparently was working, fails during periods of heavy workload.

Bottlenecks restrict our ability to stress each component to its limit. One test may be limited to one bottleneck, and the same test may later encounter another bottleneck. You need to analyze network traffic at the same time as tests occur to be aware of each subsystem's utilization level during the test. You may decide to use a variety of tests in an effort to stress test various bottlenecks.

TESTNET is included with this book to enable you to attempt various types of tests that stress your system. Try running TESTNET under the following conditions to stress various components to the limit.

Stressing Cache Buffers and Disk Performance to the Limit

You can saturate your cache buffers by generating an unrealistic load of write requests. Run TESTNET and select

> Repeat testing cycles
> Minimum delay between cycles
> Large file size (4096 to 65535 bytes per record)
> All write requests
> Sequential file requests

By running TESTNET in a multistation mode from multiple workstations, the test fills up the cache buffers and continues to request physical writes to the disk. You can observe your dirty cache buffers reach a saturation point (75 percent of Total Cache Buffers). At this point, physical write requests become the bottleneck in your system. Cache buffer saturation can be observed at the file server's MONITOR and is indicated in Figure 31.1.

FIGURE 31.1.

Cache buffer saturation.

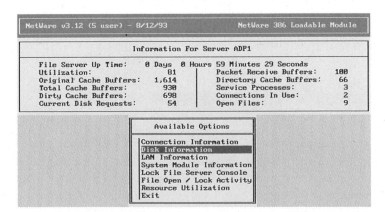

This test is run from a workstation. Therefore, you must consider that the workstation NIC, the LAN, the server NIC, the server's NCP mechanics, and the cache buffers stand between the workstation and the disk drive. The cache buffers stage the requests, however, so that the I/O between the workstations and the cache buffers are isolated from the cache buffers and the disk drive. If enough traffic is generated to saturate up the cache buffers, you can observe the raw sustainable disk transfer rate of a single disk drive.

If too few workstations are in the test, or one LAN or server NIC is saturated, then the disk may not receive requests fast enough to saturate the cache buffers. If enough workstations join the test and saturate the cache buffers, your test shows the actual physical transfer rate of your disk drive.

During this test, observe your server's CPU utilization. If at any time the CPU utilization reaches 99 percent, all subsystems are held below their true levels of capability. Momentary surges and spikes in CPU utilization may not be reported, because this statistic is polled rather than reported in real time. You can use STAT.NLM, provided on the disk that accompanies this book, to record CPU utilization over a period of time. Figure 31.2 shows the graphic results reported by STAT over the period of a test.

FIGURE 31.2.

STAT.NLM graphic time lapse reporting.

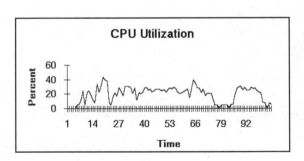

When interpreting STAT's results, observe overall averages and peaks. Average activity is usually pretty easy to spot when viewing a graph generated by STAT for a day's workload. Peaks can also be clearly seen. Network traffic is quite sporadic and bursty. Short periods of user I/O activity is spread out with infinite degrees of amplitude and frequency. You will see periodic high bursts, and frequent low bursts with various spacing between them.

Average CPU utilization level can be eyeballed or calculated. A quick look at a STAT graph, as shown in Figure 31.2, can give you an idea of what the median value would be. This estimate is good enough to indicate whether your system incurs frequent heavy activity or is lightly used. Printing may even out the flow somewhat, because print jobs tend to be long and slow. The only way to know what the load looks like is to view the graph over a full normal workday. It is best to compare very busy days and normal days to get a feel for what is normal and what can be expected. Average CPU utilization gives you a qualitative analysis of how hard your file server has to work.

Peak utilization is more concrete in its implications. When CPU utilization reaches 99 percent, no more processor time is available, and the system can handle no more I/O requests than it is currently supporting. This affects every I/O component, because they must rely on the CPU for service.

If CPU utilization ever reaches 99 percent, you should be concerned. You should evaluate the frequency and duration of such episodes. If spikes occur frequently, your server's CPU and devices do not have the capacity to handle normal workloads. If CPU utilization remains at 99 percent for more than a moment at a time, user delays are encountered. Traffic becomes backlogged, packets are lost, server busy packets are sent to workstations, and generally jams occur, which slows all work down. You should provide capacity to remain at low CPU utilization levels. Peaks hitting 99 percent should be momentary and infrequent.

> **NOTE** ▶
>
> STAT also can report disk activity over a period of time with NetWare 3.12 and 4.x versions. This option does not work with 3.11.

How to Conduct Your Own Tests

Testing software is available from several sources, or you can develop your own. Because testing is such an inexact science, you should select tests based on what it is you need to learn. Tests need to be manipulated to do the following:

- Explore component bottlenecks
- Test overall system performance
- Stress your system to unreal levels

Two testing software packages are available to help you. One is provided on the disk accompanying this book, the other is available from Novell through NetWire (see Chapter 49, "Using NetWire").

Testnet, by Scott Taylor

This package is a public-domain test utility that provides several testing options. It is simple to use, and tests can be configured to provide insights in all three testing categories. It consists of a single executable file, TESTNET.EXE. When executed, an opening screen provides clear selections for test configurations. (See Figure 31.3.) There are a few function key selections, all of which are displayed on the screen.

FIGURE 31.3.

Testnet opening screen.

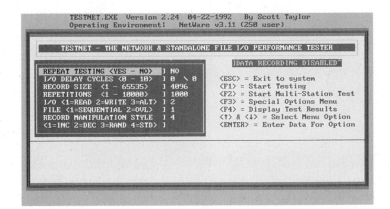

Various situations can be explored by configuring your tests from these selections. Each option is explored here.

REPEAT TESTING <YES - NO>: This option asks if you would like to run the test over again after it has completed one cycle.

I/O DELAY CYCLES <0 - 10>: This option asks how much delay there should be between repeated test cycles.

RECORD SIZE <1 - 65535>: Each record that is read or written will be this size.

REPETITIONS <1 - 10000>: This is how many times the record will be read or written.

I/O <1=READ 2=WRITE 3=ALT>: The records will be read, written, or alternate reads and writes.

FILE <1=SEQUENTIAL 2=OVL>: Each record will be written with sequentially changing records according to the next selection, or overlaid, which means the same record will be written over and over again.

RECORD MANIPULATION STYLE <1=INC 2=DEC 3=RAND 4=STD>:	If sequential is selected, the record will change incrementally (increasing), decrementally (decreasing), randomly incrementing and decrementing, or standard.
ESC =	Exit to system
F1 =	Start testing
F2 =	Start multistation test: If this selection is chosen, your station pauses and waits for other stations to join the test. Every station that joins the test locks together to start simultaneously. When all stations are paused in this mode, strike F1 to start the test with all nodes in unison. F4 will start the test and copy the selected parameters to the other workstations.
F3 =	Special Options menu
F4 =	Display test results

NOTE ▶

TESTNET.EXE can be located in your working directory or in a search drive. It will create a working file in the root of the volume in which your working directory is located. The test will explore throughput between the user workstation and this working file.

In order to lock multistations into a single test together, you should use the MAP ROOT command, be in the root directory of your mapped drive, and have rights to File scan, Create, Read, Write, and Erase files in that directory. Participating workstations share a multiuser working file located in the root of your working volume.

Perform3, by Novell

Perform3 runs timed tests for multiple workstations. Its default configuration alternately writes and reads records starting at a size of 32 bytes, and repeats the test over and over, incrementing the record size by 32 bytes each time. When the time expires, the test stops. You can adjust the starting record size, size increment, and time. Perform3 comes with a graphical reporting utility to display the performance results at the various record sizes. It also creates a data file that can be pulled into a spreadsheet or presentation graphics utility for graphing.

This test is good to gauge the capacity of the Ethernet LAN. It will also test the capacity of the server NIC. Because it is not configurable to perform write tests, it is not possible to use this test to saturate cache buffers and test disk transfer rate, as is the case with TESTNET.

Testing Server NICs

The most common type of test in industry periodicals is the comparison of server NICs. Testers have focused on maximum capacity under ideal conditions. Some testers have taken CPU utilization into consideration to assess the effectiveness of the busmastering characteristics of the NIC. In some cases, the testers even include statistics on performance at smaller packet sizes. Weighting each factor for a rating is another technique in guessing how important each of these factors is.

Perform3 is often used to test Ethernet and server NIC capacity. Many 16-bit and 32-bit Ethernet server NICs can accommodate full Ethernet bandwidth. By adjusting the record size and increment, you can compare performance characteristics of competitive server NICs at various record (and therefore packet) sizes.

Perform3 statistics give an accurate assessment of exactly how great the capacity of the LAN and the NIC are at each record size. This is because the test is timed, and all stations start together and end together. Testnet runs a selected number of repetitions for each workstation. Faster workstations finish before slower workstations, resulting in slower workstations finishing the test with less contending traffic. This skews the statistics to show the average throughput was greater than it should have been.

To fully saturate an Ethernet LAN takes between three and six nodes generating traffic at full workstation NIC capacity. Token Ring takes between 8 to 12 stations. Fully saturate your LAN, and compare throughput with other systems as advertised.

Testing Workstation NICs

Testnet and Perform3 work equally as well in assessing the performance of a workstation NIC. You should perform an alternating write and read test. You will find that the test results will be very close when the test parameters are set the same.

Run a single workstation test with a server and no other traffic. The workstation NIC will be the bottleneck in this pairing, and your performance statistic will show the actual throughput of the workstation NIC at various file read/write sizes.

Run Testnet with the following selections:

- Record size (five tests, one at each of the following record sizes: 128, 256, 512, 768, and 1024 bytes)
- Repetitions: 1,000
- I/O3, Alternate read/write

Run Perform3 with the following parameters:

- File sizes: 128, 256, 512, 768, and 1024 bytes

You will see how many bytes per second your workstation NIC can accommodate. You will find the performance of the NIC varies depending upon what type of computer it is installed in. For example, an eagle/Novell NE1000 NIC may put through about 185 Kbytes/sec in a 16MHz 386SX, and over 500 Kbytes/sec in a 33MHz 486. You can compare competing NICs by testing them in the same computer, but do not rely on statistics comparing NICs running in different workstations.

> **NOTE** ▶
>
> Do not interpret benchmark test results literally. Although a test such as this yields a precise number, you can expect actual throughput to vary substantially.

Testing LAN Capacities

Perform3 or Testnet can be run with alternating read and write tests. This is a crude approximation of normal network traffic. Alternating read/write tests mix reads and writes in a 50-percent ratio. In most NetWare software environments, this ratio is between 70 percent to 90 percent reads versus writes. Often, the ratio is higher.

Statistics from these tests therefore do not reflect an accurate match to production workload characteristics. Perform3 only runs an alternating (50 percent) read to write ratio. Testnet can run 100-percent reads, alternating reads versus writes, or 100-percent writes. Some NICs have characteristically better read or write performance.

Testing Disk Subsystems

Disk throughput is the most difficult subsystem to isolate. All interaction between user workstations and the disk subsystem is transported through NCP and the LAN. Several components lie between the user and the testfile. Each large file read or write request may be broken into packets (depending on the size). Each large file also may require an acknowledgment after a brief exchange of packets to establish file access and connection establishment. All this traffic, which must pass through both the server and workstation NICs, may encounter congestion in the LAN with other user activity, before passing through the file cache buffers. To say such a test isolates disk performance would be a gross misstatement.

However, it is possible to run a test of 100-percent write requests with large file sizes to backlog the cache buffers to saturation. This will reduce performance to a level the disk subsystem is capable of sustaining. Upon initiating the test, cache buffers will absorb the backlog of write requests. An elevated level of write performance will ensue until the number of Dirty Cache Buffers reaches 75 percent of the Total Cache Buffers. During the period the cache buffers are saturated, the transfer rate statistics reflect the sustainable transfer rate of the disk subsystem when operating under the constraints of the NCP mechanism.

You can produce these conditions by running the Testnet write sequential test with many repetitions. Start at 1,000 I/Os and a 4096-byte record size. Increase the number of repetitions and the file I/O size until the desired effect is reached. Do not pay attention to the test report once the test has ended. Instead notice the transfer rate during the period of cache buffer saturation. The desired results can be reached with one to six workstations in the test.

You can produce a condition with 50-percent read versus write activity using Perform3. To simulate similar conditions, you may need more than one server NIC with several uses connected to each one. In this case, the throughput will compete with other bus I/Os for access to the disk. This may reduce the throughput statistic. If you run the test with one disk subsystem, then run another test with another disk subsystem—and all other factors remain equal—you can compare the two disk subsystems.

Testing File Servers

Testing a file server requires more general testing to avoid isolating a bottleneck. A generalized test should alternate different types of tests that simulate production workloads. The tests can be exaggerated to test the server's ability to support heavy traffic.

You can simulate this type of test by using macros with normal software applications. Several workstations can execute word-processing, spreadsheet, database, and other applications. The macros can execute more commands than a user normally does. The tests will generate traffic consisting of the same type of activity, but at elevated levels.

Although Novell's Ghardenstone and IBM's Claire have been developed to simulate user activity, neither of these utilities is available to the general public. Ziff-Davis Labs and other testing labs have developed similar tests that can be used to stress systems in several areas.

Summary

Benchmark tests provide misleading results. Often, conclusions based on these tests are not valid. Benchmark tests need to be evaluated on the basis of which component or subsystem constitutes the bottleneck. Overall system tests need to be varied to stress and test multiple bottlenecks in a more random fashion.

Care should be taken not to interpret test results literally. Benchmarks only approximate and exaggerate production workloads and some are designed to isolate a component. Both are inaccurate, but can provide valuable comparisons for components and systems.

You should use benchmark tests in your component selection procedures. You should also stress your system to unrealistic levels to determine whether it can withstand heavy traffic. Benchmark testing can also reveal hidden defects and whether your system is operating properly. Using a protocol analyzer during a test reveals hidden inefficiencies and demonstrates the mechanics of each layer of protocol.

LAN Performance

32

by Rick Sant'Angelo

The way that you select, configure, and install your LANs can have a significant impact on performance. The type of LAN you select, how you install it, how many users are connected to it, and the server NIC are all very important considerations in networking. Monitoring and keeping traffic under maximum capacity is essential for keeping response times good. Outside of the server and the use of routers, LAN configuration is what determines performance.

LAN developers do not have control over how you implement your LAN, the quality of the cable plant, how your drivers are installed, or what other NICs and devices are in the bus of your server. You alone have the responsibility of assembling these components for optimal performance. Several factors, such as the type of LAN to be used and the number of users connected to each LAN, are decisions that the administrator must make.

This book focuses on Ethernet and Token Ring networks. These two types of LANs constitute the vast majority of LANs that are sold today; other technologies that are on the rise also are based on these same two dominant technologies. FDDI is a new generation of token-passing ring access protocol with a physical management layer added. Fast Ethernet and 100Base-VG are both based on Ethernet standards. The only other major player in the LAN game is Thomas-Conrad's TCNS (100 Mbps token-passing bus, based on ARCnet). There has been some discussion about NICs based on Asynchronous Transfer Mode (ATM), but standardized products are not yet on the market. Fast Ethernet and 100Base-VG have recently gone to committee for drafting of standards. Although we read much about these new technologies, about 95 percent of workstations today are connected by Ethernet or Token Ring.

New high-capacity LANs, similar to FDDI, are probably not going to see desktop connection for quite a while. Of the 100-Mbps products mentioned, most are being used as high-capacity backbone LANs. The high expense of NICs and the even higher expense of hubs reduces the feasibility of connected workstations with these costly products. In short, Ethernet and Token Ring are still the preferred choices for desktop connection and should remain that way for quite a while.

This chapter examines the various decisions you make that will affect performance for networked users. There are many techniques you can use to optimize performance of your network by properly implementing and configuring the products you buy. The most important of your decisions include

- What type of LAN to use
- How to determine whether your LANs have too much traffic
- How to best "segment" or divide users into separate LANs

■ What types of NICs work best in servers

■ What type of workstation NICs to use

LAN Comparison: Ethernet, Token Ring, and the Others

Many discussions have focused on whether Ethernet or Token Ring is "best." Many factors cloud the determination of which is truly the best. Often, decisions are made on the basis of loyalties. An IBM shop probably will integrate IBM Token Ring. A DEC, Sun, or HP shop probably will integrate Ethernet. Decisions are rarely made on the basis of sound performance statistics, because very few definitive comparisons have been made since 16-Mbps Token Ring entered the scene. To analyze the differences between types of LANs, a few simple facts about LANs need to be considered, and certain myths need to be exposed. Facts should replace foggy generalizations about LAN technologies.

Bandwidth Equals Capacity, Not Speed

One myth about LANs involves the concept of *bandwidth.* Quite often, you hear or read the term "wire speed" used interchangeably with the term "bandwidth." This has led many to believe that a higher-bandwidth LAN (for example, 100-Mbps) can deliver data faster than a lower-bandwidth LAN (for example, 10-Mbps Ethernet). This is not true, except when higher levels of capacity are reached. The term "wire speed" is a misnomer; it causes confusion, does not exist in any standards terminology, and should be eliminated from use when discussing LANs. Higher bandwidth translates to higher capacity, not higher speed.

Each type of cable conducts electricity at a different rate. For example, level-three twisted-pair, a voice-grade wire probably used more often for Ethernet than any other choice today, moves electrons at about 62 percent of the speed of light. Though thicknet Ethernet moves electrons faster, the difference is negligible. Because electrons travel on a wire at the same speed whether the LAN type supports a large or small capacity, when the LAN is lightly loaded there will be no difference at all in the amount of time it takes to deliver a LAN frame. For all practical purposes, bits arrive as soon as they are sent. Even if they did arrive a few nanoseconds sooner, the difference would not be noticeable to the most discriminating user. Bandwidth determines how many bits can be crammed into each second of time, not how fast the bits move.

So why, then, is everyone so enamored with FDDI and Fast Ethernet? As the bandwidth utilization of an Ethernet LAN reaches 60, 70, or 80 percent, the number of collisions reaches a high-enough level that further throughput is impossible. By increasing the bandwidth, more capacity is available so that performance will not degrade. Saturated bandwidth can affect Ethernet collisions and therefore latency (the delay in sending). Only when 10-Mbps Ethernet becomes saturated will moving to 100 Mbps improve performance by eliminating a bottleneck to sustained throughput.

A good example is the difference between Ethernet at 10 Mbps and Fast Ethernet at 100 Mbps. If a total of 500 kilobytes of data is transmitted and no other traffic is competing for use of the media, normal Ethernet should take about one-half second to deliver the data, whereas Fast Ethernet should take about one-half second. See the difference? There is none! Again, the electrons travel at the same rate. However, if 10 million bytes of data were to be sent on each, it would take 10-Mbps Ethernet about 10 to 12 seconds to deliver the data, whereas Fast Ethernet could do the job in under a second, *maybe*. Whether another bottlenecking factor, such as disk transfer rate or bus congestion, would restrict the flow of data is another matter.

Suppose a freeway near you is undergoing construction; there is one open lane and all the cars are forced into it. You are on the entrance ramp. At 5 a.m., you just drive right on, with little or no delay, and proceed to your destination at normal speed. At 5 p.m., there is a steady stream of cars going by, and you might have to wait a long time before you can get into the stream. At 5 a.m., an extra two lanes wouldn't matter at all; their expense would be wasted. However, at 5 p.m. when traffic is heavy, it would significantly speed your journey by reducing the wait time, or latency.

To anticipate that Fast Ethernet, FDDI, or other 100-Mbps LANs will make data move faster is not a reasonable assumption. For example, if you watch what is happening when Windows is loaded from a server, you will probably observe a period of 20 seconds to one minute while the disk reads the Windows files from the disk. Obviously, a larger-capacity LAN will not change this; disk transfer is the pacing factor. However, if 10 users load Windows at the same time, NetWare's caching provides reads from the cache buffers for many of the requests. Therefore, you probably will observe LAN congestion causing significant delay in loading Windows for many of the users. A higher-capacity LAN *may* reduce this delay, or it may simply shift the bottleneck to another point. Such is the game of networking: follow the bouncing bottleneck!

Your job as an integrator or system administrator is to provide enough bandwidth (capacity) to avoid latency resulting from LAN congestion. How can it be done? It's simple. When a LAN becomes congested, move some users to another LAN. Both LANs can be connected to the same server, but you can eliminate LAN congestion as a bottleneck. This will provide plenty of additional capacity, even with the same technology.

Two issues must be discussed when evaluating the performance of any LAN type: capacity and latency. Because these factors are affected by the access protocol, it is most practical to discuss these factors for each type of LAN separately.

Ethernet Capacity, Protocol Overhead, Collisions, and Latency

Specifically with Ethernet, the capacity includes overhead for carrying and delivering frames. A 10-Mbps Ethernet LAN, however, does not give you 10 Mbps of capacity; you get to use only from 7 Mbps to 9 Mbps. Of course, the difference is great between these two numbers, but they certainly do not translate to use of the full bandwidth. There are three factors that can potentially limit the effective capacity available to you: protocol overhead, latency, and, in the case of Ethernet, collisions.

Protocol Overhead

A 10-Mbps LAN can accommodate up to 10 million bits per second, including protocol overhead. The stated bandwidth includes all bits to be transmitted. That means that included in the 10 Mbps is the frame header information that each LAN frame starts with and the free space that must be left between frames.

Before a frame can be sent, there must be a sufficient amount of free space on the wire. This translates to a loss of 96 bits worth of time that the medium must be free. The frame header also reduces the amount of bandwidth available for sending data. After the frame header, an IPX packet header follows, and then an NCP packet. Table 32.1 shows the overhead for a single 802.3 or Ethernet II data transaction that is capable of transmitting 1,024 bytes of data to and from a NetWare server.

Table 32.1. Ethernet/IPX/NCP/Acknowledgment overhead per packet.

Field	Bits
Transmission	
free space	96
preamble/start delimiter	64
802.3 or Ethernet II frame header	176
IPX packet header	240
NCP packet header	128
acknowledgment	
free space	96
preamble/start delimiter	64
802.3 frame header	176
IPX packet header	240
NCP packet header	128
Totals	
total overhead per NCP packet	1408
overhead per packet (1408/(1024x8))	0.08192 percent

As you can see, the overhead to transport each packet of data is virtually insignificant, because it consumes just over 8/100 of one percent of bandwidth per packet delivered; Token Ring's access protocol overhead is insignificantly greater. If you were to transfer a large file, this would be the overhead it would take to move the file from one end to another, considering that each packet (1024 bytes times 8 bits/byte) would require one send-packet with data and headers, and one acknowledgment-packet with headers and without data.

Collisions

A large portion of Ethernet bandwidth cannot be fully utilized because of collisions. A typical 10BASE-T cable plant yields only about 70 to 85 percent net bandwidth utilization due to collisions. The likelihood of collisions increases with longer cabling segments. Benchmark tests normally use very short cables, perfectly configured (just as one would expect in a computer lab). In real-world settings, normal cabling can be quite long, and can have kinks, bends, worn connections, and quite often a few cabling violations. It also is not uncommon for the wrong type of cabling to be used, for thin-net terminators to be ungrounded, or for both terminators to be grounded at two ends of the same cabling segment.

The bottom line on this issue is that of the total theoretical capacity of 10 Mbps. Benchmark tests show as much as 92 percent bandwidth utilization, whereas you will probably only experience 70 to 85 percent under normal conditions. You can therefore expect to put through only about 800 or 900 Kbps over your LAN when running a full-capacity test. This is a substantial difference from the benchmarks of 1,000 to 1,100 Kbps obtained in most lab tests.

Latency

A common misconception is that full capacity is available under normal conditions. This is not true. The average packet size has a lot to do with how much data gets transmitted on any LAN, because of the overhead incurred in transporting each frame and in gaining access to the medium. No matter what type of access protocol is being used, some scheme must guarantee that no more than one frame will be transmitted at any given time. Latency is the delay experienced in waiting for a turn to transmit. The nature of latency varies according to what type of LAN is used and how busy the LAN is.

A busy LAN, no matter how good the access protocol, will incur latency when high bandwidth is utilized. The two major types of LANs (and access protocols) both experience latency as usage grows.

Ethernet latency, however, can become infinitely long depending on the number of nodes connected. Because it is a contention access protocol, access to the medium is on a first-come, first-served basis. In most tests, when more than six nodes run at full capacity of their NICs, full capacity is reached. All the nodes that join the contention for medium access after that point simply increase latency by increasing contention for the medium. Each node's delay is determined randomly.

Performance Variables for the Ethernet Protocol

The Ethernet access protocol is a contention protocol, which means that nodes contend for access when traffic becomes jammed. When bandwidth utilization is less than 30 percent, access is virtually immediate. This is the most impressive part of Ethernet performance. As bandwidth utilization increases, the likelihood of collisions increases until a level is reached where bandwidth is saturated, but only 60 to 90 percent of the bandwidth can accommodate data, while the remaining bandwidth is saturated with collisions and false collisions. How high this level can be depends on the quality of the cable plant and the combined length of the cabling segments. Other problems, such as a defective NIC, also can degrade performance.

Quality of Cabling Plant

Defects in your cabling plant increase the likelihood of lost or bad frames and false collisions. A kink in a cable or a frayed connection can cause reflections—impulses bouncing back when they pass down the wire (as shown in Figure 32.1). These impulses can be detected falsely as collisions by transceivers. During the first 240 bits of frame transmission, they listen for any bits on the cable. A reflected bit can cause the transceiver to shut down transmission, which would falsely sense a collision.

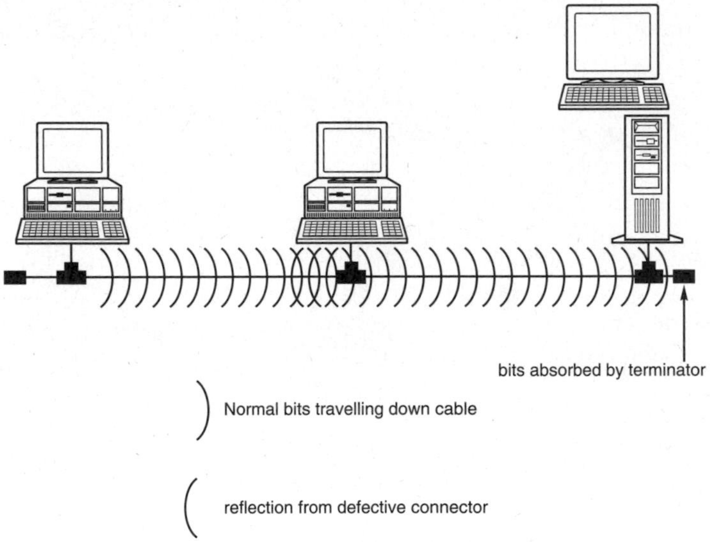

FIGURE 32.1.

A reflection resulting in a false collision.

bits absorbed by terminator

) Normal bits travelling down cable

(reflection from defective connector

Combined Length of Cable, Number of Segments, and Repeaters in Series

As stated previously, as cable length increases, the probability of collisions increases. Conversely, a very short cabling system reduces the likelihood of collisions. However, when cabling exceeds specifications, collisions can go undetected. If it takes longer for bits from one end of the cabling to reach nodes located at the other end of the cabling system, the first 240 bits of transmission can go by without a collision being detected, and both frames are lost.

This condition can be detected by the presence of frames that are too short and have bad cyclic redundancy checks (CRCs), resulting in the frames being rejected. Though the access protocol detects the bad CRC, no provision is made for resending the frame or reporting the condition. You must have monitoring software to do that.

Ethernet has cabling rules that limit the number of cabling segments and repeaters that are configured in series. Figure 32.2 illustrates the rules for limiting serial segments. You can have no more than five cabling segments in series (four repeaters), of which only three can be populated (that is, can contain more than two repeaters—one at each end). Two cabling segments can be used for distance only, or in the case of a 10BASE-T cabling system where wiring concentrators are used, each cabling segment contains only two connections and is therefore unpopulated.

Because LANs keep expanding, you have to be constantly vigilant in ensuring that these cabling rules are observed. It is common to add nodes and not be aware of any cabling violations. When cascading wiring concentrators, for example, adding one more level can affect performance for the entire LAN.

The nodes that are most often affected by these problems are located at the furthest ends of the cabling plant. To prevent these conditions from degrading the performance of a file server, it is recommended that servers be centrally located, not at the furthest ends of the cabling plant. Chapter 22, "Monitoring LANs," discusses various software that can be used to detect the presence of these and other conditions that degrade performance on your Ethernet LAN.

FIGURE 32.2.

Limiting cabling segments in series.

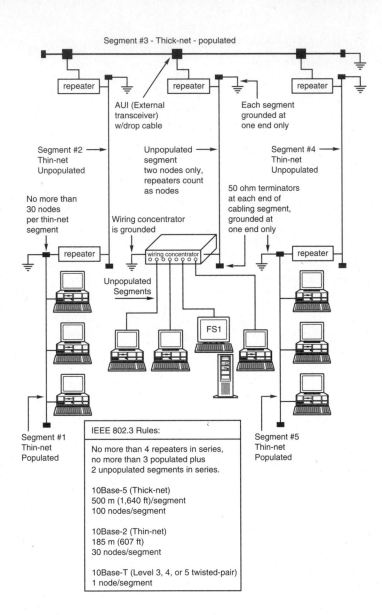

Segment #3 - Thick-net - populated

AUI (External transceiver) w/drop cable

Each segment grounded at one end only

Segment #2 → Thin-net Unpopulated

Unpopulated → segment two nodes only, repeaters count as nodes

Segment #4 → Thin-net Unpopulated

No more than 30 nodes per thin-net segment

50 ohm terminators at each end of cabling segment, grounded at one end only

Wiring concentrator is grounded

Unpopulated Segments

FS1

Segment #1 Thin-net Populated

Segment #5 Thin-net Populated

IEEE 802.3 Rules:

No more than 4 repeaters in series, no more than 3 populated plus 2 unpopulated segments in series.

10Base-5 (Thick-net)
500 m (1,640 ft)/segment
100 nodes/segment

10Base-2 (Thin-net)
185 m (607 ft)
30 nodes/segment

10Base-T (Level 3, 4, or 5 twisted-pair)
1 node/segment

Defective NICs

Defective NICs can send random signals when they are not transmitting frames. This is a condition known as a *chatty node*. These signals are detected as frames by other transceivers, causing them to falsely sense collisions and shut down transmissions. If these signals happen to occur later in the transmission of a frame, they result in data errors, and therefore bad CRCs.

This condition has been reduced with the improving quality of NIC design, but it is especially common among older NICs. Chatty nodes are not detected under normal conditions; they simply result in reduced performance at higher bandwidth utilization.

Performance Variables for the Token-Ring Environment

Token-passing ring access protocol has completely different problems than those of Ethernet, but the problems translate into more dependable service at higher levels of LAN utilization. 16-Mbps Token Ring has only 60 percent greater theoretical bandwidth; however, it can achieve over 97 percent utilization without the same problems that Ethernet experiences at high levels of utilization.

Token-passing ring access protocol is deterministic, meaning that each node is granted exclusive use of the ring as determined by receipt of the token. The token is passed by a well-determined procedure. Even when bandwidth reaches a very high level, there are no collisions. Because there is so much error detection built into the access protocol, cabling problems are far less likely to cause problems for the entire ring. Token Ring does, however, have one deficiency that may show up when bandwidth utilization reaches high levels: latency.

Token Rotation Time and Latency

The amount of time a token can take to rotate around the ring is limited. When the token is received, the node has a time allocation for sending data. The node can send as many frames as will fit into the allocated time slot, which gets smaller as more nodes enter the ring. Most benchmark tests show that performance increases as more nodes enter the test. At about 12 nodes running at full capacity, the ring maxes out. From that point on, more nodes get increasingly shorter time allocations, but the total ring performance stays level.

After the ring's peak level of throughput is reached and more nodes attempt to send data, they must each wait for a free token, which takes longer, and their time allocation is shorter; but they always get at least enough of a turn to send one frame.

Though this condition permits more data to be transmitted from all nodes, each node suffers increased latency in access to the ring, and more turns are required in order to send larger packets of data. This condition is very much affected by the design of the NIC. IBM has developed a technique it calls "pipelining," which reduces latency by eliminating buffers on the NIC. The frame is moved from the wire directly to the driver without the additional steps of being copied to a buffer and then from the buffer to the driver. This technique is employed in the LANstreamer MC 32 and is highly recommended for use in file servers, routers, and bridges where latency can affect many other user requests.

Two other factors reduce the latency factor with 16-Mbps Token Ring: priority reservations and large frame size.

Token priority reservations enable nodes to set priority levels higher on a token. If a node, such as a server, has a higher priority, it can bump the reservation bits that are on a higher token. Tokens can have three levels of priority reservations set; this enables higher-priority nodes to capture the token before lower priority nodes can. This benefits servers, which pace other nodes, because many nodes access just one (or only a few) servers.

4-Mbps Token Ring can accommodate no more than about a 4,100-byte packet in its frame. 16-Mbps Token Ring can accommodate over 17,100 bytes in each frame. This higher rate translates into less turns being required and more efficiency when a turn at sending is granted. Because the vast majority of packets are small, and a few packets are large, this results in better efficiency. The time allocation for a larger packet is extended, and each smaller transmission still gets a regular turn.

NETWARE 4 NOTE ▶

NetWare 2.x and 3.x versions limit the maximum packet size to 4096 bytes, but NetWare 4.x versions enable the larger 17,100 byte packet size.

Advantages of Token Ring

16-Mbps Token Ring is able to accommodate about 1,950 bytes per second of data on a NetWare 3.11-based network. Many benchmark tests have proven this. Furthermore, latency at each node is less random, and servers can access the priority reservation scheme, which enables greater throughput than a contention-based access protocol such as Ethernet's CSMA/CD. Even though 16-Mbps Token Ring has only 60 percent greater bandwidth than 10-Mbps Ethernet, almost twice the throughput can be expected, because the token-ring protocol is not limited by collisions.

Token Ring is not dependent on cabling conditions for its performance, as is the case with CSMA/CD. As an Ethernet cabling system grows, the likelihood of collisions increase, and total usable capacity decreases. As a Token Ring grows, more wire length and more nodes (which act as repeaters) cause the ring to accommodate more bits, and therefore it grows in capacity. It is also a far more dependable medium because all the error detection and control is built in.

Using Multiple NICs in a Server

Regardless of which type of LAN you choose, when you reach a level of bandwidth utilization on a LAN that makes you nervous, it is time to either increase bandwidth or segment your LAN into multiple LANs. You can add another NIC to your server and divide users among two LANs, thereby reducing traffic on each LAN and eliminating potential bottlenecks resulting from excessive bandwidth utilization. This is why you may never outgrow Ethernet or Token Ring as desktop connections. You can connect several LANs to a single server. However, if you do have several LANs connected to a single server, you may have shifted your bottleneck to the server's bus.

Bus Bottleneck Resulting from High CPU Utilization

Adding a second NIC to your server may simply shift the bottleneck to the bus. If you use 16-bit NICs, you may find that high levels of activity on the two NICs causes CPU utilization to reach 99 percent, thereby restricting further throughput. This is why 32-bit, bus-mastering NICs are recommended for servers. A bus-mastering NIC has its own processor, which relieves the CPU of some of the I/O processing, thereby reducing CPU utilization and alleviating a bus bottleneck. EISA and MCA servers with 32-bit, bus-mastering devices can accommodate far more I/O than 16-bit and nonbus mastering devices.

Quality of Bus-Mastering NICs

Not all EISA and MCA devices are 32-bit, and not all are bus-mastering. You may find an EISA or MCA NIC that only uses a 16-bit interface, several that are 32-bit but do not use bus mastering, and some that are less effective at reducing CPU utilization than others. A single 16-bit NIC may perform as well as a 32-bit, bus-mastering NIC, but it can use much more CPU power to move data.

The quality of the bus-mastering engineering makes a big difference if you are going to add more than two NICs into a server. With sufficient bus mastering, you can add up to four NICs to a server, and full capacity on all four LANs will not saturate the CPU. Your EISA or MCA bus can accommodate far more capacity than several NICs can give it, but CPU utilization can limit how well the bus can accommodate multiple devices.

As discussed in Chapter 4, "File Server and LAN Interfaces," the following three aspects of EISA and MCA bus mastering determine how good the NIC design is:

- Burst mode
- Streaming data mode
- Bus arbitration cycle

Bus-mastering NICs that use the burst mode and streaming data mode of EISA and MCA can move up to eight times as many bytes per address byte. The length of the cycle to access the bus can affect whether the NIC will perform better with smaller packets or larger packets. Together these factors can cause NICs to perform better when multiple NICs are in a single bus. You will find significant difference between brands of bus-mastering NICs.

You should evaluate bus-mastering NICs based on the following three factors:

- Total capacity
- CPU utilization
- Small packet size throughput

Total Capacity

Most of the published benchmark testing focuses on the total capacity of a single-server NIC with several workstations running NetWare. It is fairly simple to conclude that one card performed better than the others on the basis of total capacity. However, this does not necessarily mean that the NIC will perform better than others in your environment. You rarely will experience total bandwidth saturation, and when you do, you rarely will notice the problem, because its duration is so short.

CPU Utilization

Some benchmark tests now take the server's CPU utilization into consideration. To test this factor, CPU utilization (running under NetWare) reaches varying levels of capacity when one, two, three, and four NICs are in the server's bus, each one loaded to capacity. This is a good test of the bus mastering in each NIC. The best NICs enable you to have up to four NICs in one server, each loaded to full capacity, and still operate under 90-percent CPU utilization.

Small Packet-Size Throughput

In a true production environment, such as your office, the vast majority of packet sizes are under 256 bytes. You will see a far different performance comparison of NICs when they are tested with smaller file sizes. When tests are run with a 256-byte (or smaller) file size, you will observe different throughput and CPU utilization than you will see at 1024- or 4096-byte file sizes.

You should pay close attention to statistics in tests conducted at smaller test-file sizes, because this probably most accurately reflects the composition of traffic on your LAN. At this time, however, readers and testers seem to be more enamored with total capacity figures, even though they are less relevant than small file size tests.

> **NOTE** ▶
>
> Don't forget that 32-bit, bus-mastering disk adapters are important in reducing CPU utilization. Each bus device affects all others when it is subject to heavy loads, and uses a great deal of the processor's power.
>
> This is especially important when consolidating a number of smaller servers into a few, more powerful servers. As organizations gain experience with PC networks, there is a tendency to centralize, or at least consolidate, their servers.

Monitoring Network Utilization and Segmenting LANs

In order to determine whether your LANs are bottlenecked, you need to monitor LAN activity.

You will find that LAN activity is bursty. During busy work hours, LAN traffic includes both light and heavy packet flows from individual workstations. There are moments of heavy activity randomly overlapping, causing very short bursts of extremely high demand, sustained moderate demand, and long periods of virtually no activity at all.

During moments of high bandwidth utilization, user response is delayed for all users. These periodic delays may be frequent or infrequent. If they are infrequent, you may decide that the cost of eliminating these spikes is not justified.

To determine the typical sustained levels and whether high bandwidth levels are being reached requires monitoring devices and software. Simple solutions, such as a cabling tester or monitoring software to be used with a managed hub, can determine bandwidth utilization. A more sophisticated tool, such as protocol analyzer, also can be used. What is important is to track LAN bandwidth during heavy usage and to watch carefully for the spikes that occur because of the randomly overlapping surges in usage and data flow. (More specific detail about monitoring Ethernet and Token Ring LANs is provided in Chapter 22.)

Utilization and Performance Levels of Workstation NICs

Workstation NICs have very different utilization and performance profiles. Even the same NIC when used in a server performs differently than when used in a workstation. Selecting workstation NICs involves decisions based on performance, support, warranty, and price.

NIC Performance

Because Ethernet and Token Ring NICs mainly use controller chips made by just a few companies, performance is similar with different vendor products and may vary more among a vendor's models than between brands. Many NICs put through 220,000 to 375,000 Kbps. Prices have recently dropped so much on Ethernet NICs, you may decide that some of the very best NICs cost so little that you can afford them. Look for a good performing NIC, using the TESTNET utility or Novell's PERFORM3 (available on NetWire) to test NICs yourself.

The bus interface is not extremely important, because a single NIC limits throughput to less than the available capacity of an ISA bus. You probably will not find much difference between 8-bit and 16-bit NIC models under normal usage. However, when a workstation hosts a remote printer, a print server, or performs multitasking operations with OS/2 or UNIX, the 16-bit interface is important. A 16-bit NIC has dual-ported buffers, which provide better two-way throughput with less conflict. A bus-mastering, 32-bit NIC probably will not justify the cost differential.

Support

This should be an important factor in your selection. Some vendors provide support through the dealer that sold the NIC. Some provide direct support, and others provide extra support in the form of toll-free 800 phone lines, 24-hour support, CompuServe forums, and bulletin boards for downloading new drivers.

No matter who you purchase a NIC from, their support for that NIC will not be as good as the NIC developer can provide. So why talk to the middleman? You can get the best price through mail order, but you will still get the best support if the developer offers direct support.

Installing 100 workstations may require extensive support. If you can get good response and can download new drivers if available, it can make your job much easier. If technical support is not available when you need it, your job becomes more difficult. Later on, troubleshooting and upgrading (which can de done at night) will be easier if you can just call a toll-free line any time of the day or night.

Warranty

Many NIC vendors provide a lifetime warranty on their NICs. Others give from two- to five-year warranties. The warranty should be considered part of the cost, but more importantly it indicates the expected life of the NIC. You should avoid troubleshooting and replacing NICs over the years.

Price

Price can be an important factor in choosing workstation NICs, because you may be buying dozens or even hundreds of NICs. However, price should not rank as the most important factor; all the preceding factors are more important. For example, when you factor the price differential against the cost of replacing NICs that go bad after a few years, you might be better off paying a little more for NICs with a better warranty.

In recent years, Ethernet and Token Ring NICs have dropped tremendously in price. For example, some of the very best 16-bit Ethernet NICs in the business now retail for $129, and you can buy them for less than that if you search for a mail-order vendor. Mail-order houses have become the most popular source for obtaining the best price. Mass merchandisers or computer "superstores" often do not carry LAN products, but the ones that do are usually competitive with mail-order pricing. Corporate distributors are a good option, as they usually have competent support staffs to provide assistance in presale as well as after-sale support. They also can offer trial evaluations, so you can try before you buy.

Vendor Reliability

Probably the most important factor to consider in purchasing a NIC is vendor reliability. The brand of NIC and the vendor from whom you purchase the NIC can affect the weighted value of the other factors discussed in this chapter. Make sure you are well-informed about the factors discussed in this chapter, so you can get the most performance, with the least effort, at the best price.

Summary

The following tips briefly summarize the suggestions for optimizing LAN performance discussed in this chapter:

- Remember that increased bandwidth does not translate to faster speeds. A 100-Mbps LAN provides increased capacity, not speed. Existing LAN types (Ethernet and Token Ring) provide perfectly acceptable throughput for a limited number of users per server NIC.

- Monitor LAN bandwidth utilization. When you reach more than 30 percent of capacity on a regular basis with Ethernet, or 50 percent of capacity on a regular basis with Token Ring, you should segment your LANs, adding more NICs to your server with fewer users connected to each one. Alternatively, you can move to a higher bandwidth (100 Mbps) type of LAN, such as Fast Ethernet, 100Base-VG, FDDI, or TCNS.

- Token Ring has approximately twice the usable bandwidth of Ethernet and provides more stability and more predictable response under heavy loads.

- Under heavy loads, latency (delay) becomes a considerable factor. Six users can fully saturate Ethernet, but it takes 12 users before Token Ring's total bandwidth can be exploited. As the ring grows, so does capacity, until this level is reached. Either LAN type provides sufficient capacity under normal conditions if you segment users into separate LANs connected to multiple-server NICs.

- When using multiple NICs in a server, good bus-mastering NICs are necessary to avoid reaching 99-percent CPU utilization. Good implementation of bus mastering exploits EISA's and MCA's burst mode and streaming data modes in addition to using 32-bit bus bandwidth. Server NICs vary tremendously in bus-mastering design.

■ Small packet sizes constitute the vast majority of LAN traffic. Do not judge NICs solely on the basis of highest performance benchmarks. These are always stated using the maximum packet size for that type of LAN (Ethernet = 1024 or 1500 bytes and Token Ring = 4096 bytes in a NetWare 3.11 environment and over 17,100 bytes in a 3.12/4.x environment). For Ethernet, do not expect to see the same levels of performance on your cable plant that you see in test results. Depending upon whether you use multiple NICs in a server, judge NICs on the basis of the following:

> Small packet size performance
>
> CPU utilization under full load
>
> Full load highest capacity

■ To find the best value in purchasing NICs, judge them on the basis of the following:

> Performance
>
> Support
>
> Warranty
>
> Price

A network is a multivendor solution. No one company can do all things for you. Only you are resident with your LANs, watching their performance day in and day out. See Part IV of this book for further discussion of what tools are available and what to look for in LAN monitoring.

Monitoring and Adjusting Server Performance

by Rick Sant'Angelo

33

A system administrator should monitor the performance of each file server. Integrators should also know where to look for bottlenecks and performance opportunities. There are some excellent Novell and third-party utilities to assist with this task, although built-in NetWare utilities are sufficient to provide some of this information.

Good products to buy, products that help find bottlenecks and monitor server performance, include Novell's NetWare Services Manager, LANalyzer for Windows, and third-party packages such as Bindview NCS, Intel LANDesk, and Frye Utilities for NetWare. These products are discussed in greater detail in Chapter 20, "Third-Party System Administration Utilities," and Chapter 24, "Third-Party LAN-Monitoring and Management Products."

This chapter discusses how to monitor your server, and how to adjust and tune its operating system when circumstances require it.

Auto-Tuning and Server *SET* Parameters

As discussed in Chapter 3, "Advanced NetWare Operating System Features," NetWare 3.x and 4.x versions dynamically adjust as many OS parameters as necessary so your server runs at peak efficiency—allocating the optimal level of resources at any given time. A resource-management agent in the OS monitors resource usage, allocates more resources when necessary, and de-allocates resources when they are not needed. This enables configuration levels to drop, freeing resources for other needs when not in use. Novell calls this *auto-tuning*.

Many parameters are set to maximum levels, min/max, and fixed levels that provide the best performance under a wide variety of typical circumstances. Very few circumstances occur that would require you to manually adjust the OS parameters. There are, however, some parameters that need to be adjusted to accommodate your configuration. For example, if you are using Token Ring, you need to adjust the size of the packet-receive buffers to accommodate the larger packet size of Token Ring. The default configuration parameter is set for Ethernet.

You can adjust these levels with SET parameters. SET parameters are typed at the server's console prompt (:). They can be automated by placing them in the STARTUP.NCF or the AUTOEXEC.NCF files.

> **NETWARE 4 NOTE** ▶
>
> NetWare 4.x's SERVMAN.NLM provides a simple interface for adjusting SET parameters. Each parameter is described, and fields are provided in a

database input screen format for adjusting them. Upon exiting, this utility makes the required changes to the appropriate start-up files.

Monitoring the Server OS

Your server's MONITOR.NLM is provided to keep an eye on the server's OS and its operation. This module shows many important statistics on its main screen and has a menu where you can select several options to view other statistics. Therefore, you should load the Monitor upon booting and leave it running at all times. This section of the chapter discusses which statistics you should observe and what those statistics can tell you. (The Monitor also has a screen saver that blanks the screen when it isn't used for a while.)

Evaluating CPU Utilization

CPU utilization is a very important parameter that should be monitored on a regular basis. This statistic is shown as "Utilization" on the Monitor main screen, as shown in Figure 33.1. CPU utilization, sometimes called *processor utilization*, indicates the percentage of time the server's processor is busy.

FIGURE 33.1.

The NetWare 3.11 MONITOR.NLM.

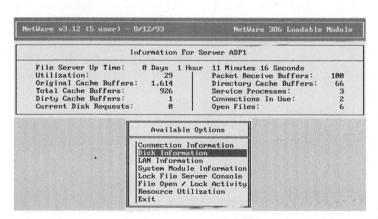

This number rarely exceeds 25 to 50 percent. As discussed in several previous chapters, if CPU utilization reaches 99 percent, the CPU is maxed out and cannot facilitate greater levels of performance. The server does not crash, but the sum total of all processes running on the server is limited to this level.

When this level is reached, you would naturally assume that you need to upgrade your CPU to push performance levels higher. This is not true, however. A faster CPU only marginally increases performance, and you will soon be up to 99-percent utilization again. You need to find out what is driving CPU utilization to this level so you can determine what to do about it.

Identifying the Offending Process

To evaluate what is using so much processor time, unload MONITOR.NLM and reload it with the P switch as follows:

```
LOAD MONITOR P
```

> **NETWARE 4 NOTE** ▷
>
> NetWare 4.x's MONITOR.NLM loads with the Processor Utilization option by default; the P switch need not be used.

If your screen freezes, be patient. When CPU utilization is high, this process is assigned a low priority, and you may not see the next screen for several minutes.

This procedure loads the Monitor with another menu selection, "Processor Utilization." Select this menu item from the main menu, and press F3 to see all the processes and interrupts in use on your server; or you can select the processes you want to view. Select such processes by using your F5 key to mark the processes to observe and then pressing Enter. An example is shown in Figure 33.2.

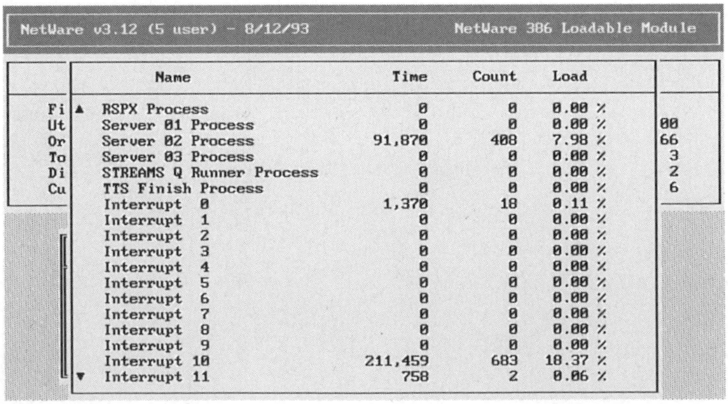

FIGURE 33.2.

*Processor
Utilization screen.*

NetWare v3.12 (5 user) - 8/12/93			NetWare 386 Loadable Module	
Name	**Time**	**Count**	**Load**	
▲ RSPX Process	0	0	0.00 %	
Server 01 Process	0	0	0.00 %	00
Server 02 Process	91,870	408	7.98 %	66
Server 03 Process	0	0	0.00 %	3
STREAMS Q Runner Process	0	0	0.00 %	2
TTS Finish Process	0	0	0.00 %	6
Interrupt 0	1,370	18	0.11 %	
Interrupt 1	0	0	0.00 %	
Interrupt 2	0	0	0.00 %	
Interrupt 3	0	0	0.00 %	
Interrupt 4	0	0	0.00 %	
Interrupt 5	0	0	0.00 %	
Interrupt 6	0	0	0.00 %	
Interrupt 7	0	0	0.00 %	
Interrupt 8	0	0	0.00 %	
Interrupt 9	0	0	0.00 %	
Interrupt 10	211,459	683	18.37 %	
▼ Interrupt 11	758	2	0.06 %	

You can watch all the processes running on your server and find which ones are taking up valuable CPU time. One process—the *polling process*—identifies the polling mechanism that this software is using. Ignore this process; it is only high when CPU utilization is low and is not active unless you access this screen.

Look at each process and notice the "load" statistic. This statistic shows the percentage of current processor utilization that this particular resource is utilizing. Each process is in use by an NLM—either a disk driver, NIC driver, or other NLM loaded on your server. When you locate which NLM is driving your CPU utilization so high, you can take steps to alleviate the source of your problem, and free up processor time to service I/O requests.

> **CAUTION** ▶
>
> On 3.11 versions, do not leave the Monitor loaded with this option turned on. Sporadic incidents may arise in which the polling process runs out of control, driving CPU utilization up, and not relinquishing processor time. This problem has been corrected on 3.12 and 4.0 versions, so the option is a default option without loading the P switch.

You can identify which NLM or driver is controlling this resource by exiting this screen and selecting "Resource Utilization" from the Monitor main menu; then select the resource in question. A list of "resource tags" that are controlling that process are displayed, as shown in Figure 33.3. Resource tags represent threads (processes) running on the server OS.

FIGURE 33.3.

Resource Utilization Listing and Tracked Resources.

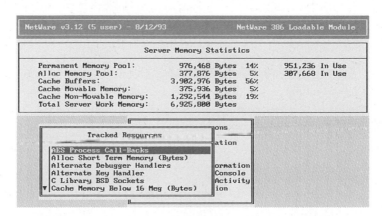

You can identify NIC drivers and disk drivers by the interrupts being used. If an NIC is on interrupt 3, check interrupt 3 for the percentage of the current level of CPU utilization being uscd by that NIC. This should be done when CPU utilization is high, close to 100 percent. You will isolate which drivers and/or NLMs restrict I/O from reaching higher levels.

Identifying Brief Bursts of High CPU Utilization

You do not need to watch your server for extended periods, hoping to see short bursts of high CPU utilization. Instead, you can load STAT.NLM on your server to monitor and graph CPU utilization over a period of time. STAT.NLM is available from Novell on NetWire and is provided on the disk that accompanies this book with Novell's permission.

Alleviating High CPU Utilization

High CPU utilization is most commonly caused by the following:

- 16-bit and non-bus mastering NICs
- 16-bit and non-bus mastering disk adapters
- Database server NLMs, such as Oracle or SQL Server
- Communications NLMs such as

    SAA Services
    NetWare for NFS
    NetWare for Macintosh
    NACS (incoming/outgoing modem lines)
    Multi Protocol Router (MPR)

- Other third-party NLMs loaded on your server

Once you identify what is driving up this statistic, you can replace those devices with 32-bit bus-mastering devices, replace the driver with a newer revision, or off-load the NLM to another server platform. Novell provides a runtime OS for NLMs that are known to be processor-intensive, such as Oracle, SAA Services, and MPR.

You do not have to go about this blindly, but the following list is an order of solutions for the most common problems:

1. **Replace 16-bit non-bus mastering NICs and disk adapters.**

    If you have 16-bit NICs that are quite active, one can drive CPU utilization to over 75 percent, and two can max out the CPU even before each NIC is saturated. This indicates a bottleneck in your bus. The interrupt controller requires CPU attention to control data flows through the bus and therefore cannot service any more I/O requests than the processor can attend to. Check out the interrupts and watch how your NICs affect the interrupt's load. Disk adapters work the same way. You can replace ISA and non-bus mastering EISA or MCA NICs or disk adapters to reduce CPU utilization.

2. **Move database server NLMs, such as Btrieve or Oracle, to another server platform.**

   Large, server-based applications can tie up your CPU to the detriment of all user requests. Other types of servers can be established that will provide a platform for such services on a server other than a file server. Some NLMs, such as NetWare for NFS and NetWare for Macintosh, need to be loaded on the file server that contains the volumes to be shared; but others, such as Oracle and SQL Server, have NetWare Runtime OS modules that can be used to establish a database server, or communications server, separate from the file server.

   Use this option only when necessary. Normally a 486DX EISA computer with 32-bit bus-mastering adapters, NetWare NFS, and NetWare for Macintosh can handle all normal activity without excessively high levels of CPU utilization.

3. **Off-load communications server NLMs to separate servers.**

   You can move communications servers to their own server platforms. MPR, SAA Services, and NACS are shipped with runtime server OSs that lack file services. Though communications services may not tie up the largest portion of CPU time, off-loading them can reduce CPU utilization, freeing up CPU time for other processes.

Evaluating Cache Buffers and the Amount of RAM Required

NetWare uses write-after cache to enhance disk-write performance. Physical write requests are held in the cache buffers and given a lower priority than physical read requests. This is because the user must wait for response from read requests that are not already in the cache buffers; but when data is written, it is immediately available for read access—regardless of whether it was physically written to the disk. If physical write requests are postponed, there is no penalty in user response. When cache buffers are updated, but not yet written to the disk, they are called *dirty cache buffers*.

However, when cache buffers become saturated, physical write requests must be written to free up cache buffers for more read requests. During the period when dirty cache buffers are allowed to accumulate, read and write requests can be handled at rates exceeding the actual physical transfer rate of the disk channel. When cache buffers become saturated, read and write rates drop to the actual sustainable physical transfer rate of your disk subsystem. Figure 33.4 shows a typical performance curve for heavy write activity that is sustained for long periods.

FIGURE 33.4.

Performance curve showing cache buffer backlog.

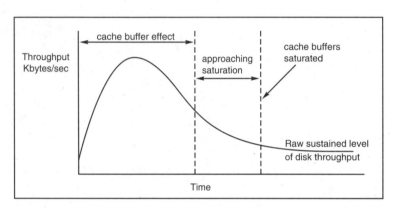

As you can see, as physical write requests are issued, immediate response is high. When more physical write requests are issued than the disk can handle, dirty cache buffers become backlogged; however, physical response does not suffer. As dirty cache buffers approach a critical level, write performance declines. When dirty cache buffers are fully saturated, disk-write performance levels out at the disk subsystem's actual sustainable transfer rate.

When you have more available cache buffers, your server can absorb more backlogged physical write requests and extend this temporary performance period further. You can determine whether you need more RAM in your server based upon whether you reach saturation level of cache buffers.

To evaluate whether cache buffers are saturated, compare the number of Dirty Cache Buffers to the number of Total Cache Buffers. When the ratio reaches 75 percent, cache buffers are saturated. To experience this condition, use TESTNET—supplied on the disk that accompanies this book. Run TESTNET with the following options:

Repeat Testing Cycles:	Yes
Repetitions:	1000
Record size	4096 (or larger)
File:	Write
I/O:	Sequential

This will cause a test to run for an infinite duration, writing a 4096 byte file 1,000 times per test cycle. Each file write will be different (sequential); each file write will fill a cache buffer and result in a dirty cache buffer. The cycle will repeat after 1,000 I/Os (Repeat Testing Cycles=Yes). As the test runs, watch your server Monitor and pay close attention to the Dirty Cache Buffers. As they reach 75 percent of Total Cache Buffers, you should watch the Testnet screen at a workstation, where you will observe a reduced level of performance. When the test cycle finishes and pauses momentarily, backlogged cache buffers will drop below saturation. When another test cycle begins, workstation performance will accelerate to a high level, again dropping as cache buffer saturation is reached. Figure 33.5 shows the Monitor screen showing cache buffer saturation.

FIGURE 33.5.

Monitor showing cache buffer saturation.

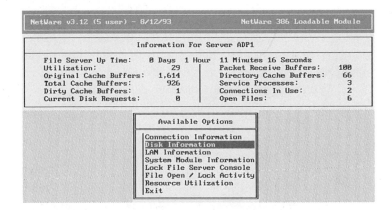

Under some conditions, cache buffers become saturated no matter how much RAM is in your server. When an extended period of sustained physical write activity continues, it is only a matter of time before saturation is reached. An example of a process that can saturate cache buffers is a large database file reorganization. In such a procedure, each record in a file is read, and a new record is written. Ultimately these write requests will be written to the disk. This type of process generally occurs much faster than the disk channel can handle, so cache buffers become backlogged further and further until they are saturated.

A software application that typically uses such a procedure is accounting software. During monthly closing procedures, entire files may be rewritten in this manner. Many database applications and record managers, such as Btrieve and dBase (Foxbase, Clipper, and so on) require this type of activity to remove deleted records from files. Files dynamically grow as records are added, but they do not shrink when records are deleted. To *pack* records, a file reorganization procedure must be executed that writes all the records to a new file, expanding as records are written. This heavy alternating read-write activity goes faster than the fastest disk subsystem and may be sustained for hours in large files. Under these circumstances, no amount of RAM can absorb the backlog, and sheer disk transfer rate is the pacing factor.

Packet-Receive Buffers

Packet-receive buffers are RAM buffers allocated to stage IPX packets after the LAN driver has stripped off the frame. They are processed according to their destination socket addresses, which are similar to an apartment number. An address identifies the type of request and where the packet should be sent. Server socket addresses are allocated for NCP, printing, routing, and other types of requests. Packets are processed on a first-in, first-out basis.

Under simple conditions, the number of packet-receive buffers is adjusted to minimum and maximum values that are sufficient, except in the case of Token Ring. The size of the buffers is set to Ethernet defaults, so they need to be adjusted for Token Ring. Adding more does not improve performance unless the maximum value is insufficient for your circumstances.

Token Ring Packet Size for Version 3.11

When any Token Ring server NIC is installed, the server's packet-receive buffer size must be adjusted. The default is 1514 bytes for the size of the packet, including NCP and IPX (or TCP/UDP and IP) packet headers. In NetWare 3.11 versions, Token Ring uses a 4096-byte packet size (plus packet headers). Even though a 16-Mbps Token Ring can have over a 17,100 byte packet size, NetWare 3.11's maximum packet-receive buffer size is 4202.

If you have a Token Ring server NIC in your server, you must place the following SET command in your STARTUP.NCF file:

```
SET MAXIMUM PHYSICAL RECEIVE PACKET SIZE = 4202
```

Failure to do so will result in packet-receive errors at the server console and errors at the workstation shells. When smaller packets are sent, everything is okay, but when larger packets are sent, they may not be able to be processed.

Token Ring Packet Size for Versions 3.12 and 4.x

NetWare 3.12 and 4.x versions support the large packet size of just over 17,100 bytes for a 16 Mbps Token Ring. Packet-receive buffer size needs to be set to its maximum size on 4.x servers, as the default packet-receive buffer size is 4202 for these versions. Like 3.11, this parameter can be expanded by placing the following command into the STARTUP.NCF:

```
SET MAXIMUM PHYSICAL RECEIVE PACKET SIZE = 17408
```

Alternatively, the 4.0 server's SERVMAN.NLM is used to adjust SET parameters with a more user-friendly interface. Figure 33.6 shows Servman's main menu. You can select "Console Set Commands" from the main menu, and you will see the settings for packet-receive buffers as well as other communications parameters as shown in Figure 33.7. Select the first field, "Maximum Physical Receive Buffer Size" and adjust it to 17408. This utility will write the changes to the STARTUP.NCF file for you.

FIGURE 33.6.

SERVMAN.NLM main menu.

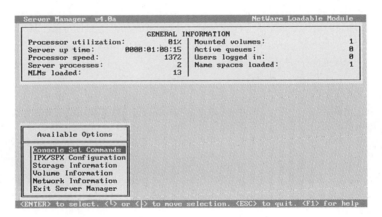

Certain conditions cause the number of packet-receive buffers to be insufficient. When the maximum number of buffers are in use, additional incoming IPX packets are discarded, causing NCP at the source to re-send packets. Of course, the result is poor performance. The problem is compounded by the extra frames that are transmitted on the LAN, which can easily cause a bottleneck in the LAN.

Ethernet is very efficient at turning buffers over, but the default number of buffers can be insufficient in large, busy Token Ring LANs. The more users that join the ring cause latency to increase, and therefore can backup into the server's receive buffer. WAN interface cards installed in the server may also cause back up in receive buffers.

FIGURE 33.7.

Servman Communications Set Commands screen.

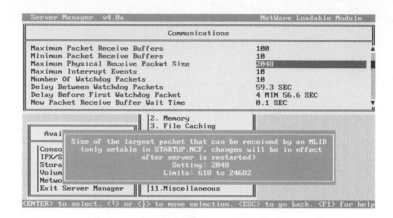

As delay on the WAN increases, receive buffers can get backed up due to delayed acknowledgments.

Normal conditions that require more than the maximum default value of 100 buffers are rare, but may affect you. You should watch the number of packet-receive buffers on the server Monitor. When the default maximum value of 100 is reached, packets are rejected, and need to be re-sent from the workstation. See Figure 33.8 for the statistic on packet-receive buffers.

FIGURE 33.8.

Packet-receive buffer statistic on Monitor.

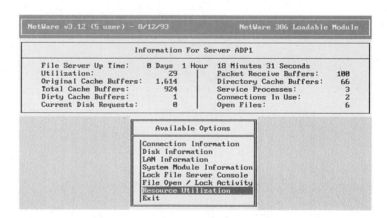

Another condition that can cause packet-receive buffers to rise to maximum values is a defective NIC driver. NIC drivers request additional packet-receive buffers and are supposed to relinquish them when no longer needed. However, drivers have been known to retain the additional packet-receive buffers and not reuse them. This causes the level of buffers in use to continually rise, until the maximum is reached, no matter how high it is. If you observe this problem, check with your NIC developer for updated drivers.

Service Processes

These are miscellaneous processes that are used by NLMs. Standard server NLMs including NetWare Streams, Pserver, the server OS itself, and Monitor commonly require one or two of these processes. However, other NLMs may use many more of them.

When combining powerful NLMs on a server, you may find that the default value of 20 may prove insufficient. For example, NetWare NFS can use as many as 15, and NetWare for Macintosh also can use about 15. Either package by itself does not require adjustment, but when combining them, you must push the maximum level to 40, which is the highest level allowed. You will find this parameter listed under the "Miscellaneous" category of parameters.

Monitoring Your Disk Drive and Driver

Your disk drive may not be performing to full capacity. You should check your Monitor and select "Disk Information" to view a list of physical disk drives that can be recognized. Select the disk drive that you wish to view information about. You will see the "Drive Status" screen as shown in Figure 33.9. This will indicate whether NetWare's Hot Fix read-after-write feature is using a software-level or hardware-level verify, or if verify has been disabled.

FIGURE 33.9.

Disk Status screen.

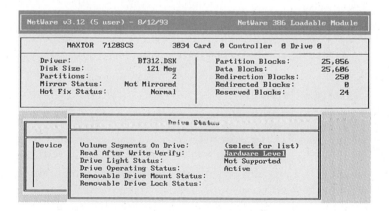

Most disk drivers communicate with the disk controller, which does a read-after-write verify. This is the appropriate state for your verification to be set. If this screen indicates that this parameter is set to a software level verify, then your driver does not direct your disk controller to communicate with NetWare and is doing a software read-after-write verify on top of the hardware verify. This can cause disk write performance to be reduced due to the extra software read after write.

From this screen, set your driver to hardware level. Many IDE drive controllers do not communicate with NetWare, so verify cannot be set to hardware level. You will find that most disk drivers automatically do this, but if your driver does not, you have no alternative except to switch it to a hardware level verify in this screen.

If you have a RAID subassembly or any other type of hardware fault-tolerant disk subsystem, you should disable read after write verify if the driver has not disabled it. You can obtain much better disk write performance when this feature is disabled. If you have enough confidence in your disk subsystem, you may consider disabling this feature, especially if your disks are mirrored.

Monitoring Your LAN Interfaces

This option can tell you much about how well your server NIC and driver are performing. Many types of problems can be detected by monitoring the statistics that are shown in this section.

To monitor NICs and their drivers, select "LAN Information" from your Monitor main menu (in 4.0 this selection says "LAN/WAN Information"). You will see a list of loaded NIC drivers. Select the NIC you want to check.

The screen you will see will be similar to the screen shown in Figure 33.10. It shows three types of information, general information about the driver, generic statistics, and custom statistics.

General Information

The top of the box showing the driver indicates what the driver name is, what physical settings are configured, and which frame type is being used by the NIC and driver. Next this screen shows the node address of the server NIC, and what protocols are bound to the NIC driver. If IPX protocol is not bound to the driver, this NIC driver will not be able to communicate with the subnetwork, or other IPX nodes.

FIGURE 33.10.

Monitor "LAN Information" screen.

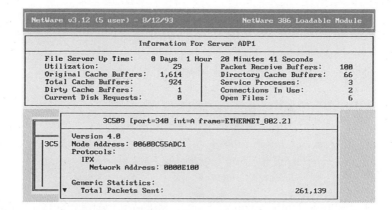

```
NetWare v3.12 (5 user) - 8/12/93                    NetWare 386 Loadable Module

                          Information For Server ADP1

   File Server Up Time:    0 Days  1 Hour  20 Minutes 41 Seconds
   Utilization:                  29     Packet Receive Buffers:    100
   Original Cache Buffers:    1,614     Directory Cache Buffers:    66
   Total Cache Buffers:         924     Service Processes:           3
   Dirty Cache Buffers:           1     Connections In Use:          2
   Current Disk Requests:         0     Open Files:                  6


              3C509 [port=340 int=A frame=ETHERNET_802.2]

         Version 4.0
   3C5   Node Address: 00608C55ADC1
         Protocols:
            IPX
               Network Address: 0000E100

         Generic Statistics:
 ▼         Total Packets Sent:                            261,139
```

> **NOTE** ▶
>
> If a workstation cannot connect with the server, check the frame type here, and at the workstation to be certain that both are using the same frame type.

Generic Statistics

These statistics are general to all drivers of similar-type LAN. The first two statistics indicate IPX packets being received from the NIC driver and sent to the NIC driver. If workstations cannot communicate with the server, you will see little or no activity on the receive field. Under normal circumstances, these values should be about the same, since every NCP packet sends an acknowledgment. They are not exactly the same because other packet types (RIP and SAP) do not require acknowledgments.

Other fields in this screen roughly indicated error conditions that you may be able to diagnose. Statistics, such as "Receive Packet Too Big Count," are self-evident if you understand information about Ethernet discussed in Chapter 2 and all of Part IV of this book.

Custom Statistics

These statistics are unique to each NIC driver. Vendors define these statistics in writing their drivers. Therefore, detailed information about these drivers are available from your NIC developer. Most NIC manuals contain descriptions of what these statistics indicate. Some developers provide a README file for this purpose.

Adjusting Protocol Defaults in 4.x

NETWARE 4 NOTE ▶

This section applies to 4.0 and 4.01 versions only. However, similar control can be effected by installing SAFILTER on 3.x versions.

NetWare 4.x allows you to adjust some of the parameters for IPX, SPX, RIP, and SAP protocols. Adjustments are made in the SERVMAN.NLM utility which can be loaded on your server OS. Context-sensitive help is pretty straightforward and simple in these screens. Before changing how these protocols work, you should be sure you understand what you are changing. Do not change for the sake of change alone; you may cause communications problems that you are not equipped to resolve. The help screens indicate the default values in case you find yourself with this problem. Press F1 to see help for each selection.

CAUTION ▶

Care should be taken when adjusting protocol parameters and when filtering protocols. Adjusting these parameters may result in loss of connection between various types of servers, and lost routes in router tracking tables. This may result in loss of ability to connect to servers, rendering their data and resources inaccessible. When adjusting protocols on one server, all other servers must be adjusted correspondingly.

To adjust parameters, load SERVMAN from your 4.x server console, and select "IPX/ SPX Configuration." You may adjust the following protocol options:

IPX Parameters

The total number of IPX sockets in the connection table can be adjusted. Unless you are running many NLMs on your server concurrently and have hundreds of users, this parameter should never need to be adjusted. IPX sockets are logical addresses and do not consume any RAM in your server, so reducing them will not save memory or optimize resources in any way.

SPX Parameters

SPX is rarely used. It is the transport protocol that provides connection-oriented acknowledgment and error-checking control. It is not used unless an application specifically makes a call to it to use it. The only NetWare utilities that use it are the print server utility (PSERVER), the remote printer (RPRINTER.EXE), and the remote console (RCONSOLE.EXE). If you experience SPX errors at a DOS or OS/2-based print server or remote printer workstation, adjust the number of SPX connections at the workstation.

> **NOTE** ▶
>
> Workstations used as print servers need to have SPX connections set to 60. Edit your NET.CFG (or SHELL.CFG) file to configure your shell for this settings.

RIP Parameters

Router Information Protocol (RIP) controls exchange of information between routers about network address information. RIP packets are issued in 30-second intervals. By default, a RIP packet is broadcasted to all other routers in two interval increments (every 60 seconds).

The only downside to RIP packets is when a large number of servers are internetworked, and WANs are involved. The bandwidth occupied by RIP packets may be of modest concern.

If you would like to reduce RIP traffic on a WAN, you can adjust the frequency of Periodic Broadcasts upward, so that they will be sent less frequently. If you adjust the frequency upward, also adjust the Aging Out Interval upward, and include at least two more intervals than you configured for the Periodic Broadcasts. When no RIP packets have been received for the number of intervals specified in the Aging Out Interval field, the network address information will be deleted from the router table. An Aging Out Interval of Periodic Broadcasts plus two, ensures that an occasional lost RIP packet will not cause the router to lose track of network addresses. If servers or routers lose network address information (check the server's router tracking screen), check your media for reliability. You may have a faulty WAN or LAN that loses data regularly.

When using WANs whose bandwidth utilization is maxed out, you can suppress all RIP traffic except for packets with changed information by changing the RIP Changed Information only field to YES. Any changes made to one server need to be made to all servers and routers that are internetworked together. When suppressing RIP information, you need to make certain that your media is reliable. If a RIP packet is lost after you have set this option to YES, other routers will not be informed of the changed network address information.

SAP Parameters

Service Advertising Protocol (SAP) packets are sent frequently (every two intervals, or 60 seconds by default) to inform other file servers about the existence and location of various types of servers. Each server broadcasts SAP packets announcing its location and type of service. This selection controls how this file server sends and receives SAP packets. These parameters work the very same way as RIP parameters discussed above.

If "Get nearest server reply" is set to OFF, this file server will not respond to workstations when they execute their workstation shell or requester. This option should not be turned off unless you specifically do not want users to connect by default to this server. If the option is set to OFF, a specific attach request will need to be issued.

TIP ▶

If you have problems with user workstations connecting to the wrong server upon execution of the workstation shell or requester, use the PREFERRED SERVER = *server_name* statement in the NET.CFG file.

This is a common problem when bridges are used instead of routers, and can be easily resolved.

SAP Filtering

A file server creates an object in the object list when a SAP packet is received. This makes the server available to users. If the server becomes aged out due to adjustment of the SAP parameters, or if the server broadcasts are suppressed, then resources that are contained in a container object controlled by that server will not be available.

This option is used to deny use of various types of servers to users connected to this file server or to isolate a server so it will not advertise its services. The option can be used to restrict SAP packets sent or SAP packets received. SAP packets from other servers can be denied on the basis of the "Service List" that can be accessed by pressing Enter when your cursor is in the Service List field.

> **CAUTION** ▶
>
> When restrictions are made to the SAP parameters or SAP packets are filtered, access to devices that are physically connected to the server will not be available.

Summary

You should monitor your server on a frequent basis to ensure that everything is running okay. Several factors indicate problems still in the development stage, other factors can be viewed to troubleshoot your server OS. The following tips can help you find where to look for opportunities to improve server performance:

1. NetWare auto-tunes itself for best performance under widely varying conditions. It is difficult to change anything that will improve performance or maximize usage of resources. Generally, the way to improve NetWare server performance is to improve or upgrade server hardware. A few SET parameters can be adjusted to improve performance and to resolve problems under specific conditions relating to use of NLMs and LAN/WAN circumstances. An administrator should frequently monitor the server to make certain that critical OS parameters are not reached.

2. Keep an eye on CPU utilization. Since the nature of network traffic is bursty, reaching peak utilization at moments, and remaining at very low levels for extended periods, run STAT.NLM, provided by Novell and included on the disk that accompanies this book to find these momentary peaks.

3. If you reach 99 percent CPU utilization on a regular basis, explore which modules of server devices are driving CPU utilization so high. To identify what is using so much power, use the "Processor Utilization" selection on your server Monitor (requires loading Monitor with the P switch for 3.11).

4. Be sure to adjust the maximum physical packet-receive buffer size for Token Ring.

5. Monitor key server parameters under heavy server load conditions. You may find resources that need to be altered changing server SET parameters.

6. NetWare 4.x has a new SERVMAN.NLM utility with menu-driven options to adjust the way IPX, SPX, RIP, and SAP protocols work. These protocols should not be adjusted unless you have a clear understanding of what they do, and how the changes can affect your internetwork. Adjusting RIP and SAP traffic can have a minor affect on bandwidth utilization of WANs when capacity is reached. NetWare 3.11 can be configured to filter SAP packets when the SAFILTER set of NLMs is installed (available from Novell). SAP filtering can be configured to remove various types of servers from use for some users. Both incoming and outgoing SAP packets can be filtered for a very flexible way of denying use of devices to users.

Workstation Performance

by Rick Sant'Angelo

34

Workstations are the most critical element of user performance. Even though you may have a powerful server and a high-capacity LAN, a faster workstation always pays higher dividends in performance. This holds true even when a bottleneck is encountered—including situations in which a LAN runs at a high level of bandwidth utilization, CPU utilization reaches 99 percent, or cache buffers are saturated. A faster workstation simply grabs a larger share of available resources and utilizes them more efficiently.

Many bottlenecks are affected by the speed of a workstation. With a faster workstation, NICs work faster, file access with a server's file system is quicker, and NCP's request-response mechanism works faster. Each component is related to others in a manner in which no single component strictly paces all the others. Performance of one affects the performance of others.

For example, a 50MHz 486 workstation may load Windows about twice as fast as a 25MHz 386. A faster server yields the same results. In this scenario, bottlenecks are all related so integrally that speed of both the server and workstation is a concern.

Even though bottlenecks restrict performance, a fast workstation is going to outperform other workstations when competing for limited resources. This is especially true in an Ethernet environment. A faster workstation attempts to send frames more frequently, and with better success. It is virtually impossible to isolate any bottleneck and say that performance is limited to a particular level. Differences in workstations, NICs, cabling, and servers obscure methods of determining exactly where bottlenecks are and where expenditures aimed at resolving them are best spent. But it's pretty hard to hide the improvement in performance a faster workstation provides.

Servers and network components are generally purchased to provide a greater level of performance than required. User workstations outnumber servers by about a 20 to 1 ratio, so any additional workstation expense has a large effect. This may not be as great a concern today, when the cost to performance ratio is so much lower than a few years ago.

This chapter discusses what you can do at the workstation to assist you in pushing performance to its highest levels. There is much you can do to optimize each workstation, no matter how limited or great the peak capacity of each workstation.

Workstation Hardware Considerations

Workstation prices have fallen so low that money hardly matters any more when it comes to workstation cost. Faster workstations make workers more productive, so management is open to upgrades.

Inside any machine, you'll find that one key component affects how well or poorly every other component works. A faster processor drives every other component faster. You might say it globally affects all other components and software applications.

A component such as a disk drive may not significantly affect some applications while dramatically affecting others. It may have little or much effect on performance under varying usage and software conditions. In most cases, however, a faster disk drive can never hurt. Today, almost all disk drives are fast and inexpensive. IDE drives are perfectly suited for workstation operations. If large volumes of local disk reads and writes are part of your software routines, you may consider a faster SCSI subsystem. Normally the expense of a faster disk subsystem is borne at the server end, so faster workstation disk drives are generally not required.

The amount of RAM required at a workstation is entirely dependent upon software requirements. You may find some applications, like Windows, work quite a bit slower when insufficient RAM is installed. In other cases, additional RAM may make no difference at all. Other workstation internal components, like video cards, affect some applications and do not affect others.

In short, the processor speed affects almost everything, and everything else depends upon the software being used. In order to determine what is required in a workstation, you need to evaluate what the software requirements are.

DOS Character-Based Applications

Older applications ran at acceptable speeds on computers that were available at the time. In many cases, older character-based applications, like Lotus 1-2-3, for the most part, ran no differently on an XT than on a 486 today. In some instances, operations like a recalculation took a little longer.

If you are using character-based applications, they are probably not workstation-intensive. This may not be true in all cases, but character-based applications generally do not require much power. For these applications, 386SX-based computers are perfectly acceptable.

Graphics, Windows, Desktop Publishing, Imaging, and CAD/CAM

This type of application is highly processor-, RAM-, disk-, and video-processing intensive. This type of application requires all the workstation you can throw at it. You need to observe workstation response and worker productivity to determine how much you should spend on upgrading hardware.

Databases and Accounting Software

These applications are generally very disk- and LAN-intensive. Accounting software is a database application, with many small program, data, and index files. In most cases, neither of these applications require much processor power for adequate performance. Of course, more processor power generally drives the applications faster.

In some instances, processor power does not greatly impact the speed of the applications. Many new database and accounting applications are Windows-based. Others have extensive screen handling. Some of the modules may need to process data and therefore require more resources than others.

Managing DOS Memory

It is important to optimize use of memory, especially conventional memory. MS-DOS 5.0 added the use of memory managers as a standard part of DOS. Memory managers are used to configure upper-memory ranges as EMS and XMS memory for application access. They also can configure upper-memory ranges as *upper-memory blocks* that TSRs can be loaded into.

Two factors can cause network administrators grief. Network drivers and shells/requesters need to be loaded TSR in memory. Also, NIC RAM buffer addresses need to be physically configured to addresses within the upper-memory range. Because the drivers/shells add overhead to the conventional memory range unless loaded into upper-memory blocks, and because the NIC RAM buffer complicates configuring and loading into these ranges, the system administrator becomes involved in managing workstation memory.

Basics of Memory Mapping

Raw memory installed in computers today is divided into two ranges: conventional and extended. Because the PC was developed around the 8086/8088 memory map, only 640K of conventional memory was available, and the top 384K of memory addresses (called the upper-memory ranges in this book) were reserved for system use. When the 80286 came along, developers added more memory—starting the 1M boundary—and called it raw extended memory. The upper-memory ranges can be configured as upper-memory blocks so you can load TSRs into them. Figure 34.1 shows the conventional and extended memory ranges of a PC.

FIGURE 34.1.
Conventional,
upper memory
range, and raw
extended memory.

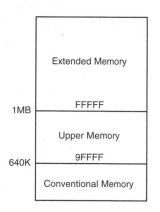

Getting-Started Tips to Get the Most Conventional Memory Out of MS-DOS 5.0

MS-DOS 5.0 added memory managers as a default option within DOS. Before that, users needed to purchase a separate memory manager to do this. Other memory managers are more efficient than MS-DOS 5.0's memory management capabilities, and are able to configure more of the upper-memory ranges into upper-memory blocks.

Loading the XMS and EMS Memory Managers

In order to configure these ranges as upper-memory blocks, you must add two standard memory managers to your CONFIG.SYS—HIMEM.SYS and EMM386.EXE. A simple standard statement looks like this:

```
Device=HIMEM.SYS
Device=EMM386.EXE
```

To disable EMS page frame, add the switch NOEMS to your EMM386.EXE statement. This will free up 64K worth of upper-memory blocks.

> **NOTE** ▶
>
> If you are not using applications that require EMS memory (expanded memory) be sure to use the NOEMS switch in your EMM386 statement (or equivalent).

HIMEM.SYS configures your raw extended memory as XMS memory so it can be used by the memory manager and other software that uses XMS memory.

Loading DOS High

To move the DOS kernel into the first range above 1M during load, you need to add the following line after your Device=HIMEM.SYS statement:

```
DOS=high, umb
```

The UMB switch allows TSRs loaded into upper-memory blocks to communicate with their conventional memory segments. The range DOS loads into is called the High Memory Area.

Here is the CONFIG.SYS after making these changes:

```
Device=C:\DOS\HIMEM.SYS
DOS=HIGH,umb
Device=C:\DOS\EMM386.EXE NOEMS
```

Loading TSRs into Upper-Memory Blocks

To load a TSR into upper-memory blocks, use the DOS LOADHI statement or its shortened form LH. The following AUTOEXEC.BAT shows loading TSRs high:

```
@ECHO OFF
PROMPT $p$g
PATH C:\DOS;C:\UTIL;
SET TEMP=C:\TEMP
cd \NWCLIENT
lh LSL
lh SMC8000
lh IPXODI
lh NETX
```

In this example, there was not a sufficient amount of contiguous upper-memory blocks to enable NETX.EXE to load high.

Checking Memory Status Before and After Making Changes

Use the MS-DOS utility MEM with the /C switch to see the status of your memory configuration. To stop the screen scrolling, add the switch ¦MORE. Type the following statement:

```
MEM /C¦MORE
```

Listing 34.1 shows two MEM reports, one with the unconfigured memory status (with no CONFIG.SYS) and the same computer with these statements added. This workstation has loaded the IPX ODI drivers with and without the benefit of these configurations.

Listing 34.1. MEM reports with and without suggested additions.

Before:

```
Conventional Memory :

    Name              Size in Decimal        Size in Hex
- - - - - - - - -     - - - - - - - - - - -   - - - - - - -
    MSDOS             57184     ( 55.8K)      DF60
    COMMAND            4704     (  4.6K)      1260
    LSL                4992     (  4.9K)      1380
    SMC8000           11136     ( 10.9K)      2B80
    IPXODI            16304     ( 15.9K)      3FB0
    NETX              48624     ( 47.5K)      BDF0
    FREE                 64     (  0.1K)        40
    FREE                 96     (  0.1K)        60
    FREE             512016     (500.0K)     7D010

Total   FREE :       512176     (500.2K)


Total bytes available to programs :               512176
                                                  (500.2K)
Largest executable program size :                 511888
                                                  (499.9K)


    4456448 bytes total contiguous extended memory
    4456448 bytes available contiguous extended memory
```

After:

```
Conventional Memory :

    Name              Size in Decimal        Size in Hex
- - - - - - - - -     - - - - - - - - - - -   - - - - - - -
    MSDOS             12864     ( 12.6K)      3240
    HIMEM              1072     (  1.0K)       430
    EMM386             3232     (  3.2K)       CA0
    COMMAND            2624     (  2.6K)       A40
    NETX              48624     ( 47.5K)      BDF0
    FREE                 64     (  0.1K)        40
    FREE             586656     (572.9K)     8F3A0

Total   FREE :       586720     (573.0K)
```

continues

Listing 34.1. continued

```
Upper Memory :

    Name              Size in Decimal        Size in Hex
- - - - - - - - -     - - - - - - - - - - - - - -     - - - - - - - - - - -
    SYSTEM          171600    (167.6K)     29E50
    LSL               4992    (  4.9K)     1380
    SMC8000          11136    ( 10.9K)     2B80
    IPXODI           16304    ( 15.9K)     3FB0
    FREE                96    (  0.1K)       60
    FREE              8480    (  8.3K)     2120
    FREE             49408    ( 48.3K)     C100

Total  FREE :        57984    ( 56.6K)

Total bytes available to programs (Conventional+Upper) :     644704
                                                            (629.6K)
Largest executable program size :                            586528
                                                            (572.8K)
Largest available upper memory block :                       49408
                                                            (48.3K)


    4456448 bytes total contiguous extended memory
          0 bytes available contiguous extended memory
    4190208 bytes available XMS memory
            MS-DOS resident in High Memory Area
```

Using the Latest VLM DOS Requester

You may use the latest VLM DOS requester instead of NETX. It will load itself into high memory as efficiently as possible. VLM is backward-compatible with all versions of NetWare and can be obtained from Novell. (Call 800 UPDATE1, obtain from NetWire, from a 3.12 or 4.0 CD-ROM, or in Novell DOS 7.0.) Listing 34.2 shows the MEM report after substituting VLM for NETX. VLM loaded most of its code high, freeing another 32.7K of conventional memory where NETX could not. The total available RAM to execute applications is increased to 605.7K after logged into the network, and there is also over 26K more room available to load other TSRs.

Listing 34.2. The MEM report after substituting VLM for NETX.

```
Conventional Memory :

    Name                Size in Decimal      Size in Hex
    -----------         --------------------    -----------
    MSDOS               14704   ( 14.4K)        3970
    HIMEM                1072   (  1.0K)         430
    EMM386               3232   (  3.2K)         CA0
    COMMAND              2624   (  2.6K)         A40
    VLM                 13200   ( 12.9K)        3390
    FREE                   64   (  0.1K)         40
    FREE                  112   (  0.1K)         70
    FREE               620096   (605.6K)        97640

Total  FREE :          620272   (605.7K)

Upper Memory :

    Name                Size in Decimal      Size in Hex
    -----------         --------------------    -----------
    SYSTEM             171600   (167.6K)        29E50
    VLM                 30768   ( 30.0K)        7830
    LSL                  4992   (  4.9K)        1380
    SMC8000             11136   ( 10.9K)        2B80
    IPXODI              16304   ( 15.9K)        3FB0
    FREE                 8592   (  8.4K)        2190
    FREE                18624   ( 18.2K)        48C0

Total  FREE :           27216   ( 26.6K)

Total bytes available to programs (Conventional+Upper) :    647488
                                                           (632.3K)
Largest executable program size :                          619952
                                                           (605.4K)
Largest available upper memory block :                      18624
                                                           (18.2K)


    4456448 bytes total contiguous extended memory
          0 bytes available contiguous extended memory
    4149248 bytes available XMS memory
            MS-DOS resident in High Memory Area
```

TIP ▶

Install the VLM DOS Requester and updated files with the INSTALL utility provided on disk with the VLM Requester. It will make all the necessary changes to your CONFIG.SYS, AUTOEXEC.BAT, and NET.CFG files.

CAUTION ▶

When executing the VLM Requester, do not use the LOADHI or LH statements. It finds available configurations and loads itself as efficiently as possible.

If you do execute VLM.EXE with the LOADHI or LH you will occasionally have problems communicating with your server.

You must update your other driver components to work with VLM. You must include LASTDRIVE=Z to your CONFIG.SYS, and other changes need to be made to your startup batch file and NET.CFG to accommodate VLM.EXE.

With these few changes and the VLM DOS Requester, it is simple to configure your system with a large amount of conventional memory. Your results may vary from the preceding ones, but manual adjustment of your computer using these techniques can make a huge difference.

How to Upgrade to MS-DOS 6.x and Optimize Memory

MS-DOS 6 can configure a little more of the upper-memory range as upper-memory blocks. It also has a memory optimizing utility, MEMMAKER.EXE, that automatically checks and edits your CONFIG.SYS and AUTOEXEC.BAT files. Unfortunately, it often screws up your AUTOEXEC.BAT files during the procedure if the batch file logic is not as expected.

To upgrade your PC to MS-DOS 6, simply boot as normal, insert the MS-DOS 6 Upgrade Disk 1 into your floppy drive, and type SETUP. You will be prompted through the procedure.

After you have upgraded your disk, you need to add the following command to your CONFIG.SYS:

```
Device=SETVER.EXE
```

> **NOTE** ▶
>
> Next, if you wish the workstation shell (NETX) to be recognized as running under version 6.0, you must include `Device=SETVER.EXE` in your CONFIG.SYS and then remove its listing from the SETVER data table. This is done by executing SETVER.EXE with the `/D` switch pointing at the file to remove. For example, if you are using NETX.EXE located in the NWCLIENT directory on C:, and you have SERVER.EXE in the DOS directory in the path, type the following command:
>
> ```
> SETVER C:\NWCLIENT\NETX.EXE /D
> ```
>
> This procedure is not necessary for use with the VLM DOS Requester. It is recognized as running under the appropriate version of DOS.

Optimizing Memory Under MS-DOS 6.x

To optimize your memory, use the MemMaker utility provided with MS-DOS 6.0. In the preceding example using the VLM DOS Requester, upgrading to MS-DOS 6.0 added another 8.4K of conventional memory—for a total of 614K. Running MemMaker did not increase available conventional memory, but it did free up 100K for loading TSRs high. However, upgrading to MS-DOS 6.0 with the NETX shell did enable NETX to load high—yielding a total of 617K conventional memory, and 102K available for loading other TSRs high. Listing 34.3 shows the MEM report after upgrading to MS-DOS 60, using the VLM DOS Requester, and running MemMaker.

Listing 34.3. MEM /C after optimizing under MS-DOS 6.0.

```
Modules using memory below 1M:

  Name        Total      =   Conventional  +  Upper Memory
  --------   -----------      ------------     ------------
  MSDOS      14845  (14K)     14845  (14K)        0   (0K)
  HIMEM       1168   (1K)      1168   (1K)        0   (0K)
```

continues

Listing 34.3. continued

```
EMM386      3120    (3K)     3120    (3K)         0    (0K)
SETVER       784    (1K)      784    (1K)         0    (0K)
COMMAND     2912    (3K)     2912    (3K)         0    (0K)
VLM        44016   (43K)     4064    (4K)     39952   (39K)
LSL         5008    (5K)        0    (0K)      5008    (5K)
SMC8000    11152   (11K)        0    (0K)     11152   (11K)
IPXODI     16320   (16K)        0    (0K)     16320   (16K)
Free      751488  (734K)   628336  (614K)    123152  (120K)
```

```
Memory Summary:

Type of Memory       Total       =     Used       +      Free
---------------   --------------    ---------------    ---------------
Conventional      655360  (640K)    27024   (26K)    628336   (614K)
Upper             195584  (191K)    72432   (71K)    123152   (120K)
Adapter RAM/ROM   131072  (128K)   131072  (128K)         0     (0K)
Extended (XMS)   4260864 (4161K)   267264  (261K)   3993600  (3900K)
---------------   --------------    ---------------    ---------------
Total memory     5242880 (5120K)   497792  (486K)   4745088  (4634K)

Total under 1M    850944  (831K)    99456   (97K)    751488   (734K)

Largest executable program size        628096   (613K)
Largest free upper-memory block        112640   (110K)
MS-DOS is resident in the high memory area
```

> **CAUTION** ▶
>
> Much of the additional memory was allocated by taking control of the
> monochrome video ROM space. If an application requires monochrome
> video mode, your workstation will lock up with this configuration. This
> option is offered in the SETUP utility and can be left out.

Conclusions About Upgrading to MS-DOS 6.0

Upgrading to MS-DOS 6.0 will pay dividends in freeing additional conventional
memory and making more space available in upper-memory blocks for TSRs. The
new VLM DOS Requester loads more efficiently into high memory. This configuration is recommended for good overall usage.

MS-DOS 6.0 is a good and stable product. Reported problems are related mainly to using the DoubleSpace utility on existing drives. IBM's PC-DOS 6.1 has resolved this problem, as has MS-DOS 6.2.

> **CAUTION** ▶
>
> When upgrading to MS-DOS 6.0, you should not convert an existing drive to a DoubleSpace drive. Many errors that cause data loss may occur.
>
> To use DoubleSpace, back up all your data, remove it from the drive, and convert the near-empty drive (you can leave your root directory and DOS directory intact) to a DoubleSpace drive. After converting the drive to DoubleSpace, restore your backups. DoubleSpace works fine, but the conversion causes problems.
>
> Also remember you cannot use Smartdrive with a DoubleSpace drive. You can choose more space or the disk caching performance, but not both.

The MemMaker utility does little more than a simple optimized memory configuration can do. What it does do is specify ranges to load TSRs so memory is less fragmented, and used more efficiently. This can free more upper-memory blocks for loading TSRs.

> **TIP** ▶
>
> Though you may be proficient at adjusting the CONFIG.SYS to optimize memory, let MemMaker do it for you. It allocates TSRs in specific ranges to more efficiently use memory.
>
> Always remember to run MemMaker after making any changes to memory configurations, such as editing the AUTOEXEC.BAT file or changing switch settings on your NIC.
>
> After running MemMaker, check your AUTOEXEC.BAT file to see if it encountered any logic it could not work with.

When you use MemMaker with the VLM DOS Requester, move your STARTNET.BAT file into the AUTOEXEC.BAT file. MemMaker does not look at other batch files and therefore will not optimize loading of your drivers and requester.

> **CAUTION** ▶
>
> Prior to using MemMaker, be sure to make a copy of your CONFIG.SYS
> and AUTOEXEC.BAT. If something does not work right, you can just put
> them back to the way they were.

Novell DOS 6.0 (DR-DOS 6.0)

Digital Research was purchased by Novell; therefore, what used to be known as DR-DOS is now known as Novell DOS. The Novell DOS 6.0 release offered many features over MS-DOS 5.0. However, MS-DOS 6.0 matched these new features and added MemMaker. Novell DOS works fine with Windows, contrary to claims Microsoft previously made that the two would be incompatible.

Novell's LAN Pack is a great step forward into managing DOS on a network. It gives you one network site license and the ability to update centrally.

Novell DOS 7.0

Novell's new version of DOS has upstaged Microsoft's new version. It even includes many of the features Microsoft promises in the upcoming "Chicago" release. Novell DOS 7.0 recovers more memory than MS-DOS 6.x. In addition, 7.0 has a ton of extra features—for example, a preemptive task manager. As for memory usage, it loads TSRs into memory starting at the 1M line (if they've been recompiled with Novell's new DPMI interface). Those without such recompilation load into UMBs. Because LSL, IPXODI, VLM and the drivers distributed with the client install package have already been recompiled, they all load into extended memory. Windows and the cache load above that. It is not difficult, using conservative techniques (as discussed previously in this chapter), to end up with 636K of available conventional memory. Additional switches recover extra video space, which can yield even more available conventional memory.

Other Memory Management Utilities

Other memory managers add features and can extract more available conventional memory and upper-memory blocks than MS-DOS 6.x. They also have utilities that perform better than Microsoft's MEM and MSD utilities.

QEMM386

Quarterdeck Systems developed memory management utilities long before they were added to MS-DOS. Most evaluations show that QEMM squeezes more memory out of a computer than any other package. It installs conveniently and is easy to use. It also suggests additional changes to help improve your computer memory configuration.

QEMM's Manifest utility is among the most comprehensive and visual reports of memory configuration you will find. It is simple to use and shows you clearly where potential improvements for memory configurations exist.

QEMM's Optimize utility is far more effective than MS-DOS' MemMaker. It generally tries thousands of configurations before choosing the best one. At best, it is difficult to manually manage memory as well as QEMM does.

> **NOTE** ▶
>
> QEMM uses Stealth to squeeze out a little more memory by claiming memory ranges allocated but not being used by hardware devices. Some hardware does not work well with Stealth. If you experience lockups, try reconfiguring your memory without the Stealth feature.

386MAX

Qualitas' 386MAX is nearly as good as QEMM in almost every way. The memory management utility in 386MAX is good, and the program's MAXIMIZE utility is perhaps even better than QEMM's. In most tests, 386MAX came very close to releasing as much conventional memory as QEMM. Most reviewers pick this package as second best.

Other Tips that Can Release More Conventional Memory

Try Loading Larger TSRs First

If a TSR will not load into upper-memory blocks, it is usually because there is not sufficient contiguous space available in upper-memory blocks. If you can get more available conventional memory by loading the larger TSR, try it. Try not loading a smaller TSR high and then loading your larger TSR high to see if sufficient space was vacated to accommodate it.

Locate NIC RAM Buffer Out of Useable Range

You might be able to free up more available upper-memory blocks by setting your NIC's RAM buffer address out of the range of usable high-memory range. Check Microsoft Diagnostics' (MSD.EXE) Memory screen (included with Windows 3.1 and MS-DOS 6.x) to see if some ranges are available, but not configurable as upper-memory blocks. You must then set your NIC switch setting for RAM buffer, change your NET.CFG, and perhaps add an exclude statement from your EMM386 driver in the CONFIG.SYS.

> **NOTE** ▶
>
> Exclude the RAM buffer range so its address space cannot be configured as upper-memory blocks. If this happens, your NIC will not work.
>
> You also can improve upper-memory block contiguous space by setting your NIC RAM buffer to the top or bottom available range. Use MS-DOS 6.x's MSD or another memory utility to see what ranges are available.

Tips on Best Performance with Windows 3.1

Windows requires the most workstation you can feed it. It relies heavily on every aspect of hardware—at the workstation, LAN, and server. It is processor-, disk-, and RAM-intensive. The popularity of Windows has been a tremendous boom for the computer hardware industry.

Video Processing

The most important component in running Windows is video. The time it takes to refresh screens punctuates almost every activity in Windows and Windows applications. A fast video accelerator card can make a big difference in any workstation that runs any Windows application. However, performance does not go hand-in-hand with price. Some less expensive cards perform well, and some expensive cards are disappointing.

Local bus cards really work fast. The speed of either the VL Bus (VESA standard) or PCI provides a perfect platform for a fast video card. However, video processing is also quite important. Some cards have on-board video accelerator processors that push video processing faster.

Video speed is often rated in Winmarks. Benchmark tests time screen updates and rate products. Compare products according to this measure. Video cards are frequently reviewed in PC magazines, and this provides the best and most accurate source for comparisons.

Processor Speed

Faster processors drive almost all components faster. Graphics instructions require extensive processor power. Internal processing speed is the most important aspect, and a math coprocessor also helps. This makes a 486DX2 processor the processor of choice for Windows.

RAM

Windows applications are large and use large amounts of RAM. Because applications can exceed the DOS 640K limit, developers exploit this capability.

Users really like switching from one application to another. Once they learn to use this feature, it is not unusual for them to keep several applications open at the same time. When this happens, unused application code in RAM gets swapped to disk to the swap file. More RAM means more swapping and less performance. Users who experience excessive disk swapping should close some of their applications and consider adding more RAM.

Workstations should have a minimum of 4M of RAM—or more if the user keeps more than two applications open at once. Eight megabytes is comfortable for most users and prevents degradation due to swapping.

Disk Drive

Many activities in Windows are quite disk-intensive. Disk caching is probably the least expensive option available to boost Windows speed.

The most prominent disk-intensive application is printing. Not only does a substantial amount of activity occur in spooling a print job, but reading the file to print is also disk-intensive. Windows applications often use temporary disk files which tax the disk drive. Most documents, spreadsheets, and databases do not fit entirely in RAM, so movement through these files also involves disk access.

All disk drives benefit from caching utilities, such as Microsoft's Smartdrive. You can use it or a competitive product to enhance Windows performance.

> **NOTE** ▷
>
> You cannot use disk caching when using Microsoft's DoubleSpace utility.

Workstation NIC

The type of LAN you use matters more than the brand of NIC. Windows has done more to convince ARCnet users to move to Ethernet. During loading Windows and Windows applications, 16 Mbps Token Ring outperforms the other LANs mentioned here. During normal usage, little difference will be noted between any of three types of LANs discussed.

If you have the opportunity, you may benchmark various NICs with Windows. Compare brands and models by switching one NIC for another to see which performs best. You'll probably find the differences are marginal under normal working conditions.

> **NOTE** ▷
>
> Use practical benchmarks when comparing NICs. Time how long it takes to load Windows or a Windows application instead of comparing performance with benchmarking utilities. The characteristics of normal Windows activity are quite different from the type of traffic generated by a benchmark test utility.

Tuning Windows for Best Performance

There are a few changes you should make to ensure you're getting the most out of Windows:

1. Disable Print Manager in Windows. Your print job must spool the server's disk; there is no need to spool it to your disk first. Spooling to your local disk slows workstation performance needlessly while printing to the printer.

2. Place a permanent swap file on local disk. A permanent swap file performs slightly better than a temporary swap file. The file should be on the local drive to prevent heavy traffic generated over the network to and from the swap file.

3. Enable 32-bit disk controller support. Under Control Panel's 386 Enhanced icon, you will find this option in the lower-left corner.

4. Use disk caching at your workstation if you use a hard drive and have the swap file located there. Disk caching improves physical read performance. The Smartdrive utility shipped with Windows 3.1 and MS-DOS 6.x is very good.

5. Run a disk defragmentation utility, such as MS-DOS 6.x's DEFRAG, on your local hard drives periodically (every few weeks). Fragmentation slows disk access. This is important for best performance where swap files, Windows, applications, and data are stored on a local hard drive.

CAUTION ▶

When using Smartdrive v4.0, flush write-behind cache by typing SMARTDRV/ C before shutting down your computer. Otherwise, data left in the cache may not be written to the disk.

Adjusting the DOS Workstation Shell/ Requester and Drivers

You can adjust the way LSL, IPXODI, NETX, VLM, and your NIC driver works with entries in the NET.CFG file. This file is a simple ASCII file that resides in the same directory with these software modules.

If no NET.CFG is present, default parameters apply. In most cases, those default parameters are fine. However, some may need to be adjusted to provide resources necessary, to configure the driver to the physical switch settings on the NIC, or to adjust parameters for better performance or functionality.

A few important parameters deserve your attention:

```
(5)File Handles (default value = 40)
```

Your shell (NETX) allows no more than 40 files open on the server for your workstation unless this parameter is adjusted upward. You may need to have more than 40 files open at any given time, especially when Windows is installed on a server.

> **NOTE** ▶
>
> The VLM DOS Requester uses the FILES= value in your CONFIG.SYS for file handles. You should set this value at around 100.

```
(5)Cache Buffers (default value=5)
```

This parameter adjusts the shell/requester buffers. Just as adjusting buffers for your disk may improve application performance of locally installed applications, this parameter can adjust performance for applications installed on your server's disk.

> **NOTE** ▶
>
> Local Cache Buffers, as discussed here, are never used with files that are flagged Sharable or Transactional.

Preferred Server

This parameter can force your workstation to attach to the appropriate server during execution of NETX or VLM. You may find that a server other than the intended server may respond first to "Get Nearest Server" NCP requests, even when they are not closer. In other cases, this attachment may result in inefficient routing.

Whenever more than one server is present on a network or internetwork, it is good policy to use this parameter.

SPX Connections (Default Value=15)

An external print server (loading PSERVER.EXE), requires this value set at 60.

Printing Performance

35

by Rick Sant'Angelo

IN THIS CHAPTER

There are two factors to consider with regard to optimizing printer performance:

1. Improving print output speed
2. Reducing I/O conflict

Although printer output has gained much attention lately, the second factor—file I/O conflict—is vastly underrated as a performance factor both for printers and for user I/O.

Because the two most-used applications on a network are word-processing and spreadsheet software, output is the most critical part of user demands. Using a word processor or spreadsheet is not server- or LAN-intensive for most functions. However, shared printer output is one of the two main reasons these applications are shared on a network. The other reason is to share files. An occasional file access or file save does not heavily tax the LAN or server, but users frequently drum their nails on the desk waiting nervously for output, glancing at the clock while deadlines come and go.

What can be done to improve print output performance? Several bottlenecks can slow output. Because the bottlenecks can vary from one system to another, the first order of business is to look at how a print job moves to its ultimate destination—a network printer.

Every time you print to a NetWare printer, your print job goes through two steps. First, the print output is spooled to a *queue*, which is a file where the print job waits in line to be printed. If no other print jobs are waiting in line, it goes straight to the printer, *after* it finishes spooling to the queue.

The second step is directed by the NetWare Print Server utility, PSERVER, where network printers can be located one of three places:

1. Printers installed on the file server, where PSERVER is running as an NLM
2. Printers installed on a stand-alone print server (not available with 4.0)
3. Remote printers, installed on workstations

Each configuration can have different bottlenecks and different solutions to printing performance. In addition to these network printer configurations, you also may have printers directly connected to a LAN cable, or you may have a small print server device with one to four printers attached. This chapter addresses both parts of network printing—spooling to a queue, and print server output—and the configurations for each.

Print Spooling to Queues

Of all the activities that dominate the disk drive, print spooling to queues is the most frequent and the most constant. This activity also requires straight physical write requests to the disk and physical read requests from the disk before being sent to a network printer. Two concerns, both grossly underrated and neglected, should be paramount to the system administrator:

1. Efficiency in spooling to the queue
2. The effect on user file I/O requests

Efficiency of Block-Oriented versus Byte-Oriented Output

There are two ways of sending your print output to a queue: by using the NetWare CAPTURE command or by using an application software driver that uses a NetWare API to activate the equivalent of a Capture. Either one works, but when print output is captured, the NetWare shell (NETX or the OS/2 Requester) intercepts output directed to a parallel port and redirects it to a queue file located on a file server.

Print output is sent to a parallel port byte-by-byte and is therefore redirected byte-by-byte to the NIC. This results in many packets being sent across the LAN, most of which are very small. Handling more and smaller packets costs you increased server CPU utilization, which can limit the performance of all the active resources on your server.

However, when a print driver uses NetWare APIs to send output to a network queue, it can be built to use block-oriented output. It is not necessary to send a stream of bytes (as it is when sent to the computer bus—each byte with an address byte). Instead, the application can send a block of data to the NIC, one full packet of data at a time. The difference is illustrated in Figure 35.1.

Block-oriented output is faster—as much as 50 times faster—in getting data to the queue. This is a pacing factor in printing, because the job cannot be sent to the network printer until the entire print job has finished spooling to the queue. Block-oriented output also puts fewer packets on your LAN and makes best use of its highest performance potential, using larger packets.It can take as many as 150 times as many packets to transport the same file to the queue.

Now consider how many print jobs go to queues every day, and how large they are. It may seem that each print job is a small matter. However, when the macro effect of many print jobs is taken into consideration, print spooling can have a huge effect on both the efficiency of your network and of print output.

This is why WordPerfect for Windows print driver is so much more efficient than the standard Windows driver. Windows uses byte-oriented output, whereas WordPerfect uses block-oriented output.

FIGURE 35.1.

Byte-oriented versus block-oriented print output.

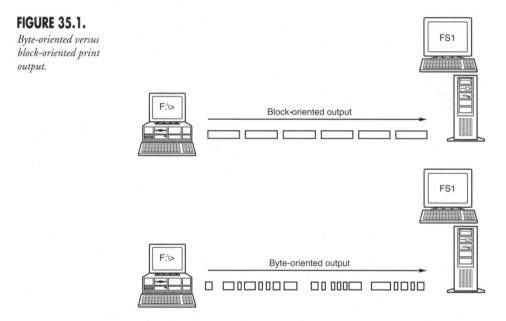

NOTE ▶

You should complain loudly to software developers who do not use block-oriented output available in NetWare APIs.

Until software developers know that software buyers are aware of this opportunity, they will not waste their time working on new drivers; they will use the same drivers they use for DOS or OS/2.

Microsoft should be your number one target because so many software applications print through Windows. Apathy on the part of software developers causes this monumental waste of network resources.

The Effect on File Server I/O

Another major factor that is overlooked by the industry is the vast amount of I/O conflict generated by print spooling to queues. Of all disk-intensive activities, printing has probably the highest volume, and it should be the highest priority. Every print job must physically spool to and from the disk. In contrast, user file I/O requests result in physical disk access only between 10 to 30 percent of the time—and often less than 10 percent of the time. As a result, print spooling has a much greater impact than user file I/O requests. Print spooling several jobs at once can cause significant disk channel bottleneck, and it can reduce performance for user file I/O requests.

Unfortunately, every network print job must first spool to a queue. The only way to avoid this bottleneck is to use a separate file server for printing. If this is a major problem in your network, next time you want to upgrade a NetWare server, buy a new copy of NetWare instead. Then use the old server as a print queue server to relieve your new file server of print queue spooling. As an alternative, you can use an inexpensive peer-to-peer NOS (such as Personal NetWare on an old 286 computer) as a print server.

> **TIP** ▶
>
> Personal NetWare server and client agents are included in Novell DOS 7.0 at no additional cost, and you can obtain the universal client software (Virtual Loading Modules) from Novell, which supports all NetWare versions from one set of drivers and shells.

Using the NetWare Print Server Most Efficiently

After your print job has finished spooling to the queue, the print server directs the print job to spool to itself before sending it to a network printer. PSERVER can be loaded as an NLM on the file server itself, or on a workstation as an EXE (DOS executable file). When loaded as an EXE, a DOS workstation is a dedicated print server, whereas an OS/2 workstation also can be used as a user workstation. This section examines each of these possibilities, plus whether the printers should be connected to the print server or to a workstation as a remote printer.

Loading PSERVER.NLM versus PSERVER.EXE

Loading PSERVER as an NLM is the most efficient way to run a NetWare Print Server. This opinion is diametrically opposed to the official Novell position that was last discussed when NetWare 3.0 was introduced. At that time, PSERVER.NLM was buggy and slow, and PSERVER.EXE was not much better. The latest software modules of the Print Server utility (available on NetWire—PSERV5.ZIP) are far better.

> **NOTE ►**
>
> You need to obtain the latest NetWare Print Server Utility if you are using NetWare 3.11. You can download it from NetWire (PSERV5.ZIP) or obtain it from Novell by calling 1-800-UPDATE1.
>
> Your distribution diskettes contain older utilities that are slower and have a few bugs.

Now it makes most sense to load PSERVER on your file server. It takes little away from your server's processing power. To verify this, load Monitor with the P switch (LOAD MONITOR P) as discussed in Chapter 33, "Monitoring and Adjusting Server Performance," and watch how little CPU utilization your PSERVER.NLM consumes. This affords a few benefits that pay dividends in performance:

- It reduces the number of trips across the LAN the print job must take
- It does not use SPX (which consumes additional resources)
- It reduces traffic on the server NIC

Print Job Trips Across the LAN

When PSERVER is not actively printing, it polls each queue that it serves every 15 seconds to see if another print job has finished spooling to the queue. When the queue file closes, PSERVER directs it to begin spooling to the print server itself. This is where you may find big differences in how you configure your network printers.

> **NOTE ►**
>
> Later PSERVER versions enable you to set the polling time previously mentioned. When loading, use the command LOAD PSERVER POLL=n (where n is the amount of time between polls).

PSERVER.NLM with Printers Connected to the Server

If the network printer is connected to the server running PSERVER.NLM, the job simply goes to the configured port, as shown in Figure 35.2.

FIGURE 35.2.

PSERVER sending a job to a print server printer.

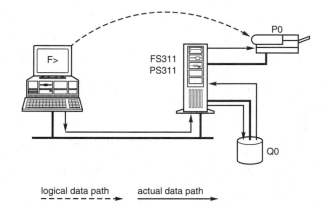

logical data path — — — — →   actual data path ——→

This is the most efficient printing configuration, requiring only one trip across the LAN. The print job spools to the queue, and then to a PSERVER port. The spooling to the printer is as fast as the slowest bottleneck between the disk and the printer output. In most cases, the pacing factor is the port output speed.

PSERVER.EXE with Printers Connected to the Print Server

When printing to a stand-alone print server, your print job must be taken from the queue and sent to the print server, as shown in Figure 35.3. Not only does this cause the print job to take a second trip across the LAN, but the print server utility uses SPX between the file server and PSERVER.EXE. SPX uses more resources because a checksum must be calculated at the sending and receiving end to ensure the accuracy of each packet. This causes more processing at each end, in addition to more traffic on the LAN.

The print output is paced by the slowest bottleneck, which is typically the printer port on the print server.

Although this configuration is not as efficient as running PSERVER.NLM on the server, it is better than using remote printers.

FIGURE 35.3.
PSERVER.EXE and printers connected to the print server.

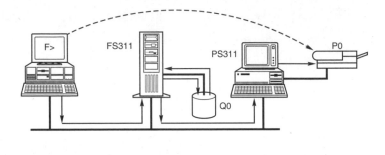

logical data path - - - - - →   actual data path ⎯⎯⎯→

Using PSERVER.EXE and Remote Printers

The least efficient configuration consists of running PSERVER.EXE on a stand-alone print server and using remote printers. This causes the print job to be spooled from the queue to the print server (PSERVER.EXE), and again from the print server to the remote printer (RPRINTER.EXE).

Not only does this cause the print job to take three trips across the LAN, but SPX is used in two of those trips, from the queue to the print server, and from the print server to the remote printer. This causes SPX checksum calculations to be done on the file server, the print server, and again on the print server and the remote printer, placing a bigger burden on the file server CPU, the print server, and the remote workstation. The additional traffic on the remote printer workstation can slow foreground processing for the user at that workstation. This affects both processing power and NIC access.

> **TIP** ▶
>
> You should use 16-bit NICs in remote printer workstations, because two-way communications are likely to be active at times when the remote printer is being used.

The print output is paced by the slowest bottleneck between the queue and the printer itself. This bottleneck is typically the printer port on the remote printer.

> **CAUTION** ▶
>
> This configuration is very common and is the least efficient method of printing. It not only puts additional traffic on the LAN; it also can bog down

the processor on the print server and remote printer workstation as well as place an additional burden on the file server CPU.

Bottlenecks can restrict print job flow at the server NIC, the print server NIC, and the remote printer NIC. Not only can this restrict flow of print jobs, it also competes with user file I/O requests at all these points.

Third-Party Print Server Software

A few companies make substitutes for the NetWare Print Server utility. In the past, this provided a more stable, bug-free utility that was more efficient and easier to learn to use. Today, Novell's improvements to the Print Server utility have closed the gap between these products and its own. It is no longer a great improvement to purchase and use one of these products. Few of them have features that NetWare does not have.

Check out these products carefully and be certain that the reason you purchase one of them is valid. In many cases, these products claim to perform functions that the NetWare Print Server also performs (but perhaps with less eloquence). For example, one utility claims to enable you to use features of your printer that are not supported by your software. NetWare print job configurations do this also—if you learn to use them. Some products do offer additional features. For example, PS-Print and Printer Assist both support Postscript banner pages and settable poll times per printer.

Using Printer Devices that Connect Directly to Your LAN

One of your best options for reducing printer performance bottlenecks is to use a device that connects printers directly to your LAN cabling. There are two types of devices: NICs that plug into a printer (normally a laser printer) and stand-alone print server devices that have ports for one to four printers. In general, any of these devices can be configured as a print server (in lieu of PSERVER) or as a remote printer driven by PSERVER.

Printer NICs

Several brands of NICs that plug into the interface slots on Hewlett Packard LaserJets are available. They enable you to directly connect a printer to the LAN cabling without using the NetWare remote printer utility (RPRINTER.EXE). A couple of other features are important in these cards.

Many of these cards can be configured as print servers in lieu of using the NetWare print server. HP and other companies make cards like this, and they generally include a software application to set up and configure the print server. In many cases, the print server is more efficient, may or may not use SPX, and takes a load off other print servers. This option also eliminates the port bottleneck, enabling printing to go through the printer NIC at faster than normal parallel port speeds.

> **NOTE** ▶
>
> The only downside to this feature is the connection limitation on your copy of NetWare. You get a few extra connections over and above the number of users you license. Each print server takes up a connection on the file server that it supports. With enough print server devices, you may find that you have reached your limit on connections, thereby reducing the number of users that can be logged in at any given time.

In many cases, these cards plug into the Modular I/O jack of the LaserJet (model IIIsi, and all LaserJet 4 models). This option enables you to print at speeds as fast as the LAN can carry them and the printer can print them. It entirely eliminates the port as the bottleneck.

Stand-Alone Print Server Devices

Several companies make little boxes that connect directly to your LAN cabling and have printer ports for one, two, or four printers. These devices normally can be configured as remote printers or as print servers, using their own internal print server software on a PROM chip in lieu of the NetWare print server utility. There are a few advantages to using such a product. Some of these devices have features that others lack.

Many of these devices have printer ports that are much faster than standard computer ports. Some of them claim as much as 10 times the throughput of a traditional parallel port. This is a distinct advantage, because the printer port is normally the pacing factor in moving the print job from the queue to output.

> **NOTE ▶**
>
> Printer developers have formed a group called Network Printer Alliance (NPA). They have proposed a new, enhanced parallel port standard based on port design already in use on some of these products.

One device can manage more than one printer. It also alleviates the necessity of using a remote printer workstation. In many cases, the print server utility is more efficient than the NetWare utility. Devices are available for Token Ring, Ethernet coaxial, twisted-pair, and thick-net models. They also can be used with almost any type of printer.

Summary

Understanding NetWare printing mechanics leads to understanding where bottlenecks occur and what to look for. Novell never withdrew its previous recommendation of moving the print server off the file server. This is an example of why you must rely on your own knowledge to optimize your network; you cannot rely on Novell for the best advice. Here are some tips that can help you improve printer performance and alleviate file I/O conflict for user requests:

1. Use application software that uses block-oriented output calling NetWare APIs. Complain loudly to your software developer, especially Microsoft, so it will provide block-oriented output drivers.

2. Update your NetWare Print Server utility to the latest version. If you have 3.11, you must obtain PSERV2.ZIP or later (available) on NetWire from Novell.

3. If print spooling to a queue causes file I/O conflict, offload print queue servicing to a separate file server. You can use inexpensive peer-to-peer software for this purpose.

4. Run PSERVER.NLM on your server, and use server-attached printers for best performance and less user file I/O conflict. Alternatively, use PSERVER.EXE, but stay away from using remote printers (RPRINTER.EXE) because that is the most costly way to print in terms of performance. Reduce the number of trips across the LAN whenever possible.

5. Use print server devices that connect directly to your LAN cabling. Most of these devices can be configured as print servers. You should use this option, because it reduces one trip across the LAN and the potential for bottleneck in your print server.

Internetwork Performance

by Rick Sant'Angelo

36

When multiple LANs are connected via NetWare routers, external routers, and bridges, an internetwork is formed. Internetworks consist of multiple LANs and/or WANs, and have routers or bridges as boundaries between them. NetWare servers have internal routers, so they also constitute boundaries between LANs and WANs. This is what is called the *physical infrastructure* of your internetwork.

When you assemble and configure an internetwork, you should conceptualize the *network address* as the center of each network. Servers and clients are both ancillary to this infrastructure. You must learn to distinguish the *logical network configuration* implemented by your system administration from your physical infrastructure. This logical configuration can differ dramatically from the physical infrastructure you must design in order to provide optimum routing of IPX and IP packets across your internetwork.

This chapter discusses in precise detail how you should configure the physical infrastructure of your internetwork for best performance. This discussion builds on previous discussions of routable protocols, including IPX and IP, in Chapter 5, "Novell's Protocol Stack," Chapter 25, "Basics of Internetwork Data Communications," and Chapter 26, "Routers and Bridges." Be sure you understand the mechanics of IPX and NCP before you proceed. The mechanics are far simpler than you might think, even though you may be an experienced NetWare professional. Nothing can substitute for this firm foundation in routable protocol mechanics. Understanding these mechanics will make troubleshooting internetworks much easier for you.

Bridges make separate physical LANs look as if they were one logical LAN. This causes NetWare's Router Information Protocol (RIP) to make poor routing decisions, as discussed in Chapter 26. Therefore, this chapter proceeds from an assumption that routers are the preferred devices to use when internetworking.

This chapter discusses the following subjects:

- NetWare routing-related limitations and improvements
- Novell's forthcoming NLSP router protocol
- Software-based versus hardware-based routers
- Internetwork configurations
- The use of T-1 versus frame relay services
- Internetwork software configurations

This chapter builds on and summarizes the discussions of mechanics and protocol in earlier chapters. It offers conclusions based on a comprehensive understanding of IPX and other routable protocols. Background information is contained in previous chapters, which you should read for best integration of these conclusions. Further depth on some issues is given in the following listed chapters, so you may want to consult specific topics there.

Chapter	Title
3	Advanced NetWare OS Features
5	NetWare's Protocol Stack
22	Monitoring LANs
25	Basics of Internetwork Data Communications
26	Routers and Bridges
Appendix A	Glossary

> **NOTE** ▶
>
> Although you may be very experienced with NetWare, you should refer to previous discussions of routable protocols. Novell's education may not have adequately prepared you for the challenges you encounter in everyday life in the area of internetworking.
>
> If conclusions drawn in this chapter do not concur with your previous impressions about the mechanics of NetWare protocols and routing, refer to previous chapters for better in-depth understanding.
>
> In many cases in our industry, terms are used indiscriminately, leaving false impressions of the mechanics of internetworking with NetWare. Whenever you are confused on an issue, look up definitions in the glossary and read supporting material in other chapters.

NetWare Routing-Related Limitations and Improvements

An internal router was incorporated into NetWare 2.0 in 1985. Since that time, very few enhancements have been made to NetWare's internal router. Even today, if you want good routing services, you must purchase a separate router. Problems have plagued NetWare internetworks for quite some time; these limitations are more fully discussed in Chapter 26, "Routers and Bridges."

Logical versus Physical Hops
The Problem

NetWare internal routers are based on Router Information Protocol (RIP). Novell's implementation of this protocol is somewhat ineffective at discerning the least-costly route. RIP determines the best way to route based on the number of logical hops. The main problem with logical hops is that physical hops, such as bridges (which constitute a physical hop, the same as a router), may not be detected.

When routes have the same logical hop count, RIP next looks for the lower tick count. However, NetWare routers estimate the tick count as the number of logical hops plus one, regardless of the cost of the hop. Therefore, one hop may be across a slower link than an alternate. Thus, at times, RIP (as implemented by Novell) fails to determine the least-cost route.

The Solution

1. Use only routers, which work best with NetWare. Do not use bridges for NetWare IPX traffic. There are bridge routers that route any (encountered) routable protocol packets and then bridge other nonroutable or unsupported protocols.

2. Carefully configure internetworks so that routers won't choose a less efficient path. Monitor expansion carefully so that router inefficiencies are not introduced.

3. Replace RIP with NLSP when available.

Small Packets Across Routers
The Problem

NetWare internal routers break down all sizes of packets up to 512 bytes. Even though you may have all Token Ring LANs connected by NetWare servers, the 4096-byte packets in the Token Ring frames must be broken into 512-byte packets to be routed. This restriction was built into the internal NetWare router to accommodate the small packet size of ARCnet. Even though you have no ARCnet, you are still bound by this restriction for all versions up to and including 3.11. Versions 3.12 and 4.x have eliminated this artificial restriction.

The Solution

On NetWare 3.11 versions, implement LIPX.NLM. There is no solution for 2.x servers. Another alternative is to upgrade to 3.12 or 4.01.

RIP and SAP Broadcasts
The Problem

The way NetWare internal routers inform one another of their existence is to broadcast RIP packets frequently. NetWare servers inform file servers and routers of their existence by broadcasting SAP packets frequently. As a result, internetworks with many LANs, WANs, and servers can have unnecessary traffic circulating on the LANs and WANs. This situation can constitute an unnecessary burden on WANs of low bandwidth.

The Solution

1. Install and configure SAFILTER for 3.11 to adjust and filter SAP traffic.
2. Upgrade to NetWare 4.x and edit protocols in SERVMAN utility.

> **NOTE** ▶
>
> Do not assume that poor response-time over a WAN is your problem. See the section in this chapter on Packet Burst NCP for a more likely explanation.
>
> The perceived problem of excessive RIP and SAP packet traffic on LANs is normally insignificant, unless you have a 9.6-kbps link with more traffic than it can handle. If you use a protocol analyzer and isolate this traffic, you will find that far too much fuss has been made over a very minor issue.
>
> Unless you have *many* servers and *very* limited bandwidth WANs, this limitation should not concern you.

NCP Acknowledgments and Packet Burst NCP

The Problem

Another of NetWare's protocols that limits internetwork performance is the "ping-pong" effect of NCP acknowledgments. Each NCP packet must be answered with an acknowledgment NCP packet. The problem with the request-acknowledgment mechanism has nothing to do with the amount of bandwidth being used by acknowledgments or even the effect of processing all those packets. The problem is how normal NCP affects flow control.

NCP acknowledgments affect only certain types of NCP requests: those requiring acknowledgment before the next packet is sent, such as a file read or write request. When this type of request requires many packets in a series, and each request must wait for an acknowledgment before the next is sent, latency can cause some serious performance degradation.

The main performance disadvantage in this scenario is that file read and write requests exceeding 512 bytes in length require an acknowledgment to come back before the next packet is sent. This is because NCP requires the read or write to be successful before the next offset of the file request is sent.

The Solution

This problem was addressed with a new version of NCP that Novell calls *Packet Burst Protocol* or Packet Burst NCP. When Packet Burst NCP is used, a series of requests, called a *burst*, can be sent without waiting for an acknowledgment, as shown in Figure 36.1.

> **NOTE** ▶
>
> This protocol was initially called "Burst Mode Protocol" when it was first developed by Novell. This terminology was changed to Packet Burst Protocol to eliminate confusion with EISA and MCA's burst modes.

FIGURE 36.1.

*An NCP file read/
write request and
acknowledgment
without and with
Packet Burst NCP.*

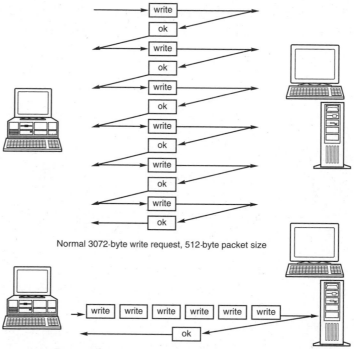

Normal 3072-byte write request, 512-byte packet size

Packet Burst 3072-write request, 512-byte packet size

When delay is introduced between transmissions, normal NCP can cause serious degradation in the process of reading or writing a long file. Ironically, this affects higher bandwidth data communications lines, such as T-1s, more than lower bandwidth lines, such as a 56-kbps line. It also affects congested routers and bridges, and LANs filled to capacity. Whenever latency increases, large file reads and writes degrade significantly. The problem with Packet Burst NCP addresses is latency, not bandwidth.

The effect of latency is most evident in satellite links. No matter how high the bandwidth is in a satellite link, latency is very high. Due to the sheer distance involved (communications satellites orbit at about 25,000 miles altitude), it takes a packet about 1/6 of a second to reach its destination, and 1/6 of a second for the acknowledgment to come back. Each packet therefore takes about 1/3 of a second to be sent and acknowledged before the next packet can be sent. With a 512-byte packet size, it takes more than 23 minutes to send a 1M file transfer, but with Packet Burst NCP, it takes less than five minutes. In this example, bandwidth is irrelevant; the latency between requests and acknowledgments causes performance problems.

When Packet Burst NCP is used, latency does not affect large file reads and writes as much because each packet can be sent without waiting for the acknowledgment.

Latency can be caused by many factors, only one of which is the transmission medium. Disk bottleneck caused by cache buffer saturation also can cause latency. So can a congested LAN or insufficient packet receive buffers in a server.

According to Novell performance tests in normal workload conditions, by using Packet Burst NCP, you can expect an improvement in throughput ranging between 10 to 300 percent. The two situations where the most improvement is experienced are on T-1 and T-3 WAN lines, and also wherever latency is an issue—for example, an Ethernet LAN that is running at full capacity.

NOTE ▶

This limitation has presented a problem on WANs and LANs where bandwidth is insufficient and where propagation delays cause some NCP procedures to run with intermittent pauses until acknowledgments are received. Because of the large numbers of packets being exchanged, these tiny delays add up to significant performance degradation.

Under normal LAN conditions, normal NCP communications do not present a perceivable problem, because they take up only a negligible portion of bandwidth and are delivered almost instantaneously.

However, installing Packet Burst NCP costs only a few kilobytes of conventional memory and seems to have no apparent cost in performance. It does not hurt to implement the NLMs in 3.11.

NetWare 2.x Problems
The Problem

NetWare 2.x versions had trouble with the network address to which the router was assigned. The address of the router was located on LAN A, the first NIC installed in the server. This caused routes on LAN A to appear to be one logical hop closer than routes on LAN B, C, or D.

The Solution

This problem was resolved with 3.x's internal network address. The internal network address became the interface point between clients and the rest of the network. Now each LAN connected to a server is configured with the same number of logical hops. This problem cannot be eliminated in 2.x versions. Whenever internetworking performance is a concern, 2.x versions should be upgraded to eliminate this problem. It can affect all routers, not just NetWare internal routers, by broadcasting inaccurate RIP and SAP packets.

Many of these problems have been addressed and resolved in NetWare 4.x. Some of these problems can be reduced by adding NLMs to NetWare 3.11, and/or by using Novell's Multi Protocol Router. These and other limitations of NetWare routers are discussed in Chapter 25, "Basics of Internetwork Data Communications."

Improvements in NetWare 3.12 and 4.x

Several of these limitations have been resolved in later NetWare versions, which also feature a long list of improvements. Only improvements relative to those limitations discussed previously are included in this discussion. The following features eliminate or reduce the previously enumerated limitations.

Large Internet Packets

The reduction of packet size to 512 bytes has been eliminated. When a client attaches to a 3.12 or 4.x file server, NCP negotiates the largest packet size it can use between the source and destination, and it configures packets to that size. This feature is billed as a plus by the Novell marketing machine, but it is the way NetWare should have worked from the beginning.

RIP and SAP Parameter Adjustment and Filtering

NetWare 4.x's SERVMAN.NLM provides an easy-to-use interface for adjusting RIP and SAP parameters. RIP and SAP packets can also be filtered to reduce traffic on limited-bandwidth WANs.

> **CAUTION** ▶
>
> Do not attempt to adjust RIP/SAP parameters or filters unless you understand the affects your changes can have, and you adjust all file servers to the same parameters.
>
> See Chapter 33, "Monitoring and Adjusting Server Performance," for specific adjustments of RIP and SAP protocols.

Packet Burst NCP

This protocol has replaced normal NCP communications in both 3.12 and 4.x versions. As discussed previously, substitution of Packet Burst NCP for normal NCP does not have an apparent downside, so Novell has included it in NetWare's later versions.

Fixes Available for NetWare 3.11

One of the very successful improvements in NetWare 3.x versions relates to the modular design of 3.x. Several fixes can be implemented by loading NLMs on the file server. The following fixes are available for 3.11 to remedy some limitations discussed previously.

LIPX (Large Internet Packets)

This NLM can be installed on file servers to eliminate the breakdown of packets to 512 bytes when traversing a NetWare internal router. The NLM must be installed on all servers that lie between the source and destination. This module is available on NetWire at no cost and is included with MPR.

SAFILTER (SAP Parameter Adjustment and Filtering)

This series of NLMs allows filtering of SAP traffic. No fixes are available for adjusting or filtering RIP traffic. This module is available on NetWire at no cost and is included with MPR.

PBURST and BNETX (Packet Burst NCP)

Packet Burst NCP can be implemented on a NetWare 3.11 server as an NLM and at client workstations by replacing the shell (NETX) with the Packet Burst Shell, BNETX. This module is available on NetWire at no cost and is included with MPR.

> **NOTE** ▶
>
> The above patches to 3.11 have become part of the core operating system features of 3.12 (except SAFILTER). It is not necessary to add these patches to 3.12.

Novell's New NetWare Link Services Protocol (NLSP)

Novell has developed a solution for the inefficiency of Router Information Protocol and Service Advertising Protocol. NLSP is a link-state routing protocol that can determine the least-cost route more effectively than RIP, and it eliminates the need for redundant "keep-alive" router broadcasts.

A link-state router queries routes instead of broadcasting packets on a frequent basis. This is the ultimate solution to adjusting and filtering RIP and SAP packets. More importantly, NLSP, like Open Shortest Path First and OSI's IS-IS routing protocol, promises to resolve many of the inefficiencies in NetWare's determination of the most cost-efficient route. Other router vendors, including Wellfleet, Cisco, and 3Com, have announced that they will support this protocol in their routing products. Although Novell has not specifically announced how this new protocol will be marketed, it should be included in future MPR updates as a standard feature and perhaps may be included as a new feature in future OS versions.

Software-Based versus Proprietary Hardware-Based Routers

To maintain low levels of departmental LAN bandwidth utilization, you should divide users into smaller LAN workgroups and link the LANs together with routers. You should monitor LAN bandwidth to detect when a LAN becomes overburdened.

(Monitoring LANs is discussed in great detail in Chapter 23, "Novell Products for LAN Monitoring.")

Quite recently, external routers have evolved into a new generation of higher-performance, lower-cost products. Novell's introduction and development of Multi Protocol Router (MPR) as a software-based router, coupled with fast 486 EISA and MCA computers and good bus-mastering 32-bit NICs, has allowed the assembly of less- expensive, high-performance routers.

Several recent studies have proven that MPR can be built to perform as well as the best hardware-based routers. Router developers have answered by producing new models with very high performance and lower prices. The industry is therefore witnessing lower router prices, more options, and better performance.

Protocol Filtering

One feature you may like to have in a router or bridge is the ability to filter specific protocols, nodes, network addresses, servers, and so on. Protocol filtering allows many options for reading a layer of protocol and using a given criterion for filtering out packets to be routed.

Novell's Multi-Protocol Router

MPR can be installed on your server, or, because it ships with a NetWare 3.x Runtime OS, it can be installed on a server or on a stand-alone router. It also can use any 3.x server driver. This also makes it an ideal platform for other NLMs that you may wish to offload from your server, such as SAA Services or SQL Server. By itself, MPR is used for local routing, and with the optional WAN Links product it can be used for remote routing.

MPR also features source-route bridging for SNA traffic. It first routes IPX, IP, OSI, and AppleTalk protocols, and then bridges SNA traffic where routing is not possible.

MPR includes SAFILTER for filtering and adjusting SAP packets and parameters. The series of NLMs is loaded on all NetWare 3.11 file servers internetworked by MPR. The LIPX.NLM also is included to eliminate the problem of NetWare internal file-server routers breaking IPX packets into 512-byte segments when crossing routers.

Novell Strategic Alliances

Two companies, NetWorth and Cisco, have signed OEM agreements with Novell to include MPR and the NetWare 3.x Runtime OS in their hardware-based routers. They also have lowered their prices to be competitive with software-based routers. This has added more credibility to MPR's performance potential. Also, more features can be packed into one device. For example, NetWorth incorporates MPR into its wiring concentrators.

Newport Systems' LAN²LAN/MPR and Intelligent Wide Area Network Interface Card (WNIC)

Newport Systems Solutions is a leading software-based router developer that produces a router and intelligent WNIC adapter matching or exceeding the performance of any proprietary hardware-based router on the market. Independent tests have indicated that its product virtually matches LAN speeds; therefore, no product could route faster.

The company's internetworking strategy differs from Novell's in the following ways:

1. Newport Systems developed its own proprietary OS specifically designed as a platform for routing and MAC-layer bridging. This OS is similar to NetWare 3.x Runtime, and it can use the same NIC drivers and run the Newport Systems MPR software.

2. Newport Systems uses parallel processing to offload some tasks to dedicated processors on their WNIC board and on daughterboards. Novell prefers to keep all functions in software and all processing on one CPU. LAN²LAN/MPR is not subject to the same types of demands on CPU utilization as NetWare Runtime.

3. LAN²LAN/MPR includes a MAC-layer bridge to accommodate non-routable traffic.

4. Newport Systems' data-compression daughterboards compress data to an average ratio of 4:1 on digital lines up to 2.048 mbps.

Newport's proprietary router OS and MPR software reduces the problem of high CPU utilization, which can limit NetWare NLM and driver performance. Dividing the processing tasks among dedicated processors means that routing never suffers as a result of heavy data compression or protocol handling. The operating system is not restricted by design features for a file system or other networking features. This provides the best features of software-based routing with hardware designed to handle routing most efficiently.

Special LAN²LAN/MPR NIC drivers are available for some Novell, 3Com, and SMC Ethernet model NICs, and also for SMC TokenCard Elite (Token Ring) NICs. Newport Systems plans to open its driver specifications to allow drivers to be written for other NICs as well.

LAN²LAN/MPR routes IPX and IP packets and bridges all other traffic. The built-in Ethernet MAC-layer bridge will not bridge IPX or IP traffic if those protocols are activated. Only nonsupported protocols, such as those for NetBIOS/NetBEUI, DEC LAT, and AppleTalk, are bridged.

LAN²LAN/MPR differs from Novell's MPR in routable protocols supported, and it does not route OSI or AppleTalk. However, the bridge feature does, and it also supports Spanning Tree Protocol for Ethernet and Source-Route Protocol for Token Ring.

This product has an SNMP agent to interface with other SNMP-compatible software products. Specific software interfaces are being developed for Hewlett Packard's OpenView, Novell's NetWare Distributed Management Services, and other products.

Putting Four Times as Much Data Through Each WAN Line

Data compression is another feature that Novell is just beginning to consider. However, Newport Systems has been using compression for some time now, with a compression daughterboard that plugs into the WNIC. Two models are available — one for up to 128 kbps lines, and another for T-1/E-1 lines for up to 2.048 kbps per port.

Compression ratios vary according to data structures, but a reasonable rate to expect is 4 to 1. Newport Systems offloads compression to the daughterboard so that it will not affect the router's performance. When the cost of leasing dedicated lines is taken into consideration, the modest investment in data compression pays for itself very quickly.

One WAN Adapter for Any Data Communication Medium

One single WNIC provides two ports with the following interfaces:

RS232C	Analog communications from 9.6 to 38.4 kbps
RS422	Digital communications from 56 to 2.048 kbps
V.32	Digital communications from 56 to 2.048 kbps

A plug-in module can adapt the board to four ports, but it cannot be used with the data compression daughterboard.

Supports Most Popular Communications Protocols

Newport Systems' intelligent WAN adapter features a dedicated processor for the following WAN protocols:

HDLC
X.25
LAPB
PPP

A frame relay upgrade is to be released soon. These transmission protocols are included in the product at no additional cost. To upgrade the transmission protocol, a binary software file can be updated locally or remotely, making hardware upgrades unnecessary.

RIP and SAP Filtering and Echo

On a 9.6-kbps link, as much as 10 percent of bandwidth can be consumed by RIP and SAP broadcasts. LAN^{2}LAN/MPR filters out redundant broadcasted RIP and SAP packets, automatically stores them at each end, then echoes them to prevent routers from dropping connections. When new information in RIP and SAP packets is discovered, they are forwarded, but all others are filtered. This reduces RIP and SAP traffic on the WAN; only the packets that change are transmitted.

Automatic Load Balancing and Downed-Line Recovery

When mission-critical connections must be maintained, or when line service is restricted, multiple lines may be used to the same destination. LAN^{2}LAN/MPR can automatically split and balance communications over one WNIC with two, three, or four lines between the two locations, thereby doubling, tripling, or quadrupling the effective bandwidth. When a line goes down, its traffic is automatically routed to the remaining lines. When the downed line returns to service, load balancing automatically resumes.

Field Upgradeable

Upgrading preserves the investment in WAN hardware, and upgrades can be performed without replacing the WNIC adapter. This adapter is designed to look to a binary file on the router's hard drive for its execution instructions instead of to a ROM, PROM, or EPROM chip. To upgrade the board, all that is required is to replace a .BIN file on the router hard drive. This enables upgrades to other transmission protocols, such as frame relay, without replacing the WNIC. Communication Interface Modules (CIMs) in chip form can be used to swap the type of port interface. Data compression is added or upgraded by adding a daughterboard. Another daughter card and cable adds more ports and changes from two on board to four.

Multiple WNICs can be used in one router, and the router PC can be upgraded very simply. After one LAN^{2}LAN/MPR is upgraded, other LAN^{2}LAN/MPRs can be upgraded remotely using communications software, which is included with LAN^{2}LAN/MPR.

This product currently has these advantages that distinguish it from competitive routers. Newport Systems has been on the leading edge of router and WAN development for several years.

Internetwork Configurations

Several considerations need to be made when configuring an internetwork. Improper configuration can cause inefficient routing and less-than-optimal performance. A few basic guidelines are suggested as follows.

Routers in Series

Unless absolutely necessary, do not put routers in series. Each router introduces latency, and when congested, latency can cause substantial delay—especially in such NCP functions as a large file read or write operation.

The best configuration for any internetwork, whether routed or bridged, has a flat superstructure, or as few levels as possible. A good example of an efficient internetwork is shown in Figure 36.2, where a backbone LAN connects several LANs. The same LANs can be linked into a less efficient configuration, as also shown in Figure 36.2.

FIGURE 36.2.

A backbone LAN versus LANs in a series.

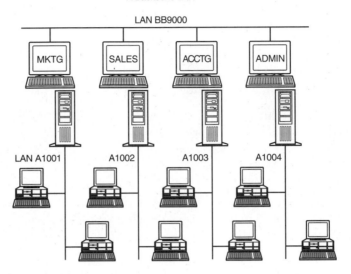

A Backbone LAN

LAN BB9000

MKTG   SALES   ACCTG   ADMIN

LAN A1001   A1002   A1003   A1004

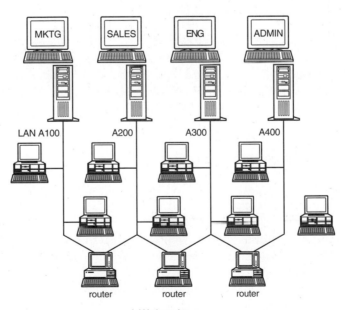

MKTG   SALES   ENG   ADMIN

LAN A100   A200   A300   A400

router   router   router

LANs in series

Using Redundant Paths

You would think that redundant paths were desirable because they introduce redundancy. However, in the case of Novell's RIP, redundant paths serve only as a backup path when one path is not available during an NCP connection request.

Providing redundant paths can be a liability when routers are used in one path and bridges in another. You should always take care not to have redundant routes that may reflect logical hop information inequitably. (This situation is fully discussed in Chapter 26, "Routers and Bridges.")

Link-state routing protocols, such as Open Shortest Path First and IS-IS, are preferred when using redundant paths. Link-state routers can reconfigure paths dynamically and determine the least-cost path more dependably. NetWare's RIP cannot be used in a link state. The problem with RIP, when redundant paths are available, is the route choice mechanism. If two paths have the same logical hop count, there is no mechanism for testing which path may be faster. If the more efficient path happens to be momentarily congested, the alternate path is chosen and that path remains for the duration of the connection. The introduction of NLSP is a step forward in resolving redundant-path inefficiencies.

Using Backbone LANs

Backbone LANs have been the preferred configuration for NetWare internetworks since 1985, because of the latency introduced in NetWare OS internal routers. Although high-performance external routers reduce this problem, you should always configure internetworks with the fewest potential hops. A backbone LAN or WAN provides the most cost-efficient (in terms of routing) internetwork configuration.

Campus-Wide Internetworks

Where local distances and right-of-ways are available, connecting all local LANs together with a high-speed LAN is the best possible configuration. Fiber optics may be necessary to span distances without having to go to a WAN. Switching hubs (concentrators) and routers are available to connect FDDI or optical-fiber Ethernet LAN segments to departmental Ethernet and Token Ring LANs. Although the cost is high, the alternative costs of restricted WAN throughput and recurring monthly charges may be far less attractive. In many cases, the cost is justified. Figure 36.3 shows a high-capacity backbone, campus-wide LAN.

FIGURE 36.3.

A high-capacity backbone campus-wide LAN.

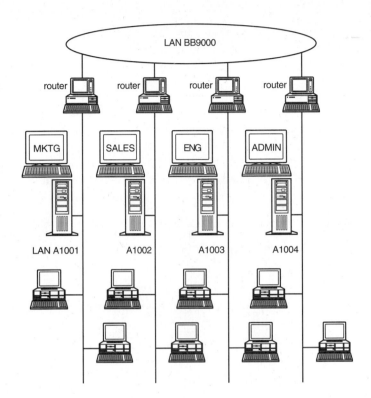

FDDI is an especially attractive LAN for this purpose. It can span distances of up to 1.2 miles between concentrators and many miles from end to end with 100-mbps bandwidth. Optical-fiber Ethernet (10Base-F) can span intermediate distances for far less cost. SynOptic's LattisNet fiber-optic facilities concentrators can span up to 4.3 miles from one end to another.

Enterprise-Wide Internetworks

Connecting facilities where right-of-ways are not available is a more difficult problem with PC-based networks than it was with mainframes and minicomputers. In an SNA network, for example, the SDLC link between a Front End Processor and a remote Cluster Controller carries only simple video and keystroke characters. Even with many terminals multiplexed, a 9.6- to 56-kbps line is normally quite adequate. Similarly, in a TCP/IP internetwork, UDP is substituted for TCP to eliminate the connection-oriented TCP acknowledgment mechanism. Higher-layer protocols such as Telnet, FTP, and SMTP restrict communications to terminal emulation and file transfers.

PC-based networks generally use interactive processing between nodes. Because of NCP's connection-oriented nature, and because PCs convey complex data (such as complex screen images) over communications links, even high bandwidth links are inadequate for many purposes.

WANs are normally point-to-point entities. Unlike LANs, a WAN cannot contain multiple nodes—only a source and destination. A multiple-point WAN must therefore be configured into a mesh topology, as shown in Figure 36.4. Connections between each point must have a direct connection. If you need to connect several points, a mesh network can become complex and expensive, which severely limits how extensively WANs can be configured for remote sites.

FIGURE 36.4.

A mesh topology WAN for connecting multiple points.

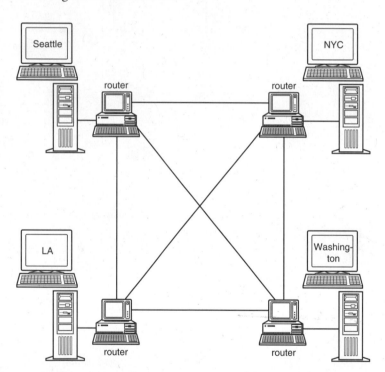

This is not altogether true for X.25 Public Data Networks (PDNs). Although each router (or bridge) has only one connection to the PDN, a new end-to-end connection is established each time communications are sent. Although potential throughput for X.25 is 384 kbps, PDNs offer service only at 56 kbps. This is still actually not a true multipoint network like a LAN.

To reduce the number of WAN lines between sites, a single router at each site is used to connect all local LANs into one WAN line. Wherever possible, it is best to directly connect one router (or bridge) to all LANs in a facility, as shown in Figure 36.5. By connecting all LANs in a site to one router (or bridge), one hop is eliminated when compared against connecting the router to a backbone LAN.

FIGURE 36.5.

One router connecting all LANs to a WAN versus connecting the router to a backbone LAN.

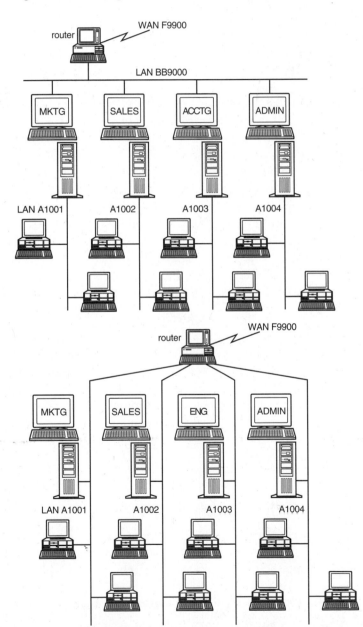

Alternatively, connecting the router to a backbone LAN may be required to reach all LANs spread across a campus, as shown in Figure 36.5. This introduces one more hop, but it makes the router available to all nodes. Although with NetWare, routers are preferred over bridges in all situations, in this illustration routers are virtually mandated. Otherwise, the additional hops may not be perceived.

T-1 Lines versus Frame Relay

Major interest in frame relay has not translated into a huge migration from T-1 lines, as some might expect. Several factors prevent this new technology from starting a stampede. First, frame-relay services are not as widely available as T-carrier service. Second, frame-relay transmission protocol has not been implemented in as many routers as other transmission protocols, so changing equipment and upgrading is an obstacle. Third, usage charges can only be compared on a case-by-case basis. T-1 lines are deregulated, so rates vary from location to location, and many find that rates are not set so firmly after all. Frame relay rates are based on usage, and what is required for access to the Point of Presence (POP) varies. T-1 lines may be required to connect some locations to frame relay POPs, and the T-1 access lines must be included in a comparison if they are not bundled with the frame relay service. With so many variables, the whole picture becomes confused.

Both T-carrier and frame-relay services provide about the same level of service—digital service at 64 kbps through 1.544 mbps—with increments in between. Products can be combined for higher bandwidths. Frame-relay providers may have services available that T-1 carriers may not offer in your area. For example, Wiltel offers bundled routers, load balancing, fault-tolerant redundant line conditions, and overflow excess capacity on demand. Although competitors are working hard to provide these services, Wiltel offers it now. Other vendors, such as AT&T, have been very competitive, working diligently to match Wiltel's offerings. Check in your area to see who offers the best service.

Frame relay is more cost effective than equivalent capacity T-carrier lines when long distances are involved and less than 24-hour usage is demanded. Many frame-relay providers offer service bundled with T-1 access and even a router, taking total responsibility for line conditions, components, and bundled services—or, you can do it yourself. T-1 providers have refused to provide such services in the past, but many are reversing their stands now. It certainly may pay to have a frame-relay provider bid on your service; it can save thousands of dollars per month in monthly charges and in lost productivity when line problems occur.

Internetwork Software Considerations

Due to the limitations of WANs and their limited bandwidth and high cost relative to LANs, you should reconsider your software system design. Electronic mail is designed to work well as-is over a WAN, and file transfers also may be practical. Interactive database-oriented systems, however, should be evaluated for more efficient design.

Application software should never be executed from a remote file server on the other end of a WAN. Executable files should be located locally with data mapped remotely to reduce the amount of traffic over a WAN, as shown in Figure 36.6. This provides centralized data and good performance.

FIGURE 36.6.

Executable files local, with data remote.

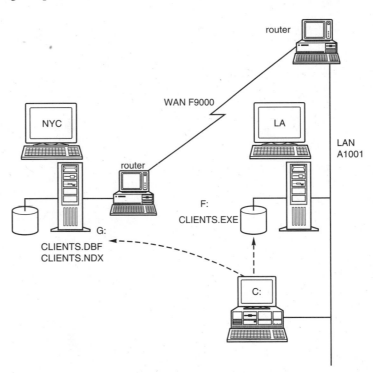

Client-server database software servers are growing in popularity for the very same reason. You should put as little traffic as possible on a WAN, redistributing processing back to the host whenever possible. A database server, such as Oracle, SQL Server, or Informix, can do some of the file searching at the data location, while the application running on the node's application is slimmed down to accommodate more records for immediate use. The client-server model in database design is more practical for remotely shared data.

This software architecture can be hierarchical to provide fast and efficient local processing, centralized data, and even batch-updated consolidation of data. The Internal Revenue Service has recently shifted to such a design, with distributed local applications on UNIX workstations, local UNIX database servers, and central servers where data is consolidated, as shown in Figure 36.7.

FIGURE 36.7.

Hierarchical client-server distributed databases and consolidation.

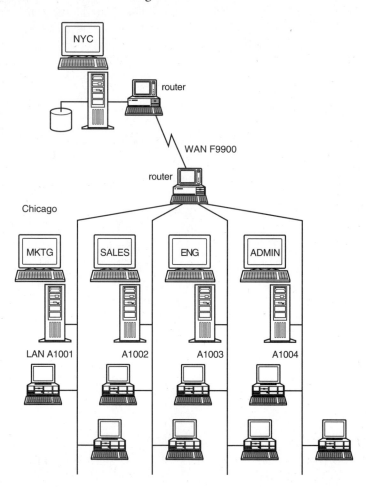

UNIX workstations run applications and process data locally. Data is shared from a local database server, with as many as 30 servers in one regional office. Every evening, data is collected from the database servers and consolidated into a central repository server. Within one day, all records are consolidated nationally into a single point. The results are quite efficient. (Run for your life, tax-dodgers!)

Although this example is not a NetWare solution, NetWare is integrated into the same LANs and WANs, and NetWare client workstations and cross-platforms can be integrated into the same databases if desired. This example can just as easily be applied to NetWare as to UNIX. Platform-independent applications can be integrated with UNIX, OS/2, Windows, DOS, and Macintosh clients, with UNIX or NetWare database servers, and with repository servers. This approach incorporates distributed real-time shared data access with batch updated centralized databases, for the best of both worlds.

With client-server database software, the technology is here today to replace large, expensive mainframes with distributed applications. The client-server database design offers distributed computing, with some computing redistributed back to centralized points. This design makes the most sense when long distances are involved. The element of flexibility is an added benefit for client workstations. They can be used locally for more than just their dedicated missions with off-the-shelf software.

Summary

It is important to stay current on internetworking developments. This area of LAN integration is the leading edge where new technology is developing daily, and new developments change the rules periodically. Read industry publications that focus on internetworking and PC periodicals that have dedicated sections for internetworking. Attend trade shows, and keep current with internetworking software and hardware updates. In this dynamic environment, you can be out of date in a flash.

You can do the following to improve internetwork performance:

1. Use routers exclusively with NetWare. Use bridges only for nonroutable protocols. Many bridge-routers (so-called *brouters*) first route routable protocols, and then bridge only nonroutable protocols, for this very reason.

2. Incorporate Packet Burst NCP for best performance over internetworks. This protocol is included in NetWare 3.12 and 4.x, but 3.11 requires the addition of an NLM at the server and new workstation shells. It is available on NetWire.

3. Monitor LAN bandwidth utilization and keep departmental LANs at low levels, routing together departmental LANs into campus-wide and enterprise-wide systems.

4. Whenever possible, configure internetworks into a flat superstructure using backbone LANs. Configure with as few hops as possible for best performance.

5. Check out frame relay to see if something is available or the cost is lower. You cannot know simply from reading on this issue; every case is different.

6. Use client-server database software designed for centralized data applications. Install applications locally, distribute database processing as close to the application as possible, and batch-consolidate distributed databases from collection points for best use of distributed and centralized software design. Combine real-time with batch updates wherever possible to avoid the necessity of building behemoth systems.

7. Keep updated. Read about the latest developments in internetworking software and hardware. Stay current on versions and releases. Internetworking is probably the most dynamic part of the industry at this time.

VII

PART

Preventing Downtime

Protecting Files with Transaction Tracking System

37

by *Rick Sant'Angelo*

Transaction Tracking System (TTS) is a System Fault Tolerant (SFT) Level II feature that is included in every current version of NetWare. Prior to 3.0 and 2.2 versions, SFT II features were included in a special SFT version of NetWare at additional cost.

TTS protects your vital operating system files to prevent their corruption. TTS also can be used to protect other data files from corruption, but only if implemented by the system administrator. The process is often as simple as adding the transactional attribute to a file using the NetWare FLAG command.

TTS protects operating system files, such as the bindery files, from corruption caused by damage during update. Previous versions of NetWare that did not have this protection could experience periodic problems, such as bindery corruption or damage to file system tables. For example, with Advanced NetWare 2.15 (without SFT II features), power loss to the file server during file update occasionally caused extensive damage to the file system. To repair the damage, you had to run VREPAIR. In many cases, the file system damage might be so extensive that you had to completely reinstall the OS to get the server running again. This is no longer a problem. TTS provides such outstanding and reliable protection that you can always count on your file system and security to work properly, regardless of any abuse the server may receive.

How TTS Works

TTS protects data files during update by creating a *transaction backout file* where all file updates are stored. These updates are not added to the original file until the transaction is completed. Upon completion of the update, TTS commits the updates by copying the updates in the transaction backout file into the original file. This reduces the exposure of the original file to damage. If for any reason the update fails, the original file is intact, and all transactions up until the failure are saved separately in the transaction backout file. You can either revert to the file as it was before the update began, or you can add the transactions stored in the transaction backout file. During the update, the combination of the original and backout files appears to your application to be one file.

A TTS file update occurs in two steps. First, updates are written to the transaction backout file. When the update is completed, the entries in the transaction backout file are written to the original data file. The process is represented in Figure 37.1.

FIGURE 37.1.

A TTS transaction.

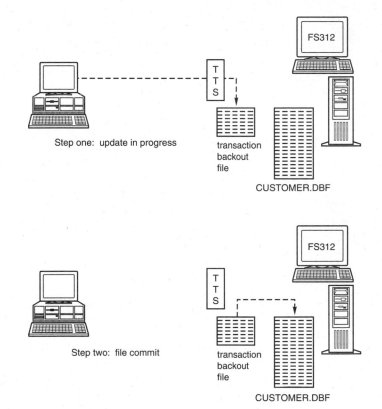

Step one: update in progress

transaction backout file

CUSTOMER.DBF

Step two: file commit

transaction backout file

CUSTOMER.DBF

Programming languages, database managers, and record managers often have similar features, which are usually called *transaction rollback.* For example, Btrieve has a transaction rollback feature that can be called from an application. Btrieve is a record manager that is used with several programming languages. At the outset of a file update a transaction is initialized, and at the end of the transaction a commit is issued. Either the entire update occurs or none at all. If the update fails, a Btrieve error is sent. When the file is opened again, its use may be blocked if, for any reason, Btrieve cannot ensure the integrity of the update.

This type of protection is most often handled in software application procedures. If such programming is in your application, TTS does not need to be activated. However, if you are running a mission-critical application that does not include this feature, and your data needs to be protected, TTS can be used to perform a similar type of file protection even during access from multiple users.

TTS might be preferred over software procedures for two reasons. First, TTS is controlled by the server OS, so it is more secure than a higher-layer procedure. The server OS is less likely to crash than the software application, and therefore damage control is lessened. Second, like other physical write requests, it can be performed as a lower-priority background function, giving priority to file read requests. Performance for other applications is therefore enhanced.

TTS is designed to be transparent to applications. During the update, the application is not aware that two files are being maintained because NetWare presents them with one file handle. This should not cause any problems or considerations for your applications, but you may notice degradation of performance during heavy read-and-write activity due to the additional file handling. In some cases, the application language or record manager may experience unexpected results and cause problems. The interaction of multiple data files, index files, and locks can cause problems specific to the application. Normally these problems can be overcome with slight programming modifications.

Implementing TTS

TTS can be activated with the NetWare FLAG command-line utility. If a file is flagged with a T (transactional attribute) when the file is opened, TTS will go to work. It initializes a transaction backout file and intercepts all physical file updates, redirecting them to the backout file. To flag a file called CUSTOMER.DBF with the transactional attribute, change to the directory in which this file is located and type FLAG CUSTOMER.DBF T.

Adjusting TTS Parameters

NetWare's dynamic allocation of resources makes TTS virtually maintenance-free. The following SET parameters can be adjusted at the server's console prompt. NetWare 4.x has a SERVMAN.NLM utility, where these parameters can be adjusted from a menu with online help available. TTS can also be temporarily disabled, as discussed in this section. The SET parameters can be adjusted at the console by typing the command, SET *SET_parameter* = *value*.

For example, to toggle the Auto TTS Backout Flag (as discussed in the next section) from its default state of OFF to ON, type the following command or place it into your STARTUP.NCF file: SET Auto TTS Backout Flag = ON.

> **NOTE ▶**
>
> Unless otherwise noted in the following sections, these commands can be automated by placing them in your AUTOEXEC.NCF file. However, some of the commands must be placed into the STARTUP.NCF file as noted in the next section.

Auto TTS Backout Flag

When this parameter is set to OFF (the default value), an incomplete transaction causes the following message to appear the next time the file server is brought up:

```
Incomplete transaction found. Do you wish to back them out?
```

By toggling the state to ON, TTS automatically backs out of an incomplete transaction during file server boot.

TTS Abort Dump Flag

This flag can cause TTS to write transactions that are backed out to a log file (TTS$LOG.ERR, located in the root of the SYS: volume). The default value is OFF, which prevents backed-out transactions from being written to the log file.

> **TIP ▶**
>
> If you use TTS, it is valuable to toggle the state of this parameter to ON.

Maximum TTS Transactions

Your system can accommodate up to 10,000 concurrent TTS sessions. During a TTS update, each open transactional file is one TTS session. Each transactional file initializes a transaction backout file. There is no advantage to be gained by adjusting this parameter. It is set to the maximum value, but resources are not tied up unless required.

TTS Unwritten Cache Wait Time

This is the maximum amount of time that an updated cache buffer can remain held before its contents must be physically written to the disk. When this time limit is reached, the physical write request is given a high priority.

The default value is 1 minute, 5.9 seconds.
The minimum value is 11 seconds.
The maximum value is 10 minutes, 59.1 seconds.

TTS Backout File Truncation Wait Time

This parameter controls the amount of time TTS waits while file-write activity is idle before it assumes the update has stopped and therefore commits the file update. Database file updates may be idle because of processing activity such as a sort or merge, or a workstation or application may have crashed. When this amount of time has expired before a file close has been issued, the update is assumed to have been abnormally terminated.

The default time is set to 15 minutes, 19.2 seconds.
The minimum value is 1 minute, 5.9 seconds.
The maximum value is 1 day, two hours, 29 minutes, 51.3 seconds.

Disabling TTS

TTS can be disabled through the FCONSOLE utility. Under the Status menu option, TTS can be toggled between Enable and Disable. A user must be the user Supervisor, a Supervisor equivalent, or a Console Operator to toggle this option.

Preventing Loss of Data Due to Disk Failure

by Rick Sant'Angelo

38

Disk failure can be the most costly type of problem you'll face. Any other hardware failure may interrupt productivity, but a disk failure also loses your data and perhaps your OS. When you lose the disk that contains your SYS volume, you must reinstall, restore your backups, and restore your security. You can expect to be down for a while.

Restoring backups involves restoring data to a previous level, perhaps the end of the previous business day. Users must then reinput all work that was saved the same day. If your server provides storage for 100 users, and each user has an average of only one hour's worth of reinput (which is unlikely), that amounts to 100 man hours of lost productivity plus the amount of time it takes to reinput the data. When this type of problem is experienced, it is almost impossible to estimate the cost related to the confusion and mistakes that occur. Worst of all, downtime disrupts efficiency and normal work flow.

Sometimes, restorations do not produce what you expect—a perfectly functioning server. You may need to restore backups from several days ago, and therefore your security may be out of date. For other reasons, restoring your security may not be successful, in which case you will need to add users and groups and rewrite login scripts before the system can be used again.

Lost revenue may also plague you during your recovery. When customers phone in orders and salespeople take orders manually, some orders may get lost or entered incorrectly. This would cause loss of revenue and dissatisfied customers. Rebuilding your system and restoring your backups may take longer than anticipated.

Even in the smallest company, loss of data costs money. Regardless of what problems you encounter, any time a disk is lost, losses accumulate quite rapidly. No matter how slight the cost may seem to be, these costs occur regardless of whether checks are written that are directly associated with the loss.

Adequate analysis of alternate costs are not generally evaluated. Though recent surveys indicate that many companies have lost millions of dollars annually due to downtime, these costs get lost in the piles of paperwork and expense account numbers. To adequately assess your losses (and therefore establish a budget item for this expense item), you may need to conduct extensive studies. After a figure has been established, some of these funds can be spent on prevention of downtime.

Fault-tolerant disk storage is one of the most cost-effective solutions in network computing today. In virtually every situation, the cost of a mirrored system disk drive is far less than the alternative costs of downtime directly attributable to loss of an unmirrored drive.

NetWare's disk mirroring in the OS has evolved over several revisions and new OS upgrades. It was initially introduced as SFT NetWare Version 2.10, but it did not work very well. Subsequent revisions improved functionality, and SFT NetWare Version 2.15 Revision C was stable and safe. Occasionally, disk drivers would cause minor problems, but by this point, virtually all disk-drive developers have learned to make their drivers function flawlessly with mirroring.

By adding another disk drive and configuring a mirrored pair, you can prevent these problems. Not only will you save your company money, but your sanity can be maintained.

Disk mirroring is not your only option. You should be aware of simpler and more complex solutions. This chapter discusses

- Disk mirroring
- Disk duplexing
- RAID subsystems
- Mirroring software

Disk Mirroring

NetWare provides options for mirroring disks. When two drives are mirrored, all files stored on one drive are also stored on the second drive. This activity is part of the NetWare server OS and is therefore transparent to applications. All configuration is done at the server, and users can see no evidence that mirroring is in process at any time.

How it Works

When two disks are mirrored, the portions of their NetWare partitions that can be allocated to volumes become physical copies of one another. One drive is designated as the primary drive and the other as the secondary drive, so that if either fails, the alternate can continue to operate without interruption of service.

Every physical write request from the OS is first sent to the primary drive, and then a duplicate write request is issued to the secondary drive. This can have obvious disadvantages to disk performance when cache buffers are saturated. However, a high level of disk-write activity is seldom experienced in typical situations, so the effect is negligible. Typically, any performance effect experienced as a result of disk mirroring can be offset by adding more RAM to your server. If you believe your performance suffers because of this factor, see Chapter 33, "Monitoring and Adjusting Server Performance," for tips on observing your cache buffers for saturation.

When a drive fails, the server OS will not be able to communicate with the drive. When a drive does not respond, the OS polls the drive, and then deactivates it if it does not respond. The following message then appears on your console:

```
Device #n (driver_name) deactivated due to drive failure.
```

Each device is assigned a number based on which adapter and drive number is connected to that adapter. In the preceding code line, *n* refers to this number. You also will get a message indicating that mirroring has been disabled. When a mirrored drive deactivates, you can verify loss of the drive in a few places:

1. The previous error message is displayed at the server console.

2. The error message is saved to the system error log, which can be viewed from SYSCON | Supervisor Options | View File Server Error Log. The error log is saved in the file SYS:SYSTEM/SYS$LOG.ERR. It is an ASCII file that can be saved with another filename or printed out.

3. You can check the server MONITOR.NLM under Drive Information, as shown in Figure 38.1. There you can select the drive and examine the Drive Status. It will show Active if it is accessible. If the drive is not listed under System Disk Drives, check for a hardware problem; the driver cannot communicate with the drive at all.

TIP ►

Whenever a drive deactivation occurs, you should check the system error log carefully for errors that you may have missed before the deactivation occurred.

FIGURE 38.1.

Checking the server Monitor Drive Information.

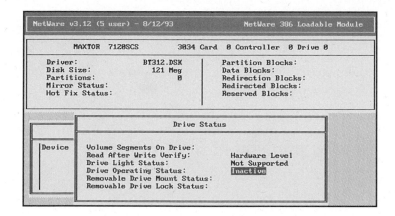

4. You can check the INSTALL.NLM. Load Install. Select Disk Options, the appropriate drive, and then the Partition table. If there are problems communicating with the drive, Install displays specific error dialog boxes (as shown in Figure 38.2) and attempts to fix the problem. If the drive does not appear during this procedure, the driver cannot communicate with the drive at all. Again, check for hardware problems.

FIGURE 38.2.

Install's Partition table screens.

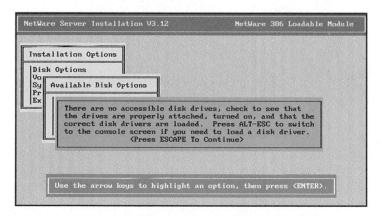

5. You also can check Install's Disk Options; select the appropriate drive and then select Mirroring. Here also, you should see whether the drives are synchronized. If the drives are not synchronized, the mirroring has been disabled.

> **NOTE** ▶
>
> When any disk problem occurs, it may cause volume on that drive to become dismounted. You can restore the volumes by running VREPAIR.NLM. See the section on Troubleshooting for instructions on running VREPAIR.NLM.

How to Implement Disk Mirroring

Disk mirroring is simple to implement. The following procedure demonstrates the process of adding a second disk and mirroring:

1. Physically install the disk.
2. Load INSTALL.NLM and create a NetWare partition.
3. Pair the two drives.

Mirroring will commence in the background. Check the server console screen (press Alt+Esc to switch screens) for messages. Be patient; it may take a long time to complete the mirror copy, especially if the server is busy. Remirroring does not affect user disk access because it is assigned a very low priority. When the drives are synchronized, a message appears at the console indicating that the drives are in synch.

What to Watch Out For

A few small "gotcha's" apply with disk mirroring. A system administrator should constantly monitor servers, watch for console error messages, and observe for proper operation. Third-party system-monitoring software, as discussed in Chapter 20, "Third-Party System Administration Utilities," is quite helpful in providing alerts and monitoring through a workstation-based utility. Using the remote console (RCONSOLE) utility enables remote monitoring from a workstation. During the server boot procedure, observing error messages is also important. Following are some factors to watch out for.

Drive Deactivation

The biggest problem with disk mirroring is that when a drive goes down, you probably will not notice it. Unless you constantly monitor your server's console, look at the error log on a frequent basis, or have a third-party utility that will inform you, drive deactivation occurs quietly.

Malfunctioning Disk Drivers

Although NetWare certification reduces potential disk-driver problems, new hardware and NetWare versions constantly throw curves at driver developers. The signs of driver bugs include the following:

- Failure to see drives during installation
- Failure to mount volumes or communicate with drive
- Loss of volumes
- Drive deactivation
- File server "abend" (crash)
- File corruption

Obviously, none of these problems is to be taken lightly. Problems, as discussed previously, occur almost immediately upon installation of the new driver, although in some cases they appear only when heavy file access occurs. Typically, if the drive cannot be seen during the installation, the disk subsystem is not physically installed properly.

When problems occur after the server has been operating properly for an extended period, you should suspect hardware failure. Always look for what has changed on the system. If nothing has changed, hardware failure is most likely.

Controller Failure

In mirroring, if the controller fails, both drives are down. This is why duplexing is more reliable. When controllers fail, the problems are often intermittent. Controller problems have been known to

- Deactivate drives
- Lose volumes
- Corrupt data

IDE Drives

> **CAUTION** ▶
>
> Mirroring IDE drives may not provide the type of fault tolerance you might expect. Under normal conditions, when one mirrored IDE drive fails, both drives go down.

When two IDE drives are mirrored, the second drive connected to an adapter becomes the slave of the first (using the primary drive's controller). If the primary drive's controller fails, both drives are disabled. IDE adapters are available that can duplex IDE drives. These are preferred for this reason alone.

If this problem happens to you, separate the drives and bring up the remaining good drive as a single drive. If the failure was in the embedded controller on the primary drive, your data will still be intact, and you will be able to bring the server up again without much downtime.

Disk Duplexing

Disk duplexing is more reliable and more fault tolerant than mirroring. The only difference in implementing disk duplexing is the fact that the drives are connected to separate adapters. Most of the time, two drivers must be loaded (or one driver must be loaded re-entrantly). In some cases, a single driver is designed to address two adapters. Each adapter must be addressed by the driver. This is done by identifying the base I/O address (port address) during driver load procedure.

> **NOTE** ▶
>
> In order for duplexing to yield improved performance, at least one of the drive subsystems must be SCSI. SCSI drives have the capability to physically read and write at the same time. Theoretically, this is not possible with ESDI, IDE, or other types of drives.
>
> No NetWare screen information indicates any difference between mirroring and duplexing. If the two drives are physically connected to the same adapter, they are mirrored; if they are connected to separate adapters, they are duplexed.

For more information about disk duplexing, see Chapter 2, "Local Area Networks."

Redundant Array of Inexpensive Disks (RAID) Subsystems

RAID technology has improved reliability when massive storage is required. Some smaller RAID systems are available, but the cost of a smaller RAID system is normally quite prohibitive when compared to disk duplexing. Conversely, duplexing 10G or 20G of disk space may be far more expensive.

Evolution of RAID Technology

RAID was first implemented for PCs by Compaq when the SystemPro was first developed. Compaq used the same type of technology that was employed in mainframe and fault-tolerant minicomputers. Once the technology was developed, other vendors followed the lead and developed their own systems. Today, RAID is fairly standard, and many vendors produce systems that are highly fault tolerant. Pricing has fallen substantially as a result.

RAID Levels

In 1987, a University of California at Berkeley publication defined RAID technology. This white paper has become a *de facto* standard in RAID systems. The levels that were defined include the following:

Level 0: Data striped across all disks in an array.

Level 1: Data mirrored on two or more disks. Failure of one drive does not disable the system.

Level 2: Data striped across drives at the bit level.

Level 3: Data striped across drives at the byte level.

Level 4: Data striped across drives at the block level.

Level 5: Data striped across drives at the block level, and a parity drive is added for fault tolerance. If any drive fails, data is reconstructed on the fly.

Most RAID subsystems are Level 1 or Level 5. Another level, defined by Storage Computer Corporation, was called Level 7, but it wasn't related to the UCB standard. In all other RAID systems, drive actuation is synchronized. Level 7 enables heads to move independently of one another for better performance.

> **NOTE** ▶
>
> NetWare disk mirroring is technically a Level 1 RAID implementation.

RAID Decision Factors

The choice for RAID is normally justified by massive storage requirements. Disk duplexing imposes a 100-percent cost for fault tolerance, whereas most Level 5 RAID systems cost from 20 to 25 percent. To mirror 1G of disk storage requires two 1G drives. To implement Level 5 RAID, three or four disks can contain striped data, whereas one drive contains parity information. The initial cost of a RAID subsystem is high, but the premium paid in disk space is lower. The balance point of which is more cost-effective changes as prices change.

Disk-Mirroring Software

Few products are available that handle mirroring of data at the source. One such product is REFLECT, from CLone Star Software. When a small DOS TSR (less than 8K) is installed at the user workstation, disk writes can be sent to two destinations. This product does not perform a background copy or send data with any delay. The same write request is duplicated and sent simultaneously to two locations with identical system calls. If availability at one location is interrupted, REFLECT automatically switches your file read operations to the alternate location without interrupting service.

REFLECT works perfectly with NetWare and other networks. Several users can mirror data, and file/record locking works normally. This product is sold as a stand-alone product or is licensed according to the number of users.

REFLECT mirrors drive letters, which can be mapped or substituted (using the DOS Substitute utility) to mirror data from any drive or directory to any drive or directory. REFLECT can therefore mirror

- One directory to another directory
- One drive to another drive
- An entire server volume to another server volume

REFLECT offers a simple, inexpensive, and flexible solution to the problem of filed disk drives. Although it can be used to mirror servers, it is used most often for duplicating data in more specific and unique situations than Novell's disk mirroring or SFT III solutions. For example, a user can concurrently write data to a server and a local disk. Data is synchronized in both locations so the user can access data in either place when the other is not available.

Alternative uses add value to this product. You can make data available for database searches without touching the primary data file. If the user updating a file is using REFLECT to mirror data to two locations, other users in distributed locations can read from either data file.

A working demonstration copy of REFLECT is included on the disk that accompanies this book. The one-hour demonstration will not damage any data, and it includes documentation. It is that simple to set up and use. All information necessary to install it, use it, and contact the developers is in the file, REFLECTB.DOC.

Summary

You have all the means necessary to ensure that disk failures do not cause downtime. This technology is not new or unproved, and it is extremely reliable. You have several choices for protecting your data. If money to purchase a second disk is a problem, consider how much your company spends each year on disk drive disabilities. You can spend money to prevent the problem, or spend it on lost productivity, downtime, and crisis management. The choice is yours.

A fault-tolerant disk subsystem does not make backups unnecessary. For many reasons, good backups stand as a separate issue. You should never let down your guard when protecting your data with every means possible. See Chapter 21, "Backup Strategies and Products," for more information.

Fault Tolerance with SFT III

39

by Rick Sant'Angelo

IN THIS CHAPTER

SFT III can provide the key link in eliminating downtime in any system. If the integrator builds redundancy into all important components, the system can be as reliable as any fault-tolerant system available today. SFT III guards the file server from potential loss of file server operation. Of course, for SFT III to be effective, you need to know how to implement it and how to take other measures to keep your network running. Common networking components can be used to provide dependability and redundancy beyond previous capabilities.

For many years, true fault tolerance was expensive and proprietary. Applications that required this type of dependability were limited to those that could support a hefty price tag. SFT III has transformed that restriction. Although some consider SFT III's price to be high, there isn't a point of reference with which to compare. Today, SFT III enables users to use common PC and LAN hardware to make a system so safe that life-support systems can rely on it. Even if the cost of all parts of a network is doubled, the value-to-cost ratio of SFT III makes true fault tolerance available to more applications than ever before.

Many say that SFT III is expensive. Perhaps in a discussion of cost, the relative cost of downtime should be considered. An hour of downtime in a large company can cost up to $500,000. Recent surveys have estimated that the average hour of downtime costs between $32,000 to $78,000 in a large company. No matter what the actual cost of downtime is in your company, it is likely that SFT III and its associated costs are less than you will spend because of downtime. You can place no monetary value on the chaos, pressure, and confusion that accompany downtime.

SFT III is simply a NetWare server OS version that maintains servers in an identical state of data update. It is a server OS that is designed to work in tandem with two servers. One server is designated as a primary server, and the other is secondary. The primary server is the main point of update, whereas the secondary server is in a constant state of readiness to take over without as much as a hiccup. Both receive all updates through a special link called a Mirrored Server Link (MSL), which is dedicated to this purpose. The servers also communicate over the Internet link (normal LAN communications) they share in common, so that one will know if the other has failed. When a failure occurs, the second server automatically takes over without interrupting communications in any user-detectable way.

SFT III also uses redundant measures to ensure reliability. Each server monitors the other server's NCP acknowledgments over their normal Internetwork links to see that all the requests are serviced, and that OSs are constantly maintained in a mirrored state. A special utility is provided to monitor the servers, their devices, and their states.

SFT III also can improve server response. Routing requests and disk reads are expedited as an added benefit of mirrored server design. SFT III can be run on dual processor computers asymetrically—that is, some of the processing can occur on one processor while the rest is executed on another.

SFT III does not prevent LAN, cabling, print server, communication server, or many other types of failures. It only provides automatic switchover to a standby server when loss of a critical component is experienced in a primary server. In addition to using SFT III, you need to shore up and monitor several critical failure points in order to provide true fault-tolerant service.

This chapter discusses how SFT III works, and it gives some direction on how to implement it and the components upon which you must rely.

How SFT III Works

SFT III was designed to mirror server OSs in an identical state. Each server, however, needs to be isolated from hardware problems experienced by the other server. To accomplish this goal, Novell engineers split the server OS into two separate parts: the Mirrored Server Engine (MS Engine) and the Input/Output Engine (I/O Engine). Both engines are loaded on both servers. The MS Engines are maintained in an identical state (mirrored), while each I/O Engine works independently of all other engines so that a fault in one server's hardware only affects that server's I/O Engine and does not halt any of the other engines. Figure 39.1 shows SFT III's separated engine design as installed on mirrored servers.

FIGURE 39.1.

SFT III mirrored and separated engines.

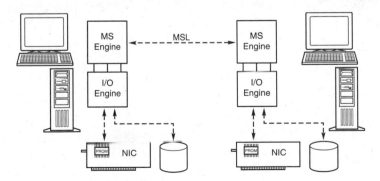

The MS Engines

This is the portion of the OS that runs the NCP functions. Each NCP request is received by the primary server, duplicated, and sent across a special link (see the section titled "The Mirrored Server Link") to the secondary server.

Most OSs use preemptive processing, where several threads may be in process at any given time. This design makes it very complex to keep two OSs synchronized in a mirrored state, because each one would need to have multiple processes, their interrupts, and memory duplicated at all times. Because NetWare uses nonpreemptive processing (explained in detail in Chapter 3), only one thread is processed at a time on the MS Engine. The requests received by the secondary server can be queued by its OS scheduler and executed, even though it may not be executed at exactly the same time. The two MS Engines receive exactly the same instructions in the same sequence, but process each separately. The two OSs therefore remain in a mirrored state without the need to simultaneously duplicate multiple states of interrupts, memory, and controls.

The MS Engine also can execute NLMs that are not hardware-related. Any NLM that can execute on the MS Engine is also mirrored.

The I/O Engine

This is a separate portion of the OS that controls only the local hardware devices, such as the disk drives, NICs, MSL, and hardware-related NLMs. NIC and disk drivers are loaded on the I/O Engine. Because this is a separate OS, the mirrored MS Engines relay the same NCP requests to their respective I/O Engines in the very same sequence. Each I/O Engine therefore executes exactly the same requests almost simultaneously. Each I/O Engine operates completely independently of the other but duplicates the other's processes, because each receives the same requests in the same sequence. This process is represented in Figure 39.2.

This total separation between I/O Engines enables each server and its OS to handle localized hardware failures without affecting the other. The MS Engines do not handle any processes that may cause faults and therefore will not crash, even though hardware may fail. A hardware failure that would normally halt a file server halts only the I/O Engine in the server on which its driver is loaded.

FIGURE 39.2.

SFT III's mirrored MS engines, with separate I/O engine operation.

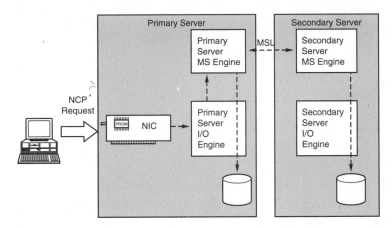

Logical Communications path - - - - - - - - - - - ▶

The Mirrored Server Link (MSL)

An MSL is a special bidirectional communication channel. Normal NICs can be used as long as they have special MSL drivers, but an MSL should be a special type of NIC-and-driver combination capable of only point-to-point communications at very high bandwidth.

MS Engines communicate with one another logically through the MSL, even though the I/O Engine physically handles the MSL requests (as illustrated in Figure 39.3). MSL drivers are loaded in the I/O Engine, connecting the two servers with a separate network. Each NCP write request is duplicated in the primary server—one issued to its I/O Engine, and one sent by the MSL to the secondary MS Engine.

FIGURE 39.3.

MSL logical versus physical communication paths.

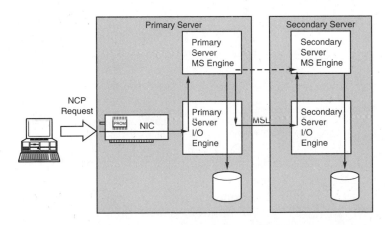

Logical MSL communication path - - - - - - ▶

Physical MSL communication path ——————▶

The access protocol and drivers for an MSL should be built to be efficient for this specific application. Normal NICs can be used, but it is far more effective to use a 100 Mbps point-to-point link. The overhead of normal LAN access protocols, and the limited capacity of most LANs, may reduce the capability of an MSL to quickly synchronize the MS Engines. The MSL should be able to respond immediately with no latency so that the link never experiences delay in synchronization. It also should have very high bandwidth (capacity) to accommodate the vast number of requests passing between MS Engines. All current MSL products communicate at 100 Mbps or greater capacity.

Eagle Technologies, Thomas-Conrad, and PlainTree Systems make MSL hardware and drivers that meet these requirements. Novell's NMSL has the greatest capacity at 143 Mbps, whereas the others run at 100 Mbps. PlainTree's Wave Bus can accommodate a 100-Mbps connection between servers of several miles using optical fiber cabling and their proprietary hardware. Each product has been Novell Labs certified, and each is proven to be stable.

Novell/Eagle NE2000 or NE2/32 Ethernet NICs can be used as a backup MSL should the primary MSL fail. Only one MSL can be loaded at any given time in each server.

Fault Recovery

SFT III recovers from four potential types of failures, discussed in the following sections.

Primary Server Hardware Failure

When the primary server fails, the secondary server detects the failure and immediately takes over as the primary server. Because the secondary server is for all purposes in an identical state, the switchover occurs transparently. NCP's connection-oriented mechanics automatically recover from communications complications of the momentary switchover. The failure is detected in one or both of two ways: The MSL link generates an error condition when no activity is noticed; and/or the servers communicate over the normal Internet link, each one monitoring the other's NCP acknowledgments.

The primary server is simply the first server of the pair that is brought up. It becomes the server that is being used at all times, and it processes all requests. When the primary server fails, the secondary server is immediately substituted as the primary server with identical configuration. User connections are in an identical state in the new primary server. The switchover is handled entirely at the server end, and work continues without any perceivable interruption.

During the switchover, a few NCP requests may be lost. NCP is a connection-oriented protocol that is designed to recover from minor losses of this nature, so it automatically recovers without user intervention. The workstation's shell or requester does not receive acknowledgments for lost requests and therefore reexecutes the missing requests. The secondary server reconfigures itself as the primary server, quickly enough to respond to the reexecuted requests before a time out occurs. The switchover therefore occurs without any connection or service interruptions as far as the workstation shell can detect.

To understand NCP's acknowledgment and reexecution mechanics read Chapter 5, "Netware's Protocol Stack," where it is discussed in greater detail.

NIC Failure in Primary Server

When an NIC failure is detected in a primary server's I/O Engine, it polls the secondary server's I/O Engine to see if it is functioning properly. If functionality is better in the secondary server, a switchover occurs, making the secondary server the primary server. If possible, the primary server starts up again as a secondary server. The administrator is notified when this condition occurs, and an entry is made in the error log.

From the time of switchover, all disk updates are recorded at the new primary server. When the failed server is repaired and brought back up, it automatically becomes the secondary server. The backlog of all disk updates is sent over the MSL until the secondary server is again synchronized with the primary. Remirroring occurs in a background mode without affecting primary server response to user requests.

Secondary Server Hardware Failure

A secondary server failure does not affect the primary server, except as discussed in the following paragraphs. However, when a secondary server fails, the primary server records all disk updates. When the failed server is brought up again, the backlog of all disk updates is sent over the MSL until the secondary server is again synchronized with the primary. Remirroring occurs in a background mode without affecting primary server response to user requests.

MSL Failure

When the secondary server detects no MSL activity but does detect activity over the normal Internet link, it notifies the primary server of the condition and shuts down, because it can no longer maintain a mirrored state.

When the MSL link is repaired and the secondary server reloads the MSL driver, synchronization is attempted. All disk updates that occured during the disablement are forwarded to the secondary server over the MSL. Resynchronization occurs in a background mode.

Performance Considerations

Better performance may be experienced under certain conditions when using SFT III. Mirrored servers provide split seeks in much the same manner as duplexed disks. Every disk write request must be serviced by the primary server and echoed to the secondary server. However, read requests are serviced by whichever server can respond first. When the primary server is backlogged with write requests, the secondary server responds by executing the read requests. The secondary server also responds to routing requests, relieving the first server of this duty if it is more efficient to do so.

Mirroring Server-Based Applications

NLMs loaded on one MS Engine are duplicated on the other MS Engine. Applications such as Oracle, Btrieve, and SQL Server therefore are executed on both servers at all times.

> **CAUTION** ▶
>
> Use only proven, certified NLMs. An unproven NLM can crash the MS Engine on both servers, resulting in total invalidation of SFT III functionality.

Planning for a Fault-Tolerant Network Based on SFT III Servers

SFT III must be implemented properly in order to be reliable. It can only respond to failure of critical components; it cannot prevent them. There is much you have to do to make your network a stable platform and to provide redundancy in other critical failure points, including the following:

1. Observe the hardware/software requirements.
2. Prevent system failures.
3. Constantly monitor the server OS.

Hardware Requirements

Table 39.1 shows SFT III hardware and software requirements.

Table 39.1. SFT III requirements.

Component	Required	Recommended
Processor	Two 386, 486, or Pentium	25 MHz or faster
Server	Identical make, model	EISA or MCA
RAM	12M	Same amount in each server
Disk storage	Any	Same amount in each server
MSL	Any certified	
NIC	Any	
Video adapter		Same type in each server (VGA/EGA/mono, and so forth)
Server DOS	v3.1 or higher	Same on both servers
MSL driver	Any	Novell Labs Certified
NIC driver(s)	Any	Novell Labs Certified
Disk driver(s)	Any	Novell Labs Certified

Dual processor servers can be used; however, a Dual Processing (DP) driver must be provided by the hardware developer for SFT III. Dual Processing drivers make asymmetric processing possible, executing the MS Engine on one processor and the I/O Engine on the other.

TIP ▶

It is necessary to have plenty of extra disk storage. To be able to remirror the servers after an incident of downtime, sufficient disk space must be available to hold the backlogged requests.

NOTE ▶

Identically configured equipment certainly reduces complexity, but it is not absolutely necessary. If one server has more RAM or disk storage than the other, the excess will not be used. Different server hardware will not significantly impact mirroring. However, complications may result from unequal configurations. For best results, make your mirrored servers identical in every way.

Preventing System Failures

SFT III servers are subject to the same weaknesses as any other server; components can fail. Having a backup server does not justify using weak or failing hardware in a server. The potential benefits of fault tolerance are eroded by weak components. A server is only as reliable as its weakest component.

Other network components and subassemblies can bring the network down. You should pay close attention to components that consititute critical failure points. A point is critical if its failure will disable or impair the network's capability to function. For example, a linear bus cabling system is a critical point of failure. A fault anywhere in the cabling segment can disable all communications coming through that segment.

Pay special attention to single points that are critical failure points, such as a server NIC. If only one NIC connects users to the server, its failure will stop communications entirely. Provide redundancy wherever a single point of failure exists. For example, when two NICs connect the server to two separate LANs, a failure of one NIC can be worked around by reconnecting the disabled cabling segments to the functioning NIC. Although some users would be down, the disability would not be global, it would be simple to recognize, and it could be overcome quickly.

A disk drive in an SFT III server is also a single point of failure (although not as critical because SFT III can recover from its loss). Disk mirroring or duplexing should still be used with SFT III to reduce the chance that a disk failure will cause SFT III to recover. Chapter 40 focuses on the issue of preventing network disabilities.

Monitor SFT Functions

SFT III's MS Engine does not monitor LAN or MSL device information. Therefore, the DEVMON.NLM must be loaded on the I/O Engine to monitor communications and should be viewed periodically.

DEVMON reports statistics on LAN and MSL interfaces. It is similar to the server Monitor's LAN Information selection. You can select each server NIC or MSL card and view generic and custom statistics. Similar to the LAN Information screen in MONTOR.NLM, generic statistics must be supported, and custom statistics show information the developer has added.

Monitor these statistics regularly, perhaps several times a day. Whenever any error statistics are reported, investigate their source. Part IV of this book (Chapters 19, 20, and 21) specifically pertains to this subject. Chapter 40 goes into further protocol analysis of LANs.

> **NOTE** ▶
>
> MSL systems currently lack support in third-party monitoring software and protocol analysis. Therefore, monitoring your MSL in DEVMON is very important.
>
> You also should protect power to your servers with separate UPSs. See Chapters 40 and 41, "Reducing Server Downtime" and "Protecting Critical Failure Points," for more discussion of protecting your servers.

Integrating SFT III

Installation of SFT III differs only slightly from that of native NetWare 3.11. The most important considerations are discussed in this section.

Installing

1. After installing all your hardware, including the servers, drives, NICs, and MSL hardware, test it all to make sure everything is working properly.

2. Put a DOS partition on your disk and make it bootable. Copy the required files to your DOS hard drive.

3. Load the I/O Engine on each server.

4. Load the device drivers (NICs, MSLs, disk drivers, and so forth).

5. Load the MS Engine.

6. Copy the SFT III files to the MS Engine.

7. Create and configure the server configuration (.CFG) files.

8. Update the workstation shells or requesters.

Configuring

Configuration files are ASCII files that automatically bring up the server. NetWare 3.x and 4.x versions require STARTUP.NCF and AUTOEXEC.NCF. SFT III NetWare does not use these files. Instead, each server—the primary and secondary—has the following configuration files:

IOSTART.NCF

This file is on the DOS partition and executes as the I/O Engine is executed. It must

- Name the I/O Engine
- Assign its internal network address
- Load and configure the disk driver(s)
- Load and configure the LAN driver(s)
- Bind IPX protocol to each LAN driver
- Load and configure the MSL driver
- Configure any SET parameters for the I/O Engine

An example of an SFT III server IOSTART.NCF is

```
ioengine name ADMIN_IO_A
ioengine ipx internal net FFFF220A
load AHA1640 port=330 int=10
load NE3200 port=300
bind ipx to NE3200 net=A2201
load TC3047 port=2E0
```

Each I/O Engine must load the same way. The other server in the mirrored pair might have the following IOSTART.NCF:

```
ioengine name ADMIN_IO_B
ioengine ipx internal net FFFF220B
load AHA1640 port=330 int=10
load NE3200 port=300
bind ipx to NE3200 net=A2201
load TC3047 port=2E0
```

> **NOTE** ▶
>
> After this file has executed, the MS Engine will load.

> **NOTE** ▶
>
> Each engine must be assigned a different name, and each internal network address must be assigned a different number. It's a good idea to design a naming and numbering system to identify, categorize, and distinguish internal network addresses, to simplify future troubleshooting.

MSSTART.NCF

This file is required only if you need to add SET commands or load NLMs into the MS Engine. SET commands that normally would go into the STARTUP.NCF would be included here if they need to be set for the MS Engine. SET commands and modules that control or monitor hardware devices must be included in the IOSTART.NCF. This file is stored in the SYS:SYSTEM directory and is executed upon loading of the MS Engine. This file becomes mirrored on both servers.

MSAUTO.NCF

This file names the MS Engine and assigns its internal network address. This file also is mirrored on both server MS Engines. As discussed in an earlier section, this makes both of the MS Engines appear to be the same engine. NCP requests are routed to both of them. A sample file might look like this:

```
msengine name ADMIN_MS
msengine ipx internal net FFFF220C
```

IOAUTO.NCF

This file is provided to load NLMs to run on the I/O Engine, or NLMs that require an active MS Engine and a mounted SYS: volume. The following NLMs are loaded in this file:

```
PSERVER
REMOTE and RSPX or RS232 remote console modules
SBACKUP
```

Reducing Server Downtime

by Rick Sant'Angelo

40

A discussion of what constitutes acceptable downtime can be divided into a few different categories. In some cases, applications and usage require virtually 100 percent uninterrupted service. In other cases, some downtime is tolerable, but generally must be severely limited. In considering downtime, systems and components can be categorized as follows:

1. **Fault tolerant** means redundancies are built in for critical components. Failure of a fault-tolerant component does not disable the system because the redundant component continues operation uninterrupted.

2. **High availability** means the system is built with a high level of reliability. Using fault-tolerant and highly reliable components, system failures should be rare, and a 99.9 percent uptime is provided.

3. **Nonstop computing** means the system must not fail at any time. Systems with this level of service are not available in a PC-base at this time. Systems that do provide this service, such as Tandem and Stratus, are totally redundant and have total fault tolerance. These are special operating systems that provide 100 percent uptime through regular repair and replacement.

Monitoring is the hallmark of systems built to provide high levels of availability. When any failure or threatening condition is detected, alarms warn the system operator.

This chapter discusses how to reduce the probability of network failures and how to recover quickly when they do occur. These two factors constitute major obstacles in the way of downsizing and reducing complexity and costs in mission-critical computing.

Today's everyday network components are often as failsafe as any expensive, proprietary components have ever been. Many Ethernet NICs that sell for less than $200 are tested to last an average of 35 years before failing. These parts are under warranty for a lifetime because they never fail during normal use. Modern disk drives are hundreds of times more reliable than models made just a few years ago. Servers often operate with power abnormalities, temperature fluctuations, and levels of static electricity that would disable any minicomputer or mainframe. However, if you expect to reduce the possibilities of downtime, each of these components needs to be carefully evaluated. In some cases, critical failure points may need to be bolstered with the most reliable equipment available, including, in some cases, redundant hardware.

This can be accomplished with minor effort and expense when compared to the expensive proprietary methods previously used. To provide high availability for mission-critical, fault-tolerant systems in the past, users had to use a proprietary operating system, hardware, and services. Today, common networking hardware and software can provide nearly the same level of service. However, the guarantee of nonstop computing is not quite here.

More frustrating than cost is the potential to make the wrong decision at the outset. When selecting a proprietary system, you put your security and dependability into the hands of an outside vendor you must trust. You pay the vendor highly and usually get the dependability you require. However, whenever contracting for high availability or nonstop computing systems with a vendor, you are handcuffing yourself to that vendor. Today's trend toward open systems is largely in response to vendors who dropped the ball, or worse, went bankrupt. Ultimately, your best form of protection is to provide fault tolerance in-house.

If you are downsizing a mission-critical application that requires a high level of system availability, you can provide it with NetWare and currently available components. If you are switching from a proprietary system, you'll probably find the financial reward worth the effort.

The burden of providing high availability falls on in-house systems analysts and administrators. These positions normally do not include making decisions. So it is up to these folks to convince management to spend a little more money to provide better equipment. It is also their job to keep the system working, even before management dictates this requirement.

The average system administrator spends far too much time responding to emergencies and far too little time managing. A good system's administrator is prepared for emergencies, but also has shored up the system's weak points and spent time on preventive maintenance. Managing a network to be bulletproof requires several considerations:

- Development of system goals
- Proper system design
- Proper selection of hardware and software
- Proper installation
- Proper configuration
- Well-trained, on-site service providers
- Excellent support off-site
- Maintenance of inventory of spare parts
- System administration that includes monitoring
- Development of a disaster-recovery plan

- Periodic auditing of actual problems resulting in review of the system design and its ability to meet system goals
- Preventive maintenance and upgrading

Each of these factors must be tailored to a theoretical worst-case scenario. A study of downtime expenses should be conducted and factored into the cost justification for implementing a system.

Though this chapter does not focus on all these factors, management and integrators should look at this chapter in context of these factors. In most cases, integration occurs out of context, and administrators and support providers must therefore constantly deal with emergencies. On a regular basis, the goals of the system need to be re-evaluated, and perhaps upgraded or redesigned. When specific problems are identified, the areas with the greatest possibility of failure must be addressed.

This chapter focuses on the second and third factors from the preceding list: proper system design and selection of equipment. Relative to these factors, this chapter discusses the following points:

- Solid server design and selection
- Server support systems
- Server LAN interfaces and LAN "segmentation"
- LAN cabling and intermediate devices
- Internetwork and WAN dependability
- Disaster recovery

Server High Availability

Several factors must be considered when selecting and purchasing a server that must be available 99.9 percent of the time. Superservers aim for this goal, but the server itself must be supplemented with the proper environment and connected to a reliable system. If you are using NetWare SFT III as discussed in Chapter 39, "Fault Tolerance with SFT III," you must use servers that provide a high level of availability.

Computer Developer and Vendor

Selecting the server brand, model, and support system is the most important step in providing a high level of availability. You must research carefully and select more than just design features. Reliance on a substantial company and support organization is essential for reducing the frequency and duration of failures.

Selecting a server based on cost is the poorest decision you can make. The server and its disk subsystem constitute the very heart of your network. Whether your server is used by a few users in a department or manages hundreds of users scattered throughout the world, it must be reliable.

Clone computers (with questionable levels of support) are no bargain. You must rely on a computer manufacturer that provides solid hardware that works out of the box, can continue to work reliably for years, and provides the highest level of support. Part of your investigation into a system should include questions such as

- Who actually produces the board-level components?
- What is your warranty?
- Who provides service?
- What is your support policy?

Server Design Features

The difference between a solid, well-designed server and a cheap one is quality. Many clone computers boast good performance and use the same components as other computers, but intermittent hardware problems often accompany cheap and shoddy manufacturing and system board components.

Construction quality often is apparent to an experienced technician immediately upon removing the cover from a computer. Computers can look as if they are well-designed and constructed, but the proof is in their reliability. You should rely on a good brand of computer from a firm with a reputation for quality. This is what elevated IBM to the leadership position it currently holds in the industry. No matter what problems face IBM, its products always have been recognized for outstanding quality. Today, several companies meet IBM's quality goals and therefore earn the business of the largest companies.

Outside of quality in general, you should evaluate several key components in servers. The following components are most important in providing high availability.

Error Correcting Code (ECC) Memory

A significant number of server disabilities arise from memory errors. Parity errors crash your server more often than almost any other type of failure. An intermittent RAM error can crash the server and, in many cases, not even leave behind a parity error. In some cases, the error is simply, "Abend: Non Maskable Interrupt." This is a general hardware failure error.

Because so many companies make RAM chips and SIMMs, you need to be certain to get RAM your server developer trusts and recommends. Some RAM does not work well with some motherboard designs and is not manufactured with good quality control. Power problems complicate RAM problems by revealing RAM weaknesses and damaging integrated circuits. Grounded surges can charge back through the ground in your computer and cause RAM to become weaker and weaker until it fails. Heat causes RAM to become sensitive, and it can cause damage. Dust buildup on chips also can insulate the chips, resulting in temperature buildups within chips that cause them to weaken and fail. When handling board-level components, take care to prevent static discharge, a condition which can easily damage RAM chips and SIMMs.

Parity errors are often intermittent and difficult to detect. The simple memory check most computers run at boot performs a very cursory test. Even more extensive RAM testing utilities are inconclusive in finding intermittent RAM errors. More comprehensive tests may be run thousands of times before the sources of some RAM errors are discovered.

Though better servers are built with very dependable RAM, the most reliable type of memory is ECC memory. ECC memory can reduce downtime significantly. Though memory errors can occur, ECC memory can prevent the server from crashing. ECC isolates memory errors and corrects them.

Internal Power Supplies

Your server should have a substantial power supply—one that supports all the internal disk drives and power equipment you desire. Power-supply failures are responsible for many system failures and can cause system board components to appear faulty. Superservers are normally equipped with redundant power supplies to guard against failure.

Superservers

Superservers are built not only to provide better performance, but also to prevent downtime. Higher-performance processors and components magnify hardware weaknesses. The design of a superserver necessarily focuses on providing the ultimate in both performance and durability.

The most important part of a superserver today is its dependability. Many superserver designs include ECC memory, redundant power supplies, redundancy, rugged components, and meticulous attention to engineering and assembly. Most are factory configured, so compatibility and performance problems have been resolved by system engineers. When moderate performance is required, the power of a superserver may not be significantly better, but factors that improve production consistency may sway your decision. You can rely on major superserver manufacturers to provide powerful and rugged equipment.

Power Protection

One of the key elements in protecting your server and its data is power protection. A few years ago, it was difficult to convince system administrators and integrators that an uninterruptible power supply (UPS) or a switch-over power supply was needed. Today, these products are used with a server. However, awareness of power problems and power-supply requirements is still lacking.

In a typical office environment, power is not as good as it should be. Electrical installations are often performed haphazardly, and other office equipment can affect computers. Servers are exposed to several potential hazards that can damage components and crash the OS, including

- Loss of power and brownouts
- Power fluctuations
- Line noise and other power defects
- Ineffective grounding

Uninterruptible versus Switch-Over Power Supplies

If facility power has been interrupted or voltage drops occur, these devices provide power to the server. Either type of device should be selected on a basis of the length of time it can maintain supplementary power during a full power loss.

These two types of devices differ significantly in another way. In this industry, terminology sometimes fails to draw a distinction between true UPSs and switch-over power supplies. The difference is quite simple. A true UPS provides AC converted from battery power to your server, while the battery is being recharged. A switch-over power supply provides AC from your electrical service, and includes a battery. When loss of power is experienced, the switch-over power supply switches to battery power. The difference is in the quality of electrical current supplied to your server.

A true UPS not only alleviates the brief loss of power experienced during a switch-over, it also conditions your power. Your server suffers damage and exposure to potential OS-crashing power fluctuations. Unless you are an electrical engineer or have substantial experience with electrical equipment, it is difficult to determine whether one specific model or brand of UPS is better than another. Generally, you can expect that a cheap model won't provide the protection your server should have. Better UPSs can be quite expensive, but they can pay for themselves by reducing downtime episodes and loss of data, and by extending server life.

Power Fluctuations

The need for surge suppression is assumed and widely recognized. Surge suppressors intercept large voltage and amperage increases, and send them to ground. This prevents a surge or spike from electrocuting an individual who is touching or is near electrical equipment. Contrary to popular opinion, however, surge suppression provides little protection to your server. In many cases, cheap or damaged surge suppressors can cause damage to your equipment.

Your computer's power supply converts and transforms 110-volt alternating current to low-voltage direct current. Surges and spikes may damage your power supply, but rarely are passed onto system boards or internal computer components. High-quality surge suppressors have capacitors that absorb some of the electricity instead of discharging surges and spikes directly to the ground. Large surges and spikes can burn out the capacitors. A cheap or damaged surge suppressor enables large power surges to go directly to the ground, thereby causing extensive damage.

Even a small surge or spike that has gone been grounded can enter your computer through the ground lead. The ground lead also grounds the system board and can enable surges and spikes to hit your system board, disk drives, and internal components.

Power Conditioning

It is not necessarily the magnitude of the power surges and spikes that damages your internal computer components. The speed at which the power fluctuations occur is a greater factor in causing damage. This significant factor in damage is called *speed edge*.

When a power fluctuation has a rapid speed edge, components can become damaged. Integrated circuits have very small conductors and thin insulation. Rapid speed-edge surges and spikes cause the integrated circuits to become internally pitted, causing shorts or open circuits. Over time, even small power fluctuations eventually damage chips on your system board.

It takes more than filtering or surge suppression to protect your server from damage. You need good power conditioning. A good power conditioner can filter and suppress surges, and condition your power to a smooth and consistent level. A good power conditioner is expensive, but it pays for itself by extending the life of your server.

Improper Grounding

In many buildings, grounding is done with sufficient skill to prevent physical harm, but can be poorly suited for sensitive electronic equipment. Though the National Electric Code gives requirements for grounding, they do not specify how the installations are to be done. Electricians often take shortcuts that pass inspection, but do not fulfill engineering design intentions.

When surge suppressors are hit with large fluctuations in current, they become damaged. Internal capacitors, designed to slow the rate of discharge, are damaged by large spikes and surges. Later surges can go straight to the ground and charge back into your server through the ground lead. Look for surge suppressors that give visual indication when their capacitors are damaged.

Physical Server Security

To provide the greatest protection for your server, you should remove it from physical harm or access. Anyone who has physical access to a server can damage it, turn it off, or otherwise disable it. It should not be placed where it can be affected by dust, cigarette smoke, heat, cold, moisture, or other environmental factors.

On Track Computing makes a product called NetUtils that enables you to access a file server's file system if you can physically access a server. Anyone with NetUtils can view all the files on disk, edit or delete filenames, edit file contents, and copy files off your server. It is a great utility for data recovery and maintenance, but it does give anyone with access to your server access to your files.

Your best advice is to lock up your server in a secure, well-ventilated, cool, and dry location. Make sure it is accessible if you need to get to it quickly.

Monitoring Your Server

Keep an eye on your server. Monitor its OS for signs of impending danger or failure. You should down the server on occasion and watch the system messages when it is brought up again. Be on guard for errors in the file system and for messages that indicate problems.

You should leave the file server Monitor up when the server is active. The screen saver protects the screen from getting an image burned in, and you have access to the server's most critical statistics at a glance. Chapter 33, "Monitoring and Adjusting Server Performance," discusses monitoring your server OS.

Novell and other software developers have software packages that monitor the server OS and LAN health. See Part IV of this book for several tips and utilities to monitor your system.

Summary

The following list offers helpful tips for keeping your server running and performing well.

- Use solid server design. Rely on a good brand and service, and select the best model and components.
- Use only proven, certified NLMs. An NLM can crash the MS-Engine on both servers, resulting in total invalidation of SFT III functionality.
- Install separate uninterruptible power supplies for each critical component. Use UPS monitoring.
- Install multiple NICs in each server, which segments larger LANs with many nodes into smaller LANs with fewer nodes. Make certain critical services are redundantly connected.
- Properly install cabling to protect from interference and damage.
- Schedule regular maintenance and testing.

■ Keep properly trained personnel on hand at all times.

■ Regularly back up data and store it off-site, with systematic rotation.

■ Perform frequent virus monitoring and scans.

■ Physically secure critical system components such as servers, wiring concentrators, bridges, and routers from potential damage or abuse. Access to these components should be severely secured and restricted. To guard against fire or burglary, consider installing mirrored servers in separate, secured rooms.

Protecting Critical Failure Points

by Rick Sant'Angelo

41

Several problems can disable a LAN. Damage to your cabling or a failed server NIC can bring LAN communications to a halt. When problems like these occur, it may take a while to fix them. In the meantime, you should enact plans that enable users to be connected to the server.

Single-Point-of-Failure Protection on a LAN

Critical failure points need to be identified and shored up with standby replacements. If it is not possible to configure the components into an online standby, replacements should be nearby and configured for quick replacement. The following are suggestions for building redundancy into your system.

Use Redundant Server NICs

When you configure your server with two NICs, and if one fails, the users connected on that LAN can be connected to the functioning LAN (as shown in Figure 41.1). You may suffer reduced performance, but at least everyone can work. This gives you time to replace the defective NIC or to fix the cabling fault.

You may decide to put the wiring concentrators or CAUs for both LANs into the same location or have a patch cable available to connect them together in case you need to join them.

Use Hot Online Backup Servers and Redundant LANs

You should have a standby server in case your primary server fails. It should be connected to the same LAN. This may not entail as much expense as you might think, because the standby server can double as a production workstation. The only major requirements for a standby server are that it be in good operating condition, and that it have sufficient RAM and disk capacity to provide satisfactory service until the primary server can be fixed.

> **TIP** ▶
>
> Instead of upgrading your NetWare version, consider buying a new copy of NetWare. You can then have a hot online server at little additional expense. You may find that purchasing a new copy does not cost much more than upgrading.

FIGURE 41.1.

Two NICs in the server.

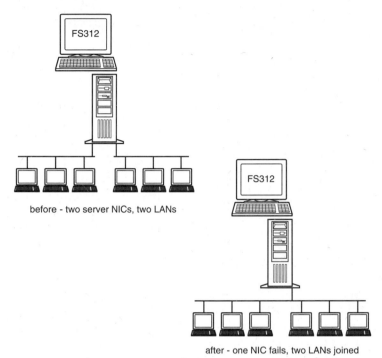

before - two server NICs, two LANs

after - one NIC fails, two LANs joined

If you have two NICs in one server, you also should have two NICs in the other server. Each LAN should be attached to each server, as shown in Figure 41.2.

FIGURE 41.2.

Hot online server and redundant LANs.

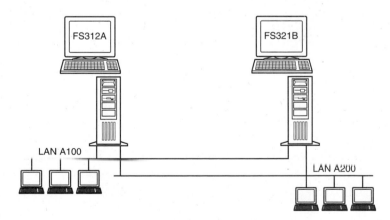

In the example shown in Figure 41.2, if either server fails, the other server is online and can be activated immediately. A failure of any NIC results in routing over the other server, but it does not interrupt service.

To prevent users from attaching to the hot online backup server, put the following command into the AUTOEXEC.NCF file:

```
SET REPLY TO GET NEAREST SERVER = OFF
```

This command prevents the server from responding when a user executes NETX or VLM. If the backup server must be pressed into service to enable the server to respond to connection requests, reverse this command by typing the following at the console's colon (:) prompt:

```
SET REPLY TO GET NEAREST SERVER = ON
```

The redundant LAN configuration gives each user direct access to each server but leaves no single point of failure. If an NIC in the primary server fails, a few courses of action can be taken. You can swap an NIC from the backup server into the online server, join the two LANs, use the backup server as a router to deliver communications from the LAN that has lost connection, or resort to using the backup server.

To keep your secondary server ready, you can frequently copy all data from one server to the other. The following command, executed as Supervisor or Supervisor equivalent, copies all files, verifies copy accuracy, and informs you of attributes that could not be copied:

```
2NCOPY FS312A/SYS: FS312B/SYS: /S /E /I /V
```

Keep Excess Capacity on Your Wiring Concentrators

You should have either a spare wiring concentrator on hand, or you should have spare ports available in case one wiring concentrator fails. If an eight-port concentrator fails, you should have eight spare ports available on other wiring concentrators. You can install patch cables to connect the orphaned nodes to other concentrators until you repair or replace the bad one.

Use Out-of-Band Monitoring

The most critical time for checking conditions on your LAN is when the LAN is down. Many wiring concentrators have built-in monitoring agents that can report error conditions to you. However, if the reporting capabilities come over your LAN, a loss of LAN connectivity not only disables your LAN, it disables your capability to find out what has happened from the wiring concentrator's management agent.

You should have wiring concentrators that have monitoring capabilities, and they should have RS-232 ports for out-of-band monitoring. You can connect to this port with a null modem cable or with a modem to receive reporting information from the concentrator, even if the LAN is down.

Redundant WAN Configurations

If you rely on your WAN for constant availability, you have even greater potential problems than you have with a LAN. You do not have total control over line availability as you do with a private wiring system. Data communications providers also suffer equipment failures and human errors, even though their up-time record may be good. To safeguard the system, you can use redundant WAN links in much the same way as redundant LAN links (as discussed earlier).

Dual Communications Lines

Duplicating your WAN links is simple, although it may be expensive. Instead of having one WAN carrying all your data, you should consider having two separate WANs, each carrying half the workload.

You may be able to accomplish this by routing some user activity to one WAN and other activity to another WAN. This configuration requires separate communications servers, which also adds redundancy to the configurations.

Load Balancing

Newport Systems' LAN²LAN/MPR multiprotocol router/bridge has a feature that is unique among software-only routers. It can be configured to automatically spread and balance the load over two data lines. One single communications board has up to four ports and can connect multiple lines from the source to the same or different points. Figure 41.3 shows how load balancing is configured.

When two LAN²LAN/MPRs are connected with two lines, as shown in Figure 41.3, this option provides fault tolerance, additional throughput, and good management of the throughput.

As an added benefit, the synchronous communications boards can be upgraded to provide data compression on digital lines from 56 kbps to T-1/E-1. Normal compression ratios average about 4:1. Between the dual lines and data compression, you can build substantial capacity into your redundant WANs.

FIGURE 41.3.
*Load balancing
with Newport
Systems'
LAN²LAN/MPR.*

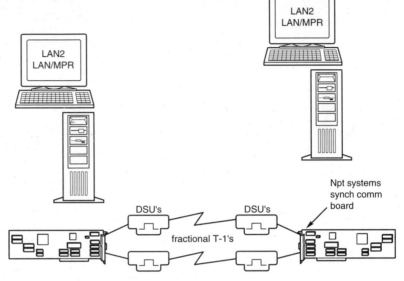

Summary

Here is a summary of how to protect the most critical failure points on your LAN:

1. Build redundancy into your LANs. Two NICs in a server can provide one good connection if either NIC fails. You can join the two LANs into one until you replace the failed NIC.

2. Configure a hot online server. Copy all files from the primary server to the hot online server frequently.

3. Install two NICs in each server. If any NIC fails, all users can still connect with little or no reconfiguration.

4. Provide spare capacity on your wiring concentrators. Provide enough spare ports to replace a failed wiring concentrator.

5. Monitor wiring concentrators out of band. If the LAN is down, you can troubleshoot with the LAN-monitoring software provided by the LAN developer.

6. Configure redundant WANs. Use two lines and four routers instead of one line and two routers.

With a few prudent expenditures, you will have shored up critical failure points and provided multiple paths if a failure of any one component occurs.

Protocol Analysis

VIII

PART

Introduction to Protocol Analysis

42

by Dan Nassar

Because of the complex network technologies that are starting to enter the local-area network (LAN) and wide-area network (WAN) environments, you must be prepared to adapt to unforeseen network events that may occur. It used to be quite simple to keep up with the basic LAN deployment; most of the time you would encounter minor problems that could be worked out easily through basic troubleshooting approaches. However, the problems encountered today are much more complex because of the overall layout of the networks that one deals with across the spectrum. There are much larger groups of users involved, who have to work along with many new and complicated network applications. These network entities have to function together through the range of intricate layout designs that are in place in today's LAN and WAN environments.

This overall complexity of new technologies, new applications, new user deployments, and vast network layouts necessitates some sort of tool that will enable us to troubleshoot these networks and help them run at their optimum level. These new technologies, applications, and layouts are increasing the complexity of the protocols that flow across the network. The actual protocols are the vehicle that transmit all of the data among these different entities within the networking environment. The only way to actually examine and troubleshoot a network's operational state and performance is by examining the protocol traffic flow on the network.

There are various tools available that enable you to view network protocols, and most of them fall into an industry product category called protocol analyzers. In the following section we discuss the theory behind protocol analyzers and introduce the main protocol analyzers that are used in the NetWare environment. It is important to understand when and why you are going to need a protocol analyzer to examine a NetWare network.

Why and When a Protocol Analyzer Is Needed

Some situations demand an immediate resolution. The ultimate tool for network problem resolution is a protocol analyzer in the hands of a knowledgeable analyst. Critical situations occur during the normal course of business in a network's life cycle. A protocol analyzer will benefit your NetWare network when the following conditions apply:

- NetWare networks are not performing well.
- NetWare networks are newly installed.
- NetWare networks have just undergone extensive growth and technical migration.
- Internetworked LANs and WANs are being sized and configured for their overall capacity, communication links, and general bridge and router implementations.

Let's examine why you would use a protocol-analysis approach in each situation.

NetWare Networks Are Not Performing Well

NetWare networks that are running slowly or are not performing to their optimum level would likely be brought to the administrator's attention by users. This may be in the complaint form of an application or in network operation system calls that aren't running fast enough for the user. Another clear indication of performance problems is when error messages such as "file server not found" and "abort retry" are generated on workstations when users are trying to communicate or connect to a file server.

These would be specifically categorized as workstation-to-file-server time-outs and are key issues that should trigger the thought, "If I use a protocol analyzer as a troubleshooting approach, I can examine why this is occurring." This is an important tool because you will have to find out if the physical layer of the network, a NetWare network shell, or a file-server configuration is causing the problem. Before you can isolate the problem to any of the main categories in your troubleshooting path, remember that a protocol analyzer will identify the area of the problem.

There will be specific times when a network is not performing well because of a configuration problem with a bridge or router implementation. A protocol analyzer enables you to identify the problem by capturing the network traffic data that comprises the bridge or router communication. You can examine the data traffic to track the problem to the bridge, the router, or even a workstation that is communicating through one of the devices. Also, you can watch specific devices communicate on the NetWare network. You can investigate a slow workstation complaint by attaching a protocol analyzer to the LAN and tracking the problem to the workstation or possibly to a traffic bottleneck within the network.

You should consider protocol analysis when the users complain about login failures or not being able to access a server within what is considered a normal amount of time. The protocol analyzer will enable you to determine whether the bandwidth on the respective network is too high, and whether the actual timing within a NetWare shell is set up properly to communicate on the network.

Newly Installed NetWare Networks

There are many product deployments that occur during a NetWare network's life cycle. When you're installing a new NetWare network, there are standard configuration parameters and setups that should work properly from the start. By using a protocol analyzer, you are able to verify that all of the technologies that are implemented are set up correctly. Also, when you load new types of protocols and workstation shells on the NetWare network, you can determine if the general traffic flow across the network is operating correctly or if changes need to be made.

For example, you can set up a NetWare network with a certain configuration and put a protocol analyzer on the network and examine the bandwidth of the respective network. Next, you can make a change to a particular shell parameter—for instance a packet size or watchdog time-out parameter—to see if your traffic flow has changed or improved. This also would be an easy thing to do with the new PBURST.NLM, which will be discussed later.

In new NetWare networks, it is useful to examine the cable wiring to determine whether the layout is working at its optimum level. You can use a protocol analyzer to look at the timing between stations, the file servers, and the devices on the network. Some protocol analyzers enable you to examine the overall quality of the cable that you're using for your NetWare network.

Probably the best reason to analyze a new NetWare network is to verify the general health of the network itself.

NetWare Networks with New Technical Migration Changes

When you examine a network that has been deployed for a while, generally it is an internetwork that is growing and changing through new network modifications, new technology implementations, and new application deployments. Altering a network requires a methodical approach, even when you just add one new device, application, file server, or make a single modification to a file server. Everything you change on a network today may affect the overall operational performance of the complete network in the future.

Network changes should be measured, and modifications to the network need to be proven effective. A protocol analyzer enables you to examine the network immediately after you modify it. Specifically, if you make a major modification to a network such as a new file server or if you segment a LAN with a bridge or a router, it is important to reanalyze the network after the modification. You can use a protocol analyzer to examine major characteristics of the network and how the modification affected the operational state and performance of the network.

General traffic-flow verification analysis for NetWare networks will be important in the next decade. There are many new NetWare products that are supposed to improve your network's performance, but you must have a calculated approach to network modifications when faced with implementing new applications and deciding which technology or product will improve performance. A protocol analyzer will enable you to categorically make changes and carefully organize and examine how the network performs with these changes.

NetWare Networks that Need Communication Link Sizing

New LANs are starting to tie in with existing LANs to create vast internetworks. As this occurs, every link that is added to the internetwork should be sized. Protocol analyzers examine communication-link sizing and help you understand the capacity of different networks and the effects of adding different bridges and routers.

For example, a protocol analyzer examines the actual timing in a cross-country data transaction between two NetWare networks. You can time-stamp a NetWare file read request from a workstation in New York to a file server in Los Angeles. You then can examine the transaction time to confirm that the link is properly configured.

Ways to Analyze a NetWare Network

There are several ways to analyze a NetWare network today. First, you can come on-site to a NetWare network and analyze its overall environment by using a protocol analyzer on the LAN. Second, you can analyze a NetWare network by dialing in from a remote site. If you're installing a remote NetWare network, you can use a standard dial-up circuit to analyze the LAN to verify the new network's health and its general bridge and router deployment, or you can perform remote troubleshooting exercises. Third, you can have all your LANs tied together through a standard protocol analysis distributed approach. You can have an online analysis occurring in all of your LANs, so you will have the ability to check the internetwork's overall performance, while you verify the health of any particular LAN at a given time.

Protocol Analyzers for NetWare: An Overview

To utilize a protocol analyzer for NetWare, you should know what the key functions of a protocol analyzer are, what protocol analyzers in the market work best in the NetWare environment, and the general theory behind a protocol analyzer.

What Is a Protocol Analyzer?

This section discusses the internal operating structure of a protocol analyzer. A protocol analyzer is a hardware and a software device that examines the overall operational state of your NetWare network. A protocol analyzer has a network interface card (NIC) that works with specific software designed by the protocol analyzer's manufacturer. The NIC and software usually are implemented within a PC platform. Some of the protocol analyzer manufacturers actually implement the product in a portable PC for your use, and some of the manufacturers ship the NIC and the software with instructions on how to implement the protocol analyzer platform in a PC of your own choosing. It should also be noted that there are many good protocol analyzers on the market today that are software-only analyzers and operate on certain types of network interface cards. These protocol analyzers come with their own NIC software drivers to enable analyzers to function as protocol analyzers.

Try to envision a protocol analyzer as a scope that can enable you to examine data traffic on your NetWare network. You can specifically look at all of the LAN frames that are traveling across your LAN cabling medium. You can become the NetWare doctor who takes a look at the health of the Internetwork Packet Exchange (IPX), Sequenced Packet Exchange (SPX), and NetWare Core Protocol (NCP) packets as they travel across the network from different workstations to different file servers (and vice versa).

Most protocol analyzers are preconfigured for the specific type of LAN (Ethernet or Token Ring) that you are going to be analyzing. If you are going to be working on an Ethernet or a Token Ring LAN, you will need a protocol analyzer that can analyze the LAN data link layer for that type of LAN. Most of the protocol analyzers designed can examine the NetWare protocols, because NetWare includes the dominant protocols in the marketplace.

An important thing to remember about a protocol analyzer is that it must be able to examine all of the data traffic on the LAN to which it is attached—not just the data traffic intended for one node. Specifically, the NIC in the PC on your desk is designed to receive information that is going from that particular PC or that is actually intended for that PC. A protocol analyzer is an indiscriminate node on the LAN that will sit on the network and examine all of the data traffic that flows through the LAN. When the protocol analyzers are configured, software is loaded on the specific disk drive within the PC platform that the protocol analyzer is configured to work upon.

The protocol analyzer is next connected to the LAN and activated in a mode where it can capture all of the data traffic of all nodes on that LAN. Novell calls this the *promiscuous mode.*

Key Functions of a Protocol Analyzer

The following sections cover some of the key functions that are internal to the operations of every standard protocol analyzer in the marketplace.

Capturing LAN Frames

A protocol analyzer must be able to operate in a capture mode. When it runs in a capture mode, it must be able to actually capture data that travels by the protocol analyzer node on the specific network. What this means is that any LAN frames that pass the protocol analyzer can be captured and stored in a buffer within the protocol analyzer. This buffer must be available for examination. A protocol analyzer must be able to display the data that is captured into the protocol analyzer—the data that is captured in the protocol analyzer in some sort of stored buffer is displayed as data on-screen or stored to a disk for printing to a printer. This enables the particular user— the protocol analyst—to examine in detail the data that the protocol analyzer has now captured.

LAN Statistical Analysis

Usually after a capture, the data is put into a mode called statistical analysis. The way statistic analysis modes are used varies with different protocol analyzers. All protocol analyzers should enable you to examine the major characteristics of your LAN by checking the levels of certain statistics. The statistics mode, which is a key function of every protocol analyzer, will enable you to examine the overall health of the LAN. If you're working on an Ethernet LAN, you can examine the overall physical and data link layer health of the Ethernet LAN by monitoring the collision rates and general data traffic at the Ethernet data link layers. If you are on a Token Ring LAN, you can examine all of the general Token Ring operations for isolating and non-isolating Token Ring errors along with the Medium Access Control (MAC) portion of the data link layer.

Trace Analysis

The next key function for a NetWare environment is a trace-analysis mode, in which you examine the header fields of the IPX, SPX, and NCP packets that you have captured into the protocol analyzer. Trace analysis is a term that clarifies that the data that has been picked up on the LAN has been traced off the network and can be examined by the protocol analyst. This is a mode in which you examine a data conversation between a NetWare workstation and file server, for example, to log on a network. If you captured all of the data traffic from the specific workstation to a NetWare file server, you could examine the overall logon sequence among the workstations that attach to the file server. This includes the workstation request for the particular logon file, along with the file server response, which is sent back to the requesting workstation. You can examine the complete conversation by capturing it in your protocol analyzer and then examining the data trace on the analyzer screen. You can decode all the IPX and NCP packet formats and understand the general details of the complete packet transmission.

Overall Traffic Error Rate

Another function of every protocol analyzer is to examine the overall error traffic on the network. At times, you'll have general packet-communication problems on the NetWare network (for example, an abort retry, a file server not found, or a bindery error). It is important to be able to examine the overall packet communication to understand why a problem occurred. Trace analysis enables you to examine such problems. This is a separate function, and every protocol analyzer that you work with will operate differently to give you error descriptions of what is occurring within your NetWare operations.

Some protocol analyzers, such as the Network General Sniffer, can tell you whether or not there has been a file retransmission or a read/write overlap condition occurring between the workstation and the file server when communicating across a particular LAN.

There are also focusing features in which you can actually work on the detail of the data that you have now captured in your trace analysis mode. One of the potential focus areas in analysis is looking at the data in the display mode of the particular analyzer. It is important to remember that on some protocol analyzers, you can look at data graphically on-screen, or you can look at it numerically. Sometimes, depending on the analysis mode you're in, it might be beneficial to look at a bar chart of bandwidth or to look at it numerically. It is important that you understand the difference and the benefits of the various display modes.

Filtering and Triggering

The two final key focus functions of every protocol analyzer should be filtering and triggering. It is important to understand the difference between these two functions. Filtering is when you only capture and examine the data on the network that you want to analyze. For instance, if you're only interested in the NetWare Core Protocol, you may filter out the IPX and SPX protocols and all of the standard data-link layer protocols, and then you can selectively examine the NCP command set conversation between the respective devices on the network. If you're just interested in examining the reply and request codes of the NetWare protocol suite, you would not need to examine and understand the IPX, SPX, and data-link layers since they would only be in the way, so you would filter them out of the trace mode.

Triggering means, basically, starting to capture data when a certain network event occurs. For example, if you want to watch the network traffic when a particular user logs into a certain NetWare application, every time that user logs into that application you would start capturing data. You will have to understand some complex filtering techniques and complex data patterns to do so, but the advantage is that you will be able to capture just the events that you want to view in the respective NetWare conversation.

All protocol analyzers should have the capability to capture and display data and major statistics, and enable you to do a complete trace decode analysis of the NetWare protocol suite. The protocol analyzer should enable you to check the overall error generation in the NetWare network conversations. The right protocol analyzer should give you the option to look at data in different ways through complex display modes and enable you to filter and trigger on certain types of NetWare protocol and breakdown packet types.

Overview of Key NetWare Protocol Analyzers

This next section will present an overview of some of the key protocol analyzers on the market that address the NetWare protocol suite. There are many protocol analyzers in the marketplace, and it should be stated that the particular analyzers mentioned in the next section are not the only analyzers that might be right for you. We have included these analyzers because they are some of the most widely used protocol analyzers for the NetWare environment.

Protocol Analyzers: A Product Comparison

There is a large range of protocol analyzers in the marketplace today. Most of the products support analysis of the NetWare protocol suite. It is essential that the analyzer you select for your NetWare network can analyze and decode all of the protocols on your particular network. For example, if your network operations include Systems Networking Architecture (SNA) communication, then you will also need a protocol analyzer that can decode SNA in addition to the NetWare protocols. This section describes several of the key analyzer products for the NetWare environment. Some of the units also have unique features that work well for troubleshooting NetWare networks.

Network General Sniffer Analyzer

Network General has a reputation for providing some of the foremost products in the LAN/WAN analyzer marketplace. The company was founded in 1986, and is the industry leader in protocol analyzers. The Sniffer Analyzer product line has excellent performance and is built with quality. Many NetWare operational features have been built into the Sniffer platform.

The Sniffer Analyzer product family is offered in a group of protocol analyzer configurations. The product line includes both standard stand-alone analyzers and intricate Distributed Sniffer configurations. The stand-alone analyzers are offered in two ways: as prepackaged PC analyzers in certain PCs or as a NIC/software package that you can configure on your own PC.

The Distributed Sniffer System (DSS) is a Network General product that enables the same analysis functions as the stand-alone product, but its main purpose is to enable the user to monitor a group of LANs from one central point. This will be a plus if your NetWare internetwork is spread out across multiple sites. The DSS system will enable you to analyze multiple networks from one site by communicating with inband protocols across your LAN cabling and WAN circuit framework.

The Sniffer Analyzers come in various LAN and WAN configurations, including Token Ring (4Mbps and 16Mbps), IBM PC Network, Ethernet, ARCnet, StarLAN, LocalTalk, and WAN synchronous links.

The Sniffer Analyzer enables you to filter NetWare network data by all of the individual NetWare protocols (IPX, SPX, NCP, and Packet Burst NCP). The Sniffer offers data pattern matches, addresses, and time relationships analysis modes.

The Sniffer Analyzer offers excellent report-generation features that can be easily imported into most NetWare network management systems.

One of the overall strengths of the Sniffer Analyzer for the NetWare environment is a new artificial Expert system that is included in the Sniffer analyzer platforms. The Expert system is a computer-aided analyzer that can be activated during protocol analysis sessions on your NetWare network. The newest Expert software release is extremely advanced in its general diagnosis of a network's NetWare operations. The Expert system automatically tracks certain NetWare packet types, packet transmission speeds, and frame types to identify and locate problems on your NetWare network. The system then offers a diagnosis and explanation of the particular problem. The Expert system can help to identify NetWare network errors, performance problems, errors, and data-link layer problems.

Telecommunications Techniques Corporation's NetLens

The NetLens protocol analyzer was originally called the SpiderAnalyzer and was developed by Spider Systems Incorporated. The Spider product line was acquired by Telecommunications Techniques Corporation. The Spider analyzer has been redesigned and is now called the NetLens.

The NetLens analyzer product line includes a stand-alone analyzer and remote NetLens Probes for multinetwork configurations. This is essentially the NetLens approach to distributed analysis

The stand-alone analyzers can work with the NetLens Distributed Analysis Probes to capture, analyze, and communicate network analysis data across multiple networks.

The NetLens products support Token Ring (4Mbps and 16Mbps) and Ethernet LANs. The protocol suites supported are

- IBM SNA
- NetBIOS
- SMB
- All NetWare
- TCP:IP
- DECnet
- Banyan Vines
- AppleTalk
- XNS
- ISO

The NetLens offers all of the basic modes of operations that you will need in order to analyze your NetWare environment. One advantage of the product is its capability to display the main capturing, decoding, filtering, and triggering features in multiple windows.

Another plus is that the NetLens has built in a group of security modes. You can set up the main capturing (Development) and Traffic Generation modes with password protection. One of the NetLens strengths is its excellent data-link layer error log, which keeps a chronological log of all LAN physical errors by network node addresses.

Azure Technologies LANPharaoh Scope

The LANPharaoh is offered by Azure Technologies. Azure is based in Hopkinton, Massachusetts and is a leader in the protocol analyzer industry.

All of the components that are utilized in the protocol analyzer NICs are designed with RISC technology for maximum packet-capture performance.

The LANPharaoh analyzer is designed to support the Ethernet, Token Ring, Coax, Twinax, and WAN layouts. Azure also offers the WANPharaoh, which supports analysis of all of the major WAN protocols.

The LANPharaoh analyzers come packaged as a hardware and software kit. The NICs are based on 20Mhz, 10 Mips RISC processors. The NIC boards have one megabyte of on-board RAM to provide a full 100-percent capture of all frames present on a network. The product offers full analysis of all the major LAN data-link layer statistics. The LANPharaoh will enable you to view all of the errors on a LAN in relation to the error-generating address. The LANPharaoh supports the following protocol suites:

- All NetWare suites
- IBM full suites
- SNA
- SMB
- NetBios
- TCP/IP
- DECnet
- DOD
- Banyan
- AppleTalk
- XNS

All of the displays on the LANPharaoh are extremely easy to utilize. The protocol-decoder menus are excellent for the NetWare packet types. The LANPharaoh provides a clear breakdown of the IPX, SPX, and related NCP packet breakdowns. The unit displays the packets in a multisplit-screen format that provides for an extremely comprehensive packet analysis. It should be noted that the LANPharaoh menu interface is now supported under the Microsoft Windows environment.

A real plus of the product is the DuoTrak feature, which views multiple networks within a single analysis session. The DuoTrak feature enables you to capture, trace, and display data for two networks at the same time. Overall, the LANPharaoh scopes from Azure Technologies are among the leading proficient scopes in the marketplace. The overall approach through high-end technology on the NICs, coupled with excellent filtering and triggering features, enables a thorough approach to a NetWare analysis session.

Triticom LANdecoder Protocol Analyzers

Triticom is based in St. Paul, Minnesota. The company provides excellent LAN monitoring, management, and modeling products. Its line includes the following protocol analyzer-type products: LANdecoder/tr, LANdecoder/e, TokenVision, EtherVision, and ArcVision.

The Vision product line comprises network monitoring tools. They are designed to monitor and display all major network environmental statistics.

The LANdecoder products are excellent software-only protocol analyzers. The LANdecoders currently support Token Ring and Ethernet.

The LANdecoders can be loaded on a variety of PC platforms that are specified by Triticom. They usually require a high-performance NIC. The LANdecoder products offer a full seven-layer protocol decode for the following protocols:

- IEEE 802.2
- IEEE 802.5 MAC
- LLC
- XNS
- PEP
- TCP/IP
- Full Netbios
- NetWare:Full
- NetWare Lite

The product offers full trace file conversions to most of the major protocol analyzers, such as the Network General Sniffer. This is a real plus because you can capture a file with the LANdecoder and then analyze the file on a Network General Sniffer.

The LANdecoder includes easy-to-use capture filters and triggers. The product supports full symbolic naming for address monitoring. LANdecoder enables you to decode most NIC manufacture codes for easy viewing of the board vendor code.

Overall, the LANdecoder provides a good value. It is an excellent protocol analyzer in the software category. A real plus is its pop-up menu system, which provides an easy-to-read picture of the NetWare protocol suite.

LANalyzer for Windows

NetWare's LANalyzer for Windows is a powerful protocol analyzer for the NetWare environment in a Windows-based software-only product. It runs on a variety of PC platforms. It supports all of the major LANs, including Token Ring and Ethernet. It was originally intended to just decode NetWare protocols but now has been broadened to support more of the major protocols.

The software can be used to fully capture and analyze the network data on your NetWare network. A real plus of the analyzer is that you can even use it on a laptop PC. It supports all of the NetWare NIC software driver sets. The menuing system is excellent and makes good use of its Windows interface. LANalyzer for Windows provides dynamic statistics on the LAN's data-link layer operations and will set off alarms when it encounters certain network problems. The statistics are displayed in a dashboard approach with gauges for the network bandwidth and error rate.

Network Communications Corporation's (NCC) LANalyzer

The LANalyzer was acquired from Novell in 1993 by Network Communications Corporation (NCC), based in Bloomington, Minnesota. NetWare and NCC have worked together to fully support the future development of the LANalyzer technology.

NCC also offers a partnering product line called the Network Probe that will work with the stand-alone LANalyzer for remote and distributed analysis. The Network Probe enables the remote monitoring and management of multiple LANs from a central point.

The LANalyzer is a full-blown, high-performance protocol analyzer that offers a decode for all major protocol suites.

The LANalyzer product is sold in an NIC-and-software kit that you configure in your own PC. The LANalyzer offers all the basic modes of operation, capturing, tracing, statistics, full decoding, triggering, and filtering. The LANalyzer has an excellent menu system.

The LANalyzer supports the following types of LANs:

- Token Ring (4Mbps and 16Mbps)
- Ethernet
- StarLAN

The supported protocol suites are

- IBM SNA
- NetBIOS
- SMB
- NetWare (including decodes for Packet Burst NCP and v3.12/4.x)
- TCP/IP

- DECnet
- Banyan Vines
- AppleTalk
- XNS
- SUN:NFS
- ISO
- EGP
- DNS
- ISIS
- SBP
- AFP2.1.

The LANalyzer is designed so you can activate a particular application test suite for the physical or upper layer that you are analyzing. A real plus with the LANalyzer is that you can define custom receive and transmit channels. This enables you to look at different categories of NetWare data in relation to each other on one screen. Receive channels are the actual filter channels for capturing during a protocol analysis session. The transmit channels enable you to generate traffic data patterns onto the network.

The real plus with the LANalyzer is the custom NetWare application test suites. The LANalyzer's NetWare tests let you capture and examine the complete NCP packet breakdown by packet type. For instance, you can look at NetWare requests, replies, print traffic, and SAP traffic in relation to each other on-screen. You also can track NetWare problem packets, such as Delays and File Failures. The NetWare menus include a group of excellent predefined application tests that are designed specifically for analyzing the NetWare network architecture.

Dolphin Network's ESP Family of Protocol Analyzers

Dolphin Networks is based in Norcross, Georgia. Dolphin Networks offers two protocol analyzer product lines: the Dolphin Expert System Protocol (ESP) analyzer and the Dolphin ESP analyzer plus.

The Dolphin ESP analyzer is a solid protocol analyzer that works on Ethernet, ARCnet, and 4/16Mbps Token Ring. The analyzer is offered in a hardware and software kit. The supported protocol suites are

- IBM Suites
- SMB
- NetBIOS
- Full NetWare
- TCP/IP
- Banyan
- AppleTalk
- XNS
- ISO

The Dolphin ESP offers all of the important LAN analysis modes, including capturing, trace analysis, statistics, filtering, and full triggering.

A real plus with the Dolphin ESP is that it has the ability to fully capture all 100 percent of data trace directly to a disk drive. This is excellent for when NetWare network problems are happening quickly and you cannot afford to miss a packet. The ESP also offers advanced real-time displays for all of the major LAN data-link layer traffic statistics. One of the real advantages of the ESP is that it includes a built-in Expert Alerts System that will enable the user to set thresholds and be alerted when a set threshold is exceeded. This will enable you to customize thresholds for certain NetWare problems that you are analyzing.

Dolphin additionally offers a more advanced analyzer, the ESP Plus. The ESP Plus analyzers are preconfigured in a 486DX/50Mhz EISA custom platform PC. The ESP Plus supports all major protocol decodes and can be used with Ethernet, ARCnet, Token Ring, and FDDI LANs. The ESP Plus can support up to 32M of RAM and 27 gigabytes of disk storage. It can decode over 140 protocols. The filtering and triggering processes on the ESP plus are powerful.

Hewlett Packard Network Advisor

Hewlett Packard offers excellent test equipment. They have now fully entered the LAN protocol analyzer market by introducing the Network Advisor protocol analyzer.

The HP Network Advisor is offered as a self-contained stand-alone analyzer that is based on the RISC architecture. Currently the Network Advisor supports Token Ring (4Mbps and 16Mbps) and Ethernet LANs.

The supported protocol suites are

- IBM SNA
- SMB
- NetBIOS
- NetWare
- TCP/IP
- DECnet
- 3Com

A real plus with the Network Advisor is its menuing system. It features interesting graphical displays where you can view, filter, and trigger the captured network data. The LAN data link layer statistics are displayed in a series of dynamic updating bar- and pie-chart screens.

The Network Advisor has an innovative feature called the Finder Expert System. It is an artificial-intelligence system that can analyze all captured data from a protocol analysis session. For example, it will attempt to give you logical suggestions for analyzing a NetWare problem. It will also identify error-related problems and recommend possible failure causes for any network physical errors encountered during an analysis session.

Features Comparison

The following chart displays the feature categories for the protocol analyzers that were reviewed in this section. The categories shown are important features that you should keep in mind when choosing your own analyzer. It should also be noted that when you make a product decision, always consult the manufacturer's documentation for the latest product enhancements and changes. It is always possible that changes can occur with product development and manufacturing.

	Full NetWare Protocol Decodes	*Full Filtering And Triggering*	*Full Error Recording*	*Expert System*	*Distributed Analysis Support*	*Report Generation Capability*
Network General Sniffer	yes	yes	yes	yes	yes	yes
TTC NetLens	yes	yes	yes	no	yes	yes
Azure LANPharaoh	yes	yes	yes	no	yes	yes
Triticom LANdecoder	yes	yes	yes	no	no	yes
NetWare LANalyzer For NetWare	yes	no	yes	yes	no	yes
NCC LANalyzer	yes	yes	yes	yes	yes	yes
Dolphin ESP Analyzer	yes	yes	yes	yes	no	yes
Hewlett Packard Network Advisor	yes	yes	yes	ycs	no	yes

Analyzing Physical and Data Link Layers

by Dan Nassar

43

This chapter discusses LAN access protocols so you can understand what to look for when using a protocol analyzer. Techniques that can be used to analyze the overall NetWare environment and its general traffic flow are discussed. Before you pick up a protocol analyzer, it is very important to understand that the best place to start is the data link layer of your LAN. Without a robust Token Ring or Ethernet platform, NetWare cannot perform properly. The efficiency of the NetWare protocol suite depends upon all the layers of protocol working properly. It controls communication between NetWare workstations and file servers.

Proper traffic flow between workstations and file servers depends primarily on dependable and error-free traffic flow in the Local Area Network, or *data link layer*. The data link layer of the Ethernet or the Token Ring LAN is the highway upon which your NetWare data flows. If it is robust, unobstructed, and operates properly, data will be consistently delivered without errors; thus, the higher-layer protocols can operate as intended.

Higher-layer NetWare protocols are designed to trap errors and retransmit data when errors occur. If the data link layer does not work properly, problems at other layers can be compounded—resulting in performance that can suffer. Much of your time spent troubleshooting will probably be a result of data link layer errors. By analyzing and maintaining the efficiency of your data link layer, you will have better performance and more up-time with NetWare.

This chapter delves into data link layer analysis of the two major types of LANs in the networking environment: Token Ring and Ethernet. Understanding data link layer analysis of Ethernet and Token Ring enables you to analyze whether the data link layer is robust.

Ethernet Data Link Layer Analysis

Ethernet, or Carrier Sense Multiple Access with Collision Detection (CSMA/CD), is a far simpler access method than Token Ring. Protocol analysis is, therefore, not as complicated as Token Ring analysis. This is mainly because Ethernet has elementary error-trapping facilities. It is not fault-redundant or as complex as Token Ring.

Ethernet is basically a LAN that listens, receives, and transmits. It is a bus LAN; only one frame can be on the LAN at a time. Ethernet has a very large bandwidth—10 mbps—but occasionally two stations attempt to transmit at the same time. When this happens, a *collision* of data might occur. The stations involved in the collision back off, and each waits before attempting to resend its frame. In the meantime, other nodes use the medium to transmit frames.

This chapter focuses on using a protocol analyzer to detect Ethernet error conditions. Chapter 2, "Local Area Networks," goes into great detail about CSMA/CD access protocol and how Ethernet operates. Before attempting protocol analysis of Ethernet, you should become familiar with how it works. Chapter 22, "Monitoring LANs," goes into extensive detail about monitoring for error conditions that can cause performance degradation or lack of connection.

General Error Types

Though Ethernet is standardized, there are four different Ethernet frame types that can be employed (as discussed earlier in this book). This chapter focuses on an 802.3 frame, but everything discussed is basic and common to all Ethernet frame types. Ethernet 802.2 and Ethernet SNAP frames have more fields that are used for bridging, and therefore can have more error conditions and analysis. Although the additional fields are present in a nonbridged LAN environment, they are not used.

A set of categorized errors can occur on Ethernet. For example, when a base 802.3 protocol frame without higher-layer data is generated, the result is a general (and nonspecific) error frame. Your protocol analyzer may group such errors and report them as statistics only, pinpoint the specific node address (or addresses) involved in the error condition, and show the error frequency. The following errors may point out certain application problems, NIC or transceiver problems, or other general hardware/software problems on the data link layer of an Ethernet LAN:

- Local collision error
- Remote collision error
- Cyclical redundancy check (CRC) error
- Long packet length error
- Short packet length error

Signal Quality Error (SQE)

Earlier Ethernet LANs used SQE to test the collision detection circuitry of Ethernet transceivers. This test is rarely employed today. Either all your NICs and external transceivers use SQE, or none can use it. Most transceivers have this option, and it is turned off by default.

> **CAUTION** ▶
>
> Most newer NICs and wiring concentrators do not use SQE, and they do not work properly if a transceiver on the LAN is sending SQE signals. SQE is never used with 10BASE-T. Unless SQE is to be globally used on your LAN, check all your LAN devices to see that SQE has been disabled.

Periodically, an SQE transmission is generated by some types of Ethernet devices and may cause certain error conditions. Most protocol analyzers enable you to monitor the SQE levels.

Local and Remote Collisions

A *local collision error* is a collision that occurs on the same physical LAN to which you are attached. The local collision rate on any Ethernet LAN should always be less than 1 percent of overall traffic. Most protocol analyzers enable you to examine the *local collision rate*. A local collision rate of more than 1 percent of overall traffic is considered excessive. This can be determined by breaking out the bandwidth allocation of the error ratios. Figure 43.1 shows the Network General *Sniffer* displaying these errors.

FIGURE 43.1.

Sniffer global statistics of the Ethernet monitor.

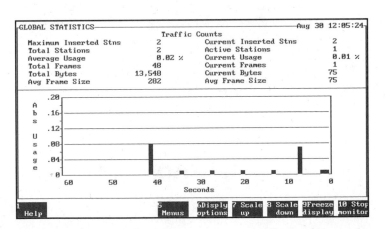

A *remote collision error* occurs on a cabling segment other than the one to which your protocol analyzer is attached. If you analyze an Ethernet LAN and notice that the remote collision error counters are increasing, you should examine those frames' node addresses to determine if a specific cabling segment is responsible for the collisions. If you suspect this, move your analyzer to that cabling segment and see if its local collision errors constitute the bulk of the collisions.

Cyclical Redundancy Check Errors

A *cyclical redundancy check* (CRC) error occurs in the general frame communication between two respective Ethernet stations. A bad CRC means that the checksum that was calculated when the frame was sent does not agree with the checksum calculated upon receipt.

This error generally indicates a bad NIC, and is easily spotted with a protocol analyzer. The analyzer shows the node address that is causing the problem. You can swap the suspected bad NIC and use the protocol analyzer to see if the error rate decreases.

Frames That Are Too Long or Too Short

There are also Long and Short frames that can be generated by NICs connected to your LAN. The frequency and number of these error types may be related to a specific node address. A Long or Short error can indicate a problem with the particular NIC, wiring concentrator, or transceiver that is generating the error. The protocol analyzer is extremely helpful here. You can examine the actual errors and observe the categorized counts. Swap the suspected bad NIC to see if you can eliminate the problem.

By examining the overall low-level Ethernet communication for the general 802.3 error types, you will be able to understand the collision and error communication exchange at the data link layer of Ethernet.

> **NOTE** ▶
>
> Because the Ethernet frame handles the actual Ethernet error communication, a robust Ethernet LAN should have a very low count of 802.3 base frames without higher-layer data. Almost all of the 802.3 frames—NetWare IPX (type 17) packets, for example—should carry higher-layer communication packets. It is important to look for a low count of such error types.

Cabling Segment Lengths and Nodes Per Cabling Segment

The next areas to examine in Ethernet are cabling segment lengths and active user node distribution across the Ethernet data link layer. As discussed in previous chapters, CSMA/CD is heavily dependent on cabling conditions to deliver error-free communications. A thin-net cabling segment can have no more than 30 nodes, and a thick-net cabling segment no more than 100 nodes. More specific rules apply. Ethernet is sensitive to improper cabling segment layouts. A protocol analyzer can be used to examine the number of active nodes on each cabling segment.

> **CAUTION** ▶
>
> Though the original cabling installation may have been done properly, it is not unusual for network growth to result in cabling rule violations.
>
> To ensure that your topology is properly laid out, follow the instructions in a cabling guide from your NIC or wiring concentrator vendor. When using a vendor's extended cabling rules, be certain that NICs and devices that cannot accept the extended rules are not mixed in. It is best to maintain IEEE 802.3 rules—regardless of whether a vendor allows extended cabling rules.

Many analyzers include a *time domain reflectometer* (TDR) function to analyze cabling segment length. If this feature is present, use your protocol analyzer to examine the proper length of the cable. Depending on the TDR's sophistication, you may be able to detect the length of a cabling segment, determine whether the cable is shorted or open, and ascertain how far the fault is from the TDR.

Bandwidth Utilization

You should determine your LAN's level of bandwidth utilization in order to assess its efficiency (which is similar to determining the bandwidth utilization for Token Ring). The capacity for an Ethernet LAN is 10 million bits per second (10 mbps). As discussed in this chapter, bandwidth equates to capacity, not speed.

CSMA/CD is a contention-oriented access protocol. This means that when a node attempts to send data, no orderly system (such as a token-passing scheme in a Token Ring or ARCnet LAN) controls exclusive use of the medium. When a node attempts to send data and 96 bit-times of free space exists, the frame transmission is initiated. If not, the node delays sending data until sufficient free space is detected. This gives each node immediate access to the medium when bandwidth utilization is low. When bandwidth utilization is high, free space is reduced, and the likelihood of collision increases. At lower levels of bandwidth utilization, more free space is available, and collisions are rare. At higher levels, collisions increase exponentially and delays increase in direct proportion. If it were not for jabber control, a few busy nodes would dominate the medium and impair all other nodes. The overall length of an Ethernet LAN also affects the level of tolerable bandwidth utilization.

> **NOTE** ▶
>
> You should look for a comfort level in an Ethernet environment. A comfort level is usually no more than 40 percent average bandwidth utilization, with a peak of less than 70 percent bandwidth utilization.

Again, depending on your network application environment and the physical size of your LAN, the proper level of bandwidth utilization can vary. Almost all Ethernet protocol analyzers include the capability to examine average and peak bandwidth utilization levels. Figure 43.2 shows the Network General Sniffer displaying bandwidth utilization readings for an Ethernet LAN.

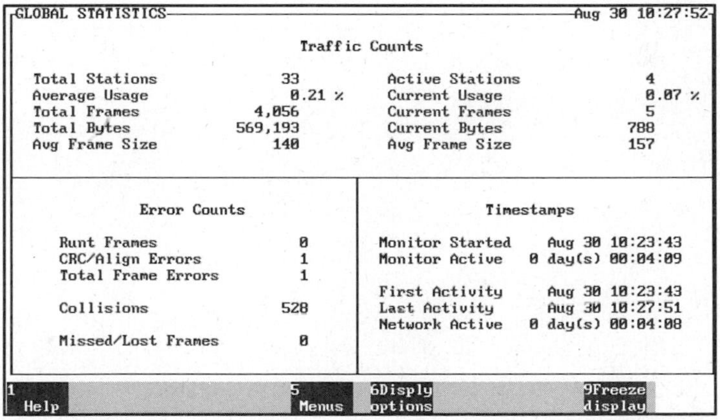

FIGURE 43.2.

Network General Sniffer Ethernet monitor global statistics.

```
┌─GLOBAL STATISTICS───────────────────────────────Aug 30 10:27:52─┐
│                            Traffic Counts                         │
│                                                                   │
│   Total Stations        33          Active Stations         4     │
│   Average Usage       0.21 %        Current Usage        0.07 %   │
│   Total Frames        4,056         Current Frames          5     │
│   Total Bytes       569,193         Current Bytes         788     │
│   Avg Frame Size       140          Avg Frame Size        157     │
│                                                                   │
├───────────────────────────────────┬───────────────────────────  │
│         Error Counts              │        Timestamps             │
│                                   │                               │
│   Runt Frames            0        │  Monitor Started  Aug 30 10:23:43 │
│   CRC/Align Errors       1        │  Monitor Active   0 day(s) 00:04:09 │
│   Total Frame Errors     1        │                               │
│                                   │  First Activity   Aug 30 10:23:43 │
│   Collisions           528        │  Last Activity    Aug 30 10:27:51 │
│                                   │  Network Active   0 day(s) 00:04:08 │
│   Missed/Lost Frames     0        │                               │
└───────────────────────────────────┴───────────────────────────  ┘
 1                     5     6Disply              9Freeze
   Help              Menus  options              display
```

Ethernet Conclusion

Ethernet's CSMA/CD access protocol is very simple. Error conditions, however, can be quite extensive. Unlike Token Ring, very little is provided in the access protocol for determining specific reasons for error conditions. It takes detective work to determine why an error condition exists. Also unlike Token Ring, cabling problems and collision-related problems have a greater effect on proper LAN performance.

Protocol analyzers categorize many types of errors and often only report statistics. You can use these statistics to locate the sources of problems. Often, the solution is to isolate the source node that generates the error condition and then swap the defective NIC, cabling, or piece of hardware.

It is also important to maintain a low level of bandwidth utilization because error conditions increase exponentially as bandwidth utilization increases. Because demands may change on a seasonal or progressive basis as your LAN grows, you should continually monitor bandwidth utilization and error conditions. Tools for monitoring Ethernet LANs are discussed in Part IV of this book.

Token Ring Data Link and Data Link Layer Analysis

Token Ring is considered to be the most complex and sophisticated technology in LANs. It is *fault-redundant*, designed with the capability to recover from minor data link layer problems, such as cabling problems and general operational problems that normally occur on the LAN. The higher-layer protocols continue to operate efficiently, even under adverse conditions at the data link layer.

Token Ring is based on the idea of consecutively passing a *token* around a ring to each user node. The token is a control frame that grants a user access to the ring. The process of controlling access in Token Ring is extremely controlled and organized. When operating properly, every station on the ring should have an equal chance to transmit on it.

Token Ring cabling rules are quite complex, and they vary according to configuration. Several configuration parameters, such as the number of users and length of cables, depend on what type of cable is being used. Such parameters also depend on the number and types of LAN components (such as Multistation Access Units, Controlled Access Units, and Lobe Attachment Modules). Because of the complexity of rules, larger Token Ring LANs often have cabling violations. As a LAN grows, its expansion often causes problems when cabling rules are violated. These problems are data link layer and physical problems; however, they may be seen in token-passing ring access protocol's extensive error control when they show up in data link layer.

This part of the book discusses how to analyze the efficiency of the Token Ring LAN's data link layer, which reflects upon the cabling medium. This part of the book includes a brief description of the Medium Access Control (MAC) data link layer of Token Ring and the general process of how it operates.

MAC Frame Types

One of the most important things that you should examine is the MAC traffic *fluency*. Fluency refers to the ability to communicate well—such as being fluent in a foreign language. At the lower data link layer of Token Ring, MAC frames need to communicate fluently between nodes. Following are the 25 MAC frame types used to control the physical ring medium; the network interface cards (NICs) on your Token Ring LAN use these frames to communicate with each other to control the physical ring medium in an efficient manner:

- Standby monitor present
- Active monitor present
- Ring station initialization
- Initialize ring station
- Lobe test
- Duplicate address test
- Beacon
- Claim token
- Ring purge
- Report neighbor notification incomplete
- Transmit forward
- Report transmit forward
- Report active monitor error
- Report soft error
- Change parameters
- Remove ring station
- Request ring station state
- Report ring station state
- Request ring station attachments
- Report ring station attachment
- Request ring station address
- Report ring station address
- Report NAUN change
- Report new active monitor
- Response

With a protocol analyzer, you can examine the communication exchange at the To-ken Ring data link layer by examining the MAC frame communication. Some MAC frames are used to recover from error conditions, so detection and encoding of MAC frames can give clues to what types of error conditions are present on your ring. Er-rors can cause complications at higher layers. When you know the operations at the data link layer are working properly, you will be able to examine whether there are truly problems at the NetWare layers.

Certain types of MAC frames may indicate problems, such as Active Monitor Error or Neighbor Notification Incomplete errors, which require immediate attention. By capturing and examining these frame types, you can identify data link layer prob-lems. If you detect the presence of Report Soft Error, Beacon Error, or Ring Purge MAC frames in large numbers, your ring is suffering from problems. When you iden-tify a problem type frame at the physical MAC layer, you need to research the prob-lem by checking the source and destination node addresses in the frame. In doing so, you can locate a possible fault domain. You need to understand token-passing ring theory to troubleshoot Token Ring MAC frame fluency.

Token Rotation Time

After examining the MAC layer communication at the data link layer and under-standing whether proper MAC processes are occurring, the next most important layer area to examine is the overall general rotational frequency of the Token frame. The statistic called *Token Rotation Time* indicates the amount of time it takes for a token to circle the ring. Normal token rotation time is between 10 and 150 microseconds. These time ranges are considered normal within the engineering environment of Token Ring, and excessive time indicates problems. Latency (delay) of the token tim-ing takes approximately between 10 and 150 microseconds (to circle the ring). If the frequency of the Token Rotation Time is higher, for example 400-500 microseconds, a problem might exist in the data link layer.

> **NOTE** ▶
>
> Excessive Token Rotation Time does not tell you where the exact problem is in the LAN. However, the rotation time is a good barometer of determining whether the ring is operating properly.

Most protocol analyzers in the marketplace enable you to examine the overall Token Ring Rotation statistic.

Soft Errors

The next category of a Token Ring data link layer analysis is the most important of all. You need to understand and monitor the *soft error* types that are nonisolating to isolating. There are 10 types of soft errors, which should be monitored with a protocol analyzer. Following is a list of soft errors and their most probable causes:

Internal Error: Reporting ring station has encountered a recoverable internal error

Burst Error: Reporting ring station—signal error detected in the Token Ring cabling medium

Line Error: Reporting ring station—checksum error

Abort Delimiter Transmitted Error: Reporting ring station—recoverable internal error

AC Error: Reporting ring station's NAUN cannot successfully set the Address Recognized or Frame Copied bits

Lost Frame Error: Reporting ring station—did not receive a transmitted frame back

Receiver Congestion Error: Reporting ring station cannot process a frame

Frame Copied Error: Reporting ring station—detects a duplicate address

Frequency Error: Reporting ring station—improper ring clock frequency

Token Error: Active monitor does not detect a token on the ring

> **NOTE** ▶
>
> Most protocol analyzers enable you to break down these errors by the soft error type and the specific node address causing the errors. Monitor the error type and then take the respective action, by either replacing the device that is causing the error, or actually making changes to your LAN to ensure that the error does not occur anymore.
>
> For example, if you captured a Token Ring internal error generated by one specific NIC, you would change the NIC in that workstation and then remonitor the LAN with the protocol analyzer. If the error is completely gone, you have isolated and fixed the problem.
>
> It is important to remember that if you make any changes to the LAN through a troubleshooting process, you should use your protocol analyzer to verify that the error has subsided.

Active User Node Count

Analysis follows a definite path. You should examine the overall MAC layer communication, view the Token Rotation Time, and look for soft errors. Then you should look at the active user node count. A higher user node translates to a higher bandwidth utilization, and therefore higher possible error effects. Under heavy usage, problems appear that you may not see at lower usage levels.

You can have as many as 260 workstations on a Token Ring LAN, but the number of user workstations permitted depends upon the type of cable being used, cabling length, the number of LAN components (such as MSAUs, CAUs, and LAMs), and several other factors. At any give time, the majority of components may be in a standby state because of workstation think time or processing delay at the workstation-input or software level. A protocol analyzer tells you the *active node count*—the number of nodes actively using or competing for use of the ring at a given moment. Therefore, the active node count is a measure of how busy your ring is.

You need to keep in mind that more intense bandwidth-consuming application environments require "segmentation" into separate rings. This technique is called *traffic balancing*. A protocol analyzer enables you to quickly key in on the user node count of a particular LAN—and to understand whether the level of traffic warrants segmentation into separate rings.

Bandwidth Utilization

The last, and probably one of the most important areas to measure, is the *bandwidth utilization*. Bandwidth utilization can be defined as the current percentage of theoretical capacity in use on the cabling medium for signaling . At any given time, some of this capacity is unused. For instance, on a 4 mbps Token Ring LAN, up to 4 million bits can be transmitted per second on the wire. If you measure data flow with your protocol analyzer, and 2 million bits are clocked per second, you have a LAN bandwidth utilization factor of 50 percent.

> **NOTE** ▶
>
> Bandwidth defines the available theoretical capacity (not speed) available on your LAN. Bandwidth utilization is therefore a measure of how much capacity is being used at any given time.
>
> A common misconception is that bandwidth (16 mbps) refers to speed. This is false. Bandwidth is a measure of how much data can be transmitted per period of time.

Bandwidth utilization can be measured by attaching a protocol analyzer to your LAN and monitoring your bandwidth utilization factors. You initiate a general monitoring test and examine the overall data link layer statistics. This is one of the most primary and simple tests to run for any type of the major protocol analyzers in the marketplace.

You may have user complaints about frequent file server disconnects. For example, if you attach an analyzer to the LAN and find that your LAN is running at 60-percent average utilization, this level constitutes what is considered to be a high average for a 4-Mbps Token Ring. Next, you can follow through and troubleshoot the problem.

Bandwidth utilization should always be measured for average and peak statistics, and is measured for a set period of time. You can have an average amount of bandwidth utilization for your complete business day, which would include many extended periods of user and software delays throughout the day. Because the nature of LAN traffic is bursty, there are going to be peaks of high levels of data traffic that can cause spikes in bandwidth utilization. If your traffic levels periodically approach the 100-percent level, noticeable performance delays can result. Such a scenario would indicate that because your data highway is filled with so much data, you periodically would encounter congested data traffic flow—and therefore latency. This is analogous to traveling on a crowded highway to or from work: too many cars on the highway cause traffic flow congestion. Just imagine what happens when an accident occurs on a crowded highway—and you can imagine how errors compound data traffic flow when bandwidth utilization is high.

NOTE ▶

A Token Ring LAN should be running no higher than an average level of approximately 55-percent bandwidth utilization, with peaks of no higher than 80 percent. If your physical bandwidth levels are normal, your NetWare data traffic flow will increase.

Though these factors can vary significantly—depending on your application and NOS—this is an acceptable level for normal conditions with NetWare. Sample bandwidth utilization as frequently as you examine your LAN. It is very important to understand your bandwidth concerns prior to decoding the NetWare protocol suite for possible problems.

Token Ring Analysis Conclusion

It is recommended to examine the following items when analyzing a Token Ring LAN:

1. MAC frame presence, type, and fluency
2. Token Rotation Time
3. Token ring soft errors
4. Active user node count levels
5. Global bandwidth utilization averages and peaks

Data link layer problems interfere with communications and complicate higher-layer protocol implementation. Without a robust LAN, the higher layers reveal errors and error-recovery procedures that wouldn't be present—without LAN problems. Far greater depth can be analyzed in a Token Ring environment to pinpoint problems and their causes; however, this is a simple and brief summary of how Token Ring analysis verifies a properly functioning LAN. If you follow the preceding five steps, you can confirm the efficiency of your Token Ring LAN—or you must resolve the problems before attempting to analyze higher-layer problems. When this is done, you can proceed to analyze the NetWare protocols.

Summary

Before you proceed to analyze the NetWare protocol layers, you should evaluate the productivity of your LAN. It is not possible for higher-layer protocols to operate efficiently when the physical medium cannot provide error-free service. Your first step in examining LAN problems is to analyze your Ethernet or Token Ring LAN.

You also should have an in-depth understanding of token-passing ring (Token Ring) and CSMA/CD (Ethernet). This chapter provided the basics of analyzing the two primary types of LANs. To become more proficient at protocol analysis, you'll need to study the details of Token Ring and Ethernet operations. Further study must go hand-in-hand with practical experience. You will probably find that a protocol analyzer significantly helps you understand what is happening inside wires; experiencing a problem and knowing how to troubleshoot it is valuable knowledge.

Analyzing Token Ring and Ethernet helps you determine whether you have a robust data highway to provide a platform upon which to base higher-layer protocols and LAN traffic.

Analyzing the NetWare Protocol Suite

44

by Dan Nassar

IN THIS CHAPTER

As discussed in previous chapters, a LAN's frames transport packets of data from source node addresses to destination node addresses. Network packets, such as Novell's Internetwork Packet Exchange (IPX) packets, are encapsulated into LAN frames for delivery. Higher-layer protocols, such as Novell's NetWare Core Protocol (NCP), are encapsulated into IPX packets, which in turn are encapsulated into LAN frames. Other types of packets are encapsulated into IPX packets in addition to NCP packets. Each packet type is provided for a certain functionality, and several functions exist for NCP, which is the main packet type used in NetWare communications. (A more detailed discussion of Novell's *Universal Network Architecture* is provided in Chapter 5, "Novell's Protocol Stack".)

NetWare Protocol Suites

NetWare protocols enable communications and ensure accurate delivery of data between servers and clients. Though NetWare protocols and packet formats were previously discussed in Chapter 5, this chapter discusses how to investigate the mechanics of the NetWare protocol stack along with details about how they should work, what types of errors can be viewed with a protocol analyzer, and some possible solutions to problems you may encounter.

The following NetWare protocols are discussed in this chapter:

- Internetwork Packet Exchange (IPX)
- Sequenced Packet Exchange (SPX)
- NetWare Core Protocol (NCP)
- NetWare Packet Burst NCP Protocol (NCPB)
- Routing Information Protocol (RIP)
- Service Advertising Protocol (SAP)

Internetwork Packet Exchange (IPX)

IPX protocol is a connectionless protocol that is designed for Network layer communication connections. (See the OSI model discussion in Chapter 5.) The protocol itself consists of one-way communications and therefore does not guarantee delivery of information across the network. It is also a routable protocol and provides for the systematic transmission of data over networks, and over internetworks through a single LAN or multiple LANs linked with routers. The goal of this protocol is to transport higher layer packets from the ultimate source to the ultimate destination node, regardless of whether they exist on the same LAN. IPX enables a set-up of communication sessions and the efficient transfer of data across a NetWare-based network. IPX also supports overall broadcast methods for most networks. It works in conjunction with NetWare Core Protocol in establishing connections.

> **NOTE** ▶
>
> You may see various writers discuss IPX as a "transport protocol." Though this makes sense to some writers, IPX is equivalent to the OSI Network layer, and is therefore called a "Network protocol" in this book.

Packet Field Description

Table 44.1 shows the IPX packet header fields and their size, as expressed in bytes.

Table 44.1. IPX Packet format.

IPX Fields	Bytes
Checksum	2
Length	2
Transport Control	1
Packet Type	1
Destination Network Address	4
Destination Node Address	6
Destination Socket	2
Source Network Address	4
Source Node Address	6
Source Socket	2

The preceding table represents the IPX packet format. Figure 44.1 shows the Network General Sniffer Analyzer displaying the detail of an IPX packet. In the following sections, each field and its purpose is described. Also, the analysis of key fields is discussed.

FIGURE 44.1.

*Sniffer screen
display showing
IPX detail.*

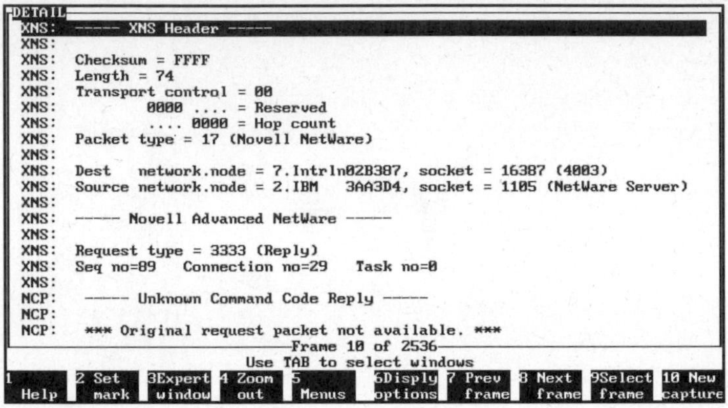

```
┌─DETAIL──────────────────────────────────────────────────────────┐
│XNS:    ─────  XNS Header  ─────                                   │
│XNS:                                                               │
│XNS:    Checksum = FFFF                                            │
│XNS:    Length = 74                                                │
│XNS:    Transport control = 00                                     │
│XNS:            0000 .... = Reserved                               │
│XNS:            .... 0000 = Hop count                              │
│XNS:    Packet type = 17 (Novell NetWare)                          │
│XNS:                                                               │
│XNS:    Dest   network.node = 7.Intrln02B387, socket = 16387 (4003)│
│XNS:    Source network.node = 2.IBM   3AA3D4, socket = 1105 (NetWare Server)│
│XNS:                                                               │
│XNS:    ─────  Novell Advanced NetWare  ─────                      │
│XNS:                                                               │
│XNS:    Request type = 3333 (Reply)                                │
│XNS:    Seq no=89   Connection no=29    Task no=0                  │
│XNS:                                                               │
│NCP:    ─────  Unknown Command Code Reply  ─────                   │
│NCP:                                                               │
│NCP:    *** Original request packet not available. ***            │
│                       ──Frame 10 of 2536──                        │
│                    Use TAB to select windows                      │
│1        2 Set   3Expert 4 Zoom  5        6Disply 7 Prev 8 Next 9Select 10 New│
│ Help     mark   window   out     Menus   options  frame  frame  frame capture│
└──────────────────────────────────────────────────────────────────┘
```

Field Descriptions

The fields within the IPX packet header function are discussed in the following paragraphs:

Checksum

This field is not normally used. It can be used to place a Cyclic Redundancy Check (CRC) on the header information. A CRC is basically a math algorithm used for bit transfer verification from node to node. Currently, NetWare does not use this field because the data link layer LAN frames also contain a CRC or checksum.

Length

The Length field represents the length of the IPX packet, including packet header fields, but exclusive of LAN frame fields.

Transport Control

The Transport Control field shows the number of routers that the IPX packet has passed through on its current network trip.

> **NOTE** ▶
>
> The Transport Control Field also is called the NetWare Hop Count field.

> **TIP** ▶
>
> A protocol analyzer can be used to monitor this field for internetwork efficiency because it shows the number of logical hops (routers) that a particular packet has passed through in transfer on an internetwork.

The importance of monitoring this field for routing performance troubleshooting on the NetWare network is discussed in detail later in this chapter.

Packet Type

The Packet Type basically indicates the type of higher-layer protocol (and therefore packet) that is encapsulated in the IPX packet. The following packet types can be encapsulated into an IPX packet:

Type 0-4: IPX and IPX-based
Type 16-31: Other NetWare packet types

There are other custom packet designations that vary from experimental to error types.

Destination Network

This particular field represents the intended destination network address for the IPX packet. See Chapter 5 for a detailed discussion on network addressing.

Destination Node

This field represents the specific node (workstation) address within the intended destination network address for the IPX packet.

Destination Socket

This field represents the type of process within the destination node to which the IPX packet is directed for operation. It is used to sort IPX packets prior to processing the packets.

The following socket types apply:

0451H	NCP
0452H	SAP
0453H	RIP

0455	NetBIOS
0456H	Diagnostic Packet
0457H	Serialization Packet
4000 to 6000H	Custom sockets for file-server processes

TIP ▶

By using a protocol analyzer to decode the destination socket, an analyst can uncover what type of network operation is actually being communicated to from the source process.

NOTE ▶

Some protocol analyzers encode the socket number into decimal, whereas others show the hexadecimal number.

Source Network

This is the network address from which the IPX packet has been transmitted. The LAN node address is used in this field, so it is identical to the source node address that is filed in the packet header.

Source Node

This is the node (workstation) address within the source network address that has transmitted the packet onto the network. The LAN node address is used in this field, so it is identical to the destination node address that is filed in the packet header.

Source Socket

This socket identifies the process within the sending node that has generated the IPX packet.

NOTE ▶

This process refers to another operation, such as NCP and others, as mentioned under the description of the Destination socket.

The preceding description of the IPX packet header fields provides the analyst with a basic but efficient summary of what needs to be known to analyze this protocol. A protocol analyzer enables you to view the information in the IPX packet headers to determine the ultimate source and destination of packets. Generally, protocol analyzers *encode* (that is, translate into plain English) the information, and then enable you to sort, filter, and otherwise view the information to determine consistency in error conditions. For example, the protocol analyzer will relay to the user in plain English whether or not the IPX packet has been through three routers, whether or not it carries an NCP request, and what source network address and node address and process spawned the packet, network address, node address, and process that the packet came from and is intended for.

> **NOTE**
>
> The key information that IPX packets provide is the identity of the networks, nodes, and processes (sockets) that are communicating with each other from different points in the network.

It is also important to understand that the Transport Control Field is actually the Hop Count field. By examining the Hop counts in an IPX packet, an analyst can understand how many routers or networks the IPX packet has traveled. As will become evident later in this chapter, it is very important to analyze the IPX Hop count when troubleshooting network traffic routes.

Sequenced Packet Exchange (SPX)

SPX protocol is a transport-layer protocol that can be used to control and guarantee connections between NetWare nodes. Although the IPX packet format is used for a general method of transferring information, the SPX is sometimes used to guarantee delivery of packets. It is connection-oriented and uses its connection type fields to guarantee a transfer of information. It also checks packets for errors.

> **NOTE**
>
> SPX is not used in most communication sessions. Novell uses SPX to maintain solid connections between print servers, print queues, and remote printers (Print Server utility), in remote console (RCONSOLE) sessions, and in various gateway products. Software developers also can use SPX for

gateways, remote connections, remote printing services, and other applications where error-free delivery of data must be guaranteed. The software developer must make a specific call to SPX to activate its services; it is not activated by any automatic process.

A protocol analyzer can be used to examine the SPX packet header fields to trouble-shoot transfers between some of the processes mentioned previously. Table 44.2 shows a breakdown of the fields and byte sizes for the SPX packet format.

Table 44.2. SPX Packet Field format.

SPX Fields	Bytes
Connection Control	1
Datastream Type	1
Source ID	2
Destination ID	2
Sequence Number	2
Acknowledgment Number	2
Allocation #1 Field	2

SPX packet header fields are described in the following section, and analysis-related information to key fields is discussed. Figure 44.2 shows the Network General Sniffer Analyzer displaying the detail of an SPX packet.

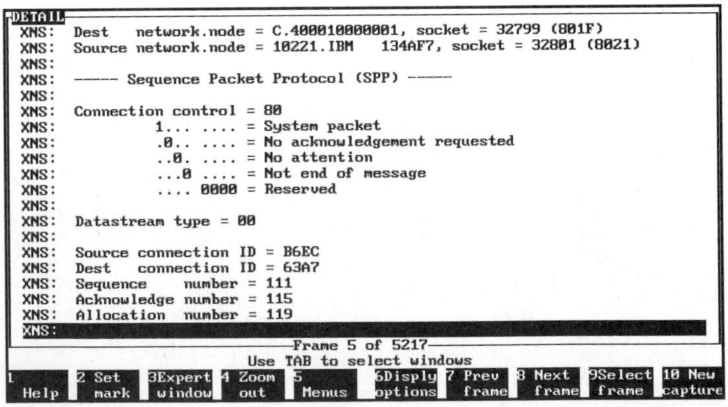

FIGURE 44.2.

Sniffer Analyzer SPX packet encoding.

```
DETAIL
XNS:  Dest    network.node = C.400010000001, socket = 32799 (801F)
XNS:  Source network.node = 10221.IBM    134AF7, socket = 32801 (8021)
XNS:
XNS:  ------ Sequence Packet Protocol (SPP) ------
XNS:
XNS:  Connection control = 80
XNS:            1... .... = System packet
XNS:            .0.. .... = No acknowledgement requested
XNS:            ..0. .... = No attention
XNS:            ...0 .... = Not end of message
XNS:            .... 0000 = Reserved
XNS:
XNS:  Datastream type = 00
XNS:
XNS:  Source connection ID = B6EC
XNS:  Dest   connection ID = 63A7
XNS:  Sequence   number = 111
XNS:  Acknowledge number = 115
XNS:  Allocation  number = 119
XNS:
                        Frame 5 of 5217
                  Use TAB to select windows
1        2 Set   3Expert 4 Zoom  5         6Disply 7 Prev  8 Next  9Select 10 New
 Help     mark   window   out     Menus    options  frame   frame   frame  capture
```

Connection Control

This field is used to control the flow of data between the source and destination NetWare nodes during each connection. Through this field, a virtual connection is established and maintained for all packets grouped into each virtual connection. This field indicates the following:

1. If an acknowledgment is required
2. Whether it is a system packet
3. End of message

> **TIP** ▶
>
> Check this field when troubleshooting workstation drop-offs, such as gateway disconnects. You can determine which station is causing the disconnect by locating a station with a consistent pattern of initiating SPX packets that result in dropped connections.

Datastream Type

This field contains the type of packet that is contained within the SPX data field.

> **NOTE** ▶
>
> This field also may contain end-of-connection information on workstation disconnects.

Source ID

This particular field contains the specific virtual connection identification for the source node that is controlling the SPX communication session.

Destination ID

This is the actual destination virtual connection identifier for the destination node communicating at the SPX layer.

Sequence Number

Though packets should arrive in sequential order, this field recovers them in case they don't arrive in order. This number indicates the order in which the packets are to be reassembled back into messages. Because the last packet contains an end-of-message marker in the Connection Control field, SPX can determine if one of the packets in a message has been lost.

> **TIP** ▶
>
> In a large SPX transfer, this field can be monitored to determine if data is flowing in a normal manner. When examining packets, check to see if the sequence was incremented in sequential order.
>
> In a normal LAN environment, packets arriving out of sequence indicate an abnormal condition, such as an intermittent loss of connectivity. In a packet-switching WAN, such as a Public Data Network, it may be normal for packets to arrive out of order.

Acknowledgement Number

This field also maintains the virtual connection during a message session. It causes the Destination ID (destination node) to acknowledge each SPX packet from the Source ID (source node) throughout the SPX transfer. Each SPX packet that requires an acknowledgment must therefore have a matching response. This is the way SPX guarantees delivery of each packet throughout an SPX virtual connection.

Allocation Number

This field indicates the number of available packet receive buffers in the destination and source workstation IDs. Flow is therefore controlled through this field.

It is important to remember that SPX communication is only utilized in specialized situations and data transfer operations where accurate delivery of data must be ensured, such as with communications gateways. When examining SPX, it is important to watch for a standard connection setup and to watch for a very fluent (error-free) communication traffic flow when workstations that are using SPX are sending data back and forth. Because the SPX protocol is used to set up and guarantee a connection, it can be monitored to determine whether the "handshaking" between a workstation and server is normal.

NetWare Core Protocol (NCP)

This protocol is used in the vast majority of NetWare packets you will encounter. NCP spans the Transport, Session, Presentation, and sometimes the Application layer between all NetWare workstations and file servers as they communicate across the network. NCP, in essence, is the overall "communication language" used between servers and clients across NetWare networks.

Transport Layer Services

NCP is a connection-oriented protocol. Every time a workstation requests information from a file server and a file server responds with the requested information, NCP is employed. Workstations may use NCP requests to request information or a service, and a NetWare file server will respond with an NCP reply. This function of NCP represents the Transport layer in normal NetWare communications dialogs. Though SPX is *sometimes* used to guarantee delivery, NCP *always* acknowledges the execution of NCP requests.

In some cases, further NCP requests cannot be executed until the previous operation has been successful, such as in a file-write request. For example, if a file-write request is larger than the packet size (for example, 1024 bytes for Ethernet), each packet must be received, written successfully, and acknowledged before the next packet in the file-write request can be transmitted.

NCP communications are therefore heavily based on the request and reply methodology. There are actually two types of NCP packets: one for NCP requests and one for NCP replies, both of which are discussed later in the chapter.

Session Layer Services

NCP is the device used to establish a connection between each client and a file server. When the workstation shell or requester is executed, it sends out an NCP request that says "Get Nearest Server." The server responds to the request and reports its name. The requester responds with a routing request, and the server in turn reports its internal network address, which becomes the point of contact for this client with the rest of the network. The file server allocates a connection in its connection table and reports the connection number to the workstation. This handshake completes the open connection between the file server and client. When the session is established, you see a screen message at the client workstation that says "You are attached to server *file_server_name.*" You also can verify the connection in the server's Monitor at the Connection Information menu selection.

> **NOTE** ▶
>
> The term "connection" is used in two ways. The type of connection discussed in the preceding paragraphs refers to the Session-layer file server's connection table, which establishes an open circuit between a server and a client.
>
> The transport layer connection-oriented service (discussed previously and under the SPX protocol) refers to a virtual circuit that is established during a brief interchange between a client and file server within a session.

Presentation Layer Services

NCP requests tell the receiver what to do with the data contained in the NCP packet. For example, a DOS function call is intercepted by the workstation shell or requester, which then creates an NCP packet, places the corresponding NCP function code in the packet header, and hands the request to IPX for transmission to the file server. NCP is therefore the device for requesting presentation layer services between workstations and servers.

Field Formats

Table 44.3 shows a breakdown of the fields and their byte length for the NCP request format.

Table 44.3. NCP Request Packet fields.

NCP Fields	Bytes
Request Type	2
Sequence Number	1
Connection Number Low	1
Task Number	1
Connection Number High	1
Function	1

NCP Fields	Bytes
Subfunction	1
Subfunction Structure	2
Data	Variable Length

Request Type

There are four request types in the Request Type field that are important for initiating an NCP conversation on a NetWare network:

1. The first important type of request is known as Create A Service Connection. This is field 1111. This particular field is used to set up a NetWare connection to a NetWare server.

2. The next field request type is a 2222. This is probably the most frequently used request type of all the subsets and is used for all NetWare reads and requests of information from all NetWare file server categories.

3. The 7777 request type is the requesting of a set-up of a Packet Burst transfer, as will be discussed later.

4. The last request type that is valid in an NCP request is a type 5555, which is actually where a NetWare connection will get disconnected. This is called a connection destroy.

> **NOTE**
>
> A protocol analyzer can be used to view the type of NetWare session in which a workstation is engaged.

Sequence Number

This is the field in which the number of transfers between a workstation and a file server are tracked for their actual sequence within the transfer.

> **NOTE ▶**
>
> The Sequence Number Field is where the user can monitor the transfer portions of information and can chart the progress of communication between a workstation and a file server.

Connection Number Low

This field has the information related to the server connection number that is assigned to a particular workstation. The user's number corresponds with the connection number assigned the client in the server's Monitor, Connection Information screen.

Task Number

This is the field that indicates what task a workstation is requesting. The file server assigns a task number to each workstation operation.

Connection Number High

Currently, this field is not used. It can be used with Connection Number Low to reference the connection number.

Function

The NCP reply format always has an attached function code. The function is the exact file direction option, such as a file read or file write.

> **NOTE ▶**
>
> By decoding the function code, the analyst can identify which discreet operation the workstation is attempting to perform.
>
> This can give clues or explain exactly why various types of operations fail. For example, when a file read is requested and it fails, the response packet will show a function code that should give a reason why the read operation failed. (Check with Novell for a listing of the function codes.)

Subfunction

This is an extension field for the definition of further operations of specific function codes.

Subfunction Length

This is the length of any data attached to the function code fields.

Data

This is where any additional data for specific functions will be kept. This field may include data on how and where to search for certain files, such as file offsets and pointers.

NCP Reply Field Descriptions

It is important to understand that an NCP Reply is issued when the actual file server replies to a particular workstation's NCP Request. With a protocol analyzer, the analyst can examine the file server reply of the workstation and the file server-related conversation by looking at the breakdown of the NCP Reply Packet Formats (shown in Table 44.4).

Table 44.4. NCP Reply Packet fields.

NCP Fields	Bytes
Reply/Response Type	2
Sequence Number	1
Connection Number Low	1
Task Number	1
Connection Number High	1
Completion Code	1
Connection Status	1
Data	Variable

Figure 44.3 shows the Network General Sniffer Analyzer displaying the detail of an NCP packet.

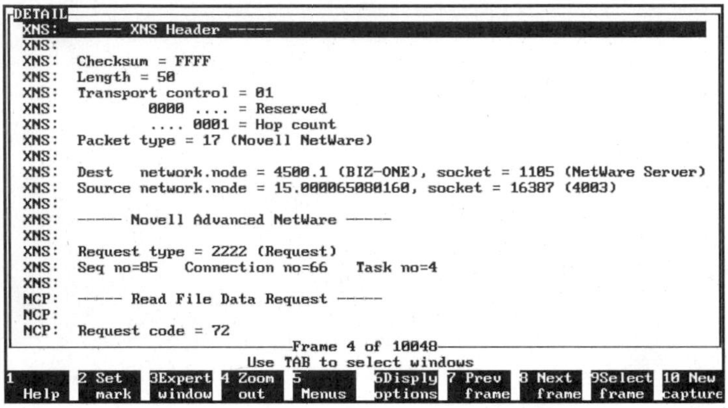

FIGURE 44.3.

Sniffer Analyzer detail of an NCP packet.

```
┌DETAIL────────────────────────────────────────────────────────────┐
│XNS: ─────── XNS Header ──────                                      │
│XNS:                                                                │
│XNS:  Checksum = FFFF                                               │
│XNS:  Length = 50                                                   │
│XNS:  Transport control = 01                                       │
│XNS:        0000 .... = Reserved                                    │
│XNS:        .... 0001 = Hop count                                   │
│XNS:  Packet type = 17 (Novell NetWare)                            │
│XNS:                                                                │
│XNS:  Dest    network.node = 4500.1 (BIZ-ONE), socket = 1105 (NetWare Server)│
│XNS:  Source network.node = 15.000065080160, socket = 16387 (4003) │
│XNS:                                                                │
│XNS:  ─────── Novell Advanced NetWare ──────                        │
│XNS:                                                                │
│XNS:  Request type = 2222 (Request)                                 │
│XNS:  Seq no=85   Connection no=66   Task no=4                     │
│XNS:                                                                │
│NCP:  ─────── Read File Data Request ──────                         │
│NCP:                                                                │
│NCP:  Request code = 72                                             │
│                    ─────Frame 4 of 10040────                       │
│                    Use TAB to select windows                       │
│1        2 Set  3Expert 4 Zoom 5        6Disply 7 Prev 8 Next 9Select 10 New│
│  Help    mark   window  out    Menus   options  frame  frame  frame capture│
└────────────────────────────────────────────────────────────────────┘
```

NCP Reply Type

The server is replying back with information to the workstation's request. There are three valid NCP reply types that can be in this field, as follows:

1. The first one is a 3333, which is a basic reply to service from a workstation.

> **NOTE ►**
>
> This is where the actual file server will be responding with the data or the information related to the data transfer for a workstation request 2222.

2. The second field that is valid is a 7777. This is the reply of a valid burst connection mode set-up attempt to an NCP request of 7777 to set up a burst mode transfer. Burst mode is discussed later in this chapter.

3. The third type field is a 9999, which is a Request Being Processed.

> **TIP ►**
>
> Field 9999 is very important for troubleshooting. This is an indication that a file server is possibly delayed and currently processing a request for information. This condition is discussed in more detail later in this chapter.

Sequence Number

This is the field in which the number of transfers between a workstation and a file server are tracked for an NCP reply.

Connection Number Low

This field has the information related to the server connection number that is assigned to a particular workstation involved in the reply.

Task Number

This is the field that indicates what the task number is, which has been assigned to the particular workstation's operation that is involved in the reply from the file server.

Connection Number High

This field can be utilized along with Connection Number Low to reference the workstation to file-server connection.

Completion Code

A completion code represents the completion of a request from a workstation to a file server. This is where the file server is telling the workstation whether or not it can complete its request.

> **TIP** ▶
>
> From a protocol analysis standpoint, this is a very important field to monitor when watching general workstation requests. Check if they are being replied to in a fluent manner from a file server. This is the field to watch for a general completion of a standard operation in a NetWare operation.

Connection Status

This is a field that indicates whether or not there is still a valid connection. For instance, if a file server were to break a connection, the status in this field would indicate whether or not a connection is valid.

NOTE ▶

Your protocol analyzer is able to encode this field, and the analyst can view whether or not the connection has been broken.

Data

This is where any additional data for specific functions is kept in relation to the reply. For example, in the case of a file read or write request, this field carries the data being read or written.

Conclusion

By analyzing the NCP communication on a network, the analyst can deduce how the core network services are functioning. All of a network's main applications have certain files that are accessed throughout the general network operations. When these files are read or written to, the NCP protocol carries direct information relating to those file reads or writes. It should become second nature for an analyst to decode the NCP headers in a protocol analysis session to see how files are actually accessed from file servers on a network. The file access information is the key data that should be examined in a NCP analysis session.

Packet Burst NCP Mode

Packet Burst NCP is a derivative of the NCP protocol itself, and NetWare has created Packet Burst to enable more efficient transfer of information through the NetWare network stream whenever latency becomes an issue.

In NetWare 3.12 and 4.x versions, Packet Burst NCP is a standard feature. In the 3.11 environment, the answer is to use PBURST.NLM coupled with the VLM shell. VLM can be acquired via purchase of NetWare 4.x or 3.12, purchase of Novell Dos 7, ordering from 800-NETWARE or by downloading from NetWire (NOVFILES).

It was developed to reduce the effect of latency (delay) during the request-response cycles of NCP requests and replies. In some situations, implementing Packet Burst NCP enables more efficient processing of NCP requests. Normally, a workstation requests a file, and the server replies by sending a portion of that file (a portion large enough to fill a packet specifically sized to the type of LAN). The workstation shell then requests another portion of the file, and the server will reply accordingly when the file portion has been read.

> **NOTE** ▶
>
> It is important to understand that certain sequential NCP requests, such as large file transfers, cannot proceed until each packet is sent, the function is executed, and an acknowledgment is received. The request-response cycle can seriously degrade performance when delay occurs because the LAN or server is backlogged or data packets are lost.

During a file-read request, Packet Burst NCP enables the file server to send several "packet fragments" in a burst without waiting between each one for a response. Instead, the burst of packet fragments can be acknowledged with a single acknowledgment packet at the end of the burst. Likewise, during a write request, the workstation can send several fragments of a write request without waiting for an acknowledgment of each one before sending the next.

Implementing Packet Burst NCP on a 3.11 network requires research and understanding of the particular network transfer methods. You should replace the workstation shell, and you also may need to modify the workstation configuration to work efficiently.

Packet Burst NCP utilizes a modified NCP packet format. Table 44.5 shows a breakdown of the NCP Packet Burst format.

Table 44.5. Packet Burst NCP field format.

Field	Byte
Request Type	2
Flags	1
Stream Type	1
Source ID	4

continues

Table 44.5. Continued

Field	Byte
Destination ID	4
Packet Sequence	4
Send Delay Time	4
Burst Sequence Number	2
Acknowledgment Sequence Number	2
Total Burst Length	4
Burst Offset	4
Burst Packet Length	2
Fragment List	2
Function	4
File Handle	4
Starting Offset	4
Bytes to Write	4

NOTE

From looking at the fields, it should be clear that Packet Burst is intended to enable large amounts of data to be transferred back and forth between a workstation and a file server, with a single request versus multiple requests.

Field Descriptions

Following is a discussion of the fields that are important for understanding the difference of the Packet Burst NCP transfer and the standard NCP transfer.

Type Field

Type 7777 indicates that this is a Packet Burst transaction, including both requests and responses.

Flags

Flags indicate whether this particular NCP packet is under standard flow control. Specifically, the flags control whether or not the particular transfer is in the beginning or in the last portion of the Packet Burst data and whether the particular workstation or file server should be waiting for the transfer. The following fields are valid:

SYS (System packet)
SAK (Transmit missing fragment list)
EOB (Last portion of burst data)
BSY (Server Busy)
ABT (Abort—Session not valid)

Stream Type

The stream type is used by the server. Its only current value to the particular server is to determine whether or not the data is going to be transferred in a standard Packet Burst transfer.

Source ID

This is the source node that has sent the data in Packet Burst format.

Destination ID

This is the destination node to which the burst is addressed.

Packet Sequence

This is a field that indicates the current sequence of the Packet Burst transaction, and it is going to be incremented throughout a Packet Burst transfer.

> **TIP** ▶
>
> Examine the Packet Sequence field for overall fluency of a general Packet Burst transaction by making sure that consecutive packets increment sequentially.

Send Delay Time

This identifies the sender to the file server, and the number of delay portions between a transfer of information back and forth on the network. Each delay portion equals 100 microseconds. With a little math, this field indicates how long it took for a response to be received from a request. Some protocol analyzers call this the *delta time*.

Burst Packet Sequence

This increments every time there is a new burst sequence within a burst mode transfer.

> **NOTE** ▶
>
> This field allows the analyst to track the Packet Burst steps throughout a total burst transfer that may include more than one burst.

Acknowledgement Sequence Number

This is the acknowledgment method for each sequence transfer in an overall Packet Burst transaction to indicate that the current connection is still acknowledged. This will only change on the last transfer within the overall Packet Burst transaction to indicate that the final Packet Burst communication transaction is completed.

Total Burst Length

This indicates the total length of a specific burst sequence.

Burst Packet Offset

This indicates where the data starts within the Packet Burst transfer.

Burst Length

This shows the overall length of a total burst transaction for consecutive Packet Burst sequence transfers.

Fragment List

This shows the current remaining fragmentation of Packet Burst sequence transfers that have to be completed throughout the total Packet Burst transaction.

Function

This indicates whether the current Packet Burst transaction is a NetWare read or write request.

File Handle, Starting Offset, Bytes To Write

These fields are utilized for specific file access and search information.

Conclusion

Packet Burst enables a workstation to make a single request and a file server to reply more efficiently in applications where long periods of latency is an issue. This transaction enables a more expedient transfer of data across NetWare networks, especially in a WAN or internetworked environment.

Packet Burst NCP should be implemented whenever an analyst determines that NCP requests have been delayed because of latency in NCP responses.

With today's faster workstations, there is apparently no downside to Packet Burst protocol; it is simply more efficient for sequential NCP file-request/reply sequences than for normal NCP communications. Novell's research and development indicated that the advantages of Packet Burst were sufficient inducement to standardize its use in 3.12 and 4.x, and you can implement Packet Burst in a 3.11 system.

NetWare Service Advertising Protocol (SAP)

The NetWare Service Advertising Protocol (SAP) is considered an application-layer protocol and enables NetWare servers to broadcast their availability and location throughout a NetWare network. From a NetWare 3.x file server, a SAP packet is generated every 60 seconds; this parameter is adjustable on 4.x servers through the SERVMAN.NLM server-based utility. A SAP packet is broadcast throughout the network to update other servers and routers of the particular server's location. NetWare file servers constantly update each other and other key information devices of their particular location in the network. In today's complex networks, this is a very important focus for routing across the network. Using protocol analysis techniques, an analyst can examine a SAP packet to find out the actual location of a server and its place in a NetWare network.

The file servers and routers throughout a NetWare network maintain routing tables of their location in the network and of other servers' locations. Inside a NetWare file server, there is a bindery where information is stored on the resources and clients throughout the network. This bindery can be considered a database of important connection points and resources throughout the NetWare network.

SAP Fields

The overall function of the SAP protocol is to update the databases within a respective server of other servers located throughout the network. This is the addressing methodology for keeping servers updated of other servers and routers throughout the network.

There are two main uses for a NetWare SAP. As mentioned, one use is as a general broadcast from a server every 60 seconds to keep other servers and routers updated of its location and its function as a server. Another use is as a SAP service request. This is where information is going to be requested of other devices through the SAP protocol. The particular SAP request can then be replied to with a SAP service response from the device from which information is being requested. The actual SAP formats are shown in Tables 44.6 and 44.7.

Table 44.6. SAP Request Packet format.

Sap Fields	Bytes
IPX Header	N/A
Packet Type	2
Server Type	2

Table 44.7. SAP Response Packet format.

Fields	Bytes
Packet Type	2
Server Type	2

Fields	Bytes
Server Name	48
Network Address	4
Node Address	6
Socket	2
Intermediate Networks	2

Figure 44.4 shows the Network General Sniffer Analyzer displaying the detail of an SAP Type packet.

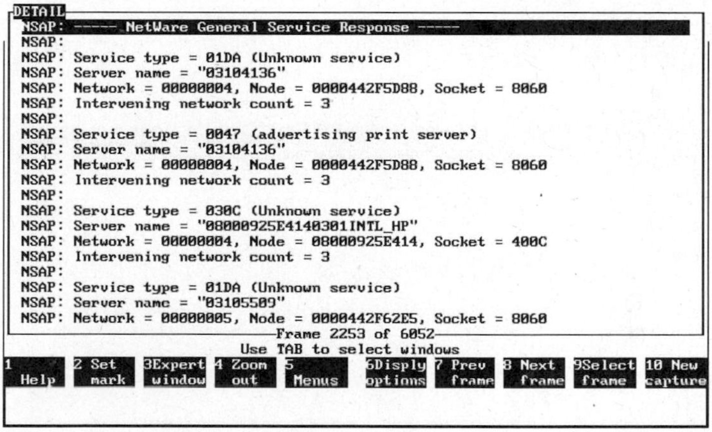

FIGURE 44.4.

Sniffer Analyzer screen displaying SAP packet detail.

```
DETAIL
NSAP: ------ NetWare General Service Response ------
NSAP:
NSAP: Service type = 01DA (Unknown service)
NSAP: Server name = "03104136"
NSAP: Network = 00000004, Node = 0000442F5D88, Socket = 8060
NSAP: Intervening network count = 3
NSAP:
NSAP: Service type = 0047 (advertising print server)
NSAP: Server name = "03104136"
NSAP: Network = 00000004, Node = 0000442F5D88, Socket = 8060
NSAP: Intervening network count = 3
NSAP:
NSAP: Service type = 030C (Unknown service)
NSAP: Server name = "08000925E4140301INTL_HP"
NSAP: Network = 00000004, Node = 00000925E414, Socket = 400C
NSAP: Intervening network count = 3
NSAP:
NSAP: Service type = 01DA (Unknown service)
NSAP: Server name = "03105509"
NSAP: Network = 00000005, Node = 0000442F62E5, Socket = 8060
                 Frame 2253 of 6052
             Use TAB to select windows
1        2 Set   3Expert 4 Zoom  5        6Display 7 Prev  8 Next  9Select 10 New
  Help     mark    window  out     Menus    options   frame   frame   frame  capture
```

Field Descriptions

The following paragraphs explain the fields and their relation to the SAP protocol.

Packet Type

This field shows the analyst the type of SAP packet. The following are considered main SAP packet types:

3H (Nearest Server Request)
4H (Nearest Server Response)
1H (Standard Server Request)
2H (Standard Server Response)

Server Type

This is the field that will indicate the type of server that is communicating on the network. The following four categories are valid for the NetWare SAP protocol:

- File server
- Specific job server
- Print server
- Backup server

> **NOTE** ▶
>
> The analyst should always note the server type.

Server Name

This is the name of the server that is involved in the SAP transmission.

Network Address

This is the network on which the particular server is located.

Node Address

This is the specific node of the server in relation to other server nodes on the NetWare network.

Socket

This is the process that is involved with the SAP transmission.

Intermediate Networks

The NetWare server itself has the capability, through the SAP protocol, to communicate with up to seven servers. Through incrementing certain bytes in the intermediate network, this enables it to advertise service on more than seven servers. The Intermediate Networks field also is used to indicate the number of network addresses, in relation to routers, between the particular requesting device and the responding server network node.

> **TIP** ▶
>
> By analyzing the Intermediate Networks that are filed, an analyst can judge the efficiency of different routes for different servers.

It should be noted that there are two packet type categories that relate to Request and Response types: a General Service Request/Response and a Nearest Service Request/Response. A General Service Request/Response is utilized mainly for broadcasts of server locations. A Nearest Server Request Response is used for specific server identification.

One important consideration of SAP traffic on a NetWare network is that, at times, a 60-second transmission of all the servers on the network from a particular NetWare server's bindery can cause excessive traffic levels. NetWare has created an NLM that restricts the number of SAPs, and this can be customized for an individual NetWare server environment. This particular NLM is called the Filter SAP (SAFILTER.NLM) and is available for filtering the amount of SAP traffic on a network. SAFILTER.NLM is available for download for 3.11 servers. There's an excellent APPNOTE that describes its use. The APPNOTE is available on NetWire as well.

> **NETWARE 4 NOTE** ▶
>
> In NetWare 4.x versions, you can edit the broadcast intervals for SAP packets with SERVMAN.NLM. Select IPX/SPX Protocols from the SERVMAN main menu. Help screens and documentation are online. Remember, however, that when you adjust one server, you should adjust all others so SAP broadcasts and listening parameters will be adjusted in sync.

> **TIP** ▶
>
> A protocol analyzer can be used to examine the frequency and bandwidth level of a SAP transmission to enable the analyst to make a decision on the particular network's SAP bandwidth allocation to broadcast level. For instance, if the SAP traffic takes five percent of overall traffic on a WAN data line, this is considered very excessive. At that point, the user should consider utilizing the NetWare SAFILTER.NLM.

NetWare Routing Information Protocol (RIP)

Novell's Routing Information Protocol (RIP) is used to broadcast key information to the network routing community about the NetWare server and router network details. It should be noted that there can be external NetWare routers and internal NetWare routing within the file servers and that all of these particular routing elements keep routing update tables within their operations. The RIP protocol is very helpful because it enables one NetWare router to notify another NetWare router of its exact network location, its length of transfer, and the respective time to transfer between the particular routers. A NetWare router keeps this type of information on all the network's possible routing channels so the network will operate in an efficient manner.

The NetWare 3.x OS routers actually update the network every 45-60 seconds (depending upon several variables). Routers also generate a RIP packet when they first start themselves on the network, and when they initialize as a router. Now and then, routers require certain information—at which point they might request a RIP across the network. There are also times when configurations are changed, or when routers go down, at which time they will generate a RIP packet.

NETWARE 4 NOTE ▶

In 4.x versions, you can edit the broadcast intervals for RIP packets with SERVMAN.NLM. Select IPX/SPX Protocols from the SERVMAN main menu. Help screens and documentation are online. Remember, however, that when you adjust one server, you should adjust all others so RIP broadcasts and listening parameters will be adjusted in sync.

Remember that the purpose of the RIP protocol is to enable NetWare routers to keep each other updated for their routing information tables on the location and function of other routers throughout the entire NetWare network. The routers, operating at the Network level, use this information to determine the best route a packet should take on its way to its destination.

RIP Fields

There are some key categories to examine for the NetWare routing environment that will be discussed in detail later in this chapter. Table 44.8 shows a breakdown of the Routing Information Protocol packet format.

Table 44.8. Routing information protocol packet format.

Fields	Bytes
Operation Packet Type	2
Network Address	4
Hops Away	2
Ticks	2

Figure 44.5 shows the Network General Sniffer Analyzer displaying the details of an RIP type packet.

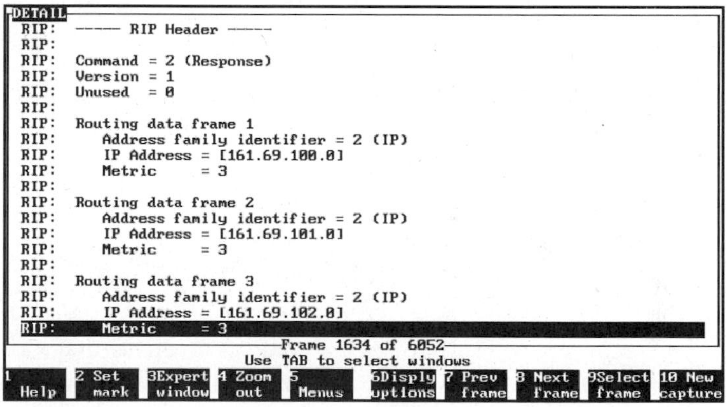

FIGURE 44.5.

Sniffer Analyzer screen with RIP packet detail.

```
-DETAIL
RIP:  ----- RIP Header -----
RIP:
RIP:  Command = 2 (Response)
RIP:  Version = 1
RIP:  Unused  = 0
RIP:
RIP:  Routing data frame 1
RIP:      Address family identifier = 2 (IP)
RIP:      IP Address = [161.69.100.0]
RIP:      Metric    = 3
RIP:
RIP:  Routing data frame 2
RIP:      Address family identifier = 2 (IP)
RIP:      IP Address = [161.69.101.0]
RIP:      Metric    = 3
RIP:
RIP:  Routing data frame 3
RIP:      Address family identifier = 2 (IP)
RIP:      IP Address = [161.69.102.0]
RIP:      Metric    = 3
                    -Frame 1634 of 6052-
                  Use TAB to select windows
1        2 Set   3Expert 4 Zoom  5         6Disply 7 Prev 8 Next 9Select 10 New
 Help     mark    window   out    Menus     options  frame  frame  frame  capture
```

Operation Packet Type

There are two major packet types in a routing information protocol:

01H (Request)
02H (Response)

NOTE ▶

At any given time, some devices, servers, and routers are going to be requesting information on the routing conditions throughout the network, and others are going to be responding with a RIP packet.

Network Address

This is the field that pinpoints the network for the respective router. It should be noted that above this particular packet field, there is always an IPX header that indicates more information about the particular router.

Hops Away

This field indicates the number of routers that still have to be passed through from the point where the RIP packets are being monitored to the point where the router actually is located.

> **NOTE**
>
> This field is extremely important for analyzing the overall placement of NetWare type routers across a network. The Hops Away field shows the efficiency of the particular route for a certain router that is involved in the RIP transmission.

Ticks

This is a time field (1/18 of a second equals one tick) that indicates how far away in time the router transmission is from transmitting to that particular router.

> **NOTE**
>
> This is the amount of time that it would take to go from the point where the analyst is actually monitoring the RIP packets to where the router is located.

> **TIP**
>
> This is a very important field to understand when troubleshooting and analyzing a NetWare network's routing efficiency and speed. An analyst can capture transmitted RIP packets across a network to measure the time delay in communicating to that particular router on the network.

Concluding Remarks on the NetWare Protocol Suite

When performing a protocol analysis session in the NetWare environment, you must examine the conversations between workstations and the file servers. The protocol analyst can be perceived as the "Big Brother" of the network, monitoring it for fluent conversations between the workstations and file servers. The analyst watches the IPX, SPX, and NCP headers for the general flow of traffic and communication and setup, looking for any problems or anomalies in the fields, or looking for data packets that do not make sense.

The foregoing was a thorough description of the packet field breakdowns of the IPX, SPX, NCP, NCP Burst, SAP, and RIP protocols throughout the NetWare protocol suite. These are the individual protocol packet formats that constitute the total NetWare protocol suite. Following is a brief description of some of the other protocols that are seen quite frequently when internetworking.

NetWare Protocols Layered with Other Protocols

Several protocols throughout the internetworking community today are seen quite frequently in the NetWare environment. The material presented earlier in this book mentions and discusses some of these protocols. Now this chapter examines how certain major networking protocols integrate with the NetWare protocol suite. It presents some of the analysis techniques related to these protocols. These protocols include the Systems Networking Architecture Protocol (SNA) from the IBM environment with the NetBIOS packet format, the Transmission Control Protocol/Internet Protocol (TCP/IP), and the AppleTalk protocol suite. These particular protocols are the ones that are seen most frequently throughout network analysis sessions on most NetWare networks, because their computing environments are the most frequently utilized for general computing on today's networks.

When analyzing a NetWare network, it is important to understand the hierarchy of the protocol layers in relation to the standard networking models that are utilized. The first protocol suite to be discussed is the SNA protocol suite.

The SNA Protocol Suite

The SNA protocol suite has its own set of rules and architecture commands that are extensive and would require more specific and lengthy study of the SNA protocol than can be provided here.

An SNA packet is usually encapsulated within a NetWare protocol analyzer trace because SNA is nonroutable and does not rely on NetWare protocols for transmission. However, SNA is seen quite frequently in NetWare environments.

The architecture comprises a transmission unit, which internally has a transmission header, plus a request and response header for the SNA protocol suite. There also is a function management header upon which the actual SNA information is layered.

When examining an SNA network within a NetWare network packetwork, you should understand that the SNA protocol suite itself is usually layered on top of other types of network- and transport-layer protocols, such as NetBIOS. Normally what can be seen first (when an analyst is decoding a captured SNA packet on a network) is the physical layer header. Then, compiled on top of the physical layer if more than one network is involved, may be a source Routing Information (RI) field. On top of the RI field, is usually the Logical Link Control (LLC) header for the particular 802.2 frame transmission. The LLC protocol usually is used for connection control at the data link layer. Next, compiled on top of that is usually a network-layer protocol for connection on the network. This is where NetBIOS usually layers in a SNA packet. On top of all that is the SNA information.

It is important to understand the possible structure for the layers in a composite SNA packet and to understand that at times an analyst picks up SNA packets with all of these layers to decode. A protocol analyzer can do most of this in a very smooth and efficient manner.

There are some packets that need to be monitored from time to time when looking at an SNA transmission. The user should be looking for a healthy physical layer communication and then be examining the SNA general communication. There is a process called Link Control Query setup, which is sometimes called a XID query setup, where the actual connection is established for the SNA network. At this point, the analyst will see what is termed a general network layer communication implementation, which could either be standard LLC or NetBIOS communications. These protocols possibly will generate some sort of connection setup that will involve either broadcast or data transfer information going back and forth. The SNA session data will finally start and be layered through the trace data. Certain information in it can be recognized as standard setup of SNA events. The analyst should be looking for standard communication that will involve an SNA Exchange ID or maybe an Active Physical Unit/Logical Unit connection. It is important to understand the SNA operations themselves in order to understand the fluency of these particular types of packets. The event to always watch for is a network layer connection and then a SNA session setup and communication session.

Figure 44.6 shows the Network General Sniffer depicting an SNA packet detailed with multiple protocol layers.

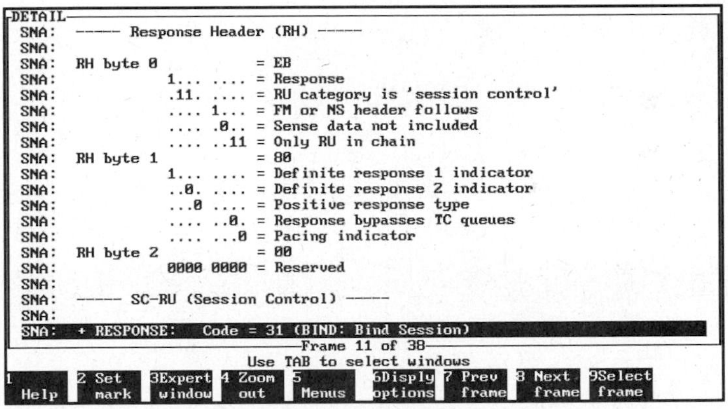

FIGURE 44.6.

Sniffer Analyzer screen display of an SNA packet.

```
┌DETAIL──────────────────────────────────────────────────────────────────┐
│ SNA:  ────── Response Header (RH) ──────                                 │
│ SNA:                                                                     │
│ SNA:  RH byte 0            = EB                                          │
│ SNA:            1... ....  = Response                                    │
│ SNA:            .11. ....  = RU category is 'session control'           │
│ SNA:            .... 1...  = FM or NS header follows                     │
│ SNA:            .... .0..  = Sense data not included                     │
│ SNA:            .... ..11  = Only RU in chain                            │
│ SNA:  RH byte 1            = 80                                          │
│ SNA:            1... ....  = Definite response 1 indicator              │
│ SNA:            ..0. ....  = Definite response 2 indicator              │
│ SNA:            ...0 ....  = Positive response type                      │
│ SNA:            .... .0..  = Response bypasses TC queues                 │
│ SNA:            .... ...0  = Pacing indicator                            │
│ SNA:  RH byte 2            = 00                                          │
│ SNA:            0000 0000  = Reserved                                    │
│ SNA:                                                                     │
│ SNA:  ────── SC-RU (Session Control) ──────                             │
│ SNA:                                                                     │
│ SNA:  + RESPONSE:  Code = 31 (BIND: Bind Session)                        │
│                        ───Frame 11 of 38───                             │
│                        Use TAB to select windows                        │
├─────────────────────────────────────────────────────────────────────────┤
│1        2 Set   3Expert 4 Zoom  5        6Disply 7 Prev  8 Next  9Select │
│  Help     mark    window  out     Menus   options  frame   frame   frame │
└─────────────────────────────────────────────────────────────────────────┘
```

When performing LAN analysis, certain packets on a network can be picked up that may indicate problems in SNA and NetBIOS communications.

In SNA communication, one of the standard packets that should be monitored with a protocol analyzer is the Receiver Not Ready packet format, which, if captured at high levels, may indicate a channel communication fluency problem in an SNA channel. One should not point a finger at any particular device or operation as a problem when immediately picking up this packet; a protocol analyzer is helpful for analyzing this particular suite.

When looking at NetBIOS communications within the SNA packetwork, it is important to remember that NetBIOS is a connection-oriented protocol that is going to set up some sort of communication session for other protocols to rely on. What the analyst should be looking for is a standard handshaking fluency at the NetBIOS protocol node level. There are certain NetBIOS packets (that are important to watch for) that may indicate session connection problems, such as Name In Conflict or No Receive packets. Overall, it is important to monitor for a connection setup, and to ensure that it is established, that data is communicated, and that the connection is properly broken. This will indicate the fluency of the overall NetBIOS transaction.

TCP/IP Protocol Suite

The TCP/IP protocol suite is probably one of the most well-known protocol suites throughout the networking industry. The following is a list of the extensive protocols that can be found in a TCP/IP environment:

> NetBIOS, File Transfer Protocol (FTP)
> Trivial File Transfer Protocol (TFTP)
> Telnet, Simple Mail Transfer Protocol (SMTP)
> Remote UNIX (RUNIX)
> Domain Name Service (DNS)
> Transmission Control Protocol (TCP)
> User Datagram Protocol (UDP)
> Internet Protocol (IP)
> Routing Information Protocol (RIP)
> Gateway to Gateway Protocol (GGP)
> Internet Control Message Protocol (ICMP)
> Logical Link Control (LLC)
> Address Resolution Protocol (ARP)
> Reverse Arp (RARP)
> Subnetwork Address Protocol (SNAP)
> Server Message Block (SMB)
> Common Management and Information Systems Protocol (CMIP)

In a NetWare environment, an analyst can capture the TCP/IP protocol suite in a variety of layered ways. The Internet Protocol (IP) layer of TCP/IP is a network- and transport-layer protocol that can set up a connection for higher TCP-related applications. When monitoring a NetWare network with TCP/IP, an analyst may capture the IP protocol suite interleaved with NCP data. This will vary depending on the type of devices and their purposes with TCP/IP on the network. Most of the time what will actually be picked up is, for instance, certain application-layer TCP/IP protocols layered on top of the IP protocol. Figure 44.7 shows a TCP/IP packet format layered on top of an IPX header.

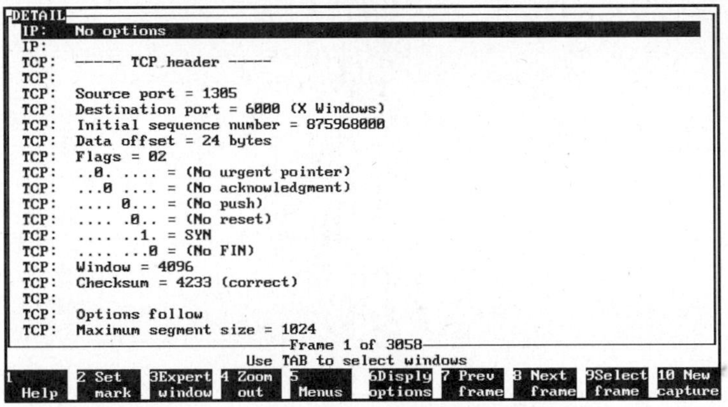

FIGURE 44.7.

Sniffer analyzer displaying a TCP/IP packet.

```
┌DETAIL┌─────────────────────────────────────────────────
│ IP:   No options
│ IP:
│ TCP: ----- TCP header -----
│ TCP:
│ TCP:  Source port = 1305
│ TCP:  Destination port = 6000 (X Windows)
│ TCP:  Initial sequence number = 875968000
│ TCP:  Data offset = 24 bytes
│ TCP:  Flags = 02
│ TCP:  ..0. .... = (No urgent pointer)
│ TCP:  ...0 .... = (No acknowledgment)
│ TCP:  .... 0... = (No push)
│ TCP:  .... .0.. = (No reset)
│ TCP:  .... ..1. = SYN
│ TCP:  .... ...0 = (No FIN)
│ TCP:  Window = 4096
│ TCP:  Checksum = 4233 (correct)
│ TCP:
│ TCP:  Options follow
│ TCP:  Maximum segment size = 1024
└──────────────────Frame 1 of 3058────────────────
              Use TAB to select windows
┌1     2 Set  3Expert 4 Zoom 5       6Displ 7 Prev 8 Next 9Select 10 New
│ Help   mark  window  out   Menus  options  frame  frame  frame  capture
```

Certain TCP/IP packets may be captured on a NetWare network that implements NetWare TCP/IP tunneling. This will vary from implementation to implementation, depending on the use of TCP/IP in its relation to NetWare. There are different types of products available to enable the TCP/IP protocol suite to flow differently on NetWare networks.

Certain types of packets monitor in the TCP/IP environment and can definitely indicate packet communication problems that need to be resolved. For instance, the following TCP/IP packet types may indicate problems at certain capture levels:

- Destination unreachable
- Source quench
- ICMP redirects
- ICMP fragments

The analyst needs to be extremely familiar with the TCP/IP protocol suite to understand the transmission at the TCP/IP layer.

Time To Live

One of the things that the user should examine closely is the standard Time To Live (TTL) value in the TCP/IP protocol suite. This can indicate the number of times that a particular packet has been passed through an IP routing network and can indicate possible routing loops in the network when the value is low.

Destination Unreachable

Another type of packet that is important to monitor is the Destination Unreachable packet on a TCP/IP network. This type of packet indicates whether a TCP/IP transmission was able to complete successfully and reach its destination.

Acknowledgments

Overall, an important area to watch in the TCP/IP communication is the acknowledgment of transactions back and forth from nodes. From time to time, an analyst must watch the acknowledgments in the TCP/IP level and look at the actual events to see if they are being responded to in a normal manner.

Internet Control Message Protocol

Internet Control Message Protocol (ICMP) is another protocol that enables a user to monitor the fluency of communication across the TCP/IP environment. The ICMP protocol enables testing information between different TCP/IP nodes through what is called a *Ping test*. Ping is a program that the administrator executes from the user's workstation. A Ping test sends a request that requires an acknowledgment and waits for a response. It is used to verify the connection between a workstation and host in a connectionless environment.

> **TIP**
>
> An analyst can utilize certain protocol analyzers to automatically activate the Ping test or can monitor a Ping through a TCP/IP station with a protocol analyzer and see whether the response is found. Specifically, the scenario is as follows: a user at a TCP/IP station "Pings" while the analyst monitors the Ping with a protocol analyzer through filtering on the TCP/IP protocol suite. The analyst then looks at the response level of the Ping. At this point, the analyst can identify possible faulty network nodes or internetwork traffic routes for the TCP/IP network Ping.

Duplicate Addresses

One last area to monitor is duplicate addresses. Because TCP/IP addresses are issued by system administrators within a company, it is possible to have duplicate addresses. This problem is frequent enough that many protocol analyzers enable you to specifically monitor and capture duplicate address packets.

AppleTalk Protocol Suite

The AppleTalk protocol itself is quite extensive. There are more than 15 possible protocols that can be discreetly involved in the AppleTalk protocol suite. The AppleTalk protocol is broken up into what is considered a Phase I and Phase II breakdown. The following is a list of the major AppleTalk protocols that can be captured on a NetWare network:

Apple share file server
Apple share print server
Apple talk filing protocol
Apple talk data stream protocol
Zone information protocol
Apple talk session protocol
Printer access protocol
Routing table maintenance protocol
Apple talk echo protocol
Apple talk transaction protocol
Name binding protocol
Datagram delivery protocol
Token talk link access protocol
Ethertalk link access protocol
Local talk link access protocol

As can be seen, the list is quite extensive. The Phase I and Phase II breakup is as follows: Phase I was originally intended for the Ethernet environment and was centered around the Ether Talk and Local Talk Link Access protocols; Phase II was developed for the Token Ring environment and involves an addition of the Token Talk Link Access protocol. Specifically, depending upon the type of LAN involved, one will encounter most of the AppleTalk protocols when examining a NetWare environment. It should be noted that the AppleTalk protocols at these higher layers, for instance the AppleTalk Filing Protocol, will usually rely upon an LLC delivery across a NetWare network. Figure 44.8 shows the Network General Sniffer Analyzer displaying an AppleTalk packet.

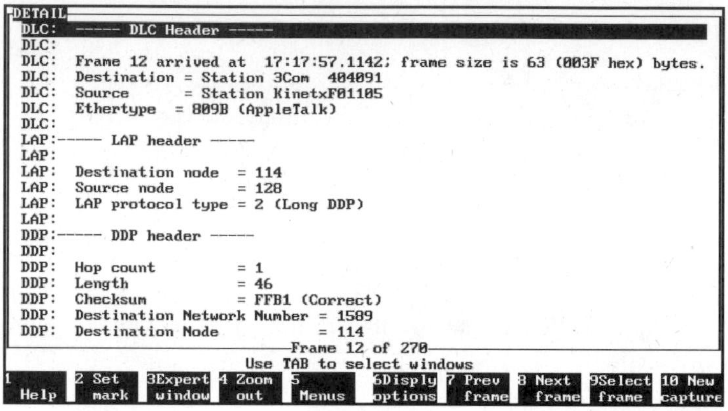

FIGURE 44.8.

Sniffer Analyzer screen displaying an AppleTalk packet.

```
DETAIL
DLC: ------ DLC Header ------
DLC:
DLC:  Frame 12 arrived at  17:17:57.1142; frame size is 63 (003F hex) bytes.
DLC:  Destination = Station 3Com  404091
DLC:  Source      = Station KinetxF01105
DLC:  Ethertype = 809B (AppleTalk)
DLC:
LAP:------ LAP header ------
LAP:
LAP:  Destination node  = 114
LAP:  Source node       = 128
LAP:  LAP protocol type = 2 (Long DDP)
LAP:
DDP:------ DDP header ------
DDP:
DDP:  Hop count         = 1
DDP:  Length            = 46
DDP:  Checksum          = FFB1 (Correct)
DDP:  Destination Network Number = 1589
DDP:  Destination Node           = 114
                      Frame 12 of 270
                 Use TAB to select windows
 1        2 Set   3Expert 4 Zoom  5        6Disply 7 Prev  8 Next  9Select 10 New
   Help     mark    window   out     Menus  options   frame   frame   frame  capture
```

There are some issues to troubleshoot in the AppleTalk environment, and through troubleshooting the Zone Information Protocol (ZIP) packets and the Name Binding Protocol packets (NBP), one can actually examine a lot of general communication problems on a NetWare and Apple network. Most problems in any type of environment are involved with either addressing or location in the transfer of data. The ZIP protocol is used and translates between network numbers and zone names within the overall Apple network environment. The NBP protocol has to do with the name relational transfer of information on the AppleTalk network. It actually permits network users to refer to different types of network services through a general process by character names.

So when troubleshooting most of the NetWare networks that involve Apple protocols, keep a very close eye on whether the ZIP packets and NBP packets at the AppleTalk layers are actually communicating in a fluent manner. Certain fields can be examined closely, such as the routing lengths and wait time in the AppleTalk layers. An analyst should pay particular attention to the AppleTalk file protocols to determine whether that particular protocol suite is fluent.

This section does not describe in detail the AppleTalk protocol, which would involve extensive study, but there are numerous references available on the subject.

Summary

This chapter gave you an overall understanding of the general packet formats for the major NetWare protocol suites and some of the related protocols that can be seen in a NetWare environment with a protocol analyzer. This text described the fields that an analyst needs to examine. However, it is important to understand and get used to the communication language on a NetWare network. A protocol analyzer enables an analyst to focus in and watch the conversation between a workstation and a file server. It will not tell the analyst what specifically is wrong; he or she will have to look into the packets themselves and observe the communication of the language. Once a language is understood, the analyst will be able to decipher whether or not there is a problem in the conversation and possibly find the source of that problem.

The next chapter discusses some specific issues and methods for analyzing and trouble-shooting certain types of NetWare-related problems with the aid of a protocol analyzer.

NetWare Analysis Methodolgy

by Dan Nassar

45

When approaching a NetWare protocol analysis session, it is important to understand that after analyzing the efficiency of the data link layer, packet formats, and workstation-to-file server communication, there are further steps to be taken. This section addresses how to analyze NetWare for specific types of problems that may occur.

This chapter examines NetWare:

- Addressing
- Traffic fluency
- Internetwork routing

Addressing is involved in all of the NetWare transfer and operation processes for sockets, destination IDs, virtual circuits, servers, and routers. NetWare addressing schemes are quite complex and should be examined at the IPX, SPX, and NCP layers. A protocol analyzer enables the analyst to examine these processes. The NetWare addressing scheme on a network can be specifically examined for fluency of the addressing.

Traffic fluency and communication over the network are other important areas to understand. The most common activity on a network is reading and writing information to a server's disk drive from a client workstation. Thus, the overall communication across the network is what should be examined most closely.

Internetwork routing from one NetWare network address to another is a third issue. Certain functions must be examined carefully. One of the functions is performance: whether a particular route is more efficient than another. For example, if five network addresses are linked together with routers and multiple routes exist, NetWare determines which route is most efficient. However, you must be certain that NetWare's routing decisions actually correspond to the best physical route. A protocol analyst can examine routing performance and related issues to find out whether routing decisions are okay or should be studied more carefully.

NetWare Addressing

NetWare addressing is based primarily on the IPX and SPX addressing fields. There are complexities that the following sections discuss.

Addressing Errors

When using NIC universal addressing (the IEEE preassigned numbers) on Ethernet or Token Ring, it is impossible to have duplicate data link layer addresses. Therefore, the search for duplicate addresses is normally confined to the IPX network addresses. When local addressing is used to assign node addresses, it's possible to have duplicate data link layer node addresses. A protocol analyzer can find these errors by searching the data link layer for addressing errors in the frame headers.

IPX addressing includes addresses for source and destination network, node, and socket. The network address is assigned by the installer. In an internetwork, every LAN, WAN, and internal network address must be assigned a unique 8-character hexadecimal address. The node address is picked up from the data link node address. In a NetWare internetworked environment, duplicate network numbers must not exist or router configuration errors appear. If this rule is violated, NetWare routers may have difficulty delivering IPX and SPX packets. If duplicate network addresses exist, the complete internal routing methodology of a NetWare network can malfunction.

By examining the information in the IPX and SPX headers, an analyst determines whether packets can be delivered as expected. When looking at an IPX transmission and response, duplicate address problems can be clearly seen by examining the node address and network address for duplicate IDs. Some packets won't be acknowledged or will be rejected with router configuration errors. Most protocol analyzers immediately report duplicate addresses. By comparing request and reply pairs, you can determine whether a problem exists in NetWare network addressing.

Client/Server Dialogs

It is also important to examine paired dialogs between NetWare clients and file servers in detail. Specifically, the analyst must isolate the communications coming from a specific client, and all replies to its requests, according to its node address. This can be accomplished by using a filter to eliminate from view all other node addresses, and therefore clients, present on the LAN

For example, by setting up a filter between the workstation and the file server, the analyst can examine the communication for a workstation login sequence. This is best accomplished by examining dialogs between a client and server that are both located on the same physical LAN. The simplest way to filter a dialog is to sort by the data link layer node address extracted from the frame header, which doesn't go across a router. When analyzing communication between a client and a server where a router connects two different network addresses, an analyst must filter IPX packet header information for specific node addresses to capture the dialog.

Take a look at an example of a communication session between a workstation and a file server on an individual NetWare network. The first thing you see by examining the conversation is an NCP query from the workstation, requesting access to the server. The closest server responds, finds a preferred server for the workstation, and gives an NCP response identifying the route to that server. At that point, the workstation performs a RIP broadcast to find the best route to that particular server, and the NetWare server or router responds with a request connection with the server. Then, the workstation requests a create connection with the server, and the server responds in an NCP response format with a connection assigned. Then, the workstation proposes a maximum packet size and the server returns with the largest common buffer size available. At that point, a particular server is connected through a general connection, and the logon is actually executed from the NetWare file server.

Figure 45.1 shows the Network General Sniffer display of the workstation connection request-response sequence and login. You can learn much by capturing a sequence like this one, filtering the frames, and observing the fluency of the sequence. Look for any retries and errors indicating that the connection can't be created. In this NCP dialog, as well as most other types of NCP dialogs, you learn to recognize multiple steps and handshaking between a client and file server. Become familiar with various types of NCP dialogs, including connection requests, read from file, write to file, login, and logout sequences. These are typical of all the types of NCP request-response sequences. If the sequence occurs promptly, and with no errors or retries, the sequence is considered fluent. If errors or retries are present, further analysis is necessary to determine their source.

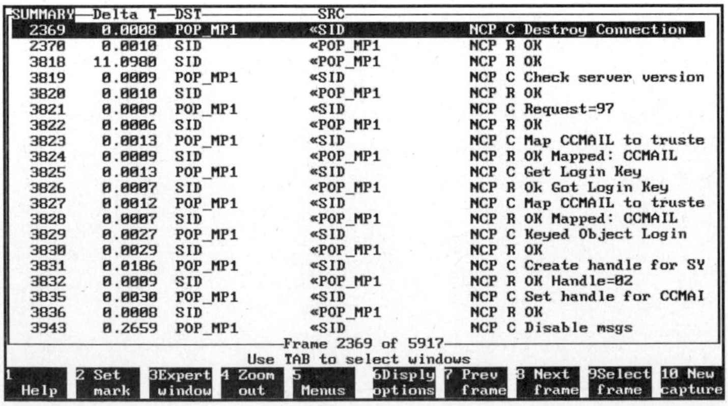

FIGURE 45.1.

Sniffer analyzer screen displaying a logon sequence.

```
SUMMARY  Delta T  DST            SRC
  2369   0.0008  POP_MP1        «SID          NCP C Destroy Connection
  2370   0.0010  SID            «POP_MP1      NCP R OK
  3818  11.0900  SID            «POP_MP1      NCP R OK
  3819   0.0009  POP_MP1        «SID          NCP C Check server version
  3820   0.0010  SID            «POP_MP1      NCP R OK
  3821   0.0009  POP_MP1        «SID          NCP C Request=97
  3822   0.0006  SID            «POP_MP1      NCP R OK
  3823   0.0013  POP_MP1        «SID          NCP C Map CCMAIL to truste
  3824   0.0009  SID            «POP_MP1      NCP R OK Mapped: CCMAIL
  3825   0.0013  POP_MP1        «SID          NCP C Get Login Key
  3826   0.0007  SID            «POP_MP1      NCP R Ok Got Login Key
  3827   0.0012  POP_MP1        «SID          NCP C Map CCMAIL to truste
  3828   0.0007  SID            «POP_MP1      NCP R OK Mapped: CCMAIL
  3829   0.0027  POP_MP1        «SID          NCP C Keyed Object Login
  3830   0.0029  SID            «POP_MP1      NCP R OK
  3831   0.0186  POP_MP1        «SID          NCP C Create handle for SY
  3832   0.0009  SID            «POP_MP1      NCP R OK Handle=02
  3835   0.0030  POP_MP1        «SID          NCP C Set handle for CCMAI
  3936   0.0008  SID            «POP_MP1      NCP R OK
  3943   0.2659  POP_MP1        «SID          NCP C Disable msgs
                          Frame 2369 of 5917
                       Use TAB to select windows
 1        2 Set   3Expert 4 Zoom  5        6Disply 7 Prev  8 Next  9Select 10 New
  Help     mark   window   out    Menus    options  frame   frame   frame  capture
```

Overall, when analyzing a network addressing situation, the analyst always should be looking for a fluent conversation. For instance, if the server were to come back and say it couldn't complete a connection because of an invalid password, this could be confirmed through a protocol analysis session. Again, the focus here is on a fluent logon connection and communication sequence between workstations and file servers. Keep in mind that the transmissions for proper NetWare network numbers, nodes, and sockets should be carefully monitored.

Traffic Flow Fluency

As previously discussed, LAN and WAN communication is based on the dialog that occurs between a pair of nodes, the client, and the server. By examining the NCP packet header information with a protocol analyzer, you can get a good idea of how efficient the traffic flow is on the LAN to which your analyzer is connected. Each LAN should be evaluated for flow statistics.

Requests to Reply Fluency

One of the flow statistics to check is the ratio of NCP requests to responses. Look for a balance between the two. The ratio isn't balanced when using Packet Burst NCP, which works differently, as discussed earlier.

> **NOTE** ▶
>
> Where Packet Burst NCP is used, the request/reply ratio should *not* be one to one.

Many protocol analyzers enable the analyst to examine the ratio of NCP requests to responses. This can be done by filtering the requests from a specific workstation to a file server according to the workstation or file server's data link layer node address. The protocol analyzer captures this information in a buffer or on the disk. Then the analyst can evaluate the ratio of NCP requests to NCP replies. Most analyzers can display the requests and responses in pairs. Once the frames are captured, the analyzer can further filter them and sort or count them. To check the ratio of requests to replies, sort by request and by reply, and then check for balance.

Fluency of Conversations

The next area to evaluate is general fluency of conversation within the NCP request and response pairs. Look at responses for valid acknowledgment or execution of functions. For example, a workstation file read request should result in a file read, data in the data field, and an NCP positive acknowledgment function call.

NCP error messages should alert you to a lack of fluency in the conversations between nodes. Examine the request for the file, the response for the file, and the actual organization of the conversation. Each workstation file read request should show an initialize, a server file open, and one or a series of data transfers from the server to the workstation. At the end of the file transmission sequence, a file close occurs, and the conversation is terminated.

NCP file requests involve a systematic set of events. A file is initialized, opened, read, and closed. This sequence is required in order to ensure delivery of data despite any connectivity problems that may occur. If errors are present, NCP normally recovers by resending the missing packets. Because problems can occur at the disk channel or over the cabling, NCP is designed to trap and reexecute requests that have suffered damage. An analyst should be searching for evidence of such problems in order to determine the source of the errors.

Request Being Processed Packets

The next area to examine is how promptly the replies come from the file server. For several reasons, instead of the normal sequence of events, Request Being Processed NCP packets may be sent from the file server. This response indicates that the file server is too busy internally to reply at this time. This type of packet tells the sender not to time-out yet, but to wait for a reply a little longer. Each Request Being Processed Reply results in latency, and is therefore sometimes called a "Delay packet." It is important to examine the ratio of Request Being Processed replies to NCP requests in order to determine if the level is too high.

In normal NCP communications (where the NETX shell is used), file read and write operations can't continue until each reply is received. Every file read request should result in a packet of data in the reply. If the file read is larger than the packet size, the next request is another file read showing the file read with an *offset*. The offset indicates where the file read or write left off and where the next should resume. When a delay occurs, the file read or write pauses until the last offset is delivered.

In Packet Burst NCP communications, the same procedure occurs differently. When a file read or write request is sent, one or several packets (called "packet fragments") come back in a burst. When the final packet is sent, the burst is acknowledged with a list of any packet fragments that are missing. Packet Burst NCP is always used by default in 4.x and 3.12 servers. In 3.11 servers, the PBURST.NLM must be loaded. In all cases, the VLM requester must be used at the workstation.

File Access Capability

The next category to examine is file access capability. When a workstation requests a particular file, the file location should be reported, a file open should be issued, and then the file read should occur, resulting in the sequence discussed previously. Periodically, there is a failed access to files (discussed in the next chapter).

Packet Size Efficiency

Another factor to look for when traversing a router is packet size. During an NCP connection request, the workstation shell (or requester) and the preferred server to which the user is connecting negotiate a packet size to be used during the term of the connection. The maximum packet size must be the smallest size supported on the LANs and WANs between the source node (the workstation) and the destination node (the preferred file server). NetWare 3.11 and earlier versions impose a maximum packet size of 512 bytes when traversing a router. This restriction is imposed to accommodate ARCnet's small packet size.

If no ARCnet is used, the packet size can be 1024 bytes; if only Token Ring LANs are used, the packet size can be 4096 bytes (over 17,000 bytes for 4.x routers and 16 mbps Token Ring). However, because this artificial restriction, you may find that your communications use a 512 byte packet size, when they could be using a larger packet size. Because of the connection-oriented (request/reply) nature of NCP, packet size can figure as an important factor in optimizing an internetwork, especially across WANs.

> **TIP** ▶
>
> This limitation is overcome by implementing LIPX.NLM at the file server and the VLM requester at the workstations in 3.11 versions. The artificial limit of 512 bytes has been removed in 3.12 and 4.x versions.

Elapsed Time Between Requests and Replies

Elapsed time between requests and replies is the most effective indicator of latency. Latency slows the flow of communication regardless of how fast your LAN or file server is. Many NCP request/reply sequences suffer dramatically because of latency, the effects of which are multiplied each time a subsequent request is held up until it is acknowledged. Most protocol analyzers time-stamp each frame as it is captured. The analyst can then examine the elapsed time between requests and replies.

The elapsed time tells you how long it took for one round trip between a workstation and a file server. The criteria for judging whether elapsed time is excessive depends upon the route and the amount of activity on the network.

For example, you might isolate a dialog between a workstation and file server by filtering out all node addresses except the two you want to observe. In observing a read request, an elapsed time of 2.3 seconds occurs between each request and reply due to the presence of a router, a WAN, and another router between two LAN segments. If you make some changes to the configuration of the WAN and the elapsed time decreases by one second, you can assume that the change has benefitted your system handsomely.

You may be able to reduce latency in your internetwork with various improvements such as LIPX and Packet Burst NCP, or by upgrading workstation shell/requester and IPX and NIC drivers.

Latency Between Requests and Replies

Long periods of elapsed time between a request and a reply can cause an IPX retry to occur. After a given number of retries, a time-out occurs, and a screen message indicates that a network error has occurred. This is a problem in a normal network environment; however, latency is the unavoidable result of slower WAN links.

If you detect many NCP requests where no replies are sent, this indicates that IPX retries have been made. You should determine the cause of excessive retries. If no WAN links are involved, you may have cabling problems, inefficient routing, or other types of communication problems. You should start by looking for problems at the data link layer, as discussed in Chapter 44, "Analysis of the NetWare Protocol Suite."

NOTE ▶

If your IPX retries are the result of slow WAN links, you can adjust your workstation shell or requester to eliminate IPX time-outs. You can adjust the IPX Retry Count or, if SPX is being used and SPX errors are reported, you can adjust your SPX Retry count.

In your NET.CFG file (or SHELL.CFG if using traditional IPX.COM drivers), increase your retry count from the default of 20. For example, to increase the retry count for IPX to 50, include the statement:

```
IPX RETRIES = 50
```

After adjusting your values, you should verify proper retry and successful reply sequences by filtering the communications and time-stamping. Increase the number of retries in increments of five until your errors disappear. In various situations, a level of 25 is sufficient, whereas in others, 50 or 60 retries are necessary to compensate for the latency that occurs in your WAN.

NETWARE 4 NOTE ▶

NetWare 4.x's SERVMAN utility enables you to adjust IPX and SPX timing parameters for the server OS. Load SERVMAN.NLM at your server console. Most parameters are apparent, and online help is available.

Watchdog Packets

Another factor to consider is the presence of watchdog packets on your network. Your server OS monitors connections and issues a watchdog packet to a workstation that hasn't transmitted any packets for a set amount of time. If the connection is still good and the user is logged in, a reply is sent, and the watchdog timer starts counting again. If the user has logged out, no reply is sent. If no reply is received for a set amount of time, another watchdog packet is sent. Again, if no reply is received, another is sent. After a given number of retries with no replies, the connection is terminated. This device is provided to free up connections after users log out.

By default, the first watchdog packet is sent after about five minutes of inactivity. There is about one minute between retries if no reply is received, and five retries before the connection is terminated. Each of these parameters can be regulated by using SET statements at your server console. To automate these SET parameters, they need to be placed in the AUTOEXEC.NCF file so they are executed every time the server boots.

If users normally log out and then log in again after the default 15-minute sequence, they need to reconnect to their server. If this is a constant hassle, you should adjust your server's watchdog parameters.

> **NOTE**
>
> You should adjust your server's watchdog parameters only if you encounter a problem with terminated connections.

Routing Inefficiency

In larger, more complex internetworks, NetWare routing may become a key issue. Routers forward IPX packets until they reach the destination network address as described in Chapter 25, "Basics of Internetwork Data Communications," of this book. As discussed in Chapter 36, "Internetwork Performance," you should design your internetwork and use routers effectively to reduce the number of hops and time it takes to forward IPX packets to their ultimate destinations.

> **NOTE**
>
> Chapter 36 pointed out various internetwork configuration problems that are inherent to Router Information Protocol, of which you should be aware. For greater detail on this topic and solutions, please refer to that chapter.
>
> If you are confused about the differences between bridges and routers, see Chapter 25.

> **CAUTION**
>
> The use of bridges in an internetwork can cause severe routing problems in a NetWare internetwork, especially when redundant paths are present, or both bridges and routers are used.

For several reasons, IPX packets coming from a remote LAN segment may be routed in a manner that is inefficient. A protocol analyzer can help you identify inefficient routing problems. To evaluate routing inefficiency, filter packets at the IPX layer to isolate those with higher hop counts. Look at the IPX Transport Control field. The number in this field reveals the number of logical hops (hops across a router) the IPX packet took to reach your analyzer. You should determine the number of hops that the packet should take and compare it to the number of hops reported in the Transport Control field.

> **NOTE** ▶
>
> Routable protocols, such as NetWare IPX, can't detect the presence of bridges, and therefore can't report physical hops across bridges in the same manner as logical hops across routers. However, bridges also introduce delay during the bridging process, which can cause NetWare routers to make poor routing decisions.

If a protocol analyzer is connected to a backbone LAN, that is in turn connected to several departmental LAN segments distributed over local and remote routers, the protocol analyzer can therefore view frames containing IPX packets that are travelling across the backbone to and from several points.

Suppose through analyzing the IPX hop count you observe many packets coming from one LAN segment to another one to reach a remote server. You may find that one physical node address is responsible for that pattern. Upon further investigation, you find that the user was relocated to another building, and was using internetwork routing to reach the server. Each user should access a conveniently located server so that routed traffic is kept to a minimum.

Just because users can access servers across routers doesn't mean this is an efficient way of working. In the case described previously, the user's performance was poor, but it also affected other user activity by placing a burden on the internal routers and creating excessive traffic on more than one LAN segment. Using a protocol analyzer, you can locate problems like this quickly and effectively.

You can evaluate proper workstation and file server placement by filtering on the IPX hop count. This technique is used quite frequently today to balance servers and workstations into LAN segments and internetwork configurations.

Routing and Bridge Loops

Keep an eye on the loops throughout the internetwork. In an internetwork with multiple LAN segments where bridges are used, there may be multiple paths to the different LAN segments. When multiple paths are present, bridges may forward frames which in turn are forwarded back, and a loop is formed. This problem was discussed in Chapter 26, "Routers and Bridges." As previously discussed, IPX is a routable protocol and can't detect physical hops across bridges. When all routers are used, they can detect multiple paths and select the best path, avoiding the possibility of loops.

In a TCP/IP environment, some routing loops are inevitable, but should be at a low level. In the TCP/IP protocol suite, the impact of loops is minimized through the Time To Live (TTL) field in a TCP/IP packet. This field says that if this packet crosses the specified number of hops, the packet will be deleted from the network. You can monitor this field to see whether a loop is occurring.

In the IPX suite, a similar mechanism is in place in the hop count. An IPX packet can traverse no more than 16 routers. If redundant routes are present, some of which contain bridges, loops may occur. Loops can cause redundant communication to a workstation or file server, and the network addressing can be confused by this transaction. If the problem can be detected by your file server, it will show console messages stating that a router configuration error is present.

Latency Between Requests and Replies

As discussed previously, inefficient routing can cause excessive latency between request and reply sequences. Each hop across a router or bridge causes some latency. The less efficient the router or the path, the longer the latency. You can use a protocol analyzer to evaluate the time between requests and replies to identify client workstations that should be connected more efficiently with a file server.

Routing Loads on File Servers

Routing loads constitute a great concern in NetWare environments. Heavy routing activity on a file server's internal router can slow both packet forwarding rates and file server performance. NetWare internal routers are less efficient than dedicated external routers. Because of the loads placed on file servers, their forwarding rates don't always perform at optimum level. Latency often occurs during routing because NetWare servers are busy and can't handle the extra load of internal routing along with other file server operations.

This isn't to say that Novell internal routing is a problem or that it can't be done. It can be done, and it can be done properly. However, you should evaluate if latency occurs because routing delays in busy servers. Several factors, including latency resulting from internal routing, have caused integrators to use external routers. This offloads the routing activity from the server and enables a router to operate more efficiently.

You can use a protocol analyzer to monitor the number of inbound and outbound packets that are being routed. For example, this can be done by filtering on the Source ID and Destination ID fields in the IPX header for packets that are being routed through a file server.

By setting up a filter to look at the Destination IDs and Source IDs in the IPX header, you can examine how much data is coming to a server from other LAN segments. By observing this packet, you can determine how heavy the routing activity is on a file server. If the routing load approaches a point where it may be affecting file server performance, you should consider using an external router or switching hub. You also can determine quite accurately what kind of performance gains you should experience by evaluating the current amount of latency.

Triggers can also be set up to halt a capture when specific data is located, such as the filter described previously. The trigger enables you to locate activity that is intermittent or hard to locate. Once the trigger stops the capture, you can evaluate what activity led up to that event. In this case, you might set a trigger for packets that are being routed. This would enable you to pinpoint which client workstations are causing the problem and exactly what activity they are performing at the time the problem occurs.

Examining RIP Packets

Keep in mind that routing tables affect router performance. One of the key things that you must understand is that these routing tables contain your Routing Information Protocol (RIP) information that is broadcasted to file servers and routers. By examining RIP packets, you can take a look at the number of timing in ticks from a particular server to another router.

> **TIP** ▶
>
> By generating and designing specialized tests with a protocol analyzer, an analyst can transmit RIP packets to all the nodes from one network to other network nodes across all of the routers that are attached to your respective LAN segment. The analyst can then wait for the RIP response packets to be returned as a response. The tick count tells you how long it took to make a round trip between your node and each router.

By examining the timing differences, you can clearly evaluate routing efficiency across the internetwork layout from router to routers. This evaluation is important when troubleshooting a possible latency problem to remote servers. Protocol analysis enables you to set up transmissions from your analyzer and then examine NetWare internetwork routing latency. It is possible through this type of troubleshooting exercise that you can identify problems with routing information tables in respective servers and routers. Large routing tables are inefficient and may contain configuration errors that slow their productivity.

Summary

This chapter discussed basic methodologies used to analyze problems throughout the NetWare environment. You should take a systematic approach to using these methodologies using filtering and triggering techniques in the NetWare environment.

The next chapter discusses the specific analysis of three types of NetWare problem packets, so you can understand the possible impacts on the overall internetwork operations in a NetWare environment.

Analyzing NetWare Problem Packet Types

46

by Dan Nasser

This chapter discusses three types of packet formats that may represent problems when certain levels are reached. An analyst can achieve a high success rate in network analysis and troubleshooting by focusing on these particular packet types and tracking any problems or addresses within the NetWare environment that are related to these types of packets.

The following types of packets will be examined in this section:

- Request Being Processed NCP packets
- File access failures
- NetWare bindery errors

This chapter also discusses the overall impact of these particular packets and how tracking them can help you isolate NetWare internetwork problems globally.

Request Being Processed NCP Packets

A *Request Being Processed* packet is reply type 9999 in the NCP command set. Certain protocol analyzers call it a *Delay Packet* and some call it a *Request Being Processed* packet. Others call it an *NCP Busy* referring to the fact that a NetWare file server's NCP processing is backlogged and cannot answer at this time. There are a range of phenomena that can cause this response from a file server.

For example, if a workstation requests a file from a certain NetWare file server, the file server normally replies immediately with the data that the workstation requests. However, assume a workstation requests a file with a request 2222 with some sort of function and function code for a certain type of data from a NetWare file server. When using a protocol analyzer, you can detect and decode delay packets where the file server responds with a NCP reply 9999 code. This means that internal file server resources are backlogged; the request has been received, but it cannot be serviced at this time because the NetWare file server is busy.

Though a low level of Being Processed replies are normal when activity is high, you should troubleshoot the cause of the high level of activity, find out how frequently this problem occurs, and determine its duration. The problem can be caused by the following factors:

1. The NetWare file server may be busy because of high levels of resource demands that cannot be met. This indicates that the file server's capacity to service requests has been exceeded. File server capacity and network design need to be aligned to accommodate the peak level of network traffic.

2. The NetWare file server may have an internal resource issue such as CPU saturation, slow bus speed, or a shortage of memory or disk space.

3. The NetWare file server may be overburdened with too many NLMs or an NLM that monopolizes resources. In NetWare's nonpreemptive environment, if an NLM or driver maintains control of the CPU for too long, other requests may become backlogged. If too many server-based applications are running, perhaps some can be moved to other servers or to a NetWare Runtime server. NetWare Runtime is provided with SAA Services, Multi Protocol Router, Oracle, and other NLMs that may require excessive resources.

The point is that a small number of delay packets indicates that capacity of the overall network was reached for short periods. A large ratio of delay packets, perhaps two to three percent of overall traffic, indicates a need for expanded internal server processing capacity. You need to plan capacity to handle the peak periods better. The analyst will have to find out if the NetWare file server is busy because of an internal issue or external issue. An example of an external issue is when the server is being flooded with more requests then it can normally handle. Maybe the application design on this particular NetWare network is not proper, and the analyst will have to look at distributing the applications among multiple file servers or moving user connections to different file servers.

Sometimes a NetWare file server's internal resources are not adequate for the overall application of the network design. In such cases, the analyst needs to examine memory capacity, disk drive capacity, internal CPU processing time, and server NIC and driver efficiency. The analyst must make a judgment about whether there is a problem based on the frequency and duration of request-being-processed episodes.

To analyze this problem, you can use a protocol analyzer to concentrate on the specific file server's node address. To capture a large amount of packets, scroll through the NCP layer headers to locate a 9999 request-being-processed packet. As soon as you locate such a packet, design a filter based on the location within the header for the pattern of the 9999 reply code. Then set your filter to eliminate all except this type of packet and the requests that they are paired with. Many protocol analyzers enable you to set a trigger to detect this pattern in the header so that no matter how infrequently it occurs, you will locate it.

You should then look at the frequency and the number of NCP responses in relation to normal NetWare traffic. Stated otherwise, of all the NCP packets received by the server, how many are request-being-processed packets?

As a rule of thumb, request-being-processed packets should not constitute more than 2 percent of traffic. If they exceed that level, this file server is too busy. The frequent appearance of request-being-processed packets indicates that the server simply does not have the power to support the activity being generated.

File Access Failures

A *Failed File Request*, also known as a file access failure, occurs when a workstation requests a file from a file server and the file server responds by indicating that the file cannot be read. This problem can be viewed with a protocol analyzer by finding the file-read request where an NCP function call initializes the file server's file-read procedure. Once the NCP file request is received, the file-server OS attempts to open the file or to search for the file. If the file is not found, it will reply with an NCP failure code that indicates why the file could not be read—in this case a completion code of 255.

File Not Found

This type of failure can occur for a variety of reasons. It might mean that the file is not in the working directory nor is it in the path (search drive). Or it could be that the file is in the path but the file is flagged as hidden, system, or not sharable while another user has the file open. It may be a software-related error wherein the workstation has not followed the proper procedure for requesting the file. An analyst can even examine a dialog box where a workstation may retry its search several times until the file is eventually located. In some cases, the file may not be accessible over a path — as is the case with some overlaid files.

Failed file requests occur normally in the course of any computing environment. It becomes a problem on a NetWare network only when the number of failed file requests reaches more than five percent of overall traffic. A high file-failure rate defeats the primary purpose of a network: to provide shared access to files. When the file failure rate exceeds a normal level, network throughput declines significantly. Under these conditions, you need to troubleshoot your network to find out why you do not have a higher success rate in file-access requests.

Print Traffic

Printer NICs and other types of printer sharing devices have become quite popular. They enable you to attach a printer directly to a LAN segment. They have been known to cause file access errors. Many such devices operate as print servers and poll the queues on a frequent basis looking for spool files that are waiting for service. If no job is in the queue, the type of request that is used elicits a completion code, indicating a file-access failure. This method of handling queue polling normally does not cause a problem. However, it should be distinguished from all other file access errors. Some protocol analyzers ignore this event because it is considered normal activity. Most experienced protocol analysts prefer to see information like this and determine for themselves whether they want to filter it out. Others think that the less information you need to screen, the easier it is to analyze protocol.

> **TIP** ▶
>
> When using this approach, examine failed file requests methodically. Expect the level of failed file requests to remain less than five percent of NCP packets. If it is determined that the level is higher than five percent, decode the frames and break down the NCP layer function codes in the replies to locate the reasons for the failed access.
>
> If you discover that a search attribute is the cause, you may be able to implement the NetWare SMODE command. SMODE affects the way DOS searches directories and on what basis files can be opened. See your NetWare Utilities Reference manual for detailed information on using SMODE. (In NetWare 4.x, SMODE has been consolidated into the FLAG command.)
>
> If a large number of file-access failure replies are being generated by print devices, it may not be easy to prevent this problem. However, you may consider locating printers on a separate LAN segment to isolate this traffic from other user requests.

There are many causes of failed file-access conditions in a NetWare environment, but these mentioned are the most common.

Bindery Errors

It should be standard procedure for an analyst to examine the NCP layer for bindery errors. Bindery errors should constitute less than one percent of overall traffic, but even that level is of concern. Figure 46.1 shows the Network General Sniffer displaying a bindery error.

FIGURE 46.1.

Sniffer analyzer showing a bindery error packet.

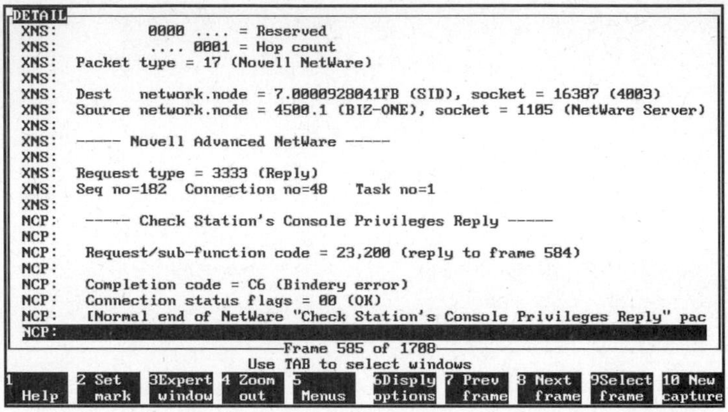

```
┌DETAIL─────────────────────────────────────────────────────────────────────┐
│XNS:          0000 .... = Reserved                                          │
│XNS:          .... 0001 = Hop count                                         │
│XNS: Packet type = 17 (Novell NetWare)                                      │
│XNS:                                                                         │
│XNS: Dest   network.node = 7.0000928041FB (SID), socket = 16387 (4003)      │
│XNS: Source network.node = 4500.1 (BIZ-ONE), socket = 1105 (NetWare Server) │
│XNS:                                                                         │
│XNS: ------ Novell Advanced NetWare ------                                   │
│XNS:                                                                         │
│XNS: Request type = 3333 (Reply)                                            │
│XNS: Seq no=182  Connection no=48    Task no=1                              │
│XNS:                                                                         │
│NCP: ------ Check Station's Console Privileges Reply ------                  │
│NCP:                                                                         │
│NCP: Request/sub-function code = 23,200 (reply to frame 584)                │
│NCP:                                                                         │
│NCP: Completion code = C6 (Bindery error)                                   │
│NCP: Connection status flags = 00 (OK)                                      │
│NCP: [Normal end of NetWare "Check Station's Console Privileges Reply" pac   │
│NCP:                                                                         │
├──────────────────────Frame 585 of 1700──────────────────────────────────  │
│                      Use TAB to select windows                             │
│1        2 Set  3Expert 4 Zoom 5        6Displa 7 Prev 8 Next 9Select 10 New │
│  Help     mark  window   out    Menus   options  frame  frame  frame capture│
└────────────────────────────────────────────────────────────────────────────┘
```

Bindery errors indicate a damaged bindery for a 3.x server. For example, if a specific workstation repeatedly requests the file server for information, and that information cannot be provided because of a bindery problem, it will respond with an NCP reply of a bindery-error failure code. A protocol analyzer can clearly identify this problem. You should then examine the NCP layer for the failure code in the context of what request was being made. An excessive level of bindery errors indicates that the file server's bindery may have become corrupted or damaged.

TIP ▶

Whenever bindery errors are detected, you should run BINDFIX while logged in as Supervisor from the SYSTEM directory.

If the bindery repair causes more problems, run BINDREST to restore the bindery to its original condition.

Bindery corruption is rare. In some instances, the user can track the frequency to determine whether it is a particular type of file or a certain area of the bindery. This can give you an idea of whether the problem is critical, whether it's network-wide, or whether it's related to just one user. It may occur when restoring a backup of security while a bindery file is open. An analyst may be able to see if the bindery failure is related to one particular file or subdirectory, or a particular type of user I.D. or process I.D by using filters. If the bindery issue is related to just one file or process or user I.D, the cause should be addressed to prevent periodic bindery corruption. You should assign another process, user I.D., or file structure name for the process.

Summary

This chapter discussed the most common network errors, many of which are difficult to detect without a protocol analyzer. You should have gained some useful insights on how protocol analysis can help you locate problems that are difficult to locate.

After years of experience with protocol analysis in the NetWare environment with a variety of different protocol analyzers, you will realize that the tool used is not the most important aspect. What is important is your understanding of the mechanics of the protocols, the protocol analysis methodology, and determining which key areas to address first so they can be researched methodically.

Protocol analysis enhances one's knowledge of the mechanics of the protocol suite and of the network. Problem assessment and the successful implementation of cures will sharpen your analysis skills. You are encouraged to utilize protocol analyzers for NetWare troubleshooting and to use this chapter as a guide to begin your search. Start by examining the network statistics, bandwidth ratios, and the breakdowns of errors in the frame header (data link layer). Next, work your way up the packet headers to the IPX, SPX, and NCP layers, examining the layers and fields of each captured frame. Look for normal communication between workstations and file servers, fluent dialogs, and internetwork traffic routing. Look for and examine the hop-count levels in internetworks. Look for NetWare request-being-processed packets and track down the actual problem behind these delay packets. Make changes to the network, and then re-examine the network with the protocol analyzer to see if the modifications have improved the overall network performance on the NetWare network.

Protocol analysis is simple if you understand what to look for. However, sophisticated skills in analysis come from actual experience. As you use a protocol analyzer, your skills will grow as you experience more problem solving. You will eliminate many more problems in the early stages when you are equipped with your protocol analyzer and the quick start this chapter provides.

IX
PART

Windows and NetWare

Installing and Configuring Windows with NetWare

by Micheal Hader and Rick Sant'Angleo

IN THIS CHAPTER

47

Apparently, Novell convinced Microsoft to allow it to help develop the Windows 3.1 network interface for NetWare. As a result, installing and using Windows 3.1 with NetWare causes only a mild headache compared to the throbbing migraine headaches that Windows 3.0 produced for millions of users. This does not mean that a system administrator does not need to take several significant steps to ensure proper operation of Windows with NetWare; it just means it can be accomplished with a little effort.

Unfortunately, Microsoft did not consult Novell in preparing Windows for Workgroups (WFW) v3.1 for market. The result was disastrous for WFW users — Novell and Microsoft alike. For the most part, it is impossible to make WFW 3.1 work properly with NetWare, although Novell developers have worked diligently on patches, fixes, and configuration adjustments. WFW sales have been disappointing, probably to a large extent due to this problem.

This chapter assumes you will not elect to use WFW 3.1 with NetWare, and it therefore discusses installing and configuring Windows 3.1 with NetWare in several parts:

- Preparing for installation and use
- Installation and configuration
- Configuration options that should be changed
- Special procedure for installing Windows with NetWare 3.12 and 4.x
- Using Windows with NetWare

The purpose of this chapter is to clarify what an administrator must do to plan, install, and configure Windows 3.1 in conjunction with a NetWare network. The following chapter goes into great detail about the mechanics of Windows and what you need to know to run Windows with NetWare after it is properly installed and configured.

Preparing for Installation and Use

You need to consider several factors when determining how you should install Windows on your network. System administrators must determine the importance of various factors in making this decision. You should consider user needs for the following:

- Simple application and file system access
- Freedom in making configuration choices
- The best reliability possible for both the network and applications

- The best network performance possible, but not to the detriment of global network performance

These needs should be balanced with the system administrator's needs:

- Simplify management as much as possible
- Control user access
- Manage the file system

In considering these needs, you will see that a system administrator must walk a tightrope in balancing the needs of the group at large, the user's desire for individual freedom, and the administrator's own need to make the system manageable. In assessing the question of where to install Windows, you must realize that your choices affect the balance of these factors.

Windows has four different sets of files associated with installing and running Windows on a network:

- Windows operational files
- Virtual memory swap files
- Windows and Windows application temporary files
- Windows .INI files

It is very important that you understand that these file sets do not necessarily have to reside in the same place. They can reside

- All at the server
- All at the workstation
- Distributed in both places

Your choice of how they are distributed affects the performance of the Windows user and of all other users who must contend for limited network resources when Windows is being used. You also must understand that neither Microsoft nor Novell has made this task an easy one for the system administrator. This chapter explains your basic options for installing and configuring Windows for use in a NetWare environment.

Hardware Requirements

Although Microsoft says Windows will run on an Intel 80286-based PC with 1M of RAM, anyone who has attempted this recognizes that this "minimum" configuration is grossly inadequate. The recommended minimum hardware to receive full benefits from Windows is at least a 386SX-based PC (the faster the better), and no less than 4M of RAM. Ideally, you will want 8M or more of RAM and the fastest PC your budget can afford. If you plan to install Windows on the user's local hard disk, you should have at least 80M of available disk space for Windows and Windows applications. Windows itself chews up 11M, and each major Windows application uses between 8 and 15M of disk space.

Where to Install the Windows Operational Files

You have two basic options for installing Windows operational files: on users' local hard drives or on the file server. Your choice reflects your strategy in managing users. In some organizations, a system administrator is a first line of support, whereas users are responsible for installing and maintaining their own software. In other organizations, a system administrator is responsible for all software installation and configuration, with few exceptions. The extent of system administrative responsibilities needs to be decided by top management.

In smaller organizations, the cost of a full-time system administrator is difficult to justify. However, as users install and configure their own software, many hours are spent that are not accounted for. Therefore, it *seems* more cost effective to have users install their own software.

Larger organizations eventually realize that each employee is assigned a specific job, and software installation and configuration reduces the employee's productivity. When difficulty is encountered in an installation or upgrade, it is obviously not cost-effective for each user to go through the process of first learning the complexities of that particular application. A full-time administrator is therefore appointed to spend the time to research, to access technical support, and to perform the upgrade for one or for all users.

When software is to be shared through installation on the file server, one person must designate where the application is to be installed, assign the appropriate trustee access rights, and edit the login script as necessary. Some of these functions cannot or should not be done by individual users. A server-based installation of Windows requires access as the user Supervisor or security equivalent. Because many decisions need to be made that require supervisory access and that affect other users, it is highly unlikely that the job of installing Windows on a server can be delegated to users.

As you can see, the decision of whether to install Windows locally or centrally reflects a decision either to support users in their own decentralized personal computing worlds, or to consolidate storage and administration into one place, relieving users to do the jobs for which they were hired. The decision has far-reaching ramifications.

Whether Windows will be installed on a server or on local hard drives dictates how to proceed from this point. Either option has advantages and disadvantages associated with it. Consider the following for each option.

Installing the Windows Operation Files on the User's Hard Disk

You can install Windows on each user's local hard disk (if each user has at least 12M of free disk space). Figure 47.1 illustrates how Windows can be installed locally and still find data located on a file server. Installing Windows in this fashion also has its own set of advantages and disadvantages.

FIGURE 47.1.

Windows installed locally.

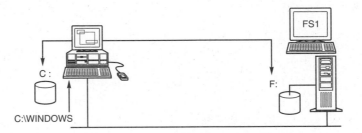

Advantages

Running Windows when not attached to a file server. Users may want to load Windows independently from the network. In some cases, attachment to a network is supplemental to operations that are almost completely decentralized. In this case, loading Windows locally is imperative. In many organizations, software is installed locally so that users can go on working regardless of whether the network is up or not. This philosophy generally gives way as the network matures and as users and management rely more heavily on it.

No usage of file server disk space. This method places all Windows files on the user's PC. This is an advantage only when this method is used for all of the Windows users on this file server. In a network installation, only one master copy of Windows has to reside on the file server, no matter how many users you have.

Reduced network traffic. Probably the most important advantage of this method is that when you load Windows 3.1 from a local disk instead of from a file server, it keeps the traffic associated with loading Windows off the LAN. Because the LAN can be a bottleneck in the network, this may be an important factor in the decision to install Windows locally. In addition to the loading of Windows, Windows uses many different dynamic link libraries (DLLs). Installing Windows locally can reduce the load associated with loading the Windows DLLs.

Improved Windows load time. If the local hardware performs faster than the combination of the file server's hardware and the underlying LAN, loading Windows from a local disk may reduce the amount of time it takes to install Windows. However, only the time needed to load Windows itself is improved, unless all the user applications are installed on local drives. In many cases, the load time from the file server is faster than loading from a local drive.

Windows hardware configuration files match the workstation. SYSTEM.INI is a hardware-specific configuration file. With a local installation, SYSTEM.INI should reflect the settings needed for the workstation.

Disadvantages

No one can work if the network goes down. Although it is true that user productivity must not be interrupted when the network or file server goes down, this philosophy is counter-productive to good networking strategies. Efforts that should be directed at keeping a network up 100 percent of the time is instead directed at multiplication of efforts on many PCs. The same effort and expense can be applied to fault-tolerant operations with better results. See Part VII of this book for information about how to make your network a more trusted environment.

A large amount of disk space is required. Windows 3.1 consumes between 9 and 11 megabytes of each user's disk space. If you are installing on a portable PC, you need disk space for the applications, as well. Each major Windows-based application requires another 8 to 12 megabytes. Multiply this by the number of users, and you will see that vast amounts of disk storage are required for local installations.

Performance improvement is offset by applications on the file server. If your motivation for installing Windows locally is to improve disk I/O performance, you may find that the gain is negligible due to traffic generated by applications that run from the file server. The only way you gain in disk I/O performance is to install every application users need on local drives. Depending upon your server's hardware and NetWare's file caching capabilities, you may not see much gain at all in loading Windows from the local drive.

Administration of user's PC is decentralized. If all Windows files are local, you cannot manage the user environments without having physical access to user workstations, in most cases. In addition, updates to the Windows 3.1 files require you to copy these files to each affected user's workstation. While this is okay for a few users, it is doubtful that you want to support several hundred users this way. This is the most important disadvantage of this method of installing Windows.

Windows Operational Files on the File Server

You can install most Windows files centrally on a NetWare volume. When installing Windows in this manner, the swap file can be located on the server or locally, as shown in Figure 47.2. In either case, centralization of resources is one of the great advantages of networking. However, there are several considerations that may persuade you to install centrally, or many reasons why you may not want to.

FIGURE 47.2.
Windows installed on a server.

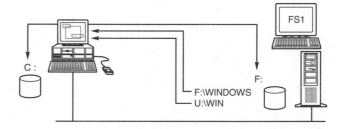

Advantages

Limited or no usage of local disk space. This method places most or all of the Windows files on the file server. User configuration files require 70K or less disk space, which can be installed locally or in user home directories. This option enables use of workstations that have no hard drives. Although hard drives have become quite inexpensive, the cost of many hard drives can be consolidated into more efficient centralized disk storage.

Centralized maintenance of Windows files. Because all Windows operational files reside on the file server, it is easier to install updated versions of these files. This is one of the more compelling reasons for networking in general. Although this is true for Windows files in general, it is especially true for Windows application files.

NetWare security controls usage. Because the bulk of the files needed reside on the file server, NetWare's trustee rights and security privileges control what the user may run or access. Users cannot run Windows unless they have been assigned appropriate NetWare access rights.

Potential improved Windows load time. Loading Windows from a file server may reduce the amount of time it takes to load Windows, if the file server's hardware performs faster than the user's local disk subsystem. However, only the time it takes to load Windows itself is improved, unless all of the user's applications are installed on a local drive. Load time from the file server is often faster than local access, but when many uses are active, performance can be erratic. On a busy network, increased performance occurs at the expense of other users.

Disadvantages

Large amount of file server disk space is required. Windows 3.1 consumes approximately 15 megabytes of the file server's disk space. Then you need disk space for the applications. Each major Windows-based application requires another 8 to 12 megabytes.

Disk I/O overhead for Windows is substantial. Because all files are on the file server, all DLLs, swap files, and temporary files must reside on the file server too. This can greatly increase the I/O demands on the file server.

Shared PCs present configuration problems. If users log in from different workstations, you have to use advanced techniques to load and maintain both user-specific configuration and workstation-specific files.

Network traffic can increase significantly. Because all Windows operational files are coming to the user's PC from the file server, network traffic is greater than it would be if these files were loaded from the user's local hard drive. The increase occurs every time Windows or a Windows application is loaded.

Installation and Configuration

Now that you understand the issues raised by running Windows on NetWare, this section discusses how to install Windows on a local hard drive or on a file server volume for use with NetWare. During Windows SETUP, you will need to

- Select workstation components and NetWare shell versions to be used
- Change the swap file size, type, and location
- Edit some or all of the following files:
  CONFIG.SYS
  AUTOEXEC.BAT
  NET.CFG or SHELL.CFG
  Login Scripts

This section provides a step-by-step overview of the installation steps you should take. More detail about the mechanics of these files and steps is provided later in the chapter. You may also consider changing some of the Windows options, such as disabling Print Manager. After installation is discussed, configuration changes are discussed in this section.

Before Running Windows SETUP for All Installations

Installing Windows to be used with NetWare can be viewed according to the chart shown in Figure 47.3.

FIGURE 47.3.
Overview of Windows installation with NetWare.

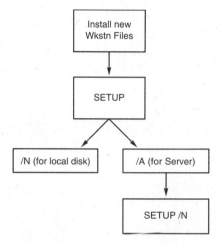

The procedure is as follows:

1. Update your workstation drivers, shells, or requesters to levels shown in Table 47.1. These files arc included in your Windows distribution diskettes. Later revisions of these files can be used.

2. Load your NetWare workstation drivers and shell (or requester).

3. Login, Map, and Capture to default user configuration settings.

Then proceed to Local Drive Installation or Network Drive Installation.

After the installation is complete, you will need to edit various files and install applications. That process will be covered later in this chapter and in the next chapter.

Table 47.1. Workstation files shipped with Windows 3.1.

File	Version #
IPX.OBJ	3.10
NETX.COM	3.26
LSL.COM	1.21
IPXODI.COM	1.20

NOTE ▶

You may elect to upgrade your workstation drivers and shells to the latest versions available. You may use the latest DOS Shell (NETX.EXE v 3.32) or the DOS Requester (VLM.EXE v1.02 + NETX.VLM). The INSTALL utility with the latest Requester, NIC drivers, support files, and Windows updates resides on three disks and is fully backward-compatible with all NetWare versions. See the section in this chapter titled "Installing Windows with NetWare 4.x and 3.12 DOS Requester" for instructions on using this utility to install Windows support.

You may order updated workstation files by calling Novell at 1-800-UP-DATE1 (cost $50). Alternatively, you may download the same files from NetWire. Currently, the files are stored on NOVFILES. Unlike other forums, you can use normal communications software; a menu will prompt you through selecting and updating to the latest files, just like a BBS. To download the DOS Shell and related files, two files need to be downloaded, totaling over 560K. If you want to download the DOS Requester and related files, they are contained in three files totalling over 1.5M. If you have a copy of 3.12 or 4.01, you should use the Requester installation diskettes created from your CD-ROM. Even at 9600 bps, this download can take over an hour.

Novell recommends using ODI/MLID drivers (see Chapter 12, "Installing Client Workstation Software," for instructions) instead of the traditional IPX drivers used with WSGEN. If you are using traditional IPX drivers, you must copy the IPX.OBJ file to your WSGEN disk or directory for inclusion in the IPX.COM file that you generate. Novell warns that IPX.OBJ will not be upgraded any more and may cause problems coping with various future software problems.

Windows SETUP utility has special provisions for installation with a network. The /N and /A switches are discussed in the following sections for installing Windows on a network.

Running SETUP for a Local Drive Installation

When installing Windows on a local hard drive:

1. Insert your Windows disk #1 into your floppy drive, switch to that drive, and type SETUP /N.

2. Select either Express or Custom setup.

3. Put the destination Windows directory on your local hard drive.

If you select Custom setup, you can edit the configuration for virtual memory (the swap file). It will be placed on a local drive, and you can select the size and whether it is permanent or temporary.

Full installation to a local drive creates a pair of directories. During installation, indicate the target directory to which Windows will be installed. The default name for this directory is WINDOWS. Beneath the target directory, the Setup program creates the SYSTEM directory. The Setup program places approximately 125 files that use about 4.5M of disk space. Into the Windows SYSTEM subdirectory, SETUP copies approximately 115 files that use about 5.5M of disk space.

The target directory contains all of the Windows-bundled programs such as Calendar, Notepad, Cardfile, and their related help and .DLL files. It also contains the bitmap wallpaper files, screen saver files, and sound files. It contains the Windows .INI files, the default and DOS .PIF files, the group .GRP files, and the program WIN.COM.

The Windows SYSTEM directory contains Windows core executable files and their .DLL files, True Type font files, fixed screen fonts, hardware drivers, screen grabbers, and NetWare drivers. These files — too numerous to list in this book — will vary based upon setup options selected.

CAUTION ▶

If Windows has been installed without the /N option (network install) and you decide to connect to NetWare at a later time, changes required for proper operation with NetWare will not have been made to several configuration files. These changes are sufficiently substantial to warrant reinstalling Windows after you have loaded the NetWare workstation shell, logged in, mapped drive letters, and captured printers. Alternatively, you can edit the appropriate configuration files.

Running SETUP for a Server Installation

Installing Windows on a file server consists of two steps. First, all files must be installed in a master Windows directory (SETUP /A), and then Windows user installations must be performed (SETUP /N).

Installing Windows Operational Files

To install all Windows files in a single directory on the server for all users to share:

1. Log in as Supervisor.
2. Create a directory on a NetWare volume to which all users will have access.
3. Insert your Windows disk #1 into your floppy drive, switch to that drive, and type SETUP /A.

SETUP prompts you to insert each disk. All files on your Windows diskettes will be expanded and copied to the directory of your choice.

After you finish installing all the Windows files:

■ Edit your login script(s). MAP ROOT a search drive to the directory in which you have installed Windows for each user who will be running Windows. To speed up file searches, the Windows search drive should be one of the first search drives — directly behind the DOS and SYS:PUBLIC search drives.

■ Grant NetWare Trustee Assignments to all users (or groups) who are to use Windows from the server.

> **TIP** ▶
>
> Always use the MAP ROOT command in both your logical and search drive mappings. Windows changes directories at times, which will confuse your drive mappings, especially if the "permanent connections" option is chosen.

[handwritten: users unique configuration but will install]

[handwritten: Easier for the administrator to manage]

Running *SETUP /N* from a Workstation

After installing all the Windows files on the file server, you must install each Windows user by running SETUP with the /N parameter. Running Windows when installed on the file server gives you the best model for making Windows easy to manage and reliable. However, Windows may load and run somewhat slower. This is the method you must use if you use diskless workstations in your network. This model also reduces your overall disk space requirements, because a single master copy of the Windows files is accessed by all users.

To install a network user

1. From the user's workstation, log in with the user's login name.

2. MAP ROOT a search drive to the Windows shared directory.

3. Switch to the user's home directory (a directory unique to the user, where all access rights are assigned).

4. Type SETUP /N.

5. Select Custom setup.

6. Install Windows into the user's home directory or into a subdirectory. This is where the user's unique configuration files will be stored.

7. Verify the hardware configuration options, making certain that the selection for Network is set to Novell NetWare (shell version 3.26 and above).

8. Change Virtual Memory settings as follows:

   Configure the swap file on a local hard drive, *or*

   Configure the swap file in the user's home directory.

CAUTION ▶

If you have a local hard drive, install the swap file on it.

If you do not have a local hard drive, configure the swap file as a *temporary* file and edit the size of the swap file to no more than 4096K (4M). A permanent swap file ties up this much space all the time for each user; a temporary swap file is erased when a user exits Windows. A swap file ties up the allocated amount of disk space for each user, which can cause serious disk storage problems and performance degradation whenever it is stored on a NetWare volume.

9. Install printers and applications as prompted by SETUP.

SETUP/N creates a set of files similar to the one shown in Table 47.2.

Table 47.2. Windows network client file set.

File	Size	Date	Time
WIN.INI	44170	06-04-92	4:18p
MOUSE.INI	28	06-04-92	4:18p
CONTROL.INI	3670	06-04-92	12:34p
WINVER.EXE	3904	03-10-92	3:10a
_DEFAULT.PIF	545	06-04-92	4:20p
DOSPRMPT.PIF	545	06-04-92	4:20p
PROGMAN.INI	309	06-04-92	4:33p
MAIN.GRP	6571	06-04-92	4:33p
ACCESSOR.GRP	11069	06-04-92	4:33p
GAMES.GRP	1488	06-04-92	4:33p
STARTUP.GRP	44	06-04-92	4:33p
WIN.COM	49950	06-04-92	4:44p
SYSTEM.INI	1672	06-04-92	12:35p
NETWARE.INI	389	06-04-92	4:29p

Note that these files are mostly configuration files (.INI), program group files (.GRP), DOS application program information files (.PIF), and two executable files (WIN.COM and WINVER.EXE). The configuration files have to be managed based on the user's needs and the type of PC used. Most .PIF files should be located in a shared directory on a NetWare volume so you can manage the files easily. Some .GRP files can stay in the user's home directory, whereas others may be in shared directories on the file server. The two executable files are not Windows itself, but are programs used to launch Windows.

Editing User Configuration Files

As far as Microsoft is concerned, you have completed your Windows installation. SETUP, however, has not finished the job for you; you must do some of it manually:

1. Edit the user's AUTOEXEC.BAT.

2. Edit the login script(s).

3. Add a search drive to the user's Windows directory.

4. Examine the AUTOEXEC.BAT file closely during execution, then edit the file. Look for any superfluous entries and lines that have errors. You also need to remove the references to Windows directories in the PATH statement.

5. Next, replace the entries that SETUP put into your AUTOEXEC.BAT with search drives. If you have a server-based installation, you need a search drive to the Windows master files directory. Add a search drive pointing at the individual's Windows directory if you want the user to execute Windows from a DOS prompt, regardless of what directory he or she may be in.

6. Edit the NET.CFG for ODI drivers. Create or edit the SHELL.CFG file if traditional IPX drivers are used. Include the following lines (not indented):

```
SHOW DOTS = ON
FILE HANDLES = 80 (or higher if necessary)
ENVIRONMENT PAD=512
SEARCH DIR FIRST=ON
```

Each of these steps is necessary to ensure users proper access to Windows and Windows resources. Some of these steps are not detailed in documents that come with your Windows distribution diskettes.

TIP ▶

To automate the process of setting up Windows clients, you can create unique user settings files. You can then log in as a user and execute SETUP, specifying which settings file to use. SETUP automatically finds the answers to its questions and creates the user configuration files without any keyboard intervention.

See the following chapter for instructions on creating and using SETUP settings files.

Installing the NetWare Popup Utility

NOTE ▶

Windows is shipped with a special NetWare Popup Utility button-bar menu. It is not, however, installed for your use unless you specifically install it using the following procedure.

This utility is very convenient, so you should take the time to install it. It enables the user to strike a hot key to invoke it, and then change drive mappings, printer captures, view or change print jobs in the queues, attach/detach servers, change the network settings, change the Windows-network startup settings, or reassign the hot key for invoking the utility — all from one menu (as shown in Figure 47.4).

If you choose to install the Client Workstation for DOS Requester (shipped with 3.12 and 4.x versions), skip this step. This installation provides a new, improved NetWare User Tools utility.

FIGURE 47.4.

The NetWare Popup utility.

To install the Popup utility button-bar menu (so it will pop up while you are in Windows), follow these steps:

1. As a logged in user, load Windows.

2. Select Control Panel.

3. Select the Network icon. (It will only be there if you have executed the workstation shell.)

4. Reverse all settings in the following sections:

Message Status at Startup

386 Enhanced

Network Warnings

> **NOTE** ►
>
> These changes are made only so that Windows will create the NETWARE.INI file the next time Windows is loaded. The changes should be reversed once the Popup utility is installed and functioning.

5. Exit Control Panel.
6. Edit the NETWARE.INI file (now located in the user's Windows directory), add the following line to the [Options] section:

```
NetWareHotKey=121
```

> **NOTE** ►
>
> You must use upper- and lowercase in the entry, as shown previously.

7. Exit Windows.
8. Load Windows.
9. Press F10 (the pop-up menu should appear).
10. Select the Network Options button and change the selections to

    NWShare Handles ON

    Restore Drives   OFF

    Network warnings OFF

> **NOTE** ►
>
> If your F10 key is assigned to another application that is loaded within Windows, the Popup Utility takes preference over the other application. You may reassign the pop-up hot key by selecting Change Hot Key from the Popup Utility, or assign another number in the NetWareHotKey setting of your NETWARE.INI file. Key assignments are sequentially 112 for F1 through 123 for F12.

Configuration Options that Should Be Changed

Windows was designed with peer-to-peer NetBIOS-based networks or LAN Manager-based networks in mind; however, NetWare works quite differently. The Windows default configuration attempts to log in and map drives if the user is not logged in, but this option does not work for NetWare. When you leave these defaults in place and do not log in prior to running NetWare, you may find drive letters and printers that appear, but also find that you have no access to files or printers. You may attempt to disconnect and reconnect them, but you will only receive error messages.

Changing Options in Control Panel

Microsoft has also assumed that users would always operate either on the network or off, but not sometimes on and other times off. Some users may use Windows locally, without being logged in, and at other times use Windows while they are logged into the network. Unless network warnings are turned off, bothersome error messages keep appearing on the users' screens.

Therefore, a few settings should be changed in Windows Control Panel for proper operation with NetWare. For all users, you will encounter fewer false error messages if you change the following options.

From Windows MAIN Program Group, select Control Panel, and then change the following:

1. Select the Network icon and set the options as follows:

   NWShare Handles ON

   Restore Drives   OFF

   Network warnings OFF

2. Close the Network icon (you may have already changed this if you installed the Popup utility, as discussed previously).

3. Select the Printers icon, and in the lower-left corner, toggle "Use Print Manager" to off. Network print jobs spool to a queue, and therefore do not need to spool to both your local disk (Print Manager) and to a NetWare queue.

4. Close the Printers icon, and close Control Panel.

As discussed previously, users must log in, map, and capture prior to loading Windows, or they will not be able to establish drive mappings or capture printers from within Windows. These functions should be established in either the User Login Script, or using variables in the System Login Script. See Chapter 17, "Login Scripts," for more information.

Updating Windows Desktops

Microsoft did not engineer Windows and Windows applications for the many variations that occur in installing and using Windows and Windows applications on networks, especially where NetWare is concerned. There are many things that, as a system administrator, you need to check or change.

TIP ▶

A very simple way to administer users is to set up all user Windows configu-rations, desktops, and applications in the very same way. You can copy one user's Windows directory to all the others, then edit his or her hardware configurations as necessary.

On very large networks with many different configurations, especially where you may want to keep user desktops uncluttered, this is not feasible. The suggestions offered in this chapter and the next are only suggestions of what you can do to manage your Windows users. You must ultimately find what works best for you. This often requires trial and error until a workable balance of configuration is achieved.

In order to edit configuration files to accommodate applications, see the next chap-ter, which goes into great detail on several aspects of these files (including location, functionality, syntax, and other factors).

Installing Windows with NetWare 4.x and 3.12 DOS Requester

The new DOS Requester INSTALL utility provided with NetWare 4.x and 3.12 versions automatically handles the job of updating Windows files. If you opt to in-stall support for Windows, the utility will ask which directory Windows is installed in, and it will update the Windows files. This utility assumes that Windows is al-ready installed before installing the DOS Requester, drivers, and workstation files.

If you have not installed Windows, you should do so before running the Client Workstation for DOS INSTALL utility. For complete instructions on installing this product, see Chapter 12, "Installing Client Workstation Software." The INSTALL utility must update your Windows files. If Windows is not already installed when you run this utility, it will not enable you to install Windows support. You will need to rerun the utility after you have installed Windows.

If Windows is installed on your local hard drive, follow the instructions in the Client Workstation for DOS INSTALL utility.

Installing Windows Support for a Windows Server Setup

INSTALL assumes that Windows is installed on a local hard drive. No provisions are made in the Client Workstation for DOS INSTALL module for installing Windows support when a shared copy of Windows has been installed on a server, as discussed earlier in this chapter. If you have installed the Windows master and user configuration files on the server, your path of least resistance is to do the following:

1. Copy the Windows user configuration files to a separate directory on the local hard drive.

2. Run the DOS Requester INSTALL utility, indicating that Windows is installed in the local hard-drive directory where the user configuration files are temporarily stored.

3. Copy the updated files in the local hard drive Windows directory back to the user configuration directory on the server.

4. Copy the files installed in the SYSTEM subdirectory to the master (shared) Windows directory on the server. INSTALL will have created a SYSTEM subdirectory under your Windows directory on your hard drive.

5. Edit the NET.CFG (in the directory where the DOS Requester is installed) to include the following lines:

```
SHOW DOTS = ON
ENVIRONMENT PAD=512 (or DOS environment size stated in CONFIG.SYS)
SEARCH DIR FIRST=ON
```

> **NOTE**
>
> In order to copy the files contained in the local Windows SYSTEM directory to the master (shared) Windows directory on the server, you will need to have NetWare Modify and Write access rights in that directory, and you will need to change the master files' attributes to read-write. Once you have copied the new files to that directory, change the attributes back to read-only.

6. To install your new NetWare User Tools (replaces the NetWare Popup utility discussed earlier in this chapter), select the group in which you want the icon to appear; then in Program Manager, select File, New, and Browse to find the XXX file in the Windows directory. Select this file; it will automatically select the NetWare User Tools icon. Name and save these file

properties. You now have access to the User Tools utility by double-clicking that icon. The options available in this utility are shown in Figures 47.5 through 47.9.

FIGURE 47.5.

Drive Connections.

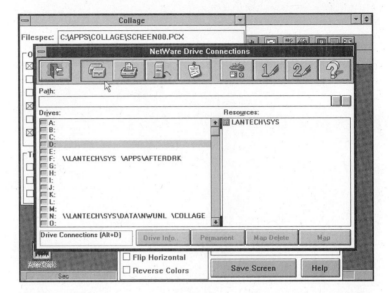

FIGURE 47.6.

Printer Connections.

#### Chapter 47

FIGURE 47.7.

Server Connections.

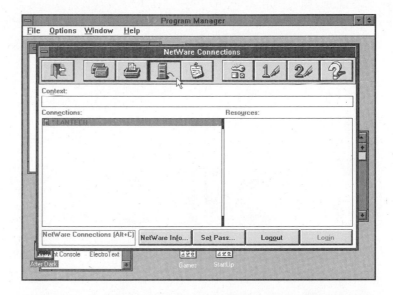

FIGURE 47.8.

Send Messages.

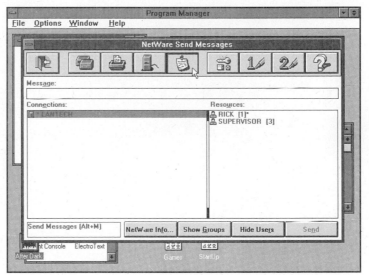

FIGURE 47.9.

Settings.

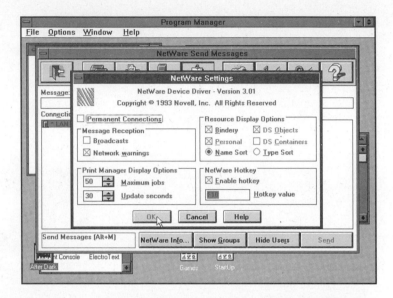

The DOS Requester and all the latest support files are backward compatible. If you have this product, you should install it on all your NetWare workstations. It is stable, has new features, and is a universal client that can be used with all versions of NetWare including Personal NetWare (NetWare Lite), 2.x, 3.x, and 4.x versions (with full functionality). It is well worth the investment and effort.

You should check for the most updated workstation files from Novell (at 800-UP-GRADE1 or the NOVFILES forum on CompuServe). You should upgrade your DOS Requester to version 1.02 or higher. All the basic rules about Windows installation and use apply equally to the DOS Requester (VLM) as they do to the DOS Shell (NETX).

Using the Windows Environment

A few particularities can plague your Windows installation if you do not understand them. For example, a logout from a DOS prompt within Windows will disconnect all network connections. The subsequent login does not reestablish your NetWare session and can result in loss of data.

> **CAUTION** ▷
>
> You must never log out and/or log in while in Windows. If you do, you will lose all network connections, which cannot be reestablished. You may therefore lose all work in process and cause damage to open data files.
>
> To log out, you must exit Windows, log in, then load Windows again.

Most importantly, you have to develop an awareness in Windows as to what settings are *global* and which are *local.* This is important because you will have to set up your DOS batch files and execute DOS Terminate Stay Resident (TSR) applications, your NetWare login scripts, and MAP and CAPTURE commands based upon these rules.

Global settings affect all applications or windows currently active, or any applications to be executed at a later time. Local settings affect only the current application or window and cease to exist when that window or application is closed. Some global settings can be changed while Windows is running; others cannot. Without a good understanding of which settings are global and which are local, you can become quite confused, because DOS acts differently according to these settings.

Settings that are affected by your actions include

■ DOS TSR applications
■ DOS environment settings
■ Drive mappings
■ Printer captures

You should always log in prior to loading Windows, so that all settings up to that point will be globally recognized. This is especially true for your initial drive mappings and printer capture settings, which must be set prior to loading Windows so they will be global.

> **CAUTION** ▷
>
> You must log in, map, and capture before loading Windows. If you don't, drive mappings and captures will not work properly within Windows, nor can they be changed. Restoring network connections upon execution does not work as Microsoft intended with NetWare, and it cannot be used to reestablish these connections.

Global access to the DOS environment is enabled because every window that is opened within Windows creates a DOS or Windows Application Virtual Machine (VM), as shown in Figure 47.10. When you execute a DOS application or double-click the DOS icon, a separate DOS Application VM is created as a real-mode window in a protected memory space. COMMAND.COM is loaded within the VM, and a copy of the global environment space is copied into the local COMMAND.COM session. Changes made in that VM address space are not copied back to the global DOS environment space and therefore apply only locally, to the current application.

FIGURE 47.10.

Windows Virtual Machines.

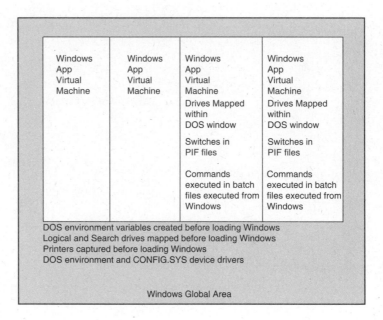

Anything that occurs prior to loading Windows globally affects Windows and any applications launched from within Windows, while *most* DOS commands and DOS applications affect only the current VM, and therefore the DOS session. This statement works as a good rule of thumb; however, some applications are specifically written to fit into Windows Global Area and therefore affect all applications.

DOS TSR Applications

Based on an understanding of VMs, it is easy to understand that when a TSR is loaded prior to loading Windows, it will be available in all Windows VMs and therefore to all DOS sessions and applications. For example, if you load MS-DOS DOSKEY application, you will find that it is loaded in each DOS window you open, and that it ties up some RAM in each DOS session launched from Windows. Another good example is loading the NetWare workstation shells. If you were to execute NETX files prior to loading Windows, connection to a NetWare server (or servers) is global and available to all Windows applications. On the other hand, if you did not execute NETX prior to loading Windows, and did so from a DOS prompt, you would find that your connection to the NetWare server would only be local and would not be available to other windows. Your connection would be terminated when you exited the DOS window. This likewise holds true for all DOS internal commands, external commands, and DOS applications.

TIP ▶

Each application that is loaded as a TSR, before loading Windows, reduces the amount of memory available within each DOS window. Therefore, you should not load TSRs that are not required globally. Instead, you can execute a DOS application from a batch file, where the TSRs can be loaded locally, not affecting other DOS applications. Keep in mind, however, that the TSR you have loaded will no longer be available if you exit the DOS window in which it was loaded.

DOS Environment Settings and Variables

If you execute a DOS internal or external command from within Windows or use a SET command from a DOS prompt, the change is accessible only to the current DOS session. Your changes are not available to any other programs you already have running, nor will they be available to any programs you run except DOS applications active in the same window (DOS session). This is true for DOS applications that change or create DOS environment variables. Programmers must specifically use Windows APIs to write to the Windows Global Area in order to affect applications globally. This is also true for most DOS commands, such as the DOS PATH command. For example, if you open the DOS prompt icon, and execute a DOS path statement, the DOS path is only altered in that DOS window you have opened.

DOS variables can be used to edit DOS environment settings. DOS variables are created and placed into the DOS environment space using the DOS internal command SET. The DOS environment space is a small amount of DOS conventional memory that is reserved for settings, such as the DOS path, COMSPEC (where COMMAND.COM is located), and the DOS prompt configuration. Variables can be set into the environment space, so that when an application looks for this variable another value can be substituted. For example, Windows SETUP places a command into your AUTOEXEC.BAT file, setting a variable TEMP equal to a directory name. When Windows or a Windows application writes working files, it places them into TEMP, which is a variable referring to the directory name mentioned in your AUOTEXEC.BAT. You can see your current environment space settings by typing SET at the DOS prompt.

> **TIP** ►
>
> Practically nothing can be accomplished with DOS environment variables that cannot be controlled in a login script.
>
> Use your NetWare login script variables and conditional statements (IF...THEN statements) to accomplish the same results. Unless you have pretty good skills with DOS variables, this strategy proves to be a more stable choice and simpler to learn.

Using DOS Environment Variables

DOS environment variables you create before you launch Windows are picked up when the Windows Global Area is initialized and are therefore global, as illustrated earlier in Figure 47.5. Global variables, for the most part, remain unchanged regardless of what happens within a DOS session. However, if you set a string for an environment variable that already exists, then the new setting is substituted for the existing local DOS environment variable. You can accomplish this from a batch file; the new variable will only apply to the current DOS setting. This variable can be different for various applications, or different for various workstations on the network. For example, the following batch file

```
COPY F:\PUBLIC\%MON%\*.* U:\
WIN
```

copies all files from the directory that bears the same name as the string to be substituted for variable MON. If the workstation's AUTOEXEC.BAT includes the line

```
SET MON=EGA
```

the files from F:\PUBLIC\EGA will be copied to U:\.

Variable names can be used in your batch files, .PIF files, and Program Properties in the same manner you used them prior to Windows, by referring to them as %variable%. If you execute any DOS commands from within Windows, or if your DOS application changes DOS parameters during execution, these changes apply only to that DOS session; they will not apply globally. Only parameters that are set prior to loading Windows apply globally, unless a utility was designed to specifically provide global changes.

TIP ▶

If you use a DOS variable to reference a global parameter, you can edit the value for the local parameter by changing the DOS variable in the environment space. The value can be changed with a SET command from a DOS prompt, or within a batch file from within a DOS Window. The DOS variable has to have been set into the environment prior to loading Windows.

CAUTION ▶

If you or your applications use the global DOS environment space to pass variables and global parameters, you may hit the DOS default limitation of 160 bytes. If this happens, you may receive the DOS error "Out of environment space," and/or your changes simply are ignored.

To resolve this problem, place the command

```
SHELL=C:\COMMAND.COM C:\ /P /E:512
```

into your CONFIG.SYS. The /P parameter makes the shell permanent; the /E: parameter adjusts the amount of RAM allocated to the DOS environment space.

Many network software applications use the DOS environment space to pass global parameters, and this is a common problem. This command should probably be standard in all CONFIG.SYS files.

Drive Mappings

> **NOTE** ▶
>
> Drive mappings created *before* loading Windows are global.
>
> When using the older set of Windows update files supplied with the DOS Shell (NETX — Novell file WINUP7.EXE or earlier) NetWare drive mappings created while in Windows are *global* if NWShare Handles are ON in the Control Panel's Network icon (same as in the Popup utility, Network Options). NetWare drive mappings created while in Windows are local if NWShare Handles are OFF.
>
> When using the newer set of Windows update files supplied with the Workstation Client for DOS Requester, all drive mappings made in the User Tools utility are global, and any mappings made within a DOS window are local.

Any changes made to drive mappings, even though they may be made within a DOS session in Windows, are global when you set NWShare Handles to ON. Changes made to drive mappings made within a DOS session in Windows are local when you set NWShare Handles to OFF.

Printer Port Capture Commands

> **NOTE** ▶
>
> All capture commands executed within Windows are global.

Use the NetWare Capture utility to redirect output from a local LPT port to a NetWare queue. You also can perform a capture using Windows Control Panel, Printers option, Print Manager, the NetWare Popup utility, or the User Tools utility. You cannot, however, send output from two running programs to different queues using one LPT port. In order to spool output to two different printers, you need to direct print output from your applications to two different LPT ports, which can be captured to two different queues at the same time.

For example, you may not have captured print output for LPT1 to any network printer, so an application printing to LPT1 will go to a local printer physically attached to your workstation's LPT1 port. You also can capture LPT2 to print to a

NetWare queue, and therefore to a network printer. When you print to LPT1, the print job prints to your local printer. When you print to LPT2, your print job spools to a queue, then to the network printer. This works the same way whether you are running Windows or not. NetWare's Capture utility simply intercepts all LPT print output if a capture is active—even output from Windows.

You do not have to have a physical LPT1, LPT2, or LPT3 port to use the capture command to redirect print output. In this manner, you can have access to up to five printers at any given time; however, only three printers can be captured to NetWare queues at any given time. Serial ports cannot be redirected, but you can use them for local printers.

> **NOTE** ▶
>
> The VLM DOS Requester enables you to capture nine LPTs instead of only three.

Summary

This chapter has reviewed in detail many of the essential issues that concern installing and using a copy of Windows on your server. The chapter started with general issues concerned with the question of where to install Windows and how to manage Windows with NetWare and multiple users. It then covered details of the installation procedures that were omitted in the Windows manuals. The chapter then examined the most common and important issues administrators encounter with Windows.

Installing Windows on a NetWare network is no simple task, but almost all problems can be resolved with a bit of effort and configuration. It requires careful planning and lots of attention to details.

Running Windows on a Network

48

by Micheal Hader

Besides installing Windows and configuring it appropriately for use with NetWare, you need to know about several other aspects of Windows. This chapter discusses the most significant aspects of Windows that an administrator needs to be concerned with, including

- Windows mechanics
- Using the Windows environment with NetWare

There are many things to consider when running Windows in a NetWare environment. The following section goes into great detail on administering and using Windows when running NetWare.

When administering a Windows environment, it is essential to know the mechanics of how Windows works, what files it uses, and how to make adjustments. This section details the use of Windows .INI files. Although Windows applications are designed for simple installation, it was never anticipated that the application would be installed once and accessed by many users. When Windows applications are installed, several changes may need to be made to Windows .INI files before they can be used on a network.

The administrator who installs Windows applications in a multiuser environment needs to do the following:

1. Run Windows SETUP to find and add applications
2. Reinstall the application from the floppy for each user
3. Learn to edit the appropriate configuration files

If this isn't done, many applications won't work properly. Even if you use the SETUP utility, it may not make all the changes that should be made. If you intend to install applications on the server's volume, you must learn to edit each user's configuration files for each application, or suffer reduced productivity and constant difficulties. For miscellaneous reasons, you may need to manually edit the user configuration files.

Windows .INI File Locations

When you launch Windows, it starts up like most other software in terms of how it locates its files. First, it looks for files in the current default directory. If it does not find a file in the current default directory, Windows uses your path to locate other files. Specifically, Windows first searches the directory where you installed Windows, and then it looks at your path. The program that performs these initial searches is WIN.COM. Windows expects to find all .INI files in the same directory.

Furthermore, Windows must find WIN.COM, PROGMAN.INI, and SYSTEM.INI in the same directory.

If you inspect all of the standard Windows .INI files, you can sort them by their function:

- ■ Hardware Information
  SYSTEM.INI
  MOUSE.INI
- ■ User Preferences
  PROGMAN.INI
  WIN.INI
  CONTROL.INI
- ■ Application Information
  WIN.INI

Alternatively, some applications create separate, application-specific .INI files.

Even though WIN.INI contains application-oriented information and a couple of hardware-specific settings, it is treated as a user preferences file for now. Other aspects of WIN.INI are discussed later in the chapter.

What Happens If Users Log In from Different Workstations

When developing Windows, Microsoft assumed the user would always log in from the same workstation—an assumption that is true only some of the time. If users log in from various PCs that do not have exactly the same hardware options and configuration, they will experience a wide variety of problems.

> **TIP** ▶
>
> You can accommodate users who move around to various workstations if you use a Windows startup batch file that copies workstation-specific files to the user's Windows startup directory before loading Windows.

Currently, the only way to manage Windows under these circumstances (without the aid of third-party software) is to develop a scheme to get the correct files to the user. Because you allow users to move around, you must store user-specific files in

*[handwritten: 1) User specific files should be stored in network home directories.
2) Workstation-specific files should be copied to users home directory.]*

their network home directories, and then copy workstation-specific files to the user's home directory prior to loading Windows. Workstation-specific files may be located either on the PC's local hard drive or in a directory on the file server designated for that workstation (or for all workstations configured in a similar manner).

Your users need the set of workstation-specific files, SYSTEM.INI and MOUSE.INI, that match the workstation they are using. These files are workstation-specific, not user-specific. However, when moving to a different workstation, the user still needs to retain the same user information files—WIN.INI, CONTROL.INI, and PROGMAN.INI. Table 48.1 shows which files are workstation-specific and which files are user-specific.

[handwritten: user specific]

Table 48.1. Windows configuration files.

[handwritten: Workstation specific]

*[handwritten: * These files should be in the users home directory or on the hard drive. You need drives mapped to both.]*

Workstation-specific	User-specific
SYSTEM.INI	WIN.INI
MOUSE.INI	CONTROL.INI
WIN.COM	PROGMAN.INI
	*.GRP

CAUTION ►

Applications or data stored on a user's local drive are not accessible from another workstation.

The WIN.INI file contains configuration information for ports, so the user also should check target printer and serial port configurations within Windows when using different workstations.

If you have the same types of workstations everywhere, you can use the same SYSTEM.INI, MOUSE.INI, and WIN.COM for everyone. If users never move to different workstations, these files never need to change. Depending on how you installed Windows, these files should be on the user's local hard drive or in the user's home directory on the file server. As long as your user's path contains this directory and a path to the Windows master directory, Windows can be loaded from any directory without any .INI file problems.

Figure 48.1 displays how workstation-specific files can be copied from a *local drive*, when Windows master files are stored in a shared directory on the server and the user configuration files are stored in the user's home directory (or a subdirectory of the home directory). Notice that the *workstation-specific* files must be copied to the Windows startup directory before loading.

FIGURE 48.1.

Copying workstation-specific files from a local drive with Windows master and user files installed on a server.

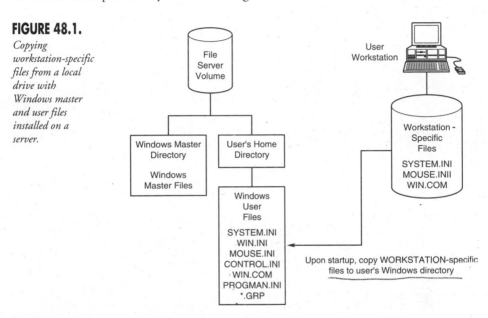

Figure 48.2 shows how workstation-specific files can be copied from another directory on the server's volume when Windows master files are stored in a shared directory on the server, and the user configuration files are stored in the user's home directory (or a subdirectory of the home directory). The workstation-specific files must be copied to the Windows startup directory before loading.

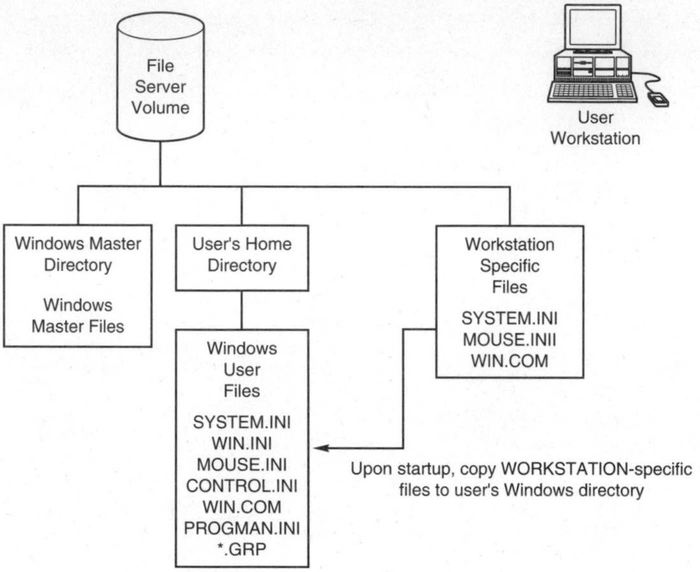

FIGURE 48.2.

Copying workstation-specific files from a NetWare directory with Windows master and user files installed on a server.

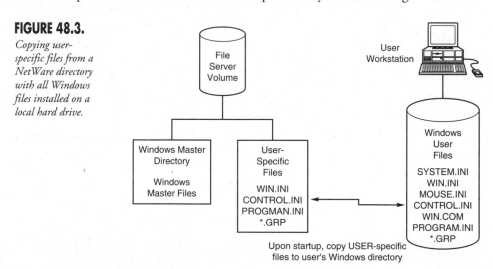

Figure 48.3 displays how the workstation-specific files can be copied from a shared directory when Windows is installed entirely on a local drive. The user-specific files must be copied to the local Windows startup directory before loading.

FIGURE 48.3.

Copying user-specific files from a NetWare directory with all Windows files installed on a local hard drive.

NOTE ▶

It does not matter if the user has a full copy of Windows on a local drive or just the user configuration files for a network installation. In a server-based installation, the user should have a search drive to the Windows directory on the file server.

If the user is allowed to make changes to the Windows Control Panel or other configurations, your Windows startup batch file should copy the changed files back to the location from which Windows is launched.

Because these files can come from the workstation itself or from a network directory, you may want to establish a DOS environment variable to identify the workstation type. For example, you may establish the DOS environment variable PC_TYPE, and establish it as PC_TYPE=VGAMSM3 for a 386-based PC with a VGA adapter and a Microsoft mouse. Then create a directory containing a WIN.COM, SYSTEM.INI, and MOUSE.INI for this workstation type, and for other workstation types. You then can use the variable PC_TYPE in a batch file, which will locate the appropriate workstation type variable that you set in your DOS environment to be equivalent to a filename. You also should use a DOS variable to store the user's login name. For example, the DOS environment variable PC_TYPE would be exchanged for the value VGAMSM3 and would reference one of the three following files:

```
VGAMSM3.SYS - SYSTEM.INI File
VGAMSM3.MSE - MOUSE.INI File
VGAMSM3.COM - WIN.COM File
```

The batch file could have a very simple copy command substituting the variable name for the filename in the source. The following example shows the lines to be placed in a batch file for a server-based installation, where the user launches Windows from the user home directory (named the same as the login name). In this case, the workstation-specific files are located in the SYS:CONFIG directory.

```
NCOPY SYS:\CONFIG\%PC_TYPE%.SYS SYS:\USERS\%LOGIN_NAME\SYSTEM.INI
NCOPY SYS:\CONFIG\%PC_TYPE%.MSE SYS:\USERS\%LOGIN_NAME\MOUSE.INI
NCOPY SYS:\CONFIG\%PC_TYPE%.COM SYS:\USERS\%LOGIN_NAME\WIN.COM
```

> **TIP** ▶
>
> You may find that using NetWare variables and login script conditional
> statements is simple and can be maintained easily, without extensive learning
> of DOS programming.

An alternative is to use NetWare login script conditional statements. A conditional
statement can branch based upon a NetWare variable configured when the workstation shell is loaded. The process has two steps. A variable such as LONG MACHINE TYPE
is set in the NET.CFG file (or the SHELL.CFG if using traditional IPX drivers).
The NetWare solution is similar to the DOS solution discussed previously, but perhaps would be a little simpler. The NetWare variable is set as follows for a VGA system with an MS mouse:

- Create or edit the NET.CFG or SHELL.CFG file, located in the same
  directory as NETX.COM (or NETX.EXE), with the following line:

  ```
  LONG MACHINE TYPE = VGAMSM
  ```

- Create separate directories for the workstation-specific files for each type of
  workstation. In this example, the directory for the VGA MS mouse system is
  SYS:PUBLIC/WIN/VGAMSM. The following line would therefore be
  placed in the login script to copy the appropriate files to the user's home
  directory:

  ```
  #NCOPY SYS:PUBLIC/WIN/%MACHINE/*.* SYS:USERS/%LOGIN_NAME
  ```

- EXIT the login script to a batch file to start Windows. You should not
  execute Windows directly from the login script, because this will needlessly
  tie up about 75K of memory. The following command can be used to call
  the WINDOWS.BAT file:

```
EXIT "WINDOWS"
```

You can see that neither option is an optimal way to manage your Windows installation. It certainly does not deliver on the promise of being easy to install and use.
These gyrations illustrate a basic problem with Windows and networks: Windows
was not designed well for networked environments. You may want to enlist the aid
of Saber LAN Workstation, by Saber Software, or NetTools/Windows Workstation
by Automated Design Systems, to give you a more coherent way of managing .INI
files and multiuser aspects of Windows in a simpler, more eloquent
manner.

> **NOTE** ▶
>
> Microsoft offers an optional $30.00 utility called WinLogin, which was supposed to be the answer to this problem. It provides little relief, however, and most feel that the product is a waste of time, effort, and money.
>
> Microsoft is developing a product called Hermes, which is supposed to resolve many network problems. Microsoft's answers for network problems often have been disappointing, and expectations should not be high for this product either.

Using Automated Settings Parameter Files (SETUP.SHH)

If you have many users to set up, the procedure of running SETUP from each work-station and answering questions interactively can be quite labor-intensive. Again, Microsoft seems to have assumed that users would each install their own copies of Windows. When a system administrator is responsible for installing Windows on dozens, perhaps hundreds of workstations, this procedure is not acceptable. An administrator can use a partial solution to reduce the work involved in adding Windows users when a master copy of Windows is installed and shared from a NetWare volume.

> **TIP** ▶
>
> You can automate network user setups by creating and using automated settings parameter files. When you run SETUP and specify which settings file to use, SETUP proceeds without pausing to ask questions. Instead, the answers are automatically drawn from the setting file that you make.
>
> Using this tool, you can easily set up dozens of users.

You can invoke a setting file by using the following syntax:

```
SETUP /h:filename [/n]
```

The filename refers to a parameter file, created by you, that contains the setup information needed for this installation. You can create several settings files for different circumstances. Your Windows disk #1 contains an example of this type of file in SETUP.SHH.

The settings file used by SETUP /h is an ASCII file that contains the sections listed in Table 48.2.

Table 48.2. The SETUP.SHH file parameters and explanations.

Section Name	Usage
[sysinfo]	Determines whether the configuration screen will be displayed during setup
[configuration]	Specifies the specific hardware devices installed in the PC
[windir]	Indicates the target directory in which to install Windows
[userinfo]	Registers the user and company information
[dontinstall]	Indicates specific Windows components that will not be installed
[options]	Specifies various setup options to run
[printers]	Determines which printer drivers will be installed
[endinstall]	Selects options for updating the user's CONFIG.SYS and AUTOEXEC.BAT and what will happen at the end of the setup

When SETUP is run with the /h option, it uses the SETUP.INF, CONTROL.INF, and SYSTEM.INI files that are in your Windows master directory.

> **NOTE** ▶
>
> The settings parameter file usually has an extension of .SHH. For more information about the settings for this file, refer to the utilities disk that accompanies this book.

The advantage of using automated settings files is that you can make installing Windows an automated, hands-off process. You can make a few automated settings files—one for each unique workstation hardware configuration. This option also provides consistency in user setups. You may find it necessary to edit a few options in the

Windows Control Panel or from the NetWare Popup utility to adjust each user's configuration for user preferences.

Restricting User Capability to Run SETUP

As the network administrator, you are normally responsible for keeping everything running. You may or may not want to allow users to run the Windows SETUP utility. The most common reason that a user might need to run this program is to edit hardware configurations. Users may physically change video adapters, or add or change printers to which they are attached.

> **TIP** ▶
>
> If your users do not need to rerun SETUP, you can remove the Windows SETUP icon in the Main group.

Users can run SETUP from the File Menu or from File Manager if the program resides in a directory to which the user has access. You could rename SETUP.EXE (located in the master Windows directory) to prevent users from running it in this manner. The only sure way to prevent the user from running SETUP is to remove SETUP.EXE from the Windows master directory.

Alternatively, you can restrict usage of SETUP where Windows is entirely installed on the server. You can change a statement in the SETUP.INF file. The [data] section has the statement:

```
NetSetup = FALSE
```

If you change this setting to TRUE, the user can run only a network setup. This limits the SETUP utility to updating the user's .INI files to reflect the driver changes needed. SETUP will recreate the user's group files, but configuration changes options should not be changed or lost. It also prevents the user from making a full workstation installation to a local disk.

Windows .INI File Configuration

Management aspects of Windows .INI files were discussed earlier in this chapter. The following sections discuss the standard Windows .INI files, including the following:

WIN.INI
SYSTEM.INI
MOUSE.INI
PROGMAN.INI
CONTROL.INI

SETUP does not edit all configuration options you might want to set. Instead, some options are normally edited from within Windows after installation. However, you can edit the defaults for some of the options in the previously listed files before adding users so that when you run SETUP, your defaults will apply. You may want to consider editing several options in the .INI files.

SYSTEM.INI

As the primary hardware configuration file for Windows, SYSTEM.INI is a critical Windows .INI file. It also controls most of the multitasking options for using Windows. Each workstation may require a unique configuration in its SYSTEM.INI file. Many of the settings in this file are not configurable; you must modify other files to change the behavior of Windows on an as-needed basis. You should carefully consider changes to this file.

Some settings in this file need to be considered for potential change. Most of these affect the [386Enh] section, because it controls multitasking when running in 386 Enhanced Mode.

> **NOTE** ►
>
> You can place commands in Windows .INI files in any order within their appropriate sections.

[386Enh] Section

The first settings change that you should consider controls how Windows uses the upper-memory area (UMA) when running DOS applications. UMA includes the memory addresses between A000 through FFFF, which are reserved for system use. Windows automatically scans the UMA for a place to put expanded memory page frames and translation buffers. Translation buffers enable Windows to translate DOS and network application interface (API) calls from protected mode (Windows) to real mode (DOS). However, if your third-party memory manager has already allocated the page frame, Windows uses the page frame that was configured in your CONFIG.SYS.

If you use only the Windows memory manager and have only HIMEM.SYS in your CONFIG.SYS, you will have to configure the UMA for the page frame location; otherwise, DOS applications that require expanded memory will not be able to find any expanded memory.

In addition, Windows scans UMA for unused memory areas that it can allocate to DOS applications that run under Windows. The problem is that Windows does not always accurately detect other device drivers and ROMs that use UMA address space. Therefore, you must tell Windows which areas to exclude by editing the following lines in this section:

`EMMExclude=`*`Starting Hexparagraph-Hexparagraph range`*

Default: The command is not included in SYSTEM.INI and there are no default settings. Example: `EMMExclude=A000-FFFF`

This setting excludes a memory range of A000 through EFFF from Windows use. The paragraph and range starting and ending addresses must be specified as even multiples of 16K. Multiple lines can be used to exclude more than one range. If you think Windows is not picking these addresses up properly, use multiple lines to avoid conflicts with ROM and RAM addresses used by other peripherals.

> **TIP** ▶
>
> You can exclude A000-FFFF on all workstations so that changes made in the UMA by the user will not affect Windows.

Several types of devices, listed in Table 48.3, have known areas that you must exclude.

Table 48.3. Upper-memory area exclusions.

Product	Memory range
AST Premium 386/25 and 386/33	E000-EFFF
Dell 386SX	C000-C7FF
	E000-FFFF

continues

Table 48.3. continued

Product	Memory range
Dell Laptops	C000-C7FF
	E000-FFFF
Epson	E000-EFFF
IBM PS/2 Laptop Model 40	E000-EFFF
NCR—All 80386 and 80486 Machines	C600-C7FF
	E000-EFFF
Toshiba 5200	C000-C7FF
Zenith—All 80386-based PCs	E000-EFFF
Almost all ARCnet Cards	D000-E000
Eagle/Novell Ethernet Remote Boot ROM	C000-DE00
Almost all VGA Adapters	C000-C7FF
Almost all SVGA Adapters	C400-C7FF
All systems using Plus Development Impulse drives	C000-DFFF

To include these ranges, add or edit the following line:

```
EMMInclude=Starting Hexparagraph-Hexparagraph range
```

Default: The command is not included in SYSTEM.INI, and there are no default settings.

This setting specifies a range of memory that limits where Windows scans when looking for unused memory in the UMA area. More than one range can be specified with multiple lines. The paragraph and range must be an even multiple of 16K.

```
EMMPageFrame=Hexparagraph
```

Default: This command is not included in SYSTEM.INI. This enables Windows to scan the UMA for a suitable location on its own. Windows uses the page frame location established by a third-party Windows-compatible memory manager.

This setting specifies where Windows will put the 64K page frame used for EMS memory if no third-party memory manager already established the location. You must use this setting if the only memory manager you have in your CONFIG.SYS is HIMEM.SYS. Otherwise, DOS applications will not receive any expanded memory.

`EMMSize=`*kilobytes*

Default: This command is not included in SYSTEM.INI. Therefore, Windows will use the maximum amount of expanded memory possible.

This limits the total amount of expanded memory that can be made available to any DOS application using expanded memory. Some applications grab all available RAM, leaving none for other applications. When this occurs, you cannot create another virtual machine, which means that other applications cannot be launched within Windows. If you have an application that behaves this way, set EMMSize to zero. This will deny use of expanded memory to that application.

`SysVMEMSLimit=`*number or kilobytes*

Default: 2048

This command establishes the maximum amount of expanded memory Windows can provide to all running DOS applications. A value of zero prohibits Windows from providing any expanded memory. A value of -1 enables Windows to create as much expanded memory as it needs until it runs out of memory. Use this setting if you have DOS applications that use extended memory. However, Windows does not have any to give because it has converted all extended memory to expanded memory for other DOS applications.

> **NOTE** ▶
>
> Few current applications need to access expanded memory, so you may not have applications that require expanded memory at all.
>
> If this is the case, use the NOEMS switch with your EMM386 driver in your CONFIG.SYS. This will enable use of the UMA but will not configure any expanded memory, nor will it tie up a 64K page frame in the UMA.
>
> If you use the NOEMS option, you will not need to edit .INI parameters referencing EMS memory.

The next set of commands you should consider deals with serial ports. Windows supports up to four serial ports, COM1-COM4. Unfortunately, whenever you go beyond COM2, the Windows defaults don't work. The defaults listed in Table 48.4 illustrate the problem.

Table 48.4. COM port defaults.

Port	I/O Port	IRQ
COM1	03F8	4
COM2	02F8	3
COM3	03E8	4
COM4	02E8	3

In Industry Standard Architecture workstations (ISA), interrupt requests (IRQs) must be unique or the workstation will crash when both devices are active at the same time. Therefore, you usually have to avoid conflicts between serial or parallel ports, NICs, and memory manager configurations of the UMA. If you reconfigure your COM ports on the PC, you must reconfigure SYSTEM.INI in Windows using the following commands:

```
COM1Base=address
COM2Base=address
COM3Base=address
COM4Base=address
```

See Table 48.4 for the defaults in the preceding code lines.

This setting controls the I/O port used for serial ports. It can be changed with the Ports option of the Control Panel.

```
COM1Irq=number
COM2Irq=number
COM3Irq=number
COM4Irq=number
```

See Table 48.4 for the defaults in the preceding code lines.

This setting controls the interrupt channel used for serial ports. It can be changed with the Advanced option of the Ports selection of the Control Panel.

The next section to consider is what devices are needed for running Windows with NetWare. Novell wrote device drivers for interfacing NetWare with Windows. If you had previously loaded the workstation's network shell software, these devices were written into SYSTEM.INI when you ran Setup.

The following is the normal line you should find in the [386Enh] section of SYSTEM.INI:

```
network=*vnetbios,vnetware.386,vipx.386
```

The first driver listed, *vnetbios, is an internal driver to Windows. There is no external file for this driver. The other drivers, vnetware.386 and vipx.386, are external files. These files should be in the user's Windows SYSTEM directory or in the master Windows directory on the file server.

NOTE ▶

Installing the DOS Requester (VLMs) will automatically add updated VNETWARE.386 and VIPX.386 files to your workstation's Windows SYSTEM directory, or it will create these files if they don't exist. If all Windows users convert to VLMs, you can copy these to the Windows directory on the file server. If not, you need to make sure that these files are found in your path before the older versions for those users who are VLM-based, and that these files are not found for those using NETX.

If your PC uses temporary swap files, the next two commands control the swap file. The temporary swap file WIN386.SWP can be on the file server or on a local hard disk.

TIP ▶

For the best performance, it is normally better to put the swap file on the local hard disk. Putting your swap file on the server will substantially increase traffic on the network and workload for the file server, and tie up excessive amounts of disk space on the server.

In addition, file servers running NetWare 2.x allocate the disk space for the swap file right away, whether or not the space is ever needed. Fortunately, NetWare 3.x does not allocate the swap file space until it is actually written.

TIP ▶

Contrary to the Windows 3.1 Setup program and the Windows 386 Enhanced Control Panel option, you can create the temporary swap file on a compressed volume.

A permanent swap file can use 32-bit disk access with some disk controllers to provide better performance. However, a permanent swap file cannot be placed on a compressed drive.

Microsoft probably discourages the use of a compressed drive so that Windows does not have to suffer the performance loss that happens when compressing and decompressing data. Because you cannot use a disk caching utility with disk compression, this further slows performance. Some of Microsoft's technical support people seem to believe that installing your swap file on a compressed volume causes strange problems, but this isn't true. With the voracious disk appetite of Windows applications, a disk compression utility such as MS-DOS 6.0's DoubleSpace or Stac Electronics' Stacker is sometimes the simplest and most cost-effective way to gain the disk space you need. This is particularly true of laptops and notebook computers.

You can specify a compressed drive by manually editing the SYSTEM.INI file:

```
MaxPagingFileSize=kilobytes
```

Default: There is no default value.

CAUTION

If Windows does not find a permanent swap file, it automatically uses a temporary swap file. If this command is missing from the user's SYSTEM.INI file, Windows uses 50 percent of the user's free disk space.

CAUTION

If the temporary swap file is placed on the file server, you might have conflicts with NetWare's User Volume and Disk Space Limitations.

Windows does not read the NetWare binderies to determine how much disk space the user has remaining. It only looks at total free disk space. Therefore, it is possible for Windows to "allocate" more space to the swap file than NetWare will enable Windows to write, which causes Windows to fail when loaded. NetWare controls all data written to the file server, regardless of how much disk space Windows estimates as available.

CAUTION ▶

If you use NetWare's user disk space limitations and place your temporary swap files on the file server's disk, you must edit the defaults SETUP offers and allocate sufficient space for each concurrent user's temporary swap file.

You also should use MaxPagingFileSize to limit the swap file size.

You still may run into problems, even after having tried to allocate enough disk space to the user. This happens because the size of the user's temporary swap file is established by SYSTEM.INI and doesn't change dynamically as the user stores more real files on the file server. Eventually, you will have a problem with the size of the swap file and the user's disk space limitations.

```
MinUserDiskSpace=kilobytes
Default=500
PagingFile=path\filename
Default=The current drive and directory when the user started Windows.
```

This command specifies the name and path for the temporary swap file (if no permanent swap file exists) and overrides the PagingDrive command. You should use this setting whenever the temporary swap file resides on the file server.

The next two commands affect how Windows handles multitasking. Use these commands to fine-tune how you want Windows to perform.

```
MinTimeSlice=milliseconds
Default=20
```

MinTimeSlice determines how much time Windows must spend on an active task before it is permitted to switch to another task or virtual machine. Decreasing this value makes the foreground task run smoother at an overall cost of less performance. This happens because Windows spends more time switching tasks and less time actually processing. On workstations with clock speeds over 25 MHz, you may find that decreasing this value is beneficial.

```
WinTimeSlice=foregound priority, background priority
Default=100,50
```

This value sets the relative priority of all Windows running applications. These values are compared to the values of any running DOS program PIF settings, in order to determine how much time is spent on Windows programs running in foreground or background.

```
WindowUpdateTime=milliseconds
Default=50
```

This command controls the length of time Windows is permitted when performing a screen refresh. Increasing this value gives your foreground DOS application more time for screen writes. If you have a fast workstation or a fast video adapter, you may find it beneficial to increase this value to between 200 to 400.

The next command is important for every SYSTEM.INI file. It addresses how Windows handles devices in the multitasking, virtual machine environment.

```
Local=device
Default=CON
```

Add another line:

```
Local=EGA$
```

You can visualize the Windows environment consisting of two components. One component is the virtual machines that contain DOS, drivers, and programs that are specific to that application and do not affect any other virtual machine; the other component is the part of Windows that is global and relevant to all virtual machines (see Figure 48.4). A simple question is, "Where do physical device drivers reside?" Because the hardware is shared by all virtual machines, Windows device drivers have to be part of the global environment so that Windows can arbitrate between different programs that may need access to a given device.

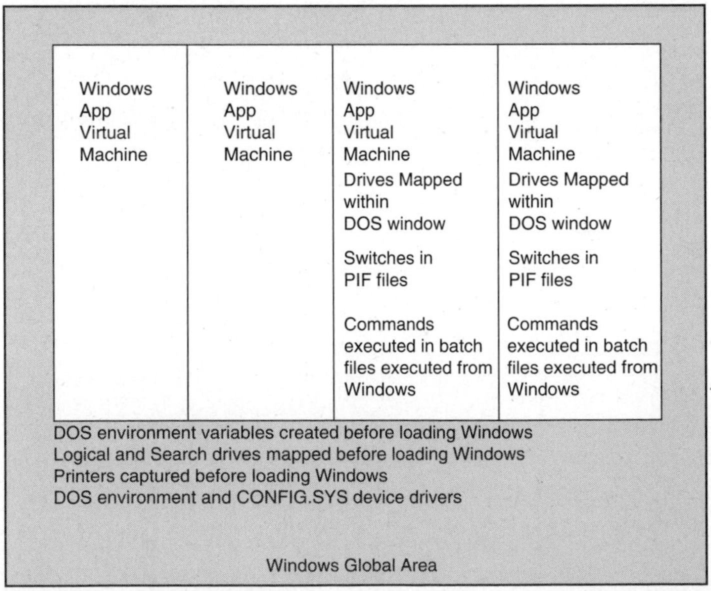

FIGURE 48.4.

Windows Virtual Machines and Global Areas.

Windows App Virtual Machine	Windows App Virtual Machine	Windows App Virtual Machine	Windows App Virtual Machine
		Drives Mapped within DOS window	Drives Mapped within DOS window
		Switches in PIF files	Switches in PIF files
		Commands executed in batch files executed from Windows	Commands executed in batch files executed from Windows

DOS environment variables created before loading Windows
Logical and Search drives mapped before loading Windows
Printers captured before loading Windows
DOS environment and CONFIG.SYS device drivers

Windows Global Area

Some DOS programs reset the monitor upon exiting. Because the monitor is global to all virtual machines, this can cause other VMs to hang. Setting `Local=EGA$` localizes any monitor settings to that VM. The DOS device name, `EGA$`, must be typed in uppercase.

The `[boot]` section of SYSTEM.INI contains one line that must be present for Novell networks:

```
network.drv=netware.drv
```

This command identifies the driver needed by Windows for NetWare. The NETWARE.DRV file must be in the user's Windows SYSTEM directory or in the master Windows directory on the file server.

The `[Boot.description]` section of SYSTEM.INI contains one line that must be present for NetWare LANs:

```
network.drv=Novell NetWare (version information)
```

Setup uses this section to display the user's current configuration when Setup is run from Windows. There is no need to edit this section.

[NonWindowsApp] Section

The `[NonWindowsApp]` section contains a couple of commands that you need to consider. Both commands concern DOS application parameters.

The first command is for users who run Windows in Standard mode. Standard mode does not permit multitasking DOS applications. It does, however, permit task switching between DOS applications.

```
SwapDisk=drive:path
```

Default: The directory established by the DOS TEMP variable. If no TEMP variable exists, Windows uses the current directory when the user starts Windows.

When a user switches out of a DOS application in foreground, the DOS application is swapped out of memory onto disk. It remains there until the user switches back to the DOS application. Windows also uses the swap area when it runs out of RAM for Windows applications.

```
CommandEnvSize=bytes
```

Default: The amount of environment space established by the `SHELL=` statement in CONFIG.SYS.

This value establishes the amount of DOS environment space created in each virtual machine running a DOS application. The valid range is between 160 and 32,768 bytes. If the value entered is smaller than that already established for the DOS environment, this setting is ignored.

The commands documented are the ones likely to need adjusting for your Windows environment. There are many other possible settings. This section discusses the SYSTEM.INI sections pertinent to NetWare system administration. For other commands in SYSTEM.INI, refer to the *Microsoft Windows Resource Kit*.

PROGMAN.INI

This is one of the critical .INI files for Windows. It contains information about the Program Manager groups. In the following example, the [settings] section displays the current settings for the user's window placements and the name of the user's display driver. The [Groups] section contains the name and path to the user's group files. Note that two of the groups in the example refer to a network volume. Shared groups can be on the file server as long as the user's PROGMAN.INI contains a valid path to the group. This enables the network administrator to update a group easily. This syntax is known as a DOS TrueName and works for referencing a NetWare file server volume.

```
[Settings]
Window=4 5 1019 673 1
display.drv=ULTRA.DRV
Order= 4 2 3 5 6 1
AutoArrange=1

[Groups]
Group1=C:\WIN31\MAIN0.GRP
Group2=C:\WIN31\ACCESSO0.GRP
Group3=C:\WIN31\GAMES.GRP
Group4=C:\WIN31\STARTUP.GRP
Group5=\\ATRIUM2\SYS\WAPPS\GRP\TOOLS.GRP
Group6=\\ATRIUM2\SYS\WAPPS\GRP\DTP.GRP

[restrictions]
NoRun=1
```

The most important change to PROGMAN.INI for networks is the addition of the [restrictions] section. This section enables the network administrator to limit some aspects of Program Manager. Table 48.5 displays the settings for this section.

Table 48.5. PROGMAN.INI `[restrictions]` settings.

Setting	Values
EditLevel	Controls what the user can modify in Program Manager:
	0—The user can make any desired changes.
	1—The user cannot create, delete, or rename groups. Disables New, Move, Copy, and Delete commands on the Program Manager File menu when a group is selected.
	2—All restrictions from 1, plus the user cannot create or delete program items. New, Move, Copy, and Delete commands are completely disabled.
	3—All restrictions from 2, plus the user cannot change command lines for program items. The text in the Command Line field of the Program Properties dialog box cannot be changed.
	4—All restrictions from 3, plus the user cannot change any program item information. None of the fields of the Program Properties dialog box can be changed.
NoClose=	0—No restrictions.
	1—The user cannot use the Exit option from the File menu. The user cannot use Alt-F4 to exit Windows. Use this option with extreme care! You have no way of making sure the user has closed all applications before turning the workstation off. This can result in lost data and corrupted files!
NoFileMenu	0—No restrictions.
	1—Removes the File menu from Program Manager. Users can run a program only by selecting its icon. However, users may still run programs from File Manager.
NoRun=	0—No restrictions.
	1—Disables the Run option in the File menu.
NoSaveSettings	0—No restrictions.
	1—The user cannot use the Save Settings on the Exit option of the Options menu. Any changes made to the arrangement of windows and icons will not be saved when the user exits Windows.

WIN.INI

This file is one of the most important files in Windows; it contains a wide array of information about the user's Windows environment. It can contain 17 sections just for Windows. In addition, application software can add sections to this file.

It is almost impossible to discuss everything found in this file. However, the most important sections for running Windows with NetWare are discussed in the section.

[Windows] Section

This section contains settings usually affected by the Control Panel program. These choices are user-specific for the most part. A couple of network-oriented settings can be found in this section:

```
NetWare = 0 or 1
```

When `NetWare=1`, Windows warns the user if he or she starts Windows and the network is not running or if the user has not loaded the workstation shell software. All network options in Control Panel will be disabled. You change this option through the Network option in Control Panel.

```
Spooler = Yes or No
```

If `Spooler = Yes`, Windows prints all jobs to a temporary file before sending them to the printer or network queue. You should make sure that this value is `No` when using a network queue. This option is changed from the Print Manager Options menu.

[extensions] Section

Windows uses this section to relate files with their source programs through the file's extension. Windows installs the default settings shown in the following code lines. Third-party Windows applications may add other settings for their applications. Note that the DOS TrueName path convention is used. The network logical drive letter was edited and replaced with the more desirable TrueName. Because applications are installed user-by-user, this section is also user-specific.

```
[Extensions]

cal=calendar.exe ^.cal
crd=cardfile.exe ^.crd
trm=terminal.exe ^.trm
txt=notepad.exe ^.txt
ini=notepad.exe ^.ini
pcx=pbrush.exe ^.pcx
bmp=pbrush.exe ^.bmp
wri=write.exe ^.wri
rec=recorder.exe ^.rec
hlp=winhelp.exe ^.hlp

wrk=\\ATRIUM2\SYS\programs\123w\123w.exe ^.wrk
wks=\\ATRIUM2\SYS\programs\123w\123w.exe ^.wks
wk1=\\ATRIUM2\SYS\programs\123w\123w.exe ^.wk1
wk3=\\ATRIUM2\SYS\programs\123w\123w.exe ^.wk3
wr1=\\ATRIUM2\SYS\programs\123w\123w.exe ^.wr1
doc=C:\WAPPS\WINWORD\winword.exe ^.doc
dot=C:\WAPPS\WINWORD\winword.exe ^.dot
rtf=C:\WAPPS\WINWORD\winword.exe ^.rtf
```

[ports] Section

This section is one of the misunderstood sections of this file. The following code lines list the default contents of this section. This section contains the configuration for serial ports as set in the Ports option of Control Panel. This section does not reflect the ports installed on the user's PC, which are the Windows driver names for the physical ports. With the exception of COM port settings, this section is the same for all users. Otherwise, you could not use a user's WIN.INI file on more than one workstation without having to reconfigure Windows every time the user runs it.

[ports]

```
LPT1:=
LPT2:=
LPT3:=
COM1:=9600,n,8,1,x
COM2:=2400,e,7,2
COM3:=4800,n,7,1,p
COM4:=9600,n,8,1,x
EPT:=
FILE:=
LPT1.DOS=
LPT2.DOS=
```

[fonts] Section

This is a real problem section. So far, WIN.INI has contained user-specific information. If this trend held true throughout WIN.INI, you could use the same WIN.INI for the user, no matter which workstation the user uses. Now, at the end of the [fonts] section, screen fonts are listed that are specific to the type of video adapter. This means that the same WIN.INI will not work on a workstation that doesn't have the same type of video adapter. These screen fonts are the fonts Windows uses for its own menus, icons, and dialog boxes. You need to solve this problem or users will not be able to use any workstation but their own.

[fonts]

```
Modern (Plotter)=MODERN.FON
Script (Plotter)=SCRIPT.FON
Roman (Plotter)=ROMAN.FON
Arial (TrueType)=ARIAL.FOT
Arial Bold (TrueType)=ARIALBD.FOT
Arial Bold Italic (TrueType)=ARIALBI.FOT
Arial Italic (TrueType)=ARIALI.FOT
Courier New (TrueType)=COUR.FOT
Courier New Bold (TrueType)=COURBD.FOT
Courier New Italic (TrueType)=COURI.FOT
Times New Roman (TrueType)=TIMES.FOT
Times New Roman Bold (TrueType)=TIMESBD.FOT
Times New Roman Bold Italic (TrueType)=TIMESBI.FOT
Times New Roman Italic (TrueType)=TIMESI.FOT
Courier New Bold Italic (TrueType)=COURBI.FOT
WingDings (TrueType)=WINGDING.FOT
Symbol (TrueType)=SYMBOL.FOT
MS Sans Serif 8,10,12,14,18,24 (8514/a res)=SSERIFF.FON
Courier 10,12,15 (8514/a res)=COURF.FON
MS Serif 8,10,12,14,18,24 (8514/a res)=SERIFF.FON
Symbol 8,10,12,14,18,24 (8514/a res)=SYMBOLF.FON
Small Fonts (8514/a res)=SMALLF.FON
```

The solution is rather simple. You have to add all of the screen fonts to all WIN.INI files that the user might invoke. Table 48.6 displays all of the screen fonts used by Windows. These have to be added to the user's [fonts] section of WIN.INI. The .FON files for the particular video display still have to reside in the master Windows directory on the file server or in the Windows SYSTEM directory on the PC.

Table 48.6. Windows screen fonts.

[fonts]	
MS Sans Serif 8,10,12,14,18,24 (EGA res)	=SSERIFB.FON
Courier 8,10,12,15 (EGA res)	=COURB.FON
MS Serif 8,10,12,14,18,24 (EGA res)	=SERIFB.FON
Arial 8,10 (EGA res)	=ARIALB.FON
Times New Roman 8,10 (EGA res)	=TIMESB.FON
Symbol 8,10,12,14,18,24 (EGA res)	=SYMBOLB.FON
Small Fonts (EGA res)	=SMALLB.FON
MS Sans Serif 8,10,12,14,18,24 (VGA res)	=SSERFIE.FON
Courier 10,12,15 (VGA res)	=COURE.FON
MS Serif 8,10,12,14,18,24 (VGA res)	=SERIFE.FON
Symbol 8,10,12,14,18,24 (VGA res)	=SYMBOLE.FON
Small Fonts (VGA res)	=SMALLE.FON
MS Sans Serif 8,10,12,14,18,24 (8514/a res)	=SSERIFF.FON
Courier 10,12,15 (8514/a res)	=COURF.FON
MS Serif 8,10,12,14,18,24 (8514/a res)	=SERIFF.FON
Symbol 8,10,12,14,18,24 (8514/a res)	=SYMBOLF.FON
Small Fonts (8514/a res)	=SMALLF.FON

Unfortunately, Microsoft does not use the TrueType fonts for its own system fonts (screen fonts). The default screen fonts must continue to work.

[network] Section

This section records the permanent network connections established by the user in File Manager. It also records the permanent queue assignments and job settings for each queue. These options are user-specific. The following code lines display an example of these entries.

[Network]

```
L:=[ATRIUM/SYS:USERS/HADER]
LPT2:=ATRIUM1/AP_LW1
LPT2-OPTIONS=128,1,8,0,0
LPT3:=ATRIUM1/HP_LJ1
LPT3-OPTIONS=128,1,8,0,0
```

[PrinterPorts] Section

This section lists the active and inactive printers installed for this user. The following code lines display an example of the entries in this section. Network printers available to a user are user-specific, but the user must have the correct drivers installed. The needed printer drivers come from this section. The drivers themselves must reside in the master Windows directory on the file server or on the local PC's Windows SYSTEM directory. If Windows was installed on the individual PCs rather than a network installation, this section can present a problem when users move around from workstation to workstation.

```
[PrinterPorts]

Apple LaserWriter=pscript,LPT2:,15,90
Canon Bubble-Jet BJ-10e=CANON10e,LPT1:,15,45
Epson LQ-2550=EPSON24,LPT1:,15,45
HP LaserJet Series II=HPPCL,LPT3:,15,45
```

CAUTION ▶

NetWare 3.11's distribution release of the print server utility has bugs that cause problems in network printing with Windows (especially with LaserJets). If you experience printing problems, you should upgrade your print server utilities files before asking for further support.

You should either request an UPDATE from Novell (1-800-UPDATE1) or from NetWire on CompuServe. You should use at least v1.27, but for best results upgrade to version 3.7.6. The latest version can be found in the NOVLIB forum in the filename PSERV*n*.EXE (*n* is a number that is incremented upward as the version is revised).

You shouldn't run RPRINTER under Windows.

[devices] Section

This section is needed if you run applications written for Windows 2.x. It lists the printers that are installed for the user.

[application] Sections

Every Windows application may make changes to WIN.INI for its own use. Most of the time, these applications add new sections to WIN.INI, which can be quite substantial. The listing below illustrates a change made to WIN.INI for Arts & Letters, from Software Support Group Inc. You can see that this application recorded its path needs in WIN.INI.

Windows application developers have the option to create their own .INI files or add their data to WIN.INI. Separate .INI files for each application are preferred because it becomes difficult to tell which parts of WIN.INI belong to each application, making it very difficult for you to uninstall a Windows application.

```
[a&l]

editor config=\\ATRIUM2\SYS\WAPPS\A&L\STARTUP.DEF
editor=\\ATRIUM2\SYS\WAPPS\A&L
backuppath=\\ATRIUM2\SYS\WAPPS\A&L
symbols=\\ATRIUM2\SYS\WAPPS\A&L\SYMBOLS
typefaces=\\ATRIUM2\SYS\WAPPS\A&L\TYPEFACE
Editor Libraries=2
Editor Library1=\\ATRIUM2\SYS\WAPPS\A&L\CUSTOM\Curves.yal
Editor Library2=\\ATRIUM2\SYS\WAPPS\A&L\CUSTOM\*.yal
Editor Activities=2
Editor Activity1=\\ATRIUM2\SYS\WAPPS\A&L\ACTIVITY\eless-b.yal
Editor Activity2=\\ATRIUM2\SYS\WAPPS\A&L\ACTIVITY\*.yal
```

CONTROL.INI

This file contains information about the Windows color schemes and other user-specific options. Table 48.7 lists the sections and what they contain. There are no specific changes needed for networks in this file.

Table 48.7. CONTROL.INI sections.

Section	Contents
[current]	The current color scheme in use
[color schemes]	Data about all of the standard color schemes
[custom colors]	Information about any user-defined color schemes created from the Colors option of the Control Panel
[patterns]	Information used for the background patterns that can be used in place of wallpaper
[screen saver.name]	Information about the user's screen saver selections from Control Panel
[userinstallable.drivers]	Information about user-installed drivers
[MMCPL]	Information about multimedia options selected from the Control Panel
[drivers.desc]	Information about the MIDI Mapper portion of the multimedia options
[installed]	Records data about the printer devices that are installed and the Windows version information

TIP ▶

Here is an undocumented tip that you really need for managing the Control Panel on your network. You can add a [Don't Load] section to CONTROL.INI and use it to limit the icons in the Control Panel. Type the name of the icon followed by =NO:.

The [Don't Load] Section

Any icon that you do not want to appear in the user's control panel can be omitted by adding a statement beneath the [Don't Load] section of CONTROL.INI. The following code lines display an example that would omit the Network, 386 Enhanced and Printers icon from the control panel. The value is a Boolean statement, so Yes, True, and 1 mean the same thing and affirm that you do not want these icons loaded into the control panel.

```
[don't load]

Network=Yes
386 Enhanced=True
Printers=1
```

MOUSE.INI

This .INI file is new to Windows 3.1. It is required if you use version 8.2 or above of the Microsoft mouse driver. This file records information about your mouse interface, and it may be used to store other mouse options. However, WIN.INI currently contains the other mouse settings.

MOUSE.COM looks for the DOS variable MOUSE= to determine where to look for MOUSE.INI. Also, MOUSE.SYS looks for MOUSE.INI in the same directory that MOUSE.SYS resides. Versions 8.0 and 8.1 of MOUSE.SYS do not read MOUSE.INI. Table 48.8 contains the valid settings for MouseType= in MOUSE.INI for the Microsoft Mouse, Microsoft BallPoint Mouse, and the Microsoft Mouse driver.

Table 48.8. Settings for MouseType=.

Value	Mouse Installed
Serial	COM1 or COM2
Serial1	COM1
Serial2	COM2
PS2	PS/2 Mouse Port
Bus	Bus Mouse
InPort	InPort Card
InPort1	InPort Card—J3 Primary
InPort2	InPort Card—J3 Secondary

MOUSE.INI is not a critical .INI file for normal Windows usage. If you delete it, Windows 3.1 re-creates it in the user's startup directory if the mouse driver is already loaded.

PART

Troubleshooting

Using NetWire

49

by Peter Kuo

Have you ever been at a client site at two in the morning and needed a driver that is not part of the standard NetWare package? Have you ever wondered if anyone else has been through what you are going through now and has some tips and tricks for you? Have you ever wondered if there is a neat utility that can save you tons of headaches? Where can you turn to in order to get the latest updates, fixes, drivers, tips, and gossips about NetWare? The answers are just a phone call away—a local call, in most cases.

Novell sponsors a set of forums on CompuServe Information Service (CIS) that provides free technical support and maintains a library of the latest drivers, patches, tips, and press releases. Novell also maintains a library of user-contributed programs and files that may be of interest to you. These forums are collectively known as *NetWire*.

Joining CompuServe and NetWire

CompuServe Information Service is operated by CompuServe, Inc., an H & R Block Company, and is based in Columbus, Ohio. It maintains a large number of public access modem ports world-wide; they are available in most major cities. CIS charges a monthly membership fee plus hourly connect rates, depending on the services you use. Currently, there are two pricing plans:

1. *Standard Pricing Plan*: The basic monthly membership fee of $8.95 (U.S.) includes unlimited connect time for a variety of services, such as news, weather, and sports. All other services, including NetWire, are priced at the following hourly connect rates:

300 bps	$6.00 (U.S.)/hour
1200/2400 bps	$12.80 (U.S.)/hour
9600 bps	$16.00 (U.S.)/hour

2. *Alternative Pricing Plan*: This carries a monthly membership fee of $2.50 (U.S.) and provides unlimited access to the membership support services free of connect time charges. All other services, including NetWire, are billed at the following hourly rates:

300 bps	$6.30 (U.S.)/hour
1200/2400 bps	$12.80 (U.S.)/hour
9600 bps	$22.80 (U.S.)/hour

TIP ▶

CompuServe has recently announced 14.4K bps support in 10 U.S. cities as a pilot project. The initial pricing for 14.4K bps service will be same as 9600 bps. Check with CIS for current rates (!GO RATES). Also see Table 49.1 later in this chapter.

These listed rates are subject to change as deemed necessary by CIS.

When you first visit a forum, you are asked to "Join the Forum." Otherwise, you will not have full access to the various forum areas, such as libraries. It doesn't cost anything to join NetWire forums. You get billed only for your connect time (according to your subscribed pricing plan) by CIS .

NOTE ▶

If you have any problems or questions regarding CompuServe software or the service itself, you can contact CompuServe Customer Service at 800-848-8990 in the United States. In other countries:

Country	Toll-free	Direct
Argentina		(+54) 1-372-7817
Australia	008-023-158	(+61) 2-410-4260
Canada	800-848-8990	(+1) 614-457-8650
Chile		(+56) 2-696-8807
Germany	0130-3732	(+49) 89-66-55-0-222
Hungary		(+36) 1-156-5366
Hong Kong		(+852) 867-0118
Israel		(+972) 3-29-0466
Japan	0120-22-1200	(+81) 3-5471-5806
New Zealand	0800-441-082	(+61) 2-410-4260
South Korea	080-022-7400	(+82) 2-569-5400
Switzerland	155-31-79	(+49) 89-66-55-0-222
Taiwan		(+886) 2-651-6899
United Kingdom	0800-289-378	(+44) 272-760-680
Venezuela		(+58) 2-793-2384
Other areas		(+1) 614-457-8650

Connecting to CompuServe

In most major North American cities, CIS access numbers are available, and dial-up speeds up to 9600 bps are supported. In September of 1993, CompuServe started installing 14.4K/sec modems in 10 selected U.S. cities as a pilot project. These sites are listed in Table 49.1. Hopefully, more 14.4K ports will be available in other cities soon.

Table 49.1. 14.4K/sec access number for CompuServe.

City/State	Telephone Number
Cambridge, MA	617/497-0014
Chicago, IL	312/857-0008
Columbus, OH	614/764-2957
Los Angeles, CA	213/623-7486
New York, NY	212/755-9080
Newport Beach, CA	714/263-0244
Orlando, FL	407/894-0199
Philadelphia, PA	215/665-0360
Rochelle Park, NJ	201/712-0479
Santa Clara, CA	408/980-1044

> **TIP** ▷
>
> You can obtain a list of all the CIS public modem ports in North America by typing GO PHONES at the command prompt.

If you are in an area with no local CIS access numbers, you can connect to CompuServe in a number of ways. The most obvious way is to call long distance to the nearest city that has a dial-in port. If you are in North America, a second method is to call toll-free:

    800-848-4480 (300, 1200, 2400 bps)
    800-331-7166 (9600 bps)

If you are not using a local access number, an additional communication surcharge is added on top of your hourly connection charges. Fortunately, there are alternatives. A number of communication networks around the world have "gateways" into CompuServe. In some cases, their communication surcharges are much lower than the CIS charge on their toll-free numbers. Table 49.2, which is a summary of communication charges for various networks, examines some available in North America.

NOTE ▶

Prime-time hours as defined by CompuServe are 0800 to 1900 weekdays. Hours other than prime-time are 1900 to 0800 weekdays and all day weekends. Prime-time and nonprime-time hours are based on local time at network location.

All prices shown in Table 49.2 are in U.S. dollars.

Table 49.2. Communication surcharges for various networks.

Network	Nonprime/hour	Prime/hour
800-number (U.S.)	$8.70	$8.70
800-number (Canada)	$34.70	$34.70
SprintNet (U.S.)	$1.70(*)	$11.70
SprintNet (International)	$49.70	$49.70
BT Tymnet	$1.70(*)	$11.70
AlaskaNet	$11.70	$11.70
LATA	$1.70	$5.70
Datapac (300-2400 bps)	$8.00	$8.00
Datapac (9600 bps)	$20.00(**)	$20.00(**)

CAUTION ▶

(*) Nonprime-time rate for Alaska and Hawaii is $11.70/hour.

(**) Datapac does not distinguish between speeds.

Therefore, if you connect through one of Datapac's 9600 bps access number at a lower modcm speed, you will be charged at the 9600 bps surcharge rate.

SprintNet

SprintNet offers dial-up access to CompuServe network at speeds of up to 2400 bps. Check your phone directory for any local access numbers. Following are logon procedures for accessing CIS with SprintNet:

1. After a connection is made, press Enter twice if you are connecting at 300 or 1200 bps. Otherwise, type @ and press Enter.

2. At the TERMINAL= prompt, type D1 and press Enter.

3. At the @ prompt, type either C 614227 *or* C 202202 and press Enter.

4. You will be connected to CIS, and the User ID: prompt will appear. Log on as usual.

After you log out from CIS, you will see <network address> Disconnected on your screen, followed by a @ prompt. Type D and press Enter to disconnect from SprintNet.

> **NOTE**
>
> If you do not automatically receive a "Disconnected" message, press Enter, type @, and press Enter again. That should display the prompt.

BT Tymnet

To access CIS through Tymnet, use the following procedure:

1. Connect to your local Tymnet access number.

2. On your screen, you should see Please Enter Your Terminal Identifier. Type A *without* a carriage return.

3. You then will be prompted with Please Log In. Type CML05 and press Enter.

4. You are now connected to CompuServe. At the Host Name: prompt, type CIS and log on as usual.

AlaskaNet

The steps for accessing CIS through AlaskaNet are very similar to those of Tymnet:

1. Connect to your local AlaskaNet access number.

2. On your screen, you should see Please Enter Your Terminal Identifier. Type A *without* a carriage return.

3. You will be prompted with `Welcome to AlaskaNet. Please Log In.` Type `COMPUSERVE` and press Enter.

4. You are now connected to CompuServe. At the `Host Name:` prompt, type `CIS` and log on as usual.

LATA

It is very simple to access CIS with LATA's gateway:

1. Connect to your local LATA access number.

2. Type ... and press Enter. For CONLATA, type `HHH` and press Enter.

3. You will see the message `Welcome to <LATA being accessed>. Please Log In:` followed by a * prompt. Type `.CPS` and press Enter . Note that `.CPS` *must* be capitalized.

4. You will get the `Host Name:` prompt. Type `CIS` and press Enter. Then log on to CIS as usual.

Canadian Datapac

In Canada, you can access CIS through Datapac. Dial-up speeds of up to 9600 bps are available. Check your phone directory's white pages for your local access number. The following logon procedures are to be used:

1. Connect to your local Datapac number.

2. For access at 300 bps, type . and press Enter; for 1200 bps access, type .. and press Enter; for access at 2400 bps or higher, type... and press Enter.

3. On your screen, you should see `<Datapac dial port address>`. Type `29400138` and press Enter for the port address. When you see the message `DATAPAC: call connected`, followed by `Host Name:`, you have successfully connected to CIS.

4. Type `CIS` and press Enter to continue logging on to CompuServe.

After you sign off from CIS, you will see the message; `DATAPAC: call disconnected`. At this point, you can hang up your modem.

NetWire Mannerisms

In order to obtain the fastest and best response possible, you should observe some rules. The tips provided here apply not only to NetWire, but also to other CIS forums and any information-related services, such as bulletin board services (BBSs).

Following is a list of rules and tips for using any information services (not just CIS):

- Use a mixture of upper- and lowercase letters when composing your message. Many times, messages are in uppercase; they are hard on the eyes and give the impression that someone is YELLING.

- Think before you write. Many times, a message is worded so badly that one can only guess what the poster means. Be concise.

- Provide enough information. When asking for a solution to a problem, make sure you include enough information, such as the name of the product, version number, and any patches that you may have applied. Don't say, "My server just abended. Why?" Nobody is psychic.

- Don't give too much information. For example, if an application hangs your workstation, it doesn't help to list your AUTOEXEC.BAT, CONFIG.SYS, NET.CFG, STARTUP.NCF, and AUTOEXEC.NCF files (and hang the workstation), and then forget to provide the name of your application and its version number.

- Post to the right area. It is important that you post your messages to the proper section within the message board. This allows the right people to see your questions and give you the best advice possible. If you are unfamiliar with the NetWire forum layouts, download WELCOM.EXE from either NOVLIB or NOVUSER forum.

- Watch your language. In most, if not all, cases, message sections are public. That means *everyone* sees your message. Therefore, it is prudent for you to pick the appropriate words when composing messages.

- Do not post the same message many times or in multiple sections. Be patient. Most message boards are not interactive. Do not expect real-time response to your messages.

- Follow up on your messages. Make sure you do a follow-up with any suggestions you receive; therefore, others can know your results.

Following are some items you should keep in mind when using NetWire; they will help you get faster and better responses:

■ For *technical* assistance, post your message in the proper section and address it to "SysOp" (*System Operator*).

■ For announcements, address message to "All."

■ For general discussions, address message to "All."

■ Do *not* send electronic mail (e-mail) to SysOps asking for technical help. NetWire policy is that no support is provided for e-mail. Using e-mail takes away the open question and answer environment; many users simply "lurk" in the forums, following the message threads.

■ Use the REPLY option to follow up a message. This keeps the thread together. Starting a new thread on the same topic makes it very hard for others to follow a discussion. Do not reply by e-mail unless you're asked to.

■ Check messages frequently. CompuServe allocates only so much message space per forum. If the traffic volume is high, messages are *scrolled off* quickly. If you are following a thread, you should check at least every other day. Traffic on certain NetWire forums is very high.

■ Check other message subject headings before you post. You may not be the only one having a particular problem, or a solution may already be out there. Novell also keeps a list of NOVLIB's "top issues" from the previous month. Check it out first. Your question may already have been answered.

■ Use relevant subject headings. Try to include the product name or utility name in your subject heading. Many people read specific messages based solely on subject heading. This also helps the SysOps as they track different products.

NOTE ▶

There are two different types of SysOps on NetWire: volunteer SysOps and Novell SysOps. Volunteer SysOps are contracted by Novell to share their extensive real-world knowledge of networks and the computer industry in general. They are identified by the name "SysOp" following their name. These SysOps do not represent Novell.

Novell SysOps are Novell employees who monitor NetWire forums full time. These SysOps are identified by the name "Novell" following their name.

If you have any Novell-specific, nontechnical issues, address your messages to a Novell SysOp rather than a volunteer SysOp.

If you want to log a complaint, use the Suggestion Box section (#2) in NGENERAL forum. You can also call 800-NETWARE or 801-429-5588 and ask for the Customer Satisfaction department.

Following are some important CompuServe specifics:

High Message Counter: CIS keeps a High Message Counter so that you do not see old messages. Often someone posts a message, goes back later, and cannot find that message. The message is not lost; it is simply hidden. If you want to see old messages (provided they have not already been scrolled off by CIS), you can use the Options menu to "crank" back the message counter.

Messages Scrolled From…: If you have not accessed a forum for some time, any messages addressed to you will be scrolled into your e-mail box by CIS. The message subject will indicate "Message Scrolled from…". In such cases, it is best not to use the REPLY option in mail; this results in a broken thread. If you replied to a message two weeks after it was addressed to you, the sender may have forgotten what it is all about (because of the nondescriptive subject line).

When addressing messages, make sure you include the recipient's CIS ID. This is how the CompuServe software can inform users they have messages waiting.

TIP ▶

If you are a first-time user of CompuServe or NetWire forums, you should observe the messages for a little while so you can learn about the proper protocol. You will find out who the regular users are and learn to respect other's views and responses. Also, download a file called WELCOM.EXE from either NOVLIB or NOVUSER; it contains the most current forum layouts.

CAUTION ▶

If you are involved in a beta program, do not discuss the product in the open forums. Usually a private forum exists for that purpose. Contact your beta coordinator to locate such a forum.

SysOps reserve the right to remove messages they deem inappropriate, such as ones involving beta software, foul language, proprietary information, and so forth.

NetWire Map

As of October 1, 1993, NetWire is organized into the forums shown in Table 49.3. Note that some of these forums are private; you need to contact the appropriate departments at Novell for access. For example, if you are a Certified NetWare Instructor (CNI), you should contact CNI Admin at Provo for access to the CNI-NAEC section in NOVPRIVATE. NDEVREL replaced NOVDEV and is a private forum.

Table 49.3. NetWire message sections.

NW 2.x (NETW2X)	NW 3.x (NETW3X)	NW 4.x (NETW4X)
1) Printing	1) Printing	1) Printing
2) NetWare Utils	2) NetWare Utils	2) NetWare Utils
3) Disk Drv/Cntrls	3) Disk Drv/Cntrls	3) Disk Drv/CDs/Cntrls
4) LAN Cards/Drv	4) LAN Cards/Drv	4) LAN Cards/Drv
	5) Migration/Upgrade	5) Migration/Upgrade
		6) ElectroText/ Documentation
		7) Directory Services
	13) SFT III	
14) 2.1x and Below/OS	14) Operating Sys	14) OS/NLM/Console Utils
15) Operating Sys		

Novell Desktop (NOVDESKTOP)	Connectivity (NCONNECT)
1) DRDOS/Applications	1) Access Services
2) DRDOS/Disk	2) NACS
3) DRDOS/Memory	3) NW for SAA

continues

Table 49.3. continued

Novell Desktop (NOVDESKTOP)	Connectivity (NCONNECT)
4) DRDOS/Utilities	4) AS/400 Connectivity
5) Customer Service	5) Host Printing
6) Programming ?'s	6) SNA Links
7) Dataclub	7) LAN/LAN Links
8) NetWare Lite	8) NetWare Macintosh
	9) NetWare VMS
	10) Portable NetWare
	11) NW NFS - TCP/IP
	12) Email/MHS/FAX
	13) LAN WorkPlace/Group
14) NetWare NT Client	14) Other Connectivity Issues

Novell Information (NGENERAL)	Novell Vendor Forum A (NVENA)
1) Product Information	1) Folio
2) Suggestion Box	2) LAN Support Group
3) Application/Utils	3) Computer Tyme
4) User Groups/Train'g	4) Infinite Tech.
5) CNE's	5) Dell Computer
6) CNEPA	6) AST Research
7) NSEPro	7) Blue Lance
8) AppNotes	8) Best Power
9) NASC Program	9) Knowzall
	10) Notework
	11) RoseWare
	12) Multi-User DOS
	13) Tri-Cord
	15) SynOptics
16) Other Information	
17) The Lighter Side	

Novell User Forum (NOVUSER)	*Networking Hardware/Components (NOVHW)*
1) General Q and A's	1) Power Monitoring
2) Help Wanted	2) Token Ring
3) Classifieds	3) Ethernet
	4) ARCnet
	5) Backups
	6) Cabling/Media

Novell Network Mgmt (NOVMAN)	*Novell Private Forum (NOVPRIVATE)*
1) Network Management	1) Indris/Conug
2) NetWare Mgmt System	2) NetWare NT Client
3) LANtern System Mgr.	3) CNEPA Leadership
4) LANalyzer for Windows	4) Folio Beta
5) NW for SAA Mgmt.	5) CNI-NAEC
	6) NUI Leadership

Novell OS/2 Forum (NOVOS2)	*Novell Library (NOVLIB)*
1) OS/2 Printing	1) LIB Questions Only
2) Client/Server	
3) OS/2 Requester	
4) NSM (OS/2)	
5) NW 4.x for OS/2	
6) GUI Tools	
7) WINOS2/DOS	

Developer Support (NDEVSUPP)	*Novell Client Forum (NOVCLIENT)*
1) General Business	1) IPX/ODI Issues
2) Btrieve	2) NETX Issues

continues

Table 49.3. continued

Developer Support (NDEVSUPP)	*Novell Client Forum (NOVCLIENT)*
3) NetWare SQL	3) VLM Issues
4) NetWare Client SDK	4) ODINSUP Issues
5) NetWare Server SDK	5) NetBIOS Issues
6) Macintosh SDKs	6) NetWare and Windows
7) Communication SDKs	
8) TBA	
9) Personal NetWare SDK	
10) AppWare Foundation SDK	
11) LAN WorkPlace SDK	
12) Telephony SDK	
13) Visual AppBuilder	

Novell Developer Product Information (NDEVINFO)	*Novell UnixWare (UNIXWARE)*
1) General Business	1) General Info
2) Btrieve	2) Product Info
3) NetWare SQL	3) Developers
4) NetWare Client SDK	4) DOS Merge
5) NetWare Server SDK	5) Installation
6) Macintosh SDKs	6) X Windows
7) Communication SDKs	7) Networking
8) TBA	8) Device Drivers
9) Personal NetWare SDK	9) Printing
10) AppWare Foundation SDK	10) Communications
11) LAN WorkPlace SDK	11) Applications
12) Telephony SDK	12) Bug Watchers
13) Visual AppBuilder	13) Updates

Novell Developer Relations Forum (NDEVREL)	*Novell Vendor Forum B (NVENB)*
1) Gen/Forum Business	1) OnTrack
2) Database	2) NetWorth
3) Network Management	
4) NetWare C Interface for DOS	
5) System Calls for DOS	
6) Client	
7) NLMs	
8) OS/2 API	
9) Mac API	
10) Windows	
11) TBA	
12) Communications Services	
13) UnixWare and TCP/IP	
14) MHS (SMF71 SDK)	
15) DOS Protected Mode Services	
16) Vertical Application Development Services	
17) Enterprise Development Services	

Table 49.4. NetWare Libraries.

Libraries for NOVLIB	*Description*
1) Novell New UPLOADS	Files Uploaded by Novell, Inc.
2) General Information	General Info, Education, Press Releases
3) NetWare 2.X Specific	Files Pertaining Only to NW 2.x
4) NetWare 3.X Specific	Files Pertaining Only to NW 3.x
5) Client/Shell Drivers	Workstation Shells, Drivers, Windows Files, and so forth

continues

Table 49.4. continued

Libraries for NOVLIB	Description
6) NetWare Utilities	Utils that pertain to NW 2.x and 3.x
7) Btrieve/XQL	Novell Development Division Products Btrieve/XQL/Xtrieve
8) MAC/UNIX/LANalyzer	Files for Macintosh, UNIX, LANalyzer
9) Communications Product	Novell's Communications Products
10) NetWare Lite	NetWare Lite-Specific Files
11) Techinfo/IMSP's	Tech Bulletins, FYIs, IMSP's, AppNotes
12) NDSG/DRDOS	Files for Novell's Desktop Systems Group and DR DOS
13) APPWARE	
14) NetWare 4.X Specific	Files Pertaining to NW 4.x

Libraries for NOVUSER	Libraries for NVENA
1) New Uploads	1) Folio
2) Disk Drv/Patches	2) LAN Support Group
3) Lan Drivers/Patches	3) Computer Tyme
4) Comm. Drv/Patches	4) Infinite Tech.
5) Host/UNIX/drivers/patch	5) Dell Computer
6) Printer Utilities	6) AST Research
7) Network (sys) Utils	7) Blue Lance
8) Client WS Utils	8) Best Power
9) Management Tools	9) Knowzall
10) Text Files/Help	10) Notework
11) Windows Utils	11) RoseWare
12) Btrieve/Pgm Utils	12) Multiuser DOS
13) Virus Detectors	13) Tri-Cord
14) General Utils	
	15) SynOptics
17) Classifieds/Jobs	

Libraries for Novell UnixWare Forum	Libraries for NVENB
1) General Library	1) OnTrack
2) Developer Tools	2) NetWorth
3) X Window Library	
4) Network Utilities	
5) Applications	
6) Device Drivers	
7) Updates	

As you can see from the previous tables, most technical support forums do not have an associated library. All Novell files are available from NOVLIB.

> **NOTE** ▶
>
> Forum sections are added and removed as needed. It is a good idea to periodically refresh your section listings.

Other NetWire Services

Other than the message and library forums, there are a number of less-known online services available. For example, you can look up recent top issues (that is, most commonly asked questions). Following is a sample dialog of the session. User inputs are shown in bold:

```
!GO NETWIRE
NetWire+ NOVELL
NETWIRE MAIN MENU
1 What's New
2 Service and Support
3 Sales and Marketing
4 Novell Programs
5 About the Network Support Encyclopedia
6 New User Information
7 Compuserve Information Service

!2
NetWire+ SUPPORT
SERVICE AND SUPPORT
```

1 Files, Patches, and Fixes
2 Messages   (Questions & Answers)
3 NetWare Application Notes
4 Novell Professional Development (NPD) Bullets
5 Novell Labs Bulletins
6 Service Providers Guide
7 Training
8 Top Issues

!8

NetWire+   NOV-39

[...lines deleted ...]
NACS

Q: After installing NACS 3.0, I received the following
error when loading COMMEXEC:

LC:UNLOAD FROM NETWARE CONSOLE OF SERVICE NACS.

How can I fix this?

A: Follow the steps listed below to resolve this problem:

1. Log in to the NACS server as SUPERVISOR. If the
NACSPORT.CFG is not in the SYSTEM directory, copy
NACSPORT.CFG from the original NACS diskette 1.

2. Make sure that communication boards/serial ports
are installed in the NACS server.

3. If a DigiBoard is being used, add <node=0> to the
load statement in the AUTOEXEC.NCF as shown
below:

load aiodgxi mem=xxxxx port=yyy node=0

The DigiBoard driver is case-sensitive and
requires all lowercase letters in the load
statement shown.

[... lines deleted ...]
!

Some lines are deleted to save space.

Effective September 1, 1994, Novell is moving its NetWare Express program from
the G.E. network onto CompuServe. This saves many users from having to search
two different networks for patches.

Also available online are

Service Provider Database: An online searchable database of all the registered Novell Service Providers.

AppNotes: For a yearly subscription fee, you can download current and past issues of Application Notes. Postscript and WordPerfect formats are available.

Buyer's Guide: An online searchable database of the Novell Buyer's Guide. You can download sections based on your keyword selection(s).

A number of other services are in planning at the time of this writing. Check the NetWire main menu (!GO NETWIRE) for latest available services.

Patches via Internet

If you are on the Internet or have access to it, you may choose to download patches with the anonymous FTP. Novell maintains two anonymous FTP sites on the Internet. There are currently seven "mirror" sites around the world:

FTP.NOVELL.COM
SJF-LWP.NOVELL.COM
FTP.RUG.NL (Netherlands)
FTP.SALFORD.AC.UK (UK)
NETLAB.USU.EDU (Logon, UT)
TUI.LINCAN.AC.NZ (New Zealand)
RISC.UA.EDU (Tuscoloss, AL)
NOVELL.NRC.CA (Ottawa, Canada)
BNUG.PROTEON.COM (Boston, MA)

Get the Most out of CompuServe

As mentioned previously, CompuServe charges by connect time and the modem speed at which you connect. There are many ways to access CIS from your desktop. People commonly use a terminal emulation program, such as Procomm to access CIS in a real-time, interactive manner. However, as many have learned, this method is cumbersome, and it quickly becomes very expensive. The following sections discuss alternative means of accessing CIS. They may not save you money, but they will make you much more efficient and productive for the same amount of money spent.

AutoSIG

AutoSIG (ATO) is the first "offline" message reader available for CompuServe. It is free of charge from the IBMCOM forum, AutoSIG section (Section 1). A number of programs are available to augment ATO:

ACL313.EXE: A program that enables you to find out how much you are spending while using AutoSIG

ATOBRO.EXE: A program that enables you to create scripts for downloading files from the Libraries (Libs)

ATOADV.EXE: A manual that documents AutoSIG's advanced functions

DLSCAN.ARC: A program that builds a catalog of files in the CompuServe Libraries of your choice and automatically downloads the ones you pick (through AutoSIG)

AutoSIG was developed by a project group consisting of the following people, all of whom are SysOps in the IBMCOM forum:

Vernon Buerg
Jim McKeown
Don Watkins

CompuServe Information Manager

CompuServe Information Manager (CIM) is a software package developed by CompuServe to provide CIS users with a Windows-like interface (see Figure 49.1). It enables you to customize a list of Favorite Places (see Figure 49.2) so you can simply "point and shoot," rather than have to remember the online commands and forum names.

FIGURE 49.1.

CompuServe Information Manager (DOS version) main menu.

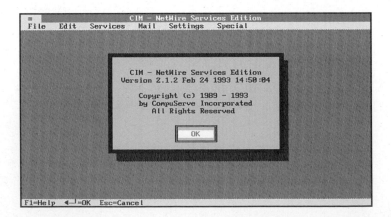

FIGURE 49.2.

An example of a Favorite Places listing.

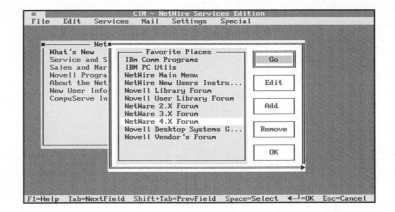

While online, you can easily get a list of all message subjects in a given section of a forum. You can read the messages online or download and file them away in your "filing cabinet" for later reference (see Figure 49.3). You also can get a listing of library files and download selected ones (see Figure 49.4).

FIGURE 49.3.

Filing Cabinet listing.

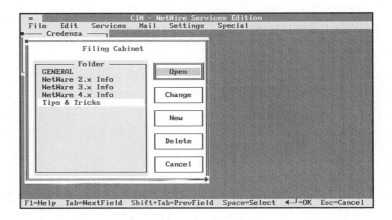

CIM is a step forward from using terminal emulation programs such as Procomm, because you don't waste your valuable online time typing commands and remembering syntax. Two versions of DOSCIM are available: v1.36 for floppy-based installation, and v2.1.2 for hard-disk based installation. With v1.36, most of what you do using the program still costs you valuable online charges, with the following exceptions:

- You can compose your forum messages offline and upload them when you connect to CIS.
- You can compose and read your mail messages offline.

FIGURE 49.4.

Online Library Files listing.

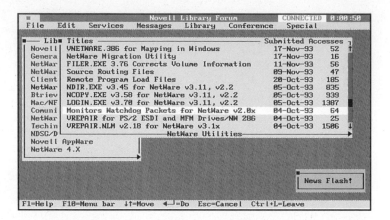

For example, you stay connected while reading messages. However, with DOSCIM's v2, you have the capability of downloading the messages and reading them offline. Versions also exist for Windows and Macintosh users. You can download these programs from the CIM forums on CIS.

> **NOTE**
>
> To download DOSCIM from CompuServe, type !GO DOSCIM at the command prompt.
>
> To download WINCIM, type !GO WINCIM. For the Mac version, type !GO WCIMSOFT.
>
> There is a one-time $10.00 (U.S.) download charge for this software. However, it is credited back to you in connect time on CIS.

In the NOVCIM forum, a special version of DOSCIM (called NOVCIM) is preconfigured especially for NetWire. You can download NOVCIM for a one-time, $10.00 (U.S.) fee, which will be credited back to you in connect time on CIS. A Windows version is also available under the same terms.

From time to time, Novell offers a special promotion, called the NetWire Starter Kit, to NetWare users. This includes a copy of NOVCIM. Bundled with it is a temporary user ID and $15.00 (U.S.) usage credit for CIS. This way, you can start using NetWire right away.

TAPCIS

Although CIM is an improvement over manual entry of commands, TAPCIS is yet another giant step forward from CIM. TAPCIS, published by Support Group, Inc., in what is known as an *offline thread/message reader*. With Procomm or CIM, you do everything online: scan for messages, read messages, reply to messages, scan libraries for files, and so forth. With TAPCIS, however, you go online only when you have to.

TAPCIS first goes online to the predesignated forums and grabs the message *subjects* from the sections that you have defined. It then signs off from CIS. You mark the messages you want to read based on the subject headings (see Figure 49.5). TAPCIS goes back online to download just those messages. You then can read and reply to the messages offline, without burning up any online charges. The same can be done with library files (see Figures 49.6 and 49.7).

FIGURE 49.5.

The TAPCIS message-marking screen.

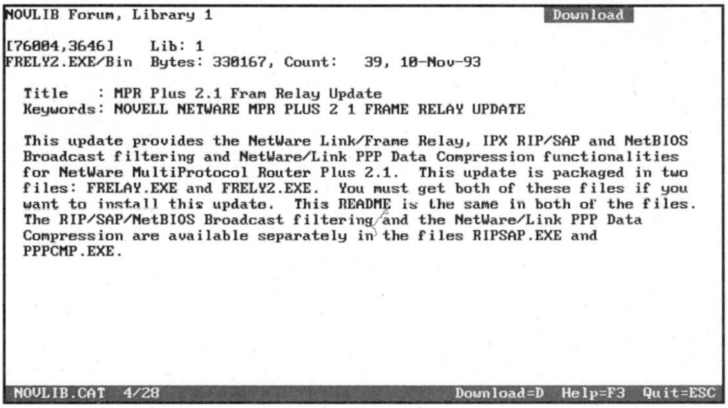

```
36657        R BBS SERVICES AVAILABLE     S 1 / LIB Questions Only!
36647 [ 1] R Where is new PS2OPT.DSK?     S 1 / LIB Questions Only!  NOVLIB
36646        R DOSGEN  qemm/ipxodi         S 1 / LIB Questions Only!
36648 [ 1] R MSM.NLM                       S 1 / LIB Questions Only!  R>ead
36650        R Windows/ARCNet/NetWare      S 1 / LIB Questions Only!  S>ection
36644 [ 1]   3.11 Memory                   S 1 / LIB Questions Only!  <Space>
36645 [ 1]   NASdrv_0.OVL                  S 1 / LIB Questions Only!  K>ill
36649 [ 1]   NFS error                     S 1 / LIB Questions Only!  Help=F3
36656        NE3200 latest drivers         S 1 / LIB Questions Only!  Quit=ESC
             ============ End of Headers ============
```

FIGURE 49.6.

The TAPCIS library file scan screen.

```
NOVLIB Forum, Library 1                              Download

[76004,3646]    Lib: 1
FRELY2.EXE/Bin  Bytes: 330167, Count:   39, 10-Nov-93

    Title   : MPR Plus 2.1 Fram Relay Update
    Keywords: NOVELL NETWARE MPR PLUS 2 1 FRAME RELAY UPDATE

    This update provides the NetWare Link/Frame Relay, IPX RIP/SAP and NetBIOS
    Broadcast filtering and NetWare/Link PPP Data Compression functionalities
    for NetWare MultiProtocol Router Plus 2.1.  This update is packaged in two
    files: FRELAY.EXE and FRELY2.EXE.  You must get both of these files if you
    want to install this update.  This README is the same in both of the files.
    The RIP/SAP/NetBIOS Broadcast filtering and the NetWare/Link PPP Data
    Compression are available separately in the files RIPSAP.EXE and
    PPPCMP.EXE.




NOVLIB.CAT  4/28                        Download=D  Help=F3  Quit=ESC
```

FIGURE 49.7.

The TAPCIS library file download screen.

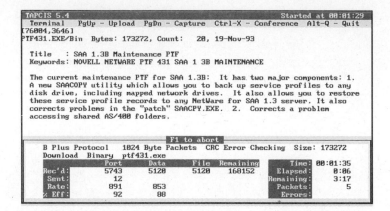

If you have to call long distance, you can program TAPCIS to call CIS when the rate is lower. TAPCIS is highly configurable. For example, you can "turn off" forums that you don't want to visit or just scan messages in particular sections within a forum. Once configured, all functions are single-character commands. For example, to scan for new messages in the "active" forum, type N (see Figure 49.8).

FIGURE 49.8.

TAPCIS Main Menu.

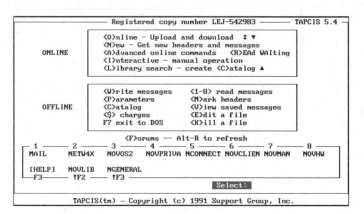

Many utilities are designed to work with TAPCIS to further help with your CIS productivity. I discuss these utilities in the next section. You can download TAPCIS from the TAPCIS forum (GO TAPCIS). It is a $79.00 (U.S.) shareware program.

Message Thread Manager

If you download and follow many message threads, you will need a way to sort and manage them. When appended to TAPCIS message files, new downloaded messages are not sorted into any particular thread order, nor do they age out old discontinued ones. There is no facility within TAPCIS to do any of this, and TACPIS doesn't have the capability to delete a single message. However, there are many add-ons available for TAPCIS, which give it added functionality. Two of the more well-known add-ons are TAPORDER and RECON.

TAPORDER and RECON can consolidate multiple TAPCIS online sessions into a single, properly threaded message collection. They both provide the capability to delete messages from within TAPCIS. They also enable removing and archiving messages/ threads of a specific age.

TAPORDER is free to registered TAPCIS users. RECON is a $36.00 (U.S.) shareware product. Both TAPORDER and RECON can be downloaded from the TAPCIS forum library.

OZCIS

OZCIS combines the functionality of TAPCIS and TAPORDER/RECON into a single program. Not command-based, it utilizes pull-down menus. Full support for the mouse gives you point-and-shoot capability. Previous versions of OZCIS were available as freeware; the new Version 2.0B is a $20.00 (U.S.) shareware package. You can download it from the IBMCOM forum library on CIS. Many new features have been added to this version, including a spell-checker.

Summary

This chapter reviewed some tips and tricks for using CompuServe Information Service and NetWire forums. It also discussed some of the tools that can make your CIS access much more easy and efficient.

Cable Troubleshooting and Certification

by Mark Johnston

50

IN THIS CHAPTER

Cabling problems account for more than 50 percent of all LAN failures and cost organizations thousands of dollars per year in lost productivity, idle resources, and lost revenues. This chapter reviews troubleshooting and certification of cabling systems typically used in NetWare applications. Most NetWare systems are running on twisted-pair or coax, though a small percentage run on fiber-optic cabling. This chapter discusses the cause and treatment of all common cabling problems, explains what's required to certify your cabling, and reviews some installation tips to help you prevent costly network downtime.

Coaxial Cable

Although it's rapidly being eclipsed by its twisted-pair rival, coaxial cabling still enjoys a large installed base and is often a good choice for small networks. Coaxial cable is familiar to most of us because of its cable TV application. Physically, coaxial cable is simple. There are several concentric layers of material surrounding a common axis, that is, the coaxis or coax. Typically, there is a central, solid-core conductor surrounded by a nonconducting material, that is in turn surrounded with a foil and/or braided shield, which is finally covered by an abrasion-resistant jacket.

Coaxial Cable Impairments

Many computer technicians believe that if they have followed their cabling guidelines and have continuity, their cabling is good. This is not the case at all. Access protocols, especially CSMA/CD, rely heavily on the appropriate cabling characteristics for proper operation. Several factors must be correct in order to ensure proper cabling and good performance.

Attenuation

Any electromagnetic signal loses strength as it moves away from its source, and LAN signals over coax are no exception! This signal loss with distance is called *attenuation*. One of the most common problems in coaxial networks is the slow and steady growth of the cabling segment that exceeds the length limitation. For 10BASE-2 Ethernet systems, this is 200 meters. (10BASE-2 means 10 Mbps, baseband, for 200 meters, which was later changed to 185 meters.) If the length is too great, the signal may have too much attenuation and you will experience degraded performance. You measure length with Time Domain Reflectometry (TDR), which is a technical term for cable radar. TDR is conceptualized in Figure 50.1.

FIGURE 50.1.
Time Domain Reflectometry (TDR).

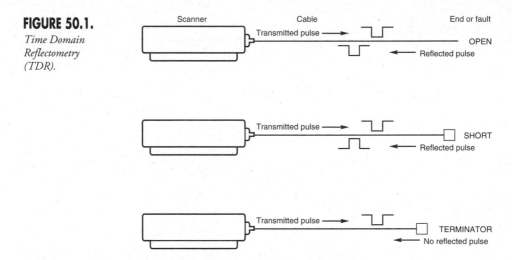

TDRs are built into almost all cable testers today, and they are invaluable tools for measuring cable length, finding cable mismatches, and finding shorts, opens, and breaks. The method is simple. A pulse is sent from the tester down the cable. When the pulse encounters a change in cable impedance (usually an open or short), it is reflected back to the tester. The tester measures the elapsed time and, detecting how fast electrons travel in the cable, calculates and displays the distance to the fault.

Cable Mismatches

Another common problem involves connecting different types of coaxial cable together. Just because the connectors mate does not mean they are suited to work together in a LAN application. It's possible to connect a 50-ohm cable to a 93-ohm cable and achieve continuity, but you will get a major mismatch in impedance. Impedance mismatches are easily found using a TDR.

CAUTION ▶

Check your cable carefully before installation. Thin Ethernet is RG58U (50 ohms). You must not substitute TV coaxial (RG59U) or ARCnet (RG62U). Although you may be able to log in, extensive LAN errors and limited capacity can occur.

Physical Problems

A stretched cable, an intermittent connection, or a cable left in a hostile environment often leads to cable breaks, opens, and shorts. Be especially careful to route cables near workstations in a way that minimizes the risk of accidental cable damage. Again, these types of faults are easily found with a TDR.

Terminators

Terminators for coaxial cables are nothing more than resistors soldered into a can. If they are dropped, it's very easy to break them. Because they are inexpensive, it's a good idea to have spares on hand. Be sure they are the right value (50 ohms for Ethernet).

> **NOTE** ▶
>
> You should check and verify terminator resistance for 50 ohms, especially if you cannot communicate over your cabling. ARCnet and TV terminators look identical and are often not marked.

Twisted-Pair Cable

By far, the most popular type of LAN cabling is Unshielded Twisted-Pair (UTP). Why? It is easy to work with, flexible, low cost, has small diameter, is lightweight, and is simple to connect and terminate. It supports wide-ranging applications including voice, ISDN, Ethernet, Token Ring, Fast Ethernet, FDDI, and even Asynchronous Transfer Mode (ATM).

UTP commonly consists of four pairs of 24 AWG solid or stranded copper wire surrounded by a thin insulating jacket. The most important standards reference for those interested in LAN cabling is the Electronic Industries Association/Telecommunications Industry Association (EIA/TIA) standard 58A. See Table 50.1.

Table 50.1. The EIA/TIA category system.

Category	Description	Typical Application	Classification
Category 1	Intended for basic communications and power-limited circuit cable. There are no performance criteria for this category. Functional equivalent of UL Level 1.	Not rated for any application.	Nondatagrade
Category 2	Low-performance UTP. Typical applications include voice and low-speed data. Not specified in EIA/TIA 568A for data use. Functional equivalent of UL Level or IBM Type 3.	IBM Type 3 Voice/PBX Alarm wiring	Nondatagrade
Category 3	Applies to UTP cables and associated connecting hardware with transmission characteristics up to 16 MHz. Functional equivalent of UL Level 3.	10BASE-T 4 Mbps Token Ring ARCnet 100BASE-VG	Nondatagrade
Category 4	Applies to UTP cables and associated connecting hardware with transmission characteristics up to 20 MHz. Functional equivalent of UL Level 4.	16 Mbps Token Ring low 10BASE-T	Datagrade

continues

Table 50.1. continued

Category	Description	Typical Application	Classification
Category 5	Applies to UTP, ScTP, or STP cables and associated connecting hardware with transmission characteristics up to 100 MHz. Functional equivalent of UL Level 5.	ATM over copper TP-PMD CDDI 100BASE-X	Datagrade

Near End Crosstalk (NEXT)

When current flows in a wire, an electromagnetic field is created that can interfere with signals on adjacent wires. In UTP, two wires are twisted together to form a pair, because this enables opposing fields in the wire pair to cancel each other. The tighter the twist, the more effective the cancellation, and the higher the data rate supported by the cable.

> **WARNING** ▶
>
> Maintaining a tight, consistent wire twist from end to end is the single most important factor in a successful UTP cable installation.

What is the impact of loosely twisted pairs, substandard connectors, and casual termination practices? The signals will experience excessive near end crosstalk. Have you ever experienced a telephone conversation in which you could faintly hear another conversation in the background? That's an example of NEXT, and it's deadly to LAN traffic. In LAN applications, NEXT occurs when the transmitting pair radiates energy, which is coupled into the adjacent receiving pair and is erroneously interpreted as the intended receive signal. The NEXT between two adjacent pairs is shown in Figure 50.2.

FIGURE 50.2.

Near End Crosstalk (NEXT).

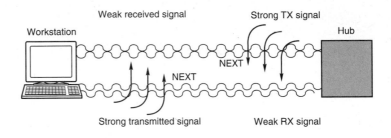

NEXT is measured as the difference between the strength of the transmitted signal and the strength of the crosstalk measured on an adjacent pair. Thus, a large number (such as 50 dB) is preferred over a small number (such as 20 dB).

> **CAUTION** ▷
>
> Be careful when someone says, "High NEXT." Do they mean a high number (which is good), or high amounts of crosstalk (which is bad)? The normal convention is to refer to the amount of crosstalk, so that "low crosstalk" means a good cable.

Note that most UTP has four wire pairs, and because NEXT occurs between all pair combinations, there are six different NEXT measurements required per cable. If you measure only the NEXT on the 12/36 pair, that won't tell you anything about how the cabling will perform for Token Ring applications (which use 36/45) or Fast Ethernet 100BASE-X applications (which use 12/78). The *worst* measurement of the six is the one used to rate the cable. If this sounds complicated, don't worry. Most test tools automate the whole process, making all the measurements, comparing the results to appropriate pass/fail standards, and then giving you a pass or fail result.

Troubleshooting NEXT problems:

Possible Cause of NEXT	Recommendation
Pairs untwisted	Examine cable for loose or untwisted cabling, particularly at connection points.
Use of silkline	Discard and replace with datagrade (untwisted) patch cables.
Split pairs	Ensure logical pairs are twisted together (see "Split Pairs" in Figure 50.3.)
Multiple applications in common sheath	Never run voice and data applications in the same sheath.

Attenuation

As discussed earlier, attenuation is a measurement of the loss of power of a LAN signal. Every six dB doubles the power. Thus, -10dB is four times the power of -22 dB, because it is 12 dB stronger.

Troubleshooting attenuation problems:

Possible Cause of Excess Attenuation	*Recommendation*
Excessive length	Check with TDR; add repeater or change to a higher grade of cable if necessary.
Inadequate grade of cable	Replace cable with higher grade (Category 5 recommended).
Nontwisted patch cable	Replace with twisted-pair cable.
Poor punch block connections	Check and reconnect if necessary.
Poor jack connections	Verify conductors are seated properly and check for tight wire twists right up to point of termination.
High-temperature environment	Attenuation increases with temperature. If cable is subject to extreme heat (>40 C), this can severely impact performance. Remove or shield from heat source.

Connector/Wiring Issues
Crossed Pairs

Crossed pairs constitute a typical installation problem and are easily detected with a cable tester that includes a wire map function. (Refer to Figure 50.3.) In this example, pins 1 and 2 have been crossed, which results in the inability to communicate.

FIGURE 50.3.

Crossed pairs (12 crossed) and Split Pairs (12/36).

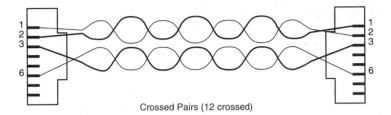

Crossed Pairs (12 crossed)

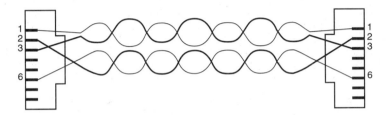

Split Pairs (12/36 split)

Split Pairs

Although crossed pairs are relatively easy to find, split pairs are a bit trickier. Split pairs occur when physical continuity is maintained but wires from logical pairs are split up. (Refer to Figure 50.4.) This error is much tougher to isolate because there is still a pin-to-pin correspondence. A wire map test would show no problem. However, with split pairs, all the benefits of twisting are lost and Category 5 cables degrade to Category 2 performance very quickly. Split-paired cabling may support 10BASE-T for short distances, but the additional NEXT that is induced will severely limit high-speed communications.

Split pairs are best found by measuring Near End Crosstalk. If you are using datagrade components and get a NEXT result of less than 22 dB, suspect split pairs.

Connector Problems

All modular 8-jacks are not the same. Careful inspection will reveal there are two main types: those designed to work with solid-core UTP and those designed to work with stranded UTP. (Refer to Figure 50.4.) In the solid-core design, the blade in the pin connection is split into two tines, which firmly grasp the solid wire. In the stranded-wire design, the blade is designed to pierce the strand. If you attach the wrong type of connector to your cabling, you are likely to get an intermittent connection.

FIGURE 50.4.

Solid-core versus stranded modular 8-jacks.

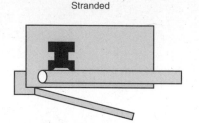

Stranded

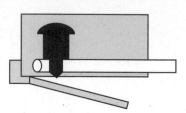

Solid

Termination Practices

Physical continuity does not guarantee high-speed performance. Using old style telephone wire installation techniques with datagrade cabling and components will give you telephony-quality performance. For example, in voice applications, it's okay to strip off 3 inches of insulation, pull the wires apart for easy access, and then connect them to the punch block or wall plate. Such techniques will clobber an intended Category 5 installation.

> **NOTE** ▶
>
> EIA/TIA 568A requires all terminations to have no more than 13mm (0.5 inches) of untwisted wire at *any* location on the LAN.

UTP Installation Tips

You will save yourself future LAN downtime if you use the following UTP installation guidelines:

- ■ Buy the best UTP you can afford.
- ■ Buy termination equipment (modular 8-jacks, punch blocks, and so on) that meet or exceed the quality of your cable.
- ■ Label cable ends.
- ■ Do not mix up modular 8-jacks designed to work with stranded UTP with those designed for solid-core UTP.
- ■ Always maintain the wire twist for all pairs up to the point of termination (within 13mm for Category 5 installations).
- ■ Never share voice and data applications in the same cable.

- Always terminate voice and data cables into different punch blocks or racks.
- Strive to minimize the number of connections between the NIC and LAN devices.
- Use a minimum bend radius of 10 times the cable diameter.
- Tie and dress cables neatly.
- Never use bridged taps (multiple appearances of the same cable pair at several distribution points).
- Allow at least one square foot of closet floor space for every 250 square feet of usable floor space.
- Allow for sufficient cooling and airflow in the wire closet.
- Put a lock on the wire closet and use it.
- On multi-floor installations, locate the wiring closet where there is common vertical access, preferably in a location less than 100 meters (328 feet) from the farthest user connection. The location is often near the center of the floor, which helps ensure cable distances don't exceed the maximum. AT&T research has shown that 99 percent of the time, user stations are located 93 meters or less from a wiring closet.
- Install sufficient power outlets for future unanticipated equipment.
- Be sure you have permission to work in the wiring closet. In some buildings, the owners of the closet are not the tenants.
- Do not use old type 66 blocks (which exhibit high-frequency attenuation and poor NEXT). Use them only for voice applications.
- Do not use screw-type terminations. Use clip or barrel IDC (insulation displacement contact) connections, such as those used in type 110 blocks.
- Pay careful attention to termination practices. Maintain a tight wire twist up to the point of termination at punch blocks, wire plates, and connectors.
- Check building and fire codes and follow them.
- Avoid routing cables near EMI noise sources, such as motors and AC power lines.
- Use the same cable throughout. Avoid mixing up cabling from different manufacturers in the same application.
- Keep patch cables as short as possible, and choose Category 5 patch cable if possible.

■ Do not use silkline (untwisted) or flat-ribbon patch cables, especially from the wall plate to the NIC.

■ Insist the installation be tested with equipment that meets or exceeds the requirements for the installation, and get a certification report for each cable. A toner or DMM is insufficient. Such tools tell you nothing about the cable's capability to reliably transfer high-speed data.

Fiber-Optic Cable

Fiber-optic cabling has a far lower incidence of trouble than copper cabling, principally because it is usually found only on the backbone, or in well-protected areas. Fiber-optic troubleshooting is done with either a power meter, which measures attenuation, or an Optical TDR, which measures distance and finds faults. Aside from catastrophic failures (such as those caused by your friendly neighborhood backhoe), most fiber-optic problems are caused by poor quality splices and connections, which can be found using a power meter.

Cable Certification

Cable certification is required when you need to be sure that the cable you intend to use will work for the intended application. Cable can be certified in either a Category classification (for example, Category 3) or for a specific LAN application (for example, 10BASE-T). To perform cable certification, a test tool runs a prescribed series of tests, stores the results, compares each result to its particular pass/fail parameter for that measurement, and then provides an overall pass/fail.

Cable certification tools are actually the best cable troubleshooting tools because they take all the effort and analysis out of the test. When you run one test, the tester determines whether the cable is OK for the application; or it tells you specifically why it failed. Such tools eliminate the guesswork of which test to run or how to interpret the results.

Cable Troubleshooting Tools

Cable troubleshooting tools fall into three broad classes with increasing price and capability: continuity testers, troubleshooting tools, and certification devices.

Continuity Testers

The simplest cable troubleshooting tools are toners and continuity checkers. These are generally less than $200 and verify end-to-end connectivity, continuity, and can check for crossed pairs. Common manufacturers are Paladin, Progressive Electronics, and the Siemon Company. Continuity checkers are useful tools, but are usually insufficient to diagnose problems on LANs. They are available from the catalog supply companies. Probably the most popular tool in this class is the ubiquitous toner from Progressive Electronics.

Troubleshooting Tools

This class of tools includes the functionality of the previous group, but adds TDR, attenuation and NEXT measurement, and the intelligence to interpret most results. Prices range from around $700 to $2500, but compared to the cost of LAN downtime, they are a bargain. They are generally easy-to-use, lightweight, and portable. Common manufacturers include Microtest, Fluke, and Wavetek. These products are generally available from VARs and large networking product distributors. The Microtest MT350 is a good choice in this class of tools.

> **WARNING**
>
> Because cable faults account for more than 50 percent of all LAN failures, a cable troubleshooting or certification tool is an essential first line of defense for any LAN greater than 25 nodes. Continuity testers tell you nothing about the cable's capability to successfully transmit *high-speed* data. Many users are surprised to find cable scanners often pay for themselves within their first 30 days.

Certification Tools

Certification tools include the functionality of the previous group, but add the additional measurements and extended range needed to completely certify LANs or cables. Prices range from $2500 to $5000. These tools are available from the same sorts of suppliers as the previous group. Manufacturers include Microtest and Hewlett Packard. The best certification tool on the market is the Microtest PentaScanner (Figure 50.5). It is capable of full Category 1-5 certification and LAN monitoring, and includes all the troubleshooting tests needed for Ethernet, Token Ring, Fast Ethernet, ARCnet, CDDI, and many other types of LANs.

FIGURE 50.5.
*The Microtest
PentaScanner.*

General Troubleshooting Procedures, Tips, and Suggestions

by Rick Sant'Angelo

51

Troubleshooting seems to be a "black art" to many, but is actually a science anybody can learn. It seems to be a black art only because users lack the knowledge to understand the mechanics involved. When you understand the mechanics of the product and its components, you are equipped to solve problems. Without this understanding, you resort to chance to solve problems. You continue to blindly try different solutions until problems disappear.

That is why this book contains detailed information about how NetWare and hardware work. You need to know about all the software, protocol, and hardware layers involved to be a good troubleshooter. When you encounter a problem, be sure you understand the mechanics of each layer involved. Find sections of this book that pertain to a problem so you can understand how it is supposed to work, and then analyze why it is not working.

Some people seem to have innate troubleshooting skills. For many, such skills are associated with good work habits and skills, so troubleshooting becomes second nature. For others, a concerted effort is needed to learn these skills. If you watch a good troubleshooter, you notice a few traits:

Good observation skills. In order to resolve a problem, you must observe the problem. Observation is an important skill that helps you detect subtle clues and symptoms.

Good concentration and the ability to focus. Concentration makes observation possible. Without it, you miss the more subtle messages and symptoms that occur. A good troubleshooter finds a quiet environment in which he or she can concentrate and focus on the problems, causes, and potential solutions.

Clear logical thinking. Logical thinking is essential to solve problems. Without logic, the connection between problems, symptoms, and solutions is not clear. You must make the connection between the problem and its resolution—and that requires logical problem solving.

Good hardware knowledge. Hardware knowledge is important because software and hardware work together. Networking hardware and software are intimately linked. When a networking software problem occurs, it is most often caused by a hardware problem. Determining why a hardware-based problem occurs requires good hardware skills. Without these skills, your job is harder.

Commitment to follow through regardless of time and effort. Commitment to follow through on a problem (not just to a solution) and verifying the problem is critically important. Many problems, some of which are simple in nature, require extensive time and effort to resolve. People who give up easily rarely get close to solutions. Those who have dogged determination are the ones who fix the problems. Quite often, solutions simply require many attempts at trying various solutions. Though more successful experience and knowledge may make solutions easier to find, diligent effort also is required. It will normally pull anyone through the maze of potential solutions.

> **TIP** ▶
>
> The most important aspect of troubleshooting is the commitment to follow through. If you are the type of person who gives up or takes a break after a few inconclusive steps, you might rarely resolve anything except the simplest of problems.
>
> If you can keep trying, you eventually find a solution. Ask anyone who runs a large network. They periodically find themselves at work after hours attempting to find solutions. With enough experience, the extra hours are typically reduced, but never eliminated.

Computers are not moody, although they seem to be at times. They are electromechanical devices that simply follow instructions. Software provides the instructions, which may be extremely complex and depend upon many variables, but the instructions are explicit. Artificial intelligence has not been applied to networking software or operating systems. So unless your system is haunted, it does what it is supposed to do — and malfunctions according to cause and effect circumstances. In other words, your network functions the way it is supposed to unless one or more things goes wrong. If you can find out what is wrong, you can fix it.

> **NOTE** ▶
>
> The most difficult problem to troubleshoot is a problem that occurs infrequently. Intermittent malfunctions cause your system to act less consistently than usual. To solve a problem, you must be able to observe and hopefully re-create the problem on demand.

Troubleshooting Methodology

To find and solve problems, you must establish a troubleshooting procedure that works for you. Basic methodology requires

- ■ Establishing work rules
- ■ Categorization
- ■ Isolation of the problem
- ■ Making changes that work around or solve the problem
- ■ Documentation of your steps
- ■ Verification of the problem and quality control

Establishing Rules

You should establish rules for yourself, perhaps even in writing, and refer to them whenever starting a troubleshooting session. In a troubleshooting session, you need to proceed with direct and positive action. You must stay on task. This requires a plan and some guidelines that keep you on task. Here are some rules that experienced troubleshooters live by:

1. Look for the obvious.

   Though it seems silly when technical support people ask us an elementary question, it is also the most effective place to start. Likewise, you should first look at the most obvious and simple potential causes before proceeding to more complex issues.

   Before you begin troubleshooting, take a moment to assess the situation. Examine the most simple and common components before concentrating on the area you suspect may be the problem. It is human nature to skip this step and proceed directly to your "hunch," but a little general fact-finding can save hours of wasted time.

   Ask questions, but ignore superstitions. For example, when something is not working, the first question to ask is, "Did it work before?" If the answer is yes, then ask, "What changed?" In order for something to work consistently, and then quit, some factor must have caused the stoppage. It may be a component failure, or some other change.

2. Look for the most common problems first.

   A relatively small number of factors cause a vast majority of problems. In many cases, a single problem can cause a variety of symptoms. By looking for the most common problems first, your success rate will be better.

For example, more than half of all network problems are related to cabling. The most common cabling problem is a damaged connection. When a connectivity problem occurs, the connector on the workstation is the most likely place to find the problem. Why not start there?

3. Observe the error and attempt to re-create it.

If you can re-create an error on demand, you can solve it. A hardware failure or configuration change that results in a consistent condition can be traced. By observing the problem, and re-creating it under differing conditions, you have an opportunity to see various symptoms or errors. With every variation of an error or symptom, your trail is more clearly defined.

If you cannot re-create the error on demand, it may not be possible to solve it at all. Intermittent problems are the most difficult to solve. You must often wait until the problem worsens until it can be observed and re-created.

4. Isolate the problem.

Troubleshooting procedure has one basic methodology: isolation. Isolating a problem and finding the problem are one in the same.

Isolating a problem is easy. You must re-create the error, change one variable, and attempt to re-create the error again. This often causes a variation of the symptom or another related error to occur. Each variation usually casts additional light upon the nature of the problem. As with geometry, this method leads you more directly to the cause.

You should change only one variable at a time. When you change two or more variables and the problem is solved, you remain uncertain about exactly what caused the problem. Without a certain solution, the problem can recur or similar problems can crop up, and you will know less about how to resolve them.

Your skill as troubleshooter improves every time you solve a problem—but only if you are absolutely certain about the cause. This certainty produces a solid foundation for solving similar problems. Guessing does not produce the same level of confidence and skill.

5. Avoid superstitions.

Many problems are not easily traced. Users and troubleshooters always attempt to associate the problem with other conditions that may have caused it. With little knowledge of the mechanics involved, this can become a game of chasing ghosts. Users often state their conclusions instead of giving facts about exactly what is wrong. You can spend hours following leads provided by others. Interview users, but be sure to isolate facts from opinions.

Categorizing

When observing a problem, various hints often provide you with clues about whether the problem is related to hardware, software, or operating system environment (drivers, configuration files, NetWare rights, drive mappings, and so on).

You should narrow your scope to one of these three areas. When you first observe a problem, it may seem that the potential number of causes is overwhelming. The only possible way to handle most problems is to limit your initial path of investigation until you have found the problem or eliminated this path.

Each of these three basic areas have several divisions beneath them. When limiting your scope, investigate each division and limit your search to that division. For example, a hardware error can be limited to LAN hardware, the server, or the workstation. The workstation is divided into memory, disk subsystem, and interface cards. Each step down this tree can either lead you closer to the solution, or help you determine that you are searching the wrong path. Figure 51.1 shows a tree structure of troubleshooting paths that you may use. Alter this to fit your personal style.

FIGURE 51.1.

A troubleshooting tree.

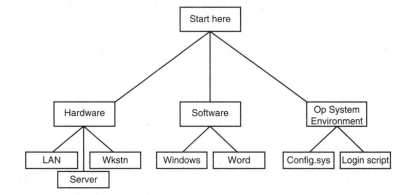

Documenting Your Work

It is essential to document your troubleshooting work. While working to isolate a problem, you may question whether you changed a particular variable, and what the outcome of that change was. When seeking technical support, you are asked to try variations that you may have already attempted. To be absolutely certain about your previous troubleshooting attempts—and the results of those attempts—refer to your documentation. It also helps you efficiently return to the point where you can resume your search.

Verification

After solving a problem, verify the exact cause and the solution. If you fixed something by changing two variables, you are not really certain of the exact cause. Your degree of certainty causes you to develop more knowledge and skill in troubleshooting. Also, by gaining a degree of certainty, you can confidently solve similar problems when facing them in the future.

For example, if you have eliminated two TSRs from an AUTOEXEC.BAT and solved a problem, you cannot be certain whether one, the other, or the combination of both TSRs caused the problem. You need to identify every problem's cause.

Quality Control

After fixing your work, you *must* test your solution to be certain it works properly. This is a step many consultants and administrators skip in the interest of saving time. It cannot be skipped. One of the most common problems users have, after someone has supposedly fixed a glitch, is that the problem recurs or another similar problem crops up. When you make a change, it often causes a ripple of other changes or problems. Be certain the problem is truly resolved.

Summary

Several tips in this chapter provide the framework for troubleshooting. You need to establish a system that works for you, including rules, categorization, process of elimination, modifications, and documenting. Troubleshooting is a science—and perhaps an art—but is not magical. Anyone can learn to be a good troubleshooter—it mainly requires confidence in approaching the problem at hand.

This chapter gave general directions for troubleshooting. The following chapters provide more significant detail on what problems occur most often, how they can be identified, and how they can be solved.

Troubleshooting File Server Disk Drive Problems

by Doug Archell

52

File server downtime can cost hundreds or thousands of dollars in lost business and staff productivity. The faster you can get the server back online, the less money your company will lose. Your file servers' disk subsystems are the most critical part of a server. It is the very heart of your system.

When a disk drive fails, your worst nightmare may come true: All your data may be gone, and you may need to reinstall the file server operating system. A critical part of your job must be to protect this data and to recover as quickly as possible from drive-related problems.

With NetWare, you have the option of providing a level of fault tolerance for the disk drives to protect yourself from these crashes. *Duplexing* and *mirroring* are an important part in the overall fault tolerance of your file server because your disk drives are the most prone to failure.

Although every potential problem cannot be documented in a single chapter, the most common problems are discussed here. These common problems are introduced and discussed by analyzing the error messages you may receive. NetWare's error messages notify you when problems are detected by the file server OS. Error messages differ significantly between 3.11, 3.12, and 4.x versions. Several general errors in 3.11 have been eliminated in favor of far more specific messages, but no discussion of error messages has been provided by Novell as yet. 3.12 and 4.x have been on the market such a short time that error message experience is not available. Therefore, if you are using 3.12 or 4.0, your error-messages may differ slightly from the discussion in this chapter. For a complete listing of 3.12 and 4.x error reports, see your NetWare Messages manual in ElectroText.

Mirroring and Duplexing

NetWare's disk mirroring/duplexing capabilities provide disk-drive dependability even when a drive fails completely. Whenever either drive fails, the mirrored drive continues to operate without any interruption of service. When a new drive is installed, the drives can be remirrored without interrupting service.

When a drive error occurs, a message is displayed on the file server console and should be written to the System Error Log. However, some errors are not written to the System Error Log. Unless you constantly observe the console, error messages are rarely noticed, because they may scroll off-screen before you have an opportunity to read them.

> **CAUTION** ▶
>
> Because NetWare's recovery from mirrored drive loss is usually so flawless, there are times when the drives will be unmirrored and you may not notice. Therefore, you should monitor the mirrored status of drives regularly by using INSTALL.NLM and by checking the System Error Log.

When mirroring is disabled and the situation is not resolved promptly, your system is exposed to downtime. If a critical error occurs on the remaining drive, service will be interrupted. Though you have backups, you may still incur a substantial amount of downtime and loss of productivity.

Mirrored drives do not have to be the same type of drive. All that is required to mirror drives is to configure the logical partition size (after Hot Fix) of both drives in the pair to the same size.

Mirroring/duplexing problems are generally caused by

- Improperly dismounted volumes
- Hard disk failure
- Disk adapter failure
- Defective disk drivers
- Cable problems

Unmirroring Drives Before Removal

There are times when you may need to unmirror your server disks (for instance, when upgrading disks, or when a drive failure is imminent). On occasion, a problem can arise wherein NetWare's automatic switchover to the remaining good drive may not work. The process of unmirroring drives is documented in the Novell manuals, but there are several potential problems that you may need to resolve.

Disk Failure: The Warning Signs

Generally, drives do not fail all at once without warning signs. You should periodically check your server MONITOR screen, under the "Disk Options" menu selection. When you select this option, you will see a list of physical disk drives.

To illustrate the recovery process after drives have been unmirrored, consider file server FS1 as shown in Figure 52.1. FS1 has two hard-drive adapters with one drive attached to each. The first adapter uses the ISADISK.DSK driver, and the second uses DCB.DSK. For increased fault tolerance, the disks have been duplexed.

FIGURE 52.1.

File server FS1.

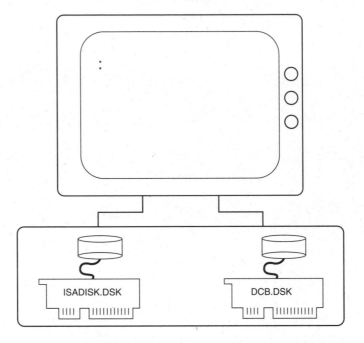

In this example, assume that on several occasions console errors have reported the need to redirect data to Hot Fix. This indicates some type of drive problem, most likely the appearance of many media defects. After examining the Disk Information screen in MONITOR, the Redirected Blocks count has been increasing steadily. At this point, a prudent course of action would be to remove the drive for testing or replacement.

Before physically removing the drive, it should be unmirrored. Using INSTALL.NLM, select Disk Options and then Mirroring from the Installation Options menu. After you select the logical mirrored partition, NetWare displays a window that lists the partitions currently being mirrored. If you select the partition on the second disk drive and press the Del key, the disks will be unmirrored. Figure 52.2 shows the Partition Mirror Status window of INSTALL after the drives have been unmirrored.

FIGURE 52.2.

*Partition Mirroring
Status window.*

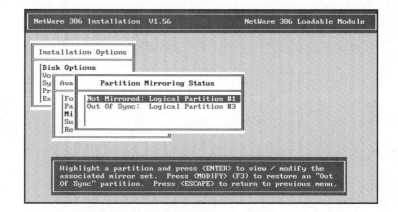

> **CAUTION** ▶
>
> Be careful about which partition that you delete. if you choose the wrong
> one, you may lose all your data on the drive. Once you press the Delete key,
> the drives are unmirrored. You will *not* be asked to confirm this process.

After you disable the drive mirroring, the file server can be brought down and the
primary drive can be removed. If the remaining drive was the secondary drive in a
mirrored pair, you should encounter a console error message similar to the following:

```
There are no accessible disk drives with NetWare Partitions. Check
to see that the needed disk drivers have been loaded and that your
disk drives are properly cabled.
```

There is no need for alarm. The secondary drive is flagged "OUT OF SYNC." To
restore operations, you must reset this drive as the primary drive and mount the SYS:
volume. Follow these steps:

1. Load INSTALL.NLM.
2. Select Disk Options and then Mirroring from the Installation Options
   menu.
3. Highlight the partition marked "OUT OF SYNC" and press F3.
4. A window will pop up stating "There are no accessible disk drives with
   NetWare partitions." You should ignore this message and press Esc.

5. Now comes the crucial part. You are presented with a window titled "Salvage Volume SYS Segment 0," and two options are available: Yes or No. If you want to bring your server back up with this drive as the SYS: volume, select Yes. NetWare will then edit the system drive table to reflect this change.

> **CAUTION** ▶
>
> Answering No will result in NetWare deleting the volume's definition table. This will destroy all the data on the volume, and your only recourse will be to restore from backups.

6. Down the file server and reboot.

Remirroring Drives

In the previous example, drive removal was accomplished with little disruption of service. To carry the example further, assume that the drive was extensively tested and that no problems were found with the drive. You must then assume that the disk adapter, controller, or cabling has caused the reported errors. In this example, the cost of a new disk controller and cables is insignificant in comparison to the threat of downtime, so you should replace all suspect components.

After replacing the disk controller and cable and reinstalling the disk drive, you must reestablish drive mirroring. As the server loads, several warning messages come up on the screen. In many cases, NetWare cannot recover from the errors and will report the following:

```
Volume SYS could NOT be mounted; some or all volume segments cannot
be located.
```

If both drives have primary mirror volumes, NetWare cannot determine which has the most recent information. If the drive you are returning to service had no data on it, this problem doesn't occur. You can create a NetWare partition, configure Hot Fix, and select the drive as a secondary drive in a mirrored pair. Assuming the data is intact on both drives and data has been updated on one of them, you need to specify which should be the new primary drive and which should be the new secondary drive in the mirrored pair.

Because the error message notes a problem with the SYS: volume, it is only natural to believe that the SYS: volume may be corrupt. At this point, if you select Volume Options from the Installation Options menu, several messages are posted on-screen related to the SYS: volume and its definition table. You should press Esc until you get to a window that asks "Delete The Invalid Volume Segments?"

At this point, you must answer No. Answering Yes to this question will delete *all* your data. Because there are two primary NetWare SYS: volumes, NetWare classifies them as invalid and deletes volume definition tables on *both* drives. You must re-mirror the drives and reestablish the installed drive as the primary one and the drive you are reintroducing as the secondary. This will enable NetWare to bring the secondary drive into synchronization with the primary drive, without the loss of current data. Obviously, you must be careful not to select the wrong drive as the primary drive, or all your updates will be lost from the time the former primary drive was removed.

To successfully reinstall the drive and establish drive mirroring, there are a few short steps to follow. Before continuing, you must know which drive has the most current data on it. In this example, the DCB drive has the most current data on it because the former primary drive, run by the ISADISK driver, was removed from the server for testing. To get everything back up and running you should do the following:

1. Unload the DCB.DSK driver.
2. Load the ISADISK.DSK driver and mount the SYS volume.
3. Load INSTALL.NLM and select Volume Options from the Installation Options menu.
4. Delete the SYS volume.
5. Load the DCB.DSK driver.
6. Using INSTALL.NLM, reconfigure drive mirroring, selecting the DCB drive as the primary drive and the ISADISK drive as the secondary.
7. Mount the SYS: volume.

You will hear a beep. If you switch to the console, you will see a message indicating that drive synchronization has started and is in progress. The system is fully operational at this point, and drive synchronization occurs as a low priority background activity. Users can log in and work; however, resynchronization slows significantly when user disk requests are serviced. It will take as long as necessary without slowing user file access.

TIP ▶

To check to see how far along the remirror process has gone, you can load the MONITOR.NLM with the -P switch. Select Processor Utilization from the Available Options menu and select the REMIRR process. (See Figure 52.3.)

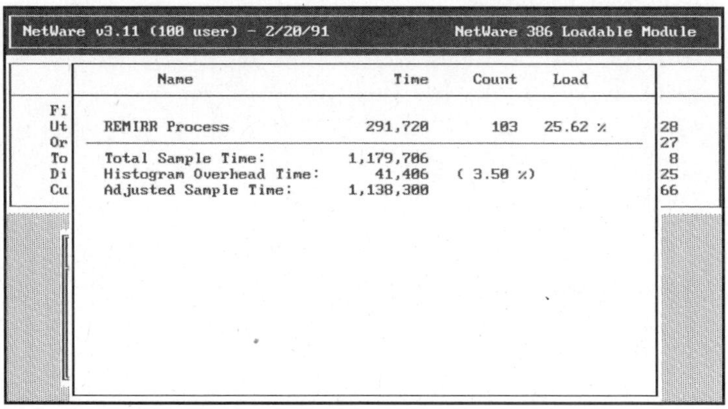

FIGURE 52.3.

*Processor
utilization.*

```
NetWare v3.11 (100 user) - 2/20/91          NetWare 386 Loadable Module

              Name                Time     Count    Load
Fi
Ut    REMIRR Process           291,720      103    25.62 %       28
Or                                                               27
To    Total Sample Time:      1,179,706                           8
Di    Histogram Overhead Time:    41,406   ( 3.50 %)             25
Cu    Adjusted Sample Time:   1,138,300                          66
```

Mirroring IDE Drives

Although mirroring or duplexing disk drives provides an additional level of fault tolerance for your file server, there is an exception to this rule. When using IDE disk drives, you should *not* mirror them.

Each IDE disk drive has an embedded disk controller. When mirroring IDE drives, the secondary drive's controller must be disabled to run as a "slave" to the primary drive. Therefore, when there is a problem with the primary drive, it is highly likely that the secondary drive also will fail. Duplexing can be used effectively with IDE drives but requires a second IDE adapter.

NOTE ▶

IDE adapters that can be used as secondary adapters are difficult to find. No matter what you do, you may not be able to implement duplexing with IDE drives because of the lack of computer BIOS support for this option.

Even if you are able to duplex IDE drives, only one drive will operate at any given time, reducing the split-seek advantage that duplexing normally provides. This option will resolve the problem of both drives going down when one fails.

Resolving Mirroring Problems

When drive mirroring is disabled by the system because of errors, the situation must be resolved as soon as possible. There are several points to consider during the troubleshooting process. Here are some questions you should ask to help locate the source of the failure:

- Does the office suffer from power problems? Loss of power can cause mirroring errors because drives may be momentarily out of sync. When mirroring or duplexing disks, it is imperative that the server is brought down cleanly using the DOWN console command or by selecting Down File Server from the FCONSOLE utility. If the server shuts down abruptly, especially during times of peak utilization, it is likely that both drives' file systems could be severely corrupted. To repair file system corruption, run VREPAIR.

- Do you encounter "Mirror Mismatch..." errors whenever you DOWN your server and reboot? A faulty hard-drive adapter can cause mirroring problems whenever the server is rebooted.

- Do you have the latest "NetWare Certified" disk driver for your disk adapter? Monitor any updates to your disk driver. It is not uncommon to find disk mirroring problems with a driver for some time after it has been released and in wide usage.

- Are your drive cables tightly secured? A loose or damaged cable can result in errors that you cannot distinguish from physical disk-drive failures.

- Are the disk drive adapters firmly seated in their slots? This is one of the most common problems in ISA adapters. EISA and MCA cards fit more securely and rarely have this problem.

- Is your disk adapter working properly? Do not hesitate to replace it. This is one critical component that can have intermittent problems. It will cost you far more than the cost of a new disk adapter to spend time wrestling with intermittent errors that you cannot find.

TIP ▶

You should be monitoring the status of your mirrored drives frequently. Using INSTALL.NLM and selecting Disk Options and then Mirroring, you may press Enter on the logical mirrored partition to check that the partitions are in sync.

Drive Deactivation

One of the most annoying drive problems to troubleshoot can be the infamous "Drive Deactivated" error. Hot Fix will usually handle media defects that are discovered during a read-after-write verification; however, any time drive communications are faulty, the OS will deactivate the drive in order to prevent potential file corruption.

It is essential that the disk driver software and the disk drive be able to communicate fluently. If the drive does not respond to driver commands, several retries will occur. Eventually, the OS will deactivate the drive. You will see the following (or similar) drive deactivation message at the console:

```
Device #0 (20100) ISA type 49 deactivated due to drive failure
```

There are several ways that you can verify that a drive has been deactivated. If the drive containing the SYS: volume goes down, user requests will be interrupted. When this occurs, you will probably find out immediately—because users will let you know in short order.

If the failed drive contains your SYS: volume, errors may scroll off-screen because several specific (or related) errors will be reported in rapid succession. Each drive error related to this type of problem is automatically saved in your System Error Log. The server will continue to function, but volumes on that physical drive will be dismounted automatically. You should check the System Error Log; however, if your SYS volume has been dismounted, this will be impossible, because the System Error Log is located on it.

NOTE ▶

When a drive fails, it is almost inevitable that some file corruption will result before the volume is dismounted. NetWare will therefore dismount volumes where drive problems surface, sometimes before file corruption results.

> Whenever a volume is dismounted by the system, you should check your drive subsystem carefully for intermittent problems.
>
> Volumes can be repaired and remounted using VREPAIR.NLM, as discussed in the following chapter. If your SYS: volume is down, however, you will not be able to run it. It should therefore be copied onto the DOS partition of your server's hard drive.

From the file server console, you can check the status of any drive by using the Disk Information option of MONITOR.NLM. Checking the drive status will inform you whether the drive is active or if it has been deactivated. (See Figure 52.4.) You should also make a point of monitoring the Redirected Blocks. When the number of redirected blocks begins to climb steadily, this generally indicates an imminent drive failure, and it is just a matter of time before the OS deactivates the drive. You should take immediate action when you notice this.

FIGURE 52.4.

Drive status.

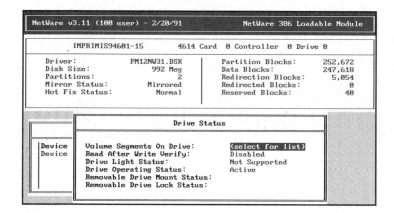

```
NetWare v3.11 (100 user) - 2/20/91          NetWare 386 Loadable Module

         IMPRIMIS94601-15      4614 Card  0 Controller  0 Drive 0

    Driver:            PM12NW31.DSK    Partition Blocks:    252,672
    Disk Size:              992 Meg    Data Blocks:         247,618
    Partitions:                   2    Redirection Blocks:    5,054
    Mirror Status:         Mirrored    Redirected Blocks:         0
    Hot Fix Status:          Normal    Reserved Blocks:          40

                              Drive Status

  Device   Volume Segments On Drive:    (select for list)
  Device   Read After Write Verify:     Disabled
           Drive Light Status:          Not Supported
           Drive Operating Status:      Active
           Removable Drive Mount Status:
           Removable Drive Lock Status:
```

Troubleshooting

Although there are many reasons for drive deactivation, generally these reasons fall into one of the following categories:

- **Physical Configuration.** Ensure that all adapter cards are properly configured and do not conflict with any other devices. Server-based backup systems or other devices (such as CD-ROM drives) can cause drive deactivation. When a conflict is present, it may not show up until the device is activated.

■ **Driver Problem.** There could be a problem with the device driver that you are using. Make it a habit to check if there have been any updates to your disk drivers and why they were updated. You also should ensure that the driver that you are using is "Novell Certified" and will operate properly in conjunction with your adapter.

> **NOTE** ▶
>
> Check with the disk drive developer's technical support personnel immediately upon discovering a problem. Report the exact error messages and conditions. You may have discovered a "known problem" (which is usually only "known" to those that have encountered it). Most developers do not publish reports of "known problems," because such problems would reflect negatively on their products.

■ **Disk Adapter Firmware.** Find the revision number of the BIOS or ROM chip firmware of the disk adapter and the drive itself. Check with the driver developer for "known problems."

■ **SCSI Configuration Errors.** Confirm that all SCSI IDs are set properly. The SCSI adapter should always be set according to vendor instructions. Each physical device attached to the adapter must be uniquely numbered. In most cases, the adapter must be set to 7, and each device must be numbered 0 through 6 sequentially. Terminators must be installed on each end of the cabling, which normally includes the adapter at one end and the last disk drive at the other end. The terminating device may be physically installed, set by a switch, or software-configured. Check the SCSI setup if a utility exists to see that factors such as the SYNC parameter are set to factory recommendations for NetWare.

> **NOTE** ▶
>
> There are several exceptions to this numbering rule. For example, IBM PS/2 systems require the disk adapter to be set to 7, and all attached devices are uniquely numbered sequentially from 6 to 0.

■ **Power Supply.** Make sure that your power supply can handle all of the equipment installed in your server.

■ **Cabling.** Examine the cabling of the SCSI devices to ensure a tight fit and that no cables have been damaged. SCSI cables are subject to electromagnetic interference and should be adequately protected and isolated if problems occur. Good-quality cables should be used, especially for Fast SCSI (SCSI-2). You should immediately replace any cables when signs of damage are evident.

■ **Disk Adapter Seating.** Adapters frequently work themselves loose because of moving, handling, or temperature fluctuation. ISA cards more commonly experience this problem, but this can happen with EISA and MCA adapters also.

■ **Potentially Defective Parts.** If your problem is not resolved after working through the preceding steps, consider replacing the disk adapter and, if problems still occur, the hard drive. Weigh the cost of troubleshooting and downtime against the cost of a new part. It may not be worth the effort or cost to try to salvage a potentially defective part. In many cases, you may find that obscure incompatibility issues or a difficult-to-diagnose problem is inherent in the design of a component. Replacing the part may be a far more direct approach than isolating and resolving the problem through extensive technical-support efforts.

CAUTION ▶

If the adapter is replaced with a different make or model, it may be necessary to reformat your hard drive. Never attempt such replacement without absolute certainty that your backups are up to date!

Examples of "Drive Deactivated..." Problems

Drive deactivations may be troublesome to resolve. You can bet that whatever problem you experience, others have experienced it too. The following are a few more common examples of problems that have been encountered in the field. While this list does not cover every possibility, it does provide some ideas on where to look for problems.

PROBLEM: *Updated ISADISK.DSK causes drive to Deactivate.*
SOLUTION: Some users have had problems after upgrading their ISADISK.DSK driver dated 02-15-92 to the updated driver dated 07-08-92.

The new driver will only attempt to write to the drive three times, whereas the older driver would continue these attempts. If the request is not successful by the third attempt, the drive is deactivated. Should your drive deactivate after upgrading, try going back to the old driver.

PROBLEM: *Using an Adaptec 1542C SCSI adapter, drives are occasionally deactivated when attached to the external port.*
SOLUTION: The problem is caused by using low-quality cables with high-performance drives. Fast SCSI (SCSI-2) especially requires excellent cable quality to function error-free.

PROBLEM: *While using an Adaptec 1510 SCSI adapter under heavy loads, the drive will deactivate.*
SOLUTION: Try setting SYNC=OFF in the load command.

PROBLEM: *Using a Maxtor 7213 IDE drive setup as TYPE 47, the drive would deactivate while running a surface test.*
SOLUTION: In the CMOS setup, try changing the SCRATCH RAM setting from 0:300 to DOS 1K.

PROBLEM: *After installing a second Ethernet card in the file server, one of the internal SCSI drives repeatedly deactivates.*
SOLUTION: Once the user checks the configuration of the server hardware, he or she may notice that the SCSI cable has a bend in it. The possibility exists that the cable was damaged when replacing the cover during the last upgrade.

Miscellaneous Errors

Drive-related problems can be very troublesome. There are so many different possibilities that, at times, it could feel as if all is lost. Luckily, many of these problems can be considered "common"—which means that somebody else has already figured out a way to solve them.

Although there are virtually thousands of different problems, here are a few of the most commons ones and how they can be resolved.

PROBLEM: *A volume is periodically dismounting. There are two drives with one volume on each. From time to time, the second volume dismounts and the drive shuts down.*
SOLUTION: The cabling being used to connect the two drives is faulty. Once the cable is replaced, everything works fine.

PROBLEM: *The user accidentally deletes the SYS: volume partition where critical company data is stored. He attempts to use INSTALL.NLM to recreate the partition and then tries VREPAIR to salvage the data. It still doesn't work.*
SOLUTION: When the partition was first deleted, it may have been possible to salvage data from the volume to a DOS partition using OnTrack's NetUtils. However, once the partition is re-created, a new volume table is established, destroying access to all previously recorded data. At this point, the only alternative is to restore from the most recent backup tape.

PROBLEM: *INSTALL.NLM is used to run a Surface Test on the disks overnight. When the user arrives in the morning, there are no messages on the screen. How does he know that there are no problems with the drive?*
SOLUTION: If a problem is encountered while running the Surface Test, the error will be noted on the console. When there are no errors on the drive, INSTALL does not confirm that everything is okay.

PROBLEM: *Using a Micropolis 1.2 gigabyte drive and DCB.DSK, the user finds that he cannot access the partition.*
SOLUTION: The driver provided by Novell, DCB.DSK, will only recognize partitions that are smaller than 1 gigabyte. If you want to use the DCB.DSK driver, you must change your partition to meet these requirements (that is, a 990M partition).

PROBLEM: *A user wants to implement disk duplexing on his server but is not sure about how to go about it. His current file server is a Compaq Systempro 386/33 with one 650M drive. He wants to duplex this drive with a larger IDA setup that is made up of 4 smaller drives.*
SOLUTION: When duplexing, it is not mandatory for the drives to be the same size, but the NetWare partitions must be the same. If dissimilar drives are used, the second drive must be the larger of the two.
In most situations you cannot duplex or mirror one drive to two or more. There is an exception to this rule when you are using a drive system (i.e Raid) that appears to NetWare as one drive.

PROBLEM: *While performing an upgrade to NetWare 3.12, an error "Partition object not found in partition mapping table" results. The user cannot get the 3.12 installation to access the hard disk.*
SOLUTION: Not all disk drivers written for 3.11 will work on 3.12. Check to see if there is an updated driver available or if your current driver will operate properly on a 3.12 server.

PROBLEM: *While using an IDE drive and ISADISK.DSK, the error "Primary Interrupt Controller Detected a Lost Hardware Interrupt" appears on the console.*
SOLUTION: In some cases, switching from ISADISK.DSK to IDE.DSK will resolve this problem.

PROBLEM: *After checking the "Disk Status" screen in MONITOR.NLM, the user notices the 'Read After Write Verify' setting was configured for 'Hardware Level Verify'. As the server uses a Procomp DCB that can provide R-A-W verifying, should the setting in MONITOR be changed to 'Verify Disabled'?*
SOLUTION: When the server boots, the driver has a default setting for this field. You should leave this setting to its default.

PROBLEM: *A file server is running with three SCSI drives and one volume which spanned across all three drives. The second drive in the chain has died. Can this volume be fixed?*
SOLUTION: Whenever you span a volume over multiple drives, it is recommended that you mirror or duplex these partitions. If a single drive fails without mirroring or duplexing, the entire volume will be lost. The only way to recover would be to restore from a backup tape.

PROBLEM: *When trying to down a file server that uses a Toshiba MK-538 1-gigabyte drive with an Adaptec 1522, the server hangs.*
SOLUTION: There is a potential problem with using the 1522 with a Toshiba drive in the server. Upgrading the adapter to a 1542 should resolve this problem.

PROBLEM: *When rebooting the file server, the system abends with the error "Logical Partition Not Found."*
SOLUTION: There is evidence that the SERVER.EXE file is corrupted. Try deleting the copy on the boot drive and make a fresh copy from the SYSTEM-1 disk.

PROBLEM: *The user is having problems increasing the size of the server's Hot Fix Redirection Area.*
SOLUTION: NetWare will not enable you to have a Hot Fix area larger that 30720 blocks. If 2 percent of your disk drive is greater than 30720 blocks, NetWare will default back to this limit.

NetWare File System Corruption and Repair

53

by Doug Archell and Rick Sant'Angelo

IN THIS CHAPTER

Your file server's physical disk drive has a logical file system that comprises partitioning information, volumes, volume definition tables, Directory Entry Tables (DETs), File Allocation Tables (FATs), and perhaps mirror tables and Name Spaces. All this is in addition to the normal DOS, OS/2, Macintosh, and/or UNIX file listing information. Chapter 3, "Advanced NetWare Operating System Features," contains detailed information about the NetWare Universal File System.

As with any file system, corruption can occur as a result of hardware failure or interruption during update. For example, if a server disk becomes full during the update of a data file, the file will be corrupted unless it is somehow protected. Another common problem is when a disk-write error occurs during an update. The file information may be corrupted or lost. An error in one of the system tables can manifest itself in many different forms, including a volume dismount, server Abend (OS shutdown) software execution errors, or missing data.

Some installations suffer extensive and frequent file corruption, while others never do. Even though intermittent hardware failure may be the essential cause, good networking software protects against file corruption. To protect your files, you can use NetWare's Transaction Tracking System (TTS), or your software may use its own file-protection techniques. For example, Btrieve uses pre-imaging, which is similar to TTS. Unlike TTS, this procedure is performed at the software level. File updates are written to a pre-image file first, and when the transaction is completed, the transactions are added to the original data file. The exposure to damage is therefore limited to the brief period when the update from the pre-image to the original file occurs.

In programming, some programming languages or record managers (such as Btrieve) can identify points in execution where transaction rollback is initialized and then committed. (Other software can suffer file corruption from the most minor hiccups that may occur.) If all software was written this way and had this type of record-management protection, you would hardly ever need to be concerned about file corruption.

This chapter provides some guidelines and troubleshooting tips for resolving various file-system errors that you may encounter. When possible, specific examples are discussed along with their solutions. Using these examples, you may be able to resolve your own problems more quickly—or avoid them entirely.

This chapter discusses the two major utilities available to repair NetWare file-system damage: Novell's VREPAIR and Ontrack's NetUtils. VREPAIR is included with NetWare, whereas NetUtils must be purchased separately. NetUtils performs the same functions as VREPAIR but also does far more. It includes data-recovery utilities. This chapter also discusses how you can scan your disk-drive surfaces for media defects.

Repairing Your File System with VREPAIR

VREPAIR.NLM is a server-based NLM utility provided to correct problems related to a disk's FAT or DET entries and to ensure the integrity of the volume's file system. Just as CHKDSK /F can repair damaged directory listings on a DOS disk, VREPAIR performs the same functionality (and more) for a NetWare file system. It cannot, however, fix the source of the problem.

VREPAIR is essentially the same for 3.x and 4.x versions, except that version 4.01 automatically executes VREPAIR when certain error conditions are detected. It also automatically repairs damaged files (the default has been changed) instead of first asking for permission to do so. This may cause loss of data at times that might otherwise be salvaged.

Though the VREPAIR that was shipped with your distribution diskettes may work fine, several fixes have been made to VREPAIR.NLM since the utility was first introduced. You should check NetWire for the latest version. You can inquire about updated releases of this utility in the NetWire forum for your version (NETW3X or NETW4X forums) in the section named "NetWare Utilities."

When Does VREPAIR Need to Be Run?

VREPAIR is not a maintenance utility—it is a tool for fixing file corruption in NetWare system tables. Most of these tables are protected by TTS, so damage does not occur easily. However, whenever you suspect that you may have file corruption, you should run VREPAIR or NetUtils.

> **TIP** ▶
>
> You can confirm your suspicions about file corruption by using the NetWare server INSTALL.NLM. When you select Volume Options in this utility and access a damaged volume, it often will give more specific error messages indicating the nature of the problem.
>
> If you have problems with a partition table, you can get more specific error messages from this utility when you access Disk Options and examine the partitions.

In many cases, INSTALL.NLM will not only diagnose the problem, but will also repair it after asking for confirmation from you.

You should run VREPAIR under the following circumstances:

■ When a volume will not mount

■ When file-related errors are reported during server boot

■ When file-related errors appear on the console during operation

■ To remove Name Spaces

■ If file-system corruption is suspected

NOTE ▶

You must dismount a volume before running VREPAIR on it. VREPAIR should therefore be installed on your server's DOS partition in case the SYS: volume must be fixed.

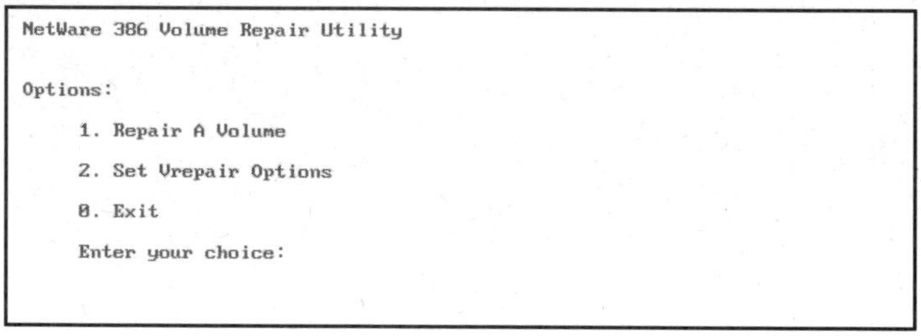

FIGURE 53.1.

*NetWare 3.12
Volume Repair
utility.*

```
NetWare 386 Volume Repair Utility

Options:

    1. Repair A Volume

    2. Set Vrepair Options

    0. Exit

    Enter your choice:
```

When loading VREPAIR, you will be presented with three options (as shown in Figure 53.1): Repair A Volume, Set VREPAIR Options, and Exit. Before starting VREPAIR, you can select Set VREPAIR Options to toggle the following four settings. (See Figure 53.2.)

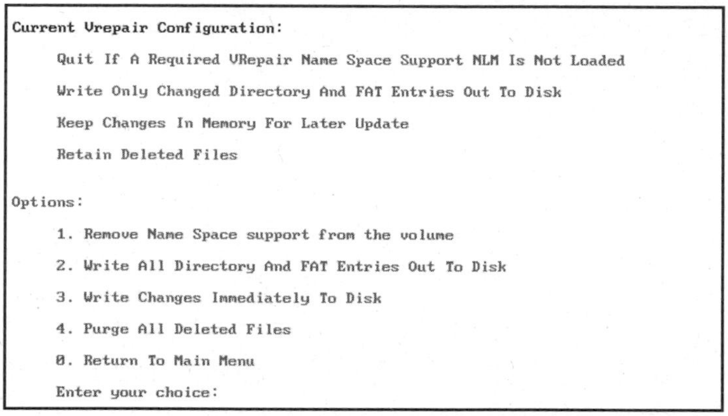

FIGURE 53.2.

Current VREPAIR configuration.

```
Current Vrepair Configuration:

    Quit If A Required VRepair Name Space Support NLM Is Not Loaded

    Write Only Changed Directory And FAT Entries Out To Disk

    Keep Changes In Memory For Later Update

    Retain Deleted Files

Options:

    1. Remove Name Space support from the volume

    2. Write All Directory And FAT Entries Out To Disk

    3. Write Changes Immediately To Disk

    4. Purge All Deleted Files

    0. Return To Main Menu

    Enter your choice:
```

1. **Remove Name Space Support from the Volume.** The default is "Quit If A Required VREPAIR Name Space Support NLM Is Not Loaded." Change this option only if you want to eliminate Macintosh, OS/2, or UNIX file support from the volume to be repaired. You may not run VREPAIR until you unload Name Spaces with a console command.

> **CAUTION** ▶
>
> Changing from the default will result in the loss of all file entries for OS/2, Macintosh, and UNIX files.

2. **Write All Directory and FAT Entries Out To Disk.** The default is "Write Only Changed Directory And FAT Entries Out To Disk." When VREPAIR is run, it stores the FAT and DET tables in memory. The default setting will write only changes that are made because of errors. Changing this setting will cause VREPAIR to completely overwrite all FAT and DET entries with what is stored in memory.

3. **Write Changes Immediately To Disk.** The default is "Keep Changes in Memory for Later Use." Unless you change this option, you will be notified when errors are detected, but the errors will not be corrected until you approve the fix. If your server is running with a minimal amount of memory, you may want to change the default setting, because the server could run out of memory.

4. **Purge All Deleted Files.** The default is "Retain Deleted Files." Changing this setting will force VREPAIR to delete all purged files from the volume.

You will not be able to salvage any files after running VREPAIR if the default is changed.

Once you have set the options as desired, you can execute VREPAIR. The process will begin by checking the FAT blocks. When VREPAIR is running, the following three options may be changed. (These options are accessible by pressing F1.)

1. **Do not pause after each error.** The default is "Pause After Each Error." If left at the default, VREPAIR will pause after every error that is encountered in order to display detailed information on the screen. When you are running VREPAIR on a large drive, this can slow the entire process down. By selecting "Do not pause...," VREPAIR will run automatically.

2. **Log errors to a file.** The default is "Do not log errors to a file." If you would like a record of the errors that occurred for the purposes of analyzing what went wrong, you can log all of the errors to a file on the SYS: volume (if you are *not* repairing SYS:) or a local drive on the server. See Figure 53.3 for an example of an error log.

3. **Stop volume repair.** You may press the number 3 to stop the VREPAIR process.

FIGURE 53.3.

VREPAIR error log.

```
/**********************************************************************/

VRepair error log file for volume SYS

/**********************************************************************/

Error at directory entry 3938
Primary and mirror copies of directory entry disagree

Primary Entry - Deleted DOS file entry
    Name: \BACKOUT.TTS
    This is a hidden file
    Size: 114688

Mirror Entry - Free entry

Corrected Entry - Deleted DOS file entry
    Name: \BACKOUT.TTS
    This is a hidden file
    Size: 114688

/**********************************************************************/
-- More --
```

When VREPAIR is running, there is a series of processes that it goes through. The progress of each task is noted by a string of dots that stretches toward the edge of the screen.

VREPAIR will display the following messages while running tests:

- **Checking FAT blocks.** FATs are mirrored on the disk; there are two copies and they should be identical. The mirrored FATs are checked for differences. Initially, VREPAIR will validate the FAT tables by looking at both FAT blocks and repairing any differences. If VREPAIR finds problems in the first FAT table but not the other, it will repair the first table using information from the second. Upon successful completion, VREPAIR will have a good copy of the FAT table stored in memory.

- **Checking mirror mismatches.** Copies of the Directory Entry Table (DET) are checked for errors and discrepancies. If errors occur, VREPAIR attempts to repair them using the same process that was used for the FAT table.

NOTE ▶

VREPAIR leaves you no option except to copy the first FAT and the first DET entries to the alternate mirrored copy whenever errors are detected. NetUtils enables you to select which FAT or DET to use, and therefore which to overwrite when a mismatch is detected. This feature enables you to save data when it would otherwise be lost.

- **Checking directory entries.** Directory listings stored in the DET are checked to ensure that they are valid. Invalid entries that cannot be fixed are freed for later use.

- **Checking file entries.** VREPAIR checks the DET again to ensure that any file listings (other than directory listings) are valid. This check is done by running a mirror mismatch check on the FAT chains for all files on the volume being repaired.

- **Checking trustee entries.** VREPAIR checks trustee-related entries for the files. The first eight trustee assignments are stored in the file entry. If more trustee assignments are required, a tnode structure is created. A tnode is an additional file listing that contains a pointer to the original file entry.

- **Checking deleted entries.** At this stage, VREPAIR does not use the DET to examine deleted files but rather confirms that the pointers assigned to a deleted file, the file name, trustee entries, and name space are all valid. When files are deleted on NetWare, they are placed in a deleted file listing. Using this listing, NetWare is able to recover these files using the SALVAGE utility. The file entries for these files are moved into a delete file or directory block that only contains deleted files. Finally, a pointer is used by the deleted file blocks to tell NetWare what directory the file originally came from.

■ **Checking Invalid Entries.** An invalid entry occurs when the link between a DOS entry pointer and the corresponding Name Space entry is not valid. VREPAIR attempts to repair these links, but if they are not corrected by this pass, the entry is altered so it will only be accessible to DOS.

■ **Checking Free Blocks.** Sometimes there can be a minor problem in the FAT or DET where these tables list a block entry and nothing exists in the block any more. VREPAIR will ensure that these blocks are marked as being free so they can be reused.

When VREPAIR Finishes

When VREPAIR is complete, and if "Write Repairs to Disk Later" was set (default value), you will be asked whether to write these changes to disk. At this stage, you must answer "Yes" or the errors found will not be corrected.

> **CAUTION** ▶
>
> When file damage is found, you should carefully consider your actions before fixing it. If the data is still accessible, you should retrieve all data possible before attempting to repair it. In many cases the repair will completely eliminate the possibility of access to the file.

At the top of the screen, VREPAIR shows a running total of the errors that have been encountered. When you run VREPAIR and it finds errors, *do not* reboot your system. After writing the changes to disk, select Run VREPAIR from the "NetWare 386 Volume Repair Utility" menu again. When file system errors are fixed, it may leave lost clusters behind or empty FAT/DET entries that will subsequently need to be cleaned up. Figure 53.4 shows the display after VREPAIR has completed.

> **NOTE** ▶
>
> Whenever errors are found, fix them and run VREPAIR again. Continue this process until no more errors are found.

FIGURE 53.4.

VREPAIR screen shown upon completion.

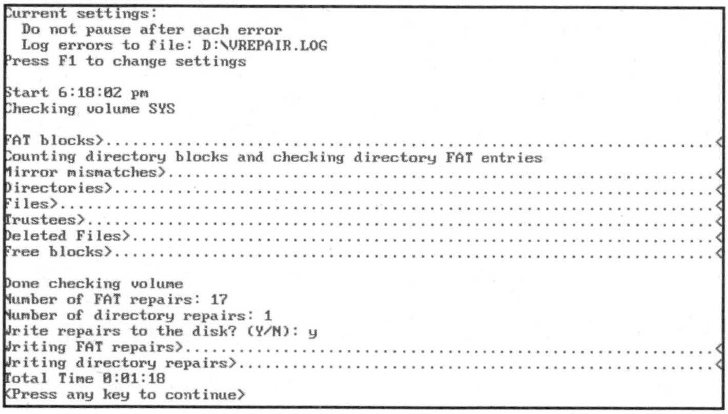

```
Current settings:
  Do not pause after each error
  Log errors to file: D:\VREPAIR.LOG
Press F1 to change settings

Start 6:18:02 pm
Checking volume SYS

FAT blocks>...............................................................<
Counting directory blocks and checking directory FAT entries
Mirror mismatches>........................................................<
Directories>..............................................................<
Files>....................................................................<
Trustees>.................................................................<
Deleted Files>............................................................<
Free blocks>..............................................................<

Done checking volume
Number of FAT repairs: 17
Number of directory repairs: 1
Write repairs to the disk? (Y/N): y
Writing FAT repairs>......................................................<
Writing directory repairs>................................................<
Total Time 0:01:18
<Press any key to continue>
```

How Effective is VREPAIR?

Although VREPAIR is usually very reliable, there are times when the damage is beyond VREPAIR's capabilities. During a repair pass, there are several areas where VREPAIR may find errors that it cannot correct. The following limitations of VREPAIR pertain to the same tests that were previously discussed:

- **Checking FAT Blocks.** If the damage to the FAT is so severe that VREPAIR cannot repair it, the operation will stop and give you an error similar to "Volume Repair was not Possible." If the damage cannot be ignored, your only alternative is to repartition and rebuild your server using the most recent backup tape.

CAUTION

When restoring backups, you may need to find an older backup copy that also did not contain the damaged file entries. In some cases, you will have to restore older backups in their entirety, and then restore undamaged files only from a more recent backup.

When file corruption is suspected, it behooves you to repair it as soon as possible for this reason.

- **Checking Mirror Mismatches.** In some instances, VREPAIR will not be able to fix a file link. If this occurs, affected files will have to be restored from a backup tape from a period prior to the file damage.

■ **Checking File Entries.** Errors in this pass could result in the truncation of a file. As such, affected files will have to be restored from a backup tape.

■ **Checking Deleted Entries.** If VREPAIR cannot confirm these entries, the deleted directory block is freed. These files will not be available to salvage.

Examples of Problems Encountered with VREPAIR.NLM

At times, you may receive errors when attempting to load VREPAIR.NLM. In most cases, these problems are easily resolved. Following are a few examples of problems you may encounter.

PROBLEM: *VREPAIR was used to remove Macintosh Name Space support. Later, it was added back to the same volume. Now Mac users are having difficulty accessing their files.*

SOLUTION: When VREPAIR is used to remove Name Space support, the Macintosh attributes are deleted. The only way to recover these attributes is through a tape restore.

> **NOTE** ▶
>
> In order to successfully restore from tape, your backup system must be designed to properly backup and restore Macintosh files.

PROBLEM: *When you try to load V_MAC.NLM, you get the error "Loader cannot find Public Symbol..."*

SOLUTION: To run VREPAIR on a volume with Macintosh Name Space, you must load VREPAIR first. Once VREPAIR is loaded, press Alt+Esc back to the system console. Then load V_MAC.NLM and press Alt+Esc to return to the VREPAIR menu.

PROBLEM: *When using IDE.DSK and running VREPAIR, an error "Could Not Read Bad Block" occurred and the volume would not mount.*

SOLUTION: Try using ISADISK.DSK with the /B and /L switches and then rerun VREPAIR.

PROBLEM: *The user was getting "Mirror Copies Of The FAT Do Not Match" errors and tried to run VREPAIR from the C: drive. The server then abended with a "GPPE: Running Process VREPAIR."*

SOLUTION: Try using ISADISK.DSK with the /B switch and rerun VREPAIR.

PROBLEM: *When booting the server, an error "Invalid Deleted Name Space" occurred while an NFS Name Space volume was loading.*
SOLUTION: The NFS Name Space volume is corrupted. Dismount the volume and run VREPAIR.

Repairing Your File System with NetUtils

Ontrack Computer Systems has developed NetUtils, a product that does everything that VREPAIR does and much more. Ontrack is a very proficient purveyor of data recovery services and for many years has provided the disk initialization software that is shipped with Seagate drives (Disk Manager).

NetUtils3

This product is a collection of three utilities, as follows:

- **NetScan**, which does what VREPAIR does, but gives clearer and more specific information and control over the process. It also includes surface scan functionality with control over how the scan is conducted.

- **NetDisk**, a sector-by-sector editor to search the disk for data, including files, specific data, and location of files or specific data.

- **NetFile**, which is used to see all files and directories on the disk, even if the server OS is not up and running. This utility can be used to recover data that is not otherwise available, copy files to a DOS device, edit files on the disk, rename and/or delete files. All this is done with a simple-to-use and clear presentation format similar to many other file-management utilities that are used for DOS.

NetUtils3 reports much information about your drives that can be valuable to you. When the utility is executed, a drive-selection screen offers comprehensive information on your disk drives, as shown in Figure 53.5. In this example, the server has four disk drives; you can select one, and its drive geometry is revealed. Most other products are specific to a particular line of drives. This is about the only general-purpose utility that can read and discover the geometry of almost any drive.

FIGURE 53.5.

*NetUtils3's drive
selection screen.*

This utility also will check for mirror consistency between mirrored/duplexed drives. The utilities can work on drives when they are mirrored and in sync or out of sync. It reports the mirror status of drive pairs, the sync status of drives, and other situations. If you have volumes that are spanned across multiple disk drives, it reports the status of the spanned volume and its volume segments.

NetDisk

This utility enables you to examine the physical structure of the file system and your disks. It is a sector-by-sector editor that gives complete information on a drive, its partitioning, and descriptor tables. It enables you to view sectors on the drive in hex format and can search the disk for hex or ASCII data and/or files. You can print data out, or copy files or sectors to another DOS device.

NetFile

This utility enables you to view the file system logically. It first checks the drive descriptor tables for

- Partitioning
- Volumes
- Hot Fix

Figure 53.6 shows information about all these items for the disk drive that was selected. These descriptor tables can become damaged, and though INSTALL can look at them and perhaps attempt to fix them, you will not know what went wrong or what got fixed most of the time. NetFile tells you exactly what your descriptor tables say and reports any errors that can be found.

FIGURE 53.6.

NetUtils3's NetFile drive descriptor analysis.

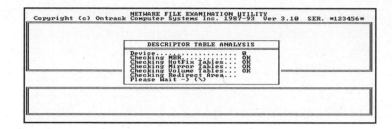

Once you select a volume on the disk to examine, this utility displays directory and file information that resides on this disk, as shown in Figure 53.7. This utility enables you to do the following:

- Navigate and view the directories and files
- Search for files
- Sort files by several parameters, such as file size, date, or extension
- Show the file data in hex and ASCII
- Modify the file data in hex and ASCII
- Copy files to floppy or local hard drive
- Rename files
- Delete files
- Change file attributes
- Print out records

FIGURE 53.7.

NetFile examining the directories in a volume.

NetScan

NetScan is similar in functionality to VREPAIR, but it goes much further in readability and control. It is a utility designed to test and repair corrupt file structures in a NetWare 3.x volume.

When all of the volume structures are valid, the Alt+F1 through Alt+F4 tests will nondestructively scan the disk surfaces for errors. Upon execution, NetScan polls the disk and reports each drive's model description and drive geometry.

You can select from the list of disk drives, and you can examine that drive's descriptor tables, testing and reporting error conditions in Hot Fix, mirroring tables, and volume tables.

After the drive descriptor tables are examined, a volume list is displayed. After selecting a volume, a file-integrity test is run much in the same way that VREPAIR does. The volume statistics are displayed, as shown in Figure 53.8.

FIGURE 53.8.

NetScan's Volume Information screen.

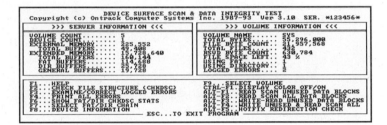

Help is displayed, indicating your various options for running some or all of the volume tests, along with media-scanning options.

When the utility is scanning drive-media surfaces, statistics and conditions of disk errors are discovered are reported in a clear, understandable manner, as shown in Figure 53.9.

FIGURE 53.9.

NetScan's Surface Scan.

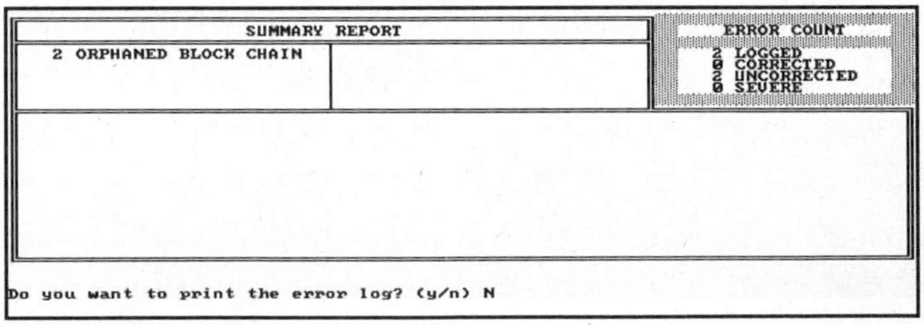

When mirror mismatches are found between DETs or FATs, NetScan's algorithms calculate which table is most likely to be correct. It informs you of the best choice and gives you the option to override it. VREPAIR copies only the primary table to the secondary, so chances of a mirror mismatch ending up in an unusable file are reduced.

The manual is well-written and gives complete descriptions of over 100 error reports. It gives examples and shows typical error conditions for the most common NetWare problems. Another section shows how to interpret the screens and gives suggestions for the probable causes and solutions.

The technical support staff is highly proficient and responsive. This alone is worth the cost of the software.

Ontrack Data Recovery for NetWare (ODRN)

A new version of NetUtils is available for all versions of NetWare. It enables the file system and disk drives to be probed while the OS is up and running. It functions as an NLM and can access disks and volumes that NetWare cannot.

This product gives you all the control and intelligent choices that NetUtils3 gives. In contrast, NetWare 4.x's VREPAIR.NLM automatically executes itself when a volume goes down and attempts to repair any damage found. In some cases, repairing the file results in irretrievable data loss. ODRN provides options enabling you to salvage data, whereas VREPAIR does not.

Ontrack Data Recovery Service

Ontrack is one of the most experienced companies in the field of disk-drive technology. Its data-recovery service can often retrieve data from drives that are no longer functional under normal use. If the data can possibly be recovered, Ontrack will recover it.

Scanning Disk Media Surfaces with NetWare INSTALL.NLM

Media defects are a significant source of file corruption. NetWare read-after-write verification checks at the time the file is written that no media defect causes file corruption. Though your disk was tested prior to or during installation and read-after-write verification tested each file block at the time it was written, it is possible that a media defect escaped detection or occurred after the data was written. This problem then manifests itself as a corrupted file or FAT entry.

It is a good policy to scan the surfaces of your disk drives for weak or bad sectors, especially if periodic file corruption occurs and no cause is found. Your

INSTALL.NLM's Disk Options selection has a function to scan the disk surface. You also can use NetUtil's NetScan utility to perform a nondestructive surface scan.

> **NOTE** ▶
>
> If errors are discovered, scan the surface again. It is standard practice to scan a surface two times without errors.

INSTALL.NLM's Surface Scan

This utility can perform a destructive or a nondestructive surface scan. A destructive scan is more comprehensive, but it destroys data. You should not perform a destructive surface scan unless you intentionally plan to wipe out all the data on your drive.

> **CAUTION** ▶
>
> When you run INSTALL's Surface Test option, you should be careful to avoid inadvertently running a destructive test. The menus are not laid out well for using this option. You should try it out and be very careful. A fully destructive test is only one keystroke away from a nondestructive test.

To run a nondestructive test, follow these steps:

1. Load INSTALL.NLM.
2. Dismount the volume(s) that you want to scan.
3. From the INSTALL Disk Options menu, select Surface Test. You will see the screen shown in Figure 53.10.

> **NOTE** ▶
>
> You will be reluctant to select this option, because it appears that selecting this option will start the test, not giving you a choice of destructive or nondestructive testing. Figure 53.7 shows the screen that will be displayed when you select Begin Surface Test. You *will* have the option to select a nondestructive test.

4. Select "Begin Surface Test." You will have a choice of destructive or nondestructive test, as shown in Figure 53.11.

FIGURE 53.10.
*INSTALL's Surface
Test Options menu
false start.*

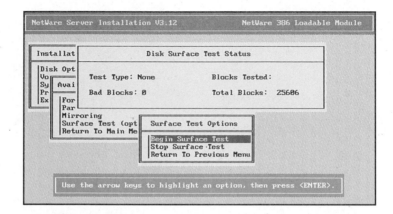

FIGURE 53.11.
*INSTALL's
destructive versus
nondestructive
selection.*

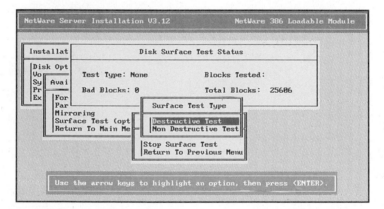

CAUTION ▷

Selection of "Destructive Test" will destroy *all* the data on your disk. Be
careful not to inadvertently select this option—it is the default.

You may halt the test at any time without file-system damage, as long as you select
"Stop Surface Test" from the screen shown in Figure 53.11.

> **CAUTION** ▶
>
> Do not reboot or turn off the power while a surface scan is in progress; you will damage the file system. You may stop the test by using a menu selection and no damage will occur if you wait until the test responds. It may take a couple of minutes for it to respond.

Summary

VREPAIR is essential for repairing file-system corruption. One other utility, NetUtils, is available that can test, diagnose, and repair file system problems.

Whenever problems appear, check your hardware carefully and scan your disk surfaces.

General Server Errors

54

by Doug Archell

File-server problems can be very stressful for the LAN administrator. While rushing around to calm down the users and assuring them that the system will be available shortly, the LAN administrator must try to decipher the cryptic server-error messages. If you do not immediately know the cause of the problem, chances are that you will contact a vendor, an associate, or someone on NetWire for help.

This chapter explains a few of the most common problems that you can encounter on your 3.11 file server. The problems discussed in this chapter may also apply to 3.12 and 4.x versions, but error messaging has been enhanced on those versions. Their error messages are more explicit. The error messages discussed in this chapter are more general, and their meanings are more elusive to the troubleshooter. Using the tips and guidelines listed in the chapter, you should be able to solve these problems more efficiently.

How to Interpret an Error Message

File-server error messages are categorized by severity level. Some errors are virtually meaningless, such as "Spurious interrupt." Other errors are terminal, such as "Abend" (abnormal-end/abort-end). You can tell how serious the error is by whether your file server crashes or if communications are interrupted. Terminal errors require immediate attention—not only do they interrupt service, but they can cause data and file-system corruption.

An error message is generally displayed at the server console, and a beep is heard (if you are in the vicinity of the server). Whenever you hear a beep, you should examine the server console, since the errors can scroll away. Though the error may be recorded in the server error message log, if the server is down you will not be able to read it.

The text of an error message generally looks like this:

```
Abend:
General Processor Protection Interrupt
                    in process:
                        DISKMUX
```

This particular error will be followed by a matrix of hexadecimal code and a message asking if you would like to dump memory to disk. Unfortunately, there is nothing you can do with the disk dump. In the early development of 3.0, these dumps were sometimes sent to the Novell developers for analysis. The purpose was to locate and fix bugs.

Now that 3.x is in its fourth revision, there is no longer a need to accumulate common error conditions; Novell *knows* you will receive GPPEs if you have hardware conflicts. You must figure this out for yourself and resolve it. The 3.12 maintenance release fixed the bugs that Novell has found since the inception of 3.0. No new enhancements were made to the basic OS, so the opportunity to introduce new bugs has been minimized. However, this does not solve many problems you may have with 3.11. However, 4.x is another matter. Although the 4.x operating system is fairly clean, it will take a while before it has proven itself as stable as 3.12.

General Protection Processor Exception (GPPE)

Many of the errors that you encounter on your file server pertain to a specific piece of hardware or software. Unfortunately, a GPPE is not one of them. A GPPE halts your server OS—no problem could be more severe than that. It is a problem that requires full attention on an immediate basis.

When you are trying to troubleshoot a GPPE error, it is imperative that you know as much about your server as possible. GPPE is an acronym for General Protection Processor Exception and it is just that: general. In the majority of cases it means that some conflict has caused the problem—either conflicts between two devices configured with the same settings, or a server-based software conflict (much like a lockup on a DOS workstation). A small percentage of the time, this error is the result of intermittent hardware failure or power problems.

Because of NetWare's nonpreemptive processing, each process maintains control over all the hardware momentarily. If release and/or suspension of resources is not accomplished in a proper manner, conflicts will result, which in turn causes the OS to stop. These errors cannot easily be pinned down to any specific piece of software or hardware in your file server. During the troubleshooting process, there are two things that will help:

- **Documentation.** A well-documented server is the key to solving any problem, especially GPPEs. Your documentation should contain detailed information on the hardware being used and its configuration (interrupts, memory addresses, and so forth), as well as the software and the versions in use.

- **Current Activity.** Try to isolate what was happening on the server when the error occurred. When trying to troubleshoot any error, knowing what caused the error will be a real time-saver.

Causes of GPPEs

The following problems cause GPPEs. These problems are listed in order from the most common to the least common.

- Improperly configured or conflicting hardware
- Faulty or corrupt NLMs
- Faulty or corrupt drivers
- Memory faults
- Faulty hardware
- Faulty utilities
- Poorly conditioned power

Some of these problems are more difficult to solve, even though they may be less common. For example, after installing a server, if it crashes repeatedly with a GPPE, you should look for a hardware conflict. On the other hand, if a server has been running faultlessly for a year, and then it periodically abends with a GPPE, you may have an intermittently bad RAM chip or hardware device. This is far more difficult to track down.

The key thing to remember when trying to solve GPPEs is that you must *never* assume anything. Why? Because almost anything can cause a GPPE. Though hardware conflicts may be the most common cause, and power conditioning may be the least common, both are possible. But all is not lost. While these errors may be confusing and mysterious, if you are armed properly, you can win the war.

Test Your Hardware

Before installing any piece of hardware in your file server, it should be thoroughly tested. Today, vendors are manufacturing more reliable equipment than they were five years ago, but faulty equipment can still slip through.

Assuming that a product will work well just because it is new is the worst mistake that you can make. Even if the testing performed by the vendor is foolproof (which it's not), the equipment passes through many different hands before it reaches your doorstep.

After a manufacturer has tested a product, it is then packaged, sent to a distributor, then sent to a vendor, and finally sent to your door. During this transition, the equipment can be exposed to various weather changes, kicked, stepped on, or even dropped.

A PC may have been working fine at the manufacturer, but after it falls 20 feet from a shelf, there could be problems. Electronic devices are usually "burned in" at the plant, but the first few hours of additional use may reveal weak components. A small snap of static electricity during installation is often to blame.

Most vendors will provide some sort of diagnostic program with their adapter cards or PCs. At a minimum, you should use these utilities on the equipment *before* installing anything into your production server. The best time to find out if a NIC is faulty is definitely *not* after it has been installed in a production file server.

Figure 54.1 is an example of the diagnostic utility provided by DCA for its IrmaTRAC cards.

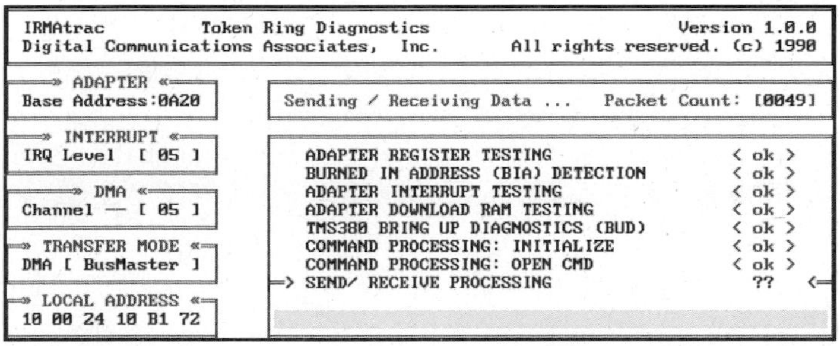

FIGURE 54.1.

DCA IrmaTRAC diagnostics.

```
IRMAtrac        Token Ring Diagnostics                    Version 1.0.0
Digital Communications Associates,  Inc.     All rights reserved. (c) 1990

==» ADAPTER «==
Base Address:0A20        Sending / Receiving Data ...   Packet Count: [0049]

==» INTERRUPT «==
IRQ Level  [ 05 ]           ADAPTER REGISTER TESTING              < ok >
                            BURNED IN ADDRESS (BIA) DETECTION     < ok >
==» DMA «==                 ADAPTER INTERRUPT TESTING             < ok >
Channel — [ 05 ]            ADAPTER DOWNLOAD RAM TESTING          < ok >
                            TMS380 BRING UP DIAGNOSTICS (BUD)     < ok >
==» TRANSFER MODE «==       COMMAND PROCESSING: INITIALIZE        < ok >
DMA [ BusMaster ]           COMMAND PROCESSING: OPEN CMD          < ok >
                        ==> SEND/ RECEIVE PROCESSING              ??      <==
==» LOCAL ADDRESS «==
10 00 24 10 B1 72
```

There are dozens of third-party packages on the market that will also test adapter cards, PCs, or SIMMs, such as TouchStone's CheckIt software. (See Figure 54.2.) Generally, these programs provide a more in-depth analysis of the equipment than the diagnostics provided by the manufacturer.

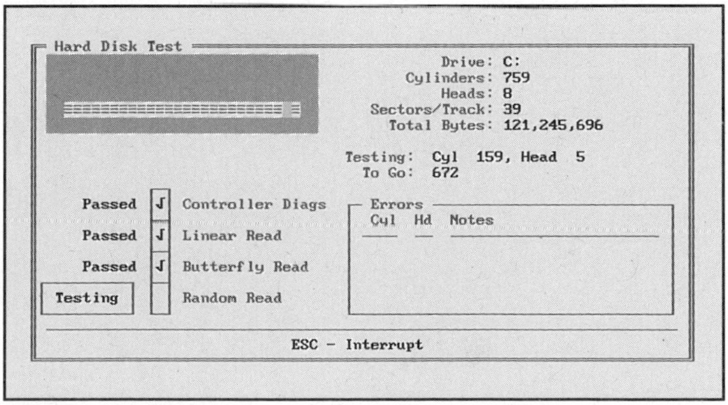

FIGURE 54.2.

CheckIt diagnostic test.

```
┌─ Hard Disk Test ═══════════════════════════════════════════════════
│                                                    Drive: C:
│                                            Cylinders: 759
│                                                Heads: 8
│  ════════════════════════════════════     Sectors/Track: 39
│                                            Total Bytes: 121,245,696
│
│                                        Testing: Cyl 159, Head 5
│                                        To Go:   672
│
│    Passed  √  Controller Diags     ┌─ Errors ──────────────
│                                    │ Cyl  Hd  Notes
│    Passed  √  Linear Read          │
│                                    │
│    Passed  √  Butterfly Read       │
│  ┌─────────┐
│  │ Testing │   Random Read
│  └─────────┘
│
│                    ESC - Interrupt
└────────────────────────────────────────────────────────────────────
```

Because GPPEs can be so difficult to troubleshoot, here are a few questions that you should ask yourself before you proceed:

1. Did the GPPE abend message make reference to any specific utility or program? If so, it is possible that the file has been corrupted. Delete the file from the server and make a copy from your master diskettes. You also should check if there are any updates available by calling the vendor or checking on NetWire.

2. What happened immediately preceding the GPPE? A GPPE abend is not always the reason why your server went down. Sometimes there were critical errors on the system before the GPPE. If you can reboot your server, take a look at the System Error Log. There may be information there that will point to a faulty adapter board or another area of the server.

3. What was happening at the time of the abend? Although the message may not mention a specific file, it is possible that a program was being run on a workstation that caused the error. In some situations, an old version of SYSCON has been known to cause a GPPE.

4. Can you recreate the error? You might wonder who in their right mind would actually want to make the server abend. A skilled troubleshooter, that's who. If you can isolate the circumstances around the GPPE, you're that much closer to solving the puzzle.

5. Is the hardware configured properly? When there are conflicting configurations in the file server, intermittent errors will arise. Verify your configuration.

6. Is the hardware faulty? It is possible that your server hardware was damaged before you installed it or that it suffered damage after months or years running perfectly.

7. Are you using any patches? There are several patches available for the NetWare OS on NetWire that may correct your problem. Check in the various NetWire forums for information on the latest available patches.

Examples of GPPEs

Following are a few examples of the circumstances surrounding some GPPEs. Although your specific case may not be shown here, you may be able to solve your problem in a similar fashion.

> **PROBLEM:** *While using INSTALL.NLM and selecting "Product Options," the file server abends with the error "GPPE: Running Process Install Process."*

SOLUTION: This problem is usually related to BTRIEVE. Although you may not be running any database applications that use BTRIEVE, NetWare uses it to keep track of the product NLMS installed in your server. To resolve this problem you should confirm the following:

- The file SYS:\SYSTEM\BTRIEVE.TRN must be flagged RW. Your server will abend if it is flagged RO.

- The file SYS:\SYSTEM\PRODUCTS.DAT must be flagged RW. Your server will abend if it is flagged RO.

- Make sure that you are using a current version of BTRIEVE.NLM. Versions prior to 02/19/91 can cause your server to abend.

PROBLEM: *Using NetWare 3.11, the file server runs for almost 30 days when it suddenly abends. No changes had been made to the file server and everything appeared to be running smoothly.*
SOLUTION: The version of MONITOR.NLM that shipped with NetWare had a bug in it that would cause the file server to abend if it was left loaded for extended periods of time. Make sure that you are using at least MONITOR.NLM version 1.75.

PROBLEM: *Whenever the administrator tries to use Alt+Esc to toggle between the various NLMs, the file server abends with "GPPE: Error Code 00180000 Running Process Sleep Process."*
SOLUTION: There could be a problem with your SERVER.EXE file. Delete the file on your boot disk and copy it from the SYSTEM-1 diskette.

PROBLEM: *When using SYSCON to create a new group, the file server abends with a GPPE.*
SOLUTION: The version of SYSCON.EXE that shipped with NetWare has been updated. Dial in to NetWire and download the latest version. You must be running at least version 3.68.

PROBLEM: *The file server is abending with a GPPE whenever a user prints to the network.*
SOLUTION: It is possible that your print queues or the print server files have been corrupted. Using PCONSOLE, try deleting the print queues and print server, then recreate them.

PROBLEM: *Whenever the file STAT.NLM is loaded, the file server abends with a GPPE.*
SOLUTION: GPPEs can be caused by corrupted NLMs. Try removing the NLM and reinstalling from a disk.

Non-Maskable Interrupt—Parity Error

If the GPPE abend is the hardest to troubleshoot, the NMI Parity Error runs a close second. Thankfully, in most cases these errors are attributable to problems with the server memory.

The difficulty in resolving this problem is that NMIs can be caused by any piece of equipment that has some sort of RAM chips (for instance, video cards).

What can cause an NMI error?

- Conflicting configuration
- Faulty SIMMs or memory modules
- Faulty memory boards
- System boards
- Network Interface Cards (NICs)
- Video controllers

As with most errors, NMI abends can be generated by configuration problems. When installing hardware in your server, be careful when configuring the interrupts, DMA channel, and memory addresses. If a conflict exists, it may not be immediately apparent.

If everything in the server is configured properly, your next step is to examine the hardware for any errors. Along with testing your NICs, disk drives, or system boards, you should ensure the reliability of your RAM.

Faulty SIMMs can be the most troublesome piece of hardware in your server. Whenever you are testing RAM, run a diagnostic program (such as TouchStone's CheckIt software, shown in Figure 54.3) through several passes. There could be problems that may not be detected in the initial pass.

Although third-party diagnostic programs are valuable tools in testing, when it comes to RAM, nothing beats a hardware-based tool. There are various hardware-based testers on the market that provide the most reliable and in-depth testing for your SIMMs. The only drawback to a hardware-based tester is the price. Compared to a software package, it can be expensive; but the security is well worth it.

Remember, however, that just because you have tested the RAM and it appears to be reliable, does not mean that it will work flawlessly in your system. The type of RAM that you install in the server can make a big difference.

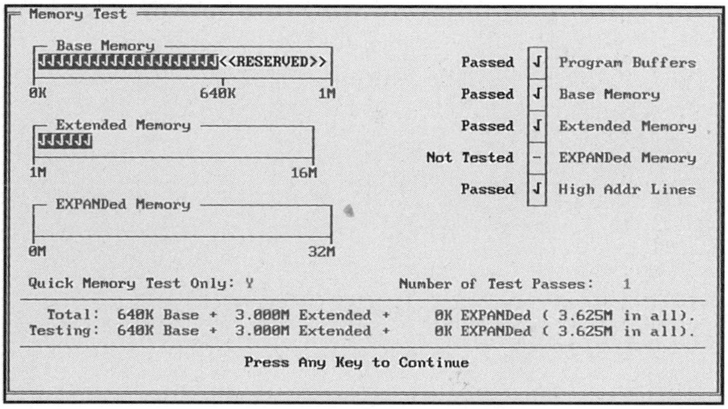

FIGURE 54.3.

CheckIt memory test.

```
┌─ Memory Test ══════════════════════════════════════════════════════════════┐
│  ┌─ Base Memory ──────────────────────────────┐                              │
│  │▐▐▐▐▐▐▐▐▐▐▐▐▐▐▐▐▐▐▐▐▐▐▐▐▐│<<RESERVED>>│    Passed  │√│  Program Buffers    │
│  0K              640K            1M            Passed  │√│  Base Memory        │
│  ┌─ Extended Memory ──────────────────────────┐                              │
│  │▐▐▐▐▐▐│                                        Passed  │√│  Extended Memory    │
│  1M                          16M          Not Tested │-│  EXPANDed Memory     │
│  ┌─ EXPANDed Memory ──────────────────────────┐    Passed  │√│  High Addr Lines    │
│  0M                          32M                                              │
│  Quick Memory Test Only: Y            Number of Test Passes:   1              │
│  ┌────────────────────────────────────────────────────────────────────────┐ │
│  │  Total:  640K Base + 3.000M Extended +   0K EXPANDed ( 3.625M in all).   │ │
│  │  Testing: 640K Base + 3.000M Extended +   0K EXPANDed ( 3.625M in all).  │ │
│  └────────────────────────────────────────────────────────────────────────┘ │
│                        Press Any Key to Continue                             │
└──────────────────────────────────────────────────────────────────────────────┘
```

Before purchasing RAM, check the vendor specifications for your server. In some systems, you must use a specific "pattern" when installing RAM. For example, in one server, you may be able to install two 8M-SIMMs for 16M of memory; in another, you may have to purchase four 4M-SIMMs.

The speed of the RAM in your server should be consistent. If your file server has two 4M-SIMMs that run at 70ns and you are adding two more SIMMs, make sure that they are also 70ns. When you mix speeds, you could be asking for trouble.

The brand of the RAM that you are using may also cause problems. Some people run into problems when mixing RAM from different manufacturers. When possible, try to avoid mixing RAM.

Unencrypted Passwords

NetWare uses an encryption routine when sending and receiving passwords. By default, NetWare will not accept passwords that have not been encrypted first.

When checking your file server console, you may see a message that states "Station *X*: attempted to use an unencrypted password call". When this happens, many people immediately assume that someone is trying to break into their network. While this may indeed be the case, most of the time the error is caused by a utility that is trying to make use of your server.

While searching for the cause of the UNENCRYPTED PASSWORD error, you should be on the lookout for any NetWare 2.x servers. Novell NetWare 2.x cannot encrypt passwords for access to the 3.x or 4.x server. As such, whenever you have a 2.x server on your network, you should upgrade the utilities from the 3.x server. Make sure to look in the PUBLIC and the LOGIN directories. An old version of LOGIN.EXE will only bring you grief.

While third-party developers do not have access to Novell's encryption algorithms, they can use Novell developer kits which will ensure that their applications will encrypt the passwords properly. When the developer does not use the kits provided by Novell, his or her application may cause UNENCRYPTED PASSWORD errors on your file server. To accommodate these systems, you can type SET ALLOW UNENCRYPTED PASSWORDS=ON at the file-server console.

Lost Hardware Interrupts

A "Lost Hardware Interrupt" error will occur when a request is made by a driver with an interrupt call, but it is dropped before the file-server CPU can respond. Whenever this happens, the OS will generate the following message on the file-server console:

```
Primary Interrupt Controller Detected A Lost Hardware Interrupt
```

There are several reasons why you may get this error. One of the main causes is related to processor speed. When one board in your server is too slow for the CPU, you may get intermittent errors of this nature. Another cause is a faulty adapter board or driver.

Although this error is not usually critical, it can affect the performance of your file server. To determine the cause, you must try to isolate the offending board or driver.

> **NOTE** ▶
>
> The Lost Hardware Interrupt error is common with IDE drivers and can usually be ignored.

To narrow down your search, DOWN the file server and restart the OS by typing SERVER -NA from the boot drive. This will load NetWare without using the AUTOEXEC.NCF file. By doing so, drivers can be loaded one at a time until the error occurs. Unfortunately, this method may not uncover the cause of the errors. Without users logged into the server and creating a load, there may not be any problems.

Your next step is to list the various disk and NIC drivers that are being loaded on the server and then to contact the vendor to see if there have been any updates. If there have not, try deleting the driver and reloading it from the source diskette; the driver may have been corrupted somehow.

After checking the drivers, determine whether there is any faulty hardware in the server. Using the utilities provided by the vendors of your adapter cards and third-party packages, run the diagnostics to check for any problems.

If you have confirmed that everything in the file server is working properly, you should also examine the network as a whole. A faulty NIC, transceiver, or cable can cause an unusually high level of traffic on the network. The network may have only 10 stations, but there could be faulty hardware in a station that is flooding the network with unnecessary traffic.

Even after checking the drivers and hardware, you may still encounter "Lost Interrupt" errors. If there are no other problems on your server, the easiest thing to do is to disable these error messages. Although the problem will not go away, it will restrain these messages from appearing. To disable these messages, type the following at the console:

```
SET DISPLAY LOST INTERRUPT ALERTS=OFF
SET DISPLAY SPURIOUS INTERRUPT ALERTS=OFF
```

TIP ▶

If you are using an IDE driver with the ISADISK.DSK driver, changing to the IDE.DSK driver may resolve these errors.

Not Logged In

NetWare is sold in various license counts to meet the needs of the customer. If you have 30 employees in your company, buying a 50-user version of NetWare is more economical than buying a 100-user version.

When the number of users on the network approaches the number of connections available, you may encounter problems with logging into the file server.

Once the network shells are loaded at the workstation, a connection is established to the file server even if the user has not logged in yet. You can view these connections by selecting "Connection Information" from the "Available Options" menu of MONITOR.NLM (see Figure 54.4).

FIGURE 54.4.

Active connections.

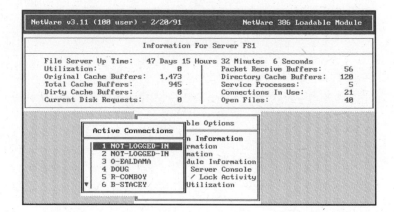

A connection that is noted as being "NOT-LOGGED-IN" is either a station that has loaded the network drivers but is not currently logged into the file server, or someone who has logged out of the server but still has the drivers loaded.

These "NOT-LOGGED-IN" connections cause problems for many people. For example, you may be running a 50-user version of NetWare, but have 55 people in your company. At any given time, you might expect to have only 40 users logged into the file server. When the first 50 people turn on their PCs and load the network drivers, MONITOR will display 50 "NOT-LOGGED-IN" connections. Assume that of these 50 people, only 30 log in. When employee 51 tries to boot his PC and log in to the file server, he will get an error that states "All connections are currently in use."

The problem is that although there are only 30 users that have actually logged in, there are also 20 other stations that are using a connection on the file server.

To solve this problem, Novell has a utility called NLICLEAR.NLM that you can load on the file server. This NLM is available on NetWire and it is also shipped on the runtime version of NetWare. NLICLEAR.NLM checks the file server on a regular basis for connections that are classified as "NOT-LOGGED-IN" and deletes them.

Although this will solve one problem, it also creates another. If the stations are using the old IPX/NETX shells to login to the server and NLICLEAR deletes the network connection, the station may need to be rebooted before accessing the network again. Before rebooting, you can try typing NETX /U and then reload NETX, but this will not always work. This problem has been solved with the VLMs.

When the network connection is deleted on a station using the VLMs, an error will occur if the DOS prompt is at a network drive. After receiving the error "Network Error Receiving on Drive F:", the user must specify a local drive for the DOS prompt. At this point, the connection can be reestablished by changing back to the network drive.

Miscellaneous Problems

PROBLEM: *The message "Time to run preventative maintenance" is being displayed on the file-server console, yet this message is not listed in the "System Messages" Novell manual.*
SOLUTION: These messages can be generated by third-party software or hardware that you add to your server. Check the documentation that came with your products to learn how to disable this message or what else may be required.

PROBLEM: *When running RCONSOLE.EXE on the workstation, there are no servers listed in the "Available Servers" window. There are five NetWare 3.11 servers on the network.*
SOLUTION: Both REMOTE.NLM and RSPX.NLM must be loaded on the file server before a workstation can access the server console.

PROBLEM: *The LOGIN directory on the file server was deleted by accident. After recreating the directory and restoring the files, users are still having problems accessing the file server.*
SOLUTION: After restoring the LOGIN directory, you must dismount the SYS: volume or down the file server before users will be able to log in.

Summary

GPPE and NMI errors with NetWare 3.11 are nonspecific and can be quite perplexing. (3.12 and 4.x error messages are far more explicit.) If you encounter any error that abends (crashes) your server, you need to resolve it immediately. This chapter may help with some of the more elusive problems that users and administrators encounter with NetWare 3.11.

XI

PART

Appendixes

Glossary of NetWare Terminology

A

access protocol (access method, access scheme)   The method of communication used between NICs on a local area network. Frames of data that contain packets of data are exchanged between NICs. (See CSMA/CD, token-passing bus, and token-passing ring.)

AppleTalk   Networking protocols and networking software proprietary to Apple Computers. (See OSI Model.)

application (application software)   Software program.

ARCnet (Attached Resource Computer Network)   A type of LAN that uses token-passing bus access protocol and (normally) 93 ohm coaxial cable. ARCnet is a trademark of Datapoint, Inc., and is proprietary, although widely licensed and used under various brand names. Standard Microsystems Corp. and Thomas-Conrad Corp. are the leading purveyors of ARCnet products, although many other ARCnet products are produced using SMC ARCnet chips.

attachment unit interface (AUI)   An IEEE term for a connector that connects an external transceiver to the AUI plug on an Ethernet NIC. (Also see DIX connector.)

boot image file   A file located in a server's LOGIN directory that works in conjunction with a remote boot chip on a NIC or diskless workstation to boot without the aid of a local disk drive.

bridge   A device that joins two separate LANs but restricts LAN frame traffic to either side of the bridge unless forwarding is required. Bridges process LAN frames (not network packets) and are governed by IEEE standards. A bridge either filters or forwards frames by reading the node address in the frame header (MAC-layer bridge), or by reading the DSAP and SSAP in an 802.2 header (LLC-bridge). A bridge should not be confused with a router, which uses an entirely different layer of protocol and information for forwarding packets (not frames). (Also see MAC-layer bridge, LLC bridge, and router.)

brouter (bridging-router, routing-bridge)   A device that can perform both bridging and routing functions.

burst mode   A mode used in MCA and EISA computers and devices to facilitate greater flow of data through the bus. When bus mastering is employed, a bus master and its slave can establish a connection and send large blocks of data without CPU intervention. Without burst mode, each byte requires CPU attention to gain control of the bus, and then to send a byte of data.

Burst Mode NCP (Burst Mode Protocol)   A variation of NCP's normal one-to-one, packet-to-acknowledgment procedure. In Burst Mode NCP, up to

64K worth of "packet-fragments" can be acknowledged with one NCP acknowledgment packet.

bus (computer)   The interface between devices in a computer. PCs incorporate bus designs that include ISA, EISA, MCA, and NuBus (Macintosh).

bus (network)   A network that includes one circuit on which data is sent and received. Bits of data are broadcasted over a bus network; only one frame of data can occupy the bus at one time.

bus mastering   A function used to off-load I/O processing to a processor on the interface card. Although some ISA boards use this technique for marginally improved performance, bus mastering is only truly effective when used with a bus design that is capable of controlling bus master access to the computer bus, as is the case in EISA and MCA computers. Bus mastering alone does not fully realize capabilities of this design unless implemented in conjunction with accessing the 32-bit burst mode and streaming data modes of EISA and MCA computers.

Carrier Sense Multiple Access with Collision Detection (CSMA/CD)   The access protocol used in "Ethernet" LANs. CSMA/CD is the foundation of IEEE 802.3 standards as well as Ethernet II standards developed by Digital, Intel, and Xerox. (Also see Ethernet and access protocol.)

centralized processing   In a minicomputer or mainframe environment, processing is conducted in one (or in a few) CPUs. User devices are "terminals" that provide multiple-user access to one centralized processing.

central processing unit (CPU)   The processor that controls a computer. In an Intel-based computer, this is the 80x86 processor that runs the operating system and controls all internal devices. In a minicomputer or mainframe environment, this is the processor (or multiprocessor computer) where processing takes place for all users.

connection   A communication session established between a server and a workstation. An NCP request issued by the DOS workstation shell or OS/2 Requester is answered by the NCP layer of the server, and the server allocates a connection for the workstation. Messages are then passed through the connection, much in the same way a mailbox is used. Once the connection is established, NCP packets communicate between workstations and servers, without regard to the layers of protocol or physical media that lie between the two. This is a session-layer function equivalent to layer 5 of the OSI model. (See OSI Model, UNA, and NCP.)

connectionless protocol   A networking protocol that communicates in one direction only, not requiring an acknowledgment. (See IPX, connection-oriented protocol, NCP, and SPX.)

connection-oriented protocol   A networking protocol that communicates in two directions, each packet being sent requiring an acknowledgment packet. (See connectionless protocol, NCP, and SPX.)

Destination Service Access Point (DSAP)   IEEE LLC protocol designates and uses a DSAP and SSAP to determine routes for LAN frames to be taken when entering a system of bridges. The DSAP designates the bridge to which the frame is to be forwarded. (Also see LLC, SSAP, spanning-tree protocol, source-routing protocol, and translating bridge.)

distributed processing   In a PC network, processing of data is conducted at each workstation instead of at one CPU.

DIX connector   The Ethernet II (Digital-Intel-Xerox) term for the connector that connects an external transceiver to the 15-pin connector on an Ethernet NIC. (See AUI.)

DOS (MS-DOS, PC-DOS, DR-DOS)   This term is used throughout this book to refer to any version of the MS-DOS operating system that is used at a workstation.

drive array   A series of intelligent disk drives linked together, for the purpose of spanning data across the drives and/or improving reliability. (Also see RAID.)

Enhanced Small Device Interface (ESDI)   A drive controller type that utilizes a hard drive as a slave unit. ESDI controllers generally drive only two disk drives and have an on-board processor to translate drive geometry, manage I/O requests, and provide caching.

Ethernet   The term generally used to refer to CSMA/CD LANs, based on 802.3 or Ethernet II standards. Though the term "Ethernet" is commonly used to refer to both Digital-Intel-Xerox Ethernet II and IEEE 10BASE-5 standards, technical differences exist in terminology and frame formatting. The differences in frame formatting make Ethernet II and 802.3 LANs incompatible, though they use the same cabling and physical specification. IEEE does not use the term "Ethernet" anywhere in their specifications. In this book, the term "Ethernet" is used as a synonym for both Ethernet II and 802.3 networks—to avoid confusion with common usage.

Ethernet II   The original Ethernet design developed by Digital, Intel, and Xerox in the late '70s. True Ethernet II design only includes thick Ethernet cabling with external transceivers, but today is compatible with all IEEE 802.3 physical specifications and devices. Ethernet II frame formatting differs from and is not compatible with 802.3 frame formatting. Ethernet II frame formatting is commonly used in TCP/IP networks and can be used with NetWare ODI drivers and some (but not all) traditional IPX drivers. Care must be taken with NetWare to observe and correct frame incompatibilities between Ethernet II and 802.3 frames on a single LAN. (Also see CSMA/CD and Ethernet.)

Extended Industry Standard Architecture (EISA)   A computer bus and interface card design based on 32-bit bus mastering. EISA is an extension to ISA bus design and enables EISA and ISA interface cards to be used in a single type of bus interface slot. (Also see ISA and MCA.)

firmware   Software that is programmed into a PROM chip to become part of the hardware function.

frame   A unit of data that is exchanged on a LAN. Frame formatting implements an access protocol for the purpose of enabling communications between nodes on a LAN (Ethernet, Token Ring, ARCnet, and so on). A frame should not be confused with a packet, which is encapsulated within a frame for transport across a LAN. The terms "frame" and "packet" often are interchanged in common usage, especially by Novell, but have distinctly different functions and use distinctly different layers of protocol. In this book, the terms always are used consistently and never are exchanged.

hub (active hub, passive hub)   A wiring concentrator or multiport repeater. (Also see wiring concentrator.)

Industry Standard Architecture (ISA)   This term was developed to describe the design of the 16-bit AT bus (sometimes called the "classic bus") developed by IBM.

Institute of Electrical and Electronic Engineers (IEEE)   A U.S. trade association. The IEEE 802 committee was formed for the purpose of standardizing Local Area Networks. It provides physical, Medium Access Control, and Logical Link Control standards for interoperability between competing vendor devices.

Integrated Drive Electronics (IDE)   A later drive design that incorporated an embedded controller on a smaller (3 1/2-inch) disk drive. IDE drives can be connected together, but the second drive must be a slave of the first, using the primary disk controller and not its own embedded controller. This type of drive is interfaced to a computer bus with an IDE host adapter, not a controller.

International Standards Organization (ISO)   A world-wide standards organization based in Geneva, Switzerland. The United States has representation in ISO through ANSI, and ISO standards are sometimes included in international treaties or trade agreements to provide worldwide interoperability of computing and data communications systems. ISO often cites IEEE, ANSI, and CCITT standards for specifications. ISO is responsible for the OSI model. (See Open Systems Interconnection 7-layer Model.)

internetwork   A network of LANs and WANs linked together through bridges and/or routers. Each individual LAN or WAN is identified with a network address (network number).

Internetwork Packet Exchange (IPX)   A network protocol developed by Novell to address packets of data from ultimate source and destination nodes located on any LAN networked with NetWare, and to provide routing services in conjunction with NetWare (and third-party) routers. IPX is a "routable" protocol based on XNS packet format, and is identified by the type 17 designation in the "type" field of an XNS packet. It is quite similar to an IP packet (XNS packet, designated by type 800). An IPX packet has information fields that identify the network address, node address, and socket address of both the source and destination, and provides the same functionality of the OSI Network layer in the OSI model. (Also see Internetwork Protocol, router, and protocol.)

Internet Protocol (IP)   A network protocol that provides routing services across multiple LANs and WANs that is used in the TCP/IP protocol stack. IP packet format is used to address packets of data from ultimate source and destination nodes (host) located on any LAN or WAN networked with TCP/IP protocol. IP provides routing services in conjunction with IP routers, which are incorporated into many computer systems and most versions of UNIX. IP is a "routable" protocol, based on XNS packet format and is identified by the type 800 designation in the "type" field of an XNS packet. It is quite similar to an IPX packet (XNS packet, designated by type 17). An IP packet has information fields, which identify the host address that includes the network number and node address that uniquely identifies both the source and destination host computers, and provides the same functionality of the OSI Network layer in the OSI model. IP packet format is supported in NetWare 3.11 and 4.0 operating systems, and is used throughout the Department of Defense Internet—a network of thousands of computers internetworked worldwide. (Also see TCP/IP, IPX, OSI Model, router, and protocol.)

interoperability   Compatibility, or the capability for equipment (usually manufactured by competing vendors) to work together. Industry standards (or *de facto* standards) are agreed upon or used by vendors to make their equipment work with other vendors' equipment. This factor has led to wide implementation of LAN equipment.

linear-bus   A network topology consisting of connections strung over the length of a cable segment. Linear-bus topology can be used in Ethernet and ARCnet LANs.

Link Support Layer (LSL)   Novell application software that dynamically interfaces MLID NIC drivers with ODI packet drivers in RAM. (See MLID and ODI.)

local area network (LAN)   A limited-distance, multipoint physical connectivity medium consisting of network interface cards, media, and repeating devices designed to transport frames of data between host computers at high speeds with low error rates. A LAN is a subsystem that is part of a network.

In this book, the term "LAN" is used differently from the way Novell uses the term in much of its training and documentation, but fully consistent with the way the term is used in operating system messages and screens. The use of the LAN in this manner is also in full compliance with IEEE and ANSI standards, which specifically discuss technical aspects of LANs.

The term LAN is commonly used elsewhere to refer to an entire network of computers; however, in this book, the term LAN refers specifically to a single Ethernet, Token Ring, or other type of LAN. It is important to accurately describe each LAN as a separate entity in a network where routable protocols are used, as is the case in a NetWare IPX network. (See the introduction of this book for more clarification, or see network, network architecture, routable protocols, IPX, UNA, and OSI Model.)

LocalTalk   A proprietary type of LAN developed by Apple Computer for Macintosh computers. LocalTalk uses flat telephone wire and AppleTalk network architecture for peer-to-peer access between nodes. LocalTalk is not used extensively with NetWare because of its limited bandwidth (230 Kbps). (See LAN, network, and OSI Model.)

logical hop   The number of hops across routers. A router detects logical hops based on how many routers a packet must traverse to reach its destination. If bridges exist, they constitute a physical hop, but no logical hop is detected because bridges do not work at the network protocol layer.

Logical Link Control (LLC)   IEEE LLC (802.2) layer defines protocol, frame header information, and methods of bridging similar and dissimilar types of LANs together. LLC includes spanning-tree and source-routing protocols and uses DSAP and SSAP addressing to determine specific bridge routes through an internetwork connected with LLC bridges. (Also see DSAP, SSAP, spanning-tree protocol, source-routing protocol, and translating bridges.)

logical partition   The remaining usable Data Area of a NetWare partition, after the Redirection Area has been allocated. No more than one NetWare logical partition can exist on a physical disk drive.

login address   A NetWare term that refers to the combination of the network address and node address. The login address is used by IPX, routers, and NetWare file servers to determine exactly where each node is located on a NetWare network or internetwork.

MAC-layer bridge   A bridge that connects two similar LANs. Each LAN must use the same frame formatting, because a MAC-layer bridge reads the frame addresses, builds a table of which node addresses exist on either side of the bridge, and either filters or forwards each frame as necessary. This type of bridge is sometimes called a *transparent* or *learning bridge*. When a bridge joins two LANs together, they appear to be one single LAN; however, traffic on each side of the bridge is limited to that specific LAN—unless forwarding is required.

media (medium)   Cabling, telecommunications medium, and electromagnetic wave media used to transport bits of data from one node to another on a network. Generally, the term *medium* refers to whatever type of cable (or electromagnetic medium) may be used in a LAN or WAN.

Medium Access Control (MAC)   The middle layer in IEEE's 802 model for LANs. The MAC layer specifies access protocol, frame formatting, node addressing, and error-control mechanisms in a LAN. The MAC layer forms the basis for the type of LAN, whereas the physical layer adds various alternative physical media for transporting the LAN frames.

Novell had misused the term "bridge" to describe NetWare routers in version 2.15 and 3.10, and in earlier documentation and training. The residual of material and impressions continues to cause confusion. A bridge processes frames only. It works at the data link layer, (OSI layer 2) is governed by IEEE standards, and is part of the LAN. A router is a distinctly different device that processes packets of data after the frame has been discarded, works at the network layer (OSI layer 3), and is exclusive from the LAN. In a bridged environment, the two LANs appear to be one network address to NetWare; whereas in a routed environment, each LAN is a separate entity and is identified with a different network address. (Also see router, IPX, network address, and bridge.)

Medium Attachment Unit (MAU)   An IEEE term to describe the device that connects an external transceiver to the 15-pin connector on an Ethernet NIC. The same device is described in Ethernet II vernacular as a DIX connector; there is no difference except in terminology.

messages   Data to be passed between nodes is first assembled as messages, which are further broken into packets appropriately sized to fit the specific frame type for the LAN. NCP provides this function, negotiating the appropriate packet size during a workstation connection request. NCP packet headers contain a sequence number, which is used to reassemble the packetized data back into messages on the receiving end. (See NCP, OSI Model, and UNA.)

Micro-Channel Architecture (MCA)   A proprietary 32-bit computer and bus architecture designed by IBM to improve bus bandwidth and facilitate bus mastering. MCA is not backward compatible with ISA and requires exclusive use of MCA devices.

microprocessor   A miniaturized processor. Previous processors were built on integrated circuit boards with many large components. Most processors today use high-tech, silicon-based technology that improves performance, reduces heat generation, and is more efficient. In this book, the term processor is used instead of microprocessor. (See processor.)

Multiple Link Interface Driver (MLID)   A Novell specification for a NIC driver interface that provides concurrent support for multiple frame types and multiple packet types and therefore network protocols such as IP, OSI, and AppleTalk. MLID drivers are to be used with Link Support Layer (LSL.COM), the IPX ODI packet driver (IPXODI.COM), and other ODI-conforming packet drivers. (See IPX, IP, ODI, packet, frame, and network protocol.)

multiport repeater   A repeater that has multiple in and out ports. (See wiring concentrator.)

Multi-Protocol Router (MPR)   A Novell server-based software product that provides high-performance routing services for IPX, IP, AppleTalk, and OSI network protocols. MPR comes with a runtime of the NetWare 3.x OS to be installed as a stand-alone router. It provides several enhancements to normal NetWare internal router functions including Burst Mode NCP, Large Internet Packet, and RIP/SAP filtering.

Multistation Access Unit (MAU)   A Token Ring LAN device that implements star-wired ring topology. The MAU is a physical switching device that connects all nodes into a single serial circuit.

multitasking   The capability of an operating system to handle multiple processing tasks apparently at the same time. (See preemptive processing.)

multiuser   The capability of an operating system (or NOS) to handle access from multiple users at the same time. (See multitasking.)

NetBIOS   An IBM protocol (and packet structure) that provides several networking functions. NetBIOS was developed by IBM and Sytek to supplement and work with BIOS in PC-DOS-based, peer-to-peer networks. NetBIOS protocol provides transport, session, and presentation layer functions equivalent to layers 4, 5, and 6 of the OSI model. The NETBIOS software that is used to implement this protocol is the NetBIOS interface.

NetWare   A trademarked brand name for the networking operating systems and other networking products developed and sold by Novell.

NetWare Core Protocol (NCP)   A NetWare protocol that provides transport, session, and presentation layer functions equivalent to layers 4, 5, and 6 of the OSI model. NCP is implemented at the NETX workstation shell and OS/2 Requester, and is internal to the server operating system.

network   A group of computers connected by a communications link that enables any device to interact with any other on the network. The term "network" is derived from the term "network architecture" to describe an entire system of hosts, workstations, terminals, and other devices. Though the term "network" often is used in the industry to describe a LAN, the terms "LAN" and "network" are used in this book specifically to differentiate an entire system (network) from a LAN (used specifically to describe one specific subsystem of a network). (See network architecture and LAN.)

network address (network number)   An eight-character hexadecimal number assigned to each LAN or WAN to which NetWare servers are attached. The network address is used in the IPX protocol, the server operating system, and in routers. The network address determines the exact location of each node on the network. It is an essential address required for a routable protocol to be able to determine the route necessary to forward packets of data to specific NICs or WAN interface cards. (See the definition in this glossary for the term "LAN." It is being used here and throughout this book in a manner that may conflict with your understanding of the term.)

network architecture   A "blueprint" or complete design of hardware and software layers of specifications, protocols, and functions that enable communications among hosts, workstations, and terminals on a network. Most notable of network architectures is the OSI Model, which sets a standardized, layered model for network design. Every networked computer system has a formalized design for network architecture, including IBM's SNA, Digital's DECnet, Xerox's XNS, Novell's UNA, and others. (See network and OSI Model.)

Network Device Interface Specification (NDIS)   A Microsoft specification for drivers that concurrently can support multiple network protocols, such as NetBIOS,

IP, AppleTalk, and IPX. This specification is equivalent to Novell's ODI and MLID specifications, but is less efficient in a NetWare environment than ODI drivers.

Network File System (NFS)   A trademark of Sun Microsystems, which comprises a set of presentation layer protocols providing operating system function calls. NFS provides a standardized interface between various UNIX and other operating systems.

network interface card (NIC)   An interface card put in the bus of a computer (or other LAN device) to interface a LAN. Each NIC represents a node, which is a source and destination for LAN frames, which in turn carry data between the NICs on the LAN.

network protocol   A packet protocol that provides routing and other information for a network equivalent to layer 3 of the OSI model. NetWare's proprietary network protocol is IPX, which is very similar to IP.

network utilization   The percentage of bandwidth in use on a LAN or WAN.

node   An intelligent device connected to a network.

node address   An address assigned to each node on a LAN. IEEE-assigned "universal addresses" for Ethernet and Token Ring are generally used for both the serial number of the NIC and node address. Alternatively, a "local address" can be assigned. ARCnet NICs have locally assigned addresses configured with switch settings. This number is picked up by the NIC driver as the node address for use in IPX protocol.

nonpreemptive processing   A multitasking operating system design feature of NetWare that yields better performance and less processor utilization over normal preemptive processing. In a multitasking operating system, multiple tasks (threads) apparently run at the same time, normally using a preemptive processing procedure. NetWare, however, uses nonpreemptive processing, in which each thread is scheduled to run exclusively on the processor in an unprotected priority ring—whereby it cannot be preempted by another thread. The scheduler assigns priorities to threads and stacks them for processing, but cannot preempt (or interrupt) any process running. Each process is designed to run for a period and then relinquish the processor if not completed. This enables short processes to run to completion. It also reduces CPU utilization, because less processor overhead is required to control and track resources of concurrently active threads. (See ring, thread, time slice, and preemptive processing.)

nonroutable protocol   A network protocol, such as IBM's SNA or NetBIOS, that uses a name for the source and destination of packets and does not identify each LAN or WAN as a separate entity. These protocols do not work with traditional nonproprietary routers the way routable protocols do, whereby network addresses (network numbers) and node addresses are used to locate the ultimate source and destination nodes (or hosts) for packets of data. Instead, the scheme for locating the ultimate destination and source of packets is contained in proprietary protocols that are part of the networking software. Therefore, "routing" usually occurs either by processing requests and repacketizing them or by using intelligent bridging techniques, such as source-routing bridging (802.2 protocol). In the past, nonroutable protocols restricted packet traffic to a specific physical LAN or WAN (network address), relying on bridges (as opposed to routers) to provide service across an internetwork. (See routable protocols, internetwork, bridges, routers, network address, and node address.)

Open Data Link Interface (ODI)   A Novell specification that provides service for multiple network packet types and for network protocols such as IPX, IP, OSI, and AppleTalk with a single NIC driver. Novell's MLID specification enables NIC drivers to interface through Link Support Layer (LSL.COM) with IPX ODI (IPXODI.COM) and multiple ODI-conforming packet drivers. (See IPX, IP, ODI, packet, frame, network, and protocol.)

Open Systems Interconnect (OSI) 7-layer Model (OSI Model) A model developed by International Standards Organization to establish a standardized set of protocols for interoperability between networked computer hosts. Each layer of the model consists of specifications and/or protocols that fulfill specific functions in a networking architecture. The OSI Model parallels DECnet, SNA, XNS, and other networking models. Novell's UNA was patterned against the OSI Model. The OSI Model consists of specific protocols that are nonproprietary and offered in the hope of unifying networking protocols used in competing vendors' systems. In this book, the OSI Model serves as a central model of traditional routable networking protocols, which helps clarify the functionality and equivalence of various network architectures. (See Chapter 5, "Novell's Protocol Stack," for a full explanation of Novell's UNA networking protocols and the OSI Model and comparisons to other network architectures.)

OS/2 Requester   NetWare workstation software that links an OS/2-based workstation to a NetWare server. The OS/2 Requester loads IPX and NIC drivers as SYS files during loading. The OS/2 Requester hears OS/2 and application function calls and echoes them to the server in the form of NCP function calls in the packet header. This software is the OS/2 workstation equivalent of the DOS shell. (See shell, NCP, and OSI model.)

packet   A limited-length unit of data that is formed by the network, transport, presentation, or application layer (layers 3-7 of the OSI Model) in a networked computer system. Packet headers contain information that is used by each corresponding layer of protocol in a network architecture. Packets may or may not contain data, as their functions are often fulfilled by one of the codes in a field of the header or trailer. In all cases, data is transported over a network, and larger amounts of data are broken into shorter units and placed into packets. Higher-layer packets are encapsulated into lower-layer packets for encapsulation into LAN frames (or in WAN frames or packets) for delivery to the ultimate host destination. The terms "packet" and "frame" should not be confused, because each has different specific functions. Novell often uses the term "packet" to describe "frames," but a clear distinction is drawn in this book, and the two terms are never used interchangeably. Novell uses proprietary packet formats including IPX, SPX, NCP, RIP, and SAP packet formats based upon Xerox's XNS network architecture. (For more complete discussion of packets and frames, see the Introduction, Chapter 5, "Novell's Protocol Stack," or the following Glossary items: frame, network, network architecture, IPX, OSI Model, protocols, and UNA.)

physical hop   A hop as counted when crossing a bridge or a router. Each physical hop incurs latency as a result of delay in processing a frame for bridging or a packet for routing.

preemptive processing   In a multitasking operating system, multiple tasks (threads) are generally controlled by a scheduler that preempts or interrupts each process, granting processor time in the form of a time slice (about 1/18th of a second). This enables multiple tasks to *apparently* run at the same time. However, each task runs for a time slice and is then preempted by the next process, which in turn is preempted— rotating processor time among active threads. In most Intel-based, multitasking operating systems, the scheduler executes in ring 0, and threads are executed in ring 3. (See ring, thread, and time slice.)

processor   The controlling device in a computer that interprets and executes instructions and performs computations, and otherwise controls the major functions of a computer. This book discusses Intel 80x86-series processors, which are miniaturized single-chip "microprocessors" that contain thousands to millions of transistors in a silicon-based, multilayered integrated circuit design.

processor utilization   The percentage of clock cycles that the processor is busy. When processor utilization reaches 100 percent, the processor cannot process more requests; it is fully saturated.

protocol   Rules of communication. In networks, several layers of protocols exist. Each layer of protocol only needs to physically hand off or receive data from the immediate layer above and beneath it, whereas virtual communications occur with the corresponding layer on another host computer. Layers between the two hosts are transparent. (See OSI Model, UNA, and access protocol.)

redundant array of inexpensive drives (RAID)   A disk subsystem that contains multiple disk drives in which data is spanned across drives for the purpose of performance or fault tolerance. RAID subsystems have several different types of configurations, but RAID 5 is most commonly used for protection of data with good performance.

remote boot chip   A chip installed on a NIC or diskless workstation that enables the workstation to boot from a boot image file on the server, without the aid of a local disk drive.

repeater A device that repeats or amplifies bits of data received at one port and sends each bit to another port. A repeater is a simple bus network device that connects two cabling segments and isolates electrical problems to either side. When used in a LAN, most repeaters take a role in reconstituting the digital signal that passes through them to extend distances a signal can travel, and reduce problems that occur over lengths of cable, such as attenuation.

ring (processor ring)   Intel 80286 and higher processors execute threads in one of four rings. Ring 0 is termed the "most favored" ring, having priority over threads running in rings 1, 2, and 3. Each lower-numbered ring has priority over higher-numbered rings. NetWare executes its scheduler and all threads in ring 0 to affect nonpreemptive processing. Most multitasking operating systems execute code in ring 3, whereas a scheduler executes in ring 0, which has the capability to preempt the thread. Ring 3 has memory protection so that memory being utilized by each thread is protected from potential corruption from other threads that are concurrently running. (See preemptive processing and nonpreemptive processing.)

ring (ring topology)   A network topology in which each node is a repeater, and nodes are physically connected into a physical ring circuit. This topology can be used for Token Ring and FDDI LANs, though star-wired ring is preferred. (See star-wired ring.)

routable protocol   A network protocol that can work with nonproprietary routers. Traditional routers use the network packet header fields to identify network addresses (network numbers) and node addresses for ultimate source and destination nodes (or hosts) for packets of data. This scheme for routing packets across internetworks is used with OSI, NetWare (IPX), TCP/IP, and AppleTalk network protocols.

Conversely, other network protocols, such as IBM's SNA and NetBIOS protocols, use a name for the source and destination resource and do not identify each LAN or WAN as a separate entity. (See nonroutable protocols, internetworks, routers, network address, node, and address.)

router   A device that reads network layer packet headers and receives or forwards each packet accordingly. A router does not in any way process LAN frames, because the LAN frame is discarded once the LAN has delivered the frame to the NIC driver. The destination network address in the header is read and checked against the routing tables the router has learned; where necessary, the header hands off the packet to the NIC driver for the destination network address. NetWare operating systems, version 2.0 and later, incorporate an internal router that enables the NetWare server to function with multiple LANs (network addresses), regardless of whether the LANs are of the same type. Novell incorrectly described internal routers as "internal bridges" in documentation up to versions 2.15 and 3.10. In version 2.2 and 3.11 documentation, they are described correctly. Routers are distinctly different devices from bridges, and integrators need to learn the difference so that they can properly configure NetWare operating systems (and routers) during installation. Many NetWare integrators and industry writers still incorrectly use the term "bridge" to describe routers, causing needless confusion in understanding routable protocols, bridges, and internetworking.

External routers (Novell and third-party) are stand-alone routers that perform the same functions as a server's internal router, except that the router itself is seldom the ultimate destination for packets. The protocol used for NetWare (and third-party) routers to communicate and function is Router Information Protocol (RIP). RIP packets are periodically broadcast by all routers to inform all other routers of their network addresses and number of hops (passes across routers to get to a network address).

Routers connect LANs and WANs into internetworks, but must be able to process the network packets for specific types of network protocol (NetWare's network protocol is IPX). Many routers process various packet types and therefore are termed multiprotocol routers. (See IPX, bridge, OSI Model, and UNA.)

Router Information Protocol (RIP)   A protocol and packet format that exchanges routing information among routers. RIP packets contain multiple information fields that include the network addresses, number of hops (traverses across routers), and number of ticks (estimate of time delay) for available LANs and WANs. RIP packet format is a subset of XNS.

segment   An electrically isolated cabling section. LAN segments are connected with repeaters. A single Ethernet LAN can have as many as 1024 segments, but no more than four repeaters can be used in series.

The term "segment" is sometimes used by Novell and industry writers to describe a LAN. To avoid confusion in this book, the term "segment" is never used in this manner. (See segmentation and repeater.)

segmentation   A term used to describe separation of a LAN into multiple LANs using a bridge or a router. The term often is used in the industry in this manner (and is therefore used as such in this book).

This term is used more accurately to mean splitting a single LAN segment into multiple LAN segments for the purpose of isolating electrical problems on a cable segment to provide improved cabling reliability. This is the primary function of a wiring concentrator.

When reading industry literature, determine whether this term is meant to convey the first meaning or second meaning described in this glossary. In this book, the term "segmentation" is used only to describe separating a LAN into multiple LANs to reduce confusion.

Sequenced Packet Exchange (SPX)   A NetWare connection-oriented protocol and packet format that provides transport layer functions for NetWare communications. SPX calculates a checksum of each IPX packet at the sending end, and again at the receiving end where the checksum is compared for accuracy. If the IPX packet is received with no checksum error, an SPX positive acknowledgment is sent. If a checksum error is detected, a negative acknowledgment is sent. If no acknowledgment is sent, IPX resends the packet again. SPX fulfills the standard functions of OSI layer 3, the transport layer.

By default, SPX is used only by NetWare's Print Server and Remote Console utilities. Unless an application specifically calls for the use of SPX through an API, it is not used. Instead, NCP acknowledges the receipt of NCP packets without calculating a checksum or verifying accuracy.

Service Access Point (SAP) (as used by IEEE)   The SAP is the interface between two layers of protocol. Each layer of protocol must communicate with the layer above it and beneath it. SAPs are also connection points between parallel layers of protocol in an internetwork. Each bridge is either a Destination SAP (DSAP) or Source SAP (SSAP) for bridged LAN communications.

Service Advertising Protocol (SAP) (as used by Novell) A NetWare proprietary protocol and packet format that provides notification between servers of their existence, service type and network address location. Each server broadcasts SAP packets to inform all file servers and routers of its existence. Each SAP packet can contain up to seven server names, service type, and routing information. SAP packets are broadcast every 60 seconds. When a SAP packet is received by a file server, an object is created in its bindery, which makes the server available for user requests.

shell The workstation software that connects a DOS workstation with the file server and provides a DOS interface with the server operating system. The NETX.COM software (or its equivalent) provides this function.

NetWare 4.0 now uses a NETX.VLM (Virtual Loading Module) and terms this same functionality a DOS requester. (See OS/2 Requester.)

Small Computer System Interface (SCSI) An ANSI standard bus design. SCSI host adapters are used to adapt an ISA, EISA, or MCA bus to a SCSI bus so that SCSI devices (such as disk drives) can be interfaced. A SCSI bus can accommodate up to eight devices, however the bus adapter is labeled as one device, thereby enabling only seven usable devices to be interfaced on each SCSI adapter.

SCSI devices are intelligent devices. SCSI disk drives have embedded controllers and are interfaced to a SCSI bus adapter. A SCSI interface card is therefore a "bus adapter," not a "controller." (See SCSI-2.)

Small Computer System Interface-2 (SCSI-2) An ANSI standard that improves on SCSI-1 standards for disk and other device interfaces. SCSI-2 bandwidth is 10 Mbytes/sec, whereas SCSI-1 is 5 Mbytes/sec. SCSI-2 also permits command-tag queuing, which enables up to 256 requests to be queued without waiting for completion of the first request. Another feature of SCSI-2 is the bus's capability to communicate with more than one type of device at the same time, where a single SCSI-1 host adapter could only support one type of device (that is, a disk drive or CD-ROM) to communicate on the bus. (See SCSI.)

socket address An extension to the ultimate source and destination in an IPX combined address. The socket identifies the type of request and therefore where the request should be forwarded in a server operating system. Separate socket addresses are assigned to NCP, routing, printing, and other types of requests.

source-routing bridge/protocol A type of LLC bridge and protocol generally used with Token Rings that use IEEE 802.2 source-routing protocol and frame header fields to identify the path a frame should take through a system of bridges. The protocol is termed "source-routing" because the source of the communications (the workstation) determines the path to be taken by a discovery process. The protocol and frame header fields identify SSAPs and DSAPs (entry and exit points) in the series of bridges. (See LLC-bridges, bridges, DSAP, and SSAP.)

Source Service Access Point (SSAP)   The entry point bridge in an LLC-bridge that uses 802.2 protocol. (See LLC-bridges, bridges, DSAP, and SSAP.)

spanned volume   A volume that spans across more than one logical partition, and therefore more than one disk drive.

spanning-tree bridge/protocol   A type of LLC bridge and protocol, generally used with Ethernet, that provides service for more complex configurations of multiple bridges using one of IEEE's 802.2 spanning-tree protocols. When multiple bridges are employed, the possibility of frame traffic entering infinite loops exists, and complications develop, such as determining the most efficient path develop. This protocol designates bridges as SSAPs and DSAPs (entry and exit points) in the series of bridges. (See LLC-bridges, bridges, DSAP, and SSAP.)

star-bus   A bus network topology configured into a star by introducing a wiring concentrator (multiport repeater/hub).

star-wired ring (star-ring)   A network topology in which connections are strung along a cable that is configured as a ring, and wired into a star. The ring is contained within a Multistation Access Unit (MAU) or Control Access Unit (CAU), with two pairs of wires extending to each connection. MAUs/CAUs can be connected together to form a larger ring.

This topology is the preferred method for configuring Token Ring LANs, because a break in a cable can be detected and corrected without losing the ring configuration and disabling the LAN.

streaming-data mode   A function of MCA and EISA bus architectures in which four bytes are transferred at a time with only one address byte, instead of the normal one address byte per data byte. Devices that access this mode can increase data transfer rates up to fourfold for short bursts of data through the computer bus. This technique is used with 32-bit bus mastering devices.

striping   Blocks, sectors, or bytes of data that are recorded to separate disk drives can be striped across the drives. Striping can produce better performance by writing or reading data from or to multiple drives at the same time. If NetWare volumes are spanned, NetWare automatically stripes sectors of blocks (of newly recorded data) across the drives, splitting seeks as it does, and reducing access time.

Systems Network Architecture (SNA)   IBM's network architecture used in mainframe systems. (See network architecture.)

terminal   An input/output device that is a slave of a CPU, such as with a minicomputer or mainframe terminal. Terminals are not used in the distributed computing environment of a PC network. The term "terminal" sometimes is used incorrectly to describe a "workstation." (See workstation.)

time slice   A brief period of time in which a process is given access to the processor. Each second is divided into 18.3 time slices; multiple tasks can be scheduled for processing in these slices, yet outwardly appear to be occurring simultaneously. (See multitasking.)

token-passing bus   An access protocol that uses a linear-bus or star-bus network, but uses a logically configured ring to pass a token for exclusive access to the network. ARCnet, Thomas-Conrad's TCNS LAN, and General Motors' MAP networks use this access protocol. The access protocol was described in IEEE 802.4 Medium Access Control specifications, which describe MAP. ARCnet and TCNS are proprietary and do not conform to IEEE 802.4 specifications.

token-passing ring   The access protocol used in Token Ring networks. Token-passing ring uses a ring or star-wired ring topology to pass bits of data around a physically wired ring. Three frame types exist, the first of which is a token which grants exclusive use of the ring when received.

Token Ring   A type of LAN that uses token-passing ring access protocol, and uses a physical ring or a star-wired ring topology and twisted-pair or optical fiber cable.

topology   The layout or design of cabling on a network. Three basic topologies are used in LANs today: linear-bus, star-bus, and star-wired ring. Variations such as hierarchical star-bus and distributed star-bus topologies are also used. Though other topologies are used in networks, including mesh and tree topologies, they are not commonly employed in LANs and therefore are not discussed in this book.

The term "topology" often is used by Novell and in the industry to identify a single physical LAN (or network address). This usage is vague, confusing, and inconsistent with industry standards. Moreover, it confounds clear and concise explanations of network addressing, and is therefore not used in this manner in this book.

transceiver   An electrical LAN device that transmits and receives bits of data from a network. In an Ethernet LAN, the transceiver acts as a gate, closing the circuit to enable data to be transmitted when the cable is free and opening the circuit to disable transmissions when other activity is sensed on the cable. It also detects collisions (transmissions from other nodes during a transmission) and stops the transmission. Transceivers also introduce "jabber control" to prevent one node from dominating the network, and Signal Quality Error (which is turned off in modern Ethernet LANs).

translating bridge   A type of LLC bridge that translates between different frame types and access protocols using 802.2 protocol. (See LLC, bridge, and frame.)

Transmission Control Protocol/Internet Protocol (TCP/IP)   A set of networking protocols developed in the 1970s and funded by the U.S. Government's Defense Advanced Research Projects Agency (DARPA). TCP/IP was the second generation of the previously established DARPANET, which had been developed for weapons research, development, and procurement by the Department of Defense. TCP/IP includes Transport Control Protocol, which is a connection-oriented transport protocol that includes transport, session, and presentation layer protocol functions equivalent to layers 4, 5, and 6 of the OSI Model and Internet Protocol, and a widely used routable network protocol that corresponds to layer 3 of the OSI Model. User Datagram Protocol (UDP) can be substituted in cases where connectionless datagram service is desired.

TCP/IP is more than these two protocols; it is an entire protocol stack that includes protocols for file transfers (FTP), terminal emulation services (telnet), electronic mail (SMTP), address resolution (ARP and RARP), and error control and notification (ICMP and SNMP).

TCP/IP is used extensively in many computer systems because it is nonproprietary—free from royalties. Its use was mandated by Congress in 1988, in computer systems for many government agencies and contract situations.

TCP/IP is used in the Internet, a huge government and research internetwork spanning North America and much of the world, which was opened to commercial use in the summer of 1991. These factors have caused TCP/IP use to grow, making it the most commonly used set of network protocols.

transparent bridge   A MAC-layer bridge. (See bridge and MAC-layer bridge.)

twisted-pair   Cabling that consists of lightly insulated copper wire, twisted into pairs and bundled into sets of pairs. The twists enhance the wire's capability to resist *crosstalk* (bleeding of signal from one wire to the next). This cabling is used extensively in phone systems and LANs.

Universal Network Architecture (UNA)   Novell's proprietary network architecture, based on XNS and very similar to TCP/IP. UNA includes protocols and packet formats that enable the system of data communications between workstations and servers on a NetWare network. The protocols and packet formats include Internetwork Packet Exchange (IPX), Sequenced Packet Exchange (SPX), NetWare Core Protocol (NCP), Router Information Protocol (RIP), and Service Advertising Protocol (SAP).

UnixWare   A UNIX System V Release 4.2 operating system developed and produced by Univel, which includes support for NetWare networking. UnixWare Application Server is an operating system that incorporates NetWare server and routing functions and support for IPX communications. UnixWare Personal Edition is a workstation UNIX operating system that incorporates NetWare workstation connectivity with the capability to run UNIX, DOS, and Windows applications at the desktop under either the X-Windows or Motif graphical user interfaces.

Virtual Loading Modules (VLMs)   Support software modules that are dynamically loaded when VLM.EXE is loaded. These files are used with the DOS Requester.

wiring concentrator   A multiple port repeating device used in Ethernet LANs to connect multiple cable segments into one LAN. Sometimes called a "hub" or "multiport repeater," this device isolates cabling problems by separating each workstation connection on an isolated cabling segment. Wiring concentrators are a required component in 802.3 10BASE-T (twisted-pair Ethernet) LANs, and improve reliability on any type of Ethernet LAN. Wiring concentrators also link together different cable types, many incorporating AUI connectors for connection to thick coaxial (10BASE-5), BNC connectors for thin coaxial (10BASE-2), RJ-45 jacks for twisted-pair (10BASE-T), and fiber-optic connectors. Some Token Ring vendors also call their MAUs wiring concentrators.

workstation   A user computer that is connected to a network. In the distributed computing environment of a PC network, workstations are user stations (not "terminals") that are clients of one or more servers. A workstation has its own processor, processes applications locally, and may access data and resources located elsewhere on the network. In some cases, partial processing may be distributed back to a server such as a database server; however, a workstation always executes applications locally. (See terminal.)

Xerox Network System (XNS)   Xerox's network architecture, which provides the basis for both Novell's Universal Network Architecture and TCP/IP network protocols and packet formats.

NetWare Capacities and Requirements

B

When planning NetWare installation or expansion, you should check with Tables B.1, B.2, and B.3. These statistics can be found in your NetWare manuals in many different places.

Table B.1. File server hardware and OS capacities.

Description	3.11	3.12	4.x
Processor	386SX or above	386SX or above	386SX or above
Min RAM	4MB	4MB	8MB
Max RAM	4GB	4GB	4GB
Max disk space	32TB	32TB	32TB
Min DOS partition	1.5MB	5MB	5MB
Min SYS volume size	20MB	45MB	45MB
Max volume size	32TB	32TB	32TB
Max volumes	64	64	64
Max volume segments/disk	8	8	8
Max disks/spanned volume	32	32	32
Min phys disks	1	1	1
Max phys disks	2,048	2,048	2,048
Min FDD	1	1	1
Min NICs	1	1	1
Max NICs	Ltd by # of physical bus slots		

Table B.2. Operating system capacities.

Description	3.x	4.x
Max # users	250	1,000
Open files	100,000	100,000
Max file size	4GB	4GB
Concurrent TTS	1,000	1,000
Dir ent/vol	2,097,152	2,097,152

Description	3.x	4.x
Subdir in pathname	10 to 100 (def = 25)	10 to 100 (def = 25)
Percent of disk space in one directory	5 to 50 (def = 15)	5 to 50 (def = 15)
Search drives	16	16
IPX hops to live	16	16
No. printers/print server	16	256
Jobs in queue at any time	(ltd. by disk space)	(ltd. by disk space)

Table B.3. Disk space provisions (MB).

Description	3.11	3.12	4.0
Min DOS partition	1.5	5.0	5.0
Min NetWare SYS volume	20	45	45
Server OS	12.5	15	35
ElectroText	n/a	30	25
BasicMHS	n/a	2.5	2.5
Full install	20	59	79

NET.CFG Configuration Settings

C

The NET.CFG file is a workstation configuration file. It is a simple ASCII file that adjusts the workstation drivers and shell or the requester. Statements in this file adjust the following software layers:

```
Link Support Layer (LSL.COM)
NIC Driver (i.e. NE2000.COM)
IPX/SPX (IPXODI.COM)
Novell NetBIOS Emulator (NETBIOS.COM)
DOS Shell (NETX.COM/NETX.EXE)
DOS Requester (VLM.EXE)
```

This appendix discusses the statements and keywords used in the NET.CFG, organized by software layer.

Link Support Layer Statements
LINK SUPPORT

This statement introduces the section of the NET.CFG file that adjusts LSL.COM.

BUFFERS *number size*
Explanation

This statement configures the number and size of packet receive buffers used by LSL.

Syntax

```
Link Support
   Buffers 10 4202     (initializes 10 buffers, 4202 bytes in size)
```

Default and Range

> default number = 0, range = 0 to 97
> default size = 1130, range = 618 to 59K

Notes

Total buffer space is limited to 59K. The number of buffers times the buffer size may not exceed 59K.

MAX BOARDS *number*

Explanation

This configures the number of logical boards LSL can manage. Each logical board handles a single frame type. The default is designed to support all four Ethernet frame types at once.

Syntax

```
Link Support
   Max Boards 2
```

Default

4

Range

1 to 16

MAX STACKS *number*

Explanation

This statement tells LSL how many higher layer protocols it can handle. Each protocol can require support for several protocols at various layers.

Syntax

```
Link Support
   Max Stacks 8
```

Default

4

Range

1 to 16

Discussion

When supporting other protocols in addition to IPX, SPX, and NCP, you should adjust this parameter upward if a protocol stack fails to load because of "out of resource" conditions. For TCP/IP workstations, read the installation guide supplied with your TCP/IP workstation software for recommended values.

MEMPOOL *number*

Explanation

Protocol stacks other than IPX, SPX, or NCP may use this option to configure the size of memory pool buffers.

Default

0

Syntax

```
Link Driver
    Mempool 12
```

Discussion

The number is specified in K (1024 bytes). See the installation guide for your TCP/IP (or other) workstation software for recommendations on use of this parameter.

NIC Driver Statements

This section configures Multiple Link Interface Driver (MLID) NIC driver parameters to communicate with the actual physical switch (or software) settings on the board. Because ML:ID drivers are executable files, written by the NIC developer specifically for their own boards, this file configures parameters such as the physical hardware settings.

LINK DRIVER *driver_name*

This statement introduces the section that specifies parameters for the NIC driver. A single NET.CFG can be used with several NICs. This heading specifies the portion of the file that pertains to the named driver.

In this section, if more than one logical board is supported, the board number is specified. The board number does not need to be specified if only one logical board is used.

DMA *#board_number channel*

Explanation

This parameter can specify the DMA channel used by the named driver.

Default

Specified by board developer.

Syntax

```
Link Driver NE2000
    DMA 5
```

Discussion

Some NICs can use DMA channels alternate to the standard DMA channel. The DMA channel used must correspond with the physical hardware settings and must not conflict with other devices.

FRAME *Frame_type*

Explanation

This statement specifies the frame type supported by this driver and by this logical board. This is used for Ethernet NICs which may use any one of four frame types.

Default

Specified by the NIC developer.

Frame Types Supported

```
Ethernet_802.2
Ethernet_802.3
Ethernet_II
Ethernet_SNAP
```

Syntax

```
Link Driver NE2000
   Frame Ethernet_802.3
```

Discussion

Your server and workstation must use the same frame type in order to communicate. MLID drivers can support multiple frame formats at the same time.

> **NOTE ▶**
>
> Novell changed the default Ethernet frame type for MLID drivers in the Fall of 1993. Unless you specify the appropriate frame type, some of your drivers may default to a different frame type from the others. If a workstation uses one frame type, and a file server uses a different frame type, they will not be able to communicate.

INT

Explanation

This parameter specifies the interrupt request (IRQ) physical hardware switch setting on your workstation NIC.

Default

Specified by NIC developer.

Range

Specified by NIC developer.

Syntax

```
Link Driver
   INT 10
```

Discussion

This parameter specifies the physical IRQ setting of your NIC.

MEM *start_memory_buffer_address*

Explanation

This address specifies where the memory buffer address space begins.

Default

Specified by NIC developer.

Syntax

```
Link Driver NE2000
   MEM C8000
```

Discussion

The memory address set for RAM that buffering can use.

> **NOTE** ▶
>
> The number used in this statement uses five hexadecimal digits, the last number equals the offset, which is usually 0.

ALTERNATE

Explanation

Uses the alternate board.

NODE ADDRESS *hex_number*

Explanation

This statement is used to assign a local address to a NIC, overriding the universal node address assigned by the NIC developer.

LINK STATIONS *number*

Explanation

This statement is used with the IBM LAN Support Program LANSUP.COM. See your IBM LAN Support Program documentation for further information.

MAX FRAME SIZE *number*

Explanation

This statement adjusts the maximum frame size that can be transmitted on the LAN. This number includes the packet and frame header/trailer. For example, an Ethernet_802.2 frame has a maximum packet size of 1501 bytes plus the frame header and trailer. Any board overhead must be included. See your NIC driver instructions for information on using this parameter. Most NIC developers write their drivers so they will default to the optimum value for the NIC.

Default

Specified by NIC developer.

Syntax

```
Link Driver NE2000
   Max Frame Size 1621
```

PORT *port_address*
Explanation

This statement configures the driver to look for the NIC at the specified base I/O address. This address must correspond with the physical switch setting of the NIC. If no parameter is entered, the NIC default will apply.

Default

Specified by NIC developer.

Syntax

```
Link Driver NE2000
   PORT 340
```

Discussion

Configure your driver to locate the base I/O address set on your NIC. If other than the factory default setting is used, this parameter must be used to initialize the NIC.

PROTOCOL *name hex_protocol_ID frame_type*
Explanation

This statement is used to configure your driver to support a protocol in addition to IPX/SPX/NCP. The protocol to be supported, such as TCPIP, must be assigned along with its hexadecimal code. If more than one frame type is being supported, the frame type to which the protocol is to be bound must be specified.

Default

IPXODI

Syntax

```
Link Driver NE2000
    FRAME Ethernet 802.3
    FRAME Ethernet_802.2
    Protocol IPXODI 0 Ethernet_802.3
    Protocol TCPIP 1 Ethernet_802.2
```

Discussion

In the previous example, IPX protocol is bound to the Ethernet_802.3 frame and therefore logical board #0, and TCPIP is bound to the Ethernet_802.2 frame and therefore logical board #1. If only IPX is used, this statement is not necessary.

SAPS *number*
Explanation

This statement specifies the number of Service Access Points needed for the IBM LAN Support Program (LANSUP.COM driver). See your IBM LAN Support Program for detail on this statement.

Default

1

Discussion

This statement is ignored if another application has already opened the board.

SLOT *#board_number slot_number*
Explanation

This parameter specifies the Microchannel slot number into which this NIC is installed and therefore identifies the board.

Default

Defined by NIC developer.

Range

Defined by vendor, limited to physical slots.

Syntax

```
Link Driver NE2-32
   Slot #1 1
```

Discussion

The driver locates the appropriate board according to which Microchannel slot the board is in. When the driver locates the board according to slot, the configuration is read from the board's memory. If more than one board is supported in this workstation, the number following the # identifies the board number to be supported, and the second number is the slot number in which the board is located. See your IBM Reference Program for information about slot numbers.

IPX Protocol Statements

This section identifies adjustment parameters for the IPX/SPX protocol. The IPXODI.COM packet driver is adjusted through the use of these supporting statements.

BIND *board_name*

Explanation

This statement binds the specified protocol to the specified board. If no board is specified, the protocol is bound to the first board encountered.

Default

IPXODI

Syntax

```
Protocol IPXODI
   Bind NE2000
```

CONFIG OPTION *number*

Explanation

Assigns a board configuration number (a set of configuration parameters) specified in the WSGEN or DCONFIG programs.

Default

0 (#0 parameters are defined by an NIC developer).

Syntax

```
CONFIG OPTION 1
```

Discussion

When using WSGEN to generate an NIC configuration, vendors define a set of default configuration options that apply when no parameters are specified and call it configuration option #0. Other sets of configuration parameters are set as option 1, 2, 3 , 4, and so on. This number identifies which set of configuration options are to be selected.

INT64 *on/off*

Explanation

This statement enables support for application calls to software interrupt 64h to maintain compatibility with applications written with older NetWare APIs (prior to version 3.10).

Default

ON

Syntax

```
INT64 OFF
```

Discussion

Applications written for previous versions of NetWare may hang when used with 3.10 or later. If your application calls this interrupt, or if the application works with previous versions, but not with 3.10 or higher, set this parameter to OFF.

INT7A
Explanation

This statement enables support for application calls to software interrupt 7Ah to maintain compatibility with applications written for NetWare 2.0a APIs.

Default

ON

Syntax

```
INT7A OFF
```

Discussion

Applications written for previous versions of NetWare may hang when used with 3.10 or later. If your application calls this interrupt, or if the application works with previous versions, but not with 3.10 or higher, set this parameter to OFF.

IPATCH *hex_address*
Explanation

This statement enables the IPXODI.COM code to be patched with any specific byte offset value.

IPX PACKET SIZE LIMIT *size*
Explanation

This statement reduces the IPX default packet size set by the NIC driver.

IPX RETRY COUNT *number*

Explanation

Adjusts the number of IPX retries.

Default

20

Discussion

IPX recommends NCP packet resends when no acknowledgment is received within a default time period. On media that is not reliable or where extensive delays occur (such as in a WAN), this number may need to be adjusted upward so that a time out will not occur. NetBIOS session establishment also may require extending this parameter.

IPX SOCKETS *number*

Explanation

This statement adjusts the number of IPX sockets.

Default

20

Discussion

The default number of IPX sockets is sufficient for the vast majority of applications. If more sockets are required, your application documentation or technical support will specify what level to set this parameter.

MINIMUM SPX RETRIES *number*

Explanation

When SPX is used (as in the NetWare Print Server Utility), this value regulates how many retries will be ignored before a time out occurs, and the send connection is considered bad.

Default

20 (adjustable through API)

Discussion

This value may need to be adjusted only under unusual circumstances. Normally, if the value needs to be adjusted, it is adjusted through the application developer's calls to SPX. See your application documentation or technical support for advice on adjusting this parameter.

SPX ABORT TIMEOUT *number*

Explanation

Adjust the time period before an SPX time out when no acknowledgment is received. Time period is specified in ticks (18.21 ticks per second).

Default

108 ticks (about six seconds)

Discussion

When SPX is used, it waits about six seconds before terminating a connection that has not acknowledged receipt of each packet. To extend this period, adjust the number of ticks upward in increments of 54 until time outs diminish or are eliminated.

SPX CONNECTIONS *number*
Explanation

This is the number of SPX connections used at any given time.

Default

15

Discussion

SPX is not normally used, so the default parameters are set low. Almost any time SPX is used, this number must be adjusted upward. For example, when your workstation printer is shared as a network remote printer, this number must be adjusted up to 50, or various SPX errors will occur.

SPX LISTEN TIMEOUT *number*
Explanation

This parameter specifies the amount of time the sending SPX waits before it requests a resend if it has not received a packet.

Default

108 ticks (about six seconds)

Discussion

When SPX is called, each message (series of packets) to be transmitted is sent within a connection that is established for this purpose. Once the connection is established, if no packets are received during this time period, the connection times out. You can extend the length of that period using this parameter.

IPX VERIFY TIMEOUT

Explanation

This statement adjusts how often a keep-alive packet is sent to keep the connection active within a message if no data is being sent.

Default

54 ticks (about three seconds)

Discussion

This time period should be observed by applications using SPX. If the application does time out when no verification is forthcoming, the time period can be adjusted to a longer period.

DOS Requester (VLM) Adjustments

Novell switched to using the VLM.EXE requester in place of NETX shell with versions 3.12 and 4.0. These products load support modules as overlaid files. The support modules can be selected for loading and adjusted through the use of these parameters.

AUTO LARGE TABLE *off/on*

Selects a large table (178 bytes) or small table (34 bytes) per connection for bindery reconnections. When a server connection is broken, it can be re-established through this table. When reconnections are not necessitated, the OFF default should remain. When disconnections occur regularly, this may be insufficient to automatically re-connect the requester upon demand without unloading and reloading the requester (VLM.EXE).

Default

OFF

Modules

AUTO.VLM, BIND.VLM

AVERAGE NAME LENGTH *number_of_characters*

This parameter adjusts the average length allocated for server names. The default is configured for maximum length server names. To save workstation RAM, if short server names are used, this parameter can be reduced.

Default

48 characters

Range

2 to 48 characters

Module

CONN.VLM

AUTO RECONNECT *on/off*

When this parameter is set to the default value of ON, the workstation reconnects to the server automatically and rebuilds the connection environment (such as mapping) if a server connection is broken. If this parameter is set to OFF, the user must reboot or unload and reload the VLM.EXE.

> **NOTE** ▶
>
> You must include the statement VLM=AUTO.VLM to re-establish AUTO.VLM stored parameters.

Default

ON

Modules

AUTO.VLM, NDS.VLM, PNW.VLM

AUTO RETRY *number*

This parameter establishes the number of retries permitted to reconnect to a file server when a fatal connection error has occurred.

Default

0

Range

0 to 3640

Modules

AUTO.VLM, NDS.VLM, BIND.VLM, PNW.VLM

NOTE ▶

Unless this parameter is set to some level, reconnection will only try once. No retries will be attempted if the reconnection attempt fails the first time.

BIND RECONNECT *on/off*

Automatically restores drive mappings and printer captures when reconnection occurs.

TIP ▶

Set this parameter to ON to ensure proper mapping and printer captures upon reconnection.

Default

OFF

Modules

AUTO.VLM, BIND.VLM

CACHE BUFFERS

Allocates the number of cache buffers used by the requester between the workstation and the server's open files.

> **CAUTION** ▶
>
> In some cases, more buffers lower performance.

Default

5

Range

0 top 64

Modules

FIO.VLM

CACHE BUFFER SIZE *size*

This parameter sets the cache buffer size. It can be adjusted for some applications that use a large page size (such as Btrieve) for better performance.

Default

512 bytes

Range

64 to 4096

Modules

FIO.VLM

CACHE WRITES *on/off*

This parameter improves performance when it is set to ON, but improves data integrity when set to OFF by recovering from disk full errors at the server.

Default

ON

Modules

FIO.VLM

CHECKSUM *value*

This parameter adjusts the NCP validation level for level of data delivery integrity required. Reliability of your LAN cabling is of the utmost concern with this parameter.

> **TIP** ▶
>
> For better I/O performance when your LAN is highly reliable, set this parameter to 0. This is a good option when using Token Ring and no error conditions are present.
>
> When network errors are present, set this level to a higher value, especially if data loss caused by connection errors occurs.

Values

0 = disabled
1 = enabled but not preferred
2 = enabled and preferred
3 = required

Default

1

Modules

FIO.VLM

CONNECTIONS *number*

This value sets the number of NCP connections available during I/O operations. If the workstation needs to attach to more than eight servers at one time, you must adjust this number upward.

Default

8

Range

2 to 50

Modules

CONN.VLM, FIO.VLM

DOS NAME *name*

This is a user definable variable that is substituted for the login script identifier variable %OS. It is generally used to enable varying versions of DOS to be supported with a single statement in login scripts.

> **NOTE** ▶
>
> DR-DOS or Novell DOS is recognized as DRDOS by the %OS parameter as part of a pathname.

Default

MSDOS

Modules

NETX.VLM, GENERAL.VLM

FIRST NETWORK DRIVE *drive_letter*

This statement specifies the first drive letter NetWare can use for drive mappings. Because the LASTDRIVE=Z command is used with the CONFIG.SYS, the old NetWare convention used with the NETX shell no longer applies.

Default

First drive letter not in use by DOS

Range

A to Z

Modules

GENERAL.VLM

HANDLE NET ERRORS *on/off*

When no response is received from a server, this parameter redirects errors to interrupt 24 for application handling if set to the default value of ON. If set to OFF, the error is reported to the workstation screen in the form of a NET_REV_ERROR *hex_value*.

> **TIP** ►
>
> When failure to connect to a server or interruption of connection to a server is encountered, set this option to OFF; then look up the generated error code in your System Messages manual.

Default

ON

Modules

IPXNCP.VLM

LARGE INTERNET PACKETS *off/on*

This statement enables negotiation of the largest packet size possible between source workstation and remote file server upon connection. It can be used to restrict the packet size to 576 bytes.

> **NOTE** ►
>
> Where a 3.11 or 2.2 server or router that does not support Large Internet Packet is between the source and the destination, packet size is forced to 576 bytes.

Default

ON

Modules

IPXNCP.VLM

LOAD CONN TABLE LOW *on/off*

This statement loads the connection table into conventional memory and does not take advantage of loading into high memory saving conventional memory. Early 4.0 releases required this statement. It is still recommended for better performance with 4.01.

> **NOTE** ▶
>
> If you see the message "Authenticating user to file server NAME, please wait" several times in a row on your screen when first requesting a service or connection to a new file server, load the connection table low to correct the problem.

Default

OFF

Modules

CONN.VLM

LOAD LOW CONN *on/off*

This statement can be set to OFF to load the connection manager into high memory. This improves memory management, optimizes conventional memory, but affects performance.

Default

ON

Modules

CONN.VLM

LOAD LOW IPXNCP *on/off*

This statement can be set to load the IPX/NCP protocol layers into high memory.

Default

ON

Modules

IPXNCP.VLM

LOCAL PRINTERS *n*

This statement can be used to configure the requester for fewer local printers. When a DOS application attempts to print to a local printer port that has not been redirected and does not have a local printer attached to it, normal BIOS error control is disabled. This may result in printer errors and locked applications unless this parameter is adjusted.

Default

3

Range

1 to 3

Modules

PRINT.VLM

LONG MACHINE TYPE *name*

This statement can be used to create a user-definable variable restricted to six letters. This variable is accessed in a login script with the %MACHINE identifier variable.

Default

IBM_PC

Modules

NETX.VLM, GENERAL.VLM

MAX TASKS *n*

Enables *n* number of tasks to be active at one time. Windows or Desqview can have more than one application active at one time. If you have problems when many programs are loaded at the same time, increase this parameter.

Default

30

Range

20 to 128

Modules

CONN.VLM

MESSAGE LEVEL *value*

This statement controls the level of screen message reporting from the requester.

Values

0 = Always display copyright and critical errors
1 = Display warning messages
2 = Display program load information for VLMs
3 = Display configuration information
4 = Display diagnostic information

Default

1

Range

0 to 4

Modules

NWP.VLM

MESSAGE TIMEOUT *time*

This statement defines the amount of time a broadcast message is left on-screen before it is automatically cleared. The time is expressed in ticks (18.21 ticks per second).

Default

0

Range

0 to 10,000 (approximately six hours)

Modules

NWP.VLM

NAME CONTEXT = "*name_context*"

This statement sets the current location in a 4.0 NDS tree.

Default

Root

Modules

NDS.VLM

NETWORK PRINTERS *n*

Adjusts the number of LPT ports that can be redirected. This statement can be used to give access to up to nine network printers at the same time using the CAPTURE command.

Default

3

Range

0 to 9

Modules

PRINT.VLM

PB BUFFERS *n*

This statement configures the number of Packet Burst buffers. Packet Burst Protocol is self-adjusting and normally should not be adjusted. For more information about adjusting Packet Burst Protocol, see Chapter 33, "Monitoring and Adjusting Server Performance."

> **NOTE** ▶
>
> Specifying a value of 0 toggles the Packet Burst Protocol off.

Default

3

Range

1 to 10

PREFERRED SERVER *server_name*

This statement is used to force attachment to a specific server by default. This is used to prevent inefficient routing and specific login.

Default

"Get Nearest Server"

Modules

BIND.VLM

PREFERRED TREE *NDS_tree*

Default

No preferred tree

Modules

NDS.VLM

PRINT BUFFER SIZE *size*

This statement configures the size of the print buffer that caches print spooling between the software output and the packet driver. Redirected printing is spooled in a byte-oriented output, resulting in many small packets. As the buffer size is increased, this parameter can reduce the number of packets in a print job, increasing the size of each packet, which makes handling across the LAN more efficient.

Default

64

Range

0 to 256

Modules

PRINT.VLM

PRINT HEADER *size*

This statement sets the size of the print header that is sent at the beginning of a print job. The print header contains printer codes if you are using print job configurations. Long printer intialization strings used in a print job configuration can be larger than the default, causing some of the printer codes to be truncated.

Default

64 bytes

Range

0 to 1024 bytes

Modules

PRINT.VLM

PRINT TAIL *size*

Sets the size of the trailer sent at the end of the print job.

Default

16 bytes

Range

0 to 1024

Modules

PRINT.VLM

READ-ONLY COMPATIBILITY *on/off*

This statement controls whether a read-only file can be opened with read-write access. Some applications require this to be set to ON to resolve software problems.

Default

OFF

Modules

REDIR.VLM

SEARCH MODE *value*

Adjusting this parameter adjusts the way executable files use the path to look for supporting files (files called from the application). Executable files are sometimes hard-coded to search for files a specific way (for example, to find only executable files such as subroutines, not overlaid files.) Some executable files search the path for data or overlaid files; other applications have no search instructions. Often these instructions are controlled by a record manager or database runtime, such as Btrieve or Foxbase.

NOTE ▶

You can execute files according to normal search conventions. This statement adjusts only how an executable file searches for support files.

CAUTION ▶

This statement can adversely affect the way applications work. You should not adjust the search mode without good reason and understanding of the effect it can have. After making changes, test your applications for proper execution.

Values

0 = No search instructions, executable files search default setting according to hard-coded instructions, DOS searches the path for .EXE, .COM, and .BAT files only.

1 = Executable files according to hard coding only. If no search instructions are hard coded, directories are searched according to normal path conventions.

2 = Search only the working directory; do not search other directories. Ignore hard-coded instructions.

3 = Search only the hard-coded path, except when reading a file flagged as read-only. If no path is hard-coded, read-only executables search working directory then search drives.

4 = Not used (reserved for future use; no effect if used).

5 = Search working directory and search drives regardless of hard-coded search instructions. Can search for any file extensions depending upon hard-coded search instructions, but DOS only searches for .EXE, .COM, and .BAT files.

6 = Not used (reserved for future use; no effect if used).

7 = If file is flagged as read-only, search the working directory and the search path for all files with all extensions, regardless of hard coding. Executable files will therefore locate all files called (regardless of extension) as long as the executable is flagged as read-only.

> **NOTE** ►
>
> Unlike previous DOS shells, this statement affects searches on local drives as well as network drives.

Default

1

Modules

GENERAL.VLM

SET STATION TIME *on/off*

This statement can be changed to ignore file server time upon initial connection, retaining its own clock time.

Default

ON

Modules

VLM.EXE

SHOW DOTS *on/off*

Displays "." and ".." directory listings for network directories (which do not exist in NetWare directory listings).

> **NOTE** ▶
>
> You must add the following statement when using Windows to see "." and ".." in Windows file listing dialog boxes.
>
> SHOW DOTS = ON

Default

OFF

Modules

REDIR.VLM

SHORT MACHINE TYPE *name*

This statement can be used to create a user-definable variable restricted to four letters. This variable is accessed in a login script with the %SMACHINE identifier variable.

Default

IBM

Modules

NETX.VLM, GENERAL.VLM

SIGNATURE LEVEL *value*

Adjusts the way Packet Signature works. Levels 2 and 3 increase security but reduce performance.

Values

0 = disabled
1 = enabled but not preferred

2 = preferred
3 = required

Default

1

Modules

NWP.VLM

TRUE COMMIT on/off

Setting this function to ON forces an NCP commit when DOS commits a file write request. Default disables this function. Default value of OFF gives better write performance under some circumstances, whereas ON may hamper performance. However, it does so with better file integrity, especially when LAN or WAN may be less than 100-percent reliable.

Default

OFF

Modules

FIO.VLM

USE DEFAULTS on/off

A default value of ON loads .VLM files that are specified in the NET.CFG listing. If this parameter is set to OFF, a default list of .VLMs will be loaded. If set to OFF, you may receive errors indicating that VLM files are loading twice, once by default, and once according to listing in NET.CFG. Set this to OFF to eliminate the list of .VLMs in your NET.CFG and to load the default list.

Default

ON

Default list of .VLMs

```
CONN
IPXNCP
TRAN
SECURITY
NDS
BIND
NWP
FIO
GENERAL
REDIR
PRINT
NETX
```

Modules

VLM.EXE

VLM = *path VLM*

This statement includes the loading of .VLMs in addition to the default listing discussed in USE DEFAULTS. This statement applies only if USE DEFAULTS is set to OFF. Otherwise, the .VLMs can be included in the list of .VLMs to load.

> **NOTE** ▶
>
> You must use the entire pathname, including the .VLM extension, for this statement to be effective.

VLMs that This Statement Applies To

```
RSA.VLM
AUTO.VLM
NMR.VLM
```

Modules

VLM.EXE

ISO (NDS) Country Codes

D

Appendix D

This list of countries is the most current that was available at the time of this writing. It may not reflect recent or ongoing geopolitical changes.

Table D.1. ISO 3166 country codes.

Country Code	Country	Country Code	Country
AD	Andorra	AE	United Arab Emirates
AF	Afghanistan	AG	Antigua and Barbuda
AI	Anguilla	AL	Albania
AN	Netherlands Antilles	AO	Angola
AQ	Antarctica	AR	Argentina
AS	American Samoa	AT	Austria
AU	Australia	AW	Aruba
BB	Barbados	BD	Bangladesh
BE	Belgium	BF	Burkina Faso
BG	Bulgaria	BH	Bahrain
BI	Burundi	BJ	Benin
BM	Bermuda	BN	Brunei Darussalam
BO	Bolivia	BR	Brazil
BS	Bahamas	BT	Bhutan
BU	Burma	BV	Bouvet Island
BW	Botswana	BY	Byelorussian SSR
BZ	Belize	CA	Canada
CC	Cocos (Keeling) Islands	CF	Central Africa Republic
CG	Congo	CH	Switzerland
CI	Côte d'Ivoire	CK	Cook Islands
CL	Chile	CM	Cameroon
CN	China	CO	Colombia

CR	Costa Rica	CS	Czechoslovakia
CU	Cuba	CV	Cape Verde
CX	Christmas Island	CY	Cyprus
DE	Federal Republic of Germany	DJ	Djibouti
DK	Denmark	DM	Dominica
DO	Dominican Republic	DZ	Algeria
EC	Ecuador	EG	Egypt
EH	Western Sahara	ES	Spain
ET	Ethiopia	FI	Finland
FJ	Fiji	FK	Falkland Islands
FM	Micronesia	FO	Faroe Islands
FR	France	GA	Gabon
GB	United Kingdom	GD	Grenada
GF	French Guiana	GH	Ghana
GI	Gibraltar	GL	Greenland
GM	Gambia	GN	Guinea
GP	Guadeloupe	GQ	Equatorial Guinea
GR	Greece	GT	Guatemala
GU	Guam	GW	Guinea-Bissau
GY	Guyana	HK	Hong Kong
HM	Heard & McDonald Islands	HN	Honduras
HT	Haiti	HU	Hungary
ID	Indonesia	IE	Ireland
IL	Israel	IN	India
IO	British Indian Ocean Territory	IQ	Iraq
IR	Islamic Republic of Iran	IS	Iceland
IT	Italy	JM	Jamaica

JO	Jordon	JP	Japan
KE	Kenya	KH	Democratic Kampuchea
KI	Kiribati	KM	Comoros
KN	Saint Kitts and Nevis	KP	Democratic Republic of Korea
KR	Republic of Korea	KW	Kuwait
KY	Cayman Islands	LA	Lao People's Democratic Republic
LB	Lebanon	LC	Saint Lucia
LI	Liechtenstein	LK	Sri Lanka
LR	Liberia	LS	Lesotho
LU	Luxembourg	LY	Libyan Arab Jamahiriya
MA	Morocco	MC	Monaco
MG	Madagascar	MH	Marshall Islands
ML	Mali	MN	Mongolia
MO	Macau	MP	Northern Mariana Islands
MQ	Martinique	MR	Mauritania
MS	Montserrat	MT	Malta
MU	Mauritius	MV	Maldives
MW	Malawi	MX	Mexico
MY	Malaysia	MZ	Mozambique
NA	Namibia	NC	New Caledonia
NE	Niger	NF	Norfolk Island
NG	Nigeria	NI	Nicaragua
NL	Netherlands	NO	Norway
NP	Nepal	NR	Nauru
NT	Neutral Zone	NU	Niue

NZ	New Zealand	OM	Oman
PA	Panama	PE	Peru
PF	French Polynesia	PG	Papua New Guinea
PH	Philippines	PK	Pakistan
PL	Poland	PM	St. Pierre and Miquelon
PN	Pitcarin	PR	Puerto Rico
PT	Portugal	PW	Palau
PY	Paraguay	QA	Qatar
RE	Reunion	RO	Romania
RW	Rwanda	SA	Saudi Arabia
SB	Solomon Islands	SC	Seychelles
SD	Sudan	SE	Sweden
SG	Singapore	SL	St. Helena
SM	Svalbard & Jan Mayen Islands	SN	Sierra Leone
SO	Somalia	SR	Suriname
ST	São Tome and Principe	SU	USSR
SV	El Salvador	SY	Syrian Arab Republic
SZ	Swaziland	TC	Turks and Caicos Islands
TD	Chad	TF	French Southern Territories
TG	Togo	TH	Thailand
TK	Tokelau	TN	Tunisia
TO	Tonga	TP	East Timor
TR	Turkey	TT	Trindad and Tobago

TV	Tuvalu	TW	Province of China Taiwan
TZ	United Republic of Tanzania	UA	Ukrainian SSR
UG	Uganda	UM	US Minor Outlying Islands
US	United States	UY	Uruguay
VA	Vatican City State	VC	St. Vincent & the Grenadines
VE	Venezuela	VG	British Virgin Islands
VI	US Virgin Islands	VN	Vietnam
VU	Vanuatu	WF	Wallis and Futuna Islands
WS	Samoa	YD	Democratic Yemen
YE	Yemen	YU	Yugoslavia
ZA	South Africa	ZM	Zambia
ZR	Zaire		

Login Script Commands, Variables, and Defaults

E

The concepts, strategies, and techniques discussed in Chapter 17, "Login Scripts," are incomplete without the detail contained in this appendix. Login script programming is simpler than most languages, but you need additional detail on each command to learn to use them.

In this appendix, each login script command and identifier variable is discussed in detail. Examples are given for each command, which is the only way most can learn to use them. This appendix goes into far more detail than your NetWare manual. You will find that using the powerful detailed options of these commands and variables can make a single login script universally usable.

For additional help on login scripts, see Chapter 17 or your NetWare installation manual.

Login Script Commands
ATTACH

Description

Attaches user to alternate file server.

Syntax

```
ATTACH server_name/user_name
```

Example

```
ATTACH FS2/%LOGIN_NAME
```

Discussion

ATTACH is an internal command that logs a user into a file server without logout from the current file server, and without executing another login script. (This command does not need to be preceded with a #.) It must be used in a login script prior to mapping to a file-server directory unless already attached. Generally, the first lines of a login script should attach to all file servers where drive mappings need to be created during or subsequent to the login script.

ATTACH bypasses the alternate server's login script. The alternate server grants a connection and restricts the user through user account security.

The user must have a user account on the alternate server. ATTACH assumes the user login name is the same unless the *user_name* is specified as shown in the preceding syntax.

ATTACH is also used to provide access to a file server's printing services, or any other account services, such as electronic mail.

BREAK ON/OFF

Description

Sets DOS BREAK function to ON or OFF.

Default

OFF

Syntax

BREAK ON

Discussion

BREAK ON in your login script enables a user to execute a Ctrl+Break or Ctrl+C to terminate the login script and exit. The default value is set to OFF, which prevents a user from breaking out of the login script during execution.

> **TIP** ▶
>
> You are advised to use this command at the very beginning of a System or Organizational login script until debugging, in case a fatal error prevents mappings. It should be removed once the login script is debugged so that users cannot interrupt the login script.

COMSPEC

Description

Inserts location of COMMAND.COM into DOS environment.

Default

As set in your DOS environment (your boot disk, that is, if your computer booted from C:, your COMSPEC is set to C:\COMMAND.COM).

> **NOTE** ▶
>
> To view your DOS environment, type SET at any DOS prompt.

Syntax

```
COMSPEC = path_name/COMMAND.COM
```

Example

```
COMSPEC=S2:COMMAND.COM
```

(assuming S2: is the DOS directory)

Discussion

This command is required when a diskless workstation or floppy-only workstation is used. A search drive must first be mapped to the DOS directory for the appropriate version of DOS located on the file server's volume, and then the COMSPEC parameter can point to that directory to find COMMAND.COM.

Proper use of COMSPEC eliminates the following errors:

```
Invalid COMMAND.COM, System Halted
Insert Disk with COMMAND.COM in Drive A:
```

This command is not required on hard disk workstations where COMMAND.COM is permanently located and available at all times.

TIP

To view your current COMSPEC variable, type the DOS command SET at a
DOS prompt.

DOS SET *variable*

Description

Sets into DOS environment (same as SET from DOS).

Syntax

```
DOS SET variable = value
```

Examples

```
DOS SET USR = RICK
DOS SET USR = %LOGIN_NAME
```

Discussion

This command enables you to add a DOS variable to your DOS environment. The
environment space is used to store user-defined variables for access by various applications and/or batch files.

CAUTION

DOS environment space is used by many network applications as well as
DOS parameters. By default, DOS limits the environment space to 160
bytes.

You may run out of environment space at times, which can cause error
messages like "Out of environment space." In other instances, applications
simply may not work properly.

> To increase your environment space, use the SHELL command in your
> CONFIG.SYS. See your DOS manual on how to use this command. An
> example that would expand your environment space to 256 bytes would be
>
> ```
> SHELL=C:\COMMAND.COM /P /E:256
> ```

DOS VERIFY ON

Description

Turns DOS verify ON or OFF for local drives.

Default

OFF

Syntax

```
DOS VERIFY ON
```

Discussion

DOS copies or backs up files without checking to be certain that what was written
was without errors unless VERIFY is set to ON. Setting VERIFY to ON does degrade write performance to local hard or floppy disk drives. It is normally left in its
default state of OFF. Even when turned on, error messages are echoed, but data is
not otherwise saved. Writing to NetWare volumes, NetWare performs a read-after-
write verification with redirection to Hot Fix if necessary. For safety and performance,
save all important data to a NetWare volume.

DRIVE d:

Description

Makes stated drive letter the default network drive letter.

Syntax

```
DRIVE drive_letter:
```

Example

```
DRIVE U:
```

Discussion

Use this command to place the user in a drive letter of your choice when exiting the login script.

> **TIP** ►
>
> Users often save files to the default directory without thinking. In the preceding example, assume U: is mapped to the user's home directory. This causes the vast majority of user files and copies to go to the user's home directory.

EXIT

Description

Terminates execution of login script.

Syntax

```
EXIT
```

Example

```
EXIT "batch_file.bat"
```

Discussion

You always should use the EXIT command to explicitly terminate the login script.

No commands are executed after an EXIT. When EXIT is used in a System or Organizational Login Script, the User Login Script or Default Login Script does not run.

> **CAUTION** ▶
>
> When exiting the login script and calling a file for execution, call a batch file to prevent the possibility of locking LOGIN.EXE in conventional memory.

(DOS Execution Symbol)

Description

Shells out to DOS and executes a DOS executable file.

Syntax

#command

Example

#CAPTURE L=1 Q=Q0 NB NFF

Discussion

Any DOS executable file (with a .COM or .EXE extension) can be executed from within your login script. Simply precede the command with the DOS Execution Symbol.

> **CAUTION** ▶
>
> Do not execute any TSR applications within a login script. It hooks memory vectors, causing LOGIN.EXE to become locked in conventional memory once the login script is terminated.

Execute only applications such as CAPTURE or MAP that affect variables, and then exit memory completely.

TIP ▶

This command does not execute a DOS internal command or batch file.

To execute a DOS internal command or batch file, use the command

```
#COMMAND /C batch_file.bat
#COMMAND /C DOS_internal_command
```

DISPLAY *path_name/file_name*
Description

Displays contents of an ASCII text file.

Syntax

DISPLAY *path_name/file_name*

Example

DISPLAY SYS;PUBLIC/UTIL/DAILYMSG.TXT

Discussion

Use this command to present a message to a user during login. Use the PAUSE command to stop the message from scrolling off the screen.

FDISPLAY
Description

Same as DISPLAY, but suppresses control characters.

FIRE PHASERS *n*

Description

Produces audible "phaser" sound *n* times.

Syntax

```
FIRE PHASERS 3
```

Discussion

This command is used to announce when a particular event occurs, such as a Supervisor login. When used with a conditional statement, it can be used to announce when one or the other condition exists.

INCLUDE *path_name/file_name*

Description

Includes contents of ASCII file as part of the login script.

Syntax

```
INCLUDE path_name/file_name
```

Example

```
INCLUDE SYS:PUBLIC/LOGIN.SCR
```

Discussion

If you prefer to use your own text editor, you can put the INCLUDE statement into your login script to point to the ASCII file you have created.

> **TIP** ▶
>
> Use the INCLUDE command with conditional statements and identifier
> variables to locate different login scripts for various groups, users, or worksta-
> tions.

MACHINE NAME

Description

Variable used to identify a workstation.

Syntax

```
MACHINE NAME = variable
```

Example

```
MACHINE NAME. = LOGIN_NAME
```

Discussion

Applications sometimes use this parameter to locate a variable. Microsoft-oriented
networking software uses this variable to identify a workstation, and this parameter
makes NetWare more compatible with applications written for other types of networks. Use this command when instructed by an application.

MAP

Description

Assigns drive letters and search drives to directory pathnames.

Syntax

```
MAP d:=file_server/volume:path_name
```

Example

```
MAP F:=FS1/SYS:PUBLIC/UTIL
```

Discussion

The MAP command is used to assign a DOS drive letter and/or a search drive to a NetWare directory name. See Chapter 14, "System Administration and Logical Configuration Strategies," for further details on using the MAP command.

> **NOTE** ▶
>
> In a login script, the MAP command is internal, and therefore does not require a DOS Execution Symbol (#) to precede it. It also must be preceded by an ATTACH, though this is not necessary when used as a command-line utility from a DOS prompt.

MAP DISPLAY OFF/ON

Description

Prevents messages from printing to screen.

Default

ON

Syntax

```
MAP DISPLAY OFF
```

Discussion

This stops commands from echoing to the screen upon execution during the login script. Messages still print to the screen.

MAP ERRORS OFF/ON

Description

Prevents login script errors from printing to screen.

Default

ON

Syntax

```
MAP ERRORS OFF
```

Discussion

This command stops errors from printing to the screen. If any commands used in your login script cause expected, nonfatal errors, this command reduces user concern over whether an error has occurred.

PAUSE

Description

Pauses and displays "Strike any key to continue."

Syntax

```
PAUSE
```

Discussion

Use this command to stop the screen from scrolling during a login script. When this command is encountered, the login script pauses, the message above is displayed, and the login script continues when the user strikes any key. If you would like a message to be displayed, or to verify error-free execution of the login script, place this command in a strategic location within your login script.

> **TIP** ▶
>
> Use this command to debug your login script. Place it after lines where errors
> may occur so you can stop the login script and verify errors or appropriate
> execution. When you have fixed your login script, remove the PAUSE state-
> ments used for this purpose.

PCCOMPATIBLE

Description

Resolves problems when %MACHINE is other than default.

Syntax

```
PCCOMPATIBLE
```

Discussion

Whenever you encounter the error message "*Application* not supported on targeted
computer," this command resolves the problem.

REMARK (* or ;)

Description

Ignore this line.

Syntax

```
REMARK text
```

Examples

```
REMARK This section MAPs Search Drives
; This section MAPs Search Drives
* This section MAPs Search Drives
```

Discussion

Documenting a login script is important because more than one person often edits them.

Use this statement to invalidate a line in your login script that you may want to use in the future.

WRITE
Description

Prints text delimited with quotes to screen.

Syntax

```
WRITE "test string"
```

Example

```
WRITE "Good %GREETING_TIME, %FULL_NAME."
```

Discussion

This command prints the message enclosed in quotes to the screen.

WRITE without any additional text sends a line feed to the screen.

> **NOTE**
>
> You can use identifier variables preceded by a % inside of quotes. The value for the identifier variable is then displayed within your text.

Conditional Statements

Conditional statements say "if" something is the case, "then" execute this command(or set of commands). Several variations can be used, and when combined with identifier variables they can provide almost any condition for all users in a single System or Organizational Login Script.

IF ... THEN

Description

Enables the use of programming logic in one statement.

Syntax

```
IF identifier_variable = "text_string" THEN statement
```

Examples

```
IF LOGIN_NAME = "SUPERVISOR" THEN MAP U:=SYS:HOME/SU
IF MEMBER OF "ACCTG" THEN EXIT "ACCTG.BAT"
```

Discussion

Using the conditional statement with an identifier variable enables your login script to execute different statements according to those variables. In the preceding example, if the user Supervisor logs in, the U: drive mapping points at the SYS:HOME/SU directory.

IF ... BEGIN/ELSE/END

Description

Enables the use of programming logic in a multiple-line statement.

Syntax

```
IF identifier_variable = "text_string" THEN BEGIN
    statement
    statement
    END
```

Examples

```
IF LOGIN_NAME = "SUPERVISOR" THEN BEGIN
     FIRE PHASERS 5
     MAP U:=SYS:HOME/SU
     ELSE
     MAP U:=SYS:HOME/%LOGIN_NAME
     END

IF MEMBER OF "ACCTG" THEN BEGIN
     MAP S3:=SYS:APPS/FOX
     MAP S4:=SYS:PUBLIC/UTIL
     END
```

Discussion

This variation of a conditional statement works the same way as the IF ... THEN conditional statement. You can use the ELSE when appropriate.

Identifier Variables

The variables (shown in Tables E.1 through E.4) can be used within a login script. They can be used as a condition within a conditional statement or can be used as part of an ASCII string or pathname.

Identifier variables can be used to make one login script do almost anything necessary without having to create a different login script for each user.

Most identifier variables are defined within the NetWare environment, but at least one (%MACHINE) can be user-defined.

> **NOTE**
>
> When using an identifier variable within an ASCII text string or pathname, precede it with a % symbol. When it is used as part of a conditional statement as shown previously, do not use the % sign.

Table E.1. Day, date, and time variables.

Variable	Value	Default	Use
YEAR	Year in four-number format		
SHORT_YEAR	Year in two-number format		
HOUR	(1-12)	Time of day	Hour of the day
HOUR24	(00-23)	Time of day	Hour of the day (24-hour clock)
MINUTE	(00-59)	Time of day	Minute
SECOND	(00-59)	Time of day	Second
AM_PM	AM or PM	Time of day	AM or PM
GREETING_TIME	(Morning, Afternoon, Evening)	Time of day	
MONTH	(01-12)	Month of year (numeric)	
MONTH_NAME	(January-December)	Month of year (ASCII)	
DAY	(1-31)	Day of month (numeric)	
DAY_OF_WEEK	(Sunday-Saturday)	Day of week (ASCII)	
NDAY_OF_WEEK	(1-7)	Day of week (numeric)	

Table E.2. User and workstation variables.

Variable	Value	Default	Use
LOGIN_NAME			User account login name
FILE_SERVER			File server name
FULL_NAME			User full name
USER_ID			User's MAIL directory name
STATION			Connection number
P_STATION	(12 hex digits)		Physical node address
SHELL_TYPE	Workstation shell version		
OS		MSDOS	Workstation OS (MSDOS or OS2)
OS_VERSION	V*x.xx*		DOS version number
<dos_variable>	Inserts the value or string of a DOS variable		
MACHINE user-defined	IBM_PC		LONG MACHINE TYPE (in NET.CFG)
SMACHINE user-defined	IBM_PC		SHORT MACHINE TYPE (limited to 4 characters)
NETWORK_ ADDRESS	(8 hex digits)		Network address/ number

Table E.3. Variables used in conditional statements.

Variable	Value	Default	Use
ERROR_LEVEL	(0, 1)	0	0 if no error occurs, 1 if error occurs
MEMBER OF "*group*"		ASCII	Workgroup identifier
ACCESS_SERVER	(True, False)	True	Returns True if Access Server is functional

Table E.4. User and workstation variables.

Variable	Value	Default	Use
LOGIN_NAME	ASCII	User account login name	Substitute variable for text
FILE_SERVER	ASCII	This one	
FULL_NAME	ASCII	User full name	
USER_ID	8 char ASCII	User's MAIL directory name Connection number	
P_STATION	(12 hex digits)	Physical node address	
SHELL_TYPE	Various	Workstation shell version	
OS	Workstation OS (MSDOS or OS2)	MSDOS	
OS_VERSION	Vx.xx	DOS version number	
<dos_variable>	Inserts the value or string of a DOS variable		

Variable	Value	Default	Use
MACHINE user-defined	IBM_PC	LONG MACHINE TYPE (in NET.CFG)	
SMACHINE	IBM_PC	SHORT MACHINE	
user-defined	IBM_PC	TYPE (limited to 4 characters)	
NETWORK_ ADDRESS	(8 hex digits)	Network address/ number	

Default Login Script

This default login executes if no user login script is present, and if no EXIT was issued from the system (or organizational) login script.

```
WRITE "Good %GREETING_TIME, %LOGIN_NAME."
MAP DISPLAY OFF
MAP ERRORS OFF
Rem:Set 1st drive to most appropriate directory.
MAP *1:=SYS:%LOGIN_NAME
IF "SUPERVISOR" THEN MAP *1:=SYS:SYSTEM
Rem: Set searchj drives (S2 machine-OS dependent).
MAP INS S1:=SYS:PUBLIC
MAP INS S2:S1 %MACHINE/%OS/%OS_VERSION
Rem: Now display all the current drive settings.
MAP DISPLAY ON
MAP
```

What's on the Disk

F

IN THIS CHAPTER

This book's disk contains many helpful NetWare utilities and support files. The following files are contained on the diskette:

FileName.EXT	Description
STAT.EXE	Novell utility for tracking CPU and disk activity
REFLECT.EXE	Working demo of mirroring software
LOGIN.EXE	AUTOEXEC.BAT, System login script, and related utilities
TOOLBOX.EXE	Several helpful Admin utilities
DSUM.EXE	Utility for reporting available disk space on all drives
NOVBAT.EXE	Batch file enhancer that can query NetWare configurations
NUTILS.EXE	35 helpful administrative utilities
SUPER.EXE	Toggles supervisor equivalences on and off
TSRUTILS.EXE	Memory management utilities, including TSR management
TESTNET.EXE	Network testing utility for throughput
ROOT.EXE	Miscellaneous sample Files

Most of the utilities are provided free by the authors of the software. A few of these packages are distributed as shareware and some are special demos—see the documentation for each program for more information.

Installing the Disk

The files on this disk are compressed using LHArc version 2.13. To install all the files to your hard drive, follow these steps. You'll need at least 3 megabytes of free space on the drive to which you choose to install.

1. At the DOS prompt, change to the drive containing the installation disk. For example, if the disk is in drive B, type B: and press Enter.

2. Type INSTALL C: to install the files to your C: hard drive. If you want to install to any other drive, substitute that drive letter for C: (for example, INSTALL P:).

The files will be automatically decompressed and installed to a directory named \NW3U.

If you want to install only one program, you can manually decompress the program's compressed archive. For example, here is the command to decompress the files in the NUTILS.exe archive:

```
NUTILS S:\BOB\
```

This command will decompress the NUTILS.EXE files to a directory named \BOB on your S: drive. Don't leave off the final \ character—it's important.

STAT

by Novell, Inc. (with permission)

STAT is an NLM to be installed on your server for tracking CPU utilization and disk activity over a period of time. It is helpful to monitor server activity over time, noting the peaks in utilization. You can dump STAT statistics to disk for import into a spreadsheet for analysis.

STAT is loaded as any other NLM, and it records activity according to your selections. You can start and stop recording or set a time to start and stop recording. DUMPSTAT is used to dump statistics in a couple different formats.

To learn more about STAT, log in as Supervisor (or equivalent), copy the file to the SYSTEM directory on your server, and execute README.

NOTE ▶

When STAT is installed with 3.x, you will need to install DPATCH first.

What STAT.EXE Contains

The STAT.EXE archive contains the following files:

```
STAT      NLM        12,449 12-09-91   2:39p
DUMPSTAT  EXE        42,779 08-12-92   6:36p
DPATCH    NLM         1,190 04-27-92   6:14p
PATCHMAN  NLM         9,111 04-16-92   2:08p
APPNOTE   TXT        37,706 08-15-93  12:02p
README    TXT         3,449 08-15-93  12:12p
   6 file(s)        106,684 bytes
```

SETUPSHH.TXT

by Michael Hader

This text file indicates how Windows SETUP.SHH file works and discusses all its options and parameters. This file specifies the configuration options when running Windows SETUP utility. When creating a user copy of Windows in a file server installation, you can specify which file to use. SETUP proceeds without pausing to ask for input. This enables a network administrator to quickly and efficiently set up users copies of Windows.

MNUSAMPL.SRC

by Rick Sant'Angelo

This file is the source code for the NetWare user menu file shown in this book. It give examples of just about every feature of the new menu system in 3.12 and 4.x, developed by Saber for Novell.

REFLECT

by permission CLone Star Software

This is a one-hour, live working demonstration of REFLECT by CLone Star Software . This software package mirrors data between two drives. Every time your data is written, it goes to two destination drive letters. REFLECT works very well with

NetWare and can effectively provide fault-tolerant mirroring of data without the complexity of SFT III and extra hardware. It will not corrupt your data, and it is simple to use. Full electronic documentation and related utilities are provided.

What REFLECT.EXE Contains

The following files are compressed into this archive:

```
INSTALL   EXE      17,510 06-01-93   12:00a
OKOKOK    EXE         733 06-01-93   12:00a
REFLECT   CFG         468 06-01-93   12:00a
REFLECT   DOC      85,208 06-01-93   12:00a
REFLECT   EXE      60,838 06-01-93   12:00a
REFLECTB  EXE      19,968 06-01-93   12:00a
REFLECTW  EXE      19,360 06-01-93   12:00a
RWFWUNLD  EXE       1,289 06-01-93   12:00a
ZCOPY     EXE      86,928 06-01-93   12:00a
 9 file(s)        292,302 bytes
```

LOGIN

by Rick Sant'Angelo

This file contains an electronic copy of the system administration example files used in the book. It also contains a few helpful utilities to use with your AUTOEXEC.BAT.

What LOGIN.EXE Contains

The following files are compressed into this archive:

```
AUTOEXEC  BAT       403 07-17-93    9:50p
YESORNO   COM       101 11-24-85    3:14p
FASTKEY   COM       512 09-13-85   12:07p
NET$LOG   DAT      2176 08-01-93    9:48p
  4 file(s)        3192 bytes.
```

NetWare Toolbox

by Wolfgang Schreiber

This toolbox of utilities enables you to do many functions that no NetWare utilities can do. The following utilities are included:

Utility	Purpose
ACCOUNT	View, change, set user accounts and account notes
APRITE	Grant rights to applications (60 days demo)
APRUN	Run applications defined by APRITE
CACHE	Show caching efficiency (NW 286)
CHANGE	Replace strings in all specified files
DOFORALL	Execute command for specified users/groups
DOFORMMB	Execute command for members of specified group
DOWN	DOWN specified file server
EQUIV	Show security equivalences of specified user
EXECONLY	Set files to 'Execute Only'
GOTODIR	Move default drive to the specified directory
GOTOFILE	Move default drive to the directory of the specified files
LIMIT	Limit number of concurrent application users
OVER32	Enable NetWare to handle more than 32 security equivalences
PAUDIT2	Replaces NetWare's PAUDIT.EXE enabling several selections
PRT_SRV	Mini-print server with some additional features
QUICK	All-around supervisor tool (60 days demo)
S-MAP	Converts standard mapping to search mapping
SAVEUSER	Inversion of MAKEUSER; converts user information to the script file
SHOWDOTS	Displays and changes the shell's 'SHOW DOTS' setting

Utility	Purpose
SWATCH	Server watch: show and trace statistics (NW 286; 60 days demo)
TRACK	Display SAP info similar to 'TRACK ON' on a file server
TR_LIST	Global TLIST: show trustees of all server volumes
UNLOCK	Solves problems with locked pservers/users
UPDATE	Compare and update two directories
VSPACE	Show space restrictions/usage of specified users
XFER	Copy users/groups between servers

Most of these tool are provided as freeware; the APRITE and Quick utilities are demo versions.

What TOOLBOX.EXE Contains

The following files are compressed into this one archive:

```
ACCOUNT   DOC          54 03-24-92    1:07p
ACCOUNT   EXE      20,752 05-05-93   11:45a
APRITE    TXT       1,785 12-29-93   11:32a
APRITE    DOC      29,689 10-22-92    1:20a
APRITE    EXE      43,760 05-05-93   11:47a
APRUN     EXE      17,744 10-22-92    1:20a
CACHE     EXE      20,768 09-25-91    4:41p
CHANGE    EXE      17,760 09-30-91    5:50p
DO-FOR    DOC       3,331 09-03-92    6:05p
DOFORALL  EXE      20,864 05-05-93   11:47a
DOFORMMB  EXE      21,008 05-05-93   11:52a
DOWN      EXE      11,088 09-25-91    4:41p
EQUIV     EXE      16,400 05-05-93   12:23p
ERR_LVL0  COM           5 01-15-91    1:15a
EXECONLY  EXC      13,008 11-29-91    7:55p
GOTODIR   EXE       9,632 09-25-91    4:42p
GOTOFILE  EXE       9,856 09-25-91    4:42p
INSTALL   US        1,057 01-15-91    1:15a
INSTALL   GR        1,152 01-15-91    1:15a
```

```
LIMIT      EXE       14,192  11-29-91    8:20p
OVER32     DOC        6,030  09-23-91   11:16a
OVER32     EXE       22,256  04-29-93    3:37p
PAUDIT2    DOC       14,708  11-24-92   10:48a
PAUDIT2    EXE       48,864  06-01-93   11:00a
PRT_SRV    EXE       13,584  09-25-91    4:42p
QUICK      TXT        1,081  12-29-93   11:34a
QUICK      EXE      128,752  05-05-93   12:56p
QUICK      MNU        6,492  01-15-91    1:15a
QUICKHLP   US        25,990  05-05-93   12:54p
QUICKHLP   GR        27,723  05-05-93    2:32p
QUICKMNU   DOC        1,062  01-15-91    1:15a
S-MAP      EXE       13,008  09-25-91    4:43p
SAVEUSER   EXE       22,656  05-05-93    2:33p
SHODOT     DOC          213  12-29-93   11:48a
SHOWDOT    LZH        8,274  12-29-93   11:47a
SHOWDOTW   LZH       12,690  12-29-93   11:47a
SWATCH     DEF        6,018  11-04-92    2:00a
SWATCH     DOC        1,321  11-04-92    2:00a
SWATCH     EXE      143,760  04-28-93   10:09a
SWATCH     HLP       41,677  11-04-92    2:00a
TOOLBOX    TXT        2,035  12-29-93   11:30a
TRACK      EXE       22,352  08-04-93   11:17p
TRACK      DOC        1,083  08-04-93   11:20p
TR_LIST    EXE       16,240  11-29-91    6:11p
UNLOCK     EXE       17,824  09-25-91    4:44p
UNLOCK     DOC          482  06-01-93   12:33p
UPDATE     EXE       22,416  10-02-91   12:11p
VSPACE     DOC          640  08-23-91    1:09p
VSPACE     EXE       15,712  05-05-93    2:39p
XFER       DOC          143  09-09-91   10:49a
XFER       EXE       32,128  05-05-93    2:40p
   51 file(s)      951,119  bytesCastaway!
```

DSUM

by Danon Software Services

This utility gives a single-screen summary of all drives and their used/available space.

What DSUM23.EXE Contains

The following files are compressed into this archive:

```
DSUM      COM      12,354 12-03-91    2:31a
DSUM      TXT       1,955 12-03-91    2:31a
DSUM      WP       13,778 12-03-91    2:31a
 3 file(s)          28,087 bytes
```

NOVBAT

by Horizons Consulting

NOVBAT (short for Novell Batch Enhancer) is a package designed to assist the system administrator in developing network intelligent batch files. Every system administrator has to write and support batch files. Many of these batch file oriented tasks are more difficult than they need to be because of the limitations in batch file programming in which some of the rules change from one version to the next.

NOVBAT simplifies batch file programming and enables you to use NetWare information within your batch files. NOVBAT supports commands such as

Command	Meaning
DoesUserExist?	Is there a user BOB in existence?
IsLoggedIn?	Is BOB currently logged into the net?
IsMemberOfGroup?	Is BOB a member of the SALES GROUP?
User@Con?	What connection is BOB at?
NodeNum?	What node number am I logged into?
IsFreeEMS@Least?	Do I have at least 300k of unused EMS?
WhatDOSVer?	What version of DOS am I using?
IsVideo?	What graphics adapter am I using?
WhatServer?	Is my current server the SALES_SERVER?

NOVBAT contains more than 50 netware-oriented commands that help the system administrator or installer develop powerful login scripts and batch files. NOVBAT is designed to operate from the batch file command-line, and returns information to your batch file through use of the ERRORLEVEL function and environment variables. This enables batch files to perform differently for varying users, environments, and applications. These utilites are evaluation versions.

What NOVBAT.LZH Contains

The following files are compressed into this archive:

```
IDLEBOOT  TXT         4,595  07-25-92   11:33a
NOVBAT    DOC        84,722  07-25-92   11:43a
NOVBAT    EXE        67,328  07-24-92   11:47p
NOVBAT    TXT         4,110  08-03-92   12:37p
OEM       TXT         1,132  07-25-92   11:42a
ORDER     FRM         2,520  07-25-92   11:49a
   6 file(s)        164,407  bytes
```

The N Utilities

by Darwin Collins

Here are some general, but helpful utilities to make a system administrator's life easier. Though many of these utilities can be used interactively, most of them are designed to be placed into batch files, menus, and login scripts to simplify NetWare object management. These utilities are distributed as shareware. The NUTIL.DOC file contains instructions for using the programs.

What NUTILS.EXE Contains

The following files are compressed into this archive:

```
NADDRESS  EXE         9,210  09-03-92    9:58p
NALLCARD  EXE        32,540  03-10-93    1:11a
NASKRPRN  EXE         7,484  12-15-91   10:24p
NCARD     EXE        17,996  10-12-91    1:14p
NCHGOWN   EXE        14,028  12-03-91   12:06a
NCHKCSYS  EXE        12,268  11-16-91    2:27p
```

```
NCHKMODM  EXE     13,990  01-26-93   12:53a
NCHKPASS  EXE     14,012  09-15-91   11:03p
NCHKRPRN  EXE     21,314  01-10-93   11:10a
NCMPDATE  EXE      7,500  02-17-92   10:39p
NCMPDRVR  EXE     13,740  04-08-92   11:45p
NCOPYIPX  EXE     15,756  04-08-92   11:54p
NCOPYNEW  EXE     13,322  05-31-92    2:36p
NCOPYSCR  EXE     10,826  02-17-93   12:40a
NCPY2SUB  EXE      8,540  10-12-91    5:17p
NDATEDIR  EXE      7,868  10-12-91    5:21p
NDELFILE  EXE     11,098  01-30-93   12:09a
NDELPRNJ  EXE      8,924  10-12-91    5:34p
NDISK     EXE      6,668  07-27-91   10:31a
NDOSVER   EXE      5,979  07-13-91    4:07p
NEMSMEM   EXE      6,508  07-27-91   10:32a
NEQUA     EXE      7,996  01-22-92    8:26p
NEXPIRE   EXE     10,426  11-30-92   11:22p
NEXTMEM   EXE      6,092  07-27-91   10:34a
NFINDMSG  EXE     14,778  08-07-93   10:43p
NGETTIME  EXE      7,228  07-21-91   11:07p
NGROUP    EXE      7,852  10-12-91    5:45p
NINVENT   EXE     19,262  02-17-93   12:23a
NLIST     EXE     11,034  07-11-93    7:59p
NLOGADDR  EXE     10,108  11-24-91    9:49p
NLOGEVT   EXE     29,130  11-29-92   12:27a
NLOGMSG   EXE      9,404  02-20-92   11:01p
NMANPCON  EXE     15,690  02-21-93    6:52p
NMEM      EXE      7,060  07-27-91   10:35a
NMHS2TXT  EXE     13,980  02-29-92    5:45p
NOPNFILE  EXE     16,010  04-12-93   11:03p
NPHONE    EXE     10,730  08-14-93   12:50p
NQUOTES   TXT      3,522  11-30-92   12:22a
NQUOTES   EXE      8,874  11-28-92   10:37p
NRPTBIND  EXE     57,638  08-08-93   11:14p
NRPTCONN  EXE     13,804  10-12-91    9:10p
NRPTEQUA  EXE     13,052  10-12-91    9:18p
NRPTMHS   EXE     14,314  07-04-93    4:38p
NRPTMHSU  EXE     13,802  01-30-93    1:26p
NRPTOWN   EXE     15,482  01-30-93    1:29p
NRPTPCON  EXE     16,586  01-30-93    1:33p
NRPTCCRP  EXE     15,914  01-30-93    1:38p
NRPTSUB   EXE     22,704  12-27-92   12:54a
NSCRIPT   EXE     29,594  04-03-93    3:08p
NSELPRNJ  EXE     16,106  12-07-92    8:27p
NSETTIME  EXE      7,564  10-12-91    9:43p
NSTRING   EXE      7,836  02-12-92   11:38p
```

```
NSUBOWN    EXE       12,186 01-30-93    1:11p
NTRAFFIC   EXE       19,164 10-12-91    9:58p
NUTIL      DOC       98,419 01-05-94   10:22a
NW_SEC     DOC        2,385 01-03-94   11:09p
NW_SEC     EXE       40,432 06-23-93    4:02p
NXMSMEM    EXE        6,188 07-27-91   10:38a
REGISTER   FRM        1,897 02-08-93    7:00a
SAMPLES    LZH        8,307 01-05-94   10:21a
SUMMARY    DOC        6,515 01-03-94   11:14p
SUPPORT    TXT        3,235 01-03-94   11:12p
ULIST      EXE       23,587 06-18-92    8:26a
UPDSHELL   TXT        4,103 03-11-92   10:02p
WHATSNEW   700        5,519 02-08-93    7:00a
   67 file(s)       945,080 bytes
```

SUPER

by Wolfgang Schreiber

This utility enables you to switch on and off Supervisor equivalences without logout and login. This saves an administrator considerable time when interactively working and administering. There are DOS and Windows versions of this SUPER.

What SUPER.EXE Contains

The following files are compressed into this archive:

```
SSUPER     DOC        5,562 12-01-93   10:43p
SUPER      EXE       14,517 12-01-93   10:28p    (DOS subdirectory)
SUPER      ICO        2,038 09-03-92    4:56p    (WINDOWS subdirectory)
SUPER      EXE       41,728 12-01-93   10:55p    (WINDOWS subdirectory)
    4 file(s)        63,845
```

The TSR Utilities

by Turbo Power Software

This is a helpful set of memory management utilities. It has utilities that enable you to remove TSRs from memory that would otherwise require you to reboot. Other utilities help you to manage TSRs and see exactly where they load and how their vectors are hooked.

What TSRUTILS.EXE Contains

The following files are compressed into this archive:

```
DEVICE    EXE      8,608 02-14-92   11:05a
DISABLE   EXE     11,904 02-14-92   11:05a
EATMEM    COM        239 10-07-91   10:02a
FMARK     COM        922 02-14-92   11:05a
MAPMEM    EXE     19,136 02-14-92   11:18a
MARK      COM        510 02-14-92   11:05a
MARKNET   EXE     10,800 02-14-92   11:18a
RAMFREE   COM        168 11-22-91    9:29a
RELEASE   EXE     13,952 02-14-92   11:52a
RELNET    EXE     20,512 02-14-92   11:52a
TSR       DOC     56,638 02-14-92   12:10p
WATCH     COM        993 02-14-92   11:05a
 14 file(s)      144,382 bytes
```

TESTNET

by Scott Taylor

This is a useful tool for performance testing on a network. This utility tests and reports I/O throughput in KBps. It can be used in a single-user test or multiple-user tests between workstations an file servers. By manipulating test parameters, it can gauge the raw throughput of the LAN, or net throughput to the disk. See Chapter 31, "Benchmark and Workload Testing," for a detailed discussion on how to use this utility.

What TESTNET.EXE Contains

The following files are compressed into this archive:

```
TESTNET   EXE     32,914 08-22-87    9:49p
TESTNET   DOC      2,895 01-06-88    2:23p
  2 file(s)       35,809 bytes
```

INDEX

I

Symbols

A

Add to Your Sams Library Today with the Best Books for Networking, Operating Systems, and New Technologies

The easiest way to order is to pick up the phone and call
1-800-428-5331
between 9:00 a.m. and 5:00 p.m. EST.
For faster service please have your credit card available.

ISBN	Quantity	Description of Item	Unit Cost	Total Cost
0-672-30382-5		Understanding Local Area Networks, 4th Edition	$26.95	
0-672-30362-0		Navigating the Internet	$24.95	
0-672-30326-4		Absolute Beginner's Guide to Networking	$19.95	
0-672-30206-3		Networking Windows, NetWare Edition	$24.95	
0-672-30026-5		Do-It-Yourself Networking with LANtastic	$24.95	
0-672-30173-3		Enterprise Wide Networking	$39.95	
0-672-30170-9		NetWare LAN Management Toolkit	$34.95	
0-672-30243-8		LAN Desktop Guide to E-mail with cc:Mail	$27.95	
0-672-30075-3		LAN Desktop Guide to Troubleshooting, NetWare Edition	$29.95	
0-672-30085-0		LAN Desktop Guide to Security, NetWare Edition	$27.95	
0-672-30084-2		LAN Desktop Guide to Printing, NetWare Edition	$27.95	
0-672-30005-2		Understanding Data Communications, 3rd Edition	$24.95	
0-672-30119-9		International Telecommunications	$39.95	

❏ 3 ½" Disk

❏ 5 ¼" Disk

Shipping and Handling: See information below.	
TOTAL	

Shipping and Handling: $4.00 for the first book, and $1.75 for each additional book. Floppy disk: add $1.75 for shipping and handling. If you need to have it NOW, we can ship product to you in 24 hours for an additional charge of approximately $18.00, and you will receive your item overnight or in two days. Overseas shipping and handling adds $2.00 per book and $8.00 for up to three disks. Prices subject to change. Call for availability and pricing information on latest editions.

201 W. 103rd Street, Indianapolis, Indiana 46290

1-800-428-5331 — Orders   1-800-835-3202 — FAX   1-800-858-7674 — Customer Service